King James Version

STANDARD LESSON COMMENTARY

2002–2003

International Sunday School Lessons

Edited by

Ronald G. Davis, Ronald L. Nickelson,
and Jonathan Underwood

Published by
STANDARD PUBLISHING

Mark A. Taylor, Vice President, Church Resources
Paul D. Learned, Managing Director, Church Resources
Carla J. Crane, Production Manager
Jonathan Underwood, Senior Editor, Adult Curriculum
Cheryl Frey, Associate Editor

Fiftieth Annual Volume

©2002
STANDARD PUBLISHING
A division of STANDEX INTERNATIONAL Corporation
8121 Hamilton Avenue, Cincinnati, Ohio 45231
Printed in U. S. A.

In This Volume

Fall Quarter, 2002 *(page 1)*

Judgment and Exile

Writers

LESSON DEVELOPMENT: Orrin Root
VERBAL ILLUSTRATIONS: Charles R. Boatman

LEARNING BY DOING: Ronald L. Oakes
LET'S TALK IT OVER: Kenneth Goble

Winter Quarter, 2002-2003 *(page 113)*

Portraits of Faith

Writers

LESSON DEVELOPMENT: Thomas Friskney (1-5),
Terry A. Clark (6-9), Michael Shannon (10-13)
LEARNING BY DOING: Alan Weber

VERBAL ILLUSTRATIONS: Robert C. Shannon (1-7),
Victor Knowles (8-13)
LET'S TALK IT OVER: Richard A. Koffarnus

Spring Quarter, 2003 *(page 225)*

Jesus: God's Power in Action

Writers

LESSON DEVELOPMENT: Dennis Gaertner (1-5),
John W. Wade (6-8), Marshall Hayden (9-13)
VERBAL ILLUSTRATIONS: Charles R. Boatman

LEARNING BY DOING: Rick Shonkwiler
LET'S TALK IT OVER: Phil Roberts

Summer Quarter, 2003 *(page 337)*

God Restores a Remnant

Writers

LESSON DEVELOPMENT: Lloyd Pelfrey (1-5)
Orrin Root (6-11), Douglas Redford (12-14)
VERBAL ILLUSTRATIONS: Jeffrey Metzger
and Ronald L. Nickelson

LEARNING BY DOING: Virginia Beddow
and Greg Delort
LET'S TALK IT OVER: David Baynes (1-7),
Simon J. Dahlman (8-14)

Artists

TITLE PAGES: James E. Seward

Cover design by DesignTeam

Lessons based on International Sunday School Lessons © 2000 by the Lesson Committee.

CD-ROM AVAILABLE

The *Standard Lesson Commentary* is available in an electronic format in special editions of the *Standard Lesson Commentary* (King James edition) and *The NIV® Standard Lesson Commentary*. These editions (order #20003 for KJV and 30003 for NIV®) contain a compact disk for use with Windows®-based computers.

System Requirements: Windows XP/2000/ME/98/95; 32 Meg RAM; 25 Meg Available Hard Drive Space; 2x or better CD-ROM drive.

If you have any questions regarding the use of this CD-ROM, please contact Technical Support by telephone at (360) 679-4496, by E-mail at tech@logos.com, or online at www.logos.com/support.

Index of Printed Texts, 2002-2003

The printed texts for 2002-2003 are arranged here in the order in which they appear in the Bible.
Opposite each reference is the number of the page on which it appears in this volume.

Cumulative Index

A cumulative index for the Scripture passages used in the STANDARD LESSON COMMENTARY for the years September, 1998—August, 2003, is provided below.

V

Fall Quarter, 2002

Judgment and Exile

Special Features

Lessons

Unit 1: Urgent Plea

Unit 2: Limited Hope

Unit 3: Final Defeat

About These Lessons

The lessons of the present quarter chronicle the sad decline of the kingdom of Judah until the fall of Jerusalem in 586 B.C. We then pick up the story of the exiles as they look in hope to their eventual return to their homeland. It is a tale of lessons taught but not learned. May we learn from the failure of God's people so that we might enjoy the blessings of the Lord.

Sep 1

Sep 8

Sep 15

Sep 22

Sep 29

Oct 6

Oct 13

Oct 20

Oct 27

Nov 3

Nov 10

Nov 17

Nov 24

Year of Jubilee!

FIFTY YEARS AGO Standard Publishing first began gathering its popular *Bible Teacher and Leader* quarterlies into an annual volume called the *Standard Lesson Commentary*. This year, then, marks the year of Jubilee for the commentary. In the Old Testament, the Year of Jubilee was a time of celebration that came every fifty years. It was a time of freedom, as servants were set free and family lands that had been sold reverted to the original families.

This is a year of celebration for us, too. What began as a convenience fifty years ago is now a major reference tool for thousands of students, teachers, and preachers of God's Word. It not only provides weekly help for Sunday school lessons, but also invaluable help for Bible study in a variety of settings.

The chart below shows the current study plan for the International Sunday School Lessons, the basis for the texts in our commentary. Journey with us to the land of Israel this fall and witness the sad decline of a once-powerful nation. In the winter come and meet some of the influential people of the New Testament. Walk—no, run—with Jesus in a springtime study of the fast-paced Gospel of Mark. And in the summer, return to the Old Testament to welcome the exiles home. What was an extended Jubilee for them foreshadows an even greater Jubilee that we anticipate when our Lord returns to set the captives eternally free!

International Sunday School Lesson Cycle
September, 1998—August, 2004

YEAR	FALL QUARTER (Sept., Oct., Nov.)	WINTER QUARTER (Dec., Jan., Feb.)	SPRING QUARTER (Mar., Apr., May)	SUMMER QUARTER (June, July, Aug.)
1998-1999	God Calls a People to Faithful Living (Old Testament Survey)	God Calls Anew in Jesus Christ (New Testament Survey)	That You May Believe (John)	Genesis: Beginnings (Genesis)
1999-2000	From Slavery to Conquest (Exodus, Leviticus, Numbers, Deuteronomy, Joshua)	Immanuel: God With Us (Matthew)	Helping a Church Confront Crisis (1 and 2 Corinthians)	New Life in Christ (Ephesians, Philippians, Colossians, Philemon)
2000-2001	Rulers of Israel (Judges, 1 and 2 Samuel, 1 Kings 1-11)	Good News of Jesus (Luke)	Continuing Jesus' Work (Acts)	Division and Decline (1 Kings 12-22, 2 Kings 1-17, Isaiah 1-39, Hosea, Amos, Micah)
2001-2002	Jesus' Ministry (Miracles, Parables, Sermon on the Mount)	Light for All People (Isaiah 9:1-7; 11:1-9; 40-66; Ruth, Jonah)	The Power of the Gospel (Romans, Galatians)	Worship and Wisdom for Living (Psalms, Proverbs)
2002-2003	Judgment and Exile (2 Kings 18-25, Jeremiah, Lamentations, Ezekiel, Habakkuk, Zephaniah)	Portraits of Faith (Personalities in the New Testament)	Jesus: God's Power in Action (Mark)	God Restores a Remnant (Ezra, Nehemiah, Daniel, Joel, Obadiah, Haggai, Zechariah, Malachi)
2003-2004	Faith Faces the World (James, 1 and 2 Peter, 1, 2, 3 John, Jude)	A Child Is Given (Samuel, John the Baptist, Jesus) Lessons From Life (Esther, Job, Ecclesiastes, Song of Solomon)	Jesus Fulfills His Mission (Death, Burial, and Resurrection Texts) Living Expectantly (1, 2 Thessalonians, Revelation)	Hold Fast to the Faith (Hebrews) Guidelines for the Church's Ministry (1, 2 Timothy, Titus)

Disaster and Hope

by Orrin Root

IN THE FALL OF 1998 we began our six-year cycle of Sunday school lessons with a swift survey of the Old Testament. This provided a framework in which later Old Testament lessons can be placed. In the fall of 1999 we traced the escape of God's people from Egypt, their wandering in the desert, and their conquest of the promised land. In the fall of 2000 we considered the time of the judges who followed Joshua, and then the reigns of Israel's first three kings, Saul, David, and Solomon. In the summer of 2001 we saw how Israel was divided into two separate kingdoms, and we followed the fortunes of the two until the northern kingdom was overwhelmed by Assyria and its people were scattered abroad. Now in the fall of 2002 we turn to the southern kingdom, usually called Judah. We shall follow it through good times and bad until we see it conquered by Babylon and taken into captivity. Here are short previews of our thirteen lessons.

Unit 1. September
Urgent Plea

Judah, the south part of divided Israel, did not fall into idolatry and kindred sins as rapidly as the north kingdom did. The temple was in Judah, and there were faithful priests to lead in God's way. But Judah wavered between true worship and idolatry, swayed by the wish of each new king. Jeremiah was God's outstanding prophet then. Through him God pleaded with the people to be true; but when a king preferred idolatry, some people were all too ready to accept it.

Lesson 1. King Ahaz led the country far into idol worship, but King Hezekiah turned it around. He restored the Passover feast that had been neglected for a long time and proceeded to encourage worship of the Lord and to banish idolatry.

Lesson 2. When Hezekiah died, his son Manasseh became king. He was as bad as his father had been good. Vigorously he promoted idolatry, and, of course, other sins grew along with it. For that God let Judah be attacked by the Assyrians, who had destroyed Israel. They captured Manasseh and took him to Babylon, which they ruled at that time. Then Manasseh saw his mistake and repented. Somehow the Lord arranged for Manasseh's return to Judah, where he spent the rest of his life trying to undo the harm he had done.

Lesson 3. Manasseh's son Amon had no sympathy with his father's reformation. But Amon ruled only two years. When he was murdered, his eight-year-old son became king. This boy began early to seek the Lord and to lead Judah in doing right. In that he was helped by the prophet Zephaniah, from whom we take the text of lesson 3. Through this prophet the Lord promised punishment for the wicked leaders in Judah, and promised a happy future for the humble and godly people of Judah.

Lesson 4. In the long reign of Manasseh and the short reign of Amon, places of idol worship were built all over Judah. King Josiah ordered them destroyed along with the idols and altars that were in them. After that was done, the king appointed a committee to clean and repair the temple of God. It had not been cared for in those years when Manasseh and Amon had been promoting idolatry. Working to clean the temple, the men found the book of God's law. Apparently it had been laid away and forgotten in those many years when no one was paying attention to it. Josiah was shocked when the law was read to him. He could see that he and his people were breaking the law in many ways. So the king called his people together. He read the law to them, and king and people together promised to obey it.

Lesson 5. After King Josiah died, Judah had no more good kings. God's law was still the law of the land, but it was not enforced. The people still went through the motions of worshiping the Lord, but their hearts were not in it. Jeremiah was God's most noted spokesman then. He warned the people that their wicked ways would bring disaster. He urged the people to mourn over the coming trouble. The truth Jeremiah brought was a test for the people, and they failed the test. They insisted on ignoring God's law, and punishment drew near.

Unit 2. October
Limited Hope

Through Jeremiah and other prophets, the Lord kept on warning that evil living would surely bring disaster. But the people did not have to go on with their evil living. They could repent; they could obey God, they could avoid disaster. But the people preferred to believe lying prophets who said no disaster was coming.

Lesson 6. Through many years God's warnings had been ignored. Now came a definite promise: an enemy army was about to strike from the north. Some of the people thought of killing God's prophet, but it seems that hardly anyone thought seriously about obeying God's law.

Lesson 7. God's warning came with increased intensity. Vigorously He denounced the growing evil in Judah and called for a return to righteousness. But the people liked their lawlessness, and kept on with their evil ways.

Lesson 8. Without withdrawing one word from the prophecy of disaster, the Lord looked beyond the disaster to a better time. The hills of Israel would be peopled with farmers and shepherds. Better still, they would be the "habitation of justice, and mountain of holiness" (Jeremiah 31:23). Then the Lord looked yet farther into the future and promised a New Covenant to replace the one given at Sinai. Announcing the crowning feature of that New Covenant, the Lord said, "I will forgive their iniquity, and I will remember their sin no more" (31:24).

Lesson 9. Habakkuk was one of the true prophets of that time when Israel's sins were monstrous and continuous. He asked, "Lord, how long will You let that go on?"

The Lord answered calmly: "Not long. The Babylonians will be here to punish them."

"Babylonians!" Habakkuk was shocked. "Lord, they're worse than we are. How can You let them punish us?"

The Lord was still calm. "Don't worry, Habakkuk. The Babylonians, too, will be punished in their turn."

Unit 3. November
Final Defeat

"The Lord is merciful and gracious, slow to anger, and plenteous in mercy" (Psalm 103:8). But persistent sinners find there is a time when His mercy gives place to wrath.

Lesson 10. When the huge Babylonian army came, the king of Judah wisely surrendered, promising to be obedient and pay tribute. But when the army was far away, the king declared independence and refused tribute. So the army came again, and it took the king and ten thousand others away. Another native was left to rule in Judah and pay the tribute, but after some years that king, too, rebelled. This time the Babylonians were angry when they returned. They leveled Jerusalem and the temple, and they took most of the survivors to captivity in Babylon. No longer was there a nation of Israel in the land of Israel.

Lesson 11. The people of Judah had been bad, ungrateful, and rebellious. Yet they did love the land they lost. Their grief found expression in "The Lamentations of Jeremiah," a collection of mournful songs designed for singing, and they probably were sung many times. The short samples in our text express deep grief, acknowledgement that their survival is due to God's mercy, and resolve to turn again to the Lord and wait for His renewed blessing.

Lesson 12. Ezekiel was among the ten thousand captives taken to Babylon when the Babylonian army came to Judah a second time. In Babylon he gave God's messages to his fellow captives. In our text he rebukes those captives for two separate but related things.

First, he rebukes the captives for trying to deny their guilt by saying they were being punished for the sins of former generations. In truth, they were not being punished because their parents sinned, but because they themselves continued the sins of their parents in their own lives.

Second, he rebukes them because they accused God of being unfair. In fact, God was fair when He punished each sinner for his own sins, not others—and when He forgave a sinner He was much better than fair.

Lesson 13. The final lesson of this series will bring a promise bright enough to dry all the tears of the long captivity. God is going to take the homesick captives back again—back to the well-loved hills of home. The fertile valleys among those hills will be full of golden grain. The fruit trees will be laden with tasty fruit. Best of all, the people who will return will not be the same sinners they were when they were taken captives. They will be cleansed, purified, made fit to be God's people.

And then comes a surprise. The Lord will not do that for the sake of the people of Israel who will benefit from it. Stay around and learn why He will do such a wonderful thing.

Then stay with us till we return to Old Testament study in the summer of 2003. At that time we shall see how fifty thousand captives led the move from Babylon back to the homeland.

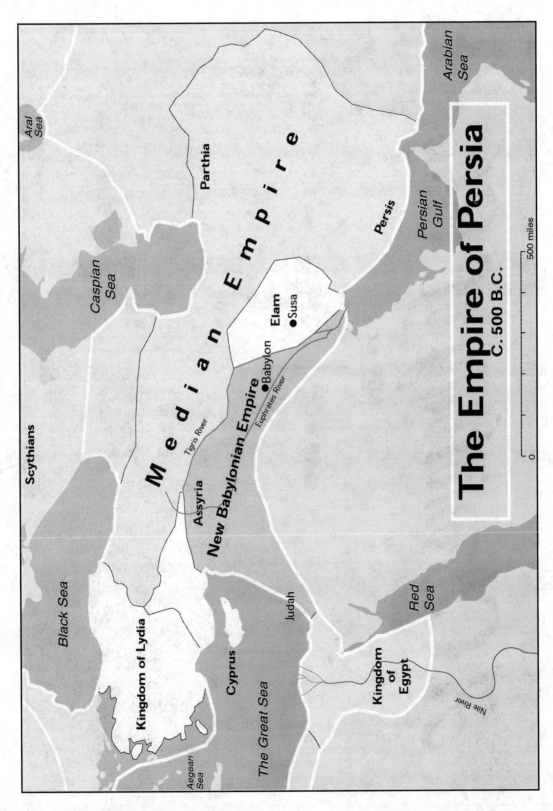

The Empire of Persia
C. 500 B.C.

Aral Sea

Arabian Sea

Parthia

M e d i a n   E m p i r e

Persis

Persian Gulf

Caspian Sea

Elam
●Susa

Scythians

●Babylon

Euphrates River

New Babylonian Empire

Tigris River

Assyria

Black Sea

Kingdom of Lydia

Cyprus

The Great Sea

Judah

Red Sea

Kingdom of Egypt

Nile River

Aegean Sea

0   500 miles

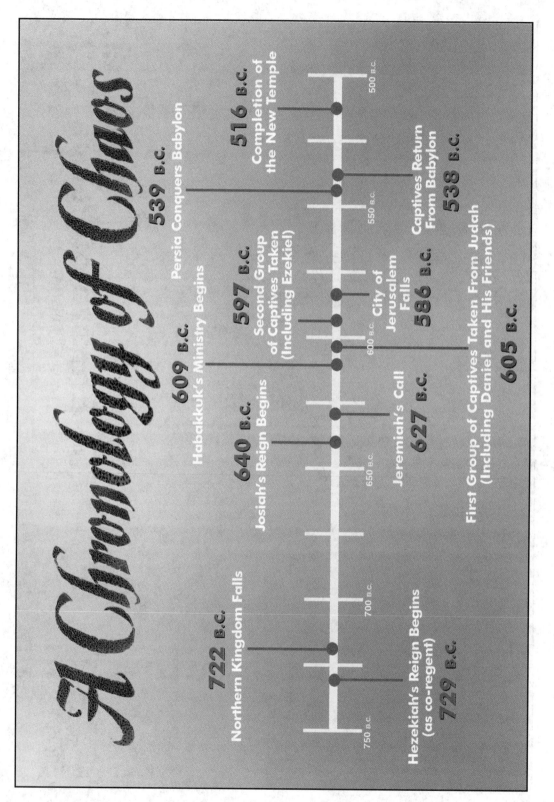

Why Study the Old Testament?

by George Mark Elliott (1897–1981)

A s the *Standard Lesson Commentary* reaches its Jubilee (fiftieth) Year as an annual publication of the quarterly *Bible Teacher and Leader*, we are honored to present an adaptation of an article by Professor George Mark Elliott that appeared in the first annual edition in 1954.

The morning class had assembled in the old Bethany College. Alexander Campbell [1788–1866] began his lecture like this: "Gentlemen: We commence properly, this morning, the consideration of a volume, surpassing all others in the blessings vouchsafed to man. It is a superlative work of transcendent value and importance. It spans the whole arch of time, leans upon eternity past and eternity to come, and comprehends time in its history and in its prophecy. It gives to man a knowledge paramount to all knowledge of the sciences of earth; yea, it involves his whole destiny, and is, therefore, the superlative study of life."

William E. Gladstone [1809–1898], the grand old man of England, once remarked that the grand old Book is "stamped with a Specialty of Origin," and that "an immeasurable distance separates it from all competitors." This Book is not just the best book in the world; it is in a class by itself, different in kind from all other books because it is the Word of God written by men as they were borne along by the Holy Spirit.

A foundational reason for studying the Old Testament is that its writings constitute an integral part of the sacred Scriptures. Since the Bible is an organic unity, a full understanding of one part necessitates an understanding of the various parts with which it stands. In a comprehensive study, the eye is not isolated from the body, or the sun from the solar system.

It is simply impossible to understand the New Testament as we ought without a corresponding understanding of the Old Testament. The Bible, of course, must be rightly divided. As a codification of law, the old covenant has been abrogated, and we are living under the new covenant. But while there are transient ordinances, methods, and symbols, revelation as such is not transient, but permanent. The lessons of the divine revelation before the cross are wondrously contemporary, and constitute one of the grand means of grace today. Paul had been referring at some length to Old Testament history, and finally explained: "Now all these things happened unto them for ensamples: and they are written for our admonition, upon whom the ends of the world are come (1 Corinthians 10:11).

It is true that the writings of the Old Testament were preparatory to the climax of revelation in the New Testament, and that without that climax those writings would be "a blind alley, and we should never have had a Bible." But a study of this preparatory activity, in both its negative and positive aspects, is of tremendous importance. Here the gospel will be found in promise, type, and prophecy. The perfect counterpart in the New Testament constitutes a grand argument for the divine origin of Scriptures that no infidel can answer. The messianic kingdom anticipated in the Old Testament finds its perfect fulfillment in the kingdom of the New Testament. Jesus claimed that He Himself stood in the converging rays of Old Testament prophecy, that He was the Messiah of the prophets. Our Lord made use of the prophets in meeting temptation, opposing error, and teaching the way of holiness. He died with the words of a Holy Spirit inspired psalmist upon His lips.

Follow the New Testament writers, and you will get some idea of the frequency and effectiveness with which they made use of the Old Testament. Here was the inexhaustible storehouse from which they continually drew. Through the prophets of Israel, God still reveals Himself to us as the all-powerful Ruler of the world. Through them, He strengthens our faith that now, as always, He is carrying forward to completion His plan for our redemption.

The Bible has been likened by Saphir to the child brought before King Solomon. The king said, "Divide it"; but the mother cried out, "By no means slay the child." "To divide Old Testament and New Testament is to take away the life of both, for they are not merely connected, nor are they merely harmonious, but they interpenetrate one another. The same breath of life and the same covenant blood of Him that died for us pervades them all." What holds the Bible together? Christ!

If the Bible be regarded as a glorious panoramic scene, then the central figure, giving meaning, animation, and exquisite beauty to the whole, is none other than Jesus, the Messiah, the expectation of the law, the hope of the prophets, the longing of the rest of the books, the Christ of the Gospels, the Lord of Acts of the Apostles, the reigning one of the Epistles, and the coming one of the Apocalypse!

Quarterly Quiz

The questions on this page may be used in several ways: as a pretest at the beginning of the quarter; as a review at the end of the quarter; or as a review after each lesson. The questions are based on the Scripture text of each lesson (King James Version). ***The answers are on page 4.***

Lesson 1

1. What king invited "all Israel and Judah" to celebrate the Passover? *2 Chronicles 30:1*
2. The invitation to celebrate the Passover was received with joy and eagerness in all parts of Israel and Judah. T/F *2 Chronicles 30:10*

Lesson 2

1. Manasseh was fifty-five years old when he became king, and he reigned for twelve years. T/F *2 Chronicles 33:1*
2. What did Manasseh sacrifice in the valley of the son of Hinnom? *2 Chronicles 33:6*

Lesson 3

1. Jerusalem's judges are criticized for being what kind of animal? (wolves, tigers, leopards?) *Zephaniah 3:3*
2. The Lord will eventually take away Jerusalem's judgment [i.e., punishment]. T/F *Zephaniah 3:15*

Lesson 4

1. Who became king of Judah when he was eight years old, and reigned for thirty-one years? *2 Chronicles 34:1*
2. What did this king do when he heard the words of the law? (laughed, took off his sandals, tore his clothes?) *2 Chronicles 34:19*
3. Where was the book of the covenant found? *2 Chronicles 34:30*

Lesson 5

1. What type of paths did Jeremiah tell his hearers to seek? (old, new, paved?) *Jeremiah 6:16*
2. Whom did God appoint to warn the people? (soldiers, watchmen, craftsmen?) *Jeremiah 6:17*
3. What type of corrupted metal did Jeremiah say the people were? (gold, silver, copper, zinc?) *Jeremiah 6:30*

Lesson 6

1. Jeremiah was a what? (prophet, priest, king, baker?) *Jeremiah 25:2*
2. The king of Babylon whom God sent to punish Judah and Jerusalem was Alexander the Great. T/F *Jeremiah 25:9*
3. If the people would do what Jeremiah says, the Lord promised He would not bring disaster on the people. T/F *Jeremiah 26:13*

Lesson 7

1. Jeremiah condemned a king who was particularly fond of what kind of wood? (cedar, cherry, oak, pine?) *Jeremiah 22:15, 23*
2. The king Jeremiah condemned was King Solomon. T/F *Jeremiah 22:18*

Lesson 8

1. God promised that the land of Judah would stay in captivity forever. T/F *Jeremiah 31:23*
2. The New Covenant would be written on the _____ of the people. *Jeremiah 31:33*

Lesson 9

1. In the midst of wrath, what did Habakkuk ask God to remember? (justice, mercy, rain?) *Habakkuk 3:2*
2. Which part of Habakkuk's body quivered? (heart, lips, hands?) *Habakkuk 3:16*

Lesson 10

1. Zedekiah was one of the most godly kings Judah ever had. T/F *2 Chronicles 36:12*
2. Zedekiah rebelled against King _____. *2 Chronicles 36:13*

Lesson 11

1. In His winepress, the Lord had trampled the virgin daughter of _____. *Lamentations 1:15*
2. The Lord's _____ never fail. *Lamentations 3:22*
3. God does not bring affliction willingly. T/F *Lamentations 3:33*

Lesson 12

1. What type of grapes did Ezekiel mention in the prophecy that the Lord condemned? (white, sour, seedless?) *Ezekiel 18:2*
2. God takes no pleasure when people die. T/F *Ezekiel 18:32*

Lesson 13

1. God, speaking through the prophet Ezekiel, associated filthiness (impurity) with idol worship. T/F *Ezekiel 36:25*
2. God promised to give the people a new _____ and a new _____. *Ezekiel 36:26*
3. When the people looked back on their evil ways, they would loathe themselves. T/F *Ezekiel 36:31*

Repentance and Renewal

September 1
Lesson 1

DEVOTIONAL READING: Psalm 122.

BACKGROUND SCRIPTURE: 2 Chronicles 29, 30; 2 Kings 18-20.

PRINTED TEXT: 2 Chronicles 30:1-12.

2 Chronicles 30:1-12

1 And Hezekiah sent to all Israel and Judah, and wrote letters also to Ephraim and Manasseh, that they should come to the house of the LORD at Jerusalem, to keep the passover unto the LORD God of Israel.

2 For the king had taken counsel, and his princes, and all the congregation in Jerusalem, to keep the passover in the second month.

3 For they could not keep it at that time, because the priests had not sanctified themselves sufficiently, neither had the people gathered themselves together to Jerusalem.

4 And the thing pleased the king and all the congregation.

5 So they established a decree to make proclamation throughout all Israel, from Beer-sheba even to Dan, that they should come to keep the passover unto the LORD God of Israel at Jerusalem: for they had not done it of a long time in such sort as it was written.

6 So the posts went with the letters from the king and his princes throughout all Israel and Judah, and according to the commandment of the king, saying, Ye children of Israel, turn again unto the LORD God of Abraham, Isaac, and Israel, and he will return to the remnant of you, that are escaped out of the hand of the kings of Assyria.

7 And be not ye like your fathers, and like your brethren, which trespassed against the LORD God of their fathers, who therefore gave them up to desolation, as ye see.

8 Now be ye not stiffnecked, as your fathers were, but yield yourselves unto the LORD, and enter into his sanctuary, which he hath sanctified for ever: and serve the LORD your God, that the fierceness of his wrath may turn away from you.

9 For if ye turn again unto the LORD, your brethren and your children shall find compassion before them that lead them captive, so that they shall come again into this land: for the LORD your God is gracious and merciful, and will not turn away his face from you, if ye return unto him.

10 So the posts passed from city to city, through the country of Ephraim and Manasseh, even unto Zebulun: but they laughed them to scorn, and mocked them.

11 Nevertheless, divers of Asher and Manasseh and of Zebulun humbled themselves, and came to Jerusalem.

12 Also in Judah the hand of God was to give them one heart to do the commandment of the king and of the princes, by the word of the LORD.

GOLDEN TEXT: The LORD your God is gracious and merciful, and will not turn away his face from you, if ye return unto him.—2 Chronicles 30:9.

Judgment and Exile
Unit 1: Urgent Plea
(Lessons 1-5)

Lesson Aims

After this lesson each student will be able to:

1. Tell how Hezekiah attempted to restore the Passover celebration for all Israel and the result of his efforts.

2. Explain why one's efforts to do the right thing are not always appreciated.

3. Commit to do this week something to share the gospel or otherwise honor the Lord even though unbelievers may oppose the effort.

Lesson Outline

INTRODUCTION
  A. Like and Unlike
  B. Lesson Background
I. PASSOVER RENEWED (2 Chronicles 30:1-4)
  A. Passover Called (v. 1)
  B. Passover Delayed (vv. 2-4)
II. PEOPLE INVITED (2 Chronicles 30:5-9)
  A. Extent of the Invitation (v. 5)
  B. Speed of the Invitation (v. 6a)
    New Methods, Timeless Message
  C. Content of the Invitation (vv. 6b-9)
III. PEOPLE RESPOND (2 Chronicles 30:10-12)
  A. Some With Scorn (v. 10)
    Satisfied With Substitutes
  B. Others With Acceptance (vv. 11, 12)
CONCLUSION
  A. Today's Drift
  B. Today's Need
  C. Prayer
  D. Thought to Remember

Introduction

A. Like and Unlike

"Like father, like son." That old adage is so often repeated and so often true that we may forget it can be false. I am the son of an Arizona farmer, but here I am writing lessons at a desk two thousand miles from the old home farm. Dad never wrote a Sunday school lesson. But yesterday on a downtown sidewalk I faced my reflection in a store window, and it was like coming face to face with Dad, who died many years ago. The hat, the face, the coat and tie, the shoulders stooped a little—it was Dad as I remember him. So am I like my father? In occupation, no. We

could hardly be more different. But in physical appearance, I am a photocopy. On a deeper level, my father's faith is my faith, and shall be till I die.

When we look at the kings of ancient Judah, we see them alike in ancestry and occupation. They are descendants of David and kings of Judah. Sometimes we see a king duplicating his father's faith and course of action as well. But sometimes we see a king forsaking his father's faith and deliberately revising his father's way of living and ruling.

B. Lesson Background

Students of Old Testament history remember that Solomon's magnificent empire was split when that king died (about 931 B.C.). It became two feeble little nations. Ten tribes, mostly in the north, kept the name of Israel. The tribes of Judah and Benjamin, with Jerusalem on the border between them, were known as Judah.

In Israel to the north, King Jeroboam I (reigned 931–910 B.C.) did not want his people to go to Jerusalem and worship with the people of Judah. He was afraid that the two nations would reunite and he would no longer be king. So he established centers of worship in his own domain, with golden calves as idols (1 Kings 12:26-33). In declaring them to be "thy gods, O Israel, which brought thee up out of the land of Egypt" (v. 28), King Jeroboam used words startlingly similar to those used by Aaron about five hundred years before! (See Exodus 32:4.) That northern kingdom sank deeper into idolatry and other sins.

Judah, for her part, wavered between the Lord and idols because different kings led in different ways. King Jotham was like his father, Uzziah (790–739 B.C.). Both "did that which was right in the sight of the Lord" (2 Chronicles 26:4; 27:2). But Jotham's son, Ahaz, was different. He did not do right; he made and worshiped idols; he killed his own children in sacrifice to an imaginary god (2 Chronicles 28:1-4).

When Ahaz died, his son Hezekiah (727–695 B.C.) became king and promptly reversed the wicked policies of his father. He reopened the Lord's temple that Ahaz had closed, having it cleaned and repaired. He gave no worship to idols, but restored worship of the Lord with abundant sacrifices and great rejoicing (2 Chronicles 29). This brings us to our printed text.

I. Passover Renewed
(2 Chronicles 30:1-4)

The Passover might be called the Jews' independence celebration, since it marks the anniversary of their release from slavery in Egypt. Having been in existence for over seven hundred years, this feast has been ignored during the sixteen-year reign of Ahaz because of that king's devotion to the imaginary gods of the pagans. Now Hezekiah intends to restore the Passover to its proper place in the life of the nation.

A. Passover Called (v. 1)

1. And Hezekiah sent to all Israel and Judah, and wrote letters also to Ephraim and Manasseh, that they should come to the house of the LORD at Jerusalem, to keep the passover unto the LORD God of Israel.

Roughly two hundred years have passed since ten of Israel's twelve tribes have stopped coming to *Jerusalem* to worship (1 Kings 12:26-33). By 732 B.C., the Assyrians have conquered "Gilead, and Galilee, all the land of Naphtali, and carried them captive to Assyria" (2 Kings 15:29). It is within this framework of religious decay and foreign threat that Hezekiah sends *to all Israel and Judah* an invitation to *keep the passover* feast at Jerusalem. Hezekiah longs to see old enmity forgotten, as all Israel once again worships *the Lord God of Israel* together. [See question #1, page 16.]

B. Passover Delayed (vv. 2-4)

2. For the king had taken counsel, and his princes, and all the congregation in Jerusalem, to keep the passover in the second month.

Hezekiah shows a great deal of prudence with his plan. In consulting *his princes* (government officials) *and all the congregation in Jerusalem* (at least the heads of the families in that city), the king acts neither hastily nor unilaterally. His consultations undoubtedly reveal that the regular, appointed time of the Passover is to be the fourteenth day of "the first month" (late March or early April to us), and is the beginning of the weeklong Feast of Unleavened Bread (Leviticus 23:5, 6). The Law further provided for an alternative date in the second month. If anyone is "unclean" at Passover time, or is far away on a long journey, that person may celebrate the Passover in the second month instead of the first (Numbers 9:9-11).

3, 4. For they could not keep it at that time, because the priests had not sanctified themselves sufficiently, neither had the people gathered themselves together to Jerusalem. And the thing pleased the king and all the congregation.

Thus the celebration was delayed a month because, first of all, *the priests had not sanctified themselves sufficiently.* When the cleansed temple is rededicated, there are not enough consecrated priests to offer the sacrifices (2 Chronicles 29:34). Hezekiah's respect for the holiness of God is such that it seems best to postpone the Passover until the priests are sanctified. After the reign of Hezekiah's wicked father, most of the

people as well as many of the priests are undoubtedly unclean in some way, and time will be required for them to sanctify themselves.

Second, the Passover cannot be celebrated at the regular time because *the people* have not *gathered themselves together to Jerusalem.* The decision to celebrate this feast must have been made while the temple was being cleaned in the first month of the first year of Hezekiah's reign (2 Chronicles 29:3-5). At that time, it was too late for invitations to be sent to all Israel and for the people to assemble at Jerusalem for a Passover in the first month. Delaying the Passover until the second month will provide time to "get the message out" regarding this upcoming celebration.

II. People Invited
(2 Chronicles 30:5-9)

As noted above, the Passover celebration is part of the Feast of Unleavened Bread (cf. Matthew 26:17). According to the Law, all adult male Israelites must be invited (cf. Deuteronomy 16:16). The godly Hezekiah makes sure this happens.

A. Extent of the Invitation (v. 5)

5. So they established a decree to make proclamation throughout all Israel, from Beer-sheba even to Dan, that they should come to keep the passover unto the LORD God of Israel at Jerusalem: for they had not done it of a long time in such sort as it was written.

Beer-sheba in the south and *Dan* in the north—about 150 miles apart—marked the limits of *all Israel* before the division of 931 B.C. The expression "from Dan even to Beer-sheba" is familiar as a designation for the entire Israelite people (e.g., 2 Samuel 3:10; 17:11; 24:2). The invitation is to be

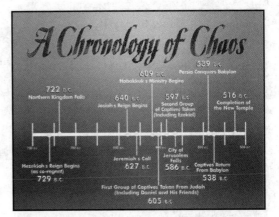

Visual for lesson 1. *Use this timeline from the Adult Visuals packet to help your students sort out the chronology of this quarter's studies.*

sent to all that territory, which now includes the two separate nations of Israel and Judah. Since *a long time* indicates roughly two hundred years, we wonder how much of any part of the *written* Word of God has been taught to the people during that period! [See question #2, page 16.]

B. Speed of the Invitation (v. 6a)

6a. So the posts went with the letters from the king and his princes throughout all Israel and Judah, and according to the commandment of the king.

The posts are swift couriers (cf. Job 9:25) who carry *the letters from the king and his princes* to every part of *Israel and Judah,* reading them in the streets and marketplaces of all the towns. There must be a great many of them to reach all the towns quickly, for now hardly a month remains until the Passover time in the second month. In Judah, the king invites his own people to come to the Passover. In Israel, Hezekiah bypasses the feeble king and makes his appeal directly to the people. [See question #3, page 16.]

NEW METHODS, TIMELESS MESSAGE

"Neither snow nor rain nor gloom of night stays these couriers from the swift completion of their appointed rounds." These words, inscribed on the New York City General Post Office building, are those of Herodotus, the ancient Greek. They describe the fidelity of the mounted postal carriers that served the Persian empire under Cyrus, about 500 B.C. Mounted couriers, trains, trucks, and planes have all been used to carry personal mail, government information, newspapers, magazines, and news of every sort. Now, with the advent of speed-of-light E-mail, these methods have all become "snail mail."

No longer do missionaries have to wrestle with the vagaries of international phone service or wait days and weeks for mail from their prayer partners and supporters. E-mail lets them communicate almost instantaneously.

There is a downside to this: anyone can send out any kind of message he wants. E-mail hoaxes are legion. Our penchant for speed tempts us to pay less attention to truth than we ought.

The message brought by Hezekiah's couriers wasn't as fast as E-mail, but it was true. In keeping with God's plea to His people in every age they said, "Return to God and He will bless you." Methods of communicating God's Word may change, but the message is timeless. —C. R. B.

C. Content of the Invitation (vv. 6b-9)

6b. Saying, Ye children of Israel, turn again unto the LORD God of Abraham, Isaac, and Israel, and he will return to the remnant of you, that are escaped out of the hand of the kings of Assyria.

This is more than an invitation to a feast. It is nothing less than a call to forsake idolatry and *turn again unto the Lord God,* the real God, the God of their ancestors. Already *the kings of Assyria* have conquered a substantial part of Israel's territory, taking captive many of the Israelites (2 Kings 15:29). In making a promise to the *remnant* Israelites that God would *return* to them if they *turn again* to Him, Hezekiah sets a theme that will be echoed frequently by the prophets (cf. Isaiah 31:6; Jeremiah 3:12; Joel 2:13; and others).

7. And be not ye like your fathers, and like your brethren, which trespassed against the LORD God of their fathers, who therefore gave them up to desolation, as ye see.

The Israelites who have escaped capture so far can *see* with their own eyes the *desolation* that has come at the hand of the Assyrians. This has come about because the Israelites have *trespassed against the Lord God of their fathers.* Will the remaining Israelites heed this "visual aid" and not repeat the sin that has brought it about?

8. Now be ye not stiffnecked, as your fathers were, but yield yourselves unto the LORD, and enter into his sanctuary, which he hath sanctified for ever: and serve the LORD your God, that the fierceness of his wrath may turn away from you.

The Old Testament refers to the Israelite people as *stiffnecked,* stubborn, or obstinate more than thirty times (also cf. Acts 7:51). This type of attitude toward God always leads to destruction.

The only way to prevent the pending destruction will be for the Israelites to *yield* themselves to the Lord. The starting point on this road back to God is to come to the Passover and *enter into his sanctuary,* the temple in Jerusalem. The Passover was one of three pilgrimage feasts adult Israelite

---

How to Say It

AHAZ. *Ay*-haz.
ASSYRIA. Uh-*sear*-ee-uh.
BEER-SHEBA. Beer-*she*-buh.
CYRUS. *Sigh*-russ.
EPHRAIM. *Ee*-fray-im.
GALILEE. *Gal*-uh-lee.
GILEAD. *Gil*-ee-ud.
HERODOTUS. Heh-*rod*-uh-tus.
HEZEKIAH. Hez-ih-*kye*-uh.
JEROBOAM. Jair-uh-*boe*-um.
JOTHAM. *Jo*-thum.
MANASSEH. Muh-*nass*-uh.
NAPHTALI. Naf-*tuh*-lye.
SEURAT. Suh-*raw*.
UZZIAH. Uh-*zye*-uh.
ZEBULUN. *Zeb*-you-lun.

males were to keep each year. (The Feast of Weeks, later known as Pentecost, and the Feast of Tabernacles were the others; Deuteronomy 16:1-17). To go to all the trouble to make the pilgrimage to observe the Passover will demonstrate action coupled with repentant faith. [See question #4, page 16.]

9. For if ye turn again unto the LORD, your brethren and your children shall find compassion before them that lead them captive, so that they shall come again into this land: for the LORD your God is gracious and merciful, and will not turn away his face from you, if ye return unto him.

The letter now returns to the promise of verse 6b. Since *the Lord your God is gracious and merciful,* He would rather bless than punish. He will not turn away from the Israelites if they *return unto him* with genuine worship and faithful obedience. If they will do that, even those already in captivity will be set free again.

III. People Respond
(2 Chronicles 30:10-12)

Drastic proposals can draw mixed responses— and it is certainly a drastic change that Hezekiah advocates. The people now living to the north in Israel have never attended a Passover celebration in Jerusalem. For generations, their government has promoted a state religion with worship centers at Bethel and Dan (1 Kings 12:26-33). Besides that, pagan worship has increased rapidly, especially during the infamous reign of Ahab (1 Kings 16:30-33).

A. Some With Scorn (v. 10)

10. So the posts passed from city to city, through the country of Ephraim and Manasseh, even unto Zebulun: but they laughed them to scorn, and mocked them.

As the *posts* travel from *Ephraim* to *Manasseh* to *Zebulun,* they are moving extensively throughout Israel, progressively northward. Asher (v. 11) is the northernmost of the tribal territories. King Hezekiah is serious that all Israelites be invited.

But in Israel the usual response to the invitation is *scorn* and ridicule. That is not surprising, for people of that area regard Judah as an enemy. They remember the bloody war in the time of King Ahaz. Israel and Syria had formed an alliance to oppose the growing might of Assyria and had tried to conquer Judah to add her to their coalition. They had failed, and that had made them hate Judah all the more. Now they howl in derision when they hear the king of Judah's invitation to come and join his people in worship.

If we take our stand for God and His Word, for Christ and the church, for right instead of wrong, we too can expect to be answered with scorn and

ridicule. People who like the drift away from God will despise us. [See question #5, page 16.]

SATISFIED WITH SUBSTITUTES

Since 1933, the community of Laguna Beach, California, has held an annual *Pageant of the Masters,* an art festival that uses live mannequins to recreate the great paintings and sculptures of the Western world. The subjects appear motionless in life-size reproductions of the art works, and are otherwise indistinguishable from the originals.

Hundreds of works have been presented, ranging from Leonardo da Vinci's *Last Supper* to Seurat's famous *A Sunday on La Grand Jatte* and even the familiar World War II photograph of the American flag being raised on Iwo Jima.

At each presentation from early in July to Labor Day, forty living reproductions are displayed at two-minute intervals. In recent summers, as many as 150,000 people have attended, many of whom probably would decline the opportunity to see the real art works!

For two centuries the people of the northern kingdom of Israel had forsaken worship of the true God. Now they were invited to attend the real thing, but their response was mixed. In worship and in art, apparently the imitation may seem more interesting than the genuine article. Does our worship indicate that we prefer religious substitutes just as ancient Israel did? Or do we continually seek for a more genuine relationship with our God?   —C. R. B.

B. Others With Acceptance (vv. 11, 12)

11. Nevertheless, divers of Asher and Manasseh and of Zebulun humbled themselves, and came to Jerusalem.

The antique English word *divers* is an adjective that means "various" or "diverse." Here it is used substantively to mean "some men," which is a more literal translation of the Hebrew word used. Apparently, the history of the nation has been passed from father to son through the generations in at least some of the households of the northern kingdom. Such households, in remaining loyal to the one true God, welcome the revival of the Passover and humbly go *to Jerusalem* to join in the worship of the Lord.

If we take our stand for God and against the drift away from Him, we shall not be surprised by the contemptuous hoots of the drifters; but we may be surprised to see how many quiet, thoughtful people will join us! [See question #6, page 16.]

12. Also in Judah the hand of God was to give them one heart to do the commandment of the king and of the princes, by the word of the LORD.

Now the focus shifts to the southern kingdom. Although the call to observe the Passover is issued by *the king* and his *princes*, it is ultimately according to *the word of the Lord*. Guided by *the hand of God*, the people of *Judah* are more unanimous in answering that call than those of the northern kingdom. And so they pour into Jerusalem at the appointed time in the second month. They are so delighted to have the Passover back that they continue the celebration for fourteen days instead of the legal seven (2 Chronicles 30:13-26). There is a precedent for such an extension in King Solomon's dedication of the temple, held in conjunction with the Feast of Tabernacles (7:9).

Conclusion

"History repeats itself." How many times that old adage has been verified by actual events! In Old Testament history, nothing is plainer than the repeated drift of God's people away from Him—and every such drift brings disaster (cf. Judges 2:6-19). No less plain are the many times when God's drifting people turn back to Him, and every return brings spiritual peace and joy. How much better it is never to drift in the first place!

A. Today's Drift

Our time is seeing a drift away from God in the European and American nations that once were called Christian. Don't you know some people who proudly run their own lives without any help from God, the Bible, or the church? Perhaps you know one or two who angrily denounce God and the Bible. The drift is seen in increasing tolerance for foul language, dirty jokes, pornography, adultery, and promiscuous sex. It is seen in churches run by men with no respect for God and His Word. It is seen in people you see as you drive to church on Sunday morning—people raking leaves in their yards, people working on their cars, people leaving home with picnic baskets. It is seen in the removal of the Ten Commandments from public places where they were posted. It is seen in the prohibition of prayer in public schools. It is seen in the clever theories that are invented to explain the origin and development of the world and the living things in it—theories that try to discredit the Genesis record.

B. Today's Need

The solution to this drift is an army of modern-day Hezekiahs to turn people and nations back to God. We need millions of Christians who make no secret of their distaste for what is obscene and evil. But more than opposition to evil, we need adherence to good. We need millions of Christians to proclaim, by what they say and what they do, the goodness of God, the truth of the Bible, and the glory of doing right. Are you one of those millions we need?

Perhaps your congregation already has a group that can spearhead a drive to bring more people to the Lord, to His church, and to doing right. It may be the elders or the elders and deacons. It may be called the committee on evangelism or the ministry of outreach. If such a group is really committed to the task of evangelism and actively working at it, others can be enlisted in the effort.

When a Christian is asked to become a winner of souls, a frequent answer is "I don't know how." And it's true; he doesn't know how. Would he like to learn? Would your minister like to collect a few eager learners and conduct an intensive course on personal evangelism, meeting every evening for a week or two weeks?

It is (again) time for the church to be serious about turning people from darkness to light, and from the power of Satan unto God (Acts 26:18).

C. Prayer

Forgive us, Father, if we have been drifting. Give us vigor of heart and boldness of spirit to hold forth the word of life to those who are lost in the way of death. In Jesus' name, amen.

D. Thought to Remember

"We must pay more careful attention, therefore, to what we have heard, so that we do not drift away" (Hebrews 2:1, *New International Version*).

Home Daily Bible Readings

Monday, Aug. 26—Hezekiah Calls for Renewal (2 Chronicles 29:1-11)

Tuesday, Aug. 27—Purify and Consecrate (2 Chronicles 29:15-24)

Wednesday, Aug. 28—The People Worship (2 Chronicles 29:25-30)

Thursday, Aug. 29—Sing to the Lord (Psalm 149:1-9)

Friday, Aug. 30—The People Bring Thank Offerings (2 Chronicles 29:31-36)

Saturday, Aug. 31—The People Celebrate Passover (2 Chronicles 30:1-12)

Sunday, Sept. 1—God Hears the People's Prayer (2 Chronicles 30:21-27)

Learning by Doing

This page contains an alternative lesson plan emphasizing learning activities.
Classes desiring such student involvement will find these suggestions helpful.

Learning Goals

After participating in this lesson, each student will be able to:

1. Tell how Hezekiah attempted to restore the Passover celebration for all Israel and the result of his efforts.

2. Explain why one's efforts to do the right thing are not always appreciated.

3. Commit this week to do something to share the gospel or otherwise honor the Lord even though unbelievers may oppose the effort.

Into the Lesson

Prior to this week's lesson, think about some item that has been restored: such items as an automobile that has been in an accident, a broken chair, a broken watch or clock, or even a tarnished silverware set. Take "before" and "after" pictures to the class, or take the object.

Begin this class by asking whether any of the students ever have had a piece of furniture or a broken item restored. Encourage members to share what was wrong with the item, how it ended up in that condition, and what was needed to restore it. After several have shared their "restoration stories," tell about and show the item you had restored. Say, "Several of us have experienced taking a broken or old item and restoring it. Today in our lesson text, we find King Hezekiah attempting to restore a broken practice among Israel and Judah. Turn to 2 Chronicles 30:1-12 and let's discover what was needed to restore it to its original purpose and glory."

Into the Word

Ask a student to read the lesson text aloud. Prior to class prepare a worksheet with questions to answer, and make a copy for each student. After the reading of the text, give a copy to each. Ask the class to work in pairs to answer the following questions:

1. What two reasons kept the Passover from being celebrated during the first month? *(The priests had not sanctified themselves sufficiently; the people had not gathered in Jerusalem, v. 3).*

2. How was the decision to celebrate the Passover made? *(King Hezekiah, after having the temple cleansed and repaired, consulted with his princes and all the congregation in Jerusalem. They established a decree, vv. 2, 5).*

3. How was the invitation to come to Jerusalem to keep the Passover communicated? *(Letters were written with the king's proclamation; the posts or couriers carried the letters and proclaimed this call to repentance, vv. 1, 6).*

4. Describe how their fathers had responded to the Lord and how that led to their desolation and captivity by Assyria. *(They trespassed against the Lord, v. 7; they were stiff-necked, v. 8).*

5. What did the proclamation call the people to do to restore the practice? *(Turn to the Lord, v. 6; yield themselves to the Lord, enter into His sanctuary, and serve Him, v. 8).*

6. What was the people's response to the king's proclamation? *(In Israel, they laughed and mocked; yet many humbled themselves and came to Jerusalem, vv. 10, 11; Judah had one heart to do the commandment, v. 12.)*

After giving the class time, ask for their answers. State: "Here was a religious practice neglected by the people. Even though they knew what to do, and when to do it, they failed to celebrate the Passover. In the same way, people neglect religious practices today, even people within the church." Ask the following questions:

1. What practices do religious people neglect today? *(Possible answers: prayer before meals; personal prayer and devotional times; attendance in worship or Bible study; personal fasting.)*

2. Why do people neglect these practices? *(Lack of time and commitment; don't see the value; pride.)*

3. Why are one's efforts to do the right thing not always appreciated by others? *(Possible answers: the others don't want to change; they ridicule because they feel guilty.)*

Into Life

State: "Now that we've understood this lesson text, let's see how it applies to us. This proclamation by King Hezekiah was a call to repentance and renewal, a call to restore the broken relationship with and personal worship of God. Think of a practice neglected in your life. Verse 9 reminds us that the Lord is gracious and merciful and that, if we humble ourselves and seek to restore our relationship with God, He will not turn His face away from us." Allow a few minutes for silent prayers of commitment to do something this week even though unbelievers may ridicule the effort. Close with an audible prayer.

Let's Talk It Over

The questions on this page are designed to promote discussion of the lesson by the class and to encourage application of the lesson Scriptures. The answers provided are only discussion starters. Let your class talk it over from there.

1. How much power or influence would a person need in order to inspire our nation to come back to God? Would this person likely be an elected official? A religious leader? A leader of some kind of grassroots movement? Why?

Name and discuss individuals and groups who have had a positive spiritual impact on our nation or in the world in the past fifty years. Consider political leaders (presidents, prime ministers, and those of lesser rank), religious leaders, civil rights leaders, and others. Include also local people of influence—schoolteachers, respected business people, or others in your own community. In reviewing how and why they were/are effective, think together about ways the church can help raise up spiritual leaders for the next fifty years.

2. In 2 Chronicles 30:5 we read that for a long time the Israelites had not observed the Passover "in such sort as it was written." In other words, they had not followed the Scriptures in their practice. How would you go about changing some long-standing tradition in your church if you became convinced the practice was not in harmony with the Word of God?

Some people will want to do nothing and allow the tradition to continue. That's the easy way out, easily justified by thinking the change is harmless. Others will want to launch a vehement crusade against the practice, painting all who want to keep it as "liberals" or "heretics." Rather, one should speak the truth in love, making a case for the biblical pattern without impugning people's motives. One could begin by asking questions, encouraging dialogue, and giving much prayer to the issue. Change is never easy, so much patience will be needed. A humble spirit is also necessary—sometimes a person might think a practice unbiblical and later find out he or she was wrong. What then?

3. If you could write a letter to the younger generation in your country to urge them to turn to the Lord, what would you write?

There was a time when the meetings of the church were also the only thing going on in the community. But times have changed. Still, young people can often be enlisted in a cause if they think their efforts can really change something.

Discuss potential methods or projects the church can adopt that would appeal to young people to become involved in church and in doing something meaningful to meet the needs in the community. (Do not just list what "should" work; include those that actually do work.)

4. Spiritually, Hezekiah was unlike his father but more like his faithful grandfather and great-grandfather. Name some people who have influenced you to choose God's way. How can we help people—especially young people—to choose to follow the positive role models in their lives and not the negative ones?

Help your students explore the ways people are influenced within families as well as the family factors that open the door to outside influence. They might note the problem of parents who are too busy to spend time with the children or whose own lifestyles and priorities are not in harmony with Scripture. Perhaps these can be contrasted with parents who consistently teach and model faith, take time to listen to their children, and lead in family devotions. Include 2 Timothy 1:5 in the discussion. Brainstorm on ways the church can equip parents and youth sponsors for effective spiritual teaching.

5. What does it take for a group to be spiritually faithful, maintain quality worship, and continue to reach out when their neighbors are responding with scorn and ridicule? How can the church teach members to stand strong today?

In response to persecution, many groups cluster away out of the public's eye. Yet in places like China, the church grows in spite of attacks against it. Compare the response by the faithful in the text with the way the church can respond in the face of today's subtle and open ridicule.

6. Hezekiah gave the people enough time to prepare themselves for acceptable worship. What preparation should Christians make in order to be ready for worship?

At various points in history, just attending church was an acceptable goal. It gave prestige or an appearance of goodness. Have the class discuss the difference between "attending" and "worshiping." Consider these verses: 1 Chronicles 29:3, Psalm 27:4; John 4:24; 1 Corinthians 11:23-30.

God Restores a Sinner

DEVOTIONAL READING: 2 Chronicles 6: 36-42.

BACKGROUND SCRIPTURE: 2 Chronicles 33:1-20; 2 Kings 21.

PRINTED TEXT: 2 Chronicles 33:1-13.

2 Chronicles 33:1-13

1 Manasseh was twelve years old when he began to reign, and he reigned fifty and five years in Jerusalem:

2 But did that which was evil in the sight of the LORD, like unto the abominations of the heathen, whom the LORD had cast out before the children of Israel.

3 For he built again the high places which Hezekiah his father had broken down, and he reared up altars for Baalim, and made groves, and worshipped all the host of heaven, and served them.

4 Also he built altars in the house of the LORD, whereof the LORD had said, In Jerusalem shall my name be for ever.

5 And he built altars for all the host of heaven in the two courts of the house of the LORD.

6 And he caused his children to pass through the fire in the valley of the son of Hinnom: also he observed times, and used enchantments, and used witchcraft, and dealt with a familiar spirit, and with wizards: he wrought much evil in the sight of the LORD, to provoke him to anger.

7 And he set a carved image, the idol which he had made, in the house of God, of which God had said to David and to Solomon his son, In this house, and in Jerusalem, which I have chosen before all the tribes of Israel, will I put my name for ever:

8 Neither will I any more remove the foot of Israel from out of the land which I have appointed for your fathers; so that they will take heed to do all that I have commanded them, according to the whole law and the statutes and the ordinances by the hand of Moses.

9 So Manasseh made Judah and the inhabitants of Jerusalem to err, and to do worse than the heathen, whom the LORD had destroyed before the children of Israel.

10 And the LORD spake to Manasseh, and to his people: but they would not hearken.

11 Wherefore the LORD brought upon them the captains of the host of the king of Assyria, which took Manasseh among the thorns, and bound him with fetters, and carried him to Babylon.

12 And when he was in affliction, he besought the LORD his God, and humbled himself greatly before the God of his fathers,

13 And prayed unto him: and he was entreated of him, and heard his supplication, and brought him again to Jerusalem into his kingdom. Then Manasseh knew that the LORD he was God.

GOLDEN TEXT: [Manasseh] prayed unto [God]: and he was entreated of him, and heard his supplication, and brought him again to Jerusalem into his kingdom. Then Manasseh knew that the LORD he was God.—2 Chronicles 33:13.

Lesson Aims

After participating in this lesson, each student will be able to:

1. Summarize the evil reign of Manasseh and how he finally came to repentance.

2. Compare the turnaround in Manasseh's life with similar changes in the lives of others.

3. Identify a co-worker, family member, neighbor, or other acquaintance who has no interest in God, Christ, or the church, and commit to praying for that person to come to repentance.

Lesson Outline

INTRODUCTION
  A. Quick Switches and Flip-flops
  B. Lesson Background
  I. ACCESSION OF THE KING (2 Chronicles 33:1, 2)
     A. A Boy King (v. 1)
     B. A Bad King (v. 2)
        "Going Zoom!"
 II. SINS OF THE KING (2 Chronicles 33:3-9)
     A. Idolatry (v. 3)
     B. Desecration of the Temple (vv. 4, 5)
     C. Human Sacrifice (v. 6a)
     D. Superstition and Witchcraft (v. 6b)
        Anyone for Witchcraft?
     E. More Desecration of the Temple (vv. 7, 8)
     F. Summary of Evil (v. 9)
III. REFORMS OF THE KING (2 Chronicles 33:10-13)
     A. Warning to the King (v. 10)
     B. Capture of the King (v. 11)
     C. Repentance of the King (v. 12)
     D. Release of the King (v. 13)
CONCLUSION
  A. Business Disaster
  B. Marriage Disaster
  C. Prayer
  D. Thought to Remember

Introduction

A. Quick Switches and Flip-flops

Last week we began by considering the time-worn maxim, "Like father, like son." It is often true, but not always. The history of ancient Judah presents a number of quick switches from good to bad or bad to good when the crown passed from father to son. Jotham had been a good king (2 Chronicles 27:1, 2), but his son Ahaz was bad (28:1, 2). Then Ahaz's son Hezekiah switched as quickly to good (29:1, 2). Today we see yet another quick switch.

In addition to such quick switches, there are some notable flip-flops. For many years Uzziah was one of the best of kings (26:3, 4). But success went to his head to the point that he became unfaithful and tried to usurp the role of the priests (26:16). For that the Lord struck him with leprosy so that he had to live in isolation the rest of his days (26:17-21). What a flip-flop!

B. Lesson Background

Last week we saw the godliness of Hezekiah. Although he suffered the temporary failings of poor judgment (2 Kings 20:12-18) and pride (2 Chronicles 32:24-26), he never faltered in his devotion to God (2 Kings 18:5, 6). His son Manasseh, at the age of twelve, quickly switched the policy of the government from good to evil. But as we shall discover in today's lesson, certain events in Manasseh's life led to a tremendous flip-flop from evil to good toward the end.

I. Accession of the King (2 Chronicles 33:1, 2)

When an ancient kingship passed from father to son, sometimes it fell to a minor child quite unprepared to rule a nation. Manasseh inherits the crown when he is only twelve, and his grandson Josiah receives it when he is only eight (2 Chronicles 34:1). Such children do not rule without powerful help.

A. A Boy King (v. 1)

1. Manasseh was twelve years old when he began to reign, and he reigned fifty and five years in Jerusalem.

Manasseh begins his reign in about 695 B.C. This is about seventeen years after the northern kingdom of Israel was taken into exile by the Assyrians, and about 110 years before his own people will be carried off by the Babylonians. Beginning so early in life, he has a long time to rule. Unfortunately, he rules badly (sinfully) for much of that time.

B. A Bad King (v. 2)

2. But did that which was evil in the sight of the LORD, like unto the abominations of the heathen, whom the LORD had cast out before the children of Israel.

Who is the "power behind the throne" that guides the twelve-year-old boy as he sets the course of his kingdom? Perhaps Manasseh is tutored by corrupt priests left over from the time of his evil grandfather Ahaz (2 Chronicles 28:1, 2). Perhaps evil politicians from that same time cleverly manage to win the confidence of the growing boy. Ultimately, we simply do not know. But surely Manasseh is not guided by the best advisers of his godly father, King Hezekiah. [See question #1, page 24.]

"GOING ZOOM!"

A three-year-old boy in Florida took the family car for a "joyride" a few years ago, and authorities remain puzzled as to how he managed it. The boy was only two-and-a-half feet tall, so how he was able to reach the gas pedal and still steer the car is a mystery.

Well, it must be admitted that his steering wasn't so good: on a journey that lasted less than a half-mile, he ran into three cars. Fortunately, no one was hurt.

In the middle of the night, he had climbed up on top of a five-foot-high dresser in his parents' bedroom without waking them. He then took the car keys and went on his little excursion. Perhaps we should give him high marks for creativity and ambition, at least. When he was caught, his explanation of what happened was, "I go zoom!"

Manasseh was a few years older than the Florida youngster was when he became king. He took Judah on a wild ride, leaving a trail of wreckage—both spiritual and moral—in his path. His immaturity kept him from understanding the consequences of "zooming" off on such a dangerous course. His adult advisors probably bear some blame for this. Good advice might have prevented this "accident." How can we exert a positive influence over the young people whom God has entrusted to our care?　—C. R. B.

II. Sins of the King
(2 Chronicles 33:3-9)

Seven of the thirteen verses in our text detail the extent and magnitude of the evil practices of King Manasseh and the nation he ruled. What a breathtaking turnaround from the godly rule of his father, Hezekiah! (See 2 Chronicles 29:1, 2.)

A. Idolatry (v. 3)

3. For he built again the high places which Hezekiah his father had broken down, and he reared up altars for Baalim, and made groves, and worshipped all the host of heaven, and served them.

The *high places* are places of worship, usually on hilltops. At times, people had worshiped the Lord in such places, but King Ahaz and his followers had worshiped idols there. King *Hezekiah*, for his part, had destroyed their altars and other

Visual for lesson 2

Use this chart from the Adult Visuals *packet to summarize the theme of each lesson this quarter.*

furnishings, making them unfit for any kind of worship (2 Kings 18:4).

Now Manasseh rebuilds the things his father had destroyed, and he devotes them to the worship of *Baalim*, idols representing an imaginary god called Baal (meaning "lord"). Most Christian scholars now agree that what the *King James Version* calls *groves* were simple poles erected beside the altars that were dedicated to Baal. Those poles represented an imaginary goddess (Asherah) associated with Baal. He also encourages the worship of stars and other celestial bodies—*the host of heaven*—which many centuries before Moses had specifically forbidden (Deuteronomy 4:19). By Manasseh's time, the northern kingdom of Israel has already been carried away into captivity for committing such evil (2 Kings 17:16), but the Judean king somehow "misses the message" there.

B. Desecration of the Temple (vv. 4, 5)

4. Also he built altars in the house of the LORD, whereof the LORD had said, In Jerusalem shall my name be for ever.

The house of the Lord is the magnificent temple Solomon had built *in Jerusalem* centuries earlier. The Lord had accepted it and had promised to put His *name* there forever (1 Kings 9:3). One of its main features was a massive altar where sacrifices had been offered to the Lord (2 Chronicles 4:1). But now Manasseh adds other *altars* for sacrifices to imaginary gods.

5. And he built altars for all the host of heaven in the two courts of the house of the LORD.

The temple has a big courtyard where anyone, Jew or pagan, could enter. It also features a smaller courtyard where only Jews are admitted. Manasseh puts *altars* for star worshipers in both of those *courts*.

C. Human Sacrifice (v. 6a)

6a. And he caused his children to pass through the fire in the valley of the son of Hinnom.

The valley of the son of Hinnom (or "Ben Hinnom") is the ravine outside the south wall of Jerusalem that serves as part of the boundary between two tribes (Joshua 15:8). The valley also serves as a center for worship of the imaginary god called Molech, a favorite idol of the Ammonites (cf. 1 Kings 11:7). A feature of their worship is the gruesome sacrifice of their own *children,* whom they burn with *fire.* The Lord, in speaking to Moses, had condemned this hideous practice vigorously (Leviticus 18:21; 20:1-5); but now Manasseh not only encourages it, he even sacrifices some of *his* own children. [See question #2, page 24.]

Later, the Lord declares that this infamous valley will come to be known as "the valley of slaughter" when the Babylonians come to sack Jerusalem (Jeremiah 19:5, 6). In New Testament Greek, "Ben Hinnom" becomes "gehenna," and is used by Jesus as a description for Hell (Matthew 5:29, 30).

D. Superstition and Witchcraft (v. 6b)

6b. Also he observed times, and used enchantments, and used witchcraft, and dealt with a familiar spirit, and with wizards: he wrought much evil in the sight of the LORD, to provoke him to anger.

All these terms taken together tell us that Manasseh practices the superstitions and magical arts the pagans use to contact the spirit world in order to predict or control future events. The *New International Version* says Manasseh "practiced sorcery, divination and witchcraft, and consulted mediums and spiritists."

Saul, Israel's first king, had banished such practitioners from Israel hundreds of years before (cf. 1 Samuel 28); but they did not disappear. Saul himself was able to find one on the eve of the battle that cost him his life.

All these pagan practices are forbidden to God's people (Deuteronomy 18:9-13). Practicing that which the Lord specifically forbids is a sure way to arouse His *anger!*

ANYONE FOR WITCHCRAFT?

Have you ever been caught in traffic when you were in a rush and it seemed the traffic signals stayed red a lot longer than they should have? Dorothy Morrison says a little "white magic" witchcraft can help! In her book *Everyday Magic,* Morrison (a so-called "Third Degree Wiccan High Priestess") suggests that you "focus on the red color of the light and inhale deeply, pulling the color in with your breath. Then exhale fully in

green, directing your breath at the bottom globe of the traffic light. The light will change to green." She also suggests trying this chant:

> *Gods of Movement and of flow*
> *Ease this mess that causes woe.*
> *Move these cars along their way*
> *And keep traffic moving through the day.*
> *Do this quickly—hurry, please—*
> *By winds of change, this traffic ease.*

The book also has chants and herbal potions for a good marriage, getting a friend to forgive you, and even for making your car get better fuel mileage. It lists dozens of deities and their specific areas of expertise (e.g., the book claims that there are nine gods that specialize in computers and peripherals).

Most of us probably are tempted to think that Manasseh's sin of dabbling in idolatry, witchcraft, and sorcery was a quaint relic of a much less enlightened age than ours. But this book of modern witchcraft is just one of a multitude to which modern Westerners are turning for spiritual assistance. It is no less a sin in our time than it was in Manasseh's.   —C. R. B.

E. More Desecration of the Temple (vv. 7, 8)

7. And he set a carved image, the idol which he had made, in the house of God, of which God had said to David and to Solomon his son, In this house, and in Jerusalem, which I have chosen before all the tribes of Israel, will I put my name for ever.

Manasseh wants the Lord to accept an *idol*—a dead lump of stone or wood or clay—as a housemate. What an insult to the living God! It implies that He is no better than that lump. Manasseh has forgotten the uniqueness of the temple and of the God who sanctified it. When Solomon completed the construction of the temple, "the glory of the Lord filled the house" (2 Chronicles 7:1). Later the Lord appeared to Solomon in a dream and told him that He had "chosen this place to myself [and to no other] . . . that my name may be there for ever: and mine eyes and mine heart shall be there perpetually" (2 Chronicles 7:12, 16).

8. Neither will I any more remove the foot of Israel from out of the land which I have appointed for your fathers; so that they will take heed to do all that I have commanded them, according to the whole law and the statutes and the ordinances by the hand of Moses.

This is not the first time that God promises to keep the people of *Israel* in *the land* He has given them (cf. Deuteronomy 28). But God does not say He will do that regardless of what the people do. Where we see the words *so that* in our text, read "if only." That is a better translation of the Hebrew, and it appears as such in several major English translations. God promises to keep His people in the land He has given them "if only" they will obey Him (1 Kings 9:1-9; 2 Chronicles 7:19-22). However, if God's people continue in the way Manasseh is leading, they surely will be removed from their homeland.

F. Summary of Evil (v. 9)

9. So Manasseh made Judah and the inhabitants of Jerusalem to err, and to do worse than the heathen, whom the Lord had destroyed before the children of Israel.

King Manasseh's activities are about as sinful as they can possibly be. But even worse is the example he sets as a leader for people to follow (cf. Luke 17:1, 2). How incredible to read that God's own people are actually *worse than the* pagans! Several small nations had lived in the land of Canaan before Israel had come there from Egypt. Those nations had been too wicked to be allowed to live any longer. Israel had been God's tool to destroy them. Now *Judah and the inhabitants of Jerusalem* have become worse than the nations that had lived there before. How, then, can *the children of Israel* live? [See question #3, page 24.]

III. Reforms of the King
(2 Chronicles 33:10-13)

The Lord does not want to destroy the last remaining fragment of the people of Abraham. He wants to preserve them as a separate and easily identifiable group until they bring a blessing to the whole world as God had promised Abraham (Genesis 22:18). Even in the depth of their depravity, He sets about to reform them.

A. Warning to the King (v. 10)

10. And the Lord spake to Manasseh, and to his people: but they would not hearken.

First God tries to reason with the sinners, to help them see that what they are doing will bring destruction. We are not told how He speaks, and it does not appear that any of the prophets known to us are active at that time. But God has had many prophets of which we know nothing. Perhaps some of them are giving God's warning. But king and people do *not hearken*.

B. Capture of the King (v. 11)

11. Wherefore the Lord brought upon them the captains of the host of the king of Assyria, which took Manasseh among the thorns, and bound him with fetters, and carried him to Babylon.

Often the Lord accomplishes His purposes by using people who do not believe in Him, people

who do not want to help Him, people who have no idea they are helping Him. Before this time, He used the Assyrians to destroy the northern nation of Israel (2 Kings 17:6-23). He had defended the southern kingdom, Judah, because good King Hezekiah was leading it in righteousness (2 Kings 19:35, 36). But now He does not stop the Assyrians from invading Judah and capturing King Manasseh and making an example of him. The phrase *among the thorns* seems to refer to some item of weaponry or fetters that the Assyrians used to humiliate or torture Manasseh. [See question #4, page 24.]

C. Repentance of the King (v. 12)

12. And when he was in affliction, he besought the Lord his God, and humbled himself greatly before the God of his fathers.

Manasseh the king had been an evil tyrant; Manasseh the prisoner is a humble worshiper of *God*. What a flip-flop—and what an improvement! But how much better it would have been for everyone if Manasseh could have learned such humility without the hard lesson of capture. [See question #5, page 24.]

D. Release of the King (v. 13)

13. And prayed unto him: and he was entreated of him, and heard his supplication, and brought him again to Jerusalem into his kingdom. Then Manasseh knew that the Lord he was God.

The Lord hears Manasseh's prayer and answers it. Somehow—we are not told the details—He secures this captive's release and brings him back to his home and to his throne. Assyrian inscriptions mention *Manasseh* by name and also reveal

---

How to Say It

AHAZ. *Ay*-haz.
AMMONITES. *Am*-un-ites.
ASHERAH. Uh-*she*-ruh.
ASSYRIA. Uh-*sear*-ee-uh.
BAAL. *Bay*-ul.
BAALIM. Bay-uh-*leem*.
CANAAN. *Kay*-nun.
GEHENNA. Geh-*hen*-uh (*G* as in *get*).
HEZEKIAH. Hez-ih-*kye*-uh.
HINNOM. *Hin*-um.
JOSIAH. Jo-*sigh*-uh.
JOTHAM. *Jo*-thum.
MANASSEH. Muh-*nass*-uh.
MOLECH. *Mo*-lek.
PHARAOH NECO. *Fay*-ro *nee*-ko.
UZZIAH. Uh-*zye*-uh.
WICCAN. *Wih*-kun.

a parallel case where they sent Pharaoh Neco back to his own throne in Egypt.

Undoubtedly, Manasseh pledges some cooperation with the Assyrians and agrees to pay tribute as part of his release agreement. Regardless of that, the king is a changed man spiritually. He knows *that the Lord* is *God* and that idols are worthless. The king demonstrates the change by material and spiritual rebuilding projects (vv. 14-17). In so doing, he tries to correct the evil he has done and to make the people of Judah again the people of God.

Manasseh's repentance, however, is ultimately a case of "too little, too late" in terms of the sobering *results* that his earlier, sinful actions continue to have on the nation of Judah. As events in Judah and Jerusalem unfold, the evil that Manasseh has done will outweigh any correction that he tries to bring about (see 2 Kings 24:3, 4 and Jeremiah 15:4).

Conclusion

Manasseh's capture is ultimately the best thing that ever happened to him. It makes him into the man God wants him to be. More than that, it puts the nation of Judah back on the path where God wants her to be, even if only temporarily.

A. Business Disaster

Prosperity was high in Milltown. About half of its employed people worked for the mill, the town's only industry. There was plenty of overtime work for as many employees as wanted it. Business was also booming at Murphy's little hardware store, and Murphy built a fine new home for his family.

Then the mill moved to an area where labor was cheaper, taxes were lower, and electric power was almost free. Some employees went with it; the rest were unemployed. Milltown's prosperity turned to poverty. Without customers, Murphy's store went into bankruptcy. The mortgage holder took his new home.

Murphy had no money, but he had friends. One of them found him a job as maintenance man with the high school. The pay was low, but it provided a frugal living for the Murphy family. Another friend rented them a house for half of what it had earned in the prosperous time.

Murphy is unhappy. He has turned his back on God and the church. "What is God doing for me?" he grumbles. "My friends are helping me, but God isn't."

Is Murphy right? Is God doing nothing for him, or is He doing what He did for Manasseh?

B. Marriage Disaster

Steve and Jean were the happiest honeymooners in town—until that frightful crash on the highway. Steve was not badly hurt, but Jean was paralyzed from the neck down. Motionless on her bed, she could smile or she could cry, but she could not speak. She could eat if food was put in her mouth, but she could not lift a spoon.

In her presence Steve was quiet and moody. Outside it he was furious. "I'm out of here!" he vowed often and loudly. He snarled at the minister who came to call, "Preacher, tell me about your God. What a monster! Does He really enjoy seeing Jean like that?"

The minister was irritated. "Maybe God is trying to make a man out of you," he snapped. "You have a contract, Steve. In the presence of God and a houseful of people, you promised to love, cherish, and keep Jean as long as you both would live. Men keep their promises, but you keep talking about getting out of here."

"Nuts!" Steve's voice dripped disgust. "I married a woman. I'm not going to spend the rest of my life with a houseplant."

So Steve drew his money out of the bank and vanished into the night. Jean's parents gave her tender, loving care until she died a year later.

What do you do with your disasters—and what do they do to you?

C. Prayer

Our Father who art in Heaven, in trouble there is no solace as the sure knowledge that You are also here on earth with us. We know Your goodness is unfailing. May we face every difficulty with confidence in our hearts and You at our side. In Jesus' name, amen.

D. Thought to Remember

You can't be wrong when you stand with God.

Learning by Doing

This page contains an alternative lesson plan emphasizing learning activities.
Classes desiring such student involvement will find these suggestions helpful.

Learning Goals

After participating in this lesson, each student will be able to:

1. Summarize the evil reign of Manasseh and how he finally came to repentance.

2. Compare the turnaround in Manasseh's life with similar changes in the lives of others.

3. Identify a co-worker, family member, neighbor, or other acquaintance who has no interest in God, Christ, or the church, and commit to praying for that person to come to repentance.

Into the Lesson

For class this week, prepare a transparency sheet or poster with the following statement: "A person can become so evil that God will not save him!" In addition, prepare four signs with the following words: "Strongly Agree," "Mildly Agree," "Mildly Disagree," "Strongly Disagree." Prior to class, hang the four signs in the four corners of the room. Place the "strongly" signs opposite diagonally; do the same for the "mildly" signs.

To start the class session, say, "Today we are going to begin class with an agree/disagree statement. By now you have noticed the four signs in the four corners. I am going to reveal a statement for you to consider. I would like you to stand after I read the statement; I will give you thirty seconds to decide whether you strongly agree, mildly agree, mildly disagree, or strongly disagree with the statement. Then I would like you to go stand in the corner under the sign that best represents your opinion." Reveal the statement to the class; read it audibly. After the class has moved to the various corners, ask each group to explain why they chose that position. *(Agree: God will not save because the evil person does not want to be saved; Disagree: God will save when the evil person turns to Him.)* After each group has shared, have all return to their seats. Say, "It is not the amount of evil in a person's life but one's response to God that matters. God will save when one turns to Him, regardless of how wicked that one has been in the past. Today we study a man who was so evil he was described as being worse than the pagans. Turn to 2 Chronicles 33:1-13 to read how God restores a sinner."

Into the Word

Ask the class to move into groups of three. State: "I would like one of you in each group to read the lesson text to the others in the group. I want each group to answer the questions I show you. After several minutes, we will hear answers from each." Prior to class, prepare the following questions on an overhead transparency or poster. While the students read, reveal these questions:

1. Why was Judah's behavior described as being worse than the pagans? *(The depth of evil was extensive: idolatry led to sacrificing children, witchcraft, enchantments, wizards, v. 9.)*

2. How was the temple of the Lord desecrated? *(Altars built for the host of heaven, vv. 4, 5.)*

3. Describe the circumstances that led Manasseh to turn to the Lord. *(Taken captive by Assyria to Babylon, bound with fetters, and in affliction, vv. 11, 12.)*

4. How did Manasseh turn to the Lord? *(Sought the Lord, humbled himself, prayed, vv. 12, 13.)*

5. What was the turning point in his life? *(Captivity, affliction, v. 12.)* After several minutes, ask each group its answers. Say, "Manasseh had rejected the Lord for years, but there was a turning point where he humbled himself, sought the Lord, and prayed to God. What are some of the turning points you have seen in others? In other words, what circumstances have led others to repent and turn to God?" *(Possible answers: death of a loved one; personal crisis event; broken marriage; loss of a job; changed life of a friend.)* While the class is still in the groups of three, ask each group to develop a single answer to the following question: What one principle do you think this passage is teaching us today? Give each group a large sheet of paper (flip-chart size) and a marker. Ask each group to write on the paper the one principle this passage is teaching. Have each group tape their paper on the wall for all to see. *(There will be several possible answers. Among those should be: God restores a sinner who turns to Him!)*

Into Life

State: "Regardless of how evil a person becomes, God can restore him!" Ask the class to think about someone they know who is evil: a family member, a co-worker, a neighbor, someone who cares little for God. Give a three-inch by five-inch card to each. State: "Write a memo to yourself to remind you to pray for this person daily." End the class with a prayer of commitment.

Let's Talk It Over

The questions on this page are designed to promote discussion of the lesson by the class and to encourage application of the lesson Scriptures. The answers provided are only discussion starters. Let your class talk it over from there.

1. It has been suggested that evil advisers encouraged Manasseh toward evil. Others might assume Manasseh himself is more to blame, behaving as a rebellious teenager. Whether by poor advisers or their own rebelliousness, teens can find themselves in a great many evil situations. What can the church and parents do to help teenagers through the maze of evil present in the world today?

Teenagers often are lumped together by older adults. The church needs to find ways to challenge those who are diligent in their faith to become leaders. The church can establish neighborhood programs (recreation, tutoring, vocational training) to reach many of the disenfranchised teens or their parents. Sometimes the best method is to work alongside established churches in poorer neighbors. Have the class discuss how local churches can get started on these endeavors.

2. No one is sacrificing children to the god Molech today. How does our culture today "sacrifice" children to modern "gods"? How can the church work to destroy these "gods"?

Lead the class in making a list of the "gods" to which children are sacrificed, such as athletics, beauty, abortion, sexual exploitation, and others. Discuss how these "gods" are appeased, such as through soccer on Sundays, beauty pageants for all ages, child pornography—and the list goes on!

One of the best ways to combat these is through education of the evil and the danger of what the world is doing. Sometimes the church and individual Christians must take an activist stand in the community and at the ballot box.

3. How is it possible that one person in leadership can influence an entire nation to change so radically in just one generation? What psychological, sociological, and spiritual factors make it easier to move away from God when the top leader dishonors God? How important is it for Christians to be involved in the political arena?

Discuss the significance of each of the following—and others you might suggest: modeling or imitating the leader, the leader's giving permission (by his or her own actions) for others to behave in a certain way, legislation that allows evil places (strip clubs, gambling establishments, etc.) within neighborhoods. Discuss to what de-

gree Christians have a responsibility to lobby elected leaders, to vote wisely, and to run for office in order to influence the climate within the culture.

4. In this text, God held the main leader responsible and punished him specifically. Would you expect that God always would respond in this way? Or might God hold all the people responsible? Support your position.

Second guessing the righteous actions of God can be dangerous. We can at least conclude that God used a variety of methods in trying to turn the hearts of the people back to Him. However, the Bible does confirm that leaders are held accountable for the way they exercise their responsibilities. See Hebrews 13:17; James 3:1. Ezekiel 33:1-9 also is a warning to leaders, but at the same time it confirms that each individual is responsible for his or her own behavior as well. The bottom line is that God will hold every person responsible for his or her sins unless that person is covered by the saving blood of Christ.

5. Should the church pray for God to act swiftly and strongly to humble our nation so people will be more receptive to the gospel? What would keep Christians from praying this way? How much change would people have to suffer before they turn to God?

Certainly it is right to pray that our nation would humble itself and turn to God, but shall we tell God how to do that? He may choose to exercise strong measures, as He did with Manasseh in particular and the nation as a whole later. If we pray for a humbling, however, we ought to anticipate some "hard lessons." And that anticipation is one reason we are hesitant. If we value our comfort more than our relationship with God, praying such prayers will be difficult. Ask your class which comforts and possessions the average Christian would find the hardest to give up.

The last part of the question suggests another reason we might be hesitant to pray for a humbling. Just how much will it take to turn our nation back to God? Would they even make the connection between their suffering and their need for God? It is easy to become pessimistic about such matters, but we must pray in faith and act in faith, always seeking to glorify the Lord.

The Lord Promises Future Glory

DEVOTIONAL READING: Isaiah 55:6-11.

BACKGROUND SCRIPTURE: Zephaniah.

PRINTED TEXT: Zephaniah 1:12; 3:1-7, 11-15.

Zephaniah 1:12

12 And it shall come to pass at that time, that I will search Jerusalem with candles, and punish the men that are settled on their lees: that say in their heart, The LORD will not do good, neither will he do evil.

Zephaniah 3:1-7, 11-15

1 Woe to her that is filthy and polluted, to the oppressing city!

2 She obeyed not the voice; she received not correction; she trusted not in the LORD; she drew not near to her God.

3 Her princes within her are roaring lions; her judges are evening wolves; they gnaw not the bones till the morrow.

4 Her prophets are light and treacherous persons: her priests have polluted the sanctuary, they have done violence to the law.

5 The just LORD is in the midst thereof; he will not do iniquity: every morning doth he bring his judgment to light, he faileth not; but the unjust knoweth no shame.

6 I have cut off the nations: their towers are desolate; I made their streets waste, that none passeth by: their cities are destroyed, so that there is no man, that there is none inhabitant.

7 I said, Surely, thou wilt fear me, thou wilt receive instruction; so their dwelling should not be cut off, howsoever I punished them: but they rose early, and corrupted all their doings.

. . . .

11 In that day shalt thou not be ashamed for all thy doings, wherein thou hast transgressed against me: for then I will take away out of the midst of thee them that rejoice in thy pride, and thou shalt no more be haughty because of my holy mountain.

12 I will also leave in the midst of thee an afflicted and poor people, and they shall trust in the name of the LORD.

13 The remnant of Israel shall not do iniquity, nor speak lies; neither shall a deceitful tongue be found in their mouth: for they shall feed and lie down, and none shall make them afraid.

14 Sing, O daughter of Zion; shout, O Israel; be glad and rejoice with all the heart, O daughter of Jerusalem.

15 The LORD hath taken away thy judgments, he hath cast out thine enemy: the King of Israel, even the LORD, is in the midst of thee: thou shalt not see evil any more.

GOLDEN TEXT: The just LORD is in the midst thereof; he will not do iniquity: every morning doth he bring his judgment to light, he faileth not; but the unjust knoweth no shame.—Zephaniah 3:5.

Judgment and Exile
Unit 1: Urgent Plea
(Lessons 1-5)

Lesson Aims

After participating in this lesson, the students will be able to:

1. Describe the situation in Jerusalem when Zephaniah prophesied and why it warranted the prophet's stern warning, and tell of the future hope he described.

2. Compare the Jerusalem of Zephaniah's day with their own community and suggest some spiritual and social changes that need to be made.

3. Plan a specific project that can make a difference in the community, turning hearts to God.

Lesson Outline

INTRODUCTION
  A. Obedience Becomes Complicated
  B. Lesson Background
 I. THE LORD AND HIS THREAT (Zephaniah 1:12)
  A. Thorough Search (v. 12a)
  B. Just Punishment (v. 12b)
 II. THE SINNERS AND THEIR SINS (Zephaniah 3:1-7)
  A. Filthy City (vv. 1, 2)
  B. Princes and Judges (v. 3)
  C. Prophets and Priests (v. 4)
    Something Really Stupid
  D. Warnings Ignored (vv. 5-7)
III. THE FUTURE AND ITS DELIGHT (Zephaniah 3: 11-15)
  A. Farewell to Shame (v. 11)
  B. Welcome of Survivors (vv. 12, 13)
    A Blessing for the Remnant
  C. Song of Joy (v. 14)
  D. King of Kings (v. 15)
CONCLUSION
  A. Not in Old Jerusalem
  B. In the New Jerusalem
  C. Prayer
  D. Thought to Remember

Introduction

Automobile repair was simple in the 1920s. In the backyard with just a few tools I gave my little car whatever it needed—anything from adjusting the carburetor to installing a crankshaft. But things are different now. When I lift the hood of a modern car, I am baffled. I can't even find the carburetor. (In fact, it probably doesn't even *have* a carburetor!) But no matter how complicated and sophisticated cars become, they still need proper adjustment.

A. Obedience Becomes Complicated

Obedience to God was simple when the world was young. "You may eat from all the trees except that one. If you eat from it, you die." Adam and Eve violated the only prohibition in the world, and they paid the price.

In later centuries obedience became more complicated. God gave commandments and prohibitions by the dozens through Moses, but His people seemed intent on breaking them all. Even so, a simple principle remained: obedience brought spiritual prosperity; disobedience brought disaster. Why were God's people so slow to learn that? And why haven't people in general, with all their knowledge and sophistication, learned it yet?

B. Lesson Background

In the two previous lessons we have seen bewildering changes in the government of Judah. Godly King Hezekiah was followed by evil King Manasseh—who did a thorough flip-flop and finished his reign in noble style. When his son Amon became king, he promptly switched back to his father's earlier style. After only two years, Amon was murdered by his servants. Then "the people of the land" took charge: they executed the killers and put Amon's son Josiah on the throne (2 Kings 21:19-26). Josiah's thirty-one year reign was not marked by any quick switch, but by a gradual progression from bad to excellent.

Josiah was only eight years old when he became king (2 Chronicles 34:1). No doubt his father's counselors became his counselors, and his reign was as bad as his father's had been. But in the eighth year of his reign he began to seek God (2 Chronicles 34:3a). In the eighteenth year Josiah ordered his men to clean and repair the temple as his great-grandfather Hezekiah had done about a century earlier (2 Chronicles 29:3; 34:8). Perhaps this work was spurred on by the preaching of Jeremiah, who by that time had been at work for about five years (Jeremiah 1:2). As that was being done, the long-lost book of God's law was found (2 Chronicles 34:14). Apparently it had been totally forgotten during the evil years of Manasseh's reign. Now the king and the people renewed the nation's promise to obey that law (2 Chronicles 34:31, 32). So true worship and obedience to the Lord were restored (2 Chronicles 35:1-19). This week we take our lesson from the prophecies of Zephaniah, which were given while Josiah ruled (Zephaniah 1:1).

I. The Lord and His Threat (Zephaniah 1:12)

Zephaniah 1 is devoted to the Lord's threat to Judah, a threat of destruction (vv. 2, 3). Our text takes a single verse as a sample.

A. Thorough Search (v. 12a)

12a. And it shall come to pass at that time, that I will search Jerusalem with candles.

That time is "the day of the Lord" (v. 7), a common theme in Zephaniah's writing. It is the time when God's lordship will be evident, the time when His enemies will be defeated. No enemy can hide in that day, since every dark corner in Jerusalem will be searched figuratively *with candles*. Since the widespread use of wax candles came along at a later time, we probably should understand these "candles" to be oil lamps. Still, the meaning is clear: there will be no place to hide, and there will be no escape (cf. Jeremiah 5:1; Revelation 6:15-17).

More than two hundred years after Zephaniah's time the Greek philosopher Diogenes will become legendary as he prowls the streets of Athens with a lamp in broad daylight in search of "an honest man."

B. Just Punishment (v. 12b)

12b. And punish the men that are settled on their lees: that say in their heart, The LORD will not do good, neither will he do evil.

Lees are the worthless and offensive dregs that settle in wine as it is fermented and aged. The clear, sparkling wine is carefully removed from that sediment; but the men of Judah are quite content to remain with their dregs of sin. They are not afraid of punishment, for they think that *the Lord will not* intervene in worldly affairs, either to bless the faithful or to punish the wicked. But He will indeed intervene, and people who are content with their sins will be punished. [See question #1, page 32.]

II. The Sinners and Their Sins (Zephaniah 3:1-7)

In Zephaniah 1 we considered the promise of punishment to those who were content to keep on sinning. Now we pause to take note of some of the sinners and their sins.

A. Filthy City (vv. 1, 2)

1. Woe to her that is filthy and polluted, to the oppressing city!

Zephaniah is not talking about a sanitation issue or a problem with Jerusalem's air quality. It is her morals that are *filthy and polluted*. She is

oppressing—that is, the rich and powerful are trampling the rights of the poor and helpless. This, of course, is not a new problem!

2. She obeyed not the voice; she received not correction; she trusted not in the LORD; she drew not near to her God.

Jerusalem cannot plead ignorance. God has been speaking to her through the voices of Zephaniah and other prophets, but *she obeyed not the voice.* She prefers filthiness. God is eager to correct her wrongdoing, but she refuses correction. The Lord is ready to bless and help the city where He has put His name, but she does not trust in the Lord. God longs for closer fellowship with His people, but Jerusalem chooses to go her own unclean way.

B. Princes and Judges (v. 3)

3. Her princes within her are roaring lions; her judges are evening wolves; they gnaw not the bones till the morrow.

Princes are officials of government, not necessarily men of the royal family. They ought to be servants of its people, managing the city for the common good. Instead, they are beasts of prey. By graft and extortion they enrich themselves.

Jerusalem's *judges* are the same kind of people, dispensing injustice rather than justice, selling their decisions to the highest bidder. *Evening wolves* are ravenous. After lying hidden all day, they cannot wait to get their teeth into some prey. The phrase *they gnaw not the bones till the morrow* is a bit difficult. It seems to mean that the judges make quick work of exploiting their victims. Where a beast might chew leisurely on the bones of its prey days after the meat has been eaten, these wicked judges take everything at their first opportunity. There are no "bones" left to chew on by the morrow.

C. Prophets and Priests (v. 4)

4. Her prophets are light and treacherous persons: her priests have polluted the sanctuary, they have done violence to the law.

This verse does not speak of God's prophets, such as Zephaniah and his contemporary Jeremiah. Jerusalem's *prophets*, the ones she actually listens to, are like her princes and judges. They care nothing for truth and right, but only for what they can get for themselves. *Light* here means "wanton" or "reckless." The *New International Version* translates the Hebrew word as "arrogant," and no doubt it was their arrogance that produced the wanton recklessness they displayed.

Jerusalem's *priests* are like her princes, judges, and prophets: their interest is in what they can get for themselves. Many people like to make sacrifices and offerings to the idols and imaginary

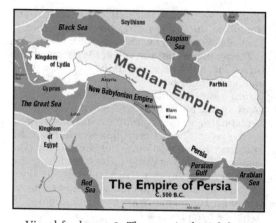

The Empire of Persia
C. 500 B.C.

Visual for lesson 3. *The map in the* Adult Visuals *packet will be helpful today and throughout the quarter. See page 13 for ordering information.*

gods promoted by King Manasseh at his worst (2 Chronicles 33:1-5). So with appropriate ceremony, the priests accept every offering that is brought, and happily keep the priests' part of it for themselves. In so doing, they *polluted the sanctuary* with pagan idolatry.

Zephaniah's words seem to fall on deaf ears, however. Some forty years later, as Jerusalem's collapse approaches, the prophet Ezekiel offers similar descriptions of the ungodly prophets, priests, and princes (Ezekiel 22:23-29). [See question #2, page 32.]

"SOMETHING REALLY STUPID"

"Every once in a while you want to do something really stupid." With these words John Quincy, a Texas "catapulteer," explains his hobby.

Catapults were first used as weapons of ancient warfare. "Greek fire"—a sort of early-day napalm—was hurled over city walls. In medieval times, dead horses infected with the plague and baskets of snakes and scorpions were catapulted into besieged castles.

Catapulteers today choose from a variety of missiles. Hew Kennedy, who lives near London, England, has a sixty-foot catapult that has thrown grand pianos (in two and one-half seconds they are moving at ninety miles per hour), cars, and dead livestock of various kinds. Caskets, bowling balls, and toilets are also favored today, tossed into empty fields or lakes.

Zephaniah's description of the leaders of Jerusalem makes it seem as if they had decided collectively to "do something stupid!" The priests polluted the temple, the rich and powerful extorted and stole from the poor, and the prophets were arrogant in their treachery, thinking not at all of the consequences. Eagerly and actively they

flouted God's laws and values, "catapulting" them over the city wall, from the inside out! Sin is the ultimate stupidity. Not even Christians are immune to participating in it.   —C. R. B.

D. Warnings Ignored (vv. 5-7)

5. The just LORD is in the midst thereof; he will not do iniquity: every morning doth he bring his judgment to light, he faileth not; but the unjust knoweth no shame.

The just Lord has not abandoned unjust Jerusalem; He is right there in the middle of it, but having no part in its *iniquity*. On the contrary, *every morning*, through His faithful prophets, He announces *his judgment* against the iniquity that fills the city. *But the unjust* ignore that unfailing warning. Despite periodic reforms (see 2 Chronicles 29:1–31:21; 33:15-17; 34:1–35:19), the city on the whole continues its shameless rush to destruction.

6. I have cut off the nations: their towers are desolate; I made their streets waste, that none passeth by: their cities are destroyed, so that there is no man, that there is none inhabitant.

Already God has brought about the destruction of some wicked *nations*. These judgments, particularly that against the northern kingdom of Israel, should have been a plain warning to the wicked in the kingdom of Judah. [See question #3, page 32.]

7. I said, Surely, thou wilt fear me, thou wilt receive instruction; so their dwelling should not be cut off, howsoever I punished them: but they rose early, and corrupted all their doings.

No doubt God knows from the beginning what the result will be, but He pictures himself reasoning as a man reasons. The people of Judah have eyes and minds. They have seen how God has *punished* the wicked nations. Isn't it reasonable to suppose that they will get the message that wickedness is intolerable to God? Shouldn't they realize that Judah, too, will be destroyed if it continues in wickedness? The people of Judah should have drawn that conclusion from their own observation. In case they missed it, God confirmed it by His written law and His speaking prophets. But still they failed to take the warning, to reform their lives, and to enjoy God's blessing. [See question #4, page 32.]

One reason for this seems to be that the unrepentant princes, judges, false prophets, and priests of Jerusalem count on the presence of the temple as something of a "good luck charm." Less than a hundred years previously, the Assyrians had threatened the southern kingdom of Judah with annihilation. But in 701 B.C., God destroyed the Assyrian army and rescued Jerusalem. This rescue had more to do with the Assyrians' own sin than Jerusalem's goodness—see 2 Kings 19. But the Judeans apparently believed that it was the presence of the temple that had saved them (Jeremiah 7:4, 14; cf. 21:2).

So they continued in their sin, pursuing it vigorously. The expression *they rose early* is a traditional Hebrew way of saying they are eager and active. Sometimes it is used in a positive sense (cf. Jeremiah 7:13, 25). Here, of course, it is a very negative quality.

III. The Future and Its Delight (Zephaniah 3:11-15)

Now the Lord looks beyond all the turmoil of sin and punishment to the time when His people will offer genuine worship, serving Him with one heart and one voice. With that holy time in view, the Lord's word on the lips of Zephaniah rises to a hymn of triumph and delight.

A. Farewell to Shame (v. 11)

11. In that day shalt thou not be ashamed for all thy doings, wherein thou hast transgressed against me: for then I will take away out of the midst of thee them that rejoice in thy pride, and thou shalt no more be haughty because of my holy mountain.

While "the unjust knoweth no shame" (v. 5), there must be a few in Jerusalem who are ashamed of what is happening. They themselves do right, but they are ashamed of the sins of their city. But there is coming a *day* when these will *not be ashamed* anymore.

The phrase *in that day* reflects the word "then" of verse 9. It refers to the future time when people will call upon the name of the Lord. In that day of the Lord's triumph, the Lord will have taken away the shameless sinners and their sins. At that time, there will be no *haughty* people in Jerusalem—only the humble and godly. God's *holy mountain* is Mount Zion, where Jerusalem stands. His holy nature is intolerant of any sin (cf. 1 Peter 1:15, 16).

B. Welcome of Survivors (vv. 12, 13)

12. I will also leave in the midst of thee an afflicted and poor people, and they shall trust in the name of the LORD.

When the arrogant sinners are taken away with their sins, the people left in Jerusalem will be *poor* and destitute of power and prestige. Instead, they will be rich in *trust*, for their trust will be in *the name of the Lord*. The kingdom of God consists of such as these (cf. Matthew 5:1-12). [See question #5, page 32.]

13. The remnant of Israel shall not do iniquity, nor speak lies, neither shall a deceitful tongue be found in their mouth: for they shall feed and lie down, and none shall make them afraid.

What a change! After the sinners described in verses 1-7 are seen no more, the holy *remnant of Israel*, the survivors, will do right and not wrong. They will not speak lies, but will speak truth. Like sheep feeding in abundant green pastures, this remnant will find every want supplied (Psalm 23:1). They will *lie down* to sleep with no more fear or anxiety, for their shepherd will keep them secure. Tormented Jerusalem at last will be at peace, and from spiritual prosperity will flow physical prosperity (cf. Micah 4:4).

A BLESSING FOR THE REMNANT

The blame for the European portion of World War II may be placed on the leaders of the Axis powers—Germany and Italy. These deluded men translated their own selfish ambition into the language of nationalistic pride, resulting in the deception of countless numbers of their citizens. The results were horrific. One-sixth of Poland's pre-war population had died by the time the war was over. Russia lost fourteen million people, equally divided between military personnel and civilians. And, of course, six million Jews were slaughtered in the Holocaust.

However, the Allied victory proved the Axis' nationalistic pride was both evil and misplaced. There was a brighter side: for most of Europe, the years following the war brought greater prosperity than before. In large part, this was due to the benevolence of the Allied conquerors, who offered aid to both the conquered nations and their victims.

God destroyed Judah's wicked leaders. When the nation had been purged of its misplaced pride, those who remained would find their judgments removed and replaced with the blessings of their benevolent God. We who are Christians may take hope in the promise that better days are ahead—if not soon, then in the ultimate future God is preparing for us at the return of Christ. —C. R. B.

How to Say It
AMON. *Ay*-mun.
ASSYRIANS. Uh-*sear*-e-unz.
DIOGENES. Die-*ah*-gin-ees.
EZEKIEL. Ee-*zeek*-ee-ul or Ee-*zeek*-yul.
HEZEKIAH. Hez-ih-*kye*-uh.
JEREMIAH. Jair-uh-*my*-uh.
JERUSALEM. Juh-*roo*-suh-lem.
JOSIAH. Jo-*sigh*-uh.
JUDEANS. Joo-*dee*-unz.
MANASSEH. Muh-*nass*-uh.
ZEPHANIAH. Zef-uh-*nye*-uh.

C. Song of Joy (v. 14)

14. Sing, O daughter of Zion; shout, O Israel; be glad and rejoice with all the heart, O daughter of Jerusalem.

In that ultimate, glad day when all is well, what can the survivors do but burst into song? From grateful hearts that have been relieved of stress will rise a ringing hymn of pure delight. Those survivors, free from sin and free from fear, will be the true progeny of *Zion*, which is also called *Jerusalem*. This remnant will be the real Israel, for they will be what Israel was called originally to be—a people in harmony with the Lord (cf. Romans 11:5).

D. King of Kings (v. 15)

15. The LORD hath taken away thy judgments, he hath cast out thine enemy: the King of Israel, even the LORD, is in the midst of thee: thou shalt not see evil any more.

Now we see the reason for that anticipated season of pure delight: it is the coming of *the King of Israel, even the Lord,* who is to dwell in their *midst* (see also vv. 5, 17). Kings Hezekiah and Josiah tried earnestly to usher in such a season, but their efforts were undone by others. But in a time to come, the greater *King of Israel* ultimately will do what those righteous kings could not: He will permanently *cast out* the *enemy.*

Through all the dark days of Israel, members of a righteous remnant try to be what they ought, but sometimes they fail. God's Word encompasses all of history when it says, "All have sinned" (Romans 3:23). The best people of ancient Israel were less than perfect (e.g., Deuteronomy 32:48-52), as are the best people of today's world. Their sins were under the judgment of God, even as ours are. They could not make personal atonement for their sinful failures any more than we can personally atone for ours. But they and we both have the assurance that *the Lord hath taken away thy judgments.* Though we are guilty and have a "judgment" against us, that judgment has been set aside.

Conclusion

The prophet Zephaniah did not live to see the fulfillment of the bright promise he recorded. Neither did good King Josiah, though he labored earnestly to bring in such a time. Then where and when *is* the promise realized?

A. Not in Old Jerusalem

Throughout her history, Jerusalem has known times of great sorrow and times of great joy. Sorrow and agony are seen when she is reduced to rubble in 586 B.C., and her people are taken captive to Babylon. Return from the Babylonian exile, in 538, is a time of great joy (Nehemiah 8:17). But in A.D. 70, her citizens are again scattered among many countries. And since the time of Zephaniah, Jerusalem has never reached the zenith of delight promised in our text. Even today, the inhabitants of Jerusalem do not enjoy perfect safety, with none to make them afraid (cf. Zephaniah 3:13). Indeed, fear is common.

B. In the New Jerusalem

But think of the New Jerusalem, which John the apostle saw "coming down from God out of heaven" (Revelation 21:2; cf. 3:12). What a city this will be! God lives there with His people (21:3), and His Son, the Lamb of God, is enthroned beside Him (22:3, 4). God will make sure that there will be no sorrow, pain, or death in that place (21:4). There are three gates in each of the four walls (21:13), and these stand open at all times to welcome God's people (21:25).

However, the presence of those open gates does not mean that all the people of earth are welcome to enter. The unrepentant are permanently shut out. Their place is the lake of eternal fire (21:8). The New Jerusalem is only for those who reject sin and follow God's plan of salvation.

C. Prayer

How gracious You are, gentle Father! How gracious is Jesus, who died for our sins! By Your grace and His we are Your people and the sheep of Your pasture. By grace we feed on Your bounty, and by grace we lie down with none to make us afraid. Thank You, Lord. In Jesus' name, amen.

D. Thought to Remember

Our names are written in the book of life!

Home Daily Bible Readings

Monday, Sept. 9—Seek the Lord (Zephaniah 1:12–2:3)

Tuesday, Sept. 10—Wait for the Lord to Work (Zephaniah 3:1-10)

Wednesday, Sept. 11—The Remnant Will Find Refuge (Zephaniah 3:11-20)

Thursday, Sept. 12—Plans for a Future (Jeremiah 29:10-14)

Friday, Sept. 13—Surely There Is a Future (Proverbs 23:15-23)

Saturday, Sept. 14—A New Thing (Isaiah 43:14-21)

Sunday, Sept. 15—Hope in the Lord (Psalm 130:1-8)

Learning by Doing

This page contains an alternative lesson plan emphasizing learning activities.
Classes desiring such student involvement will find these suggestions helpful.

Learning Goals

After participating in this lesson, each student will be able to:

1. Describe the situation in Jerusalem when Zephaniah prophesied and why it warranted the prophet's stern warning, and tell of the future hope he described.

2. Compare the Jerusalem of Zephaniah's day with his own community and suggest some spiritual and social changes that need to be made.

3. Plan a specific project that can make a difference in the community, turning hearts to God.

Into the Lesson

On a large poster board, write the words "Complacency is. . . ." Mount the poster just inside the door into the classroom. Have several markers available. Prepare instructions on a regular sheet of paper and attach it above the poster. Write on the paper: "Before you sit down, take a marker. Complete the statement below by writing a word or words describing what complacency is." *(Possible answers include self-satisfaction, smugness, indifference, unwillingness to change.)* As students arrive, make certain they see the sign and write an answer before finding their chairs. When it is time to begin class, move the poster to the front of the room for all to see. State: "As you can see by your definitions of complacency, it's a word expressing the attitude of contentment with what is, an indifference—not wanting to change. Today's text describes the Lord's attitude toward those who are complacent. The book of Zephaniah reveals a complacent people."

Into the Word

Ask a class member to read aloud Zephaniah 1:12; 3:1-7, 11-15. Afterward, ask the following:

1. How are the complacent people described in verse 12? *(Settled on their lees.)*

2. What is the meaning of "settled on their lees"? *(This is a metaphor from wine, where it coagulates at the bottom; they were content and satisfied, believing the Lord would not intervene.)*

3. What four ways did God accuse Jerusalem for failing? *(Disobeyed; received no correction; trusted not; drew not near to God, 3:2.)*

4. What leaders of Judah have failed God? *(Princes, judges, prophets, priests, 3:3, 4.)*

5. What does God specify that His people do? *(Fear Him and receive instruction, 3:7.)*

6. What does the Lord promise (v. 11)? *(A day is coming when one will no longer be ashamed for transgressions against Him.)*

7. Describe the characteristics of the people of God in the promised future glory (vv. 12, 13). *(Afflicted; poor; trust in the Lord; do not do iniquity, not lie; no deceit; eat and lie down unafraid.)*

8. Identify emotions God's people will have at that time. *(Gladness and rejoicing, v. 14.)*

9. Why should God's people be so full of joy? *(Judgments against them have been removed; their enemies have been removed; and the Lord is in their midst, v. 15.)*

State: "The complacency in Jerusalem received a stern warning. In much the same way, the warning could be directed toward our own community." Then ask the students to move into three groups and answer the assigned questions.

Group 1: What similarities are there between Zephaniah's Jerusalem and our community?

Group 2: What are some spiritual changes that need to be made in our community for it to have the future hope Zephaniah described?

Group 3: What are some social changes that need to be made in our community for it to have the future hope Zephaniah described?

Give the students about eight to ten minutes to work; then ask for their answers.

Into Life

State: "Both spiritual and social changes need to be made in our community. We may not be able to change everything in the community, but as a class we can make a difference." Prior to class prepare a worksheet to be passed out at this time. The worksheet, to be entitled "Project: Make a Difference," is a chart listing five questions down the left: What? When? Where? How? Who? The first three questions will have one column to the right for space to write in the answers to the questions. The last two questions will have three columns to the right, labeled "Phase 1: Planning," "Phase 2: Preparation," and "Phase 3: Performance." Use the class time to decide on a project. (For example: organizing a special collection of donated coats from the community to take to a homeless shelter, or other.) Answer the remaining two questions. Close the class session with a prayer circle, making a commitment to the class project and requesting God's blessing on those who accept responsibilities.

Let's Talk It Over

The questions on this page are designed to promote discussion of the lesson by the class and to encourage application of the lesson Scriptures. The answers provided are only discussion starters. Let your class talk it over from there.

1. The people of Jerusalem believed the Lord would not do anything, either good or bad. In today's culture, what wrong beliefs about God are held and taught? How can we address these wrong views and help people know the truth?

The same statement made by those in Jerusalem could summarize the beliefs of many today. Some believe there is no God to act. Others believe there is a God, but that He will not act. Either way, they expect nothing from God. Their prayers, if they pray at all, are more ritual than conversation.

Other people, however, see things very differently—but just as wrongly. They not only expect God to act, they believe they can determine how He will act. They take promises of answered prayer out of context and claim to be able to determine how God will—even *must*—respond. They need to learn to be servants and let God be Lord.

2. Read verses 1-4 again. From this list of sins, which ones are common in our community today? What can we do to address these issues?

The text refers to the sins of government and judicial leaders. It would be easy for your class to use this to note the failings of the modern political system. But call attention to the fact that the text addresses the sins of people entrusted with God's truth. Could it be that the sins of church leaders are more parallel to this list than those of political leaders? Have Christians come to accept a certain level of sin as "normal"? Discuss what impact a righteous congregation could have on its community if it refused to accept sin as the norm.

3. Words of "doom and gloom" bring feelings of fear and depression. Rescue and salvation words soothe those feelings. But how much comfort do you think the people of Judah took from the prophet's words of hope while witnessing the pruning hand of God chopping everything around them? Could this happen again in our lifetime? Why or why not?

Probably there were few in Jerusalem who took comfort from the prophet's words because few gave heed to his words at all! Discuss to what extent we today should see difficult circumstances as God's "pruning." Is *every* bad thing an act of God's discipline, or are there other answers to some? Either way, do we not take comfort from

the promises of the Bible? Discuss ways of sharing Biblical hope with those in distress—without minimizing their trying situations.

4. Many of the people in today's lesson do not seem to be listening to a spiritual message. Is there any way to phrase the message so people will listen to it even when their lives seem to be going smoothly?

Finding a way to grab the attention of listeners has been the quest of believers from the beginning. Noah preached for 120 years without any converts. Jesus preached and worked miracles for over three years and many of His first "converts" deserted him as they learned their spiritual walk would require sacrifice. Even when people do not seem to be listening, the church must continue to search for meaningful ways to communicate the good news. Ask for ideas about what might attract the attention of people in your locality. Be specific and positive.

5. The poor seem often to have a closer relationship with God than the wealthy. Why? Do spiritual riches really compensate for the material riches they are missing? Would today's Christians be willing to give up material riches in order to have a better spiritual connection with God? If they tried it, do you think they would be happy?

Sometimes the poor learn to place their hope of a better life in God's promise of Heaven. Many realize they will not have "the good life" on earth. At the same time, poverty cannot be equated with spirituality. Some poor people spend their energy hoping to "strike it big." Some of them use their meager resources for lottery tickets or other risky ventures hoping to cash in without expending any real effort. As a result, their plight only worsens.

As for whether spiritual riches really compensate for material riches, the "Sunday school" answer is obviously yes. None of your students will miss that! But ask how many would be willing to slash their incomes in half if they could be guaranteed a closer walk with God—any takers? It is hard to live in a materialistic culture without being affected. It may take a serious economic downturn—a depression—for some of us really to appreciate the nonmaterial blessings that are not dependent on wealth.

Josiah Makes a New Beginning

September 22
Lesson 4

DEVOTIONAL READING: Psalm 119:1-8.

BACKGROUND SCRIPTURE: 2 Chronicles 34, 35; 2 Kings 22, 23.

PRINTED TEXT: 2 Chronicles 34:1-4, 19-21, 29-33.

2 Chronicles 34:1-4, 19-21, 29-33

1 Josiah was eight years old when he began to reign, and he reigned in Jerusalem one and thirty years.

2 And he did that which was right in the sight of the LORD, and walked in the ways of David his father, and declined neither to the right hand, nor to the left.

3 For in the eighth year of his reign, while he was yet young, he began to seek after the God of David his father: and in the twelfth year he began to purge Judah and Jerusalem from the high places, and the groves, and the carved images, and the molten images.

4 And they brake down the altars of Baalim in his presence; and the images, that were on high above them, he cut down; and the groves, and the carved images, and the molten images, he brake in pieces, and made dust of them, and strewed it upon the graves of them that had sacrificed unto them.

. . . .

19 And it came to pass, when the king had heard the words of the law, that he rent his clothes.

20 And the king commanded Hilkiah, and Ahikam the son of Shaphan, and Abdon the son of Micah, and Shaphan the scribe, and Asaiah a servant of the king's, saying,

21 Go, inquire of the LORD for me, and for them that are left in Israel and in Judah, concerning the words of the book that is found: for great is the wrath of the LORD that is poured out upon us, because our fathers have not kept the word of the LORD, to do after all that is written in this book.

. . . .

29 Then the king sent and gathered together all the elders of Judah and Jerusalem.

30 And the king went up into the house of the LORD, and all the men of Judah, and the inhabitants of Jerusalem, and the priests, and the Levites, and all the people, great and small: and he read in their ears all the words of the book of the covenant that was found in the house of the LORD.

31 And the king stood in his place, and made a covenant before the LORD, to walk after the LORD, and to keep his commandments, and his testimonies, and his statutes, with all his heart, and with all his soul, to perform the words of the covenant which are written in this book.

32 And he caused all that were present in Jerusalem and Benjamin to stand to it. And the inhabitants of Jerusalem did according to the covenant of God, the God of their fathers.

33 And Josiah took away all the abominations out of all the countries that pertained to the children of Israel, and made all that were present in Israel to serve, even to serve the LORD their God. And all his days they departed not from following the LORD, the God of their fathers.

GOLDEN TEXT: Because thine heart was tender, and thou didst humble thyself before God, when thou heardest his words against this place, and against the inhabitants thereof, and humbledst thyself before me, and didst rend thy clothes, and weep before me; I have even heard thee also, saith the LORD.—2 Chronicles 34:27.

Lesson Aims

After this lesson each student will be able to:
1. Tell how Josiah "walked in the ways of David his father."
2. Suggest some positive benefits that would derive from the efforts of a few key people to walk in the right way.
3. Cite two personal changes to make this week to be God's man or woman in the community.

Lesson Outline

INTRODUCTION
  A. Who's in Charge?
  B. Lesson Background
 I. GROWING IN GOODNESS (2 Chronicles 34:1-4)
  A. The Facts Are Positive (vv. 1, 2)
  B. The Facts Become Even Better (vv. 3, 4)
    Destroying the Symbols
 II. APPEALING TO THE LORD (2 Chronicles 34:19-21)
  A. An Outpouring of Grief (v. 19)
  B. A Searching for Answers (vv. 20, 21)
    Curious? About What?
III. OBEYING THE LAW (2 Chronicles 34:29-33)
  A. Gathering the People (vv. 29, 30)
  B. Renewing the Covenant (vv. 31, 32)
  C. Serving the Lord (v. 33)
CONCLUSION
  A. God's Man
  B. God's Nation
  C. God's People at Work
  D. Prayer
  E. Thought to Remember

Introduction

A. Who's in Charge?

Do you work for a big corporation? If you do, what would you think if a boy were chosen from the third grade of your local elementary school to be CEO of your company?

First of all, you would know that a child was not really going to run the company. So you would want to know who really would be shaping the policies and directing the operation. If the subordinate officers of the company were the same ones who had worked with the former CEO, you would not expect much change. But if a group of officers who had been very vocal in

opposing the former leader's policies moved into the subordinates' offices, you would be wise to anticipate some drastic changes.

B. Lesson Background

In this lesson we are looking at a country rather than a corporation and a king instead of a CEO, but there are parallels. The country is Judah, and the king is Josiah. Last week we briefly noted some facts about Josiah's era (he reigned 640–609 B.C.) because we were studying prophecies that Zephaniah made during that time. Now we will look more closely at the king and what he did, but first we need to review again the background of Josiah's reign.

Josiah's grandfather Manasseh, in embracing and promoting all kinds of pagan practices, was one of the worst of Judah's kings (2 Chronicles 33:1-7). He led his people in these evil ways until they became worse than the pagans around them (33:9). But this evil king changed in his latter years. He supported the real God as vigorously as he had supported the fakes. Earnestly he tried to undo the evil he had done (33:11-16), but was not completely successful (2 Kings 24:3, 4).

The next king was Amon, Manasseh's son and Josiah's father (cf. Matthew 1:10). He liked the riotous religious feasts of the pagans, the things his father once had promoted. He was not pleased at all with his father's repentance and reformation. So when Amon became king, he promptly reverted to the evil ways of his father's earlier years (2 Chronicles 33:21-23). This continued for only two years, but that was long enough for him to dismiss his father's godly helpers and surround himself, instead, with evil men from Manasseh's early days.

Having no specific information about Josiah's early helpers, we can suppose those same evil men to have been the "cabinet" that he inherited at age eight. If so, then they undoubtedly were the rulers "in fact" during Josiah's early years, continuing Amon's evil policies. But ultimately the boy king was not seduced by them. As the boy became a man, he became God's man.

I. Growing in Goodness (2 Chronicles 34:1-4)

At the age of eight, the king is a "zero" in the government of Judah, but the recorder can hardly mention him without writing of his goodness. As we read, our admiration will grow, too.

A. The Facts Are Positive (vv. 1, 2)

1. Josiah was eight years old when he began to reign, and he reigned in Jerusalem one and thirty years.

A news writer is taught to include the main facts of a story in the lead paragraph so a hasty reader can get a quick summary of the whole. The writer of Chronicles begins the record of each king with just such a summary. This opening verse records the length of Josiah's reign, while the next offers an estimate of its character. With *Josiah* at age *eight*, the year is 640 B.C.

2. And he did that which was right in the sight of the LORD, and walked in the ways of David his father, and declined neither to the right hand, nor to the left.

David, now dead for some three hundred and thirty years, is the patriarch of the royal family in Judah. He is considered to be a role model for all the later kings, even though he fell into terrible sins of his own. Josiah has the good judgment to copy David's right *ways*, but not his sins.

B. The Facts Become Even Better (vv. 3, 4)

3. For in the eighth year of his reign, while he was yet young, he began to seek after the God of David his father: and in the twelfth year he began to purge Judah and Jerusalem from the high places, and the groves, and the carved images, and the molten images.

Josiah is about sixteen years old *in the eighth year of his reign* (v. 1)—about 632 B.C. We wonder exactly how he begins *to seek after the God of David.* He cannot simply sit down with his Bible at home. It seems he has no Bible there, as we shall see later. Though the law requires that the king have a copy of it and read it daily (Deuteronomy 17:18, 19), probably Josiah has never heard of that requirement nor has ever laid eyes on a copy of the law. We wonder whether Manasseh in his evil days had destroyed the king's copy, and perhaps others, but we have no information about that. But some faithful remnant has kept alive the truth of God's Word, and one of them has apparently influenced the king. Or perhaps Josiah has been tutored by Jeremiah, who will begin his own prophetic ministry in about five years (Jeremiah 1:2). However the instruction has come about, Josiah has been able to learn something about God and His will. [See question #1, page 40.]

In the twelfth year, four years after starting his search for God, twenty-year-old Josiah begins to act on what he has learned. He begins to *purge Judah and Jerusalem*, destroying the places and things used in the worship of idols. *The high places* are worship sites, usually on hilltops. The *groves* are poles erected to represent Asherah, the fictitious goddess associated with the equally fictitious Baal. *Carved images* are idols sculpted from wood or stone; *molten images* are idols made by melting metal and pouring it into molds that are usually made of clay.

4. And they brake down the altars of Baalim in his presence; and the images, that were on high above them, he cut down; and the groves, and the carved images, and the molten images, he brake in pieces, and made dust of them, and strewed it upon the graves of them that had sacrificed unto them.

King Josiah is there to watch personally as his men destroy the paraphernalia of idol worship. *Baalim*, the plural of *Baal*, were various images depicting that imaginary god of the Canaanites. The phrase *high above them* indicates that certain *images* were on platforms above the altars, while the *New International Version* says that incense altars were above the altars to Baal. The difference in translation is not important, for both versions make it plain that all the things used in idol worship were destroyed.

As we see Josiah beating the idols into powder and scattering it on *the graves of them that had sacrificed unto them*, we recall that graves are regarded as "unclean" in Numbers 19:16. What fitting places for the remnants of the unclean idols! To bring the process "full circle," 2 Kings 23:16 tells us that Josiah also did the opposite: he dug up the bones from those graves and burned them on the idolatrous altars to defile them. Like other religious reforms, Josiah's was violent, even to the point of bloodshed (2 Kings 23:20; cf. 1 Kings 18:40; 2 Kings 10:25-27; 11:18).

King Josiah carries this clean-up beyond the borders of Judah into the territory once occupied by the northern kingdom of Israel (2 Chronicles 34:6, 7), but now claimed by Assyria. By this time, Assyria is in a weakened state and does not move to oppose Josiah. Josiah's destruction of the altar at Bethel in this territory fulfills a prophecy

---

How to Say It

ABDON. *Ab*-dahn.
AHIKAM. Uh-*high*-kum.
AMON. *Ay*-mun.
ASAIAH. As-uh-*hye*-uh.
ASHERAH. Uh-*she*-ruh.
ASSYRIANS. Uh-*sear*-ee-unz.
BAAL. *Bay*-ul.
BAALIM. Bay-uh-*leem*.
CANAANITES. *Kay*-nun-ites.
HEZEKIAH. Hez-ih-*kye*-uh.
HILKIAH. Hill-*kye*-uh.
HULDAH. *Hul*-duh.
JOSIAH. Jo-*sigh*-uh.
LEVITES. *Lee*-vites.
MANASSEH. Muh-*nass*-uh.
SHAPHAN. *Shay*-fan.
ZEPHANIAH. Zef-uh-*nye*-uh.

that is now about three hundred years old (see 1 Kings 13:2, 31, 32; 2 Kings 23:15-18). [See question #2, page 40.]

DESTROYING THE SYMBOLS

When James I became king of England in 1603, Roman Catholics were hoping he would be tolerant of their faith. When he was not, some of them vowed to destroy this Protestant king, whom they saw as a symbol of heresy.

A small group of Roman Catholics stashed thirty-six barrels of gunpowder in a cellar under the government buildings in London. They planned to blow them up when the king opened Parliament in November of 1605, killing both the king and members of Parliament. But shortly before it was to happen, Guy Fawkes, one of the dissidents, was arrested. He named his fellow conspirators, and all were executed.

November 5 is still celebrated annually as the day when the king and Parliament were saved from death. With typical British whimsy, the day is named after Guy Fawkes.

King Josiah and Guy Fawkes had one thing in common: the desire to destroy the symbols of what each considered to be false religion. But there were two significant differences: first, Josiah was getting rid of a religion that was definitely contrary to God's word on every level, and second, God guided Josiah in his quest.

When we feel led to stand up for truth (or purge evil from our society), we must be sure we are acting in the spirit of Josiah and not upon our own misguided feelings.   —C. R. B.

II. Appealing to the Lord (2 Chronicles 34:19-21)

When King Josiah is about twenty-six years old, he appoints a committee of his officials to repair the temple (v. 8), as his great-grandfather Hezekiah had done at about the same age (29:1-3). As Josiah's orders are being carried out, a priest finds a book containing the law that God had given to Moses more than eight hundred years before. A scribe takes the book and reads the law to King Josiah (34:14, 15, 18). The next part of our text takes up the account at this point.

A. An Outpouring of Grief (v. 19)

19. And it came to pass, when the king had heard the words of the law, that he rent his clothes.

Tearing one's clothing is a traditional way of expressing extreme grief and dismay. [See question #3, page 40.] Hearing *the law,* the king knows he has seen it broken continually—all his life and in many ways. Furthermore, the law

prescribes terrible punishment, even national destruction. The king is appalled. Are all his reforms in vain? Is Judah still doomed? Must it be destroyed, as northern Israel already has been?

B. A Searching for Answers (vv. 20, 21)

20. And the king commanded Hilkiah, and Ahikam the son of Shaphan, and Abdon the son of Micah, and Shaphan the scribe, and Asaiah a servant of the king's, saying.

The king needs answers to the desperate questions that assail him. He has spent years in wiping out idolatry. We do not know how much time and money he has invested in repairing the temple to make it fit for its proper use. But the people still are ignoring God's law because they are ignorant of it, breaking it every day in many ways. Does this mean that Judah is about to be destroyed as the law indicates? The king appoints a committee to find out, a committee as prestigious as the one that he had formed to repair the temple.

21. Go, inquire of the LORD for me, and for them that are left in Israel and in Judah, concerning the words of the book that is found: for great is the wrath of the LORD that is poured out upon us, because our fathers have not kept the word of the LORD, to do after all that is written in this book.

Only *the Lord* has the answers that are needed by the king and all his people, so the committee must *inquire* of Him. They are sent to a prophetess named Huldah, of whom we know no more than what is written in this chapter (v. 22). Apparently she is well-known in Jerusalem, and none of the committee doubts that she really speaks for God.

Huldah's reply is direct. Yes, Judah will be destroyed for her sins, as the law indicates (vv. 23-25). But because Josiah is doing his best to lead

Visual for lessons 4 and 5. *This poster issues a challenge for all believers. You may want to post it outside the classroom after this quarter.*

the nation in true worship and righteousness, the destruction will not come in his time (vv. 26-28; 2 Kings 22:18-20). The historical record verifies this prophecy. Four kings follow Josiah. All of them are evil, and the sinning of the people is not checked. About a quarter of a century after Josiah's death, the Babylonians destroy Jerusalem and take most of its people captive (2 Chronicles 36:1-21). [See question #4, page 40.]

CURIOUS? ABOUT WHAT?

Since 1901, the Nobel Prize has been awarded annually to people whose inquiring minds have led them to great accomplishments in the fields of peace, literature, chemistry, physics, and physiology and medicine.

On the other hand, some minds inquire into much less noble matters. To give appropriate jeers to such endeavors, each year the Society for Basic Irreproducible Research presents an Ig Nobel prize in (dis)honor of achievements that "cannot or should not be repeated." Among the winners have been a Harvard University study on the reaction of cats to bearded men, a group of researchers who taught pigeons to distinguish between the paintings of Picasso and Monet, and a Pennsylvania zoologist who tried to make clams happier by feeding them the drug Prozac.

Obviously, many people are curious about things that have no readily apparent significance (or perhaps no significance at all). Not so with Josiah! When he heard the words of the law, his curiosity was aroused, and he commanded that its meaning for him and his kingdom be determined. How *unlike* so many Christians today who are far more interested in sports statistics or soap opera plots or a multitude of other matters than they are in what God has to say about their lives! Are *we* curious about what God has said to us? Does it show in the way we live?   —C. R. B.

III. Obeying the Law (2 Chronicles 34:29-33)

Cheered by the promise God sends through His prophetess, Josiah moves promptly to make the whole nation aware of the law that he has heard for the first time. He wants to lead all his people to pledge their allegiance to that law.

A. Gathering the People (vv. 29, 30)

29. Then the king sent and gathered together all the elders of Judah and Jerusalem.

The elders are heads of families—highly respected and very influential in their family groups. Apparently *the king* assembles them to explain his plan and secure their help in calling the larger convocation described in the next verse.

30. And the king went up into the house of the LORD, and all the men of Judah, and the inhabitants of Jerusalem, and the priests, and the Levites, and all the people, great and small: and he read in their ears all the words of the book of the covenant that was found in the house of the LORD.

Now the whole nation gathers in a mass meeting *in the house of the Lord,* the temple in Jerusalem. There the king reads to his people the book recently found in the temple. As a result, they agree to obey the laws written in that book.

B. Renewing the Covenant (vv. 31, 32)

31. And the king stood in his place, and made a covenant before the LORD, to walk after the LORD, and to keep his commandments, and his testimonies, and his statutes, with all his heart, and with all his soul, to perform the words of the covenant which were written in this book.

The king apparently has a certain *place* to stand (see 2 Chronicles 23:13). After taking that place, he leads the way by embracing the covenant Moses had received at Mount Sinai more than eight hundred years before. We need not try to press distinctions among *commandments, testimonies,* and *statutes.* Taken together these terms form "the book of the covenant" of verse 30 and *the words of the covenant* here. Josiah's promise to obey *with all his heart, and with all his soul* is borne out by the events of his life.

32. And he caused all that were present in Jerusalem and Benjamin to stand to it. And the inhabitants of Jerusalem did according to the covenant of God, the God of their fathers.

The king asks all the people to follow his lead, and they do. The commitment they make is the same made by their forefathers in centuries long past (Exodus 24:3).

C. Serving the Lord (v. 33)

33. And Josiah took away all the abominations out of all the countries that pertained to the children of Israel, and made all that were present in Israel to serve, even to serve the LORD their God. And all his days they departed not from following the LORD, the God of their fathers.

This verse presents a quick review, a summary of what Josiah achieved in his reign of thirty-one years. First, he took away all the *abominations.* These were the idols, the altars, and whatever other things were used in pagan worship. We read about Josiah's campaign against them in verses 3 and 4 of our text. An even longer account is seen in 2 Kings 23:4-20.

Second, King Josiah *made all that were present in Israel to serve . . . the Lord their God.* It was not enough to stop the worship of idols. This king did not want a godless or irreligious nation. He wanted everyone to worship and obey the real God. This short summary does not explain how he made them do this, whether by persuasion or by coercion. Those people had just heard God's law for the first time. No doubt many of them were enthusiastic about it. They obeyed it gladly, with all their heart and soul, as did their king (v. 31). But many of the people had recently seen their cherished idols destroyed violently. Probably some of them were resentful and angry. We can imagine the police were kept busy enforcing the law among them. Whether gladly or resentfully, the people did serve God as long as King Josiah lived—about thirteen years after the book of the law was found in the temple. [See question #5, page 40.]

Conclusion

As the boy king becomes a man, he becomes God's man. But young Josiah does more than turn his own life away from idolatry. He also turns his idolatrous nation into God's nation. Josiah's faith became the nation's faith.

A. God's Man

Josiah wanted to be God's man. Though he was initially surrounded by people who gave their worship and service to imaginary gods, somehow, at the age of sixteen, he "began to seek after the God of David his father" (v. 3).

Perhaps his initial "instruction" came from creation itself (cf. Psalm 19:1-6; Romans 1:20). Around us and in us is evidence that all creation is planned by one supreme mind. We do not know how much the evidence from creation persuaded Josiah. Most likely he was taught by those who cherished in their memory parts of God's law and parts of Israel's history. If the young king learned even the first of the Ten Commandments, he knew that the idols about him were sinful.

Do you want to be God's man or God's woman? You have a head start. You do have God's written Word in your home, both the law and the gospel. Are you reading them daily, as the king of Israel was required to do? Are you constantly improving your obedience to God's Word? Are you teaching it diligently to your children, discussing the keeping of it both at home and away? This is the way of God's man in ancient times, and now, and as long as the world stands.

B. God's Nation

Recently I heard an American Christian express concern about the drift of the United States away from God. This believer was anxious about God's judgment coming against the country as it had come against Israel. Another Christian tried to reassure the anxious one, replying that the United States is not God's "chosen" nation, and God's dealing with Israel was unique.

That is true, but it is not the whole truth. Israel and Judah were not the only nations that were destroyed because of their wickedness. The nations that lived in the land of Canaan before Israel came out of Egypt were destroyed so Israel could take their land—not because of Israel's goodness, but because the other nations were too evil to be allowed to live (Deuteronomy 9:5).

In addition to those tiny nations we can cite the huge empires of the Assyrians, the Babylonians, the Persians, the Greeks, and the Romans. One by one they became corrupt, and one by one they passed into the dustbin of history. History testifies that nations that become enemies of God do not survive.

C. God's People at Work

God's people today must protect the holiness of their own lives, even as they hold forth the Word of life to the unbeliever who lives across the street or across the ocean. We share the Word personally, and we support missionaries in every country where spiritual darkness reigns. Jesus instructs us to do this (Matthew 28:19, 20). People of God, get busy!

D. Prayer

Heavenly Father, thank You for Your grace that has saved us from evil to be Your children. Give us the will and wisdom to protect our holiness and to serve You faithfully. In Jesus' name, amen.

E. Thought to Remember

People need holiness, people need Jesus.

Home Daily Bible Readings

Monday, Sept. 16—Josiah Does Right (2 Chronicles 34:1-7)

Tuesday, Sept. 17—Hilkiah Finds the Law Book (2 Chronicles 34:8-18)

Wednesday, Sept. 18—The Words Grieve Josiah (2 Chronicles 34:19-28)

Thursday, Sept. 19—Josiah Makes a Covenant (2 Chronicles 34:29-33)

Friday, Sept. 20—Josiah Keeps the Passover (2 Chronicles 35:1-10)

Saturday, Sept. 21—No King Like Him (2 Kings 23:24-30)

Sunday, Sept. 22—Be Renewed (Ephesians 4:17-24)

Learning by Doing

This page contains an alternative lesson plan emphasizing learning activities.
Classes desiring such student involvement will find these suggestions helpful.

Learning Goals

After participating in this lesson, each student will be able to:

1. Tell how Josiah "walked in the ways of David his father."

2. Suggest some positive benefits that would derive from the efforts of a few key people to walk in the right way.

3. Cite two changes that he or she can make this week in order to be God's man or woman in the community.

Into the Lesson

In preparation for this week's lesson, make a copy of the acrostic puzzle below for each class member. (Replace the words in the right column with blanks to be filled in by the students.) Make certain the first letters of all correct words will align vertically.

1. Not OUT but. . . .	*IN*
2. Not EVERYTHING but. . . .	*NOTHING*
3. Not PAST but. . . .	*FUTURE*
4. Not HATE but. . . .	*LOVE*
5. Not OVER but. . . .	*UNDER*
6. Not DIFFICULT but. . . .	*EASY*
7. Not OLD but. . . .	*NEW*
8. Not RARE but. . . .	*COMMON*
9. Not WEST but. . . .	*EAST*

Open today's session by saying, "This week we begin by introducing a basic theme from our text. Complete this acrostic by writing the letters of the correct word on the spaces provided. When you complete the puzzle, the theme should become obvious."

Give the students time to complete the puzzle. Then say, "The basic theme of this week's lesson is *influence*. Turn to 2 Chronicles 34 and we'll see the influence one man had on the nation of Israel."

Into the Word

Ask the class members to move into groups of at least three students each. This newspaper article activity is designed to help the students understand the events that led to Josiah's new beginning. The groups will each be given a slip of paper containing one of the following categories and Scripture passages to read: Josiah interview, 2 Chronicles 34:1-4; Interview of a Baal worshiper, 34:1-4; Article on temple repairs, 34:8-13; Article on ancient discovery, 34:14-21; Article on the town meeting and the influence of reform initiatives, 34:29-33. Give the groups approximately ten to fifteen minutes. State: "Imagine that you were a reporter for the *Jerusalem Gazette*, the local newspaper at the time of our text. You have received information about the reform initiatives that have taken place, and your editor has assigned a topic for you. Gather the facts from the assigned Scripture passage and write an article describing the events as they might have been told in the imaginary *Jerusalem Gazette*. Remember, news stories must answer who, what, when, where, why, and how. Work in your group and write your article on the paper provided. When finished we will ask you to read the reports to the class."

After sufficient time has elapsed, ask the groups to read their news articles to the class. Say: "These articles reveal how much influence Josiah had on Israel. As a result of his influence, there were a number of positive benefits. Let's list benefits you see." After writing on the board the various benefits from Josiah's covenant with the Lord, state: "Of course, the greatest benefit was found in verse 33: the people served the Lord and 'departed not from following the Lord, the God of their fathers.'"

Into Life

Say: "In much the same way, we have influence on other people. Imagine what would happen if Christian people in your neighborhood or in your place of employment made a similar covenant with the Lord and did not depart from it for the rest of their lives. What would be some positive benefits that would result from their efforts at walking in the right way for God?" Write suggested answers on the chalkboard as they are given. Then ask: "What are two key changes that you believe most Christians need to make to be God's man or woman in the community?" Again write these specific ideas on the chalkboard for all to see. Discuss why Christians seem to have the most trouble in these areas.

Next guide the students to think about their own personal walk with the Lord. Ask: "What two changes do you need to make this week to follow the Lord?" Close the class period by giving them stationery and an envelope and asking them to write a reminder note to themselves to enact those two changes in their lives this week.

Let's Talk It Over

The questions on this page are designed to promote discussion of the lesson by the class and to encourage application of the lesson Scriptures. The answers provided are only discussion starters. Let your class talk it over from there.

1. Someone must have had a positive influence on Josiah during his first ten years on the throne. Who in your congregation has a knack for positively influencing teenagers? What are some ways the church can encourage young people and the people who influence them for good?

Have the class name some people who have a knack for encouraging the youth. Note what makes them influential—why do they have credibility with the youth when other adults do not? Can any of these traits be taught? For those who do have influence with youth, perhaps the church can budget money for advanced training. These leaders can also be asked not to take on any responsibilities in the local church that would drain energy away from the all-important task of reaching youth. Ask the class for additional ideas. Challenge your class members to take the lead in activities at home as well as in the church and community that will be a positive influence on young people.

2. If we attempted to tear down pagan or other sinful places in our culture, what would we be allowed to do? What strategies or approaches might be effective in eliminating pagan or sinful practices? How difficult would this task be?

Today it would be illegal to harm individuals or to destroy specific buildings. But Christians can unite to lobby for laws to limit or remove immoral businesses. It would be wise for each Christian to state publicly that he or she is standing up for what will be good for the community rather than acting as a representative of a specific church. In some communities, protest lines have been effective. Christians should not expect this to be an easy task. They will have to shoulder a lot of ridicule and abuse.

3. It was a custom in Josiah's day to tear one's clothes when that person was deeply troubled or grieved. In our time, what are some signs that indicate a person is deeply troubled or repentant? Do you think church members should be more open or apparent about such feelings? Why or why not?

In most Western countries it is not customary to be so open about one's feelings. In fact, it is usually more important to maintain composure and "just be cool" about everything. Still, there are signs that the discerning person can look for. Facial expressions tell much about what a person is feeling. The eyes are especially telling. Nervous motions with the hand or foot may also suggest something about a person's feelings. Still, none of these is a precise determinant, so we need to be careful not to read too much into them or assume we "know" what a person is thinking or feeling. We cannot with certainty read people's motives. At the same time, it is okay to be a fruit inspector (Matthew 12:33) to discern if one's actions are indicating that repentance has truly taken place.

4. When Josiah first heard God's Word read, his reaction was, essentially, "It is no wonder we are in this national danger. God warned us and we did not listen!" Do you think the average Christian reacts the same way upon hearing God's warnings? Why or why not?

This passage was new to Josiah, and the message clearly made an impact on him. Perhaps those who have heard the warnings so often today have a different reaction born of complacency. They have read God's warnings, but nothing has happened yet, so they assume nothing will happen anytime soon. Thus, they put off taking any action until a more convenient time. (Compare Acts 24:25.) At the same time, there are still Christians who take seriously what they read in the Bible. Sometimes a new insight will pop out from their reading or from a sermon or lesson, and they will pull up short. Maybe the class will have some ideas about how to cultivate an attitude that anticipates such insights.

5. Josiah's spiritual response to God's Word was commendable. If we rate it a "100," how do you think we should rate the average church member's response to God's Word? How about some noted church leaders? How about you?

Most of your students will rate the average response below 100—perhaps well below. Discuss some ways to bring up that score. As for church leaders, it's probably best not to rate your own church leadership; that could get too personal. Suggest some well-known national leaders. Let the students think about their own scores privately. Challenge them to make a commitment to improve their scores.

Rebellion and Judgment

DEVOTIONAL READING: Psalm 16:5-11.

BACKGROUND SCRIPTURE: Jeremiah 6.

PRINTED TEXT: Jeremiah 6:16-21, 26-30.

Jeremiah 6:16-21, 26-30

16 Thus saith the LORD, Stand ye in the ways, and see, and ask for the old paths, where is the good way, and walk therein, and ye shall find rest for your souls. But they said, We will not walk therein.

17 Also I set watchmen over you, saying, Hearken to the sound of the trumpet. But they said, We will not hearken.

18 Therefore hear, ye nations, and know, O congregation, what is among them.

19 Hear, O earth: behold, I will bring evil upon this people, even the fruit of their thoughts, because they have not hearkened unto my words, nor to my law, but rejected it.

20 To what purpose cometh there to me incense from Sheba, and the sweet cane from a far country? your burnt offerings are not acceptable, nor your sacrifices sweet unto me.

21 Therefore thus saith the LORD, Behold, I will lay stumblingblocks before this people, and the fathers and the sons together shall fall upon them; the neighbor and his friend shall perish.

. . . .

26 O daughter of my people, gird thee with sackcloth, and wallow thyself in ashes: make thee mourning, as for an only son, most bitter lamentation: for the spoiler shall suddenly come upon us.

27 I have set thee for a tower and a fortress among my people, that thou mayest know and try their way.

28 They are all grievous revolters, walking with slanders: they are brass and iron; they are all corrupters.

29 The bellows are burned, the lead is consumed of the fire; the founder melteth in vain: for the wicked are not plucked away.

30 Reprobate silver shall men call them, because the LORD hath rejected them.

GOLDEN TEXT: Thus saith the LORD, Stand ye in the ways, and see, and ask for the old paths, where is the good way, and walk therein, and ye shall find rest for your souls.—Jeremiah 6:16.

Judgment and Exile
Unit 1: Urgent Plea
(Lessons 1-5)

Lesson Aims

After participating in this lesson, each student will be able to:

1. Summarize God's complaint against the people of Judah.

2. Contrast true worship with the worthless worship of the people of Judah.

3. Suggest one specific way to make his or her own worship of God (either personal or corporate) more meaningful.

Lesson Outline

INTRODUCTION
    A. Choices Have Consequences
    B. Lesson Background
I. SIN AND PUNISHMENT (Jeremiah 6:16-21, 26)
    A. Plea Resisted (vv. 16, 17)
        Unheeded Warnings
    B. Punishment Promised (vv. 18, 19)
    C. Worship Condemned (vv. 20, 21, 26)
        Stumbling Blocks
II. TEST AND FAILURE (Jeremiah 6:27-30)
    A. The Tester (v. 27)
    B. The Tested (v. 28)
    C. The Test (v. 29)
    D. The Test Result (v. 30)
CONCLUSION
    A. Decisions We Make
    B. Leaders We Follow
    C. Prayer
    D. Thought to Remember

Introduction

We live in a time of "tolerance." Nothing is intolerable, it seems, except intolerance itself. "The right to choose" one's own path and destiny is exalted to the skies.

A. Choices Have Consequences

God does let us choose, but He warns that we must accept the consequences of our choices. Adam and Eve chose to disobey, and they died as God had warned that they would. Instead of learning from that sad experience, humanity continued to disobey so persistently that "every imagination of the thoughts of his heart was only evil continually" (Genesis 6:5). So most of hu-

manity died in the flood. In the dawn of the Hebrew nation, God set before it "life and good, and death and evil. . . . therefore choose life" (Deuteronomy 30:15-19). How disappointing it is to see that Israel chose death! Likewise Jesus set before His disciples the way that leads to destruction and the way that leads to life, and He warned that the popular way is not the best choice (Matthew 7:13, 14). But consider how many are choosing the popular way today.

B. Lesson Background

In our two previous lessons, we considered the life and work of Josiah, Judah's last godly king. After four years of seeking the Lord, in the twelfth year of his reign that young king launched a vigorous campaign to rid his people of idolatry (2 Chronicles 34:3). In the following year the prophet Jeremiah began to proclaim God's word in Judah (Jeremiah 1:1, 2). We can imagine that his eloquent preaching lent power to the king's effort. Jeremiah's laments for Josiah following the king's untimely death were memorable to the people (2 Chronicles 35:25). In the years following that death, Jeremiah's preaching could not prevent a return to idol worship.

Today's text offers us two segments from the sixth chapter of the book of Jeremiah. This prophet's ministry lasted over forty years (from 626 B.C. to beyond the fall of Jerusalem in 586 B.C.). We do not know exactly when Jeremiah delivered these particular messages.

Chapter 6 begins with a warning of hostile forces that would overrun Judah from the north. This prophecy was fulfilled by the Babylonian army. While Babylon is actually east of Judah rather than north, there is a vast, waterless desert between the two. The Babylonians had to go north to get around the desert, so they approached Judah from that direction. In Jeremiah 6:1-15, prophecies of disaster mingle with declarations of Judah's sins to be punished by the disaster. This brings us to the first part of today's text.

I. Sin and Punishment
(Jeremiah 6:16-21, 26)

The sinners in Judah cannot complain that they have no way of knowing what is right, since God's prophets are constantly among them. But the people refuse to pay attention and repent.

A. Plea Resisted (vv. 16, 17)

16. Thus saith the LORD, Stand ye in the ways, and see, and ask for the old paths, where is the good way, and walk therein, and ye shall find rest for your souls. But they said, We will not walk therein.

There are many roads in Judah, many ways of living and acting. Many are bad, but among them are *the old paths*, the ways followed by good people and good kings like David and Hezekiah. Such a path can be called *the good way* because it leads to peace with God, to spiritual prosperity and happiness. The result of walking in this ancient path, God promises, is that *ye shall find rest for your souls.* [See question #1, page 48.]

But the people refuse to walk in that good way. If a man is getting rich by lending money at exorbitant rates of interest, or by cruelly foreclosing mortgages, or by fraud and deception, or by outright stealing, he might think that is the good way. So the people reject what God is teaching them through Jeremiah. They choose ways that are immoral and illegal, but profitable.

The priests, who should be strongly supporting what Jeremiah says, are no better than the people. There are also false prophets to contradict the true prophets and approve the sins of the people (Jeremiah 2:8). So the sinners can find plenty of so-called teachers to praise them when they rejected the true teaching of Jeremiah. The people should look at the record. The evil ways they are following have brought disaster again and again in Israel's history; the good way that Jeremiah favors has brought success and happiness.

17. Also I set watchmen over you, saying, Hearken to the sound of the trumpet. But they said, We will not hearken.

A city that is in danger of attack might post *watchmen* on its highest towers so they can see an approaching enemy from a distance (e.g., 2 Samuel 18:24-27). A watchman is to *sound* a *trumpet* to warn the people of the city to get ready to meet a foe. Likewise the Lord has set prophets as watchmen for His people (cf. Ezekiel 3:17).

Visual for lessons 4 and 5. *Use the same visual from the* Adult Visuals *packet that you used to illustrate last week's lesson.*

By divine inspiration, Jeremiah foresees the attack of the Babylonians while it is still years in the future. But his message of repentance, his trumpet call of warning, ultimately falls on deaf ears. By changing their ways of living, by doing right instead of wrong, Judah can forestall the Babylonian invasion. Tragically, the people reply not with repentance, but with a flat refusal.

UNHEEDED WARNINGS

For decades scientists have warned that Lake Tahoe is in danger, but the warnings have not been heeded. Forty years ago this lake on the California-Nevada state line was so clear that a white disc such as a dinner plate could be seen more than one hundred feet below the surface. Today the disc is visible only as deep as sixty-five feet, and another foot of visibility is lost every year. Experts say the lake is "gravely imperiled."

Steps have been taken to curtail the problem, but there is no prospect of a return to the region's former purity. In 1960, there were only five hundred houses on land surrounding the lake. Now there are some twenty thousand. Silt from construction sites runs into the lake, and ash from wood fires drops into it, as do other airborne pollutants from the increasing number of people who want to live in the Tahoe basin. These pollutants act as nutrients for algae, which continues to grow and cloud the water. So, despite the warnings, a pristine environment is being destroyed by the people who enjoy it.

The people of Judah ignored numerous warnings about the moral pollution that gravely imperiled their society. They were told how to cure it, but they were too busy enjoying life. Sometimes we are like Judah, ignoring warnings until it is too late, thinking, "Surely, it won't happen to *me.*" But the Bible says a society can become so polluted that there is no cure. Is that happening to *our* society?   —C. R. B.

B. Punishment Promised (vv. 18, 19)

18. Therefore hear, ye nations, and know, O congregation, what is among them.

Therefore, because the people of Judah refuse to act in God's way and refuse to heed His warnings, He will have all the other *nations* take notice. This verse offers some difficulties to translators, and so the English versions are not all alike. But in any translation the main thought is clear: God wants the whole world to be witness to the fact that rebellion against Him will be punished. The following verse tells how.

19. Hear, O earth: behold, I will bring evil upon this people, even the fruit of their thoughts, because they have not hearkened unto my words, nor to my law, but rejected it.

God is going to *bring evil*, or disaster, to the *people* of Judah—not because He wants to but because *the fruit of their thoughts* (i.e., their action) requires it. For some reason they think that they need not pay attention to God's *words* and *law* as spoken through His genuine prophets. When confronted with those words, they either turn a deaf ear (Jeremiah 5:21; 6:10), or choose to listen to false prophets instead (28:15; cf. 2 Timothy 4:3). In short, they hear only what they want to hear.

Consequences now must follow. The armed invaders, instruments of the Lord's vengeance, will come from "the north"—a notable reference in Jeremiah (1:14, 15; 4:6; 6:1, 22; 10:22; 13:20; 16:15; and others). Later, the prophet specifically identifies this northern invader as Nebuchadrezzar (also spelled "Nebuchadnezzar"), king of Babylon (25:9). His forces will destroy Jerusalem and take most of its survivors into captivity. Interestingly, even the pagan Babylonian commander Nebuzaradan will know why the exile occurs (40:2, 3). [See question #2, page 48.]

C. Worship Condemned (vv. 20, 21, 26)

20. To what purpose cometh there to me incense from Sheba, and the sweet cane from a far country? your burnt offerings are not acceptable, nor your sacrifices sweet unto me.

Incense represents the same Hebrew word that is translated "frankincense" in Exodus 30:34-36. In that passage we learn that frankincense is a part of the sacred perfumed incense used in the Lord's tabernacle and later in the temple (cf. Matthew 2:11). Likewise, *cane* represents the word that is translated "calamus" in Exodus 30:23. This is an aromatic oil extracted from a certain kind of reed. It is a part of the holy oil used in anointing people and things for the service of God (Exodus 30:22-30). The incense is imported from *Sheba*, probably southwest of Arabia. The calamus likewise comes from a *far country*, perhaps India. Therefore both of these substances are expensive.

Thus the disobedient people in Judah are still "going through the motions" of worship, even at a high cost. Adding to the expense are the *burnt offerings* and other *sacrifices* that require valuable livestock. But all of this pretended worship is worthless because they are wicked in their daily living (cf. Isaiah 1:13-17). Going to church and putting money in the offering plate cannot win God's favor while we are disobedient in the way we live our daily lives. [See question #3, page 48.]

21. Therefore thus saith the LORD, Behold, I will lay stumblingblocks before this people, and the fathers and the sons together shall fall upon them; the neighbor and his friend shall perish.

The *stumblingblocks* will be the Babylonians that the Lord will use as His instruments to bring

about the "physical" downfall of a people that already has collapsed morally. The people of Judah and Jerusalem have rejected the rest that God offers (6:16). The suffering will come upon all—no one will escape.

STUMBLING BLOCKS

A stumbling block might be an issue of morals a spiritually weak person trips over, but more often it is something we seize upon as an excuse for failure. However, sometimes a person comes along who shows us how puny our excuses are for failing to conquer life's obstacles.

Erik Weihenmayer *(VI-en-mai-er)* is one such person. At the age of thirteen, he became totally blind at about the same time his mother was killed in a car accident. But rather than stumbling over this significant impediment, Weihenmayer accepted his blindness as a challenge. After a brief (and understandable) bout with self-pity, he set about to overcome the setback life had given him. He eventually became a schoolteacher, skydiver, skier, marathon runner, and a wrestler with membership in the National Wrestling Hall of Fame. Even more amazing, he is a "world-class" mountain climber, well on his way to his goal of climbing the highest mountain on *every* continent on earth. On May 25, 2001, he reached the summit of Mt. Everest, the world's highest mountain!

Judah no doubt had excuses as to why they could not live by God's will. So God said (in effect), "I will really give them something to trip over." And because of their lack of spiritual will, God's challenge to them to repent turned into a stumbling block. Are the challenges in our lives excuses for failure or stepping-stones to faith?

—C. R. B.

26. O daughter of my people, gird thee with sackcloth, and wallow thyself in ashes: make thee mourning, as for an only son, most bitter lamentation: for the spoiler shall suddenly come upon us.

O daughter of my people is a figurative way of addressing the whole population of Judah. The prophet might just as easily have said, "O my people" (some English versions actually render it that way), but the *daughter* image is more poetic. We may compare this phrase to verse 23, where the "daughter of Zion" is the whole population of Jerusalem. Everyone in Judah should mourn, for everyone will suffer in the coming disaster.

Sackcloth is a rough kind of fabric, uncomfortable to wear and unattractive to look at. Wearing it is a traditional way of indicating the discomfort and ugliness one feels in a time of deep mourning (cf. 4:8; 49:3). Sprinkling oneself with *ashes* is an added way of showing how debased and worthless the mourner feels, but sprinkling is not enough for the mourners of this disaster. They should also *wallow* in those ashes (cf. Ezekiel 27:30, 31).

In ancient times it was considered a disgrace to have no children, no one to carry on the family name. Thus, the grief over the loss of *an only son* was the deepest, most inconsolable kind of sorrow. Mourning over the coming disaster should (and will) be like that. The *spoiler* is the army of Babylon. It will *come* in 605 B.C. and take a few captives, but it will not yet plunder the city. It will return in 597 to steal the gold articles of the temple and seize the best and brightest of the people (2 Kings 24:13, 14). It will come yet again in 586 B.C., and the city will be destroyed (2 Kings 25:1-21; Jeremiah 52). [See question #4, page 48.]

II. Test and Failure
(Jeremiah 6:27-30)

Now the Lord speaks directly to Jeremiah to describe the prophet's work in another way: Jeremiah is administering a test. The test will demonstrate whether the people of Judah are indeed the people of God. But there can be no grade of "B–" or "C+" here. This test is strictly pass/fail.

A. The Tester (v. 27)

27. I have set thee for a tower and a fortress among my people, that thou mayest know and try their way.

In calling Jeremiah to be a prophet, God had warned earlier that he would face strong opposition by powerful men. But God has also promised that Jeremiah will become "a defensed city, and an iron pillar, and brazen walls"; Jeremiah will become so strong that his opponents will be unable to overcome him or stop his preaching (Jeremiah 1:17-19). Now that promise seems to be repeated here as *I have set thee for a tower and a fortress.*

The parallel between the first half of the verse before us and the description in 1:17-19 seems so clear that we are startled to see the *New International Version* offer us the translation, "I have made you a tester of metals" here instead. How can the same line be translated so differently?

The answer lies in understanding the ancient Hebrew way of writing without vowels. Usually this is no problem, since the native reader of the Hebrew language instinctively knows which vowels to supply. An example in English is the exhortation, "Prch th wrd," which the Christian reader can read instinctively as, "Preach the word." But what about a phrase such as, "Gt m ct"? Should this be, "Get my coat"? How about, "Got my cat"? Or perhaps, "Get me a cot"? The final choice will depend on context—what the

overall idea is, based on all the other words and sentences around it.

For the Hebrew word at issue here, *tower* is one potential translation, just as the *King James Version* has it. (This same Hebrew word is also translated that way in Isaiah 32:14.) This is consistent with the idea of being a *fortress*, also in this verse. The other potential translation, with different vowels, is "tester of metals" as the *New International Version* suggests. This is consistent with the last part of the verse (*try* is the same verb) and with the next three verses. So in addition to being "a defensed city . . . against the whole land" (Jeremiah 1:18), the "tower" is now also Judah's "tester."

B. The Tested (v. 28)

28. They are all grievous revolters, walking with slanders: they are brass and iron; they are all corrupters.

The people of Judah are miserable failures when tested against the faultless law of God. As *grievous revolters*, they shamelessly turn away from God's commands to do as they please. Instead of "speaking the truth in love" (Ephesians 4:15), they participate in spreading malicious lies in violation of Leviticus 19:16. They are *brass and iron*. That does not mean they are strong and durable. It means they are inferior to what God wants of them. God wants His people to be precious metal, gold and silver; but they are made of cheaper stuff. They are *corrupters*, not only acting corruptly themselves, but making others corrupt (cf. Matthew 23:15).

C. The Test (v. 29)

29. The bellows are burned, the lead is consumed of the fire; the founder melteth in vain: for the wicked are not plucked away.

How to Say It

BABYLON. *Bab*-uh-lun.
BABYLONIAN. Bab-ih-*low*-nee-uh.
CALAMUS. *ka*-luh-mus.
EZEKIEL. Ee-*zeek*-ee-ul or Ee-*zeek*-yul.
FRANKINCENSE. *frank*-in-sense.
HEZEKIAH. Hez-ih-*kye*-uh.
JEREMIAH. Jair-uh-*my*-uh.
JOSIAH. Jo-*sigh*-uh.
NEBUCHADNEZZAR. *Neb*-yuh-kud-*nez*-er (strong accent on *nez*).
NEBUCHADREZZAR. *Neb*-uh-kad-*rez*-er (strong accent on *rez*).
NEBUZARADAN. *Neb*-you-zar-*a*-dun (strong accent on *a*).
SHEBA. *She*-buh.

Now Jeremiah's testing of Judah is pictured as an assayer's testing of certain metals. In ancient times, a precious metal such as silver would be heated to remove impurities. But before the silver is heated, *lead* is added. Then as both are heated together, the molten lead carries off the impurities from the silver. But the precious silver in this case—the people of Judah—is so thoroughly corrupt that the lead cannot do its job of taking *away* the *wicked*, no matter how hot *the bellows are burned.* The wicked are just too numerous. [See question #5, page 48.]

D. The Test Result (v. 30)

30. Reprobate silver shall men call them, because the LORD hath rejected them.

The wicked people of Judah go through the motions of worship (v. 20) and pretend to be pure *silver,* the unsullied people of God, but God is not fooled. He has *rejected them* because they are disobedient in their daily living. Soon disaster will come to them, and then everyone will know that they do not really belong to God. They will be known as *reprobate silver,* rejected silver—mere pretenders. As the nation rejects God, so God rejects the nation.

Conclusion

Those of us who attend Sunday school and worship services regularly: are we really God's people, or are we only silver-plated vessels masquerading as sterling? The answer is not found in our thoughts and actions on Sundays alone.

A. Decisions We Make

We face decisions every day. In business, for family activities, for social life, for community service, for fun—in all these areas, we have to

Home Daily Bible Readings

Monday, Sept. 23—Look for the Good Way (Jeremiah 6:16-21)

Tuesday, Sept. 24—People Tested as Silver (Jeremiah 6:22-30)

Wednesday, Sept. 25—Amend Your Ways (Jeremiah 7:1-7)

Thursday, Sept. 26—People Will Not Listen (Jeremiah 7:16-28)

Friday, Sept. 27—Return and Rest (Isaiah 30:15-19)

Saturday, Sept. 28—Those Who Enter God's Rest (Hebrews 4:1-11)

Sunday, Sept. 29—Christ Will Give Rest (Matthew 11:25-30)

make choices. Here are some questions to guide us in our choosing, from least important to most important:

Question 5. What is easiest?

Question 4. What do I like best?

Question 3. What is best for me?

Question 2. What is best for those I do business with, for my family, for friends and neighbors, for the community?

Question 1. What is pleasing to God?

B. Leaders We Follow

The false prophets of Judah told the truth sometimes—that's partly what made them so dangerous. They approved the worship of the Lord that was carried on in the temple, even though it was costly. But they didn't speak up to confront idolatry.

False prophets of our time tell the truth sometimes, too. As this lesson is being written—long in advance to allow time for printing and distribution—it happens to be the Thanksgiving season in the United States. Among the soap operas on television, viewers are hard pressed to find one that does *not* center on the theme of Thanksgiving. Here are the main points I remember from one "informative" program.

1. The Pilgrims came to the New World because they wanted to be free.

2. After the Indians taught the Pilgrims how to grow corn, they all celebrated the harvest together.

Point number one is partially true. The Pilgrims did indeed come to the New World because they wanted to be free. But the Pilgrims were not slaves in England. They were free citizens of a magnificent free nation. The freedom they were looking for in the New World was one specific freedom only: they wanted to be free to worship God in the way they thought was right. Why didn't the program say that?

Point number two is true as far as it goes: the Pilgrims and Indians did indeed celebrate the harvest. But this inadequate statement does not mention the thanks the Pilgrims offered to God!

So, shall we listen to modern false prophets or to Jeremiah? Shall this coming Thanksgiving Day be renamed Turkey Day and devoted to football, or shall we truly thank the Lord?

C. Prayer

Father in Heaven, we owe You life, breath, and every good thing we have. Help us to smother our selfishness and really give You first place in our lives. In Jesus' name, amen.

D. Thought to Remember

Follow your leaders, but make sure they're worth following.

Learning by Doing

This page contains an alternative lesson plan emphasizing learning activities.
Classes desiring such student involvement will find these suggestions helpful.

Learning Goals

After participating in this lesson, each student will be able to:

1. Summarize God's complaint against the people of Judah.

2. Contrast true worship with the worthless worship of the people of Judah.

3. Suggest one specific way to make his or her own worship of God (either personal or corporate) more meaningful.

Into the Lesson

To focus attention on the themes from the lesson text prepare either a transparency sheet with the following scrambled words or a poster board. (You could write them on chalk- or marker board.) In big letters write: ILEREBOLN (rebellion), NGEJTUDM (judgment), and PHOSWRI (worship). Say: "To begin class this week, I am going to reveal three words that have been scrambled. They represent the basic themes of this week's lesson. You will have only one or two minutes to unscramble the words."

When time is up, ask the students to identify the words. Write the unscrambled words for all to see. Say, "The one word that does not seem to relate with the other two words is *worship*. We think that if people rebel against God, they don't worship Him. Yet, the people of Judah worshiped in spite of their rebellion and coming judgment. Turn to Jeremiah 6, and let's see the worthless worship of the people of Judah as they rebelled against God."

Into the Word

Ask your learners to keep their copies of today's text closed while you complete this first activity. Give each learner an index card, and ask him or her to draw a large curving line, as a smile. Tell the students you are going to read today's text and that every time you stop, you want them to hold their cards up either as smiles or as frowns, based on what you have just read. For example, the first verse (6:16) can be read in three parts: one, "Thus . . . walk therein"; two, "and ye shall find rest for your souls"; and three, "but they said, We will not walk therein." Expect to get smiles for the first two, but frowns for the third. Verse 17 lends itself to two parts; verse 18, one; verse 19, two (from "Hear" to "thoughts," and from "because" to "it"). Once you've read all the text verses, it will be clear that this text is dark and negative. Point out, though, the positive way the text begins. State: "God has light and hope in the midst of darkness and gloom . . . if only people will hear and obey Him."

Verse 16 speaks of the "old paths," but the people had chosen "new paths." Assign responsibility for looking at Jeremiah 2, 3, 4, and 5 to four groups within your class. These chapters give a clear picture of how far the people had fallen. Direct the groups to find within their assigned chapter examples of the "new paths" chosen by the people, in contrast to the "old paths" God laid out for them. For example, in chapter 2, "broken cisterns" have replaced the "fountain of living waters" (2:13); in chapter 3, divorce and remarriage rather than faithfulness to a spouse (3:1); in chapter 4, using wisdom to plot evil rather than good (4:22b), and in chapter 5, lying replaces truth (5:1, 2). You may want to draw lines on the board or transparency to represent a highway with a fork off to the left, writing righteous deeds on the throughway, corresponding sins on the crooked road veering off. At the end of your listing, write *GOD* at the end of the "old path"; write *DOOM* at the end of the "new."

After these activities are completed, ask the class to summarize why God was so displeased with Judah. Write suggested answers on another transparency or on the chalkboard. Say: "We've seen now how displeased God was with Judah. But we need to look more closely at Judah's worship. Let's look again at the text and contrast their worthless worship with what we know to be true worship." In preparation for this activity make a two-column chart on a transparency or draw it on the chalkboard. Label the left column "Worthless Worship" and the right column "True Worship." Make at least four rows below the title row and write one of the following verse numbers on each row: 16, 17, 20, 20. Ask each to work with a neighbor to fill the left column.

Into Life

Next, ask the class to describe the qualities of true worship and write them in the right column. Conclude class by asking them to suggest one specific way that their own worship could be more meaningful. Ask neighbors to share that way and to end class by praying a prayer of commitment for each other.

Let's Talk It Over

The questions on this page are designed to promote discussion of the lesson by the class and to encourage application of the lesson Scriptures. The answers provided are only discussion starters. Let your class talk it over from there.

1. Do the "old paths" and the "good way" always coincide? What methods must be employed to find out what God wants? How would a message to seek the old paths go over today? Is it right to call Christianity an "old path"? Why or why not?

If you have a class of older adults, the consensus may be that the older ways are always better. If you have young adults, they might say the new ways are always better. The truth is somewhere in between. Who would like to return to the days before indoor plumbing, air conditioning, automobiles, or electric lights? But with all our technology and conveniences, are we really better off? Do we feel safer than our parents did? Are our neighbors as friendly as Grandma and Grandpa's were?

Christians do not follow the same "old paths" that Jeremiah called for—the Old Testament laws. But we do follow the "faith which was once delivered" (Jude 3). Christians must "rightly [divide] the word of truth" (2 Timothy 2:15) in an effort to find out what Christ wants for and from His followers. In some churches, traditions are followed more faithfully than are the standards of the Scripture. We must be faithful to the Word of God first, holding to traditions when they are helpful and adapting to new challenges with new methods when appropriate.

2. When a car alarm sounds today, people often ignore it. Why? Does the same reaction hold true when spiritual warnings are sounded? For example, how effective are the posters that say, "The end is near"? Is there another way to communicate God's warnings? How?

An old proverb says, "Familiarity breeds contempt." The Christian message and warnings of judgment to come have been sounded so many times that many people today do not even notice. Placards and billboards may reach a few. But a Christian's own personal testimony shared with a friend is much more believable. Talk with the class about how to do this effectively in one-to-one encounters.

3. The people in the text continued to burn incense and offer sacrifices. They believed they were faithful in their "worship services." So why was God so upset with them? To what extent would God have the same reaction to worship practices today? Why?

God always has been very clear that worship without a contrite and humble heart is not acceptable to Him. (See 1 Samuel 15:22, 23.) A life committed to God is always a prerequisite for praise and adoration. If Christians today believe just showing up at church, participating in Communion when it is served, and giving an offering is enough to please God, they need to reread this passage as well as others that criticize fickle hearts.

4. If God's promise in this passage had been full of positive news of future greatness instead of warnings of punishment, do you think the people would have been more willing to embrace the message? Why or why not? What are the differences in people's perspectives when they hear positive and negative messages? What does that say about the work of the church as it speaks locally and to various cultures around the world?

Ask how class members react to good news and bad news, to promises versus threats. Maybe some can give recent examples. List the pros and cons of which to present to non-Christians first: the positives of Christ or the dire warnings for those who reject Him. The truth is, both kinds of messages are needed, and both appear in Scripture. Talk about when to use positive and negative messages in personal evangelism.

5. In verse 29 Jeremiah is demanding a major change from the people—and change is necessary for people today as well. For which age group is change the most difficult? Why? What implications does this have in how long a message needs to be taught before results can be expected?

People in every age group probably would argue they are the most flexible. The truth is that change is usually hard for all of us. We do not change our decisions, convictions, biases, or prejudices easily. For this reason, the church must be tireless as it presents the message of Christ. It is difficult to predict when an individual is almost ready to make a change. One more source of encouragement may be all that is needed to make the difference.

God Issues a Strong Warning

DEVOTIONAL READING: Proverbs 4:20-27.

BACKGROUND SCRIPTURE: Jeremiah 25, 26; 2 Chronicles 36.

PRINTED TEXT: Jeremiah 25:1-9; 26:12, 13.

Jeremiah 25:1-9

1 The word that came to Jeremiah concerning all the people of Judah, in the fourth year of Jehoiakim the son of Josiah king of Judah, that was the first year of Nebuchadrezzar king of Babylon;

2 The which Jeremiah the prophet spake unto all the people of Judah, and to all the inhabitants of Jerusalem, saying,

3 From the thirteenth year of Josiah the son of Amon king of Judah, even unto this day, that is the three and twentieth year, the word of the LORD hath come unto me, and I have spoken unto you, rising early and speaking; but ye have not hearkened.

4 And the LORD hath sent unto you all his servants the prophets, rising early and sending them; but ye have not hearkened, nor inclined your ear to hear.

5 They said, Turn ye again now every one from his evil way, and from the evil of your doings, and dwell in the land that the LORD hath given unto you and to your fathers for ever and ever:

6 And go not after other gods to serve them, and to worship them, and provoke me not to anger with the works of your hands; and I will do you no hurt.

7 Yet ye have not hearkened unto me, saith the LORD; that ye might provoke me to anger with the works of your hands to your own hurt.

8 Therefore thus saith the LORD of hosts; Because ye have not heard my words,

9 Behold, I will send and take all the families of the north, saith the LORD, and Nebuchadrezzar the king of Babylon, my servant, and will bring them against this land, and against the inhabitants thereof, and against all these nations round about, and will utterly destroy them, and make them an astonishment, and a hissing, and perpetual desolations.

Jeremiah 26:12, 13

12 Then spake Jeremiah unto all the princes and to all the people, saying, The LORD sent me to prophesy against this house and against this city all the words that ye have heard.

13 Therefore now amend your ways and your doings, and obey the voice of the LORD your God; and the LORD will repent him of the evil that he hath pronounced against you.

GOLDEN TEXT: Therefore now amend your ways and your doings, and obey the voice of the LORD your God; and the LORD will repent him of the evil that he hath pronounced against you.—Jeremiah 26:13.

<table>
<tr><td>

Judgment and Exile

Unit 2: Limited Hope

(Lessons 6-9)

</td></tr>
</table>

Lesson Aims

After this lesson each student will be able to:

1. Tell what God said would happen to Judah and the reasons He gave for this punishment.

2. List some ways our society is like that of Judah in Jeremiah's day.

3. State his or her own commitment to "choose life," following the Lord and His commands.

Lesson Outline

INTRODUCTION

    A. Getting Attention

    B. Lesson Background

I. GOD'S MESSAGE INTRODUCED (Jeremiah 25:1-3)

    A. When (v. 1)

    B. Who (v. 2)

    C. What (v. 3)

II. GOD'S MESSAGE REVIEWED (Jeremiah 25:4-7)

    A. A Message From Many (v. 4)

    B. A Message Repeated (vv. 5, 6)

    C. A Message Spurned (v. 7)

III. GOD'S MESSAGE ENHANCED (Jeremiah 25:8, 9)

    A. Reason for Punishment (v. 8)

    B. Method of Punishment (v. 9)

IV. GOD'S MESSENGER DEFENDED (Jeremiah 26: 12, 13)

    A. Jeremiah Presents His Authority (v. 12)

    B. Jeremiah Presents a Way of Escape (v. 13)

    Clear, Understandable Communication

CONCLUSION

    A. That Was Then

    B. This Is Now

    C. Prayer

    D. Thought to Remember

Introduction

Jeremiah walks where the people of Judah walk, probably in the big court of the temple. But Jeremiah is different from the rest. On his neck he wears a yoke, such as oxen wear to pull a wagon or a plow. You can imagine the comments of careless observers:

"Hey, guy, what's up with the yoke?"

"Are you looking for a donkey?"

"No, a donkey can't get into the temple. He's unclean."

"Maybe this guy is just a donkey in disguise."

So the banter may have gone on while a curious little crowd gathers. Then Jeremiah lets them have it: "Every one of you will be wearing a yoke soon enough. You'll all be beasts of burden for the king of Babylon."

A. Getting Attention

The above dialogue is imaginary, but the yoke is real. The Lord told Jeremiah to wear it. He even had the prophet send replicas to the kings of other nations near Judah. You can read about it in chapter 27 of the book of Jeremiah.

That device was useful in calling attention to a message the people did not care to hear. At ease and comfortable, they were inclined to scoff at prophecies of doom and gloom. Some were angry with the prophets. Few took God's messages seriously. Three times in the first seven verses of our text we read, "Ye have not hearkened." The people of Judah simply were not listening!

B. Lesson Background

The book of Jeremiah contains many messages that God gave through that prophet. Some of them are dated and some are not. Last week we considered one that was undated, but we suppose it was given while Josiah was king of Judah, and it strongly supported that king's effort to turn Judah back to true worship and obedience to the Lord.

Now let us pause for a quick look at the larger picture of world events. By the time Jeremiah began his prophetic ministry in 626 B.C. (Jeremiah 1:3), the Assyrian empire had been greatly weakened. They had carried the northern kingdom of Israel into exile about a hundred years before (722 B.C.), but about twenty years after that event, God had stopped their invasion of Judah by killing 185,000 of their troops (2 Kings 19:35).

Since then, it seems to have been pretty much downhill for the Assyrians. Nineveh, their capital city, fell to the Babylonians and others in 612 B.C., or about fourteen years after Jeremiah came on the scene. Three years later, Pharaoh Neco (also spelled "Necho," 2 Chronicles 35:20, 22, or "Nechoh," 2 Kings 23:34) II of Egypt led an expedition up the Judean coastline to link up with what was left of the Assyrian army in an attempt to stop the Babylonian expansion.

Josiah, the last godly king of Judah, rashly led his army out to stop Neco's northward march. Perhaps Josiah hoped to curry the friendship of the up and coming Babylonians with this maneuver, but he ended up losing both the battle and his life (2 Chronicles 35:22-24).

After this battle, Pharaoh Neco briefly took charge of Judah. He allowed Josiah's son and successor to rule for only three months. Then he was deposed and taken captive to Egypt. The Egyptians then put his brother on the throne and named him Jehoiakim. He was allowed to rule Judah and was compelled to pay tribute to Egypt.

Josiah's ill-conceived action in intercepting the Egyptian army had another important effect: it delayed the Egyptian army long enough for the Babylonians to defeat the Assyrians thoroughly first. When the Egyptians finally completed their trip up to the Euphrates River to join their Assyrian allies, they were too late. They suffered a devastating defeat at the hands of the Babylonians at the epic battle of Carchemish in 605 B.C.—the very year that Jeremiah delivered the message in our lesson text for today (see 2 Chronicles 35:20; Jeremiah 46:2). From this time onward, the Babylonians were the force to reckon with, as the Assyrians and Egyptians faded away (2 Kings 24:7; Nahum 3:18, 19).

This background sets the stage for a message that God gave to Jeremiah in the fourth year of the new king, Jehoiakim. In the first three years of his reign, that king had shown clearly that he was not interested in the reforms made by his godly father, Josiah. Swiftly he was leading the nation back to idolatry and all the sins associated with it. God and His prophet were not pleased by this turn of events.

I. God's Message Introduced (Jeremiah 25:1-3)

This time, Jeremiah tells us a little about the message before delivering it. He specifies the date, identifies the speaker and the hearers, and gives a bit of background.

A. When (v. 1)

1. The word that came to Jeremiah concerning all the people of Judah, in the fourth year of Jehoiakim the son of Josiah king of Judah, that was the first year of Nebuchadrezzar king of Babylon.

The message that follows is spoken by *Jeremiah*, but it is not his own. It *came* to him from the Lord. It is about *all the people of Judah*, both good and wicked together. *The fourth year of Jehoiakim* is 605 B.C., also *the first year of Nebuchadrezzar king of Babylon.* What a monumental change in the course of history has occurred in the short time Jehoiakim has been king.

Nebuchadrezzar (also know as Nebuchadnezzar) will come calling on Judah three times over the next nineteen years. The first will be in 605 B.C., an invasion that will take the prophet Daniel into captivity (see Daniel 1:1-6). The second would be about eight years later, in 597 B.C., when the Babylonian king will carry off much

more, including much of the temple treasure and probably the prophet Ezekiel (2 Kings 24:10-17). The third will be eleven years after that, as the city and the temple are destroyed and Judah is carried into exile in 586 B.C. (2 Kings 25).

B. Who (v. 2).

2. The which Jeremiah the prophet spake unto all the people of Judah, and to all the inhabitants of Jerusalem, saying.

The message is spoken by *Jeremiah*, but again we note that Jeremiah is *the prophet*, the spokesman for the Lord. Jeremiah does not make up the message he speaks. He may have spoken it more than once to reach *unto all the people of Judah, and to all the inhabitants of Jerusalem;* but probably he can address most of them when they gather at the temple for worship. Those people continue their worthless "worship" of the Lord (Jeremiah 6:20). [See question #1, page 56.]

C. What (v. 3)

3. From the thirteenth year of Josiah the son of Amon king of Judah, even unto this day, that is the three and twentieth year, the word of the LORD hath come unto me, and I have spoken unto you, rising early and speaking; but ye have not hearkened.

Jeremiah is now in "mid-career." He had begun proclaiming God's word in Judah in the thirteenth year of Josiah's reign (Jeremiah 1:1, 2), and has continued through the rest of Josiah's thirty-one year kingship (2 Chronicles 34:1), the three-month reign of Jehoahaz (2 Kings 23:31-35), and on into the fourth year of Jehoiakim's reign. That adds up to a total of twenty-three years. [See question #2, page 56.]

Rising early is a Hebrew expression that means being eager and diligent—Jeremiah has not been

---

Home Daily Bible Readings

Monday, Sept. 30—The Lord Has Spoken Persistently (Jeremiah 25:1-7)
Tuesday, Oct. 1—Jeremiah Speaks the Lord's Warning (Jeremiah 26:1-6)
Wednesday, Oct. 2—The Lord Sent Me to You (Jeremiah 26:7-13)
Thursday, Oct. 3—Officials Believe Jeremiah (Jeremiah 26:14-19)
Friday, Oct. 4—Turn From Evil (Proverbs 4:20-27)
Saturday, Oct. 5—Listen, Stubborn of Heart (Isaiah 46:8-13)
Sunday, Oct. 6—People Hear but Do Not Understand (Matthew 13:10-16)

slack in bringing his message! The people of Judah have had ample opportunity to hear God's messages. But they *have not hearkened*. Instead, the people use their own eagerness in rising early to do evil. (See Zephaniah 3:7 and page 29 above.)

II. God's Message Reviewed (Jeremiah 25:4-7)

Jeremiah is not the only prophet speaking for the Lord during these twenty-three years. We do not know for certain exactly how many others were active then, but we are sure God is not sending any contradictory messages.

A. A Message From Many (v. 4)

4. And the LORD hath sent unto you all his servants the prophets, rising early and sending them; but ye have not hearkened, nor inclined your ear to hear.

The Lord has been diligent in sending His messengers. Also active (or very close to starting their prophetic activities) are Zephaniah, Uriah (also spelled "Urijah," Jeremiah 26:20), Daniel, Habakkuk, and Ezekiel. No one in Judah can complain that he or she does not know what God wants. But the stubborn wrongdoers ultimately turn deaf ears to every message from Heaven.

B. A Message Repeated (vv. 5, 6)

5. They said, Turn ye again now every one from his evil way, and from the evil of your doings, and dwell in the land that the LORD hath given unto you and to your fathers for ever and ever.

Stop doing *evil!* That is the consistent message sounded day by day from uncounted prophets. Why is such preaching still needed? After King Josiah read the law to his people (2 Chronicles 34:29, 30) and everyone pledged to obey it, they should have been following it without any prompting. But they ignored the law as easily as they ignored the prophets!

The people are still living in the good *land* that God had promised them long before. They can live there forever if they will obey Him. God has promised just that. But just as plainly He has promised that they will lose that good land if they do not obey—in other words, the promise is conditional. The people are claiming the promise, but ignoring the conditions. (See Deuteronomy 8:6-20; 28:36, 37, 63-68; 29:28; 30:1-4, 17, 18.). Each one continues in his or her own *evil way*—especially in the worship of "other gods" (v. 6).

6. And go not after other gods to serve them, and to worship them, and provoke me not to anger with the works of your hands; and I will do you no hurt.

Idols and imaginary gods sometimes are worshiped with merry feasting and revelry (cf. Exodus 32:5, 6; Daniel 5:1-4). God knows that the people of Judah will be tempted to join their pagan neighbors at such times, but that will break the very first of the Ten Commandments (Exodus 20:3). Such behavior, worshiping idols that are nothing more than *the works of* their own *hands*, as well any other evil that they might do, will *provoke* the Lord, stirring Him to *anger* (e.g., Jeremiah 32:37; 44:3). If the people of Judah are careful not to disobey God, He will bless them in many ways. Deuteronomy 28 sets forth some of the ways God will bless His people if they are obedient, and some of the ways He will *hurt* (punish) them if they are not.

C. A Message Spurned (v. 7)

7. Yet ye have not hearkened unto me, saith the LORD; that ye might provoke me to anger with the works of your hands to your own hurt.

No doubt the prophets have been calling attention to God's promises and threats, such as those written in Deuteronomy 28, but the people pay no attention. They go right on worshiping their hand-made gods and doing anything else that appeals to them. That kind of behavior will result in their *own hurt.* They will be punished. [See question #3, page 56.]

III. God's Message Enhanced (Jeremiah 25:8, 9)

Now God adds another message. It is more specific about the punishment that is hinted at in verses 5 and 6.

A. Reason for Punishment (v. 8)

8. Therefore thus saith the LORD of hosts; Because ye have not heard my words,

For twenty-three years Jeremiah and other prophets have been delivering God's messages faithfully. For twenty-three years the people of Judah have been ignoring them. For that, punishment is demanded.

B. Method of Punishment (v. 9)

9. Behold, I will send and take all the families of the north, saith the LORD, and Nebuchadrezzar the king of Babylon, my servant, and will bring them against this land, and against the inhabitants thereof, and against all these nations round about, and will utterly destroy them, and make them an astonishment, and a hissing, and perpetual desolations.

The families of the north may include people groups such as the Syrians and Phoenicians, but most likely this phrase refers to the Babylonians, who will eventually attack Judah from the north. *Nebuchadrezzar the king of Babylon* is God's *servant* without knowing it (also Jeremiah 27:6; 43:10). He intends to conquer Judah for his own selfish purposes, but God will use him to punish Judah for ignoring God's leading and doing evil persistently. (Interestingly, this foreign king humbles himself before God toward the end of his own life; see Daniel 4:34-37.)

Also to be punished are the pagan *nations round about* Judah, such as Ammon, Moab, and Edom. These nations will not submit quietly to Babylonian rule. They will be so stubborn in resistance and rebellion that the Babylonians will find it necessary *utterly* to *destroy them.* That end of once prosperous nations will be an *astonishment* to all who see it. *Hissing* represents the sound to be uttered by those who would see the nations destroyed—a sound of surprise mingled with contempt for the helpless victims.

The phrase *perpetual desolations* describes the result of the Babylonian conquest. Cities are to become heaps of rubble, and fertile fields will become wasteland or grazing country. Jeremiah uses descriptions of "desolation" more than twenty times in his book. [See question #4, page 56.]

How to Say It

AHIKAM. Uh-*high*-kum.
AMMON. *Am*-mun.
AMON. *Ay*-mun.
ASSYRIAN. Uh-*sear*-e-un.
BABYLONIANS. Bab-ih-*low*-nee-unz.
CARCHEMISH. *Kar*-kuh-mish.
EUPHRATES. You-*fray*-teez.
EZEKIEL. Ee-*zeek*-ee-ul or Ee-*zeek*-yul.
HABAKKUK. Huh-*back*-kuk.
HEZEKIAH. Hez-ih-*kye*-uh.
JEHOAHAZ. Jeh-*ho*-uh-haz.
JEHOIAKIM. Jeh-*hoy*-uh-kim.
JEREMIAH. Jair-uh-*my*-uh.
JOSIAH. Jo-*sigh*-uh.
JUDEAN. Joo-*dee*-un.
NAHUM. *Nay*-hum.
NEBUCHADNEZZAR. *Neb*-yuh-kud-*nez*-er (strong accent on *nez*).
NEBUCHADREZZAR. *Neb*-uh-kad-*rez*-er (strong accent on *rez*).
NECO, NECHO, or NECHOH. *Nee*-ko.
NINEVEH. *Nin*-uh-vuh.
PHARAOH. *Fay*-ro.
PHOENICIANS. Fuh-*nish*-unz.
URIAH. Yu-*rye*-uh.
SYRIANS. *Sear*-ee-unz.
URIJAH. Yu-*rye*-juh.
ZEPHANIAH. Zef-uh-*nye*-uh.

IV. God's Messenger Defended (Jeremiah 26:12, 13)

Added predictions of disaster fill the rest of chapter 25 and continue into the first part of chapter 26. This message is not popular. People who are enjoying their wrongdoing do not want to hear anything against it. The priests, who should be teaching as Jeremiah does, seem content to go along with the new king's lapse into evil (2 Chronicles 36:5). They get their share of an offering whether it is made to the Lord or to Baal, so why not be "tolerant"? Then there are the self-appointed, false prophets who teach what people like to hear (cf. 2 Timothy 4:3). To them, Jeremiah is a real threat to their cozy arrangements.

So corrupt priests and false prophets seize Jeremiah as he teaches in the temple. They are supported by a crowd of the "tolerant" people—people ready to tolerate anything but Jeremiah's intolerance. To them, Jeremiah seems to be taking the side of Judah's enemy (Jeremiah 25:9); he is a traitor and must die! (See 26:8, 9.)

News of this soon reaches the government officials, who come as a body to deal with the disturbance in the temple court. In their presence, the accusers repeat their charge against Jeremiah (26:10, 11). The final verses of our text bring us a bit of Jeremiah's defense against this accusation.

A. Jeremiah Presents His Authority (v. 12)

12. Then spake Jeremiah unto all the princes and to all the people, saying, The LORD sent me to prophesy against this house and against this city all the words that ye have heard.

This house is the temple and *this city* is Jerusalem. Jeremiah has indeed spoken *against* both of them. He has said they will be destroyed. But he has said this by the authority of the Lord God Almighty. God's people had better listen! [See question #5, page 56.]

B. Jeremiah Presents a Way of Escape (v. 13)

13. Therefore now amend your ways and your doings, and obey the voice of the LORD your God; and the LORD will repent him of the evil that he hath pronounced against you.

In the face of a death sentence, Jeremiah's message does not change: *evil* is indeed coming, but it's not too late to escape this pending disaster. If the people of Judah will only do right instead of wrong, they will be safe. Wouldn't that be better than killing God's messenger and going on to destruction?

As the rest of the chapter unfolds, we see precedents cited. Back in the time of King Hezekiah, a prophet of disaster had been tolerated and even heeded. In the time of King Jehoiakim, a similar prophet had been put to death. But a statesman named Ahikam defends Jeremiah and has enough influence to win the argument. Jeremiah is allowed to live and continue his preaching until the predicted disaster becomes a fact.

CLEAR, UNDERSTANDABLE COMMUNICATION

If you are one of the increasingly large numbers of people who have a computer that is connected to the World Wide Web, you have a ready supply of words available to you in many languages. At www.spanishdict.com, you can find the translation and pronunciation of nearly fifty-five thousand Spanish words. Or check out www.yale.edu/swahili if you're planning a trip to Africa. There you'll find translation and pronunciation of Swahili words and phrases. Various Chinese dialects, Greek, German, and other languages have Web sites dedicated to them.

If you just want to speak English, but need plain-talk explanations of medical terms, go to www.medterms.com. "Surfer"-talk, rap music, computer tech-speak, and various sports all have their Web sites as well.

When it comes to our faith, most of us have some passages of Scripture that are not clear to us. However, most people also have very little difficulty understanding the basics of what God expects. In fact, we probably understand very clearly what God says about the sins that may trouble us the most.

The same was true of Judah in the distant past. Their problem was that Jeremiah was speaking all too plainly (for their comfort) about what God demanded of them. His clear call to repentance made them very uncomfortable, and also made them wish he would go away and leave them alone.   —C. R. B.

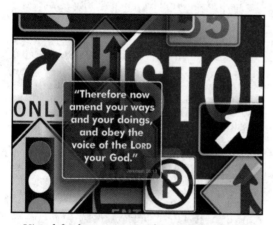

"Therefore now amend your ways and your doings, and obey the voice of the LORD your God."

Visual for lesson 6. *Use this poster to illustrate Jeremiah 26:13. You will find it in the* Adult Visuals *packet. (See page 13 for ordering information.)*

Conclusion

A parallel between Jeremiah's time and ours is clear in the growing exaltation of people's wills and desires over God's. Those who insist on what the Bible says are likely to be branded as narrow-minded, intolerant, and "out of touch." But God's way is still right—to the exclusion of all others.

A. That Was Then

When Jeremiah issued his warning, people scoffed. The people of Judah were God's people, they said. God would keep them secure. There was nothing to worry about. After all, Jerusalem was where the temple is located (Jeremiah 7:4, 14; cf. 21:2).

With such contradictory leading, how could the people know who was telling the truth and who was lying? One way to tell was to wait and see whose prophecies actually came true (Jeremiah 28:9). Another way was to compare the messages with God's previously revealed Word. Isaiah, in warning against false fortune-tellers of various kinds, said, "To the law and to the testimony: if they speak not according to this word, it is because there is no light in them" (Isaiah 8:19, 20).

The law and the testimony! The written Scriptures give all the help that is needed.

B. This Is Now

As Christians, we are not under the law, but under grace (Romans 6:14). But does that mean we are lawless? Not at all. Like the apostle Paul, we are under the law of Christ (1 Corinthians 9:21). The fact that we follow Jesus requires no less goodness in thought, word, and action than lawkeeping does. In fact, it takes more. The law forbade adultery; Jesus warns against even lust (Matthew 5:27, 28). The law required the keeping of oaths; Jesus advocates truth without an oath (5:33-37). The law enjoined love for neighbors; Jesus teaches love for enemies in imitation of the heavenly Father's love (5:43-48). We could give many other examples.

If you were to grade yourself on following Jesus, would it be "pass" or "fail"?

C. Prayer

Father in Heaven, it is discouraging to read how many people through the ages have chosen death rather than life. But when we recall that Your Son died in our place, discouragement vanishes in the glory of Your grace. In gratitude, we pledge ourselves to put Your will above our own. In Jesus' name, amen.

D. Thought to Remember

The choice is yours. Choose life!

Learning by Doing

This page contains an alternative lesson plan emphasizing learning activities.
Classes desiring such student involvement will find these suggestions helpful.

Learning Goals

After participating in this lesson, each student will be able to:

1. Tell what God said would happen to Judah and the reasons He gave for this punishment.

2. List some ways our society is like that of Judah in Jeremiah's day.

3. State his or her own commitment to "choose life," following the Lord and His commands.

Into the Lesson

Begin this week by asking the learners to rearrange their chairs into a circle. For classes with more than twelve students, move the class into several circles of eight to ten students each. When the students are arranged in circles, say: "Today's lesson is called 'God Issues a Strong Warning.' I'd like you to think about the many ways we receive warnings. Starting with the person in each group who would be first if last names were alphabetized, I'm going to ask each of you to state a type of warning device. No one can speak unless it's that person's turn. See how many warning devices you can list in your circle." *(Possible answers include smoke or radon detectors, ambulance siren, flashing light, messages on prescription medicines, computer virus detector, car or house burglar alarms, lighthouse, and foghorn.)* In smaller classes, write the suggested warning devices on an overhead transparency or board for all to see. In larger classes with several circles, ask one person in each circle to record the suggestions.

After several minutes, go over the many different warning devices and say, "These devices alert us to possible danger. Sometimes these warnings are given by a brilliant light, sometimes by a loud sound, and sometimes by strong words. Our text today is a strong warning to God's people. Turn to Jeremiah 25 and let's see why Judah is receiving this warning."

Into the Word

Prior to class, prepare the following true/false quiz from the lesson text. Make enough copies so every student will have one. Ask the students to read Jeremiah 25:1-9 and Jeremiah 26:12, 13 to prepare. Then distribute the quizzes and ask each student to work with a neighbor to respond to the quiz. Allow about eight minutes for them to read the quiz and to indicate whether each statement is true or false.

1. Jehoiakim was the grandson of Amon. *(True.)*

2. Judah worshiped other gods and provoked the Lord to anger. *(True.)*

3. Nebuchadrezzar, King of Babylon, started to reign in Josiah's fourth year. *(False.)*

4. Judah's obedience could reverse God's planned punishment for them. *(True.)*

5. Time and again, the prophets spoke God's warning to Judah. *(True.)*

6. Jeremiah began speaking the Word from the thirteenth year of Josiah. *(True.)*

7. The people of Judah provoked God to anger by rising early. *(False.)*

8. The Babylonians were coming from the south. *(False.)*

9. Jeremiah and Nebuchadrezzar were both God's servants. *(True.)*

10. The Word has come to Jeremiah for a period of twenty-three years. *(True.)*

After the time is up, ask for correct answers from the class. Then ask the following questions:

1. Why was God warning Judah of coming judgment? *(They had not listened to the prophets, vv. 3, 4; their ways are evil, v. 5; they are idol worshipers, v. 6.)*

2. What will the Babylonians do when they go against Judah? *(Go against the inhabitants, the nations round about; they will be destroyed, a hissing, and perpetual desolation, v. 9.)*

Say: "Now let's consider some ways this passage relates to our lives."

Into Life

Establish groups of three and ask each group to list as many ways as possible that our society is like that of Judah in Jeremiah's day. Give several minutes. Then ask for suggested answers from the class. As these ways are given, write them for all to see. Say: "Our society is much like that of Judah, isn't it? And just like in Jeremiah's day, we need people to rise up and choose life in God. Each of us needs to rise up and be committed to following the Lord and to obeying His commands. I challenge you to be a Jeremiah."

Conclude class with a directed prayer time. Pray that God will give us Jeremiah's boldness and ability to stand for God in an evil age. Pray for a personal commitment to follow the Lord.

Let's Talk It Over

The questions on this page are designed to promote discussion of the lesson by the class and to encourage application of the lesson Scriptures. The answers provided are only discussion starters. Let your class talk it over from there.

1. Even during the most wicked years, worship in the temple continued for the weekly and annual celebrations. God was displeased because their worship had more form than substance. How can we ensure that our worship is acceptable to God?

Going through the motions of worship may give people comfort for one of at least two reasons. Some feel good about keeping the traditions. Others do so out of the mistaken view that it earns them "credit" with God. Jesus said there would be a time in which people would worship "in spirit and in truth" (John 4:23, 24). This needs to be more than a keeping of tradition or an attempt to earn merit. Ask class members to share the helpful things they or others do to keep focused on worship when they are being distracted (noise, thoughts, fatigue, busyness, hurt feelings, and the like). Since many people have a tendency to "trance out" during routine activities, talk about innovations that can be introduced into services to help worshipers stay focused.

2. Jeremiah warned Judah for twenty-three years, but he was ignored by almost everyone. That can be discouraging! Christian leaders may also become discouraged when their ministries seem to show little or no fruit. List specific ways Christians can encourage their leaders to remain faithful in preaching and teaching God's truth.

Jeremiah remained faithful because he was convinced about the person and authority of God. He knew that only by continually speaking God's message could the people understand the truth. There were a few faithful people in his day who must have been an encouragement to him.

Have the class make a list of the many ways church members can encourage their leaders (cards, comments, gifts, testimony of how a sermon or lesson helped, etc).

3. The people in our text preferred prophets using pleasant words and predicting positive outcomes. They rejected messages condemning their actions or warning of impending doom. How can we keep ourselves open to all parts of God's message? If Christians see each other becoming complacent, what methods can they use to awaken each other?

People, including many Christians, have always preferred to believe God was happy with their actions. As a result, the full truth about God's expectations is ignored. Every Christian daily needs to seek to know the character and message of God and then live accordingly.

Read James 5:19, 20. Lead the class in a discussion about how they can encourage and/or confront each other if there is evidence of anyone's becoming complacent or wandering from God. If each Christian would give others permission to intervene, there would be less tendency to accuse each other of being judgmental when confrontation becomes necessary.

4. When Christians see a street preacher yelling, "The end is near," they often are embarrassed and resolve never to do anything that can be ridiculed. As a result, Christians become fearful and do not even share with their neighbors. What does the church need to do to help members get over this reluctance to speak about their faith?

Christians need to differentiate between method and message. Some methods are not as effective as others. Some methods bring ridicule while others are highly effective. The Christian's role is to learn effective skills for sharing the gospel. Discuss how the class can use lesson time to move beyond its comfort zone and learn new ways of sharing the message of life (special speakers, evangelism material, role-play sessions, etc.).

5. The people seemed to hold on to faulty theological beliefs like "We are God's chosen people. Therefore, God will always protect us." Their misbeliefs about God increased their difficulty in recognizing their sin. What methods can Christians employ to protect against letting faulty religious or cultural beliefs distort their walk with God?

Today's faulty beliefs may not be the same as those in Old Testament times. Have the class name the modern faulty beliefs about God (there is no God, God is love and would not punish those He loves, all gods are the same, etc.). Take each belief separately and list the specific reasons it is faulty. Develop strategies to remember these reasons as a way of protecting against the subtle eroding power present in an ungodly culture.

God Demands a Just Society

DEVOTIONAL READING: Ephesians 5:8-17.

BACKGROUND SCRIPTURE: Jeremiah 22.

PRINTED TEXT: Jeremiah 22:13-17, 21-23.

Jeremiah 22:13-17, 21-23

13 Woe unto him that buildeth his house by unrighteousness, and his chambers by wrong; that useth his neighbor's service without wages, and giveth him not for his work;

14 That saith, I will build me a wide house and large chambers, and cutteth him out windows; and it is ceiled with cedar, and painted with vermilion.

15 Shalt thou reign, because thou closest thyself in cedar? Did not thy father eat and drink, and do judgment and justice, and then it was well with him?

16 He judged the cause of the poor and needy; then it was well with him: was not this to know me? saith the LORD.

17 But thine eyes and thine heart are not but for thy covetousness, and for to shed innocent blood, and for oppression, and for violence, to do it.

.   .   .   .

21 I spake unto thee in thy prosperity; but thou saidst, I will not hear. This hath been thy manner from thy youth, that thou obeyedst not my voice.

22 The wind shall eat up all thy pastors, and thy lovers shall go into captivity: surely then shalt thou be ashamed and confounded for all thy wickedness.

23 O inhabitant of Lebanon, that makest thy nest in the cedars, how gracious shalt thou be when pangs come upon thee, the pain as of a woman in travail!

GOLDEN TEXT: I spake unto thee in thy prosperity; but thou saidst, I will not hear.
—Jeremiah 22:21.

Judgment and Exile
Unit 2: Limited Hope
(Lessons 6-9)

Lesson Aim

After participating in this lesson, each student will be able to:

1. Cite some of the ways the king of Judah failed to follow the good example of his father.

2. Tell why the example of a person in leadership is important to those who follow.

3. Suggest some specific way to influence people around him or her with the power of the gospel.

Lesson Outline

INTRODUCTION
  A. A Prophet's Task
  B. Lesson Background
I. THE KING AND HIS SINS (Jeremiah 22:13, 14)
  A. Injustice to the Workers (v. 13)
  B. Luxury for the King (v. 14)
II. THE KING AND HIS FATHER (Jeremiah 22:15-17)
  A. A Sharp Contrast (v. 15)
  B. The Father's Way (v. 16)
  C. The Son's Way (v. 17)
    Like Father, Like Son?
III. JUDAH AND HER DESTINY (Jeremiah 22:21-23)
  A. The Problem (v. 21)
  B. The Punishment (vv. 22, 23)
    The Placebo Effect
CONCLUSION
  A. About Nations
  B. About People
  C. Prayer
  D. Thought to Remember

Introduction

Freedom of speech is high among the liberties people cherish. Wise or foolish, right or wrong, true or false, people like to be able to say what they think. There was no such freedom of speech, however, in ancient monarchies where the king's word was law. The prophet Urijah (also spelled Uriah) spoke against Judah much as Jeremiah did, and he lost his life as a result. He had hoped that fleeing to Egypt would guarantee his safety, but King Jehoiakim sent men to bring him back and had him killed (Jeremiah 26:20-23). Whether he was extradited legally or simply kidnapped, we do not know.

A. A Prophet's Task

As we saw last week, Jeremiah also came close to being killed (Jeremiah 26:11). With a message similar to Urijah's, Jeremiah may have preferred to speak softly or not at all. But the Lord's prophet does not choose what he will say—or how, when, where, or to whom he will say it. The Lord sent Jeremiah straight to the royal palace with an unwelcome message for the king and his cronies (22:1-9)—and this is the same king who had killed Urijah.

B. Lesson Background

Let us review the events in Judah that provide a background for our lesson. Josiah, Judah's last godly king, was defeated and killed in battle with the Egyptians (2 Chronicles 35:20-24). The next king was his son Jehoahaz, also called Shallum. But soon the victorious Egyptians took charge of Judah, carrying this new king to captivity in Egypt, and putting his brother Jehoiakim in his place to rule Judah and to pay tribute (36:1-4).

Last week, we noted one of the king's advisers defending the prophet Jeremiah, allowing him to escape from the murderous hands of corrupt priests and false prophets. This week we see the Lord sending Jeremiah on a mission even more daring. He must take his message of destruction directly to the king, his officials, and his counselors (Jeremiah 22:1, 2). We take a part of that message for our text.

I. The King and His Sins
(Jeremiah 22:13, 14)

Jeremiah's message at the royal palace sounds much like his message to the common people: Judah must stop doing wrong—she must worship God and obey Him. Otherwise, disaster is coming (Jeremiah 22:3-9). But the text at hand focuses on the king himself.

A. Injustice to the Workers (v. 13)

13. Woe unto him that buildeth his house by unrighteousness, and his chambers by wrong; that useth his neighbor's service without wages, and giveth him not for his work.

King Jehoahaz, also called Shallum, is now a captive in Egypt (vv. 11, 12; also 2 Kings 23:31-33; 2 Chronicles 36:2-4). This message is for the next king, Jehoiakim, who is named in verse 18. He is noted for his evil in general (2 Chronicles 36:5), but the verse at hand singles out one specific sin: he is building his house *by unrighteousness* and *by wrong*.

It is fitting for a king and his family to have "above average" living quarters. Any monarch needs an impressive throne room where he can hold court and receive ambassadors from foreign countries. A banquet hall for state dinners is also appropriate, as are adequate offices for the government officials. Building such things is not necessarily wrong in and of itself, but the way this king is going about it is highly unethical. He is apparently drafting citizens to do the work without pay. [See question #1, page 64.]

Perhaps the tribute Jehoiakim has to pay to Egypt is creating a cash-flow problem for the king (2 Kings 23:34, 35). In spite of that, the king will not settle for second-best where his comfort or image is concerned. But while the king indulges himself, imagine the dismay of a man who toils in the stone quarry for a month, or makes the long trip to the mountains of Lebanon for cedar, only to receive no payment to provide for his family. There will be *woe* for that worker, of course; but there will be *woe* also for the king who is disobeying a law of God (Leviticus 19:13; Deuteronomy 24:14, 15). This is neither the first nor last time that God notices such exploitation (cf. Isaiah 58:3; Malachi 3:5).

B. Luxury for the King (v. 14)

14. That saith, I will build me a wide house and large chambers, and cutteth him out windows; and it is ceiled with cedar, and painted with vermilion.

This verse lists items of luxury in the king's palace: spacious *chambers*, many *windows*, expensive *cedar* from Lebanon to cover the cold stone walls inside, and costly *vermilion* (a reddish paint) for decoration. Rather than cut back on his own luxury items, the king cuts costs by making the builders work without pay. [See question #2, page 64.]

II. The King and His Father (Jeremiah 22:15-17)

King Jehoiakim's wickedness outweighs any good that he does. "He did that which was evil in the sight of the Lord his God" (2 Chronicles 36:5). Such behavior is all the more inexcusable because his father, King Josiah, "did that which was right in the sight of the Lord" (34:1, 2). Jehoiakim had had that noble example before him through all the years of his young adult life. But as king he ignores the good example and turns to his own greedy and godless way. Jeremiah draws a sharp contrast between the father and the son.

A. A Sharp Contrast (v. 15)

15. Shalt thou reign, because thou closest thyself in cedar? did not thy father eat and drink, and do judgment and justice, and then it was well with him?

What does it take to make a king? What does a man need if he is to *reign?* Jehoiakim seems to think that the true marks of a king consist of a *cedar*-lined palace and all the luxury that he can get away with (v. 14). So he oppresses and robs his people to provide such a lifestyle.

By contrast, his father Josiah thought the true marks of a king to be doing right in providing *judgment and justice* for his people. He had had all he needed to *eat and drink* without robbing anyone. *It was well with him:* both he and his people were prosperous and happy. Jehoiakim was about twelve years old when his father initiated his shattering reforms and reinstituted the Passover celebration. So why doesn't Jehoiakim follow the same path?

B. The Father's Way (v. 16)

16. He judged the cause of the poor and needy; then it was well with him: was not this to know me? saith the LORD.

King Josiah had provided justice for all—*the poor and needy* as well as the rich and powerful. In his court, there was no special treatment for a man who could support him with money and influence: he did what was right. And he paid his workers (2 Chronicles 34:9-11).

The result was that *it was well with him*. More than that, the king's way of judging had shown that he knew God, for God also cares for the poor and needy, and He gives no special favor to the rich just because they are rich. Josiah had included "all the people, great and small" in his reforms (2 Chronicles 34:30), and he gave freely to the people from his own possessions (35:7). This set a good example that others followed (35:8, 9).

How to Say It
AHAB. *Ay*-hab.
BABYLON. *Bab*-uh-lun.
BABYLONIAN. Bab-ih-*low*-nee-un.
EZEKIEL. Ee-*zeek*-ee-ul or Ee-*zeek*-yul.
JEHOAHAZ. Jeh-*ho*-uh-haz.
JEHOIACHIN. Jeh-*hoy*-uh-kin.
JEHOIAKIM. Jeh-*hoy*-uh-kim.
JEREMIAH. Jair-uh-*my*-uh.
JEZEBEL. *Jez*-uh-bel.
JOSIAH. Jo-*sigh*-uh.
NEBUCHADNEZZAR. *Neb*-yuh-kud-*nez*-er (strong accent on *nez*).
SHALLUM. *Shall*-um.
URIAH. Yu-*rye*-uh.
URIJAH. Yu-*rye*-yuh.
VERMILION. ver-*mill*-yun.
ZEDEKIAH. Zed-uh-*kye*-uh.

C. The Son's Way (v. 17)

17. But thine eyes and thine heart are not but for thy covetousness, and for to shed innocent blood, and for oppression, and for violence, to do it.

King Jehoiakim, on the other hand, cares nothing for the poor and needy. What could they do for him? His care is for himself and what he can get. The last of the Ten Commandments says, "Thou shalt not covet" (Exodus 20:17), but this king's *covetousness* makes him break any command or law that stands in the way of his gain. He resorts to oppression, compelling citizens to work without wages (v. 13). He will use *violence* and *shed innocent blood*. Over two hundred years before, evil Ahab had used perjured testimony to convict and execute a man in order to confiscate his property (1 Kings 21). Perhaps Jehoiakim does the same. [See question #3, page 64.]

The disgraceful end of this evil king is foretold in verses 18 and 19, which are not included in our printed text. For him there will be no state funeral, with mourners bewailing their loss. His burial will be like that of an unclean animal, which is no burial at all. His dead body will be dragged away from human habitations and left for the buzzards (cf. Jeremiah 36:30).

Jehoiakim dies in 597 B.C. Although historical records do not record the fulfillment of the details of this prophecy, there is no reason to doubt that it is indeed fulfilled. Perhaps King Jehoiakim is killed in some skirmish with the Babylonians or their agents, and when the skirmish is over those invaders perhaps drag his body far from their camp and leave it unburied. He may even have been assassinated by his own people during the Babylonian siege of 597 B.C., with his body being thrown over the wall as a message of surrender. In any case, his death is as dishonorable as that of Jezebel (1 Kings 21:23; 2 Kings 9:30-37).

LIKE FATHER, LIKE SON?

Historically speaking, most national leaders have tried to pass their position on to their offspring. Leaders of many nations in the modern Middle East have passed on power to their sons. It has been so for centuries in England also (although some of these sovereigns were women). In the United States of America, two father-son pairs have been elected as president. George H. W. Bush and his son, George W. Bush—the forty-first and forty-third presidents—follow in the train of John Adams and John Quincy Adams, the second and sixth presidents.

In Judah, it was common for son to follow father to the throne. We have seen this in our earlier studies. Occasionally, this turned out to be good for the kingdom (at least for a time), as in the case of David and Solomon. More often, however, it was to the detriment of the kingdom. This was certainly the case with Josiah and Jehoiakim. Josiah was one of the best kings ever to reign over the Israelites, in large part because of his love for God's law. His son, Jehoiakim, was among the worst of Judah's kings. He disregarded God's concern for judgment and justice for His people. It should have been clear that the nation prospered when God's word was followed. It should also be clear that the principle still holds true. Unfortunately, even Christians sometimes forget the principle when their stomachs and purses are full.   —C. R. B.

III. Judah and Her Destiny (Jeremiah 22:21-23)

The prophecy about King Jehoiakim ends with verse 19. The remaining verses of our text are addressed to the nation of Judah, not to the king. We know this because the pronouns *thee* and *thou* in these remaining verses are feminine in the Hebrew text. In the earlier verses, addressed to the king, those pronouns are masculine in form.

A. The Problem (v. 21)

21. I spake unto thee in thy prosperity; but thou saidst, I will not hear. This hath been thy manner from thy youth, that thou obeyedst not my voice.

Through the written law and the speaking prophets, God has been speaking to His people through all the centuries from Moses to Jeremiah. But in the history of those centuries, they have turned away from God repeatedly in times of *prosperity* and security—the times when it seemed that all was well with the nation. From the youth of the nation, from its very infancy, its response to God's speaking has been a refusal to listen and obey. For example, when Moses was receiving the law from God on Mount Sinai, the people on the plain below were worshiping a golden calf (Exodus 32:1-6). [See question #4, page 64.]

B. The Punishment (vv. 22, 23)

22. The wind shall eat up all thy pastors, and thy lovers shall go into captivity: surely then shalt thou be ashamed and confounded for all thy wickedness.

The Hebrew word translated *pastors* is more often translated *shepherds*. Of course Judah has literal shepherds taking care of sheep; but the pastors mentioned here are the rulers, leaders, and teachers of the people. They are the king and other officials of government, the corrupt priests, and the false prophets. They should be concerned about the welfare of the people, but they are "shepherds . . . that do feed themselves" (Ezekiel 34:2; cf. Jude 12)—they are eager for their own gain. All those greedy pastors will be gone with the *wind*. Like dry leaves in a storm, they will vanish before the Babylonian invaders. [See question #5, page 64.]

Judah's *lovers* are her allies, the other little countries of that region. They will join in resisting the Babylonians, but they will be defeated and made captives. Without leaders and without helpers, Judah will be *ashamed, confounded,* and utterly defeated. She, too, will become captive of Babylon as we see in verses 25 and 26, which are not included in our printed text. All this will be the result of Judah's wickedness.

THE PLACEBO EFFECT

Good medical science requires that new drugs be tested against placebos to determine their effectiveness. Placebos are commonly referred to as "sugar pills" in layman's terms. Doctors have found that even the color of pills—whether placebos or genuine drugs—sometimes can make a difference in their effectiveness.

In one test, one hundred people were told they would be given either a stimulant or a sedative. Actually, all were given identical placebos, except that some were blue in color, some pink. In the group taking the blue pill, 66 percent reported feeling less alert and were sure they had taken the sedative. Only 26 percent of those taking the pink pill felt less alert. The rest of that group was confident they had received the stimulant!

Thus it is obvious that what we may think about our situation is not necessarily the case. In Judah, the people were blindly following their

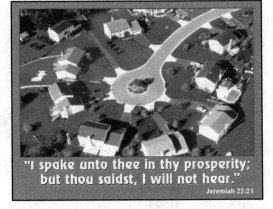

"I spake unto thee in thy prosperity; but thou saidst, I will not hear."

Jeremiah 22:21

Visual for lesson 7. *Use this visual to prompt some application discussion on verse 21. See page 13 for information on ordering visuals.*

leaders, trusting the neighboring nations, and reveling in their good fortune and luxurious surroundings. All the while, they were thinking—in the terms we are using here—that they must have been taking a wonder drug that brought them a long-lasting dose of the good life. Little did they know that this was merely a placebo. There is no "success pill," and the fake drug they had consumed would soon prove to have no power to save them from the deadly disease of sin that was destroying them.   —C. R. B.

23. O inhabitant of Lebanon, that makest thy nest in the cedars, how gracious shalt thou be when pangs come upon thee, the pain as of a woman in travail!

For hundreds of years, Lebanon has been famous for its cedar trees (Judges 9:15; 1 Kings 4:33; 5:6; etc.). Even today, the flag of Lebanon displays the image of a cedar tree prominently in its center. Here, Judah is called an *inhabitant of Lebanon,* not because her people have moved north to that country, but because they have brought so much cedar from Lebanon to build their homes in Judah. They make their *nest,* their dwelling place, *in the cedars*—not the standing trees in Lebanon itself, but in the cedar-lined houses in Judah.

Living in such homes was *gracious,* luxurious living. But the Hebrew word for *gracious* is a word of varied meanings. Many scholars think Jeremiah's thought is represented better by *miserable* or *pitiable* instead of *gracious.* This understanding is reflected in the *New International Version's* "how you will groan." Of course, the present translation, taken as sarcasm, represents the same concept. The people thought they would have gracious living, but how gracious will it be when those lovely homes are destroyed and the inhabitants dragged away to captivity?

However we translate that one line, the prediction is clear: the Babylonians will come, and all Judah will be in pain—pain comparable to that suffered by a *woman* in childbirth. The pain will come because Judah has rejected the Lord's leading and has insisted on doing wrong.

In 597 B.C., the Babylonians will return as the prophet has predicted (Jeremiah 22:25). They will come in overwhelming numbers; it would be madness for Judah's little army to try to fight them. They will come because a few years before that time King Jehoiakim will rebel against Babylon (2 Kings 24:1).

Jehoiakim's rebellion will come at a time when the Babylonian army is busy elsewhere. But by then the little nations around Judah will belong to Babylon's empire, and Babylon will send them to harass Judah. Raiding parties from those nations probably sweep into Judah to drive off the livestock, steal the grain of harvests, destroy villages, and kill or enslave people (2 Kings 24:2). And when King Nebuchadnezzar of Babylon is able, he will bring his huge army back to subdue Judah as he had in 605 B.C. It is sometime during this troubled period that King Jehoiakim dies (or is killed), and his dead body mistreated as Jeremiah predicts (Jeremiah 22:18, 19).

When Nebuchadnezzar's army comes back in force, the new king of Judah is Jehoiachin, son of Jehoiakim (2 Kings 24:6). Wisely he decides not to resist the Babylonians. He is made prisoner and taken to Babylon, along with his family, the officials of government, the military commanders, and the smiths skilled in making weapons. Thousands of captives are taken, including leaders, skilled artisans, and soldiers. This leaves behind a weakened nation that the captors hope will not be able to revolt again (2 Kings 24:10-17). The conquering Babylonians install Zedekiah, brother of King Jehoiakim, to be king of Judah and pay the tribute (2 Kings 24:17).

For eleven years Zedekiah rules Judah and pays the tribute. Toward the end of that time, Zedekiah seems to forget both the power of Babylon and the weakness of Judah, so he rebels (2 Kings 24:18, 20). For the third time, Nebuchadnezzar comes with his army to subdue Judah, and he does not intend to have to come again. In 586 B.C., his men smash Jerusalem into heaps of rubble and take most of the surviving people to Babylon and captivity (2 Kings 25:1-12).

Already the people of Judah have been subject to Babylon for some twenty years. Now they have to live as captives in Babylon for about fifty more. In addition to the book of Lamentations, Psalm 137 records their homesick wail:

> By the rivers of Babylon,
> There we sat down,
> Yea, we wept,
> When we remembered Zion.

Conclusion

People seem to be such slow learners! From the loss of paradise in Eden to the collapse of the Soviet Union and beyond, history itself cries out to all who will listen. It says that obedience to God brings spiritual peace and joy, while disobedience brings distress and disaster. When will we learn?

A. About Nations

In this series of lessons, we have noted that Judah was prosperous and blessed when the people followed King Josiah in true worship and obedience to God. But the kings who followed him chose to do evil in the sight of the Lord, so Judah became captive in Babylon. Has anyone learned from this tragedy? As the exile was taking place, the pagan Babylonian commander knew why this disaster was happening even while the Jewish people remained stubborn (compare Jeremiah 40:2, 3 with chapter 44).

The English-speaking countries of Europe and North America grew great when they were known as Christian nations. Now a trend away from God is so evident that ours is a "post-Christian era." Will we learn in time?

B. About People

When the Babylonians took charge of Judah in 605 B.C., they took some of the finest Hebrew young men to be trained in Babylon (Daniel 1:1-7). These young men remained loyal to the Lord in a time when most of the nation had turned away from Him. God showed His power by delivering them; other faithful men showed their faith by their martyrdom (Acts 6:8–7:60; 12:1, 2; Hebrews 11:35-38) To them and to us Jesus says, "Be thou faithful unto death, and I will give thee a crown of life" (Revelation 2:10). Have you and I learned to trust Him?

C. Prayer

Our Father, God Almighty and all-merciful, thank You for the long record that tells us it is best for us to obey You. Thank You for all the spiritual heroes who have trusted You and obeyed You even when their promised joy had to wait for the reality of Heaven. Give us wisdom to learn what is taught in history and Scripture, and give us strength to obey You today, tomorrow, and forever. In Jesus' name, amen.

D. Thought to Remember

Obeying God is best for me.

Home Daily Bible Readings

Monday, Oct. 7—Act With Justice and Righteousness (Jeremiah 22:1-9)

Tuesday, Oct. 8—A House Built by Injustice (Jeremiah 22:13-23)

Wednesday, Oct. 9—The Shepherds Scatter the Sheep (Jeremiah 23:1-6)

Thursday, Oct. 10—Do Justice (Micah 6:3-8)

Friday, Oct. 11—The Faithful Have Disappeared (Micah 7:1-7)

Saturday, Oct. 12—Judge According to Righteousness (Psalm 7:1-11)

Sunday, Oct. 13—Righteousness in Christ (1 John 2:28–3:7)

Learning by Doing

This page contains an alternative lesson plan emphasizing learning activities.
Classes desiring such student involvement will find these suggestions helpful.

Learning Goals

After this lesson each student will be able to:

1. Cite some of the ways the king of Judah failed to follow the good example of his father.

2. Tell why the example of a person in leadership is important to those who follow.

3. Suggest some specific way to influence people around him or her with the power of the gospel.

Into the Lesson

Prior to the students' arrival, write on the chalkboard the phrase: "The power of example." When it's time for class to begin, say, "I'd like us to consider the phrase on the board. Think of someone in your past who served as an example for you. It may have been positive or negative."

Ask for some volunteers to tell their stories. Then say: "All of us can think of people who have influenced us by their examples. Now think about people in the Bible who set positive examples to follow."

Prior to class, prepare an "Examples to Follow" chart on which to list Bible leaders who set positive examples. Make one copy for every three students. Design the activity by making a three-column chart with these headings: "Who?" "To Whom?" and "Of What?" Make five rows under those headings. Say: "You have five minutes to list in the left column up to five Bible characters who set a positive example for someone to follow. In the middle column, write the name of the person or group who saw the example. Then in the right column describe what the example was."

After the time is past, ask each group to give the name of one example, to whom it was given, and what it was about. Observe that today's lesson focuses upon a king who failed to follow the good example of his father. Ask the students to turn to Jeremiah 22 to see who those kings were.

Into the Word

Ask someone to read Jeremiah 22:13-17, 21-23 aloud. State: "Our lesson text skips verses 18-20, but verse 18 tells us who the good king was and the son who failed to follow the example. Who were they?" *(Josiah and his son Jehoiakim.)*

Ask the following questions:

1. What were some of the ways that Josiah set a good example for Jehoiakim? *(Judgment and justice, judged the cause of the poor, vv. 15, 16.)*

2. What was Jehoiakim building (vv. 13, 14)? *(A house with large chambers and windows.)*

3. What was Jehoiakim doing wrong? *(Not paying his builders for their work.)*

4. Identify the terms in verses 13-17 that describe Jehoiakim's character. *(Unrighteous, wrong, covetous, shed innocent blood, oppression, violence.)*

5. Describe Jehoiakim's character in light of verse 21. *(Rebellious from youth; did not obey.)*

6. What does Jeremiah mean by the terms "pastors" and "lovers?" *("Pastors" were the rulers, leaders, and teachers of the people; "lovers" were her allies, other countries.)*

7. Why is Judah called "O inhabitant of Lebanon" in verse 23? *(They had brought so much cedar from Lebanon to build their homes.)*

8. How is God's judgment on Judah described in verse 23? *(Painful, like that suffered by a woman in childbirth.)*

9. Why is it important for leaders to be an example? *(People follow their leader. Example influences people to act. Josiah led a national repentance and reform, 2 Chronicles 34:31, 32.)*

Into Life

Point out that Jehoiakim's sins were quite a contrast to the lifestyle of his father Josiah, who humbled himself before the Lord and did what was just. Challenge your students to follow Josiah's example of justice and ministry to the poor and needy.

Prior to class prepare a worksheet entitled, "Gospel: Power to Influence People." Make two columns: "Justice" and "Poor and Needy." Place five rows under each heading. Move the class back into the groups of three that you used earlier. Give a copy of the worksheet to each person. Say: "Josiah knew God, and as a result he executed justice and he judged the cause of the poor and needy (Jeremiah 22:16). Take each of those terms and identify some specific ways that people can be influenced with the power of the gospel."

Give about ten minutes for this activity. Then list on the chalkboard some of the various suggestions under each term. Say: "Select one way under each term for you to influence people with the power of the gospel." Close the class session by having a prayer of commitment in each group."

Let's Talk It Over

The questions on this page are designed to promote discussion of the lesson by the class and to encourage application of the lesson Scriptures. The answers provided are only discussion starters. Let your class talk it over from there.

1. Some segments of our culture are very suspicious of the rich, believing their wealth must have been gained through unscrupulous means. What must Christians do to insure they do not develop a prejudice against any group, which in turn might have a negative impact on evangelistic efforts toward that group?

God's Word never condemns a person for being rich. In today's lesson, God only condemns personal gain at someone else's expense. He warns that wealth can lead one to believe he or she is self-reliant and has no need for God (Luke 12:13-21). In contrast, a godly rich person can use the resources entrusted to him or her in many ways to enhance all aspects of God's work. Christians need to share Christ with those in every socioeconomic strata.

2. Jeremiah pronounced woe against those who said, "I will build me a wide house and large chambers." Is it wrong to want a bigger house? What standards can a Christian use to decide whether his or her desire for a new house or other possessions is excessive? How can a Christian insure that he or she views possessions from a spiritual perspective?

It is essential to remind oneself that God owns everything, that we came into the world with nothing and take out nothing (1 Timothy 6:6, 7), and that we are commissioned to be good stewards (Matthew 25:14-31). Having a nice house is not a sin. But do we live in it with the recognition that it is God's house, given to us to use in ways that honor and glorify Him? Loving wealth—seeing it as an end in itself or as a means to self-centered goals—draws us away from God (1 Timothy 6:8-10). When wealth gets in the way of doing our part in caring for those in need, we are guilty of sin (Luke 16:19-31; James 1:27; 5:1-7; Proverbs 19:17; 21:13; 29:7).

3. In the text (v. 17), four sins are listed: coveting, murder, oppression, and violence. With which of these four sins is the average Christian most likely to become entangled? Why? What steps can a Christian take to avoid this trap?

Christians are constantly reminded about the potential that sinful behavior will interfere with their witness to others. As a result, they often monitor their outward behavior more than their thought life. The last three in the list above require an outward action. Christians are perhaps less likely to be caught up in this type of activity. However, coveting is an internal sin. Thought-life sins (see Matthew 5:28; 1 Corinthians 6:9-11; 1 John 2:9-11, 15, 16) can keep a person from Heaven just as surely as outward-action sins. Philippians 4:8 provides a great formula for focusing one's thought life on good things. Once we finish the list of thinking about things that are true, honest, just, pure, lovely, of good report, virtuous, and praiseworthy, we will have used our mental energy well and will be ready for a good night's sleep—ready to resume a good thought pattern in the morning.

4. How does God speak to us "in [our] prosperity"? What does He say? What evidence is there, if any, that anyone is listening?

God's clearest communication with us is through His Word, and in it He has much to say about the use of wealth. He says, "Seek ye first the kingdom of God" (Matthew 6:33). He says, "He which soweth sparingly shall reap also sparingly" and "God loveth a cheerful giver" (2 Corinthians 9:6, 7). He says, "Let him that is taught in the word communicate unto him that teacheth in all good things" (Galatians 6:6).

Unfortunately, few people are listening. Our society is driven by an insatiable appetite for more material wealth, more convenience, more luxury. Too often, professed Christians use their resources in the same manner as non-Christians.

5. If government, business, or even church leaders are responsible for actions that oppress the poor, what responsibility do Christians have to take a stand against the practice? What steps can Christians take when it is apparent these leaders are mistreating people?

One of the most important things Christians can do is to take positive actions to undo the harm that is being done. They can provide tangible help to those who are mistreated; they can speak up and defend those who are abused. Some may be able to convince other influential persons to take direct action against the wrongdoer. Most of all, these Christians must constantly ask God to grant them ample courage for these difficult situations.

God Offers Hope for the Future

DEVOTIONAL READING: Hebrews 10:11-18.

BACKGROUND SCRIPTURE: Jeremiah 30, 31.

PRINTED TEXT: Jeremiah 31:23-34.

Jeremiah 31:23-34

23 Thus saith the LORD of hosts, the God of Israel, As yet they shall use this speech in the land of Judah and in the cities thereof, when I shall bring again their captivity; The LORD bless thee, O habitation of justice, and mountain of holiness.

24 And there shall dwell in Judah itself, and in all the cities thereof together, husbandmen, and they that go forth with flocks.

25 For I have satiated the weary soul, and I have replenished every sorrowful soul.

26 Upon this I awaked, and beheld; and my sleep was sweet unto me.

27 Behold, the days come, saith the LORD, that I will sow the house of Israel and the house of Judah with the seed of man, and with the seed of beast.

28 And it shall come to pass, that like as I have watched over them, to pluck up, and to break down, and to throw down, and to destroy, and to afflict; so will I watch over them, to build, and to plant, saith the LORD.

29 In those days they shall say no more, The fathers have eaten a sour grape, and the children's teeth are set on edge.

30 But every one shall die for his own iniquity: every man that eateth the sour grape, his teeth shall be set on edge.

31 Behold, the days come, saith the LORD, that I will make a new covenant with the house of Israel, and with the house of Judah:

32 Not according to the covenant that I made with their fathers, in the day that I took them by the hand to bring them out of the land of Egypt; which my covenant they brake, although I was a husband unto them, saith the LORD:

33 But this shall be the covenant that I will make with the house of Israel; After those days, saith the LORD, I will put my law in their inward parts, and write it in their hearts; and will be their God, and they shall be my people.

34 And they shall teach no more every man his neighbor, and every man his brother, saying, Know the LORD: for they shall all know me, from the least of them unto the greatest of them, saith the LORD: for I will forgive their iniquity, and I will remember their sin no more.

GOLDEN TEXT: This shall be the covenant that I will make with the house of Israel;
After those days, saith the LORD, I will put my law in their inward parts,
and write it in their hearts; and will be their God,
and they shall be my people.—Jeremiah 31:33.

Judgment and Exile
Unit 2: Limited Hope
(Lessons 6-9)

Lesson Aims

After participating in this lesson, each student will be able to:

1. Summarize God's promise to restore the exiles and to give a New Covenant.

2. Contrast the Old Covenant with the New.

3. Praise God for the forgiveness of sins available in the New Covenant.

Lesson Outline

INTRODUCTION

Introduction

A. Broken Promises

Dwight and Mary had to get a divorce. That was the one thing they agreed on. But before calling a lawyer, they decided they would talk with the minister who had married them eight years before.

"Dwight, Mary," the minister said, "you have a contract, a covenant. Let me remind you." He rummaged in his files and found a sheet of paper, from which he read the marriage vows. "Remember what you said to that, Dwight?"

Dwight grunted, "I said, 'I do.'"

"So did I," Mary added.

"Now," the mister said thoughtfully, "do you suppose you can postpone your divorce for a week? Call it a favor to me."

Dwight grunted again, "I can do that."

"So can I," Mary added.

"Here's what I'd like to have you do for a week. Take this home with you." He handed Dwight the sheet with the marriage vows printed on it. "Every evening after the dishes are washed, I want you to sit down together and read this again. Then, Dwight, you are not to say anything about Mary. But if you can remember a time when you broke your promise, make note of that."

"I don't get the point," Dwight complained, "but if it's a favor to you, I'll do it."

"And you, Mary," the minister went on, "not a word about Dwight, remember. But if you can remember a time when you broke your promise, write it down."

"All right," Mary agreed unwillingly, "but I'm not much of a promise breaker."

A week later the two sat facing the minister again. "Well," he began after the greetings, "did either of you remember a time when your promise was broken?"

"Did I ever!" Mary burst out sadly, "And you knew it all the time, you old smoothie. I can't believe I've broken my promise as many times as I know I did." She waved her written list and looked at Dwight. "I'm sorry."

"You ain't seen nothin' yet," Dwight grumbled, waving his own list. "Take a look at this. What a scum I turned out to be! I'm sorry, too."

The three sat in silence while long seconds ticked away—five seconds, six, seven, eight, nine, ten. Then the minister spoke softly: "Want to try again?"

"I do," said Dwight.

"I do," said Mary.

This week's lesson is about two marriage covenants of a different kind. According to one, God was a husband to His people (Jeremiah 31:32), but they broke that covenant long ago. According to the other, the holy Jerusalem (the church) is the Lord's bride and wife (Revelation 21:2, 9, 10). That covenant needs to be kept today.

B. Lesson Background

In recent lessons, we have considered the sinful actions of Jehoiakim, king of Judah, when Nebuchadnezzar came with his huge Babylonian army to annex that country to his empire. Lacking the strength to resist, Jehoiakim accepted the annexation in 605 B.C. and promised to pay tribute; but after three years, he rebelled.

But Nebuchadnezzar was busy elsewhere at the time. However, since the little nations around

Judah also belonged to his empire, he sent them to harass Judah until he could come to put down the revolt. In those troubled times, Jehoiakim died.

The next king of Judah was Jehoiachin, also known as Jeconiah and Coniah. He ruled only three months before Nebuchadnezzar took him prisoner and sent him to Babylon. Along with him went ten thousand citizens of Judah, including the civilian and military leaders, plus the blacksmiths who could make weapons of war. It seems plain that Nebuchadnezzar was trying to make Judah incapable of another rebellion. He left Zedekiah to rule that feeble nation and pay tribute. All this is recorded in 2 Kings 23:1–24:17.

Loss of those leaders in 597 B.C. was, of course, a severe blow to Judah. But cheerful false prophets were ready with encouragement. For example, Hananiah promised that the power of Babylon would be broken and the prisoners would be back home within two years (Jeremiah 28:1-4). Jeremiah countered with the Lord's true message. He wrote to the captives (recorded in Jeremiah 29), advising them to settle down for a long stay in Babylon. They would not be released until seventy years were completed (29:10).

Even so, the Lord's true message was a message of hope, a hope better than that brought by the lies of false prophets. The seventy years of Babylonian dominance would end; the captives would be set free. Those who were devoted to the Lord could then return to the homeland with His blessing. This is declared at length in chapters 30 and 31 of Jeremiah, from which we take a few verses for our text.

I. Promise of Homecoming (Jeremiah 31:23-26)

Even those of us who have been terribly homesick probably cannot truly grasp the anguish of the Judeans as they are driven over weary miles to be captives of the most powerful empire in the world. To the sinners in Judah, the voice of Jeremiah has been the voice of doom. But now Jeremiah is the voice of hope. Jeremiah writes from Jerusalem some time after the deportation in 597 B.C., but before the "final" exile of 586 B.C.

A. Spiritual Renewal (v. 23)

23. Thus saith the LORD of hosts, the God of Israel, As yet they shall use this speech in the land of Judah and in the cities thereof, when I shall bring again their captivity; The LORD bless thee, O habitation of justice, and mountain of holiness.

For modern ears, the phrase *When I shall bring again their captivity* is stated more clearly in the *New International Version* as, "When I bring them back from captivity." How the homesick hearts must have leaped at that promise! They will go back to Judah. They will again see Jerusalem, the city that is their chief joy (cf. Ezekiel 24:25). More than that, they will not be as they had been, a "sinful nation, a people laden with iniquity" (Isaiah 1:4). Restored Judah, as a *habitation of justice*, will reflect God's own nature (Psalm 89:14). The *mountain of holiness* refers to Jerusalem and its temple (cf. Psalm 2:6; Isaiah 66:20). The people coming back from Babylon will pray for God's blessing on their holy homeland. And it is none other than *the Lord of hosts, the God of Israel* who makes this promise.

B. Physical Renewal (v. 24)

24. And there shall dwell in Judah itself, and in all the cities thereof together, husbandmen, and they that go forth with flocks.

Husbandmen are farmers. Men to be freed from captivity will be happily working in the tilled fields of Judah; shepherds no less happily will lead their *flocks* on the unplowed ground of the open range. Before the captivity, many Judeans eagerly had sought unjust gain; when they come back, they will prefer to earn an honest living. At that time, the desolation of Judah's towns and *cities* will be reversed (cf. Jeremiah 10:22). [See question #1, page 72.]

C. Total Renewal (vv. 25, 26)

25. For I have satiated the weary soul, and I have replenished every sorrowful soul.

The spiritual rejuvenation of verse 23 combined with the earthly well-being of verse 24 results in the total renewal of the *weary*. Every *soul* tired of captivity will be rested and refreshed by liberty; every soul that mourns in Babylon will be filled with delight in Judah. God has decreed it. He will supply whatever is needed to make everyone satisfied, content, and blessed. [See question #2, page 72.]

26. Upon this I awaked, and beheld; and my sleep was sweet unto me.

Apparently, Jeremiah is sleeping when God reveals the message of verses 23-25 to him in a dream. The *sleep* he has just finished seems *sweet* because the message revealed in it was sweet: a promise of return and renewal for the captives. We can speculate that Jeremiah especially treasured the pleasantness of this moment given the harshness of his life as a whole. In the Old Testament, no one suffers more than Jeremiah (see chapters 37, 38, etc.).

COMING HOME TO FREEDOM

Saddam Hussein's Iraqi forces invaded the tiny nation of Kuwait in the late summer of 1990. Acting on a United Nations resolution condemning the invasion, a coalition of Western nations responded on January 17, 1991.

On the second day of Operation Desert Storm, Lieutenant Colonel Cliff Acree, USMC, was on an air mission over Iraq when his plane was hit by a ground-to-air missile. Acree survived and was captured. The war was short, but Acree and other Allied airmen endured weeks of torture and solitary confinement. Finally, on March 10, Freedom One—the plane bringing the captives home—landed at Andrews Air Force Base in Maryland. Acree appeared in the plane's doorway, and his wife burst from the waiting crowd to greet him in an emotional embrace.

Over several months, Colonel Acree's emotions and body would heal, but the real change was seen in his statement about freedom: "Freedom is precious. You don't fully realize its value until it's taken away."

Jeremiah's prediction of Judah's homecoming probably sounded too good to be true, but God's word described it accurately. Weary souls would find the joy of freedom replacing the sorrow of captivity. We *also* are captives—enslaved to sin. But the promise of the gospel is that one day God shall bring us home, and inexpressible joy will replace our sorrow and hurt.   —C. R. B.

II. Promise of Prosperity (Jeremiah 31:27-30)

God is going to restore the captives to their homeland, not as the sinners they are now, but as true worshipers, purified and obedient to God. In their own land they will grow, being built up in the knowledge of God and in their own godly character.

A. God's Replanting (v. 27)

27. Behold, the days come, saith the LORD, that I will sow the house of Israel and the house of Judah with the seed of man, and with the seed of beast.

The overall thought here echoes that of 31:24 above, but now *Israel* is also included (as in 30:3). The ultimate result of God's reuniting and replanting of Israel and *Judah* will be, of course, the coming of Christ (Hosea 1:11).

B. God's Rebuilding (v. 28)

28. And it shall come to pass, that like as I have watched over them, to pluck up, and to break down, and to throw down, and to destroy, and to afflict; so will I watch over them, to build, and to plant, saith the LORD.

God would rather *build* and *plant* than *destroy*. Contrary to the people's belief, *the Lord* is indeed watching *over them*, both in the current punishment as well as the coming restoration (cf. 12:4 and 23:24). And when the restoration comes, the people should make no mistake that it is the Lord who is bringing this about, thus putting the lie to the false prophets and their idols.

C. God's Justice (vv. 29, 30)

29, 30. In those days they shall say no more, The fathers have eaten a sour grape, and the children's teeth are set on edge. But every one shall die for his own iniquity: every man that eateth the sour grape, his teeth shall be set on edge.

Many of us can recall the sharp and very unpleasant sensation felt in our teeth when we bit into a very sour grape. The Jews in captivity know that sensation, and they use it in a popular proverb. In claiming that *the fathers have eaten a sour grape, and the children's teeth are set on edge*, they make the claim that the bitter captivity they suffer is not their own fault, but is due to the sins of former generations.

This false conclusion perhaps is due to a misapplication of Exodus 20:5, 6. But God, speaking through both Jeremiah and Ezekiel (himself among the captives in Babylon), forbids this proverb (cf. Ezekiel 18:1-4). Even so, the Lord's command here is nothing new. It merely brings back the clear precept of Deuteronomy 24:16. The whole of Ezekiel 18 expands on the correction that *every one shall die for his own iniquity*. (See more discussion of this in lesson 12.) The returning exiles must be ready to face the facts honestly. They must admit that they are suffering for their own sins, and not for the sins of their parents. [See question #3, page 72.]

III. Promise of Covenant (Jeremiah 31:31-34)

Looking more than five hundred years into the future, the Lord promises a new covenant to replace the old one He had made with Israel at Mount Sinai more than eight hundred years previously. That New Covenant is the one God has made with all of us who now are Christians; it is the same one He offers to every non-Christian in the world.

A. New and Different (vv. 31, 32)

31. Behold, the days come, saith the LORD, that I will make a new covenant with the house of Israel, and with the house of Judah.

The house of Israel and *the house of Judah* are the two parts into which the larger nation of Israel was divided after the death of King Solomon in 931 B.C. More than a century before Jeremiah's writing, *the house of Israel* had been scattered among foreign lands (2 Kings 17:6). As Jeremiah writes, *the house of Judah* has been partially taken into captivity in Babylon—with a much more extensive exile to follow in a few years. Yet the New Covenant is intended for both of these broken parts, for the whole house of Israel (cf. Romans 9–11)—and for the rest of the world, too (see Isaiah 42:6; 49:6). For this reason, many scholars consider Jeremiah 31:31-34 to be one of the most important sections in the entire Old Testament! (See also discussion of 31:27 above.) [See question #4, page 72.]

32. Not according to the covenant that I made with their fathers, in the day that I took them by the hand to bring them out of the land of Egypt; which my covenant they brake, although I was a husband unto them, saith the LORD.

The Old Covenant presents a multitude of rules—rules for individual action, rules for family living, rules for interaction in the community, and the like. If all the Israelites had kept the rules, surely their society would have been the most orderly, the most peaceful, and the most pleasant the world had ever known. But that covenant failed to produce such a society, simply because the people failed to keep the rules. The problem was not with the Old Covenant itself, but with the people who broke it. *I was a husband unto them* recalls similar statements in 3:14, 20.

NEW, NOT JUST RESTORED

Most of us have seen an old tractor, its days of usefulness long past, sitting broken and rusting beside a barn. The farmer has replaced it with a new, larger, and more powerful machine. However, some people like old tractors. Don Dahlinghaus, an Ohio farmer, is one such person. His collection of fifty antique tractors contains examples dating back into the 1920s. Photos and descriptions of many of them can be seen at his Web site www.dondatractors.homestead.com. Each winter Dahlinghaus restores another tractor or two. When he is finished with the task, he uses them in parades and occasionally does some token farm work with them.

The Old Covenant was somewhat like these old tractors. It served its purpose for its time, but a "new and better model" was eventually needed—a covenant with "more power," power to meet the needs of the human race in a way the old one never could. The New Covenant that God promised through the prophet would do the job so much better than the old one. The Old Covenant (like the old tractors) had become broken and useless. But rather than attempt to restore what had been broken (as some people still do), God offered a New Covenant that comes with a divine guarantee that it will perform the task it was designed for: to bring us salvation and forgiveness through the blood of Christ, the Son of God.   —C. R. B.

B. Hearts and Minds (v. 33)

33. But this shall be the covenant that I will make with the house of Israel; After those days, saith the LORD, I will put my law in their inward parts, and write it in their hearts; and will be their God, and they shall be my people.

Twice God had inscribed the Ten Commandments on slabs of stone (Exodus 31:18; 32:19; 34:1). Moses had written the whole Law in a book (Deuteronomy 31:24-26); the people had been told to keep it in their hearts (Deuteronomy 6:6). Sadly, they broke this Covenant repeatedly through the course of the centuries and continue to break it, so they go into captivity as a result.

Home Daily Bible Readings

Monday, Oct. 14—The Lord Will Restore Jacob (Jeremiah 30:18-22)

Tuesday, Oct. 15—An Everlasting Love (Jeremiah 31:1-6)

Wednesday, Oct. 16—God Will Satisfy (Jeremiah 31:23-30)

Thursday, Oct. 17—God Will Make a New Covenant (Jeremiah 31:31-37)

Friday, Oct. 18—God Will Bring Healing (Jeremiah 33:1-13)

Saturday, Oct. 19—You Have Made Me Hope (Psalm 119:49-56)

Sunday, Oct. 20—Eternal Hope (Titus 2:11-15)

But now God says that He Himself will write His New Covenant in *their inward parts* and *in their hearts*. The *New American Standard Bible* translates "their inward parts" as "within them," while the *New International Version* uses the freer "in their minds." But under any of these translations, the idea is obvious.

Also obvious is the fact that He will write the New Covenant only in willing hearts. To a person who stubbornly resists, it will be no more effective than the Old Covenant was when it was broken. But those who open their hearts to the New Covenant will be God's *people,* and He will be *their God.* [See question #5, page 72.]

C. Knowledge and Forgiveness (v. 34)

34. And they shall teach no more every man his neighbor, and every man his brother, saying, Know the LORD: for they shall all know me, from the least of them unto the greatest of them, saith the LORD: for I will forgive their iniquity, and I will remember their sin no more.

In the time of the New Covenant, *teach no more* means that people will have direct access to God without needing to go through the human intermediaries—the priests of the levitical system—that were a feature of the Old Covenant (cf. Isaiah 54:13). Of course, a teaching function still exists under the New Covenant as the New Testament makes clear (1 Corinthians 12:28, 29; Ephesians 4:11, 12). [See question #6, page 72.]

An outstanding feature of this New Covenant is God's forgiveness. Because Christ takes the sin penalty upon Himself, God takes away the sins of His people: He forgives and forgets. To remind us of these facts, the writer of Hebrews quotes from this section of Jeremiah in Hebrews 8:8-12 and 10:16, 17 (see also Romans 11:27 and

"They shall all know me, from the least of them unto the greatest of them," saith the Lord.
Jeremiah 31:34

Visual for
lesson 8

The visual for today's lesson illustrates verse 34. See page 13 for ordering information.

1 Thessalonians 5:9). When Christ returns, *all* Christians will *know* Him in the fullest sense of Jeremiah's prophecy.

Conclusion

Christians, He is our God, and we are His people according to His New Covenant. Our sins are forgiven and forgotten because of the death of Christ. Praise the Lord!

A. God's Holy People

Through the blood of animals and the will of God, the Old Covenant was a physical deliverance from earthly oppressors. Through the blood of Christ, the New Covenant is eternal deliverance from the oppression of sin and the wrath of God. With God's New Covenant written in our hearts (2 Corinthians 3:3), we obey God because obeying Him is our chief joy. We do not continue in sin (Romans 6:2). But if we do sin—and even God's holy people do—then "if we confess our sins, he is faithful and just to forgive us our sins, and to cleanse us from all unrighteousness" (1 John 1:8, 9). Praise the Lord again!

B. Our Holy Calling

The problem is that God's law is not the only thing in our hearts. Also crowded in there are our daily concerns that result in selfishness, pride, greed, and other impure motives. Even so, God calls us to holiness (1 Peter 1:15, 16). The word *holy* means "set apart," or "dedicated." God calls us to dedicate ourselves to His service, and He has dedicated us, too, in writing His law in our hearts. It is God who empowers us to resist sin, and live a holy life (cf. 1 Corinthians 10:13; James 4:7). Although the temptation to sin is inevitable, our surrender to that temptation is not. It is possible to live a life that is not characterized by a pursuit of sin. If you have God's law written in your heart and you use it well, you can defeat Satan every time. And if you do not know the law of Christ that is in your heart well enough to use it properly, whose fault is that?

C. Prayer

How good You are, our Father, how merciful and gracious! How You loved us to give Your Son! How He loved us to give His life! Grateful for Your grace, we promise to live daily by the new covenant You have written in our hearts; and we pray for wisdom and strength to keep our promise. In Jesus' name, amen.

D. Thought to Remember

Let God's New Covenant rule your heart and your life.

Learning by Doing

This page contains an alternative lesson plan emphasizing learning activities.
Classes desiring such student involvement will find these suggestions helpful.

Learning Goals

After participating in this lesson, each student will be able to:

1. Summarize God's promise to restore the exiles and to give a New Covenant.
2. Contrast the Old Covenant with the New.
3. Praise God for the forgiveness of sins available in the New Covenant.

Into the Lesson

Begin this week's lesson with a word-find activity. Prior to the lesson, prepare this activity on a regular sheet of paper. Design a grid eight columns across and eleven rows down. Fill the cells of the grid with the following letters:

```
T U S E R G B A
K N O W A W T Z
O W A B E I S E
R I T N J F O Q
H O B A E X T U
I V G X Y V A D
G S I N Q N O G
M L E C U V L C
E P A U B E D O
R O G W D H I Z
E V I G R O F E
```

Eight words of three letters or more are to be found: *covenant, exile, forgive, know, law, new, old, sin.* Copy the puzzle so that each student will have a copy. Say: "We begin today's lesson with a word-find activity that contains eight hidden words. These words help focus our thinking on today's lesson from Jeremiah 31:23-34. [Give a copy of the puzzle to each person and make certain each one has a pencil or pen.] The words may be spelled in any direction. Circle each of the eight words of three letters or more."

Give a few minutes for this activity and then ask for the hidden words. Say: "Under the *Old Covenant* of *law*, the people of Judah *sinned* and were *exiled* to Babylon. But God promised a *New* Covenant. They will *know* the Lord and receive the *forgiveness* of sins. Let's read the text and see their hope."

Into the Word

Ask a class member to read the lesson text aloud. Distribute copies of a worksheet with the following questions.

1. With what groups will the New Covenant be made (v. 31)? *(The houses of Judah and Israel.)*

2. When the exiles return to Judah, what two trades will occupy many? *(Husbandmen or farming, and shepherding, v. 24.)*

3. Describe how God indicated He would restore them to their homeland (v. 23). *(They will use the speech again, "The Lord bless Thee O habitation of justice, and mountain of holiness.")*

4. Contrast the ways that God did watch over the people of Judah with the ways He will watch over them. *(Pluck up, break down, throw down, destroy, afflict; build and plant, v. 28.)*

5. What is the meaning of the phrase, "the fathers have eaten a sour grape and the children's teeth are set on edge"? *(The children of Judah and Israel have been subjected to captivity in Babylon due to the sins of their fathers, v. 29.)*

6. In the New Covenant, how will that phrase be changed and properly understood? *("Every man that eateth the sour grape, his teeth shall be set on edge"; people suffer for their own sins, not their parents' sins, v. 30.)*

7. Why do people under the New Covenant not have to teach one another to know the Lord? *(Entrance into the New Covenant comes with knowing the Lord, vv. 33, 34.)*

8. How will sins of people in the New Covenant be regarded by God? *(Forgiven, forgotten, v. 34.)*

9. Contrast the Old Covenant with the New Covenant. *(Old: external, on a stone tablet; New: internal, on the heart. Old: people claimed to be punished for their fathers' sins; New: punishment recognized as for their own sins. Old: sin was punished; New: sin is forgiven.)*

Go over the answers with the whole class.

Into Life

Say: "If Jesus is your Lord and Savior, listen to the words of the Lord in Jeremiah 31:34, 'I will forgive their iniquity, and I will remember their sin no more.' God has forgiven us our sins and He no longer remembers them. When we truly understand that, what type of response to God should we make? We should praise Him! Let's brainstorm some practical ways that we can praise Him this week."

Write suggested ways on the chalkboard for all to see. Say: "Now, I want you to select one of those ways to do this week as an expression of your praise to God for forgiving your sins."

Close with prayers of commitment in groups of three.

Let's Talk It Over

The questions on this page are designed to promote discussion of the lesson by the class and to encourage application of the lesson Scriptures. The answers provided are only discussion starters. Let your class talk it over from there.

1. When the older people learned that God would take His people back to Jerusalem after the captivity, what stories might they have told the younger captives about their homeland? What hopes might they have shared? In what ways can older Christians guide and challenge younger Christians today?

Paul, in Titus 2:1-6, urged those who were older to find ways to teach the younger individuals. The goal should be to prepare the less trained for their lives in the future. To be successful, the older adults will not have the luxury of just telling stories from the past, but they must have also thought ahead to the potential opportunities and struggles of the future to be able to share wisdom that will lead the church through the coming decades. Have the class discuss ways of not getting stuck in the past and how to view the prospects of the future.

2. Suppose a new Christian comes to you for advice. He is facing some chronic health problems that have put him into a financial bind. His marriage is tense, and recently his employer informed him that layoffs are imminent. He asks you, "Where is all this rest for the weary and comfort for the sorrowful?" How will you answer?

The immediate context, of course, is addressed to Jewish exiles and not to believers. Still, the New Testament makes similar promises, so more needs to be said. You might refer such a one to verses about perseverance and endurance (e.g., Hebrews 12:3). This person needs to realize that these promises find ultimate fulfillment in Heaven, and not on earth. Then we will enter the true rest.

3. In what ways do people like to blame someone else (spouse, parent, boss, other drivers, etc.) for their sins? How can we learn to inspect our own behavior for needed changes instead of blaming someone else?

Jesus warned against finding fault with someone else before seeing one's own faults (Matthew 7:1-5). Have the class speculate on what would happen if every Christian made a conscious effort not to blame anyone for any of his or her own problems. Discuss how youth group and family life programs might be developed to address ways

of teaching the ability to correct one's faults before blaming someone else.

4. The New Covenant was to be made with the people of both the northern and southern kingdoms. God wanted all to come together again under His leadership and salvation. What can churches do to bring about God's goal of spiritual unity?

In John 17, Jesus prayed that His followers would be united. Sometimes churches are more comfortable finding what should separate them rather than discovering what they have in common. In countries where another religion is dominant, Christians are happy to find another believer with whom to share the joy of Christ. When Christians seek to help each other grow ("iron sharpeneth iron," Proverbs 27:17) based on the truth of God's Word rather than hacking each other to pieces, then there will be a greater likelihood of Christ's prayer being answered.

5. The New Covenant is to be more than a set of codes and rituals. It is a covenant of the heart, expressed in heartfelt devotion. How can we insure that our class or church is protected from practicing an empty and ceremonial religion? What can fellow Christians do to encourage their brothers and sisters in the Lord to deepen their relationship with God?

Christians need to understand that a continuous routine can lead people to want to keep the format rather than hold strong to the reason the practice began in the first place. Variety for variety's sake is not the answer. However, variation in class routine or in corporate worship can help individuals stay alert. Dividing the group into small groups and training Christians in effective ways to challenge each other to a deeper spiritual walk will benefit everyone who participates.

6. How can the church's teaching ministry maintain an effective balance between imparting facts about God and leading people to know God Himself more intimately?

Knowledge of Bible facts is not the same as spirituality. Such knowledge makes spiritual growth easier, but there must be a heart change in Christians as well as an increase in Bible knowledge. The wise church will insist on both.

Living in Faith

DEVOTIONAL READING: Hebrews 11:32–12:2.

BACKGROUND SCRIPTURE: Habakkuk.

PRINTED TEXT: Habakkuk 3:2-6, 16-19.

Habakkuk 3:2-6, 16-19

2 O LORD, I have heard thy speech, and was afraid: O LORD, revive thy work in the midst of the years, in the midst of the years make known; in wrath remember mercy.

3 God came from Teman, and the Holy One from mount Paran. Selah. His glory covered the heavens, and the earth was full of his praise.

4 And his brightness was as the light; he had horns coming out of his hand: and there was the hiding of his power.

5 Before him went the pestilence, and burning coals went forth at his feet.

6 He stood, and measured the earth: he beheld, and drove asunder the nations; and the everlasting mountains were scattered, the perpetual hills did bow: his ways are everlasting.

. . . .

16 When I heard, my belly trembled; my lips quivered at the voice: rottenness entered into my bones, and I trembled in myself, that I might rest in the day of trouble: when he cometh up unto the people, he will invade them with his troops.

17 Although the fig tree shall not blossom, neither shall fruit be in the vines; the labor of the olive shall fail, and the fields shall yield no meat; the flock shall be cut off from the fold, and there shall be no herd in the stalls:

18 Yet I will rejoice in the LORD, I will joy in the God of my salvation.

19 The LORD God is my strength, and he will make my feet like hinds' feet, and he will make me to walk upon mine high places.

Oct 27

GOLDEN TEXT: O LORD, I have heard thy speech, and was afraid: O LORD, revive thy work in the midst of the years, in the midst of the years make known; in wrath remember mercy.—Habakkuk 3:2.

Judgment and Exile
Unit 2: Limited Hope
(Lessons 6-9)

Lesson Aims

After participating in this lesson, each student will be able to:

1. Tell what Habakkuk saw in his vision of the destruction of Jerusalem, and how his faith sustained him in the face of disaster.

2. Compare/contrast Habakkuk's response of faith with the responses many people today have toward disaster.

3. State one specific lesson he or she can learn from a current difficulty in life.

Lesson Outline

INTRODUCTION
    A. How Is Justice in Your Town?
    B. Lesson Background
 I. THE PROPHET'S PRAYER (Habakkuk 3:2)
    A. Awe at God's Work (v. 2a)
    B. Plea for God's Power and Mercy (v. 2b)
      In Our Time
 II. THE PROPHET'S VISION (Habakkuk 3:3-6)
    A. Vision of Glory (v. 3)
    B. Vision of Power (v. 4)
    C. Vision of Destruction (vv. 5, 6)
III. THE PROPHET'S RESPONSE (Habakkuk 3:16-19)
    A. Fear (v. 16a)
    B. Faith (v. 16b)
    C. Joy (vv. 17, 18)
      Holding On to Our "Stuff"
    D. Strength (v. 19)
CONCLUSION
    A. Disaster Now
    B. Our Reaction
    C. Prayer
    D. Thought to Remember

Introduction

The ideal of the U.S. government is carved in stone on the front of a local courthouse: EQUAL AND EXACT JUSTICE TO EVERY MAN. But everyone in the government or out of it knows that this ideal is far from being reached.

A. How Is Justice in Your Town?

Do you know someone who has lost money in a scam of some kind? Do you have to pay more for your groceries because your grocer loses thousands of dollars each year to shoplifters? Have you been treated unjustly because you are a "minority"? Did the person who fixed your car overcharge you? Do you suspect that the justice system wrongly sets criminals free on a regular basis? Are you suspicious of political leaders at every level from local to national? Are there unsolved crimes on your local police department's books, so that thieves and murderers are apparently walking around free?

Injustice can work the other way around, too. While most Christians would protest that they never would be guilty of injustice, think about it. When you bump another car in the parking lot, do you volunteer to pay for the damage even if no one knows you did it? Do you ever lie to your spouse? What do you do when the clerk at the checkout counter gives you too much change?

Injustice may be bad in our country today, but it was worse in ancient Judah when Jehoiakim was king (609–597 B.C.). This king took the lead in wrongdoing, and most of his people were glad to follow.

B. Lesson Background

Habakkuk had a problem. King Jehoiakim of Judah was leading his people into idolatry, evil, and injustice, and the people were following him. Perhaps some of them were even "running ahead" of him in committing evil. How could a just and holy God let all that go on?

Habakkuk was a prophet. He was used to getting revelations directly from God, so he took his problem directly *to* God. The conversation between the prophet and the Lord fills the first two chapters of Habakkuk's book, but the following condensed paraphrase captures the main points.

Habakkuk: How can You tolerate all this wickedness, Lord? How long must I live in the midst of it?

The Lord: Take it easy, Habakkuk. I'm going to bring the Babylonians to punish evil Judah.

Habakkuk: But Lord, the Babylonians are worse than the people of Judah! How can You let those scoundrels punish people better than they are?

The Lord: Take it easy, Habakkuk. The Babylonians will be punished in their turn. They are going to lose their empire.

I. The Prophet's Prayer (Habakkuk 3:2)

Our text this week is from chapter 3 of Habakkuk, which offers a prayer of that prophet. The term *Shigionoth* in verse 1 perhaps names a tune to which that prayer is to be sung. When the Babylonian captivity is over and the people of Judah live again in their homeland, perhaps the temple choir will put this inspired composition to music. As such, chapter 3 of Habakkuk can be thought of as a psalm.

A. Awe at God's Work (v. 2a)

2a. O LORD, I have heard thy speech, and was afraid.

Here, the *New International Version* helps us better understand Habakkuk's frame of mind: "Lord, I have heard of your fame; I stand in awe of your deeds, O Lord." These two translations come together when we remember that in the Old Testament God's deeds say something about Him, and thus become a form of *speech* (see Psalm 19:1, 2).

Habakkuk knows about the deeds and awe-inspiring power of the Lord. Perhaps the prophet had been taught the history of his people in the time when godly King Josiah was encouraging such teaching. Such teaching would have included instruction on how the Lord freed His people from slavery in Egypt—providing for them through forty years of wandering in the desert, granting them victory in the promised land, and even punishing them when they fell (or "jumped"!) into sin as the prophet now sees them doing again. Habakkuk's fear *(I . . . was afraid)* is the "fear of the Lord" spoken of frequently in the Old Testament (cf. Proverbs 1:7). It is a deep sense of reverence and awe.

B. Plea for God's Power and Mercy (v. 2b)

2b. O Lord, revive thy work in the midst of the years, in the midst of the years make known; in wrath remember mercy.

Habakkuk begs the Lord to show His awe inspiring power again by doing marvelous things *in the midst of the years*, in those very years in which Habakkuk is living. He wants the Lord to make known His power and justice, even if He has to do it by punishing His people in Judah. But he wants the Lord to temper His *wrath* with *mercy:* to limit their punishment and then to grant forgiveness when they repent and obey Him again. (Compare with Psalm 77, particularly v. 9.)

Issues of wrath and mercy are expressed together back to the earliest days of the Old Covenant. See Exodus 32:10-12; Deuteronomy 4:31; and 29:20-28. [See question #1, page 80.]

IN OUR TIME

Neville Chamberlain was the British Prime Minister when Adolf Hitler and Benito Mussolini began their siege of Europe. He signed a treaty accepting Italy's invasion of Ethiopia on the basis of Mussolini's promise to stay out of the Spanish Civil War.

Hitler's invasion of the German-speaking areas of Czechoslovakia brought another crisis. At a conference in Munich, Chamberlain allowed Hitler's claims to those territories in exchange for Hitler's pledge not to take the rest of Czechoslovakia. He came back to Britain with the words that his concession to Hitler had brought "peace in our time," as he phrased it. We now know that he was terribly naïve in compromising with the evil Nazi regime.

We all want things to be right "in our time." It makes life so much easier when we don't have to deal with the evil that surrounds us in society. Habakkuk prayed that God would remove the idolatry and wickedness in Judah, and that God would bring righteousness to his people, *within his lifetime.* But Habakkuk had to accept the divine timing rather than his own, just was we do. A line in an old hymn says, "God doesn't always come when we call Him, but He always comes on time." And often, when God comes, He comes with a challenge for us to assist Him in His work. Haven't you found it to be so in your life?

—C. R. B.

II. The Prophet's Vision (Habakkuk 3:3-6)

It seems that the Lord answers Habakkuk's prayer with what theologians call a "theophany": a tremendous vision of Himself. (Compare his vision with that of Isaiah in Isaiah 6.) Habakkuk sees the Lord coming with visible glory: enough to fill earth and sky, with hidden power; enough to punish Judah as He has promised to do, and with mercy; enough to preserve some of Judah's people and give them another chance to be His people.

Visual for lesson 9

The visual for today's lesson suggests one application of verse 2.

A. Vision of Glory (v. 3)

3. God came from Teman, and the Holy One from mount Paran. Selah. His glory covered the heavens, and the earth was full of his praise.

Teman is a city in the region of Seir (also called Edom). Both the city and *mount Paran* are south of Judah. Mount Paran is mentioned in the Old Testament only here and in Deuteronomy 33:2. Since the wording of that passage is similar to this one (but with "Seir" instead of "Teman"), we get the idea that Habakkuk is reflecting back to the time of Moses when the Old Covenant had its beginning. The God who guided Moses and the Israelites so many centuries ago is the same God who lives and guides now!

Selah appears seventy-one times in Psalms and three times in Habakkuk (3:3, 9, 13). Many students believe it to be a musical direction. Perhaps it calls for an interlude on the instruments. When the choir announces the coming of the Lord (v. 3a), can't you imagine that the singers will be interrupted by a great flourish of trumpets?

The words *glory* and *praise* are not always synonymous, but sometimes they are. For example, giving glory to God is the same as giving Him praise. If the two words have the same meaning here, they tell us that the light of God's glory flooded both earth and sky as God came "from Teman." Again noting the similarity to Deuteronomy 33:2, we see Habakkuk looking to the future by connecting with the past.

B. Vision of Power (v. 4)

4. And his brightness was as the light; he had horns coming out of his hand: and there was the hiding of his power.

Brightness was as the light emphasizes the brilliance of the glory of God. It must have been truly dazzling (cf. Acts 26:13).

The *horns coming out of his hand* gives us a bit of a challenge in interpretation. The horns of cattle give them power in conflict, and so horns become a symbol of power. In Jeremiah 48:25, for example, "the horn of Moab is cut off" means the power of Moab is taken away. If we take the word *horns* with that meaning, the reference in this vision is to the tremendous power in God's hand.

But as Habakkuk looks on, that power is hidden: it is not visibly at work. Thus, many students think Habakkuk had a different picture in mind. Sometimes in a cloudy sunrise we see bright beams of light like long straight *horns* (or projections) across the sky. The ancient Hebrews saw them too, and when they made their word for horn into a verb, it meant "to emit light." In Exodus 34:35, the word for the shining or radiance of Moses' face is actually derived from this same word for horn.

With that meaning of *horn* in mind, the translators of the *New International Version* wrote, "Rays flashed from his hand," instead of *he had horns coming out of his hand*. Under this translation the beams of light from God's hand must have been even brighter than the glory light that filled earth and sky.

With either interpretation, we are reading that God's hand is the hiding place of power. In Habakkuk's time, it is not showing God's limitless power in some tremendous work. As with verse 3 above, the connection with Deuteronomy 33:2 is important.

C. Vision of Destruction (vv. 5, 6)

5. Before him went the pestilence, and burning coals went forth at his feet.

Now we are reminded that God is coming in judgment to punish the wicked people of Judah. The Babylonian army will be His instrument to do that. At the final onslaught of that army, the people of Judah will take refuge behind the strong walls of Jerusalem, to be besieged for a year and a half. Undoubtedly, certain diseases will become rampant as bodily immune systems are compromised because of starvation and declining sanitary conditions. The *burning coals* may refer to the fact that, when the city eventually falls, everything combustible will be burned (2 Kings 25:1-10).

On the other hand, the burning coals may have a figurative meaning. Hebrew poetry very frequently uses a second line simply to repeat a first line, using different words. Thus the *New International Version* renders this verse: "Plague went before him; pestilence followed his steps." It seems strange to see *pestilence* where the *King James Version* has *burning coals;* but the Hebrew word at issue here can have either of those meanings. The *King James* translators chose the primary meaning—something burning. The *New International* translators chose *pestilence* as a synonym for *plague* in the line above it. [See question #2, page 80.]

6. He stood, and measured the earth: he beheld, and drove asunder the nations; and the everlasting mountains were scattered, the perpetual hills did bow: his ways are everlasting.

Now the tremendous power of God is demonstrated. With a mere look He changes the face of the earth. *Measured the earth* may mean He surveyed it, measured it with His glance. Or the Hebrew may be translated "stretched out the earth," spread it in its place before changing it as stated here. The *New International Version* says, "shook the earth." This is an adaptation of the old Greek version of the Old Testament, which was made about 200 B.C. It seems to be in accord with the rest of the verse, which says the mountains and hills, supposed to be everlasting, are changed by the glance of God. In contrast with those changeable things, God's own *ways* really *are* everlasting. Verses 7-15, which are not included in our printed text, continue with the demonstration of God's tremendous power. Judah is indeed to be punished severely by that power; but God's ultimate purpose is actually the salvation of His people, not their destruction (v. 13). [See question #3, page 80.]

III. The Prophet's Response (Habakkuk 3:16-19)

Who could be unmoved by such an imposing vision of God coming with earth-shattering power, especially when He is coming with punishment on His mind? Certainly Habakkuk is moved, and the next verses of our text reveal his reaction.

A. Fear (v. 16a)

16a. When I heard, my belly trembled; my lips quivered at the voice: rottenness entered into my bones, and I trembled in myself.

Now it appears that the prophet has *heard* a *voice* in connection with the vision, and he is terrified. Sometimes fear brings a flow of adrenaline and rouses a person to fight or flee, but obviously no human can either oppose or escape the all-powerful God when He comes in wrath to punish His people. Habakkuk is paralyzed. He can only wait and tremble. [See question #4, page 80.]

B. Faith (v. 16b)

16b. That I might rest in the day of trouble: when he cometh up unto the people, he will invade them with his troops.

Habakkuk's fear is for his *people* rather than for himself. Personally, he expects to *rest in the day of trouble.* He trusts God; he is confident God will do right. Judah has been deep in sin for a long time, so God is coming *with his troops*—the Babylonian army. There will be a terrible siege; Jerusalem will be taken and destroyed; most of the surviving people will become captives.

Even so, Habakkuk's faith is bright and clear. The captivity will end; God's people will be liberated; and God's prophet will be secure through it all. The Babylonians trust in their own strength as their "god" (Habakkuk 1:11). But the prophet knows better.

Hebrew poetry is often difficult to understand and to translate. At this point the translation of the *New International Version* is strikingly different: "Yet I will wait patiently for the day of calamity to come on the nation invading us." Even given this difference, however, the two translations tell us the same thing: it is God who is in control, whether we are talking about His pending judgment against Judah, or the judgment against Babylon that will follow.

C. Joy (vv. 17, 18)

17. Although the fig tree shall not blossom, neither shall fruit be in the vines; the labor of the olive shall fail, and the fields shall yield no meat; the flock shall be cut off from the fold, and there shall be no herd in the stalls.

This picture is of Judah's total desolation as a result of the Babylonian invasion (cf. Jeremiah 5:15-17). The *fruit* trees and *vines* and *fields* will *yield no* fruit (*meat* here means food of any kind) because they have been trampled and destroyed by the invaders. (And even if they did yield their fruit, the people of Judah would not enjoy them, because they would be far away, captives in Babylon.) But nothing can destroy the joy of God's prophet. See the next verse.

HOLDING ON TO OUR "STUFF"

Nearly every person or family has something stored away in the basement, attic, or garage that they do not need. But most of us aren't like Ann Jones (as we'll call her), who has a real problem with holding on to her "stuff."

Ann's home is piled so high with junk mail, unread newspapers, broken appliances, empty food containers, and dirty dishes, that the place is nearly uninhabitable. The front door can hardly be opened. Even her bed is piled with junk except for the narrow patch on which she sleeps.

Ann is an intelligent, clean, outgoing, active person, involved in community and church work. She has many friends. But her hoarding disorder is out of control. It has made her home a dysfunctional place; its systems don't work for her. Only a regimen of radical therapy might possibly release her from her pathology.

How to Say It

BABYLON. *Bab*-uh-lun.
BABYLONIANS. Bab-ih-*low*-nee-unz.
HABAKKUK. Huh-*back*-kuk.
JEHOIAKIM. Jeh-*hoy*-uh-kim.
JEREMIAH. Jair-uh-*my*-uh.
JOSIAH. Jo-*sigh*-uh.
PARAN. *Pair*-un.
SEIR. *See*-ir.
SELAH (Hebrew). *See*-luh.
SHIGIONOTH (Hebrew). Shig-eh-*oh*-noth.
TEMAN. *Tee*-mun.
THEOPHANY. thee-*ahf*-uh-nee.

Judah's inability to rid itself of its hoard of stuff—its religious and moral perversion—was making the nation a dysfunctional place. Habakkuk saw that even the food supplies on which the nation relied would wither away, and its support systems would no longer work for it. Judah was suffering from a pathological spiritual condition. The only solution was the radical "therapy" God would provide when Babylon took Judah away into captivity. What kind of moral or spiritual "stuff" are we holding on to that keeps us from living life as God intended?　　—C. R. B.

18. Yet I will rejoice in the LORD, I will joy in the God of my salvation.

The Lord is in control, and His prophet is glad. The mighty God who comes in majesty to punish His people is not only the God of disaster to the wicked; He is the *God of salvation* to His prophet and to all who will repent and obey Him. Perhaps Habakkuk recalls the ancient promise of restoration as well (see Deuteronomy 30:1-10; 32:34-43). [See question #5, page 80.]

D. Strength (v. 19)

19. The LORD God is my strength, and he will make my feet like hinds' feet, and he will make me to walk upon mine high places.

Those who follow God do not depend on their own *strength*. Such a person—whether an ancient prophet or a modern Christian—does God's will and depends on God to supply whatever spiritual strength, wisdom, or ability is needed to keep on doing that will. In our English language, *hinds* are deer, though some scholars think the Hebrew word may mean wild goats instead. Both deer and goats are gifted with *feet* that seem to have a magical ability to cling to the ground in places that are steep and dangerous. Likewise,

God's man or woman seems to have a miraculous ability to survive whatever difficulties and dangers are encountered in service to God. With God on our side, who can be against us? (See Romans 8:31.)

Conclusion

Habakkuk knew the worst. His beloved country was going to be destroyed, and he was scared. But he knew the best, too. After the destruction, Judah would emerge as a smaller but godlier nation. So Habakkuk rejoiced in the Lord.

A. Disaster Now

Disasters did not cease when ancient times were past. These lines are being written in the closing months of a year that has brought a record number of forest fires in North America. Hurricanes are more numerous than usual, too. Japan experienced a typhoon, and India is suffering a lengthy monsoon. Europe and Africa continue to suffer small wars of extreme savagery. AIDS threatens to decimate the entire African continent.

Are such tragedies to be seen as God's punishment on people all around the world? We do not have inspired prophets today such as Habakkuk and Jeremiah to provide a direct answer from God to this question. A much more useful question is, "How should I react?"

B. Our Reaction

In commenting on two minor disasters of His own time, Jesus cautioned against concluding that the victims were people whose sin was worse than others (Luke 13:1-5). He drew His audience to a different conclusion: unless they repented, they would all perish as well.

Jesus' words and this year's deadly disasters remind us that life is uncertain, and the time to repent is now. Death is our destiny (Hebrews 9:27), but whether it will come by an earthquake tomorrow or by old age in later years, we cannot say. The important question is, have I repented? The choice is ours, and the time to choose is now.

D. Prayer

Father in Heaven, we know some disasters are the result of human sin, but we cannot think that all who suffer are being punished for their own sins. Even in suffering we rejoice because we still can trust You, and Your love never fails. In Jesus' name, amen.

E. Thought to Remember

In good times and bad, continue to trust God.

Home Daily Bible Readings

Monday, Oct. 21—I Stand in Awe (Habakkuk 3:2-6)

Tuesday, Oct. 22—The Lord Is My Strength (Habakkuk 3:8-19)

Wednesday, Oct. 23—My Heart Trusts in God (Psalm 28:1-9)

Thursday, Oct. 24—I Will Trust in God (Isaiah 12:1-6)

Friday, Oct. 25—Trust in God (Isaiah 26:1-6)

Saturday, Oct. 26—Acknowledge God's Plan (Isaiah 26:7-13)

Sunday, Oct. 27—The Fight of Faith (1 Timothy 6:11-16)

Learning by Doing

This page contains an alternative lesson plan emphasizing learning activities.
Classes desiring such student involvement will find these suggestions helpful.

Learning Goals

After this lesson each student will be able to:

1. Tell what Habakkuk saw in his vision of the destruction of Jerusalem, and how his faith sustained him in the face of disaster.

2. Compare/contrast Habakkuk's response of faith with the responses many people today have toward disaster.

3. State one specific lesson he or she can learn from a current difficulty in life.

Into the Lesson

Begin this week's lesson with an art activity to focus attention and to introduce the subject of disaster. Provide a variety of colored felt-tip markers and paper or poster board cut to four and one-fourth inches high by eleven inches wide. Write on the board prior to class time the following message: "Bumper Sticker 'Disaster Response.' Take paper and felt pens on the table to create a 'bumper sticker' that expresses a non-Christian's response to personal disaster. When you complete the sticker, use the tape to put it on the wall." (Provide masking tape for students to tape their bumper stickers on the wall.) Sample responses might be: "How could it have happened? It's not fair!" or "I'm gonna sue!" or "I'm going to get even!"

When students arrive, direct their attention to the message on the board and encourage them to participate. After the bumper stickers have been taped to the wall, state: "Disasters come in various ways: weather-related disasters such as tornadoes or hurricanes; mechanical-failure disasters such as plane crashes; accidental disasters such as automobile crashes; and wickedly intentional disasters such as terrorist bombings. People respond to disasters in different ways."

Review the various bumper stickers the class prepared. Say, "Today, we want to focus on disaster and, in particular, the way God-serving believers react when they face a disaster. Turn to Habakkuk 3, and let's read verses 3-6 and the prophet's description of God and the impending disaster on Judah."

Into the Word

Ask a class member to read Habakkuk 3:2-6 aloud. Go over the lesson background pointing out the two impending disasters, one on Israel and the other on the Babylonians. Prior to class time, prepare a four-column chart of four rows and title the chart, "In the Face of Disaster: A Study of Godly Responses to Personal Disaster." Label column two, "Habakkuk 3:2-10"; column three, "Daniel 2:47–3:29"; and column four, "Acts 27:13-44." The first column contains the labels for rows two, three, and four. Label row two, "Personal Disaster"; row three, "Faith Response"; and row four, "Personal Principles to Apply." Make a photocopy for each learner.

Move the class into three groups of no more than ten. (If you have more than thirty students, divide the class into six equal-sized groups.) Give a copy of the chart to each person. Assign one Scripture passage in the column headings to each group. Ask the group to appoint someone to read the passage aloud. Then, ask each group to identify from the passage the personal disaster, the faith response, and the personal principles to apply. Allow about fifteen minutes. When time has elapsed, ask each group to reveal their answers to the class. Ask: "What was the common element of these three events?" *(Belief and faith in God to protect and deliver.)* Now ask the groups to tell both the faith response and the personal principles to apply to life today.

Into Life

Say, "We may not face an impending disaster as Habakkuk did, but we may be facing some personal difficulties and struggles. Think about a current difficulty that you face. In consideration of the godly responses to personal disaster that we have just studied, what one specific principle can you take from today's lesson and apply to a personal difficulty that you face?"

Give several minutes for them to select a difficulty and a personal principle to apply. Then have each student write on a three-inch-by-five-inch card the difficulty that he or she faces and a principle from Scripture that he or she can apply in the face of disaster. Tell the students to write their difficulties in such a way as to keep their identities secret. Then collect the cards and shuffle them. Read aloud as many as time permits.

State: "As you can see, we all face difficulties and struggles. Yet, I want you to remember that faith overrides despair." Form a prayer circle and ask for several students to lead the class in a prayer of commitment to applying those principles to their personal lives.

Let's Talk It Over

*The questions on this page are designed to promote discussion of the lesson
by the class and to encourage application of the lesson Scriptures. The answers
provided are only discussion starters. Let your class talk it over from there.*

1. Righteous Habakkuk would suffer along with the wicked of Judah. How can righteous people sustain their faith when they suffer because of the misdeeds of the unrighteous? What can Christians do to keep their faith strong during trying circumstances?

Most of the people who heard Habakkuk's message deserved punishment because they tolerated and/or practiced evil. Yet we can surmise that there were still a few righteous individuals in addition to Habakkuk. It can be helpful if the righteous remember that God is God and does not have to tolerate *any* sin. Only God's longsuffering allows any of us to escape His immediate judgment on us. We can be thankful for God's patience that allows us the opportunity to accept God's method for us to escape God's eternal judgment.

2. Many in Judah would not have connected their trouble with their sin. But the prophet Habakkuk declared the one to be a result of the other. Is every tragedy a judgment from God? If some unfortunate circumstance falls on a group of people today, is there any way to know whether the action was an example of God's punishing that group for their wickedness? Explain.

The three men who visited Job claimed Job's misfortune was God's punishment for his sin. Obviously they were wrong. Christians have to be careful in making claims for which there is no direct verification. After all, there have been many famines, some of which perhaps were caused by God as punishment. But we have no way of knowing if all storms serve this purpose. If Christians present God as being an angry punisher, it is possible that many will be turned away from Him as a result of His being misrepresented.

3. Today's church seems to prefer happy messages of God's love. Not too many years ago, some churches served a constant menu of "hell-fire and brimstone." How can today's church accurately represent both sides of God's nature—His mercy and His justice—as Habakkuk did?

The church today seems to have tempered its message to the circumstances of life in which it finds itself. The pain and suffering experienced by most people as a result of two world wars and a worldwide depression over the course of forty years made it easy to cast the gospel message in harsh and judgmental terms. Recently, the culture's emphasis on tolerance has led the church to emphasize God's loving nature. But God has not changed His character to match the cultural transformation. God is both pure love and pure justice. The just nature of God requires that people avoid sin or suffer the consequences of their actions. The loving part of God is "not willing that any should perish, but that all should come to repentance" (2 Peter 3:9). This loving part made Him willing to send His only Son to pay the penalty for our sin, so that His justice could be satisfied. When Jesus took on our sins and paid their penalty, He then was able to give us His righteousness. Only by being seen as righteous could any of us have hope of entering the holiest of holies, Heaven, and be with God for eternity.

4. When the average Christian gets a real sense of the majesty and power of God, can we expect him or her to tremble in awe as Habakkuk did? Can you tell of a time when you or someone you know has been significantly influenced by coming to a full understanding of the awesomeness of God?

Encourage class members to tell how they first grasped something of the awesome nature of God. How did they come to that realization? What was the result?

5. Sometimes believers become impatient because evil seems to go unpunished. In Habakkuk's day God took His time in bringing judgment on His rebellious children. What must a Christian remember about the nature of God so that he or she does not become cynical, believing that God really does not care if evil seems to have the upper hand?

Some court cases take ten or twelve years to come to trial and finish the appeal process. We can become very frustrated with that timeline, since we want justice to be served. We would be alarmed if God punished us for our sin every ten or twelve years, especially if we received what we deserved (Romans 3:23). It is often good to remember that God's timetable does not match ours (2 Peter 3:8-13). Perhaps we should intensify our prayers for both God's patience and a time of revival for the entire land.

Jerusalem Falls

DEVOTIONAL READING: Psalm 75.

BACKGROUND SCRIPTURE: 2 Chronicles 36:9-21; 2 Kings 24:8-25; 26.

PRINTED TEXT: 2 Chronicles 36:11-21.

2 Chronicles 36:11-21

11 Zedekiah was one and twenty years old when he began to reign, and reigned eleven years in Jerusalem.

12 And he did that which was evil in the sight of the LORD his God, and humbled not himself before Jeremiah the prophet speaking from the mouth of the LORD.

13 And he also rebelled against king Nebuchadnezzar, who had made him swear by God: but he stiffened his neck, and hardened his heart from turning unto the LORD God of Israel.

14 Moreover all the chief of the priests, and the people, transgressed very much after all the abominations of the heathen; and polluted the house of the LORD which he had hallowed in Jerusalem.

15 And the LORD God of their fathers sent to them by his messengers, rising up betimes, and sending; because he had compassion on his people, and on his dwelling place:

16 But they mocked the messengers of God, and despised his words, and misused his prophets, until the wrath of the LORD arose against his people, till there was no remedy.

17 Therefore he brought upon them the king of the Chaldees, who slew their young men with the sword in the house of their sanctuary, and had no compassion upon young man or maiden, old man, or him that stooped for age: he gave them all into his hand.

18 And all the vessels of the house of God, great and small, and the treasures of the house of the LORD, and the treasures of the king, and of his princes; all these he brought to Babylon.

19 And they burnt the house of God, and brake down the wall of Jerusalem, and burnt all the palaces thereof with fire, and destroyed all the goodly vessels thereof.

20 And them that had escaped from the sword carried he away to Babylon; where they were servants to him and his sons until the reign of the kingdom of Persia:

21 To fulfil the word of the LORD by the mouth of Jeremiah, until the land had enjoyed her sabbaths: for as long as she lay desolate she kept sabbath, to fulfil threescore and ten years.

GOLDEN TEXT: The LORD God of their fathers sent to them by his messengers, rising up betimes, and sending; because he had compassion on his people, and on his dwellingplace: but they mocked the messengers of God, and despised his words, andmisused his prophets.—2 Chronicles 36:15, 16.

Judgment and Exile
Unit 3: Final Defeat
(Lessons 10-13)

Lesson Aims

After participating in this lesson, each student will be able to:

1. Tell how Judah "drifted" toward its sad end and how thorough was that end.

2. Compare Judah's "drift" with the changing morality evident in modern culture.

3. Suggest a specific way to confront society's "drift" with the gospel.

Lesson Outline

INTRODUCTION
  A. The Naming Game
  B. Lesson Background
I. PERSISTENT EVIL (2 Chronicles 36:11-16)
  A. Stubborn Defiance (vv. 11, 12)
  B. Repeated Rebellion (v. 13)
    Do You Really Know What Time It Is?
  C. Increasing Idolatry (v. 14)
    Looking for Answers in All the Wrong Places
  D. Mocked Messengers (vv. 15, 16)
II. JERUSALEM FALLS (2 Chronicles 36:17-19)
  A. The People Killed (v. 17)
  B. The Treasures Looted (v. 18)
  C. The City Destroyed (v. 19)
III. UNHAPPY ENDING (2 Chronicles 36:20, 21)
  A. The Remnant in Exile (v. 20)
  B. The Land at Rest (v. 21)
CONCLUSION
  A. The Drifters Then
  B. The Drifters Now
  C. Prayer
  D. Thought to Remember

Introduction

A. The Naming Game

In certain times and cultures, babies receive meaningful names. This was especially true in antiquity. When Eve's first child was born, she named him Cain, which means "gotten" or "brought forth" (Genesis 4:1). We may suppose the birth of her next boy was easy, for she named this one Abel, which means a breath, a puff of air, a mere trifle (Genesis 4:2).

Of special interest are names that are changed. In Ur, a baby was named Abram, which usually is translated "exalted father." At age ninety-nine, the Lord changed his name to Abraham, which means, "father of a multitude" (Genesis 17:4, 5). The current series of lessons calls our attention to two kings of Judah whose names were changed, not by the Lord, but by victorious enemies who made the changes for political reasons.

When Pharaoh Neco (or Nechoh) II of Egypt defeated Judah and took charge of it, the king he appointed was Eliakim, which means "God (Elohim) will establish." But Neco changed that name to Jehoiakim, "The Lord (Yahweh) will establish" (2 Kings 23:34). Although seemingly a slight change, Neco's ability to control the king's name demonstrates his ability to control Judah as well—a sign of vassalage.

A little later, Nebuchadnezzar, king of Babylon, conquered Judah. The king he appointed to rule Judah was Mattaniah, whose name means "gift from the Lord." Nebuchadnezzar changed it to Zedekiah, meaning "the Lord is righteous" (2 Kings 24:17). Again, the name change appears harmless on the surface, but Nebuchadnezzar's ability to do this shows that he was in control (cf. Daniel 1:6, 7).

B. Lesson Background

In previous lessons, we have seen bits of the teaching of three prophets: Zephaniah, Jeremiah, and Habakkuk. We have seen repeated rebukes of the evil that was widespread and persistent in Judah about six hundred years before Christ. We have seen repeated predictions of disaster because of the continuing evil.

Apparently, few people of Judah took the predictions seriously. Happy with idol worship and sinful living, the people preferred to listen to false prophets who assured them that all was well—telling them what they wanted to hear. Judah was God's own nation, the false prophets said, and God would always protect it from harm.

So Jeremiah and other prophets continued their predictions of disaster until they saw those predictions proven true. See 2 Kings 24:18–25:21 and Jeremiah 52:1-30 for parallel accounts to today's text.

I. Persistent Evil
(2 Chronicles 36:11-16)

When we last visited 2 Chronicles six weeks ago, we saw King Josiah trying earnestly and successfully to restore exclusive worship of the Lord and obedience to His law (chapter 34). But Josiah is the last godly king that Judah will have. The kings who follow ignore God's law and prophets, and most of the people follow right along. We now return to 2 Chronicles for a summary of the prevalent evils in Judah and the disaster that God sends as punishment and correction.

A. Stubborn Defiance (vv. 11, 12)

11. Zedekiah was one and twenty years old when he began to reign, and he reigned eleven years in Jerusalem.

Zedekiah begins *to reign* when Nebuchadnezzar removes the previous king, Jehoiachin, and takes him prisoner to Babylon (vv. 9, 10). Judah is now a tiny part of Nebuchadnezzar's great Babylonian Empire, but Jehoiakim (Jehoiachin's father) had rebelled against Babylonian rule (2 Kings 24:1). So Nebuchadnezzar came and took Jehoiachin and ten thousand leading citizens, along with the treasures of the king's house and the temple (2 Kings 24:10-16).

12. And he did that which was evil in the sight of the LORD his God, and humbled not himself before Jeremiah the prophet speaking from the mouth of the LORD.

Zedekiah cannot claim ignorance of the difference between good and *evil* since *Jeremiah the prophet* has been giving him instructions straight from *the Lord*. As king, Zedekiah apparently thinks he is entitled to do as he pleases, so he defies both *the prophet* and *the Lord*. But ultimately Zedekiah continues in the sins of his predecessors (52:2), for which the Lord already had delivered ten thousand leaders of Judah into captivity (2 Kings 24:14). [See question #1, page 88.]

B. Repeated Rebellion (v. 13)

13. And he also rebelled against King Nebuchadnezzar, who had made him swear by God: but he stiffened his neck, and hardened his heart from turning unto the LORD God of Israel.

Zedekiah has defied God, and apparently (by earthly standards) he has gotten away with it. Now he goes on to defy Nebuchadnezzar, the Lord's instrument (Jeremiah 21:4-7). Zedekiah had sworn allegiance to that king, but he breaks his oath (cf. Ezekiel 17:13-15). Arrogantly he turns away from Nebuchadnezzar, but in the process does not turn to *the Lord God of Israel*. With a *stiffened neck* and *a hardened heart*, he simply goes his own way. This type of attitude is, of course, nothing new—either then or now (cf. Proverbs 14:12; 16:25). But for a king, the consequences are more serious because he leads others by example down the same path (e.g., Jeremiah 44:15-17).

DO YOU REALLY KNOW WHAT TIME IT IS?

Is your life just out of control when you don't know the time to the exact minute? Relax! Now there is hope for you. The National Institute of Standards and Technology (Time and Frequency Division) for several years has had a clock that measures each second of time as 9,192,631,770 vibrations of a cesium-133 atom in a vacuum. It's accurate to within one second in a *million* years!

But here's the really good news for everyone who worries about being on time: for less than $200, you can buy a wristwatch that "listens" to a radio signal broadcast. At 1:00 A.M. each day, the watch corrects itself to a millisecond, thus assuring that when you arise in the morning you will know exactly what time it is.

King Zedekiah didn't know what time it was. He didn't know that Judah's time as a free nation was drawing short, or that it was time to yield to King Nebuchadnezzar, or that it was time to turn back to the God of Israel. The reason for his ignorance was not due to the inaccuracy of his clock (or sundial), but because he would not "tune in" to God and listen to what His prophets had been saying. There is a lesson here for us, if we will only hear it.   —C. R. B.

C. Increasing Idolatry (v. 14)

14. Moreover all the chief of the priests, and the people, transgressed very much after all the abominations of the heathen; and polluted the house of the LORD which he had hallowed in Jerusalem.

Priests in earlier times were dedicated to the service of the Lord; but in Zedekiah's time it seems that the priestly leaders are devoted to "freedom of religion." If someone wants to worship Baal, Ashtoreth, or Molech, these priests do not discriminate in helping out. Apparently, they will conduct whatever unholy pagan ceremony the worshiper asks. In today's politically correct language we would say the priests were "tolerant" of other religions. [See question #2, page 88.]

So priests and people together *transgressed very much after all the abominations of the* pagans. *The house of the Lord* is the temple Solomon had built for the one true God—the God of Israel. God had *hallowed* (consecrated) it by accepting it as His (2 Chronicles 7:16). Now the priests and people have *polluted* that sacred place with the worship of idols and imaginary gods. (See Ezekiel 8.)

LOOKING FOR ANSWERS IN ALL THE WRONG PLACES

In October 1347, the worst mass killer in history started on its awful (and awe-inspiring) course. In less than four years, twenty-five million people in Europe—one-third of the population—had died from the Black Death. Most of its victims died within a week, their skin bearing the black blotches that gave the plague its name.

Some physicians blamed an unfortunate alignment of the planets; others said the plague came from poisonous fumes released by earthquakes.

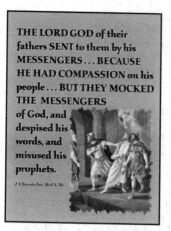

THE LORD GOD of their fathers SENT to them by his MESSENGERS... BECAUSE HE HAD COMPASSION on his people... BUT THEY MOCKED THE MESSENGERS of God, and despised his words, and misused his prophets.

2 Chronicles 36:15, 16

Visual for
lesson 10

The visual for today's lesson illustrates the tragic truth of verses 15 and 16.

Not knowing that being bitten by fleas (which transmitted the disease from infected rats) was the source of the disease, doctors recommended various avoidance regimens, such as eating figs and filberts in the morning or not sleeping on one's back so "evil airs" would not run down the nose into the lungs. The doctors were looking in all the wrong places. Religious leaders were no better: to avoid the Black Death, Pope Clement VI isolated himself and rubbed an emerald ring.

In Zedekiah's time, the priests and the people together practiced the idolatrous and immoral follies of their neighbors rather than looking to God for answers to the troubles their nation was having. We do the same today: after each news-making tragedy, we pass more laws or sanction some rogue dictator or take some other external action. What we need is a moral regeneration that only God can provide.
—C. R. B.

D. Mocked Messengers (vv. 15, 16)

15. And the LORD God of their fathers sent to them by his messengers, rising up betimes, and sending; because he had compassion on his people, and on his dwelling place.

God has not accepted silently the worship of imaginary gods and the polluting of His house. He has sent *his messengers*, Jeremiah and other prophets, to protest the wrongs that were done. *Rising up betimes* is similar to the *rising early* figure we have seen before (see page 51), which means being eager and diligent. The word *betimes* adds repetition to this diligence. Again and again God's prophets have been there to warn the people. They have protested continually against the idolatry, have reminded the people that the Lord is the only real God, and have exhorted them to worship and obey Him only.

God has kept such messages before Judah because of His *compassion*. He wants to save *his people* from the punishment that their wrongdoing demands. God also has compassion on His dwelling place, the temple. He is hurt when that holy place is polluted by pagan ceremonies. He wants His people to stop that pollution before it is too late to avert their just punishment. [See question #3, page 88.]

16. But they mocked the messengers of God, and despised his words, and misused his prophets, until the wrath of the LORD arose against his people, till there was no remedy.

The people of Judah have no regard for God's message or His *messengers*. In fact, just the opposite is true! The *prophets* are *misused* in various ways (cf. Hebrews 11:32-38). In an earlier lesson, we noted that corrupt priests and false prophets wanted Jeremiah put to death for delivering God's message (Jeremiah 26:8-24). They also tortured him with imprisonment and starvation (37:16; 38:6). In the Old Testament, no one suffers more than Jeremiah. [See question #4, page 88.]

II. Jerusalem Falls (2 Chronicles 36:17-19)

Let us very briefly review the three phases of Babylon's dominion over Judah.

Phase One. Judah surrenders without a fight when Nebuchadnezzar first comes. A few young Hebrews are taken to be trained in Babylon and to become advisers to Nebuchadnezzar (Daniel 1:1-7). Jehoiakim is left to be king in Judah and pay tribute. The year is 605 B.C.

Phase Two. While Nebuchadnezzar and his army are busy elsewhere, Jehoiakim rebels, refusing to pay tribute. When the Babylonians finally come, Jehoiachin is king instead of Jehoiakim. The new king is taken to Babylon along with ten thousand leading citizens of Judah. Zedekiah is left to be king of Judah and pay the tribute (2 Kings 24:8-17). The year is 597 B.C.

Phase Three. In the ninth year of his eleven-year reign, Zedekiah refuses to pay the tribute (2 Kings 24:18-20). The king and his people take refuge behind the strong walls of Jerusalem when Nebuchadnezzar and his army return. For a year and a half, the Babylonians camp around the city so no food can be brought in. In 586 B.C. the Babylonians break through the wall to take the starving city (2 Kings 25:1-3; Ezekiel 4:16, 17). Our text relates what happens next.

A. The People Killed (v. 17)

17. Therefore he brought upon them the king of the Chaldees, who slew their young men with the sword in the house of their sanctuary, and

had no compassion upon young man or maiden, old man, or him that stooped for age: he gave them all into his hand.

The Babylonians are also known as *Chaldees* (or Chaldeans), and Nebuchadnezzar is their *king*. He thinks he is acting in his own interest, but actually the Lord is using him to punish the sinful people of Judah. The Lord gives all the people of Judah into Nebuchadnezzar's *hand:* that is, into his power. When at last his troops break into Jerusalem, they kill all who get in their way, and some who do not. Young people, old people, men, women, and children are slaughtered without mercy.

B. The Treasures Looted (v. 18)

18. And all the vessels of the house of God, great and small, and the treasures of the house of the Lord, and the treasures of the king, and of his princes; all these he brought to Babylon.

The invaders loot the temple, the king's palace, and the houses of the subordinate officials. Some of *the vessels of the house of God* are made of gold and silver, but most of the stuff taken as booty is made of less valuable bronze (2 Kings 25:13-17; Jeremiah 52:17-23). Nebuchadnezzar had taken all the gold items in 597 B.C. (2 Kings 24:13), so most of the gold items taken now must have been made only within the previous ten years. The Babylonians keep these items as trophies of victory, eventually using them in their own drunken, idolatrous feasts (Daniel 5:1-4). The exiles who return several decades later will be able to bring some of these items back (Ezra 1:7-11).

Besides the sacred vessels, the looters take money from the temple treasury and from the homes of the king and his subordinate officials. In leaving nothing of value in the hands of those rebellious leaders of Judah, the chance of a future rebellion is diminished.

C. The City Destroyed (v. 19)

19. And they burnt the house of God, and brake down the wall of Jerusalem, and burnt all the palaces thereof with fire, and destroyed all the goodly vessels thereof.

No city will remain where *Jerusalem* now is. Everything combustible is burned. With much effort, the massive stone walls around the city are broken down. Probably the walls of the temple and palaces also are reduced to rubble. No rebellious citizen of Judah will find shelter in Jerusalem. Even after the exiles return, the walls will not be rebuilt for quite some time (Ezra 4:6-23). About one hundred and forty years will have to pass after their return before the Judean people once again feel the security of walls (Nehemiah 1–4). [See question #5, page 88.]

III. Unhappy Ending (2 Chronicles 36:20, 21)

The end of Jerusalem is a time of wailing in the streets. Even God, who has decreed it, takes no pleasure in it (Ezekiel 18:32).

A. The Remnant in Exile (v. 20)

20. And them that had escaped from the sword carried he away to Babylon; where they were servants to him and his sons until the reign of the kingdom of Persia.

If the record of Jerusalem's fall had ended with verse 17, we might think that everyone in the city has been killed. Now, however, we see that there are many survivors. Perhaps the killers have spared the unarmed people who surrendered humbly without trying to fight or to run away (cf. Jeremiah 39:9). We can only guess how many survivors there are. Some of these are left in the land of Judah (39:10), but many thousands are driven over the miles to Babylon. Interestingly, Jeremiah himself receives better treatment by the Babylonians than by his own people (see 39:11-13; 40:1-5).

How to Say It

ABRAM. *Ay*-brum.
ABRAHAM. *Ay*-bruh-ham.
ASHTORETH. *Ash*-toe-reth.
BAAL. *Bay*-ul.
BABYLON. *Bab*-uh-lun.
BABYLONIAN. Bab-ih-*low*-nee-un.
CHALDEANS. Kal-*dee*-unz.
CHALDEES. *Kal*-deez.
CYRUS. *Sigh*-rus.
ELIAKIM. Ee-*lye*-uh-kim.
ELOHIM (Hebrew). El-o-*heem*.
EZEKIEL. Ee-*zeek*-ee-ul or Ee-*zeek*-yul.
HABAKKUK. Huh-*back*-kuk.
JEHOIACHIN. Jeh-*hoy*-uh-kin.
JEHOIAKIM. Jeh-*hoy*-uh-kim.
JEREMIAH. Jair-uh-*my*-uh.
JOSIAH. Jo-*sigh*-uh.
JUDEAN. Joo-*dee*-un.
LEVITICUS. Leh-*vit*-ih-kus.
MATTANIAH. Mat-uh-*nye*-uh.
MOLECH. *Mo*-lek.
NEBUCHADNEZZAR. *Neb*-yuh-kud-*nez*-er (strong accent on *nez*).
NECO or NECHOH. *Nee*-ko.
PHARAOH. *Fay*-ro.
UR. Er.
YAHWEH (Hebrew). *Yah*-weh.
ZEDEKIAH. Zed-uh-*kye*-uh.
ZEPHANIAH. Zef-uh-*nye*-uh.

The subjugation of the people is total, as *they* become *servants* to Nebuchadnezzar. It will last until *the kingdom of Persia* conquers Babylon in 539 B.C., and Cyrus issues his decree allowing the exiles to return (2 Chronicles 36:22, 23; Ezra 1:1-4).

B. The Land at Rest (v. 21)

21. To fulfil the word of the LORD by the mouth of Jeremiah, until the land had enjoyed her sabbaths: for as long as she lay desolate she kept sabbath, to fulfil threescore and ten years.

Not only is the destruction and captivity a fulfillment of the prophecy of *Jeremiah* (25:11, 12; 29:10; cf. Daniel 9:2), it also fulfills Leviticus 26:34, 35. God's law had provided that one year of seven should be a sabbath for the land. The ground was not to be plowed or planted that year; grapevines were not to be pruned (Leviticus 25:1-5). Harvesters in the sixth year would accidentally drop some seed in the field, and a bit of wheat or barley would grow from that. Grapevines produce some fruit even if they are not pruned. Those bits of produce in the seventh year were to be for the poor of the land, not for the owners of the field (Exodus 23:10, 11). Greedy landholders had been breaking that law for a long time, planting and reaping in the seventh year as in the other six. This was part of the injustice of which the Judeans were guilty. Now the farmers were taken away. To make up for all the sabbaths that had been missed, every year will now be a sabbath for the land until the exiles return.

Conclusion

Captivity in Babylon was a climax in the history of Israel. It was the culmination of what the Israelites had been doing for eight hundred years. They had been drifting.

A. The Drifters Then

The people of Israel were not drifters when they entered the promised land and took possession of it. They were dynamic, aggressive, determined, powerful. Better still, they trusted God. They knew He gave them victory over the wicked pagans. Happily and obediently, they settled down to enjoy the land.

Years went by. Joshua and the heroes who had fought with him died. They were replaced by a generation who had grown up in times of peace. They did not suddenly rebel against the Lord; they just began to drift away from Him. They began to ignore His law; they began to deceive and cheat and mistreat each other for gain. In the pursuit of pleasure, they began to eat and drink in pagan feasts. Drifting farther, they actually participated in pagan worship.

Then suddenly their peace, prosperity, and pleasure were gone. Armed bands invaded their land to steal livestock and harvests, killing anyone who stood in their way. Then the people prayed, imploring God to help them. They worshiped in sincerity and truth. They respected God's law and obeyed it. So God raised up from among the people a leader to rally them to defeat the invaders. Peace and prosperity returned. But the next generation began another drift away from God.

The same cycle was repeated over and over in the history of Israel. Honoring God and obeying Him brought success; drifting away from Him was drifting into disaster. Still Israel drifted till the nation was split, till north Israel was destroyed by the Assyrians, till Judah was captive in Babylon.

B. The Drifters Now

In previous lessons, we noted a drift away from God in the countries of Europe and North America. The only way to reverse this drift is for Christians to take the gospel to every creature (Mark 16:15). We must make disciples, baptizing them in the name of the Father, and of the Son, and of the Holy Ghost, and teach them to do all that Jesus has commanded (Matthew 28:19, 20). It's the only way—for a nation or for an individual.

C. Prayer

Almighty God, ruler of people and of nations, with gratitude we cherish the privilege of being Your children. Help us to be faithful; and help us also to reach out to win others to the same precious faith we hold. In Jesus' name, amen.

D. Thought to Remember

Take the gospel to all nations.

Home Daily Bible Readings

Monday, Oct. 28—No Remedy (2 Chronicles 36:9-16)

Tuesday, Oct. 29—Jerusalem Falls (2 Chronicles 36:17-21)

Wednesday, Oct. 30—Weeping Over Jerusalem (Psalm 137:1-6)

Thursday, Oct. 31—How Long, O Lord? (Psalm 79:5-13)

Friday, Nov. 1—Will the Lord Keep Silent? (Isaiah 64:6-12)

Saturday, Nov. 2—Daniel's Prayer (Daniel 9:1-10)

Sunday, Nov. 3—O Lord, Forgive (Daniel 9:11-19)

Learning by Doing

This page contains an alternative lesson plan emphasizing learning activities.
Classes desiring such student involvement will find these suggestions helpful.

Learning Goals

After participating in this lesson, each student will be able to:

1. Tell how Judah "drifted" toward its sad end and how thorough was that end.

2. Compare Judah's "drift" with the changing morality evident in modern culture.

3. Suggest a specific way to confront society's "drift" with the gospel.

Into the Lesson

Begin this week's lesson with a half-page worksheet titled, "Simile Completion." Prior to class prepare this worksheet with the following uncompleted simile: "A free-floating rowboat and present-day morality are similar in that. . . ." Photocopy enough so each student will have one. Say, "This week we begin with a Simile Completion. [Pass out the worksheet.] Read the statement and then write how these two items are similar." *(Possible answers include: "They are not connected to a standard"; "They both keep drifting farther away.")* After time for students to complete the statement, ask for volunteers to share theirs. When all those who wanted to share have done so, make the transition to Bible study by saying, "As an untied rowboat drifts out to sea, present-day morality not tied to a standard drifts farther from God. Our text today describes how Judah drifted away from God and how the erosion of morality led to destruction. Turn to 2 Chronicles 36:11-21, and let's read how they drifted away from God."

Into the Word

Ask a class member to read 2 Chronicles 36:11-21 aloud. Say: "First of all, let's go over a number of basic facts. As I ask the following questions, call out the answers and give verses where they are found."

• How old was Zedekiah when he became king, and how long did he reign? *(Twenty-one years old, and he reigned for eleven years, v. 11.)*

• What words describe Zedekiah's move away from God? *(Did evil; humbled not himself; rebelled, stiffened his neck, hardened his heart, vv. 12, 13.)*

• What did King Nebuchadnezzar get Zedekiah to do so he would obey him? *(He made Zedekiah swear by his God, v. 13.)*

• How did King Zedekiah's behavior affect both priests and people? *(They transgressed in the same ways as the pagans and polluted the house of the Lord, v. 14.)*

• Why did God send His messengers to Judah again and again? *(He had compassion on His people and His dwelling place, v. 15.)*

• What did the people do to God's messengers? *(Mocked them, despised God's words, and misused his prophets, v. 16.)*

• Describe how Jerusalem was destroyed by the king of the Chaldees (Babylonians). *(Slew both male and female, old and young in the house of the sanctuary, v. 17; took all the vessels and treasures of the house of God and of the king, v. 18; burned the house of God and all palaces, broke down the wall of Jerusalem, v. 19.)*

• What did the Babylonians do to those who escaped the sword? *(Took them to Babylon to become slaves, v. 20.)*

• How long did the desolation last? *(Seventy years, v. 21.)*

Into Life

Say: "Just like a rowboat loosed from its mooring post, Judah drifted farther and farther away from God—even to the point of 'no remedy' (v. 16). This 'drifting' has also occurred both in our society and in Christian people. Let's see how this passage relates to us." Move the class into small discussion groups. Give each group the following questions:

• In what specific ways has the morality of society eroded or drifted away from God? *(Growing acceptance of improper sexual relationships, increased violence, and others.)*

• What would help Christians not to drift away from God? See Ephesians 4:13, 14. *(Not being influenced by "every wind of doctrine," by "sleight of men, and cunning craftiness," because of growing "unto the measure of the stature of the fulness of Christ.")*

• What ways can Christians confront society's drift with the gospel? *(Grow strong in faith; share Christ and our faith; become active in voting for God-serving individuals running for public office.)*

Give several minutes for the groups to discuss. Then have a reporter from each group reveal the group's answers to the entire class. Write these answers on a poster or chalkboard so all students can see them. Ask each student to select one specific way to confront society's "drift." End the class in a prayer of commitment.

Let's Talk It Over

The questions on this page are designed to promote discussion of the lesson by the class and to encourage application of the lesson Scriptures. The answers provided are only discussion starters. Let your class talk it over from there.

1. Jeremiah the prophet confronted King Zedekiah about his evil behavior. If a Christian knows of solid evidence of an official's corrupt behavior in office, what should he or she do?

Since most people are hesitant to become an activist in this type of situation, the corrupt leader simply continues to hold office and act in a corrupt manner. A Christian can report evidence to the prosecutor or other overseeing authority. Failing in that, he or she might detail information for the news media, run in opposition to the candidate or support another candidate, and help get out the vote on election day. Many communities would be better places to live if good people would become more involved in politics.

2. It is politically correct to speak with tolerance and even be supportive of the varied beliefs of all people. Teaching anything as "absolute" truth is considered bigotry. What methods can the church and average Christians use to overcome cultural barriers that work against the freedom to openly teach the truth of God's Word?

The tolerance zealots want all groups to be heard without being judged by any other group. When Christians proclaim there is one way to live, they are labeled as sinning against others through intolerance. One good rebuttal to that is to comment on their intolerance. They argue that all groups have the right to speak their mind and then disallow Christians the same privilege. "You can't have it both ways" is a statement worth repeating every time they object to the Christian message.

3. The text points out that God's condemnation of Judah's sin was an act of His compassion. But when Christians point out how different groups either tolerate or subtly embrace progressive evil, they are accused of being too restrictive, even hateful. How can the church continue its work when it is being unfairly characterized in the community?

The people of Judah did not appreciate the prophet's message anymore than people today do. That did not change the facts: they were wrong, and it was a loving thing to point that out and encourage repentance.

Whenever the church starts deciding its course of action based on community opinion, the cause of Christ is doomed to defeat. Jesus praised the prophets for their faithfulness in the face of disfavor and persecution. The early church faced the same kind of pressure within weeks of its beginning. We should follow the lead of the early church and pray for courage to work and speak as we have been instructed (Acts 4:23-29).

4. The people mocked God's prophets, but the prophets continued to proclaim the sacred message. Today's church is ridiculed in the media, at school and in the workplace, and even in the neighborhood. Which is the greatest threat— direct or indirect ridicule? Why? What can the church do to help young people stand strong in their belief in the face of ridicule?

An important way to help young people take a stand is to model it! This is especially true in regard to the indirect pressures of moral "drift." Christian adults need to demonstrate that they follow God's Word in spite of what the culture or society does. If they merely accommodate themselves to every trend and practice of the society, then young people will not see any need to take a stand themselves.

Beyond setting an example, the church can equip young people to deal with both subtle and direct pressure through its educational activities. Youth need to learn who God is in all His power. They need to understand the outcome of the final judgment of God. The church can train them in how to assess the claims made against Christianity as well as in the best ways to respond to persecution. Have the class suggest specific methods for reaching these goals.

5. When all of the items of the temple were carried off, it would have been very hard for the few people who remained to continue with their regular worship routine. Recently a Christian college in Myanmar was seized and bulldozed to the ground. If that happened to our church, what would the members do to survive and thrive?

Have your class discuss what steps your church could take if the present building were forcefully taken and destroyed. Use the discussion to note it is the attitude and actual worship that are important, not the physical trappings.

Grief and Hope

DEVOTIONAL READING: Psalm 42:5-11.

BACKGROUND SCRIPTURE: Lamentations.

PRINTED TEXT: Lamentations 1:12-16; 3:22-26, 31-33, 40.

Lamentations 1:12-16

12 Is it nothing to you, all ye that pass by? Behold, and see if there be any sorrow like unto my sorrow, which is done unto me, wherewith the LORD hath afflicted me in the day of his fierce anger.

13 From above hath he sent fire into my bones, and it prevaileth against them: he hath spread a net for my feet, he hath turned me back: he hath made me desolate and faint all the day.

14 The yoke of my transgressions is bound by his hand: they are wreathed, and come up upon my neck: he hath made my strength to fall, the Lord hath delivered me into their hands, from whom I am not able to rise up.

15 The Lord hath trodden under foot all my mighty men in the midst of me: he hath called an assembly against me to crush my young men: the Lord hath trodden the virgin, the daughter of Judah, as in a winepress.

16 For these things I weep; mine eye, mine eye runneth down with water, because the comforter that should relieve my soul is far from me: my children are desolate, because the enemy prevailed.

Lamentations 3:22-26, 31-33, 40

22 It is of the LORD's mercies that we are not consumed, because his compassions fail not.

23 They are new every morning: great is thy faithfulness.

24 The LORD is my portion, saith my soul; therefore will I hope in him.

25 The LORD is good unto them that wait for him, to the soul that seeketh him.

26 It is good that a man should both hope and quietly wait for the salvation of the LORD.

. . . .

31 For the Lord will not cast off for ever:

32 But though he cause grief, yet will he have compassion according to the multitude of his mercies.

33 For he doth not afflict willingly, nor grieve the children of men.

. . . .

40 Let us search and try our ways, and turn again to the LORD.

Nov 10

GOLDEN TEXT: It is of the LORD's mercies that we are not consumed, because his compassions fail not. They are new every morning: great is thy faithfulness.—Lamentations 3:22, 23.

Judgment and Exile
Unit 3: Final Defeat
(Lessons 10-13)

Lesson Aims

After participating in this lesson, each student will be able to:

1. Summarize the dismay of fallen Jerusalem and the hope that God still gave her for the future.

2. Explain how disaster or hardship can sometimes help turn a people to the Lord.

3. Suggest one or two ways to put into practice the message of Lamentations 3:26.

Lesson Outline

INTRODUCTION
  A. How
  B. Lesson Background
  I. THE CRUEL FACE (Lamentations 1:12-16)
  A. Sorrow and Helplessness (vv. 12, 13)
     Is It Nothing to You?
  B. Bondage and Trampling (vv. 14, 15)
  C. Tears and Desolation (v. 16)
 II. THE KINDLY FACE (Lamentations 3:22-26)
  A. Survival and Comfort (vv. 22, 23)
     God Still Loves Us
  B. Hoping and Waiting (vv. 24-26)
III. SUMMARY (Lamentations 3:31-33, 40)
  A. God's Reprieve (vv. 31, 32)
  B. God's Wish (v. 33)
  C. Our Duty (v. 40)
CONCLUSION
  A. Don't Drift
  B. Hope and Wait
  C. Prayer
  D. Thought to Remember

Introduction

The titles of books may be chosen for various reasons. The title, *Robert Kennedy and His Times*, for example, seems designed to tell me what the book is about. On the other hand, *Gone With the Wind* gives me scarcely a hint of the book's contents; but it makes me want to read the book and see what it is about.

No such purpose is seen in the titles of the books in the Hebrew Scriptures. Instead, the first word of a book becomes its title. Looking at the first word of the first book of the Hebrew Bible and trying to put the sound of it in English letters instead of Hebrew, we have *bereshith*. That

same word appears as the title of the book. It means "In the Beginning." Certainly that is an appropriate name for the first few chapters of the book, but the fifty chapters take us far beyond the beginning. Centuries later the Greek translators titled that book *Genesis*, which means "Origin." That, too, is an excellent name for the first part of the book, and the Greek word *Genesis* is brought into our English translation.

A. How

This week we take our text from a book whose original title is the Hebrew word for *How*, because that is the first word of the book. The ancient Hebrews used that word as a cry, wail, or lament at funerals. From this fact, the ancient Greek translators gave this book the title *The Lamentations of Jeremiah*. We see this same title in the *King James Version*, although other versions shorten it simply to *Lamentations*.

That book is a collection of sorrowful songs arising from the end of Jerusalem, the tragic death of many of her people, and the sad captivity of others in Babylon. Jeremiah himself was not one of those captives. He stayed in Judah and soon went to Egypt with the others who did not go to Babylon. So he, too, was an exile from his beloved homeland. For years he had tried earnestly to turn his people back to God and so to save them from defeat and captivity. No one mourned more deeply and sincerely than he did when that effort failed.

B. Lesson Background

The background of this lesson lies in the destruction of Jerusalem that we read about last week. Through many years God's people had done wrong. They had ignored God's will, disobeyed His laws, and scorned His prophets. At last God sent the mighty army of Babylon to punish His heedless people.

The first time that army came, Judah surrendered, promising to obey the king of Babylon and pay tribute. But when the army was far away, Judah rebelled and refused to pay until the army came back. After a period of submission Judah rebelled again, and the army came yet a third time. This time, instead of surrendering, the people of Judah hid behind the strong walls of Jerusalem. The Babylonians camped all around the city so no one could escape and no one could bring in food. The siege continued for a year and a half. Inside the walls many died of disease and starvation. The rest were weak with hunger when the invaders broke into the city and poured in with swinging swords. Anyone who stood against them was cut down; some surrendered abjectly enough to be made prisoners.

The temple and palaces and homes of Jerusalem were burned. Stone walls were torn apart and scattered over the landscape. The captives were marched a thousand weary miles to Babylon.

Imagine the sorrow over loved ones who had died. Imagine the grief over Jerusalem, lovely and beloved, now only a field of rubble. Imagine the horror of captivity in a strange and cruel land. All of these find expression in *The Lamentations of Jeremiah*. These lamentations are lyric poetry, poetry designed to be sung. Perhaps they were sung by mourning captives "by the rivers of Babylon" (Psalm 137:1). When the captivity was over, perhaps in restored Jerusalem they were sung in memory.

In the disaster at Jerusalem, everyone in Judah could see the cruel and ugly face of captivity and death. But with the guidance of the Holy Spirit, God's prophet could see another face of disaster, a kindly one. God did not design this horrible event to destroy His people, but to help them. Some thoughtful people now would listen to God's prophets. Some would see that the horrible disaster was the result of their own wrongdoing. Some would repent. They would worship God in sincerity and truth. They would obey Him. Then they and their children could return to rebuild Jerusalem and be what God wanted them to be—His chosen people.

In the brief sample of the lamentation before us, we shall catch a glimpse of that kindly face along with the more obvious face of horror and death.

I. The Cruel Face
(Lamentations 1:12-16)

The siege of Jerusalem is now past. Those who had been trapped within her walls had died slowly of hunger and disease. When the enemy finally had broken into the city, many had died quickly by the edge of the sword (Jeremiah 21:9).

A. Sorrow and Helplessness (vv. 12, 13)

12. Is it nothing to you, all ye that pass by? Behold, and see if there be any sorrow like unto my sorrow, which is done unto me, wherewith the LORD hath afflicted me in the day of his fierce anger.

The "singer" of this doleful song is Jerusalem herself, not Jeremiah. The prophet puts into words and music the feeling of that crushed city, the feeling of its people driven over the weary miles to an uncertain future in Babylon. With one voice those people call every observer to testify. In the entire world, is there any sorrow like the sorrow of desolate Jerusalem? [See question #1, page 96.]

And with divine insight, the prophet puts into the song more than all of the people yet realize: it is not just Babylon that is inflicting this monstrous sorrow, it is the *Lord*. The reality of *the day of his fierce anger* reflects the prediction of Jeremiah 4:26. That anger is just, and so is the sorrow inflicted on the captive people.

IS IT NOTHING TO YOU?

The most famous photograph from the Vietnam War may well be that of Kim Phuc, a child running naked and badly burned down the street after her village had been napalmed. After shooting the picture, the American photographer took Kim to a hospital for treatment—a series of ordeals that would go on for many years.

The picture of Kim pained the hearts of many who saw it. One man, especially, was touched by it. Chuck Colson, a White House aide at the time, says, "No person can look at such a picture and not be deeply moved. And because I was part of the administration prosecuting this war, there was no escaping a sense of personal responsibility, which made my agony deeper."

Years later, Kim—by then a grown woman—married a Christian man and became a Christian herself. They wanted to go to Bible college but lacked the means to do so. Colson heard of their plight, told her story, and solicited help for them on his daily radio broadcast. Several colleges immediately offered them scholarships. The actions of both the photographer and Colson said, in effect, "Yes, it does mean something to me that I was in some way involved in Kim's tragedy, and I will do what I can to change things for the better." This is the task of all who have been touched by the gospel: to feel the pain of those who suffer and do what we can to redeem their situation.

—C. R. B.

13. From above hath he sent fire into my bones, and it prevaileth against them: he hath spread a net for my feet, he hath turned me back: he hath made me desolate and faint all the day.

Bones give shape and firmness to a person's body. Without them we would sink into shapeless and helpless lumps of flesh. Now the bones of Jerusalem are gone as if destroyed by fire *from above*—fire from the Lord Himself. He has made His people helpless before the might of Babylon.

The rest of the verse pictures that helplessness in different ways. *A net* is a favorite way of catching a bird or small animal. The net is cleverly spread and weighted so it will enclose and capture the small body that touches it. In turning Jerusalem *back*, the Lord had stopped her mad course of sinning. The image of being *desolate and faint* indicates that the Lord has made Jerusalem weak and helpless, as if from being inflicted with a serious disease. Often a person in such a condition can do little but lie on a sickbed—and think.

B. Bondage and Trampling (vv. 14, 15)

14. The yoke of my transgressions is bound by his hand: they are wreathed, and come up upon my neck: he hath made my strength to fall, the Lord hath delivered me into their hands, from whom I am not able to rise up.

In the book that bears his name, Jeremiah uses *yoke* imagery more than a dozen times. Using the same kind of figurative language, the song now says the Lord has fashioned Jerusalem's countless sins into a yoke for her *neck.* Her sins are the reason for her captivity and servitude. In plainer language, the text goes on to say that the Lord has taken away Jerusalem's *strength* and has *delivered* her into the power of the Babylonians. In describing Jerusalem as being *not able to rise up,* the text gives no hope for the future. This distress seems to be "open ended," with no relief in sight.

15. The Lord hath trodden underfoot all my mighty men in the midst of me: he hath called an assembly against me to crush my young men: the Lord hath trodden the virgin, the daughter of Judah, as in a winepress.

Jerusalem is still speaking or singing this mournful song. She recognizes that it is *the Lord* Himself who has overwhelmed the *mighty men,* her soldiers. [See question #2, page 96.]

Once her protection is *trodden underfoot,* then the city itself is open to being trampled. However, the Lord has not done that all without the help of human feet. The *assembly* He had called

Visual for lesson 11. *The visual for today's lesson, with its lovely picture of a desert sunrise, illustrates the daily newness of God's blessings.*

was the army of Babylon. This army had squeezed out the very lifeblood of the city and its people, as if *in a winepress.*

C. Tears and Desolation (v. 16)

16. For these things I weep; mine eye, mine eye runneth down with water, because the comforter that should relieve my soul is far from me: my children are desolate, because the enemy prevailed.

Jerusalem is weeping uncontrollably. After the people return from exile, they will weep tears of repentance over what they had done (Ezra 3:13; 10:1; Nehemiah 8:9). But right now, there seems to be no one anywhere nearby to give comfort to her *soul,* not even God. Her *children,* her people, *are desolate, because the enemy prevailed:* the army of Babylon broke into the fortified city and crushed all the people who were there. About six centuries later, Jesus will weep over Jerusalem as He foresees another destruction of the city, this time at the hands of the Romans (Luke 19:41-44). [See question #3, page 96.]

II. The Kindly Face
(Lamentations 3:22-26)

In chapter 3, we no longer hear the voice of Jerusalem. It is now the voice of a man who has suffered much (3:1). Are we hearing Jeremiah himself? For years he has faithfully delivered God's message, and his payment has been cruel persecution.

Most of the people of Jerusalem can see only the cruel face of the monstrous calamity that has crushed Jerusalem and transported her people to an enemy land. But Jeremiah is God's prophet. He can see a kindly face in that same calamity. He writes it into his song so that we can see it, as well.

A. Survival and Comfort (vv. 22, 23)

22. It is of the LORD's mercies that we are not consumed, because his compassions fail not.

The captives fretting in captivity are still alive. That is more than they deserve. In simple justice, God could have wiped them out for their long years of stubborn sinning. It is God's *mercies,* not His justice, that keep them alive. The captives can see this for themselves if they can set aside their emotions and think reasonably. God's *compassions* have not failed in the disaster just past. He is grieved with their grief; He will be glad when again their obedience will be such that He can give them gladness. More than that, God had chosen this people centuries earlier to bring a blessing to "all families of the earth" (Genesis 12:3). For the sake of His own purpose, the Lord will preserve the descendants of Abraham until they bring into the world the Christ who will offer the blessing of salvation to all. [See question #4, page 96.]

23. They are new every morning: great is thy faithfulness.

God's mercies and compassion (v. 22) are as sure as the dawn. Deserved or not, they are with His people in each new day. The Lord is faithful to His people even when they are not faithful to Him. He is faithful enough to punish them when nothing else will turn them from their evil way.

GOD STILL LOVES US

Most golfers think of a hole-in-one as a marvelous stroke of good luck. Not so in Japan, however! Noriaki Yamashita described his feelings when he shot a hole-in-one with these words: "I knew something terrible had happened." What was terrible was that, according to Japanese custom, he had to buy drinks, dinner, and other gifts for club members and friends when he got his hole-in-one. It is a custom that cost him almost $10,000!

To prevent such "good luck," Japan's four million golfers spend considerably more than $200 million annually to insure themselves against hole-in-one expenses as well as damages or injuries caused by shots that go astray. Yamashita was carrying only $5,000 on that day, so he immediately doubled his coverage. It was a wise decision: a year later he hit another hole-in-one, and this time he was covered fully.

When "bad luck" or "misfortune" (or whatever we want to call life's calamities) strikes us, we don't have to worry about the need to "pay off" our best friend—our heavenly Father. On the contrary, even when (or if) calamity comes as part of God's judgment on sin, God is standing by, offering us the compassion, love, and support that we need to survive and overcome the sins that have beset us. As our text says, "[God's] compassions fail not. They are new every morning."

—C. R. B.

B. Hoping and Waiting (vv. 24-26)

24. The LORD is my portion, saith my soul; therefore will I hope in him.

Like other people of Judah, this solemn singer has lost much that he held dear. He no longer has wealth or property, friends have died, and the city he has loved is nothing but scorched and tumbled stones. All he has left is his *portion* in *the Lord*. And so he has *hope*. Fallen Jerusalem will rise again; the captives will walk free; God's people will worship Him and obey Him; Judah will live to fulfill her destiny, to bring a blessing to all the world.

How to Say It

BABYLON. *Bab*-uh-lun.
BABYLONIAN. Bab-ih-*low*-nee-un.
BERESHITH (Hebrew). beh-reh-*sheet*.
EZEKIEL. Ee-*zeek*-ee-ul or Ee-*zeek*-yul.
JEREMIAH. Jair-uh-*my*-uh.
JUDAH. *Joo*-duh.
JUDEANS. Joo-*dee*-unz.
KIM PHUC. Kim *Fook*.
LAMENTATION. Lam-en-*tay*-shun.
NORIAKI YAMASHITA. Nor-ee-*ah*-kee Yahm-ah-*shee*-tah.

---

25. The LORD is good unto them that wait for him, to the soul that seeketh him.

The nightmare that keeps replaying in their heads won't go away. Weeping in captivity, the people find it hard to believe that *the Lord is good*. The Babylonians have leveled Jerusalem, slaughtered thousands of its people, dragged other thousands away—and *the Lord* sent them to do that.

But *wait*. The Lord has not finished what He is doing with the Judeans. After this horrible captivity brings them to their senses, the Lord will send them back to rebuild Jerusalem. When He does, they will move on toward the purpose for which the Lord has made them His people—to bring a blessing to the whole world. That is the *good!*

26. It is good that a man should both hope and quietly wait for the salvation of the LORD.

The captives are not to give way to despair. The prophets who foretold the captivity also foretold also the end of it. The captives should not try to escape from their captivity by flight or rebellion. The Lord has brought them into subjection, and has promised that it will last for seventy years (cf. Jeremiah 29:4-14). He will rescue them when that time is up. In the meantime, their task is to *both hope and quietly wait for the salvation of the Lord*. This is not the "wishful thinking" kind of hope. This kind of hope has a definite object and basis. [See question #5, page 96.]

III. Summary
(Lamentations 3:31-33, 40)

In a few words, the final verses of our text sum up the teaching of this lesson for the captives.

A. God's Reprieve (vv. 31, 32)

31. For the Lord will not cast off for ever.

As the years and decades of captivity roll by, the unhappy captives may think that the Lord has abandoned them. They would have a hard time praying that, "God is our refuge and strength, a very present help in trouble" (Psalm 46:1). In their present trouble He actually has been on the side of their enemy. But that is only temporary.

32. But though he cause grief, yet will he have compassion according to the multitude of his mercies.

The *grief* the Lord has caused matches the greatness of His wrath and the greatness of their transgression. But that grief will accomplish its purpose in bringing the people to repent and obey God. Their God then will have *compassion* to match the greatness of His *mercies*. The Lord will end their grief by leading them back to Jerusalem in joy (cf. Ezra 1:11).

B. God's Wish (v. 33)

33. For he doth not afflict willingly, nor grieve the children of men.

The Lord finds no pleasure in afflicting and grieving His people (Ezekiel 18:23, 32; 33:11). He does it with regret, not *willingly*. He is driven to it by their persistent wrongdoing and His own holiness. He has tried milder ways of guiding them: His law given centuries earlier and the living voices of His prophets in recent times. His people have ignored those, rushing madly on in their evil ways. Now disastrous affliction and grief will stop this mad rush and turn them back to godly ways. God's wish for His people is that they glorify Him and enjoy His goodness. He afflicts them with suffering and grief because at this point there is no other way to bring this about.

C. Our Duty (v. 40)

40. Let us search and try our ways, and turn again to the LORD.

The people have been living in *ways* that have brought them to loss and captivity. They need to examine those ways, to *try* them, test them by God's written law and the teaching of His living prophets. That examination will show clearly that it is their own actions that have brought on the calamity (cf. Jeremiah 31:29, 30; Ezekiel 18), although those born while in captivity can make a good case for their own innocence (Lamentations 5:7).

Conclusion

The twofold message of this lesson is as loud and clear to us as it is to the people of Judah long ago. First, don't drift away from God. That way leads to disaster. Second, if disaster strikes, if we suffer loss or grief or pain, "it is good that a man should both hope and quietly wait for the salvation of the Lord" (Lamentations 3:26).

A. Don't Drift

We avoid drifting by spending time in His Word and by doing what we find God says there (James 1:22). Drifting seems so harmless at first. Telling a dirty joke here, looking at a pornographic Web site there—what's the big deal? The drift of the Jewish people occurred over decades and centuries. But finally God showed them that sin certainly was—as it still is—a big deal! (Compare Hebrews 2:1-3.)

B. Hope and Wait

Sometimes we, like the people of Judah, can see that disaster is the result of our own mistakes or misconduct. Then we work to repair the damage while we hope and wait for better times. We can pray while we work, and find that God is "faithful and just to forgive us our sins" (1 John 1:9). Praise the Lord!

Sometimes disaster is not our fault, but comes because of circumstances beyond our control. If what is lost can be replaced, our grief is lightened as we work to replace it while we pray, hope, and wait. If what is lost cannot be replaced, then we work to adjust ourselves to the loss realizing that God Himself is our ultimate "portion" (Lamentations 3:24). Either way, we find ourselves growing stronger spiritually. Praise the Lord!

C. Prayer

Whatever happens, Father, we know that You are good. We trust You. In every time of trouble, help us to work and wait for what we hope for, secure in the confidence that You will do all things well. In Jesus' name, amen.

D. Thought to Remember

God knows best.

Home Daily Bible Readings

Monday, Nov. 4—Comfort Is Far From Me (Lamentations 1:12-16)

Tuesday, Nov. 5—Great Is God's Faithfulness (Lamentations 3:19-24)

Wednesday, Nov. 6—God Will Have Compassion (Lamentations 3:25-33)

Thursday, Nov. 7—Lift Hearts to Heaven (Lamentations 3:34-41)

Friday, Nov. 8—God Heard My Plea (Lamentations 3:49-57)

Saturday, Nov. 9—Restore Us (Lamentations 5:15-22)

Sunday, Nov. 10—Sow in Tears, Reap in Joy (Psalm 126:1-6)

Learning by Doing

This page contains an alternative lesson plan emphasizing learning activities.
Classes desiring such student involvement will find these suggestions helpful.

Learning Goals

After participating in this lesson, each student will be able to:

1. Summarize the dismay of fallen Jerusalem and the hope that God still gave for the future.

2. Explain how disaster or hardship can sometimes help turn a people to the Lord.

3. Suggest one or two ways to put into practice the message of Lamentations 3:26.

Into the Lesson

Begin class by simply writing the words "waiting for . . ." on the board or overhead transparency for all to see. Say: "Today, I'd like you to think about the various situations in which people find themselves waiting for someone or something. As you think of those situations, call them out and I'll write them on the board." Possible situations may include: birth of a baby; company coming to your house; doctor's appointment; stuck in a traffic jam; getting tickets for a show. Say: "Now, I'd like you to think with me about what people do when they are waiting in these situations. Once again, call them out and I'll write them on the board." Possible actions may include: pacing; looking out the window; glancing through magazines; looking at the clock; blowing the horn; worrying about not getting tickets. Say: "People often find themselves waiting for someone or something. And, they engage in all kinds of behavior while they are waiting. In today's lesson, God instructs Judah to wait and to do so quietly. Turn to the book of Lamentations and let's read about the situation they were in when they were told to wait."

Into the Word

Prior to class time, prepare a Bible study chart activity entitled, "Making Sense From the Senses." Label three columns from left to right "Senses," "Lamentations 1:12-16," and, "Lamentations 3:22-26, 31-33, 40." Label five rows from top to bottom "Color," "Texture," "Sound," "Taste," and "Smell." Photocopy the chart for each student and distribute it to the class.

State: "To help us make some sense of this passage of Scripture, I'd like the class to move into groups of four." Appoint someone to read the first passage of Scripture aloud. Then say, "I would like each of you to describe the situation in terms of your five senses. In other words, what color do you see in this situation; what texture, and so forth. Write your answers in the spaces provided. Then tell the people in your group your answers and the reasons you answered the way you did."

Allow about twelve minutes for this activity. Then briefly go over the five rows, asking for answers from the whole class. Say: "Now have someone in each of your groups read the Scripture from the third column aloud. Once again, describe the situation in terms of your five senses and share those with your group." Allow another twelve minutes for this section and then call for both their answers and the reasons for their answers.

Prior to class time, ask four members of the class to serve on a panel. Assign the following Scriptures, one to each person: Luke 8:43-48; Mark 9:15-27; Luke 17:12-19; 2 Corinthians 12:7-10. State: "Now we are going to have a panel tell us Biblical examples of people who turned to the Lord when in hardship or trouble." Ask the four to present a brief summary of their texts.

Into Life

Say: "God's message to Judah, and to us as well, is to 'hope and quietly wait for the salvation of the Lord,' Lamentations 3:26. What are some ways God expects people to put this message into practice?" As ideas are shared, write them either on the board or on an overhead transparency. *(Possible answers may include trust God to take care of you, remember that God is faithful, stop worrying about your hardship.)* Also, prior to class time, make a learning activity page called, "Quietly Wait for the Salvation of the Lord." Place a sketch of a comfortable chair on the page with places available for answers of several lines' length. Give a copy of this activity to each person. Provide the following directions: "Today we've seen both the grief and the hope of Judah. In spite of God's judgment, God gave them encouragement for their future. They were told in Lamentations 3:26 to 'quietly wait for the salvation of the Lord.' We've also suggested ways for people today to put this message into practice. Now, I'd like you to suggest ways you personally can put this message into practice. Write them on the lines provided." After several minutes have passed, end the class time with a prayer of commitment and dedication to waiting quietly for the salvation of the Lord.

Let's Talk It Over

The questions on this page are designed to promote discussion of the lesson by the class and to encourage application of the lesson Scriptures. The answers provided are only discussion starters. Let your class talk it over from there.

1. "Is it nothing to you?" cries Jerusalem over her sad condition. Sometimes people in grief feel that no one cares about their situation. What can we do to express support for our brothers and sisters in grief and hardship?

It's easy to say to someone, "If you need anything, just call." And most people who say that really mean it—they would do virtually anything for the troubled person. But that one never calls, and we're "off the hook." Discuss some specific ways to help, and suggest the potential helper say, "Let me do this," or, "May I do that for you?" Bringing food, running errands, or cutting the grass are tangible ways to lighten one's burden, allowing the suffering person to focus on other everyday responsibilities. What are some others?

2. Jerusalem rightly saw its troubles as sent by God as discipline. Should we see our difficulties as God-sent? Why or why not? Perhaps some are and some aren't—how do we know the difference?

Not every disaster is a result of sin in our lives. The lesson of Job is plain on that point. (See also John 9:1-3.) At the same time, we ought not to dismiss the idea of God's discipline entirely, either. Read Hebrews 12:4-11.

The issue of God's will is complex, and not everyone agrees on every point. But one thing is clear. God can control as much of the course of human events as He wants to. How He factors in our free will is something of a mystery, but His sovereignty is not compromised. So whatever happens is at least *allowed* by God, even if He does not directly cause it. So rather than worry or fret over whether God has caused our situation, we should try to see what we can learn from it, how we can grow, and how we can glorify Christ. Whether God causes or merely allows a situation, He expects us to respond to it with faith and grace.

3. "Survivor guilt" often happens to individuals who have lived through a very tragic situation in which others were severely hurt or killed. How can Christians keep their spiritual equilibrium when things just do not seem to be fair—either to themselves or for others?

It is easy to get lost in trying to bring fairness to life. Why did I survive and someone else die? The only way to answer this is to move away from trying to understand everything from the vantage point of fairness. The silliness of asking God to make things fair becomes apparent when one remembers the unfairness of the death of Jesus, a righteous man, dying in the place of unrighteous people. Giving up the quest for fairness in life frees a Christian to see every situation as an opportunity for experiencing the goodness of God or a chance to call the attention of others to His love and mercy.

4. God used strong measures to punish Jerusalem, but because of His mercy He tempered that punishment. Many parents, knowing the necessity of punishing their children, are emotionally torn by their desire that their children not have to experience pain from the punishment. How can parents use the times when they have to administer corrective measures as a means to teach their children about the nature of God and His reaction to punishment?

It is important that children do not learn to expect God to be either a big "Santa Claus" always giving out treats or a monster who is just waiting to inflict pain. Telling Bible stories from this series of lessons and sharing a Scripture like 2 Peter 3:9 can help a child see that God punishes only when necessary. It is important to stress that God's hope is that the person will see his or her sin and turn back to God, who is waiting to welcome His child back (Luke 15:11-24).

5. Some people have difficulty experiencing the daily newness of God's compassion. Others tend to become cynical or pessimistic and lose hope. How can a Christian learn to recognize God's daily blessings while also quietly waiting on the Lord for another deeply desired blessing?

Waiting on the Lord is a common Biblical theme. It does not mean, however, that one merely sits in a rocking chair twiddling his thumbs. It is important to be active. "Waiting" on the Lord involves watching for His daily blessings, opening ourselves to His providence as He works with us and through circumstances to bring ultimate good (Ephesians 2:8-10), and being flexible enough to go with His plan (and not insisting His actions match our plans). Over time, it is possible to see what God has been doing! He deserves our praise for each of His daily mercies!

Turn and Live

DEVOTIONAL READING: Romans 6:17-23.

BACKGROUND SCRIPTURE: Ezekiel 18.

PRINTED TEXT: Ezekiel 18:1-4, 20, 21, 25-32.

Ezekiel 18:1-4, 20, 21, 25-32

1 The word of the LORD came unto me again, saying,

2 What mean ye, that ye use this proverb concerning the land of Israel, saying, The fathers have eaten sour grapes, and the children's teeth are set on edge?

3 As I live, saith the Lord GOD, ye shall not have occasion any more to use this proverb in Israel.

4 Behold, all souls are mine; as the soul of the father, so also the soul of the son is mine: the soul that sinneth, it shall die.

. . . .

20 The soul that sinneth, it shall die. The son shall not bear the iniquity of the father, neither shall the father bear the iniquity of the son: the righteousness of the righteous shall be upon him, and the wickedness of the wicked shall be upon him.

21 But if the wicked will turn from all his sins that he hath committed, and keep all my statutes, and do that which is lawful and right, he shall surely live, he shall not die.

. . . .

25 Yet ye say, The way of the Lord is not equal. Hear now, O house of Israel; Is not my way equal? are not your ways unequal?

26 When a righteous man turneth away from his righteousness, and committeth iniquity, and dieth in them; for his iniquity that he hath done shall he die.

27 Again, when the wicked man turneth away from his wickedness that he hath committed, and doeth that which is lawful and right, he shall save his soul alive.

28 Because he considereth, and turneth away from all his transgressions that he hath committed, he shall surely live, he shall not die.

29 Yet saith the house of Israel, The way of the Lord is not equal. O house of Israel, are not my ways equal? are not your ways unequal?

30 Therefore I will judge you, O house of Israel, every one according to his ways, saith the Lord GOD. Repent, and turn yourselves from all your transgressions; so iniquity shall not be your ruin.

31 Cast away from you all your transgressions, whereby ye have transgressed; and make you a new heart and a new spirit: for why will ye die, O house of Israel?

32 For I have no pleasure in the death of him that dieth, saith the Lord GOD: wherefore turn yourselves, and live ye.

**Nov
17**

GOLDEN TEXT: Behold, all souls are mine; as the soul of the father, so also the soul of the son is mine: the soul that sinneth, it shall die.—Ezekiel 18:4.

Judgment and Exile
Unit 3: Final Defeat
(Lessons 10-13)

Lesson Aims

After this lesson each student will be able to:

1. Explain the principles of justice and personal responsibility as illustrated in Ezekiel's message to the exiles of Judah.

2. Tell how repentance can avert the condemnation that one's actions might otherwise merit.

3. Express repentance for some action or attitude that he or she needs to eliminate from his or her life.

Lesson Outline

INTRODUCTION
    A. Varied Voices of Complaint
    B. Lesson Background
  I. MISTAKEN PROVERB (Ezekiel 18:1-4)
    A. The Proverb Quoted (vv. 1, 2)
    B. The Proverb Denounced (vv. 3, 4)
      Whose Responsibility?
 II. SOUND TEACHING (Ezekiel 18:20, 21)
    A. Responsibility Stressed (v. 20)
    B. Repentance Required (v. 21)
III. ANTICIPATED OBJECTION (Ezekiel 18:25-32)
    A. Complaint and Answer (v. 25)
      What Is Fair?
    B. Change and Results (vv. 26-28)
    C. Complaint and Answer Repeated (v. 29)
    D. Just Judgment (v. 30a)
    E. Repent and Live (vv. 30b-32)
CONCLUSION
    A. Popular Standards and Proverbs
    B. God's Standards
    C. Prayer
    D. Thought to Remember

Introduction

"It's not fair!" Perhaps you recall that plaintive cry from childhood, uttered by someone who had lost a game, was intimidated by a bigger child, or found himself in a minority overruled by a majority. Or perhaps you remember uttering that plaintive cry yourself when a teacher imposed some rule that you found oppressive.

A. Varied Voices of Complaint

Adults have the same complaint when misfortune strikes, but they voice it in various ways.

The favorite cry, "Why me?" means, "I don't deserve this misfortune—it's not fair." Another way of protesting is, "It's not my fault." The implication of this one is that someone else should bear the blame.

In the opening verses of our text, we see the victims of a disaster trying to blame their parents and grandparents. Perhaps they fooled themselves with that deception, but they could not fool God or His prophet. Even worse is the self-deception when we tell ourselves that God is at fault. In the last part of our text today we shall hear people of Judah doing just that.

But God certainly knows something about what is "unfair." Remember that His own Son suffered and died in the most unfair act ever done by human beings against another. Even in spite of that, God is always fair—or better than fair—toward us. Think about His forgiveness of our sins even though we are unworthy. He is generous. He gives us more than we deserve. In time of distress or disaster, we must not let our discomfort put an end to our straight thinking in this regard. God is good, just, right, and fair. "Justice and judgment are the habitation of thy throne" (Psalm 89:14; cf. 97:2). Whenever we doubt that, we are wrong.

B. Lesson Background

For this lesson and the next, we take our text from the book of Ezekiel, who may be called "the captive prophet." These studies will be helped by a review of what we already know about the Babylonian captivity and by learning a little about Ezekiel's book. You might find it helpful at this point to review the three phases of the Babylonian captivity discussed on page 84 in lesson 10 (also see the lesson background to lesson 11, pages 90, 91).

Two prophets are outstanding during the Babylonian captivity. Ezekiel is among the ten thousand taken to Babylon in the second phase of the captivity. In the fifth year of that captivity (about 593 B.C.), he began to proclaim God's word among the captives (Ezekiel 1:2, 3). Meanwhile, Jeremiah was carrying on a similar ministry back in Jerusalem (and, later, in Egypt). Thus the two prophets were speaking to two segments of Judah in the same time of peril. Their messages are similar, although the life situations of the two segments are different. Past lessons have brought us Jeremiah's blunt warning of disaster (Jeremiah 25:1-9 in lesson 6) and his bright gleam of hope (Jeremiah 31:23-34 in lesson 8). This week's lesson brings us Ezekiel's own blunt warning that each sinner must bear the guilt of his or her own sin. Next week's lesson will bring us Ezekiel's gleam of hope.

I. Mistaken Proverb
(Ezekiel 18:1-4)

We cherish the God-inspired wisdom that the book of Proverbs gives us in easily remembered bits. But we should not jump to the conclusion that all proverbs are inspired of God or written by godly men. Ungodly men can make up proverbs, too, and use them to deceive. We come now to a proverb devised to make people believe a lie. The Lord quotes that proverb only to denounce it.

A. The Proverb Quoted (vv. 1, 2)

1. The word of the LORD came unto me again, saying,

This statement or a similar one occurs more than four dozen times in the book of Ezekiel (e.g., 6:1; 18:1). The prophet wants us to be sure that what follows is not his own *word*, but God's.

2. What mean ye, that ye use this proverb concerning the land of Israel, saying, The fathers have eaten sour grapes, and the children's teeth are set on edge?

What the captives *mean* by the *proverb* is plain enough. They mean to say, "This captivity is not our fault. Our fathers and grandfathers did wrong, and we are being punished for their sins." God did say He would punish all Judah for the sins of Manasseh, and He said it long after Manasseh was dead (Jeremiah 15:4). [See question #1, page 104.]

But God did not mean Manasseh's descendants would be punished because Manasseh himself sinned. It meant they would be punished because they were continuing Manasseh's sins in their own time and in their own lives. If God punishes a sinner, it is for his own sins, not the sins of his parents or anyone else. That will be made abundantly clear in the latter part of our text. But the sinners of Judah are trying to blame their ancestors. That is true in the homeland as well as among the captives in Babylon. (Consider again Jeremiah 31:29, 30 from lesson 8, where we found the same mistaken proverb mentioned of those in Jerusalem.) Both groups could be misusing Exodus 20:5 and its parallel Deuteronomy 5:9.

Now, thousands of years later, sinners still try to blame their parents or their teachers or someone. And the effort is still futile. All of us are sinners, responsible for our own sin (Romans 3:23; 1 John 1:8). Let us confess our sins, stop our sinning, and beg God to forgive us (1 John 1:9).

B. The Proverb Denounced (vv. 3, 4)

3. As I live, saith the Lord GOD, ye shall not have occasion any more to use this proverb in Israel.

What God is saying might best be explained in this expanded way: it will not be appropriate, it will not be just or proper or right, for the captives to keep on repeating this proverb. It simply is not true. When the captives get their thinking straightened out, they no longer will promote that falsehood. God makes this emphatic by the preface *as I live.* God's own life is no more certain than the assurance that the misleading proverb will no longer be used in Israel.

4. Behold, all souls are mine; as the soul of the father, so also the soul of the son is mine: the soul that sinneth, it shall die.

God created all the people of the world; the lives of all the people of all generations are in His hand. He is not squeamish about taking the lives of those who are guilty. Consider the countless sinners who drowned in the great flood (Genesis 6–8), the many people of Judah who die by the sword when Jerusalem falls (2 Chronicles 36:17), and the false prophet who dies for his own falsehood (Jeremiah 28:15-17). The God who gives us all the breath of life in the first place is the same One who has the right to take that life back whenever He so chooses (e.g., Numbers 31:17; Deuteronomy 2:34). [See question #2, page 104.]

But the Lord does not kill one soul unjustly. A son does not die for the sins of his father unless the son also commits those sins. This truth is reaffirmed at length in verses 5-18, which are not included in our printed text. Still the people were not convinced, and still the Lord repeated the truth (Ezekiel 18:19).

WHOSE RESPONSIBILITY?

Talk about life's ironies! The house in Braunau *(brow-now),* Austria where Adolf Hitler was born is now the home and workplace of about forty Austrians with mental and physical handicaps who make handicrafts for sale. The chief propagator of the "master race" philosophy would have had such people exterminated (along with the six million other "undesirables" killed by his regime) if his Nazis had won World War II.

Hitler's family moved from the house when he was only two years old, but more than 110 years later, it still carries the stigma of his residence. It is a run-down eyesore, referred to by local people as the "Hitler house."

Leaders in the city of Braunau want to do something about "the burden," as they refer to this awful reminder of the past. They are trying to raise funds to turn the building into a "House of Responsibility" to teach visitors about atrocities in wars past with hope of deterring them in the future. They are hoping to remind the citizens of Austria that each person bears some responsibility for the prevention of evil in the community.

It is a lesson the citizens of Judah had to learn. God was not punishing them because of what

---

How to Say It

BABYLON. *Bab*-uh-lun.
BABYLONIAN. Bab-ih-*low*-nee-un.
EZEKIEL. Ee-*zeek*-ee-ul or Ee-*zeek*-yul.
HAGGAI. *Hag*-eye or *Hag*-ay-eye.
JEREMIAH. Jair-uh-*my*-uh.
LAMENTATIONS. Lam-en-*tay*-shunz.
MANASSEH. Muh-*nass*-uh.

---

their ancestors had done; His wrath was coming upon them because they did not accept responsibility for their own sins. It is a timeless principle we all must learn.   —C. R. B.

II. Sound Teaching
(Ezekiel 18:20, 21)

These two verses are chosen for our text because they summarize the teaching of the chapter. The two truths they present are repeated emphatically because Ezekiel's hearers were not willing to accept them.

A. Responsibility Stressed (v. 20)

20. The soul that sinneth, it shall die. The son shall not bear the iniquity of the father, neither shall the father bear the iniquity of the son: the righteousness of the righteous shall be upon him, and the wickedness of the wicked shall be upon him.

The Bible repeatedly stresses personal responsibility (e.g., Genesis 2:17; 4:7; Deuteronomy 24:16; 2 Kings 14:6). But the captives in Babylon are resisting this truth. Trying to believe a lie and deny the truth, they claim they are innocent—suffering unjustly for the sins of their ancestors. [See question #3, page 104.]

Perhaps they are looking to Exodus 20:5 and its parallel Deuteronomy 5:9 to bolster their belief. Those passages warn that God extends His punishment for a father's sin to the children down to "the third and fourth generation." But when harmonized with other Scripture, these passages simply indicate that God's wrath on the fathers is bound to have some indirect or "collateral" effect on their children.

The captives find help in the fact that sons do often suffer for their fathers' sins. For example, children may suffer poverty because their father is in jail and cannot provide the necessities of life. Such hardships are a natural result of the father's sin, but they are not God's punishment on the child. This fact also applies, of course, to the innocent children who are later born to the captives in Babylon (cf. Lamentations 5:7). Jesus dealt with a similar question in His day (John 9:1-3).

B. Repentance Required (v. 21)

21. But if the wicked will turn from all his sins that he hath committed, and keep all my statutes, and do that which is lawful and right, he shall surely live, he shall not die.

Here is the second great truth of this chapter, and it is good news indeed. Even the sinner does not have to *die*. He or she can repent, can stop sinning and become devoted to doing right. Then he or she will be treated as righteous. (The reverse can also happen; see v. 26 below.)

The phrase *he shall surely live* may be a reflection of Leviticus 18:5, but the world would have to wait several centuries for the full explanation. Now we understand that a sinner can escape his just punishment because Jesus the Savior has taken that punishment in his place. What is revealed to Ezekiel is only a dim preview of the Christian gospel, but it gives encouragement to sinners who are honest enough to see their sin and concerned enough to stop it. [See question #4, page 104.]

III. Anticipated Objection
(Ezekiel 18:25-32)

Ezekiel presents God's truth to people who are addicted to their own lie. They want to continue thinking that they are innocent victims of their fathers' sins. But God is not willing for any to perish. He wants all sinners to repent (Ezekiel 18:23; 1 Timothy 2:4; 2 Peter 3:9). So God continues earnestly to reason with the sinners.

A. Complaint and Answer (v. 25)

25. Yet ye say, The way of the Lord is not equal. Hear now, O house of Israel; Is not my way equal? are not your ways unequal?

In modern English, we would probably use the word *fair* or *just* where our text has *equal*. Despite what the Lord has just said, He now anticipates that the captives will raise an objection concerning His justice. They will continue to say that He is not fair in punishing them for their fathers' sins. God's answer is a challenge for them to look again at the facts. Wouldn't an honest examination show that it is God's way that is fair, and it is their ways that are unfair?

WHAT IS FAIR?

Alvin Cullum York has been called "the most celebrated G.I. in America's military history." York was drafted for service in World War I and sent to Europe. His actions in just four hours on October 8, 1918, gained him the fame that lives today. In that one battle, he is credited with leading about a half-dozen men in killing 25 German soldiers, neutralizing numerous machine-gun batteries, and capturing 132 German soldiers! For his efforts that day, York received the Medal of Honor and a hero's welcome back home. His story was made into a 1941 movie starring Gary Cooper in an Academy Award-winning role. For the rights to his story, York received $150,000. He gave it all away, but he was still hit with a bill for $172,000 in taxes and interest!

Few people would argue that it was not fair for a patriot like York to be treated in such a manner. But fairness is not necessarily a common quality in the workings of governmental bureaucracy. God, on the other hand, is fairness personified. Twice in our text today, Ezekiel challenges us to acknowledge God's fairness in dealing with our sins on a personal basis. He holds us all accountable only for our own sins, and not for the sins of others. Who can argue with that?   —C. R. B.

B. Change and Results (vv. 26-28)

26. When a righteous man turneth away from his righteousness, and committeth iniquity, and dieth in them; for his iniquity that he hath done shall he die.

The first step in exposing the weakness of their arguments is to state an obvious truth: when a *righteous man* becomes evil, he will be held accountable for that evil. What's wrong with that?

27. Again, when the wicked man turneth away from his wickedness that he hath committed, and doeth that which is lawful and right, he shall save his soul alive.

If an evil man repents and turns to the good, God grants him life. What's wrong with that?

This, of course, is not to say that living a righteous life "earns" eternal life. That would be inconsistent with what Scripture has to say elsewhere. Under the Old Covenant, a righteous life is characteristic of one whose faith looks ahead to the coming of God's Messiah (John 8:56).

28. Because he considereth, and turneth away from all his transgressions that he hath committed, he shall surely live, he shall not die.

Because he considereth is the key to turning away from the wrong and to the right. God's law is very plain with promises of blessing for obedience and punishment for disobedience (Deuteronomy 4:1-40). The history of Israel shows that God always has kept the law's promises. Anyone who considers that fact should know that He will continue to keep them. The captives are far from obedience to God's law, and they have been so for years. Anyone who stops to consider his or her own lifestyle would know that.

But those captives are not considering, not thinking. They find pleasure in doing wrong, and someone applies a silly proverb to excuse their behavior. The people treasure that proverb and keep repeating it to comfort themselves. Even after the people return from exile, the Lord will find it necessary to challenge their thinking processes to get them to reconsider what they are doing (Haggai 1:5, 7; 2:15, 18).

C. Complaint and Answer Repeated (v. 29)

29. Yet saith the house of Israel, The way of the Lord is not equal. O house of Israel, are not my ways equal? are not your ways unequal?

Again, God anticipates that the people will be unconvinced. Even after the arguments of verses 26-28, they will repeat the complaint we just saw in verse 25. This demonstrates the stubbornness of their hearts (see Ezekiel 3:7; 18:31 [below]; and 36:26). A little reasonable thinking will show that they deserve all the punishment they are getting.

D. Just Judgment (v. 30a)

30a. Therefore I will judge you, O house of Israel, every one according to his ways, saith the Lord GOD.

Even while in exile, there is more judgment to come upon the *house of Israel*. God's judgment will be fair, just, and right, whether the people choose to see it that way or not. Judging *every one according to his ways* means that no one will be held guilty because someone else has done wrong; and no one will be held innocent because someone has done right.

E. Repent and Live (vv. 30b-32)

30b. Repent, and turn yourselves from all your transgressions; so iniquity shall not be your ruin.

Iniquity indeed has been their *ruin* up to this point. But it need not continue to be this way. Although the people must now obey their captors, it

Home Daily Bible Readings

Monday, Nov. 11—The Righteous Will Live (Ezekiel 18:1-9)

Tuesday, Nov. 12—The Person Who Sins Will Die (Ezekiel 18:19-24)

Wednesday, Nov. 13—Turn and Live (Ezekiel 18:25-32)

Thursday, Nov. 14—Why Will You Die, Israel? (Ezekiel 33:7-11)

Friday, Nov. 15—Without Excuse (Romans 1:16-25)

Saturday, Nov. 16—God Will Repay (Romans 2:1-8)

Sunday, Nov. 17—Belief in the Son Brings Life (John 3:16-21)

Visual for lesson 12. *Today's visual is a stark image that speaks to our need for repentance. Use it to illustrate verse 32.*

seems that the treatment in captivity is not as severe as it could be. From this point on, they could be reduced to poverty and hunger, treated with extreme cruelty, or killed outright, as many of their countrymen will be when Jerusalem is razed (Ezekiel 33:21-29). To avoid further ruin themselves, they had better *repent.* They should settle down to productive and holy living. While in captivity, they should do all they can for the welfare of Babylon because the Lord promised them, "in the peace thereof shall ye have peace" (Jeremiah 29:4-7). [See question #5, page 104.]

31. Cast away from you all your transgressions, whereby ye have transgressed; and make you a new heart and a new spirit: for why will ye die, O house of Israel?

The call to repentance goes on. Disobedient for many years, these people now must obey God. Ezekiel in the midst of the captives is speaking the very words of God. Jeremiah in Jerusalem is writing God's will and sending it across the miles (Jeremiah 29:1). God is saying, *Cast away from you all your transgressions!* Vigorously fling them out of your lives. Throw them on the garbage heap of discarded evil, never to be picked up again. Set your heart on doing God's will; cultivate within you *a new spirit* of obedience. *Why will ye die?* This is a matter of life and death, and you can choose. Will you choose to die? What insanity!

32. For I have no pleasure in the death of him that dieth, saith the Lord GOD: wherefore turn yourselves, and live ye.

If God could do the choosing, He would choose life for all those captive people; but they themselves must make the choice. They can obey God and live, or disobey Him and die. Why is it so hard to choose life?

Conclusion

God's standards of right and wrong have been plain for centuries. Jesus reinforces those standards when He teaches us to control our thoughts, motives, and wishes as well as our actions. With eternity at stake, how can anyone ignore these standards and substitute others?

A. Popular Standards and Proverbs

I like it; therefore it is good. Ancient Hebrews enjoyed themselves at pagan festivals (Numbers 25:1-3), so they thought there was nothing wrong in such activities. People today think the same way. The modern proverb might be, "It can't be so wrong if it feels so right."

Everybody does it; therefore it is good. You're driving along the interstate highway. The speed limit is sixty-five, but everyone seems to be going seventy-five or more. So you speed up, too, in violation of the law. The proverb here is, "You have to go with the flow or you'll get run over."

It is bad; therefore it is good. There is something attractive about doing what is forbidden. It shows you are independent enough to do as you please. So people take up smoking, drug use, and immorality. Being bad makes them feel so good! The proverb here might be, "It's important to live life on your own terms."

I need it; therefore it is good. Why do workers in shops and offices go outside in midwinter to smoke? Because they need it—they're addicted. Without it they will be nervous, irritable, unable to do their best work. If they work better, that's good, isn't it? The proverb here might be, "It works for me."

B. God's Standards

An old story tells of a man who is examining yesterday's shirt, hoping to find it clean enough for one more day. Not quite sure, he appeals to his wife: "Honey, is this shirt dirty?"

The wife tosses it into the laundry hamper without a second glance. She says, "If it's doubtful, it's dirty."

Undergirded by the Word of God, perhaps that would be a safe principle to apply to any number of practices that are popular today!

C. Prayer

Thank You for Your Word, Lord. May we have the will to read it, the wisdom to understand it, and the courage to obey it. In Jesus' name, amen.

D. Thought to Remember

"Beware lest any man spoil you through philosophy and vain deceit, after the tradition of men" (Colossians 2:8).

Learning by Doing

This page contains an alternative lesson plan emphasizing learning activities.
Classes desiring such student involvement will find these suggestions helpful.

Learning Goals

After participating in this lesson, each student will be able to:

1. Explain the principles of justice and personal responsibility as illustrated in Ezekiel's message to the exiles of Judah.

2. Tell how repentance can avert the condemnation that one's actions might otherwise merit.

3. Express repentance for some action or attitude that he or she needs to eliminate from his or her life.

Into the Lesson

Prior to class time, write on the board: "That's Not Fair!" Begin this week's lesson by stating: "I'm sure all of us have heard the statement on the board at one time or another. You may have said it yourself. Today, I'd like to start by asking you to think about this statement and the different situations in which you have heard it." *(Possible scenarios include a punishment that did not match the crime, a whole class punished for one person's action, or something similar.)*

Move the class into groups of four or five students each. Give each group about seven to ten minutes to develop a skit that illustrates the phrase, "That's Not Fair!" When the groups appear to be ready, ask them to give their skits one at a time. Say: "We all understand this phrase and the different situations when we've heard it. But isn't it interesting that the people of Israel said it to God? That's right! They accused Him of being unfair and said, 'The way of the Lord is not equal.' Let's turn to Ezekiel 18 and read about their brash challenge to God's integrity."

Into the Word

Ask a class member to read Ezekiel 18:1-4, 20-32 aloud. Then, ask the following questions:

1. What is meant by the proverb, "The fathers have eaten sour grapes, and the children's teeth are set on edge" (v. 2)? *(The children inherit their parents' sins and are suffering because of them.)*

2. Why does God reject that proverb in Israel (vv. 3, 4)? *(All souls belong to God, both the father and the son. The soul that sins shall die.)*

3. Describe the principle of justice seen in verse 20. *(People bear their own iniquity, not the iniquity of the son or of the father.)*

4. Describe the principle of personal responsibility seen in verse 20. *(Each person's righteous-*ness or wickedness will be upon him. Each is accountable for his or her own actions.)*

5. What is required for the wicked to live and not die (v. 21)? *(Turn from his sins, keep God's statutes, do that which is lawful and right.)*

6. On what basis will God judge the house of Israel (v. 30)? *(Everyone according to his ways.)*

7. What did God specifically want the house of Israel to do (v. 30b)? *(Repent and turn from their own transgressions.)*

8. What is meant by the phrase, "iniquity shall not be your ruin" (v. 30b)? *(The ruin would be cruel treatment and death by the Babylonians.)*

9. Describe the inner transformation God requires (v. 31). *(A new heart and a new spirit of obedience to God; a new beginning.)*

After the questions state, "Repentance and inner transformation are required not only of the house of Israel, but for all who have committed sin. Even those who have experienced the salvation by God's grace need to repent of actions or attitudes that should not be a part of their lives."

Prior to class time prepare a worksheet, "Actions & Attitudes: Laying Them at the Cross." Write the word ACTIONS on the left side of the cross, and the word ATTITUDES on the right side. Below the words, make at least five blank lines. Distribute the worksheet and ask the class to move into their previous groups. Say: "In your groups, on the lines provided, make a list of actions and a list of attitudes that Christians need to eliminate from their lives." After several minutes, ask the groups to reveal their answers to the class. Write the answers on the board or transparency. *(Possible actions include lying, gossip, stealing, judging. Possible attitudes include prejudice, hate, greed, lack of forgiveness.)*

Into Life

Prior to class time prepare a "Repentance Response" worksheet on a half-sheet of paper. Under that title write, "Lord Jesus, I confess that my attitude and my actions have not always glorified you. I now repent of [leave blanks for the students to write the attitude or action of which they want to repent] and ask you to transform my heart and my spirit."

Prepare enough copies so that each student will have one, and pass them out at this time. After a few minutes, close the class session with a prayer of commitment and surrender to God.

Let's Talk It Over

The questions on this page are designed to promote discussion of the lesson by the class and to encourage application of the lesson Scriptures. The answers provided are only discussion starters. Let your class talk it over from there.

1. Some of the captives in Babylon could have perceived of God as a big bully because they (with their "little" sins) were being punished for the big and repeated sins of their ancestors. How can the church teach so people will understand that any sin is big enough to deserve the full punishment for disobedience?

Perhaps every culture creates its own list of little sins and big sins. While there is a difference in the earthly consequences of various sins, God sees all sin the same. Every sin disqualifies a person from the righteous category (Romans 3:9-12). The person who tells a "little white lie" and a serial murderer each merit eternal punishment (Romans 3:23). The church must stress this point. The church must also live what it teaches by taking the gospel to all no matter what their sin. Furthermore, the church must not act differentially to people (e.g., being friendly to a gossip and snubbing the alcoholic).

2. God's answer ("I made them; I can kill them") seems to bother some today. They want a God who will act in a manner that does not disturb their own sense of justice. How important is it for every believer to carry a firm picture that God is sovereign and has the right to do whatever pleases Him?

Why worship a God whose wisdom is inferior to ours? Why honor a deity who makes mistakes? Why give credence to any entity lacking ultimate power and rights? If we do not understand that God is sovereign, then we simply do not know God! He is the Creator—He can do as He pleases with His creation (Romans 9:20, 21). Even if God were capricious, He would have the right to do as He pleased, whatever He pleased.

But He is not capricious. God is just. And it is His just nature that demands that sin be punished. At the same time, His compassion recognizes the need of the sinner. His mercy and grace led Him to send His Son to pay the penalty (death sentence for sin) for everyone. God has a right to do as He pleases. Because He has all these other characteristics (love, mercy, grace), what He pleases is in our best interest. Our job is to remember we are the creatures and we are to worship the Creator, Sustainer, Author of salvation, Judge, Redeemer, and Savior. (Compare Ephesians 1:3-14.)

3. People in every culture have a way of inventing their own "truth." How can the church help believers not to fall for these self-deceiving conclusions?

Some of the statements invented by mistaken minds include the following. "If Christ has not returned yet, He is not coming back." "All religions will ultimately take you to the same place." "Since he lived a good life, there is no way God could send him to Hell." (Ask the class to list others.) It is important to measure every statement by the entire truth of God. The captives preferred their conclusion more than they preferred to hear what God was saying to them about their captivity as well as His ultimate plan for His people. But, as is always the case, God's plan for them was better than their own wisdom could devise.

4. Some Christians have been heard to say when "a very sinful person" comes to Christ, that "it won't stick." How can the church help its members mature so they realize they are responsible to help every new convert to remain faithful to his or her commitment?

Skeptics not only talk negatively, they often act in ways that discourage the new convert. The church can teach all members how to be friendly and encouraging to new members. Mature leaders in the church need to lovingly confront other members who have not learned God's attitude about sinners (see the parable of the prodigal in Luke 15). Perhaps members can be encouraged and trained to be mentors for new believers.

5. The sign says, "Repent! The end is near!" Do most people even know what that means? How can the church help people understand the need to repent and turn from their sinful ways?

Drivers pass church signs and cannot decipher their meaning. Sometimes the wording consists of phrases familiar only to believers. The driver is not taught or convicted. The concept of repentance makes no sense to the unchurched. They do not know that there is a holy God who states He will not tolerate sin forever and will eventually cast away all sinners. Most of the time, the best way for the sinner to learn about the nature of God and the consequences of sin is through the consistent personal testimony ("here is what Christ has done for me") of a Christian friend.

Look to the Future

DEVOTIONAL READING: Jeremiah 32:36-41.

BACKGROUND SCRIPTURE: Ezekiel 36, 37.

PRINTED TEXT: Ezekiel 36:22-32.

Ezekiel 36:22-32

22 Therefore say unto the house of Israel, Thus saith the Lord GOD; I do not this for your sakes, O house of Israel, but for mine holy name's sake, which ye have profaned among the heathen, whither ye went.

23 And I will sanctify my great name, which was profaned among the heathen, which ye have profaned in the midst of them; and the heathen shall know that I am the LORD, saith the Lord GOD, when I shall be sanctified in you before their eyes.

24 For I will take you from among the heathen, and gather you out of all countries, and will bring you into your own land.

25 Then will I sprinkle clean water upon you, and ye shall be clean: from all your filthiness, and from all your idols, will I cleanse you.

26 A new heart also will I give you, and a new spirit will I put within you: and I will take away the stony heart out of your flesh, and I will give you a heart of flesh.

27 And I will put my Spirit within you, and cause you to walk in my statutes, and ye shall keep my judgments, and do them.

28 And ye shall dwell in the land that I gave to your fathers; and ye shall be my people, and I will be your God.

29 I will also save you from all your uncleannesses: and I will call for the corn, and will increase it, and lay no famine upon you.

30 And I will multiply the fruit of the tree, and the increase of the field, that ye shall receive no more reproach of famine among the heathen.

31 Then shall ye remember your own evil ways, and your doings that were not good, and shall loathe yourselves in your own sight for your iniquities and for your abominations.

32 Not for your sakes do I this, saith the Lord GOD, be it known unto you: be ashamed and confounded for your own ways, O house of Israel.

GOLDEN TEXT: A new heart also will I give you, and a new spirit will I put within you: and I will take away the stony heart out of your flesh, and I will give you a heart of flesh.—Ezekiel 36:26.

Judgment and Exile
Unit 3: Final Defeat
(Lessons 10-13)

Lesson Aims

After this lesson each student will be able to:

1. Cite the kinds of restoration God promised to the exiles for the sake of His own name.

2. Cite some ways the restoration of the exiles—in purity as well as in residence in their homeland—would honor the Lord.

3. Suggest ways we today can honor the Lord by our lifestyles.

Lesson Outline

INTRODUCTION
    A. Evidence
    B. Lesson Background
I. GOD'S OWN HONOR (Ezekiel 36:22-24)
    A. God's Name Profaned (v. 22)
    B. God's Name Sanctified (vv. 23, 24)
II. GOD'S HOLY PEOPLE (Ezekiel 36:25-28)
    A. Purity Renewed (v. 25)
        "Stuff Washes Off"
    B. Heart Replaced (v. 26)
    C. Spirit Received (v. 27)
    D. Relationship Restored (v. 28)
III. GOD'S RENEWED BLESSINGS (Ezekiel 36:29-32)
    A. Bountiful Harvests (vv. 29, 30)
    B. Sobering Remembrance (vv. 31, 32)
        Painful Reminders
CONCLUSION
    A. Larger Homecoming
    B. Dangerous Drifting
    C. Prayer
    D. Thought to Remember

Introduction

A. Evidence

Charlie was a friendly man, but he never went to church. Cheerfully, he explained his skepticism to the preacher. "If God is up there," he said, pointing a bony finger toward the sky, "He's got to let me know. Me personally. Understand?"

The preacher pointed to the first verse in the Bible. "God created the heaven and the earth. Doesn't that prove He is up there?"

"Maybe," Charlie replied. "But how do *I* know He did it?"

Charlie had time on his hands, and he really did think about God. He was lost in thought as he drove home one day—so lost that he didn't hear the train whistle. His car rolled onto the track just in time to be hit broadside by the powerful locomotive. The car's passenger side was mangled, and the car was crushed to half its width. In that condition it rode the cowcatcher for a few seconds. As the train slowed, the car finally broke free and rolled over and over, battering the left side. Finally it came to rest on its roof, leaning against a pole, with Charlie dangling upside down in his seat belt.

In time, help arrived. When someone pried open a mangled door, Charlie stepped out jauntily, apparently unhurt. Declining to be taken to the doctor, he was taken home instead.

The next day was Sunday. When Charlie stepped through the church door, the preacher was speechless, but Charlie was not. "He let me know," said Charlie, pointing a finger skyward. "He's up there all right."

It took a remarkable escape from death to convince old Charlie. What makes *you* sure God really is "up there"?

B. Lesson Background

In the sixth chapter of Ezekiel, we hear the Lord shouting to the mountains of Israel. He has tried talking to the people, to little avail. In Jerusalem, some people want Jeremiah killed for bringing the Lord's message (Jeremiah 38:4), but it seems that no one thinks seriously about doing right instead of wrong. Over in Babylon, the captive Israelites listen to Ezekiel as they might listen to an entertainer. They, too, have no thought of changing their way of living (Ezekiel 33:30-32). So the Lord calls to the mountains, which were no more unresponsive than the people.

The mountains of Israel were not like the Asian Himalayas or the Rockies of North America. Compared with those majestic mountain ranges, we would refer to the mountains of Israel as "hills." Wheat grew in the valleys between them; grapevines and olive trees grew on their slopes. But God said those hills would be deserted and desolate (Ezekiel 6:1-7). There would be no one to plant wheat or prune grapevines.

That is exactly what happened, as we have seen in earlier lessons. Jerusalem was destroyed with a great slaughter, most of the survivors were taken to Babylon, and the rest fled to Egypt (2 Kings 25:1-26). The hills of Israel were deserted and desolate.

In chapter 36 of Ezekiel we hear the Lord shouting again to the mountains of Israel (v. 1). Those hills would be inhabited again, and recovered from those who had taken possession of them illegitimately (vv. 2-7). They would be cultivated; they would be fruitful (vv. 8-12).

I. God's Own Honor
(Ezekiel 36:22-24)

Our text begins by explaining why God is going to return the people of Israel to their promised land and make that land fruitful again. The promised restoration goes beyond a reclaiming of land, however. Cleansing from sin, empowerment by the Holy Spirit, and renewal and prosperity are included. Some commentators suggest that the last three of these ultimately are fulfilled in Jesus' shedding of His blood, the outpouring of the Spirit on the Day of Pentecost (Acts 2), and our future life in Heaven.

A. God's Name Profaned (v. 22)

22. **Therefore say unto the house of Israel, Thus saith the Lord GOD; I do not this for your sakes, O house of Israel, but for mine holy name's sake, which ye have profaned among the heathen, whither ye went.**

God is not going to end the captivity for the sake of the captives. They deserved nothing less. But God had His own *holy* name to think about.

From the time of Abraham, and more notably from the time they left Egypt to become a nation among nations (Deuteronomy 28:9, 10), the people of Israel were God's people. God compelled the Egyptians to set Israel free. God gave His people His laws to guide them. He gave them a good land, abundant crops, and healthy livestock.

In this unique relationship with the Lord, the people of Israel had a unique opportunity and duty. They ought to be completely obedient to the Lord who blessed them so abundantly. Thus they could show to the whole world that it is good and wise and profitable to obey the Lord.

In that duty the people of Israel failed miserably. In the midst of the Lord's blessings they disobeyed Him. Through centuries they disobeyed more and more, until they were actually worse than the surrounding nations (2 Chronicles 33:9; Jeremiah 7:26; 16:12; Ezekiel 5:9). Thus the people not only disgraced themselves; they also dishonored God. They made it seem that He was giving rich blessings to gross sinners, and therefore that He was no better than Baal or Molech or any of the imaginary gods of the pagans. "The Lord is merciful and gracious, slow to anger, and plenteous in mercy" (Psalm 103:8); but He could not let His people go on enjoying His blessings while they disgraced both themselves and Him. So He punished them with captivity in Babylon.

That punishment let them know that their disobedience was not acceptable, but it did not renew respect for God's name among the pagans. Now the pagans merely suppose the Lord to be a feeble deity, unable to protect His people against Babylon. To correct that false notion, the Lord is going to crush mighty Babylon and take the people of Israel back to their homeland. Then who will be able to doubt His power? [See question #1, page 112.]

B. God's Name Sanctified (vv. 23, 24)

23. **And I will sanctify my great name, which was profaned among the heathen, which ye have profaned in the midst of them; and the heathen shall know that I am the LORD, saith the Lord GOD, when I shall be sanctified in you before their eyes.**

Names were important in the Old Testament, since they usually had a particular meaning and significance. God is so concerned about the significance of His own name that He explicitly forbids its misuse (Exodus 20:7; Deuteronomy 5:11). God is holy. That means He is separated, "set apart," from all that is evil, and even from what is common or ordinary. Since His identity cannot be separated from His *name*, it, too, is holy.

But God's holy name has been *profaned*, made to seem unholy, common, or ordinary. In their own country, God's people had profaned God's name by their wickedness—by child sacrifice (Leviticus 18:21), by swearing falsely (19:12), in their dress and appearance (21:5, 6), and in their disobedience (22:31-33). They have profaned God's name in their idol worship (Ezekiel 20:39) and sexual immorality (Amos 2:7). Now God promises to *sanctify* His name. That means to make it holy, to make observers see that the Lord is different from any of the make-believe gods of the pagans. [See question #2, page 112.]

24. **For I will take you from among the heathen, and gather you out of all countries, and will bring you into your own land.**

Home Daily Bible Readings

Monday, Nov. 18—Israel Shall Soon Come Home (Ezekiel 36:8-12)
Tuesday, Nov. 19—The Lord's Holiness (Ezekiel 36:16-23)
Wednesday, Nov. 20—A New Heart (Ezekiel 36:24-28)
Thursday, Nov. 21—God Will Save From Uncleanness (Ezekiel 36:29-33)
Friday, Nov. 22—They Shall Know Who God Is (Ezekiel 36:34-38)
Saturday, Nov. 23—Can Dry Bones Live? (Ezekiel 37:1-6)
Sunday, Nov. 24—God's Spirit Within (Ezekiel 37:7-14)

And here's how He is going to make His name holy: God is going to crush Babylon and take His people back home. Won't that convince every observer that the Lord is supreme in power? As our next verses show, the Lord will offer other evidence to demonstrate His goodness in addition to that power.

II. God's Holy People
(Ezekiel 36:25-28)

Obviously, the captivity will be useless if the people who come back to the homeland are no better than those taken into captivity. But the Lord promises to restore His people to godliness as well as to the land of Israel.

A. Purity Renewed (v. 25)

25. Then will I sprinkle clean water upon you, and ye shall be clean: from all your filthiness, and from all your idols, will I cleanse you.

Sprinkling with blood or water is frequent in Old Testament ceremonial cleansings (e.g., Leviticus 14:7, 16, 17, 27, 28, 51, 52; Numbers 8:7; 19:18-21). This is so well known that even in New Testament times "sprinkled" is used figuratively to mean "cleansed" (Hebrews 10:22).

Literally, of course, neither a sprinkling nor a deluge of water can wash away the kind of *filthiness* the captives have wallowed in for years. The primary instrument of God's cleansing is the captivity itself. Homesick in Babylon, perhaps a few of them begin to think seriously when they hear the same kind of preaching from Ezekiel that they had heard in Jerusalem from Jeremiah. Where the pagan practices of their neighbors had seemed enticing in Judah, the pagan practices of their captors are repulsive. They learn to cleanse

A new heart also will I give you, and a new spirit will I put within you.

Ezekiel 36:26

Visual for lesson 13. *The visual for today's lesson illustrates verse 26 of the printed text. Display it as you begin to discuss that verse.*

themselves of such practices. [See question #3, page 112.]

"STUFF WASHES OFF"

What is the dirtiest, most loathsome job you can imagine? Please pardon the repulsive suggestion, but have you thought of cleaning out a city's sewer lines? Whatever goes down the toilet, the sink, and the storm drains (including such things as bicycles and hypodermic needles) ends up in the city's lines. And sometimes, they get plugged up.

Roy Parrino has cleaned out sewer lines for more than a dozen years, and he does it for $25 per hour. His work uniform consists of hip waders, rubber gloves, a hard hat, and goggles. He braves the dangers of rancid water, bacteria, disease, toxic fumes and, of course, *the smell!* As Parrino says, "You really have to psych yourself up for it. It's about as dirty as you can get. You've got to look at it one way: 'Stuff washes off.'"

Yes, stuff washes off, but the kind of pollution in which ancient Israel had immersed herself took more than a simple bath to remove. The spiritually toxic environment of idolatry and immorality had nearly killed Israel as a nation, but God used their captivity in Babylon as the cleansing agent that restored them to life. Even today, God sometimes allows us to wallow in the depths of our chosen "sewer" in order to make us seek His cleansing power.   —C. R. B.

B. Heart Replaced (v. 26)

26. A new heart also will I give you, and a new spirit will I put within you: and I will take away the stony heart out of your flesh, and I will give you a heart of flesh.

For years, Jeremiah had been delivering God's message back in the homeland. Those who heard with their ears but not their hearts wanted that prophet killed (Jeremiah 26:8, 9). The hearts of those people are *stony*, hard as flint. God's teaching does not penetrate them (cf. Mark 3:5).

Now God promises to give the captives *a new heart*, and as history unfolds we see God doing exactly that. That softer heart receives God's teaching through Ezekiel, and the people respond with hearty obedience. God gives also *a new spirit*. The spirit of stubborn rebellion long had ruled them in the homeland. Now it is replaced by the spirit of loving obedience, and God's people are ready to go home. [See question #4, page 112.]

C. Spirit Received (v. 27)

27. And I will put my Spirit within you, and cause you to walk in my statutes, and ye shall keep my judgments, and do them.

When the captives receive their new hearts and willing spirits, God will complete their transformation by putting His own *Spirit within* them (also Ezekiel 37:14; 39:27-29). With that Spirit to guide them, they will have a renewed commitment to obey God's law. They will worship God in spirit and in truth, as God always wants His people to do (John 4:23, 24).

D. Relationship Restored (v. 28)

28. And ye shall dwell in the land that I gave to your fathers; and ye shall be my people, and I will be your God.

Beginning with Abraham, in about 2000 B.C., God repeatedly made known His wish for the children of Abraham to become a nation and to possess the country at the east end of the Mediterranean Sea. From the time of Joshua in about 1400 B.C. to the fall of Jerusalem in 586 B.C., they actually did possess that land. They lost this homeland in the time of Jeremiah, Ezekiel, and Daniel, however, because of their long and constant disobedience to God—especially with regard to idolatry. But God makes them ready to go back home by means of their captivity in Babylon. More than that, He makes them ready to be restored to their proper relationship with Him. Back in the homeland they will be His people, knowing His will and taking delight in doing it.

III. God's Renewed Blessings (Ezekiel 36:29-32)

The final verses of our text reveal that God is ready to give His restored people even more than they need. Long after they return home, He will ask them again to obey Him and receive His blessing. "Prove me now herewith," He will add, "if I will not open you the windows of heaven, and pour you out a blessing, that there shall not be room enough to receive it" (Malachi 3:10).

A. Bountiful Harvests (vv. 29, 30)

29. I will also save you from all your uncleannesses: and I will call for the corn, and will increase it, and lay no famine upon you.

The mention of *famine* must have stirred painful memories in the minds of the captives. They had suffered through famine just before their captivity (Ezekiel 5:16). A quick death by the sword is certainly preferable to the slow death of starvation! (See Lamentations 4:9.) Famine can be a result of drought, diseased crops, insects, or, as in this case, an enemy invasion that stole the crops and ravaged the land (cf. Deuteronomy 28:49-51).

But captives restored to their homeland are made spiritually pure (Ezekiel 36:25); they will

no longer need this type of punishment. Instead, God will give them abundant harvests of grain for their food. In the *King James Version,* the word *corn* means grain of any kind. The kind of grain now called corn in North America was unknown in ancient Israel. The grains most used were wheat and barley. Both of these were made into bread. We should remember in passing that as bad as a "physical" famine is, a "spiritual" famine is worse (Amos 8:11, 12).

30. And I will multiply the fruit of the tree, and the increase of the field, that ye shall receive no more reproach of famine among the heathen.

The increase of the field was the abundant grain harvest (v. 29). Now God promised that the fruit trees also would have abundant fruit. If the people who returned to the homeland would be faithful and obedient, never again could the pagan people around them look down on them—or on their God—because they were suffering from a famine.

B. Sobering Remembrance (vv. 31, 32)

31. Then shall ye remember your own evil ways, and your doings that were not good, and shall loathe yourselves in your own sight for your iniquities and for your abominations.

The captives are going back—back to the dear familiar hills of home. Fields long desolate will be planted and will yield tremendous harvests. Fig and olive and pomegranate trees will bow down with the weight of their fruit. What joy! And yet the homecomers will find a shadow on their bliss. They will have to *remember.* Those fruitful fields have been ravaged by invaders and have long lain desolate; and that is due to the sins of many of these very ones returning home.

Lovely Jerusalem is gone. It will have to be rebuilt, along with its magnificent temple; that destruction, too, is due to the sins of the very people who will participate in the rebuilding. When this happens, many of those folks will weep aloud (Ezra 3:12). Hundreds of their countrymen had died in the fall of Jerusalem, and the sins of these now returning—those not born in captivity—had contributed to that debacle. Many of us know what it means to *loathe* ourselves for what we have been and what we have done. [See question #5, page 112.]

PAINFUL REMINDERS

The image of the "suffering artist" is a staple of modern folklore: actors, singers, painters, or sculptors whose work goes unnoticed by critics and public alike, who struggle for years before being "discovered" and gaining fame and fortune.

Now the new health discipline of "arts medicine" is treating artists for more tangible forms of suffering. Violinists can develop a form of dermatitis called "fiddler's neck" from friction of the violin on their skin. Bagpipers may get lung infections from the mold and bacteria that grow in the bagpipe skins. Ballerinas get stress fractures and foot deformations from standing on their toes. (As one wag put it, "Why don't they just get taller girls?") And, of course, athletes—"artists" of another sort—live with painful reminders of their sports injuries long after their careers come to an end.

Israel was "healed" of its spiritual diseases by the captivity in Babylon. God sent them back to their land with the promise of bountiful yields from their fields. However, He also pronounced a statement of fact: they would never be able to forget the sins that had brought them so low. It is a timeless truth: even after forgiveness and restoration have come, we still must live with the effects of what we have done and who we have been.   —C. R. B.

32. Not for your sakes do I this, saith the Lord GOD, be it known unto you: be ashamed and confounded for your own ways, O house of Israel.

Our text ends as it began (v. 22): God is not freeing the captives for their own sakes. Rather, the Lord is giving them and the pagans around them a demonstration of His own power, His own mercy, His own goodness. He is the Lord, the only true God (v. 23).

Conclusion

There has been much sadness in the series of lessons that we are completing. But the series ends with a bright gleam of hope in the promise of return—return to godliness and to the homeland. When we return to Old Testament study in June, we shall see fifty thousand captives lead the return to the land of Israel. The Babylonian exile and return will become one of the truly watershed events in Israelite history (cf. Matthew 1:11, 12, 17).

A. Larger Homecoming

After the initial return of the fifty thousand (Ezra 2), smaller groups will move back to the ancient homeland as the years pass. In the New Testament we read that Anna is of the tribe of Asher (Luke 2:36) and Barnabas is a Levite (Acts 4:36). Paul says "our twelve tribes" are serving God "day and night" (Acts 26:7). The return of captives from Babylon is only the beginning of the restoration that the Lord promises.

B. Dangerous Drifting

The people of Israel were defeated and taken captive because they rebelled against God, but they did not plan out that rebellion in any systematic way. They did not intend to rebel. When they were prosperous and comfortable, they just drifted into wrongdoing—drifted so slowly that they gave hardly a thought to the change taking place (cf. Judges 2:10, 11).

At several points in this lesson series we have taken note of a similar drift away from God in the post-Christian countries of Europe and North America. A thoughtful student can hardly fail to see the drift that has occurred in the prosperous years since World War II.

So again we ask, are you drifting? Consider the week just past. Did you have a definite plan to have a part in God's work? Or have you simply been floating along—taking everything "one day at a time"?

Is your congregation drifting? Is it too easily satisfied with itself as it is? Is it failing to keep its members growing "in grace, and in the knowledge of our Lord and Saviour Jesus Christ" (2 Peter 3:18)? Is it failing to keep each member growing more Christlike (Ephesians 4:15)? Is the congregation itself growing in number? A church that is failing to add citizens to the kingdom of God is failing in its mission! (See Matthew 28:19, 20.) As these lines are being written, one church in the outskirts of a certain city is making definite plans not only to stop its drift, but to turn it into fervent and continuing activity for the glory of God and the salvation of people on earth. Prayer will be fervent, plans will be made, tasks will be assigned, methods will be taught, and God will grant the increase (cf. 1 Corinthians 3:6). Does your church need something like that?

C. Prayer

Lord, grant us clear sight to see ourselves as You see us, and the will and wisdom to do what You want us to do. In Jesus' name, amen.

D. Thought to Remember

"Be ye doers of the word, and not hearers only" (James 1:22).

Learning by Doing

This page contains an alternative lesson plan emphasizing learning activities.
Classes desiring such student involvement will find these suggestions helpful.

Learning Goals

After this lesson each student will be able to:

1. Cite the kinds of restoration God promised to the exiles for the sake of His own name.

2. Cite some ways the restoration of the exiles—in purity as well as in residence in their homeland—would honor the Lord.

3. Suggest ways we today can honor the Lord by our lifestyles.

Into the Lesson

Prior to class, prepare an opening activity called, "Shield of Promises." Draw a shield (the shape of a coat of arms) and draw a diagonal strip from bottom left to upper right. Write the word "Promises" in the strip. Photocopy the activity so that each person in class can have one. Also make an overhead transparency of the activity to project. Say: "This morning we want to start by focusing on the topic of promises. Move into groups of three, and for the next several minutes generate characteristics and/or qualities of promises. Write them in the blank areas of the shield. Then we'll share our answers." While they are working on this activity, project the image of the shield on the screen or wall. After several minutes, ask the class to share their answers. As they are given, write them on the transparency for all to see. *(Possible answers include future-directed, expectation, inheritance, assurance, commitment, oath, vow.)* Once the answers have been reported, say: "Promises—we've all experienced them, either in making them or in getting the benefits of waiting for them. Today's lesson text focuses on promises God made to Israel. Turn to Ezekiel 36:22-32 and let's see the promises Israel received from God."

Into the Word

Ask a class member to read Ezekiel 36:22-32 aloud to the class. Say: "While still in your groups of three, identify the promises that God gave to Israel that are reported in this text." After a few minutes, ask each group to report its answers to the entire class. As the answers are given, write them on the board or on an overhead transparency. *(Answers will probably include the following: to restore them to their land; to cleanse them from sin and idolatry; to give them a new heart and a new spirit; to give them abundant harvests.)* Then ask the following questions:

1. For whose sake was God going to restore Israel and fulfill His promises to them (v. 22)? *(For the sake of God's holy name.)*

2. What had Israel done to God's name among the heathen (v. 23)? *(Profaned His name.)*

3. How was God going to sanctify His great name (v. 24)? *(He would gather the Israelites from all the countries and bring them to their own land.)*

4. What would be the practical benefits to the people of Israel of God's sanctifying His great name (vv. 25-30)? *(They would be cleansed from sin and idols; they would walk in His statutes and keep His judgments; their corn would increase and there would be no famine; fruit of the tree and of the field would be multiplied.)*

5. What did God expect would happen after Israel became so abundantly blessed by God in their own land (vv. 31, 32)? *(They would remember their evil ways and loathe themselves for their sin and iniquity; they would become ashamed.)*

Say: "All of these promises that God made to Israel were in the context of sanctifying, or making holy, His great name. And, we've seen how Israel benefited from the promises He fulfilled. In the same way, giving honor to God is something Christian people need to do. What are some ways Christians today can honor the Lord?" *(Answers include regularly participating in worship, sharing Christ with non-Christians, setting a sterling example, loving God and people, and respecting God and His Word.)*

Into Life

Say: "Christians can honor the Lord by their lifestyles. How can you honor the Lord in your life today?" Prior to class, prepare a learning activity sheet called, "How Can I Honor the Lord?" On half a sheet of paper sketch a wavy banner like one being pulled by a small plane. Photocopy this so that each student can have a copy.

Distribute the activity sheet and say, "Reflect on the lifestyle you are living before God. Think about specific areas in which you need to honor God more than you do. Decide one special way that you will honor the Lord this week. Write it on the banner on the worksheet, and take it home to remind you to honor the Lord this week."

After everyone has completed this activity, ask the class to stand together in a circle and have a prayer of commitment to give the Lord the honor due Him.

Let's Talk It Over

The questions on this page are designed to promote discussion of the lesson by the class and to encourage application of the lesson Scriptures. The answers provided are only discussion starters. Let your class talk it over from there.

1. An unbeliever reading today's text might accuse God of being selfish or conceited because He says He redeems people for His own "holy name's sake." How would you respond? How can Christians make sure they are giving God all the honor He deserves?

A world that has rejected absolutes is appalled at declarations of absolute sovereignty, but God is worthy of such claims. Christians, like Israel before them, must admit that God's acceptance of them is a credit to God, not to them. No one deserves God's love or acceptance. The first three Commandments (Exodus 20) declare that God and God alone is worthy of our worship. In the first half of the model prayer (Matthew 6:9, 10), Jesus places the Father above all. Christians need to live out Colossians 3:17 so that every word and deed gives praise to God.

2. God says Israel had "profaned [His name] among the heathen" but that He would once again sanctify His name. How has the church profaned God's name among the pagans of today? What can we do to sanctify His name?

How many times have Christians evaluated a movie they have seen by saying something like, "It was pretty good—a little bad language, but nothing too terrible"? Was that language taking the Lord's name in vain? Does God find that "nothing too terrible"? But His name is profaned in action as well as by words. We who wear the name of Christ (Christ-ians) have a duty to honor that name by our behavior. When surveys indicate no difference between Christians and non-Christians in sexual immorality, cheating on income taxes, speeding, and a host of other issues, something is wrong.

Profanity is making common that which is holy. Perhaps our desire to fit in—to be like everyone else—is at the root of profaning His name. To sanctify His name, we must be willing to stand up, stand out, and be different for His sake.

3. God said, "[I will] cleanse you." What must believers do to allow God to complete His work of cleansing?

It is easier to submit to a generic forgiveness as opposed to the removal of favorite or besetting sins. We love to claim the promise of 1 John 1:9 that God is faithful to forgive us from all our sins.

It is more difficult to apply the first part of the verse and confess our specific sins to God and/or to confess our sins to another Christian (James 5:16) who will hold us accountable for removing those sins from our lives. God wants to cleanse completely as much as He delights in forgiving us.

4. God wants His people to have a new heart. How does a person receive a new heart? What does a believer's new heart look like?

We live in an age of heart transplants. The patient is rolled into the operating room, a surgeon removes the old heart and replaces it with a new one. Spiritually, only God can give us a new heart. We must humbly seek Him, offer ourselves to spiritual surgery, and then exercise our new heart to make it stronger and stronger each day. This new heart is focused on God and His righteousness. This heart is loving. This heart aches for others to have a similar transformation. This heart seeks to do good. (Read Deuteronomy 6:5; Psalms 42:1, 84:2; Proverbs 3:5; Jeremiah 29:13; Joel 2:12.)

5. Some people are counseled just to forget the past and go on. The advice assumes focusing on past sins will poison the soul. How does remembering one's past, as God advises in today's text, help a person to become more righteous? When should a person forget, and when should one remember?

In 2 Corinthians 7:8-11, Paul discusses the cleansing power of "godly sorrow." Godly sorrow is different from feeling inconvenienced over being caught doing something wrong. It is more than desiring to be good and win approval from neighbors. Godly sorrow recognizes that one's sins have been an insult to the righteousness of God. The desire is to become righteous like God (Leviticus 20:7). Remembering one's sins helps spur the individual on to a higher goal. And remembering how evil sin is and that God cannot abide in the presence of evil allows the Christian to seek a way of life that is free from personal sin.

In Philippians 3:13 Paul writes of "forgetting those things which are behind." In that passage he is focused on accomplishments rather than sin. Anything that takes our attention away from God is to be forgotten; anything that helps us to keep or renew our dedication to Him needs to be remembered.

Winter Quarter, 2002–2003

Portraits of Faith
(New Testament Personalities)

Special Features

Lessons

Unit 1: Personalities Involved in the Messiah's Coming

Unit 2: Personalities in Jesus' Life and Ministry

Unit 3: Personalities in the Early Church

About These Lessons

How much better to have a guide than a map! In the present quarter, we have real people portrayed before us to act as guides. Their faith and their failures alike serve to point the way for us to follow. If you and your students will follow closely, they will take you nearer to the Master!

Dec 1

Dec 8

Dec 15

Dec 22

Dec 29

Jan 5

Jan 12

Jan 19

Jan 26

Feb 2

Feb 9

Feb 16

Feb 23

Quarterly Quiz

The questions on this page may be used in several ways: as a pretest at the beginning of the quarter; as a review at the end of the quarter; or as a review after each lesson. The questions are based on the Scripture text of each lesson (King James Version). **The answers are on page 116.**

Lesson 1

1. Herod was the Roman Emperor when the angel appeared to Zechariah. T/F *Luke 1:5*
2. What was Zechariah doing inside the temple when the angel appeared to him? (sacrificing a goat, burning incense, or driving the merchants out with a whip?) *Luke 1:9, 10*
3. Who visited Elisabeth during her pregnancy? (Joseph, shepherds, or Mary?) *Luke 1:39-41*

Lesson 2

1. The name of the angel who visited Mary was _____. *Luke 1:26, 27*
2. Mary predicted that all generations would call her what? (lucky, cursed, or blessed?) *Luke 1:48*

Lesson 3

1. Joseph was a just man. T/F *Matthew 1:19*
2. To what country did Joseph take his family? (Egypt, Spain, or Greece?) *Matthew 2:13-15*
3. Joseph eventually brought his family back to live in a city called (Jerusalem, Nazareth, or Hebron?) *Matthew 2:23*

Lesson 4

1. Mary placed the infant Jesus in a manger because there was no room for them in the _____. *Luke 2:7*
2. To whom did a great number of angels appear to announce the birth of Jesus? (Pharisees, shepherds, or Zechariah?) *Luke 2:8, 13*

Lesson 5

1. John the Baptist preached that the _____ of heaven was at hand (or near). *Matthew 3:2*
2. What did John the Baptist call the Pharisees and Sadducees? (pagans, friends, or vipers?) *Matthew 3:7*

Lesson 6

1. Jesus told the rich man to sell his possessions and give to the _____. *Mark 10:21*
2. Jesus said that it is easier for a camel to go through the eye of a _____ than for a rich man to enter into the kingdom of God. *Mark 10:25.*

Lesson 7

1. Mary and Martha were sisters whom Jesus visited. T/F *Luke 10:38, 39*

2. Which sister sat at Jesus' feet to listen? (Mary, Martha, or Priscilla?) *Luke 10:39*
3. Martha believed that her dead brother would rise again. T/F *John 11:24*

Lesson 8

1. Pilate asked Jesus if he was the King of the Jews. T/F *John 18:33*
2. Pilate ended his conversation with Jesus by asking "What is truth?" T/F *John 18:38*
3. The chief priests claimed to have no king but whom? (Caesar, Pilate, or Jesus?) *John 19:15*

Lesson 9

1. Who wanted to sift Simon Peter like wheat? (Pilate, Satan, or Zechariah?) *Luke 22:31*
2. After Jesus was arrested, he was taken to the high priest's house. T/F *Luke 22:54*

Lesson 10

1. Barnabas was from _____. (Antioch, Bethlehem, or Cyprus?) *Acts 4:36*
2. Before going on any missionary journeys, Barnabas and Saul met for an entire year with a church in what city? (Antioch, Alexandria, or Nazareth?) *Acts 11:25, 26*
3. Because Mark had served them so well on their first missionary journey, Paul and Barnabas decided to take him along on a second trip. T/F *Acts 15:37-40*

Lesson 11

1. Paul gave an account of his Heavenly vision, to what king? (Agrippa, Alexander the Great, or Augustus?) *Acts 26:19*
2. The light of the gospel is for Jews and _____. *Acts 26:23*

Lesson 12

1. Both of Timothy's parents were of Jewish descent. T/F *Acts 16:1, 3*
2. Timothy's grandmother's name was _____ and his mother's name was _____. *2 Timothy 1:5*

Lesson 13

1. Paul's customary place to preach on the Sabbath Day was the _____. (amphitheater, marketplace, or synagogue?) *Acts 18:4*
2. Aquila and Priscilla instructed a man from Alexandria named _____. *Acts 18:24-26*

Portraits of Real People

by Thomas E. Friskney

IN 1975 AFTER THE DEATHS of my parents, the seven of us siblings were faced with the task of disposing of the property so that division could be made for each. The majority of our parents' belongings would be placed in public auction, but some personal items would be appropriated to the next generation by lot. Seven groupings were prepared to make all as equal as possible. These items even included the family pictures and portraits collected over many years. We drew numbers, and my group included a portrait of the old log house where my father was born. Dad was born in 1892, and the picture was made within the year that followed. Dad, his two brothers, and his twin sisters are there with their parents. They are real people.

Portraits are pictures with such details that the viewer sees or conceives the dimensions that show life and character, times, places, and events. These pictures can be graphically presented in words. The Scriptures are replete with sufficient details to enable the reader to comprehend the real persons and the roles God has entrusted those persons. It is the responsibility of the reader to form these properly and to imitate the models as they demonstrate the response that is pleasing to God: faith and obedience.

This quarter's lessons give the readers ample opportunity to identify with several real people as we examine their responses in the portraits presented in the New Testament. When we are reading a novel, the story becomes more interesting to us when we begin to identify with one of the characters. If we can do that with a novel, how much more value and interest are waiting for us in the true stories in the Bible? The Bible is the book about God's people who contributed in God's working out His divine plan of redemption, as well as reflecting personalities who opposed God's work. All these are portraits of real people—real people with whom we can readily identify.

When we open God's picture album to see the portraits of some of those who had significant roles in the transition from the Old Covenant to the New Covenant, we look upon an attractive couple, a devoted husband and wife—devoted to one another and to God. They loved and served God in the roles that were theirs. They are Elisabeth and Zechariah, and both were of the priestly family lines and understood the promises of God found in the Old Covenant, even though they did not anticipate what their personal involvement would be.

There are two lessons that give us glances at portraits of Mary. Her beauty attracts us as in humble servant-faith she yields herself as the handmaid of the Lord. We have the privilege to place that portrait alongside that of Elisabeth to see how the faith of these two beautiful women reinforce one another. It is good to see when faith is put to the test that God often brings another person into the picture in a very meaningful way to strengthen both. The second picture of Mary brings into reality that she is the mother of the long-awaited Messiah, the hope of Israel. "But when the fulness of the time was come, God sent forth his Son, made of a woman, made under the law, to redeem them that were under the law, that we might receive the adoption of sons" (Galatians 4:4, 5).

We find it easy to place the next portrait with that of Mary, for it is that of Joseph her husband. Joseph's faith, too, was put to the test. It is so hard sometimes to put the immediate complex circumstances in proper perspective with God's ongoing plan. Joseph's courage, faith, and commitment combined to let the reader see that he was not afraid to take Mary as his wife, to protect and care for the divine Child, and to give people of all generations an example of righteousness.

As we ponder the portrait of John the Baptist, we connect him with the first portrait of Elisabeth and Zechariah, for they were his parents. Then we connect him with the Messiah, the son of Mary. As the forerunner of the Messiah, he introduced Jesus as the Lamb of God who takes away the sins of the world. When he baptized Jesus, he heard the affirmation of God, "This is my beloved Son, in whom I am well pleased" (Matthew 3:17). He was motivated as a fearless preacher of repentance in his role of forerunner of the Messiah and preparer of the hearts of people to receive the Messiah and His kingdom.

There were some who struggled in catching the significance of the kingdom Jesus taught. When our eyes look upon the portrait of the rich young ruler, we have mixed emotions. On the one hand, as Mark notes in his account, Jesus loved him; yet we see the young man go away sorrowful because he did not want to part with his possessions. The demand of the spiritual kingdom on the lives of young and old is a most telling matter—then and now.

The portrait of Mary and Martha of Bethany comes alive as we consider them when Jesus and the disciples are in their home. They fulfill roles as hosts, even though there was difficulty in balancing being hostesses and in being listeners, especially for Martha. Then came the test when their brother Lazarus was sick, and Jesus delayed His coming so that Lazarus died. When Jesus did come, love was restored, faith strengthened, and resurrection became a reality.

The portrait of Pontius Pilate is most thought provoking. Who is on trial, Jesus or Pilate? Jewish leaders had one thing in mind: to put Jesus to death. But such action would have to come from the Roman government. Pilate was the representative of Roman authority. He tried to display his authority only to have his words come back to taunt him. He did not see Jesus as a threat, for His kingdom was not of this world. However, Jesus made it clear that He was a king. He also made clear that Pilate would have no power except it were given to him from above.

Among the twelve apostles, one who rises to the forefront often in the final days of Jesus' ministry on earth is Peter. His portrait is worthy of careful examination. (We might even find ourselves looking in a mirror; therefore, we are careful with our criticism.) The picture we see at the last supper is attractive and yet foreboding, especially when Jesus told Peter that Satan was after him and that Jesus had prayed for him in this regard. The test was real: when the time came at the fire, Peter denied knowing the Lord, and then he heard the rooster crow—as Jesus had foretold. We like the closing part of the picture better. We find it in John 21 when Peter stays by his commitment to love Jesus, feed His sheep, and follow Him.

After the beginning of the church, the spiritual kingdom, we are given the occasion to see the personality of Barnabas. We don't know the details concerning the property that he owned and sold, giving the money to the apostles so that means were available for the needy among the believers. Barnabas was genuine not just in his giving, but he was also trustworthy in his presentation of Saul of Tarsus to the apostles. Later the church at Antioch of Syria sent Barnabas and Paul (formerly Saul) out on their first missionary journey by taking the gospel to Asia Minor. As plans were made for a second tour, the team divided; so two teams continued spreading the gospel.

A convert on Paul's first missionary journey was Timothy. His real portrait takes form as we see him joining with Paul and Silas on the second missionary journey. This was the beginning of his role as a helper with Paul. Paul could trust him in

preaching and guiding the new churches. Whether it was among the churches in Macedonia, Achaia, or Asia, Paul commended him highly and equipped him for his role. In Paul's final imprisonment, Timothy is the one he called for.

Another welcome portrait we find among Paul's companions and helpers is a husband and wife team, Aquila and Priscilla. Their first meeting with Paul was at Corinth on his second missionary journey, for they were all tentmakers by trade. Before long more than tentmaking brought them together. Wherever Priscilla and Aquila were, the church was "in their house." When Paul left Corinth after about a year and a half, he took the couple with him and left them at Ephesus on his way back to Jerusalem so they could lay the groundwork for the church that he would establish on the third missionary journey. From time to time and place to place they were always helpers to Paul and the work of the gospel.

All of us through the years have imitated models. These may have been our parents, our brothers or sisters, our teachers, or others whom we have admired. I still recall fondly the Sunday school teacher I had when I was four or five, almost seventy years ago. People are real to us when we like what we see. Later on, it may be easier for us to look back and recognize how God was using their lives in a way that had a real impact on us. We learn from these and we give thanks. We also reflect on the fact that there may be those who look to us as models.

It is interesting to observe that things that seem so natural in family life presented in portraits take on an added dimension when we see them fit into God's whole design of providing salvation for people. The natural and the supernatural have a way of blending when we examine the portraits of real people demonstrated in faith and obedience.

Answers to Quarterly Quiz on page 114

Lesson 1—1. false. 2. burning incense. 3. Mary. **Lesson 2**—1. Gabriel. 2. blessed. **Lesson 3**—1. true. 2. Egypt. 3. Nazareth. **Lesson 4**—1. inn. 2. shepherds. **Lesson 5**—1. kingdom. 2. vipers. **Lesson 6**—1. poor. 2. needle. **Lesson 7**—1. true. 2. Mary. 3. true. **Lesson 8**—1. true. 2. true. 3. Caesar. **Lesson 9**—1. Satan. 2. true. **Lesson 10**—1. Cyprus. 2. Antioch. 3. false. **Lesson 11**—1. Agrippa. 2. Gentiles. **Lesson 12**—1. false. 2. Lois, Eunice. **Lesson 13**—1. synagogue. 2. Apollos.

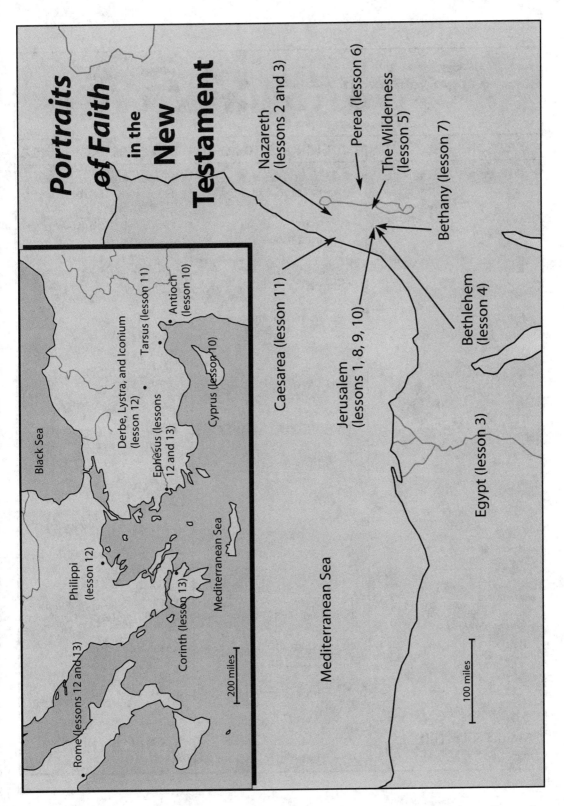

Portraits of Faith in the New Testament

Nazareth (lessons 2 and 3)
Perea (lesson 6)
The Wilderness (lesson 5)
Bethany (lesson 7)
Caesarea (lesson 11)
Jerusalem (lessons 1, 8, 9, 10)
Bethlehem (lesson 4)
Egypt (lesson 3)
Mediterranean Sea
100 miles

Black Sea
Derbe, Lystra, and Iconium (lesson 12)
Tarsus (lesson 11)
Antioch (lesson 10)
Ephesus (lessons 12 and 13)
Cyprus (lesson 10)
Philippi (lesson 12)
Corinth (lesson 13)
Mediterranean Sea
Rome (lessons 12 and 13)
200 miles

Portraits of Faith

Person	Challenges to Faith	Level of Response
Elizabeth & Zechariah	Advanced Age and Unanswered Prayer	Compliance, With Some Temporary Doubt
Mary	Youth and Humble Circumstances	Complete Submission
Joseph	Sense of Justice and Unique Circumstance	Full Obedience
John the Baptist	Personal Popularity and Political Consequences	Early Belief and Later Doubt
The Rich Man	Dependence on Wealth; Self-confidence	Sad Refusal
Mary and Martha	Human Familiarity With Jesus; Personal Jealousies	Devoted Service and Acquiescence
Pilate	Political Correctness and Egotism	Capitulation and Rejection
Peter	Rashness and Overconfidence	Repentant Recommitment and Enthusiasm
Barnabas	Family Loyalties and National Pride	Christlike Generosity and Persistence
Paul	Legalism and Intellectualism	Total Surrender
Timothy	Family Background and Youth	Lifelong Self-Denial
Aquila & Priscilla	Roman/Greek Culture and Mobility	Contentment in Service

Yes or No?

The Eternal Choice

by Ronald G. Davis

THIS QUARTER OF STUDIES looks at people who said yes or no to God's call on their lives. Though we have a tendency to stereotype people—to picture them one-dimensionally—in literature and in the Bible, these "Portraits of Faith" are of real people. They are people who are a blend of inconsistencies—of knowledge and ignorance, of discernment and foolishness, of objectivity (logic) and emotionalism. They are, in fact, just like us. Some will cry, "Yes!" with vigor; some will stutter, "Y-y-yes," with trepidation. A few will boldly and foolishly blurt, "No!" Some will say nothing, and their silence will register as a no. As we diligently compare and contrast them with God's ideal, with one another, and with ourselves, we want ourselves and our learners to learn how to say "Yes" to God unreservedly.

Is It a Yes or a No?

One of the ways to see the multifaceted humanness of a person in literature is to decide what attributes can be appropriately applied, based on that person's words and deeds. A teacher of the lessons that follow can have his learners do just that. For example, in lesson 9 of this series—for January 26—the apostle Peter is the object of the "Portrait of Faith." Give the learners a sheet of attributes, evenly spaced in two columns on a page, with the directions that the sheet be folded and torn (or cut) into separate pieces, each with one descriptor. Then ask the learners to make two piles: a "yes" pile and a "no" pile; the yes pile will contain all the attributes appropriate to the person; the no pile, the inappropriate ones. Try the following list of adjectives and nouns for Peter (with sample references for discussion): BRUSQUE, CONFIDENT (Luke 22:33), COWARDLY, DECEITFUL, FAITHFUL, FOOLISH, GALILEAN, HUMBLE, IMPULSIVE, JEALOUS, LIAR (Luke 22:56, 57), LONELY, SENSITIVE, SELF-DECEIVED, REPENTANT, SPECIAL. Once each learner has established two piles, have someone read each pile he or she has established; then discuss differences others have determined. Let learners explain why they have placed any words differently from other learners.

Paul would make an interesting second choice for such an activity. (Not only are his person and life worthy of study on their own merit, but they also serve as an important comparison/contrast to Peter.) Lesson 11 on February 9 highlights Paul as "Obedient Messenger." Such words (with sample references for discussion) as the following could be useful: BOLD, CONTENT, FEARFUL, FEARLESS, HUMBLE, IMPARTIAL (Acts 26:22), JEWISH, LAW-ABIDING (Acts 26:12), OBEDIENT, PERSUASIVE, PREJUDICED, UNPREPARED, VIOLENT, ZEALOUS. A richer, fuller concept of the person under study should emerge.

Such a look at one of the negative examples of faith in the series could be interesting as well. Try the rich man of Mark 10:17-22 with the following descriptors. (Be sure to have your learners looking also at the parallel passages in Matthew 19:16-22 and Luke 18:18-23.) Descriptors for the attributes sheet may include the following: DECEITFUL, DEMANDING, EAGER, GENEROUS, GENTILE, HEAVEN-BOUND, JOYFUL, LOVABLE, MISTAKEN, OLD, PERCEPTIVE, RICH, RUDE, SELF-CONFIDENT. As in any occasion of using such an activity, there will be disagreement for several as to whether they truly represent the man. But that disagreement will allow a helpful discussion of the text and the person.

A teacher may have a class that would like to approach such an activity in a more compositional way. Give each learner a sheet with the heading, "_____ was definitely. . . ." (Fill in the blank with the name of the Bible character you want to study.) Below that, have ten rectangles in two columns of five. Direct the class to fill in ten attributes or character traits of the character named, one per box. When boxes are filled, have class members swap sheets with one another and explain their different choices.

Can I Say Yes?

Of course, one of the reasons the Spirit has highlighted certain people in Biblical history is so that women and men in every generation and in every geography can see the Spirit at work—either being welcomed and nurtured or being rejected and quenched. It behooves the Bible student to compare and contrast himself with the individuals coming face to face with God's truth in Biblical settings. A simple, personal yes-or-no response to the behaviors of lesson heroes and heroines helps the fruit of the Spirit to ripen.

Priscilla and Aquila, Christian wife and husband, are the subjects of Lesson 13 in this series, "Partners in the Gospel." Consider giving your class—either in print or orally—a series of statements characterizing the godly lifestyle of Priscilla and Aquila, asking them to respond yes or no to each. (If done orally, you are asking only for meditative, silent responses.) Use statements such as these: (1) I carry my faith with me everywhere I go; (2) My vocation serves the noble needs of fellow citizens; (3) I welcome people into my home in the spirit of hospitality; (4) I encourage Christian evangelists and missionaries on their way; (5) My house is open and available to the functions of the church; (6) My commitment to the success of the gospel is long-term; (7) I am confident enough and bold enough to correct one who mistakenly misrepresents the gospel; (8) I will "stick my neck out" for a brother or sister under attack; (9) I have a good reputation among the churches where I am known; (10)—For married learners—My spouse and I are united in godly priority. During the introduction or the conclusion, you may want to discuss how each of these statements was true of Priscilla and Aquila; for example, take a look at Acts 18:24-26 in reference to number seven.

Similar statements might be prepared and used for other lessons in the series; such as the one on Timothy. Statements that could be used for him—based on texts used—include the following. (1) I learned the gospel from a believing mother; (2) I never use my family background as an excuse to avoid ministry; (3) I have a good reputation locally; (4) I submit readily to that which is expedient, even if it is not essential; (5) I can "play second fiddle" to a strong leader; (6) My goal is to extend Christ's reputation, not my own; (7) I can be trusted to fulfill a ministry delegated to me; (8) I can be counted upon to correct false doctrine in others; (9) I care enough about others to shed tears for their difficulties; (10) My faith could truly be called unfeigned/sincere; (11) I use the gifts God has given to me.

In the discussion, call for your learners to identify relevant text verses for their decisions. (You may prefer to give your learners a graded scale for their responses:

• Yes, always/totally.
• Yes, most of the time.
• No, most of the time.
• No, never.

Such a choice may make responding easier.)

The God Who Says Yes

Ideally, in every unit of study, the class member's prayer life will reflect the truths being learned from session to session. In this series of "Portraits of Faith," the learner will see images of the kind of person God wants him or her to be or not be. Sincere, persistent petition to God for His help to those ends is always appropriate.

Two lessons in this series have dominantly negative examples: lesson 6, on the foolish rich man, and lesson 8, on Pilate. Though adults must see a bit of themselves in those two, no one truly wants to be compared with either one. Suggesting a format of prayer expression for those lessons could be very helpful. Consider: "God of justice and righteousness, I am sorry that I am like ____. Help me to resist the temptations to be ____. Give me the grace to become ____. Be merciful to me, a sinner." Fill in the first blank with the name of the character. A group reflection on words that fill the other two blanks could well be profitable. For the rich man, words such as *materialistic* and *generous* could fill the blanks respectively. For Pilate, the words *purely pragmatic* and *a person of godly integrity* are possible.

Of course, a similar pattern could be used in lessons on those who have a positive witness. For example, the first lesson on Elisabeth and Zechariah would lend itself to a prayer with the following form: "God who hears and answers prayer, help me to be like ____ in my ____. Help me to avoid the appearance of ____." If done for Zechariah, such words as "in my faithful service," and "the appearance of doubt." For Elisabeth, the words could be "in my submissiveness," and "the appearance of shame at Your work in my life" (see Luke 1:24).

(You could provide a small tablet for each class member as this lesson series begins. Suggest that each learner use this tablet as a prayer "log" for the whole series, recommending that they compose and enter such a simple prayer after each study. If you do so, be certain to work on a model pattern in lesson one. Ask them to label the tablet, "Becoming a Portrait of Faith.")

The Simple and Profound Choice

James Russell Lowell (1819–1891) expressed it poetically and perfectly in the nineteenth century:

Once to ev'ry man and nation
　Comes the moment to decide,
In the strife of truth with falsehood,
　For the good or evil side;
Some great cause, some great decision,
　Off'ring each the bloom or blight,
And the choice goes by forever
　'Twixt that darkness and that light.

Yes or no? That is the question each must ask. That is the decision each must make. The Christian teacher's job is to help all students within his or her sway to make the right one.

Elisabeth and Zechariah

December 1
Lesson 1

DEVOTIONAL READING: Isaiah 40:3-11.

BACKGROUND SCRIPTURE: Luke 1:5-66.

PRINTED TEXT: Luke 1:5-14, 39-45, 57, 58.

Luke 1:5-14, 39-45, 57, 58

5 There was in the days of Herod, the king of Judea, a certain priest named Zechariah, of the course of Abijah: and his wife was of the daughters of Aaron, and her name was Elisabeth.

6 And they were both righteous before God, walking in all the commandments and ordinances of the Lord blameless.

7 And they had no child, because that Elisabeth was barren; and they both were now well stricken in years.

8 And it came to pass, that, while he executed the priest's office before God in the order of his course,

9 According to the custom of the priest's office, his lot was to burn incense when he went into the temple of the Lord.

10 And the whole multitude of the people were praying without at the time of incense.

11 And there appeared unto him an angel of the Lord standing on the right side of the altar of incense.

12 And when Zechariah saw him, he was troubled, and fear fell upon him.

13 But the angel said unto him, Fear not, Zechariah: for thy prayer is heard; and thy wife Elisabeth shall bear thee a son, and thou shalt call his name John.

14 And thou shalt have joy and gladness; and many shall rejoice at his birth.

. . . .

39 And Mary arose in those days, and went into the hill country with haste, into a city of Judah;

40 And entered into the house of Zechariah, and saluted Elisabeth.

41 And it came to pass, that, when Elisabeth heard the salutation of Mary, the babe leaped in her womb; and Elisabeth was filled with the Holy Ghost:

42 And she spake out with a loud voice, and said, Blessed art thou among women, and blessed is the fruit of thy womb.

43 And whence is this to me, that the mother of my Lord should come to me?

44 For, lo, as soon as the voice of thy salutation sounded in mine ears, the babe leaped in my womb for joy.

45 And blessed is she that believed: for there shall be a performance of those things which were told her from the Lord.

. . . .

57 Now Elisabeth's full time came that she should be delivered; and she brought forth a son.

58 And her neighbors and her cousins heard how the Lord had showed great mercy upon her; and they rejoiced with her.

GOLDEN TEXT: The angel said unto him, Fear not, Zechariah: for thy prayer is heard; and thy wife Elisabeth shall bear thee a son, and thou shalt call his name John.
—Luke 1:13.

Lesson Aims

After participating in this lesson, each student will be able to:

1. Describe the character and faithfulness of Elisabeth and Zechariah.

2. Tell how submission to God's will was critical for Elisabeth and Zechariah and remains so today.

3. Express a commitment born of faith and hope to do what God is wanting to accomplish in his or her life.

Lesson Outline

INTRODUCTION
   A. Portrait of Elisabeth and Zechariah
   B. Lesson Background
 I. GOD'S CALL OF ZECHARIAH (Luke 1:5-14)
   A. Character and Opportunity (vv. 5-9)
     A Sense of Timing
   B. Conversation With an Angel (vv. 10-14)
 II. GOD'S MISSION FOR ELISABETH (Luke 1:39-45)
   A. Mary's Visit to Elisabeth (vv. 39, 40)
   B. Elisabeth's Message to Mary (vv. 41-45)
     Standing on the Promises
 III. GOD'S FULFILLMENT OF THE PROMISE (Luke 1:57, 58)
   A. Birth of John the Baptist (v. 57)
   B. Occasion for Rejoicing (v. 58)
CONCLUSION
   A. They Are Changed, We Are Changed
   B. Prayer
   C. Thought to Remember

Introduction

A. Portrait of Elisabeth and Zechariah

Elisabeth and Zechariah knew the Old Testament, for that was the Word of God there was at that time. They knew the requirements of the law of Moses. They knew what it meant to minister for God. We do not know all the aspects of Zechariah's particular ministry, but the window that is opened for us in Luke 1 enables us to go with him into the temple for a once-in-a-lifetime experience. This experience also enables us to connect a religious act with a circumstance in their own home. Elisabeth was unable to bear children, a role she wanted very much. In fact,

both Elisabeth and Zechariah had desired to be parents for years to the point that they knew only God could make it possible. (Childless couples today can empathize very well with their anxiety.)

In our mind's eye we see the people, and we recreate the time and place for the important events in their lives. But more importantly, our thoughts move to consider their son John, the supernatural events in the lives of his parents, and John's ministry in introducing the Messiah. John is the one to preach repentance so that the hearts of the people of Israel would be prepared for the coming of the Messiah and His kingdom.

B. Lesson Background

We need to stretch our imaginations back some two thousand years to place ourselves into the setting in which Elisabeth and Zechariah rose to the forefront. With the close of the book of Malachi, it had been about four hundred years since there had been a direct revelation from God. Devout Jewish people used whatever opportunity was theirs to hear Old Testament messages, especially as those messages nourished their hope for the coming of the Messiah. Elisabeth and Zechariah had an advantage in this regard, since they both were of priestly family lines.

They did not squander the benefit of their heritage. They responded positively to the personal roles with which God had entrusted them. God had chosen this couple to play a significant part in preparing the way for the Messiah. Their son John would be the one to introduce the Messiah. At the time they did not comprehend what all this meant.

From the lesson, we have opportunity to examine the kind of people God uses. The time frame of Elisabeth and Zechariah was that of the Old Covenant. They knew and kept the laws and regulations of that Covenant, but their relationship with God also was limited by these same statutes. Zechariah's ministry in the temple with his particular duties was central in their lives. We may consider Elisabeth to be a homemaker, taking care of the priestly vestments of her husband and helping with his needs pertaining to his service as she was able. It is easy for us to note that God challenges people to serve "where they are."

How much Elisabeth and Zechariah were aware of the prophecy in Isaiah 40, we have no way of knowing. What did they think when they heard, "Behold, the Lord God will come with strong hand" (Isaiah 40:10)? However, we can be sure it would take on greater dimension after the birth of their son John, for they would then be involved personally with what God was doing in the blessing that would come with the Messiah.

I. God's Call of Zechariah
(Luke 1:5-14)

In writing his account of the life of Christ, Luke gives Elisabeth and Zechariah an honored role in introducing his Gospel. The portrait of their faith is real, and a model for us today. [See question #1, page 128.]

A. Character and Opportunity (vv. 5-9)

5. There was in the days of Herod, the king of Judea, a certain priest named Zechariah, of the course of Abijah: and his wife was of the daughters of Aaron, and her name was Elisabeth.

Herod the Great was *king* over *Judea* from 37 to 4 B.C. He is Jewish in background, but his faith is nil. His place of power in the Roman Empire allows him to be as selfish, ruthless, and corrupt as he desires (cf. Matthew 2:16). But *Zechariah* and *Elisabeth* are two people with different roles and very different qualities from those of the evil king. The impact of their lives on history ultimately is greater than that of Herod.

Zechariah (whose name means "God remembers") is a *priest* descended from *Abijah,* one of the grandsons of *Aaron.* There are twenty-four divisions, or courses, of the priesthood, based on the families of Aaron's descendants (cf. 1 Chronicles 24). Each division serves twice a year for one week, and the priests consider their ancestral positions as trusts from God. All of us can learn from this example and be more aware of the trusts we have from God—our family backgrounds, our abilities, and the time and place in which we live.

6. And they were both righteous before God, walking in all the commandments and ordinances of the Lord blameless.

The lifestyle of this couple is pleasing to *God;* they are the kind of people He can use to have an impact on human affairs. If God uses people to the extent that they have prepared themselves to be used by Him, then Elisabeth and Zechariah have prepared well. [See question #2, page 128.]

This passage reminds us that "real people" are participating in bringing about God's plan of redemption. Their response to God's law is exemplary, but is not complete. Their obedience to Old Testament law and Zechariah's ministry as a priest are central in their lives. They anticipate the time when sin will be forgiven. Only then will their relationship with God be complete. They expect the Messiah to provide this blessing. These two apparently have some spiritual insight into God's coming redemptive work.

So Elisabeth and Zechariah watch, learn, and serve as they wait for that plan to unfold. Faith and patience are necessary companions for servants of God. As we look forward to the second coming of Christ, we, too, faithfully watch, learn, and serve.

7. And they had no child, because that Elisabeth was barren; and they both were now well stricken in years.

Having *no child* is heartbreaking to would-be parents today. To an ancient Jewish family, it was even more so. In fact, it was often viewed as a judgment of God (cf. Genesis 20:18; Hosea 9:14).

For *Elisabeth* and Zechariah, what may have seemed "unfair" actually becomes the occasion for demonstrating the power and purposes of God. Their situation demonstrates that God's people can be His servants regardless of age. God gives Elisabeth and Zechariah the chance for their faith and patience to develop. [See question #3, page 128.]

Various situations in Scripture awaken us to occasions where human limitations serve as God's time to bring together the human and the divine. Think of the testimonies that Sarah and Abraham (Genesis 17:15-19), as well as Hannah and Elkanah (1 Samuel 1:1-20), give us concerning their own childless states.

8. And it came to pass, that, while he executed the priest's office before God in the order of his course.

Each member of the *course* takes his turn at serving in the temple, where God had revealed His presence among the people in the past. For Zechariah, ministering *before God* on behalf of the people is a high and holy service. It is a time of being close to God, of sensing His presence.

We may do well to consider if we ever have trouble worshiping or serving Christ, our problem could be solved by an awareness of the presence of Christ. This matter is a central feature in the

Visual for lesson 1

The first visual gives an overview of the personalities to be studied this quarter.

book of Revelation as John pictures Christ in the center position of the seven churches of Asia, knowing their situations and ready to be their provider and protector. We live in the presence of Christ! Our relationship is even greater than what Zechariah had; so there ought to be even a greater response. "Unto whomsoever much is given, of him shall be much required" (Luke 12:48).

A SENSE OF TIMING

The baseball player describes his success by saying, "It's all in the timing." The one who invests in stocks or real estate says, "It's all in the timing." We are impressed with the timing of the angel's visit in today's lesson. Of course, in the Bible angels brought messages at various times, and they appeared in various places. Sometimes they delivered their message through dreams while people slept, sometimes as people walked along the way, and sometimes when they were at work. Still, it is instructive to read that the message came to Zechariah when he was serving! Many have received their greatest blessings when they were serving. Many have received insights into life when they were serving. Many have found a fresh spiritual joy when they were serving.

There is something about serving God that clears the mind, opens the heart, and softens the will. God could have delivered His message to Zechariah at any time, but He chose to do it when Zechariah was serving—and serving in the temple.

Today, we do not regard any place as truly a holy place. We speak of holy places only because there is no other way to describe them. We believe that any place becomes a holy place when we meet God there. Church conventions used to appoint a time and place committee for the next convention. Such a committee could not have improved on the choice God made. Those who forget to serve, or will not serve, may miss out on a very special blessing that God has for them. We do not serve in order to receive, but when we serve we often do receive.   —R. C. S.

9. According to the custom of the priest's office, his lot was to burn incense when he went into the temple of the Lord.

The opportunity to minister at the altar is determined by drawing lots. Moreover, this occa-

VISUALS FOR THESE LESSONS

The *Adult Visuals* packet contains large, full-color visuals designed for use with the lessons in the Winter Quarter. The packet is available from your supplier. Order No. 292.

sion to offer *incense* ordinarily is allowed once in a lifetime because of the large number of priests. So for Zechariah, this is "his hour"—long awaited and long desired. But Zechariah cannot anticipate all that is in store. How can anyone know the full mind of God or what the future will hold as God's will is being accomplished?

B. Conversation With an Angel
(vv. 10-14)

10. And the whole multitude of the people were praying without at the time of incense.

Under the Old Covenant, priests are considered to be "go betweens" in bringing the peoples' sacrifices to God. The worshipers, on behalf of whom Zechariah is ministering, are assembled outside the temple and are *praying* silently. (The rising smoke of the *incense* signifies those prayers.) Incense is burned twice a day in the temple, in the morning and in the evening—Luke does not tell us the time of day here. It is certainly appropriate for Zechariah to pray at this once-in-a-lifetime service, especially since it is a time when he must be feeling closer to God than at any other time. Surely he prays for various needs of *the people,* and we would be surprised if he did not petition God for the desire of his own heart, as well. But does he ask for a child? Has he long since given up hope, or does he still pray?

11. And there appeared unto him an angel of the Lord standing on the right side of the altar of incense.

What a distinct privilege this is to Zechariah that *an angel of the Lord* should appear to him! It has been four centuries since any Heavenly messenger has walked the earth. The Word does not tell us what the angel looks like. (Whenever angels appeared on earth, they took a form appropriate for their mission.) For Zechariah there is no mistaking who he is. And the important thing is his message. The angel appears *on the right side of the altar of incense* between the altar and the golden lampstand. Being in a situation where God's communication is so personal is a real test to one's faith.

12. And when Zechariah saw him, he was troubled, and fear fell upon him.

Zechariah thinks he is alone, but to his amazement someone else is there, representing God with a personal communication. This is the angel Gabriel, as verse 19 tells us (see also Daniel 8:16; 9:21). Will this be judgment or blessing? Awe surrounds him as one in the presence of God. His *fear* is a godly fear. But what will be next?

13. But the angel said unto him, Fear not, Zechariah: for thy prayer is heard; and thy wife Elisabeth shall bear thee a son, and thou shalt call his name John.

This answer to his *prayer* is probably not what *Zechariah* expects! The announcement of the birth of John is very similar to the announcement given to the parents of Samson in Judges 13:3-5. The child to be born in each situation is empowered from birth for a special task. John means "the Lord's gift" or "the Lord is gracious." And so He is!

14. And thou shalt have joy and gladness; and many shall rejoice at his birth.

Truly the child's birth will be a time for rejoicing by his parents; yet, what is implied by *many*? The angel tantalizes Zechariah's hope and faith with the additional assurance that the child will "be great in the sight of the Lord" (v. 15). What does that mean? Zechariah can only wait for more of the divine message—and the unfolding events of history—for his answer!

II. God's Mission for Elisabeth (Luke 1:39-45)

The angel Gabriel appears to Mary about six months later (v. 26). He tells her that she will give birth to Jesus. Quickly Mary goes to see Elisabeth.

A. Mary's Visit to Elisabeth (vv. 39, 40)

39. And Mary arose in those days, and went into the hill country with haste, into a city of Judah.

Elisabeth and Zechariah live in *the hill country* of *Judah*, probably in the *city* of Hebron, the city of priests (Joshua 21:11). This is about forty miles from Jerusalem and seventy miles—a four- or five-day journey—from Nazareth. The visit will be an occasion to strengthen the faith of both *Mary* and Elisabeth and to heighten their hope concerning the Messiah. Again we note that God does not always reveal all details quickly. He does it in ways that develop faith, patience, and hope.

40. And entered into the house of Zechariah, and saluted Elisabeth.

The meeting of the two women is surely special. A unique spirit of joy and expectation fills the heart of each one, for each has a significant ministry in the work God is doing. For each of them, it is important to share some time together. We all know what comfort it brings when we can share our blessings, sorrows, or hopes with those who understand us and our circumstances.

B. Elisabeth's Message to Mary (vv. 41-45)

41. And it came to pass, that, when Elisabeth heard the salutation of Mary, the babe leaped in her womb; and Elisabeth was filled with the Holy Ghost.

In so many ways we are reminded of the quality of individual that *Elisabeth* is for the role that is hers. On this meeting with *Mary* God divinely

---

How to Say It

ABIJAH. Uh-*bye*-juh.
ABRAHAM. *Ay*-bruh-ham.
ELISABETH. Ih-*lih*-suh-beth.
ELKANAH. El-kuh-nuh or El-*kay*-nuh.
GABRIEL. *Gay*-bree-ul.
HANNAH. *Han*-uh.
HEBRON. *Hee*-brun or *Heb*-run.
HEROD. *Hair*-ud.
JUDEA. Joo-*dee*-uh.
MESSIAH. Meh-*sigh*-uh.
ZECHARIAH. *Zek*-uh-*rye*-uh (strong accent on *rye*).

---

equips her by the power of the *Holy* Spirit to speak even more than she understands. Even the movement of her unborn child communicates to encourage her in her poetic proclamation.

42. And she spake out with a loud voice, and said, Blessed art thou among women, and blessed is the fruit of thy womb.

Mary is greatly honored as the chosen of God. Elisabeth's words strengthen Mary and challenge her faith as well. It will be a message to reflect upon later as she ponders her role and that of her unborn son. What will it mean to be the earthly mother of God's child? What responsibility, what trust from God! [See question #4, page 128.]

43. And whence is this to me, that the mother of my Lord should come to me?

To what extent Elisabeth understands that Mary's son will be the Messiah is hard to know. But God has revealed some semblance of that fact through Elisabeth to reassure both women. Her use of the phrase *my Lord* is similar to David's calling the Messiah "my Lord" in Psalm 110:1 (quoted numerous times in the New Testament). What confidence this is for them that God is fulfilling His promises! Perhaps Elisabeth reflects on the meaning of her own name, "God is an oath." His word will come to pass!

44. For, lo, as soon as the voice of thy salutation sounded in mine ears, the babe leaped in my womb for joy.

Elisabeth testifies to Mary the personal witness of her unborn son concerning Mary's arrival with her own unborn son—both sons are from the promise and power of Almighty God. Although the two women cannot anticipate what is ahead for each, they can patiently trust God.

45. And blessed is she that believed: for there shall be a performance of those things which were told her from the Lord.

Faith is the foundation of hope and happiness. Whatever God promises, He intends to accomplish in His time. Sometimes we get in a hurry, only to find it is not yet the fullness of time (cf. Galatians 4:4). Whenever we try to "push" God's timetable, we run a big risk! God's own authority is sufficient reason that we should believe His promises. We see models in the portraits of Mary and Elisabeth. Even though we do not have the roles of these two women today, God provides us with happenings that both test and develop our faith. [See question #5, page 128.]

STANDING ON THE PROMISES

All of life is built on promises. Marriage begins with promises. And before those vows are said, sometimes someone sings that lovely song "Oh, Promise Me!" Business is built on promises, as everyone who has ever signed a promissory note knows. It begins with, "I promise to pay." People who enter the military must first make promises. Elected officials are inducted into office with promises. And in recent years large numbers of men have come together with a group called Promise Keepers to strengthen their resolve to be faithful husbands and fathers.

God, of course, is the ultimate promise keeper. You can see His track record in the Old Testament and mark it in the New Testament. You can observe it in the lives of others, and you can experience it in your own life. God keeps His promises. He always has and He always will. Many products are advertised on the basis of their performance, from automobiles to kitchen devices. God's performance record is perfect.

Elisabeth believed this. Mary believed this. The whole history of the church is the record of men and women who believed this. It is the kind of faith that will cheer you on your worst day and calm you on your best day. The old song is right: we are standing on the promises. In truth there is no other place to stand. We who serve a promise-keeping God must respond by keeping our own promises—to Him, to others, and to the world.
—R. C. S.

III. God's Fulfillment of the Promise (Luke 1:57, 58)

Mary stays with Elisabeth about three months (v. 56), probably long enough to see John born.

A. Birth of John the Baptist (v. 57)

57. Now Elisabeth's full time came that she should be delivered; and she brought forth a son.

During the three months that Mary is there, the two women undoubtedly share the burdens and the joys on their hearts. The common experience of approaching motherhood is not a time to talk of age difference, but to praise God and pray that they will have the faith to fulfill their roles in God's plan. These are days of preparation.

B. Occasion for Rejoicing (v. 58)

58. And her neighbors and her cousins heard how the Lord had showed great mercy upon her; and they rejoiced with her.

What a time for rejoicing! Many of the relatives and friends present would think, "God has taken away her disgrace" (compare Luke 1:25). However, the event has much more meaning than that. Here is a great demonstration of God's mercy. Here is divine evidence that the Messianic hope is still alive in this baby. Even greater things are ahead! It is noteworthy that Zechariah's first words after the return of his speech are to praise *the Lord*. Is there a better way to rejoice?

Conclusion

A. They Are Changed, We Are Changed

We no longer are the same if we are able to identify with the faith of these real people. Our faith is stronger because of their models. We look forward with desire to the work God is doing, and we offer ourselves ready to serve Him, knowing He trusts real people to do His work, regardless of their ages or the eras in which they live. There is always a place for faith, patience, and hope in the promises of God.

B. Prayer

Father, just as we trust You for the air we breathe and the food we eat, may we show our faith in trusting You to use us in Your ongoing work. In Jesus' name, amen.

C. Thought to Remember

God will give you opportunities to serve, no matter what your life situation.

Home Daily Bible Readings

Monday, Nov. 25—An Angel Visits Zechariah (Luke 1:5-13)
Tuesday, Nov. 26—Zechariah Questions the Promise (Luke 1:14-20)
Wednesday, Nov. 27—Elisabeth Conceives (Luke 1:21-25)
Thursday, Nov. 28—His Name Is John (Luke 1:57-66)
Friday, Nov. 29—Zechariah Prophesies (Luke 1:67-75)
Saturday, Nov. 30—John Will Go Before the Lord (Luke 1:76-80)
Sunday, Dec. 1—Prepare the Way of the Lord (Isaiah 40:3-11)

Learning by Doing

This page contains an alternative lesson plan emphasizing learning activities. Classes desiring such student involvement will find these suggestions helpful.

Learning Goals

After this lesson the student will be able to:

1. Describe the character and faithfulness of Elisabeth and Zechariah.

2. Tell how submission to God's will was critical for Elisabeth and Zechariah and remains so today.

3. Express a commitment born of faith and hope to do what God is wanting to accomplish in his or her life.

Into the Lesson

Ask each student to identify a person who was or is a leader. It may be a person who was influential in the development of his or her spiritual life. Or a student may choose someone who serves as a good model of faith in today's world. Ask students to create a "verbal portrait" of this person by answering the following questions:

1. What was (is) the person's name and occupation?

2. How was (is) faith or faithfulness to God demonstrated in this person's life?

3. How did (does) this person serve in his or her church?

4. Choose three words that describe this person's spiritual life.

Allow each student to share his or her "verbal portrait" with at least one other person. Remind the class that godly lives and experiences of real persons often serve as models for our lives. We are embarking on a study of New Testament models for life today. These verbal portraits are intended to inspire and give confidence to today's follower of Jesus Christ. (This activity is also included in the student book, *Adult Bible Class*.)

Into the Word

Early in the week give a class member a special assignment. Ask him or her to prepare a brief report on the Jewish priesthood in the first century. This person should identify the primary tasks of priests and tell how they were divided or organized. Give this person a copy of the lesson commentary and a copy of an article on priests from a Bible dictionary.

Begin the class by reading Luke 1:5-14, 39-45, 57, 58. Say, "There are many questions we could ask of Elisabeth and Zechariah. Suggest some questions we might ask the couple if we could interview them. For example: 'What emotions did you feel when it became apparent you were not going to have children?'" Have class members call out questions for the interview. Ask one member to be the "scribe" and write these questions on the chalkboard. Develop a list of several questions. Then have learners work in small groups to suggest potential answers to the questions listed.

Tell the class that it is often encouraging to discover characteristics of effective servants of God. Ask learners to look for clues to the character of Zechariah and Elisabeth from today's text. (Examples: "Priest," "Righteous before God," "Feared God.") Have the "scribe" list these on the chalkboard.

Call for the report on the tasks and organization of priests at this time.

Into Life

Make two columns on the chalkboard. Label one "Priests or Religious Leaders"; the other should be headed "Laymen." Say, "Zechariah was a priest, a religious leader. Who were other religious leaders God used to accomplish His will in the Bible?" List the answers in column one. *(Examples may include Eli, Saul/Paul, and others.)* Then say, "God also uses people from ordinary walks of life as His special servants." Ask for names and list them in the second column. *(Examples could include Moses, Abraham, Jacob, Peter, Andrew, Priscilla, and others.)* Discuss how both groups were useful to God only as they submitted to His will.

Give each student a piece of paper with a picture frame on it (from a computer program or clip art). Near the bottom of that frame write, "Dear Lord, help me to learn to be always ready to accept responsibilities and opportunities you provide in my life. Signed, _____."

State: "We are going to create another verbal portrait. We want to list as many characteristics of great and humble servants of God as possible and to learn from this model." Brainstorm names of some of God's servants and the characteristics that made these people great servants. Ask the learners to write the characteristics of these servants in the open part of their picture frames.

After reviewing these characteristics, ask them if they would be willing to sign the prayer at the bottom of the page. Close with prayer.

Let's Talk It Over

The questions on this page are designed to encourage review of the lesson Scriptures and to promote discussion of the lesson by the class. The answers provided are only discussion starters. Let your class talk it over from there.

1. In what ways are Christian role models important to the ministry of the church?

One of the most important ministries of the church is *discipleship*. New and young Christians need to be trained to mature in their faith and in their ability to minister. When young Christians see positive role models in their Bible school teachers, youth sponsors, deacons, elders, and ministers, they are more likely to want to fulfill the same kinds of ministry. That assures the church that it will have qualified, dedicated leadership in the years to come. Another benefit of positive role models is in *evangelism*. Most people are led to Christ by those whom they trust and respect in the faith. When the church has strong role models in positions such as Bible school teacher, youth sponsor, and church-camp counselor, it will be more likely to reach and retain its young people with the gospel.

2. Since all people sin, we might be surprised to read that Elisabeth and Zechariah were "righteous before God" and "blameless." These terms obviously are not absolute, then, but describe the couple's lifestyle. They pursued a course of righteousness even though they were not perfect. Of whom would you apply the terms *righteous* and *blameless* today? Why? What can you learn from their example?

John tells us that "Whosoever is born of God doth not commit sin" (1 John 3:9). Yet he also says, "If we say that we have no sin, we deceive ourselves" (1 John 1:8). The only way to harmonize these two passages is to understand that godly people do not, *as a matter of course*, participate in sinful activities. Occasionally, however, they do err. With that understanding, encourage learners to name specific people who vigorously pursue a righteous lifestyle and have modeled some aspect of discipleship for them. It may be a current leader in the church or someone from a student's past. It might be a parent or former Sunday school teacher. Encourage the learners to be specific about lessons learned.

3. What are some ways that the church can use the talents and experience of senior members to enhance its ministries?

Seniors can serve very effectively in a variety of ministries. They have the time, patience, and experience to minister to shut-ins, retirement community and nursing home residents, and hospital patients. Paul speaks of elderly widows who could minister by showing hospitality to strangers and assisting those in distress (1 Timothy 5:10). Seniors can also use their occupational experience to serve the church. Retired teachers can teach in and administer the Sunday school or Vacation Bible School. Retired ministers can make evangelistic calls and counsel church members. The possibilities are limited only by the willingness of the seniors to serve and the church to use them.

4. How has an older believer challenged and/or encouraged you in your walk with Christ? How have you done the same for a younger believer?

As Elisabeth encouraged Mary, so older saints can encourage younger ones today. Sometimes it is experience in a specific ministry or situation that is particularly helpful. Note, however, that in Elisabeth's case, she had only three months' more experience at pregnancy than Mary had. It was her character and general life experience—not her experience in the specific situation—that blessed Mary. Encourage younger adults not to turn away from the potential lessons they can learn from adults who do not know computers or pagers or other technological gadgets of our day. They still have lifetimes of serving the Lord!

5. Elisabeth said, "Blessed is she that believed." What blessings have come to you because of your faith? What problems have resulted when you got in a hurry and did not wait, in faith, on God's timing?

"Seeing is believing," the old adage goes. But many of your students probably can tell of times when believing was seeing. They could not see how God would work out their situations for good, but they believed and trusted. Then they saw. Perhaps some can tell of trusting God with their tithe first, and their financial problems were erased. This probably took some time, but they worked through it. They may have been tempted to skip their giving on occasion, but God finally saw them through the crisis. Others may tell of God's faithfulness in comforting their grief, healing a relationship, or beating a bad habit.

Mary: Handmaid of the Lord

DEVOTIONAL READING: Psalm 146.

BACKGROUND SCRIPTURE: Luke 1:26-56.

PRINTED TEXT: Luke 1:26-38, 46-49.

Luke 1:26-38, 46-49

26 And in the sixth month the angel Gabriel was sent from God unto a city of Galilee, named Nazareth,

27 To a virgin espoused to a man whose name was Joseph, of the house of David; and the virgin's name was Mary.

28 And the angel came in unto her, and said, Hail, thou that art highly favored, the Lord is with thee: blessed art thou among women.

29 And when she saw him, she was troubled at his saying, and cast in her mind what manner of salutation this should be.

30 And the angel said unto her, Fear not, Mary: for thou hast found favor with God.

31 And, behold, thou shalt conceive in thy womb, and bring forth a son, and shalt call his name JESUS.

32 He shall be great, and shall be called the Son of the Highest; and the Lord God shall give unto him the throne of his father David:

33 And he shall reign over the house of Jacob for ever; and of his kingdom there shall be no end.

34 Then said Mary unto the angel, How shall this be, seeing I know not a man?

35 And the angel answered and said unto her, The Holy Ghost shall come upon thee, and the power of the Highest shall overshadow thee: therefore also that holy thing which shall be born of thee shall be called the Son of God.

36 And, behold, thy cousin Elisabeth, she hath also conceived a son in her old age; and this is the sixth month with her, who was called barren.

37 For with God nothing shall be impossible.

38 And Mary said, Behold the handmaid of the Lord; be it unto me according to thy word. And the angel departed from her.

. . . .

46 And Mary said, My soul doth magnify the Lord,

47 And my spirit hath rejoiced in God my Saviour.

48 For he hath regarded the low estate of his handmaiden: for, behold, from henceforth all generations shall call me blessed.

49 For he that is mighty hath done to me great things; and holy is his name.

GOLDEN TEXT: Fear not, Mary: for thou hast found favor with God. And, behold, thou shalt conceive in thy womb, and bring forth a son, and shalt call his name JESUS.
—Luke 1:30, 31.

Lesson Aims

After participating in this lesson, each student will be able to:

1. Cite the details concerning God's call of Mary and her significant response.

2. Express confidence that seemingly impossible tasks undertaken in submission to God's will are possible.

3. Express a commitment born of faith and hope to do what God is wanting to accomplish in their lives.

Lesson Outline

INTRODUCTION
  A. Portrait of Mary
  B. Lesson Background
  I. MARY VISITED (Luke 1:26-33)
    A. Mary Introduced (vv. 26, 27)
    B. Mary Greeted (vv. 28-30)
      "We'll Understand It Better By and By"
    C. Mary Instructed (vv. 31-33)
      Kingdoms Rise and Wane
 II. MARY'S RESPONSE (Luke 1:34-38)
    A. The Question (v. 34)
    B. The Answer (vv. 35-37)
    C. The Commitment (v. 38)
III. MARY'S MESSAGE (Luke 1:46-49)
    A. Her Praise (vv. 46, 47)
    B. Her Status (v. 48)
    C. His Power (v. 49)
CONCLUSION
  A. His Call+Our Willingness=His Means
  B. Prayer
  C. Thought to Remember

Introduction

A. Portrait of Mary

When I was in my teens, I corresponded with a cousin of my sister-in-law in New Orleans, Louisiana. I never met her. I did not talk to her on the telephone—and that was long before the computer age and E-mail. She sent me her picture and wrote me several letters. Still it was possible, with what evidence I had, to know that she was a pretty, young woman. She was real.

Sometimes it is hard to think of people in the Bible as being real. Like the evidence that my

correspondent was real, the Holy Spirit-inspired Word removes all doubt of the reality of Mary. With the details recorded in the Scriptures, Mary the mother of Jesus can come to life in our understanding. We all can form a portrait of Mary as we bring those details together.

B. Lesson Background

The Lesson Background dovetails with last week's lesson. As we continue reflecting on New Testament personalities involved in the Messiah's coming, some of these have common connections. Luke 1:24 tells us that Elisabeth has conceived a child and hidden herself for five months. Our attention then is focused quickly on a betrothed virgin, Mary, living in Nazareth in Galilee. The text leads us to consider the type of person she is and the role she has in God's plan in sending the Messiah as Savior.

I. Mary Visited (Luke 1:26-33)

Gabriel is mentioned by name four times in the Bible (Daniel 8:16; 9:21; Luke 1:19, 26). That may not seem like much, but he is one of only two angels mentioned by name at all. Apparently, his role is very significant. Certainly, his announcement to Mary is!

A. Mary Introduced (vv. 26, 27)

26. And in the sixth month the angel Gabriel was sent from God unto a city of Galilee, named Nazareth.

It is one thing to have an unexpected visit from a friend or a neighbor. It is quite another thing to be visited by an *angel . . . from God.* What an occasion this visit of *the angel Gabriel* is to Mary! The meaning of the name *Gabriel,* "man of God," may have come to her mind. Here in her very presence is the "man of God," God's messenger.

The visit of the angel to Mary is about six months after the appearance to Zechariah (see last week's lesson). One might expect an angel to appear to a priest in glorious Jerusalem. But to have Gabriel appear in Nazareth—and to a young peasant woman (cf. Luke 1:48)—is most surprising. In Mary's time *Nazareth* is an insignificant village of fewer than two thousand inhabitants. Though we know little of her past, it is Mary's future role that is at issue in the angel's message from the Lord.

27. To a virgin espoused to a man whose name was Joseph, of the house of David; and the virgin's name was Mary.

For a Jewish family in Bible times, the parents normally arrange the marriages for their children. Such marriages have three segments. *Mary* is in the first part: she has become *espoused*, or pledged, to Joseph. The espousal agreement is as binding as we think of marriage itself. It requires divorce to break it. The next segment is a time of testing. During this period the groom or his representative will negotiate the dowry with the bride's father, and the dowry money will then be paid. Then, finally, comes the marriage feast, which is a public recognition of the agreement that already has been established. The couple does not live together until then. The betrothal usually precedes the wedding by about a year.

The groom, *Joseph,* can claim King *David* as an ancestor. Thus the child to be born of Mary will have by adoptive right the legal connection with the royal heritage of *the house of David.* (Next week's lesson will focus on Joseph and his role.)

Finally, this verse emphasizes that Mary is *a virgin.* As readers from a distance of two thousand years, we may think first of the purity of her life as she is looking forward to her marriage. We may also reflect on the fact that God knows the quality of the one He is calling to be His handmaid. Most importantly, we recall the prophecy of Isaiah 7:14, "Therefore the Lord himself shall give you a sign; Behold, a virgin shall conceive, and bear a son, and shall call his name Immanuel."

B. Mary Greeted (vv. 28-30)

28. And the angel came in unto her, and said, Hail, thou that art highly favored, the Lord is with thee: blessed art thou among women.

The divine communication becomes real and clear with the greeting to Mary, *Hail.* This is the Heavenly greeting to the noble virgin who is to become the mother of the Messiah, Jesus. What is about to be offered is by the grace and favor of God. She is chosen in preference to all other *women* on earth at the time.

It means something to be chosen. Do you not recall those times as children when the group you were a part of was going to play ball? The teacher appointed two to choose their teams. What a thrill it was if you were the first one to be chosen! But that thrill was by no means to be compared with the favor that God displays in choosing Mary. Nor does it compare with the blessing that we Christians have as the chosen people of God. Being "chosen" brings with it the important responsibility of personal response. This point for Mary will come later in our text. [See question #1, page 136.]

29. And when she saw him, she was troubled at his saying, and cast in her mind what manner of salutation this should be.

Mary's full emotional mind-set is impossible to know. Nothing like this has ever happened to her, nor has she heard of anything like it for anyone of her acquaintance. Mary finds herself on center stage, but she definitely has not asked for such an honor. Mary knows that with blessing comes responsibility. What will be the responsibility expected of her? Such honor she cannot immediately grasp. [See question #2, page 136.]

"WE'LL UNDERSTAND IT BETTER BY AND BY"

Some years ago, a teenage girl went to church camp. She was asked to sing a solo for the vesper service. The campers and the counselors knew that her father had died a few months before, suddenly and unexpectedly. So they were greatly moved when she sang a song of assurance that God would someday make everything plain to her.

Mary could have sung such a song. She was perplexed at the visit of the angel. She was perplexed at the visit of the shepherds in Bethlehem (Luke 2:19). She was perplexed at the wisdom of the boy Jesus when He was in the temple at age twelve (Luke 2:42, 51). No doubt she was perplexed often during His ministry and certainly at His crucifixion. Eventually, however, she did understand. The disciples also were sometimes perplexed, but later they came to understand as well (John 12:16).

Often, we are like Mary and the disciples. We do not understand things that happen to us or to someone whom we love. Sometimes, years later perhaps, we come to understand. In other cases we will not understand until we get to Heaven. But still we believe that the old songs are correct. We believe that we *will* understand it better by and by, and we believe that someday He *will* make it plain to us. Until then we live simply by trusting Him.

We live in an age when people want to understand everything fully. It takes faith, and a lot of patience to wait for the answer to our perplexity.

How to Say It

ARAMAIC. *Air*-uh-*may*-ik (strong accent on *may*).

ELISABETH. Ih-*lih*-suh-beth.

GABRIEL. *Gay*-bree-ul.

GALILEE. *Gal*-uh-lee.

ISAIAH. Eye-*zay*-uh.

JEREMIAH. Jair-uh-*my*-uh.

JOSHUA. *Josh*-yew-uh.

MAGNIFICAT. Mag-*nif*-ih-cot.

MESSIAH. Meh-*sye*-uh.

NAZARETH. *Naz*-uh-reth.

ZECHARIAH. *Zek*-uh-*rye*-uh (strong accent on *rye*).

But such faith and patience will be rewarded. If it is not at some time later in this life, then certainly it will be in the life to come.   —R. C. S.

30. And the angel said unto her, Fear not, Mary: for thou hast found favor with God.

The additional greeting does not resolve the entire puzzle, but it does bring some assurance. Some kind of assurance to be unafraid is common in Old Testament revelations (e.g., Joshua 1:9; Judges 6:23; Jeremiah 1:8; cf. Luke 1:13). Mary joins the list of those in the Old Testament who have received the *favor of God* in connection with the roles He has given them. These men and women of faith become models for us.

C. Mary Instructed (vv. 31-33)

31. And, behold, thou shalt conceive in thy womb, and bring forth a son, and shalt call his name JESUS.

Here the angel reveals a new and more amazing dimension. Mary, a virgin (vv. 27, 34), is to *conceive* a child! To Mary's Aramaic ears, the name *Jesus* is the equivalent of "Joshua." This Old Testament name means "the Lord is salvation" or "the one who saves."

The full import of this name probably is more than young Mary can grasp. The message of the Old Testament has brought the knowledge of sin but not of the means by which God will solve that problem. Bringing together the concepts of the Messiah, His kingdom, and the forgiveness of sin is more than Mary or any of her contemporaries can do at the time. Therefore, it is necessary for Mary to receive this revelation with some amplification (cf. Matthew 1:21). God gives as much information as He deems sufficient at the time, enough to strengthen Mary's faith as His special servant. [See question #3, page 136.]

32. He shall be great, and shall be called the Son of the Highest; and the Lord God shall give unto him the throne of his father David.

From her training in the home, Mary knows that there had been a continuous line of kings descended from *David*—first for the united kingdom and then for Judah after the kingdom was divided—until the Babylonian captivity in 586 B.C. Perhaps Mary can see the angel's message as a prediction that this *Son* will complete that succession, and bring the kingdom to a climax! Somehow, this one will uniquely be the *Son of the Highest*. (See Jeremiah 23:5, 6.)

33. And he shall reign over the house of Jacob for ever; and of his kingdom there shall be no end.

The hard part for Mary and others at that time is catching the spiritual meaning. It is a spiritual kingdom that is envisioned for the Messiah and His people, the true Israel of God (cf. Galatians 6:16). (Even after Jesus spends more than three years with His disciples, this overriding spiritual element will be hard to grasp; see Acts 1:6.) The concept of an everlasting *kingdom* is hard to fathom. Again, here is where faith steps into the picture.

KINGDOMS RISE AND WANE

Those of us who grew up singing four-stanza hymns may remember that we often skipped the third one. However, the third stanza of the hymn "Onward Christian Soldiers" may be the most important of the entire song. Part of it says, "Crowns and thrones may perish, Kingdoms rise and wane. . . ." History bears out that truth. The kingdom won by Alexander the Great did not last as long as it took him to win it. The Roman Empire is gone.

In the heyday of the Austro-Hungarian Empire, the design for the Hofburg Palace in Vienna featured the letters a, e, i, o, and u. Not only are they our vowels, they also stood for a phrase that translates as "Austria Will Live Forever." But that great empire is no more, and today Austria is one of the smaller countries in Europe. Once it was said that the sun never set on the British Empire, but that empire is gone as well. Hitler's "Third Reich" is only a bad memory. The mighty Soviet Union fell apart in the late 1980s.

Against the background of these fleeting earthly kingdoms stands the promise of today's lesson: "of his kingdom there shall be no end." It began with 120 people (Acts 1:15) and now numbers millions. It speaks a thousand languages, is seen on every continent, and includes people of "every tribe and tongue and nation." No movement has ever spread so far, or grown so fast—and no kingdom will endure except His kingdom. So it is good to set Luke 1:33 of today's lesson alongside the entirety of the third stanza of that old hymn:

> Crowns and thrones may perish,
>   Kingdoms rise and wane,
> But the church of Jesus
>   Constant will remain;
> Gates of hell can never
> 'Gainst that Church prevail;
> We have Christ's own promise,
>   And that cannot fail.
>   —Sabine Baring-Gould (1834–1924)
>   —R. C. S.

II. Mary's Response (Luke 1:34-38)

Some people in the Bible were speechless in the face of heavenly messages—or nearly so. (See Isaiah 6:5; Daniel 5:6; 10:15-17; Acts 9:7.)

Zechariah the priest became speechless as a *result* of a heavenly message (Luke 1:20). Neither is true of Mary!

A. The Question (v. 34)

34. Then said Mary unto the angel, How shall this be, seeing I know not a man?

Mary's question confirms the statement that she is a virgin (v. 27). There has been the contractual agreement (a "betrothal"), but she and Joseph have not yet completed the marriage process. Nor have they had relations outside the marriage bond. She knows that no conception of a child could have taken place yet—it is not humanly possible. Such a reaction from Mary is very understandable. Thus, she needs further explanation before she can give *the angel* her full reply.

B. The Answer (vv. 35-37)

35. And the angel answered and said unto her, The Holy Ghost shall come upon thee, and the power of the Highest shall overshadow thee: therefore also that holy thing which shall be born of thee shall be called the Son of God.

Gabriel answers Mary's "how?" by telling "Who." The *Holy* Spirit will bring this about. Mary knows there have been occasions when God has equipped His people for special tasks by *the power* of His Spirit (Exodus 31:3; Numbers 11:17, 25; Judges 6:34; 1 Samuel 10:6, 10). By enabling Mary to conceive a child while she is still a virgin, God's Spirit brings together the physical and the spiritual means to cause what we call "the incarnation": God in the flesh (John 1:14). The whole matter is another way of God's demonstration of His presence among His people (Matthew 1:23).

All of this helps us as readers to know that this *Son of God* has His beginning now only in the sense that this is a unique manifestation of God as Son. He has existed from all eternity (John 1:1). He becomes flesh (John 1:14) in Mary's womb to be a unique manifestation of God as Son (1 Timothy 3:16). There never has been a greater communication of who God is and of His care for us. The divine and the human will now be teamed together to accomplish God's purposes. Praise God!

36. And, behold, thy cousin Elisabeth, she hath also conceived a son in her old age; and this is the sixth month with her, who was called barren.

To help Mary understand this whole setting, the angel Gabriel gives additional revelation concerning the status of her relative *Elisabeth*. Their exact relationship is not clear by the term in the text. What our printed text calls a *cousin* is a

"Mary, you have found favor with God."

"Mary treasured up all these things and pondered them in her heart." —Luke 1:30; 2:19, NIV

Visual for lesson 2. *Display this visual at the beginning of your session. Leave it on display until after lesson 4.*

general term. The age difference suggests that the two women are not first cousins—daughters of siblings. Since Elisabeth is of the tribe of Levi and Mary of the tribe of Judah, their kinship is on the mother's side for at least one of the women. Perhaps Elisabeth is Mary's mother's aunt or some other more distant relative.

The important thing is not the human aspect, but the divine. God has acted for Elisabeth; He has nullified that which had been impossible for her. He can still do anything, even something greater. He can cause a virgin to conceive a child!

37. For with God nothing shall be impossible.

Words with the very same impact are given to Sarah in Genesis 18:14: "Is any thing too hard for the Lord?" Probably Mary knows these words. Still, it must be hard for her to think of having such a place of favor with God. As an outcome, we notice in the next verse that Mary demonstrates greater faith than either her ancestor Sarah (Genesis 18:12-14) or her contemporary Zechariah (Luke 1:18-20).

C. The Commitment (v. 38)

38. And Mary said, Behold the handmaid of the Lord; be it unto me according to thy word. And the angel departed from her.

Mary states her submission to the Lord's will in words similar to that found in some Old Testament settings. (See the responses of Hannah in 1 Samuel 1:18 and Abigail in 1 Samuel 25:41.) In place of potential shame and embarrassment over a premarital pregnancy stands faith and submission. She has been God's servant in the past, and she is ready for God's role for her in the future. Mary surrenders her whole being to God's will. [See question #4, page 136.]

III. Mary's Message (Luke 1:46-49)

After Mary accepted the angel's announcement with faith and commitment to God's will, she went to visit Elisabeth. Knowing what the angel had told her about Elisabeth's pregnancy, this would be an occasion to strengthen her faith. Still, she did not know how all this revelation would fit together in God's plan. When she arrived, she was further amazed at the special greeting given by Elisabeth (cf. last week's lesson).

A. Her Praise (vv. 46, 47)

46, 47. And Mary said, My soul doth magnify the Lord, and my spirit hath rejoiced in God my Saviour.

Just as Elisabeth has delivered a message by a power more than her own, *Mary* responds with a declaration that shows that her thoughts and longings are ever directed toward *God* (Luke 1:46-55). This hymn of praise—often called "the Magnificat" from the first word in the Latin translation—shows us a wide range of spiritual comprehension. There are elements here that reflect thoughts presented in the Psalms and in the song of Hannah (1 Samuel 2:1-10).

Verses 46 and 47 show the Hebrew parallelism that is common in the Psalms. Notice how the second line (v. 47) essentially repeats the first line (v. 46) in different words.

B. Her Status (v. 48)

48. For he hath regarded the low estate of his handmaiden: for, behold, from henceforth all generations shall call me blessed.

Mary sees herself as a nobody whom God has made into a somebody by His grace. Her faith, reflected in her utterance, gives her the courage to accept her role. So sure is she of God's promises

---

Home Daily Bible Readings

Monday, Dec. 2—Joseph Believes God (Matthew 1:18-25)
Tuesday, Dec. 3—Visitors From the East (Matthew 2:1-12)
Wednesday, Dec. 4—Joseph Moves the Family to Egypt (Matthew 2:13-18)
Thursday, Dec. 5—The Family Returns to Galilee (Matthew 2:19-23)
Friday, Dec. 6—The Righteous Please God (Proverbs 15:1-9)
Saturday, Dec. 7—The Lord Watches Over the Righteous (Psalm 1:1-6)
Sunday, Dec. 8—The Branch of Righteousness (Isaiah 11:1-5)

---

she speaks as if everything is already completed. (In that her statement is like the messages of the Old Testament prophets.) God's plan is in motion!

Mary knows she is *blessed*, and that results in obvious joy. But this joy is not the type that is connected with entertainment or social events that delight one's ego. It is a deeper satisfaction, for it is the Spirit of God that brings true joy: "The Spirit itself beareth witness with our spirit, that we are the children of God" (Romans 8:16).

C. His Power (v. 49)

49. For he that is mighty hath done to me great things; and holy is his name.

Mary knows the reality of God's goodness and greatness. She knows the message of Psalm 103:17, "But the mercy of the Lord is from everlasting to everlasting upon them that fear him, and his righteousness unto children's children." In spite of human frailty, God's servant can know God's greatness as she yields herself to His power. Thinking on her own insignificance, she acknowledges that God alone is all in all. How is He to be identified? *His name*, reflecting His whole character, is beyond expression! The spiritual insight in the Magnificat reassures us today of the power of the Almighty.

Conclusion

A. His Call+Our Willingness=His Means

When Mary responds to God's call with willingness, the result is a means for God to accomplish His purposes. Mary is a great model as a servant of the Lord. [See question #5, page 136.]

In that respect, this event in the life of Mary is not an end in itself. We are made aware that there is an enduring principle involved because the Word of God confronts us, too. This Word contains a personal message for us. Our response to that message will reflect our commitment to Christ and His purposes for the church. As with Mary's life as a whole, there may be both joy and sorrow connected with our willing response. Each of us has our own unique part to play in God's plan as we prepare ourselves for "every good work" (2 Timothy 2:21).

B. Prayer

Almighty God, Your workings are beyond our comprehension. Yet help us, through the model of Mary, to see how You can work through us in accomplishing Your purposes in Your kingdom. In Jesus' name, amen.

C. Thought to Remember

God does His work today through willing hearts and hands.

Learning by Doing

This page contains an alternative lesson plan emphasizing learning activities.
Classes desiring such student involvement will find these suggestions helpful.

Learning Goals

After this lesson students will be able to:

1. Cite the details concerning God's call of Mary and her significant response.

2. Express confidence that seemingly impossible tasks undertaken in submission to God's will are possible.

3. Express a commitment born of faith and hope to do what God is wanting to accomplish in their lives.

Into the Lesson

Prepare a visual with the following open-ended sentences. (These are also included in the student book *Adult Bible Class*.)

1. A very difficult time for me to be submissive to God is when _____.

2. A person who models a submissive spirit to God is _____ (name) because _____.

3. Being submissive to God's will is easier to talk about than to do because _____.

4. It is easier/harder (choose one) for me to be submissive to God today than ten years ago because _____.

Ask class members to work in groups of three or four. Each person may choose to respond to any of statement numbers 2, 3, or 4. Allow about six to eight minutes for them to report. Then ask everyone to identify an answer to statement 1. They do not need to reveal this to the group. Make the transition to Bible study by stating, "We all have areas of our lives that we may find difficult to submit to God. However, as we glimpse Mary's spirit, we may find encouragement and help in learning this godly trait."

Into the Word

Give three readers a copy of today's text, Luke 1:26-38, 46-49. They are to read the parts of the narrator, the angel, and Mary. Have the Scriptures highlighted that each person is to read.

Explain how this lesson dovetails with last week's study of Elisabeth and Zechariah.

Lead a discussion of the following questions. (Those with asterisks are also in the *Adult Bible Class* workbook.)

*1. The lesson commentary says, "One might expect an angel to appear to a priest in glorious Jerusalem. But to have Gabriel appear in Nazareth—and to a young peasant woman (cf. Luke 1:48)—is most surprising." What do you think the writer meant by this distinction? What does this say to you?

2. Verse 27 speaks of Mary's engagement. What can you tell us about the process of engagement and marriage in this culture? How did this cause concern for Mary and Joseph? (Use the lesson commentary to clarify answers.)

*3. It was prophesied that the Messiah was to be born of a virgin. (Write Isaiah 7:14 on a poster board and display it.) Why do you think God decided to make Jesus' birth supernatural?

Ask the class to put themselves in Mary's place. Mary must have been surprised, puzzled, honored, humbled, and frightened. Read Luke 1:28-37. Then, in pairs or small groups, jot notes on the questions you imagine were in Mary's mind. Allow groups to report their answers.

Remind the class of Mary's response: "Behold the handmaid of the Lord." Ask what Mary was implying by calling herself that. After their responses, identify two Old Testament women who used that title for themselves: Hannah (1 Samuel 1:18) and Abigail (1 Samuel 25:41).

Ask the class, "How did Mary's willingness to be God's handmaid make it possible for the 'impossible' to happen—the virgin birth?" Ask also, "Why does God not work apart from the will of the person He chooses as His servant?"

Into Life

Prepare and display two posters. The first should say "God's Angel + Willing Women = Means for God to Accomplish His Purpose." Explain the meaning of this statement as you display the poster. Then put up the second poster reading "God's Word + Committed Christian = Vessel for God to Use." Use the commentary for ideas to emphasize how Mary's experience reveals this abiding principle for life today. Remind the class of the opening exercise, where they identified times when they had difficulty submitting to God's will. God calls us, like Mary, to take risks and to let Him work though us.

Ask small groups to pray together. Ask for one person in each group to pray about one of the following: (1) thank God for speaking to us through His Word, the Bible; (2) offer God your promise to try to trust Him and His wisdom more and more in your daily life; (3) ask God to work in our lives, helping us to learn to be submissive to Him and willing to do His will.

Let's Talk It Over

*The questions on this page are designed to promote discussion of the lesson
by the class and to encourage application of the lesson Scriptures. The answers
provided are only discussion starters. Let your class talk it over from there.*

1. Our lesson writer notes that "it means something to be chosen." It means someone thinks highly of you for some reason. It means you must respond in some way. What do you find most significant about being among the "chosen people of God"?

The New Testament uses terms like "elect," "called out," and "chosen" to describe Christians. God chose to act to save us, to redeem us by the blood of His Son. That speaks volumes about how much God loves us. (See John 3:16.) It also places demands on us. We must respond to His call. We must respond initially to accept His gift of grace. But we must also continue to accept the call. Jesus said the disciple must take up his cross *daily* and follow Jesus (Luke 9:23). That is a responsibility not to be taken lightly.

2. What honor or position have you received that created a sobering responsibility? How did your faith help you to handle both the honor and the responsibility in a successful manner?

Parenthood is an obvious answer to this one. The joy of becoming a parent is hard to duplicate. At the same time, it is a life-and-death responsibility. Teaching is another example (see James 3:1), as is any leadership position in the church. Hebrews 13:17 reminds leaders that they will have to give an accounting for the exercise of their responsibility. Encourage the students to be specific about their ministries and other positions of responsibility.

3. Mary probably did not grasp the significance of Jesus as Savior—at least, not right away. Many people today do not grasp the significance either. The concept of sin is foreign to many today, so they do not realize their need to be saved from it. How can we impress on people the need for salvation and the truth that Jesus is the only one who can provide it?

One of the challenges facing the church today is the idea that there are no absolutes. To label something as "sin" or "wrong" is about the only thing this culture sees as "wrong." Whatever ideas your class has to challenge that misguided thinking needs to be explored and used if at all possible.

Perhaps one way to do this is with personal testimonies. The "story" seems especially impor-

tant in this culture. Christians can tell their own stories. They can tell how they were on the wrong path and found the Lord. This makes the statement of absolutes more a confession than a condemnation, and it may be better received.

4. Mary's obedience and submission challenge us. What risks are we willing to take in order to comply with God's commands to live the gospel and to take the gospel to others?

You can begin by noting the risks Mary took. Her pregnancy could have destroyed her relationship with Joseph. (It nearly did! See Matthew 1:18, 19.) It could have ruined her reputation in her community and spoiled her relationship with her own family. Still, she obeyed, and she trusted God to work things out.

Have any of your students risked family relationships for their faith? How about a job—has anyone had to stand up to a boss and say, "That's not right. I won't do that." Perhaps some have been fired or voluntarily left a job because they refused to participate in unethical dealings. Encourage each one who shares, especially if the risks are still active and the students' trials not completed!

5. As the mother of the Messiah, Mary stands apart from all other women in history. Even so, the details about her are amazingly brief. God's regard for her shows she has His approval. With that approval there is the understanding that she will be remembered beyond her death because of the part she has in His plan to bring salvation to the world. What encouragement does that offer us today in our service?

Most of us will never be famous. We may be like Mary before the arrival of Gabriel—faithful and pure, but relatively unknown and unheralded. We do for the Lord what no one ever could pay us enough to do for anyone else. We do it for God. But sometimes we think it would be nice if someone noticed and said thank you. We wonder whether we are making any difference. We can rest assured that, as God had noticed Mary, He knows us, and He knows our faithfulness. Our work for Him is not in vain (1 Corinthians 15:58; Galatians 6:9). As we serve Him, helping others to find the way of salvation, we too will be remembered (Hebrews 6:10).

Joseph: A Righteous Man

DEVOTIONAL READING: Isaiah 11:1-5.

BACKGROUND SCRIPTURE: Matthew 1:18-25;
2:13-23.

PRINTED TEXT: Matthew 1:18-21, 24, 25;
2:13-15, 19-21, 23.

Matthew 1:18-21, 24, 25

18 Now the birth of Jesus Christ was on this wise: When as his mother Mary was espoused to Joseph, before they came together, she was found with child of the Holy Ghost.

19 Then Joseph her husband, being a just man, and not willing to make her a public example, was minded to put her away privily.

20 But while he thought on these things, behold, the angel of the Lord appeared unto him in a dream, saying, Joseph, thou son of David, fear not to take unto thee Mary thy wife: for that which is conceived in her is of the Holy Ghost.

21 And she shall bring forth a son, and thou shalt call his name JESUS: for he shall save his people from their sins.

· · · · · · · · · · ·

24 Then Joseph being raised from sleep did as the angel of the Lord had bidden him, and took unto him his wife:

25 And knew her not till she had brought forth her firstborn son: and he called his name JESUS.

Matthew 2:13-15, 19-21, 23

13 And when they were departed, behold, the angel of the Lord appeareth to Joseph in a dream, saying, Arise, and take the young child and his mother, and flee into Egypt, and be thou there until I bring thee word: for Herod will seek the young child to destroy him.

14 When he arose, he took the young child and his mother by night, and departed into Egypt:

15 And was there until the death of Herod: that it might be fulfilled which was spoken of the Lord by the prophet, saying, Out of Egypt have I called my son.

· · · · · · · · · · · ·

19 But when Herod was dead, behold, an angel of the Lord appeareth in a dream to Joseph in Egypt,

20 Saying, Arise, and take the young child and his mother, and go into the land of Israel: for they are dead which sought the young child's life.

21 And he arose, and took the young child and his mother, and came into the land of Israel.

· · · · · · · · · · · ·

23 And he came and dwelt in a city called Nazareth: that it might be fulfilled which was spoken by the prophets, He shall be called a Nazarene.

GOLDEN TEXT: Joseph . . . did as the angel of the Lord had bidden him, and took unto him his wife: and knew her not till she had brought forth her firstborn son: and he called his name JESUS.—Matthew 1:24, 25.

Portraits of Faith
Unit 1: Personalities Involved
in the Messiah's Coming
(Lessons 1-5)

Lesson Aims

After participating in this lesson, each student will be able to:

1. Recall the details of God's call to Joseph and his significant response.

2. Tell how the responses Joseph made to divine direction typify how modern believers should respond to the will of God.

3. State one way he or she can view the challenge to one's faith to follow the model of Joseph.

Lesson Outline

INTRODUCTION
    A. Portrait of Joseph
    B. Lesson Background
I. JOSEPH'S CRUCIAL DECISION (Matthew 1:18-21, 24, 25)
    A. Pondering a Sober Reality (vv. 18, 19)
    B. Receiving Divine Direction (vv. 20, 21)
    C. Responding With Humble Obedience (vv. 24, 25)
      Out of the Script
II. JOSEPH'S PARENTAL ROLE (Matthew 2:13-15, 19-21, 23)
    A. Second Divine Direction (vv. 13-15)
    B. Third Divine Direction (vv. 19, 20)
    C. Parental Response and Divine Confirmation (vv. 21, 23)
CONCLUSION
    A. Joseph, a Model
    B. Prayer
    C. Thought to Remember

Introduction

A. Portrait of Joseph

Getting to know Joseph, the carpenter of Nazareth, is important. The portrait given us in the Scriptures may seem sketchy. It lacks many of the details that our twenty-first-century minds might desire. But the picture presented is clear in that he is the proper man to be Mary's husband and the guardian of her child Jesus. His genealogy emphasizes that he is descended from the line of King David. Such lineage is very important to the Jewish people because of their heritage and their hope. Their redemption lies in this promised one, even though for the most part

they think in terms of a political, earthly deliverance (cf. Acts 1:6).

Who is the person you have as the model of a righteous person? What woman? What man? Since we desire to be righteous before God, we need to seek out models in whose lives we see that the gospel really produces desired results. If we have had God-fearing parents, they were our first models. As we grew, our experiences have resulted in contacts with many others who have become important as we admired their lifestyles. Today's lesson offers us another role model. It is Joseph, a "just" or righteous man. His responses toward God's message for him challenge us to be righteous as well.

B. Lesson Background

Flesh-and-blood people, with all their strengths and weaknesses, are important to God in achieving His plans for humanity. In fact, it is impressive to observe that Matthew begins his account of the life of Christ with due consideration for the role of Joseph. We are not told his age, his education, the details of his parents and home life, or other matters that our curiosity might desire. Those issues are not significant to Matthew's purpose.

What Matthew wants to bring to our attention is the quality of man that Joseph is. That quality is revealed by the way he deals with issues that call for decisions on his part. In these matters, Matthew lets us know that God trusts Joseph with divine direction. Such direction does not always take the same form, but in each circumstance Joseph shows himself to be a man after God's own heart. By his responses, Joseph's portrait is that of a righteous man.

I. Joseph's Crucial Decision (Matthew 1:18-21, 24, 25)

Living in a fallen world as we do, we are sometimes forced to choose between uncomfortable alternatives. Joseph faces just such a sobering choice.

A. Pondering a Sober Reality (vv. 18, 19)

18. Now the birth of Jesus Christ was on this wise: When as his mother Mary was espoused to Joseph, before they came together, she was found with child of the Holy Ghost.

Newer translations say Mary was "engaged" or "pledged to be married" instead of using the older word *espoused*. This sounds more contemporary to modern ears, but it does not adequately describe Mary's relationship *to Joseph*. This pledging is much more than what we commonly think of as an "engagement." For the ancient Jew, marriage vows are exchanged at the time of the betrothal, and divorce is required to break them. There is usually about a year until the bride takes residence at the husband's house. During this time, her purity is established and the dowry paid. Residency with the husband—and physical union that consummates the marriage—does not take place until after the wedding feast.

During this interval Mary is found to be *with child*. We know from Luke's account how this has come to be. (See last week's lesson.) But Matthew delays explanation, and the reader puts him- or herself in Joseph's place to wonder how it has happened.

19. Then Joseph her husband, being a just man, and not willing to make her a public example, was minded to put her away privily.

Joseph evidently believes that Mary has been with another man. This would be adultery under the laws of betrothal. Has Mary not explained the situation to Joseph? Has she explained but Joseph found the story incredible? These are questions we cannot answer. Either way, at this point Mary can do nothing but trust God to ensure her safety and well-being.

While adultery carries the death penalty under the Law of Moses (Deuteronomy 22:23, 24), such a penalty is rarely invoked in Joseph's day. As the New Testament era dawns, Joseph is freer in his options and can give Mary either a public or a private divorce. By choosing a private, quiet divorce, Joseph will be conforming to the law while being compassionate at the same time.

Joseph's compassion in not wanting *to make* Mary *a public example* is now at odds with the fact that he is *a just man*. On the one hand, he wants to make the situation as easy for her as possible because of his concern for her well-being. But on the other hand, the fact that he is just (or righteous) makes him unwilling to go ahead with the marriage, because then others would logically (but wrongly) conclude that he is the other guilty party in this out-of-wedlock pregnancy. [See question #1, page 144.]

Surely Joseph prays much about all this before he acts. As his son James will later write, "The effectual fervent prayer of a righteous man availeth much" (James 5:16). God's answer follows.

B. Receiving Divine Direction (vv. 20, 21)

20. But while he thought on these things, behold, the angel of the Lord appeared unto him in a dream, saying, Joseph, thou son of David, fear not to take unto thee Mary thy wife: for that which is conceived in her is of the Holy Ghost.

Joseph has decided already on his course of action (v. 19) when an *angel* intervenes with a message from God. There are several elements in

that message that catch his attention. First, the angel addresses him as *Joseph, . . . son of David*. This reminder of his lineage to King David perhaps will bring to Joseph's mind (after he awakens from the sleep and its *dream*) the ancient promise of a Messiah to solve Israel's despair—a Messiah from David's line (Isaiah 16:5; 55:3; Jeremiah 33:14-17). But he undoubtedly does not yet have the comprehension to put all the circumstances together in a way that results in a clear understanding for him in his dilemma with *Mary*.

Joseph must clearly see, however, that this divine announcement is a means to reinforce his faith and to help him to act with confidence in doing God's will. Perhaps Joseph's faith will be strengthened after he awakens and recalls the accounts of divine messengers that God has sent to others in times long past (cf. Genesis 16:7-12; 22:11-18; Exodus 3:1–4:17). His fear of what other people might say will not be as important as what God communicates. God reassures him that Mary is pure, even if she is pregnant. He is to take her as his *wife*. He is to provide for and protect her as her husband. He is to accept the fact that God is the one who has brought about this conception.

21. And she shall bring forth a son, and thou shalt call his name JESUS: for he shall save his people from their sins.

The unfolding revelation provides Joseph with greater insight regarding his role in God's plan. Joseph is to have parental responsibility as reflected in the instruction on naming the Child *Jesus*. Joseph knows, of course, that this name means "the Lord is salvation." But how will it be possible for this Child to *save his people from their sins?* The divine messenger doesn't say.

Visual for lesson 3. *Post this visual at the beginning of the session. Note how Joseph's life demonstrates righteousness.*

Only God knows how it will all be resolved. He gives Joseph only what he needs to know at this point in the unfolding life of Christ.

In the verses not included in the printed text, Matthew reminds the reader of the Messianic promise in Isaiah 7:14 concerning the virgin birth. God provided deliverance from enemies in Isaiah's time. Such a deliverance becomes a "type" of the deliverance God provides in sending Jesus as Savior. He is also Immanuel, "God with us" (Matthew 1:23). [See question #2, page 144.]

C. Responding With Humble Obedience (vv. 24, 25)

24. Then Joseph being raised from sleep did as the angel of the Lord had bidden him, and took unto him his wife:

As Mary obeys in Luke 1:38, so *Joseph* responds in faith based on a message from God. The betrothal period ends, and Joseph takes Mary to live with him in his home. Jesus will thus be the legitimate son and heir to the throne of David (Matthew 1:1, 16; cf. Deuteronomy 23:2).

Joseph's actions are like those of other men and women of the Old Testament who obeyed God's call. Such responses may seem out of harmony with common sense. But Matthew wants his readers to catch a clear portrait of Joseph, an obedient and righteous man, as evidenced by his response to God's call. [See question #3, page 144.]

Joseph thus serves as a model for us in how we can respond properly to God's message. Our roles are not the same as his, and today God communicates His will for us in the pages of Scripture rather than dreams. Even so, we also have a place in God's plan to bring His saving gospel to all the world today. People are still the instruments to accomplish God's saving work.

OUT OF THE SCRIPT

A little church was having the final rehearsal for the Christmas pageant. Then distressing news came to the director. The little boy who was to play the part of Joseph was sick and would not be able to be in the pageant. The director said, "I guess we'll just have to write Joseph out of the script."

Sometimes that is what we do. We focus entirely on the other "players" in the drama and fail to pay attention to Joseph. If God chose Mary with care, we may be certain that He took into consideration the man to be her husband. After all, he would be the man who would fill the role of father through the years of Jesus' childhood. If the character of Mary was the first consideration in God's choice, the character of Joseph must have been the close second. So we do well today

to pay attention to Joseph. What a great example he provides for a Father's Day sermon! What a great role model! What a great example for family life and for the godly home! What a great example he is for anyone, father or not.

All of us face situations where we need to show kindness, where we must trust even when we cannot understand. We all face situations where we must take the first step without knowing what the next step is going to be. We know so little about this carpenter from Nazareth, but what we do know warms our hearts, and encourages us to be better than we are.   —R. C. S.

25. And knew her not till she had brought forth her firstborn son: and he called his name JESUS.

The phrase *knew her not* makes clear that Joseph did not have any sexual relations with Mary until after the birth of *Jesus.* The phrase that begins with the word *till* lets us safely assume that Mary and Joseph enjoyed a normal husband and wife relationship after Jesus' birth. (Jesus' siblings are mentioned in Mark 6:3.) Joseph "officially" gives Jesus His *name* eight days after His birth (Luke 2:21).

II. Joseph's Parental Role (Matthew 2:13-15, 19-21, 23)

The birth of Jesus now draws the ire of a petty tyrant. Although this threat is a deadly challenge to the young family, it is also an occasion for a new father to demonstrate his obedience to God once again.

A. Second Divine Direction (vv. 13-15)

13. And when they were departed, behold, the angel of the Lord appeareth to Joseph in a dream, saying, Arise, and take the young child and his mother, and flee into Egypt, and be thou there until I bring thee word: for Herod will seek the young child to destroy him.

They refers to the wise men (or "Magi") of Matthew 2:1-12. After these men conclude their visit to see the *child,* the one who is "King of the Jews" (2:2), Joseph receives a second divine direction. *Herod* the Great has interviewed the wise men about their quest, and he is greatly troubled (2:3). When Herod is upset, everyone knows that someone will pay. Herod is a ruthless ruler, caring for no one but himself. His position of power is paramount. If that is threatened, not even his wives or his sons are safe.

God providentially directs the wise men not to return to Herod, but to go to their own country another way (2:12). Failing in his attempt to get the information he desires through the wise men,

Herod is furious. To "play it safe," he decides to get rid of any baby who could be a future threat to his throne: he orders the death of all infants two years old and younger in Bethlehem and the surrounding area (2:16).

Yet there is a power in place greater than that of Herod. God takes care of His Son by sending an *angel* to Joseph *in a dream* with specific instructions. The border of *Egypt* is about sixty miles from Bethlehem, or a three-day journey. At this time a colony of about a million Jews lives there. They may be descendants of those who settled there in Jeremiah's time and at other periods (1 Kings 11:40; Jeremiah 26:21-23; 43:7).

Egypt, once a place of refuge (Genesis 46), became a place of oppression for God's people prior to Moses' day. But for Joseph and his family, it is once again a safe haven. God is making sure of that, but it is still important for Joseph to carry out his parental role as family protector and provider.

14. When he arose, he took the young child and his mother by night, and departed into Egypt.

Having received the instruction, Joseph knows he must react immediately. They begin their journey at *night* because delay can mean the death of the *child*, for whose care he is responsible. Providentially, the gifts from the wise men will provide for their needs in the days ahead. Sometimes it is only "after the fact" that we have the insight to recognize the providential hand of God in meeting our needs and in providing wisdom. The importance of this Child is seen in the fact that He is mentioned before His *mother* (also in 2:13, 20, 21). [See question #4, page 144.]

15. And was there until the death of Herod: that it might be fulfilled which was spoken of the Lord by the prophet, saying, Out of Egypt have I called my son.

The Jewish settlement in *Egypt* will welcome Joseph and his family, but that place is not to be a permanent residence for them. Just how long they will stay we cannot tell. *The death of Herod* can be dated as March of 4 B.C., probably within just a few months of Jesus' birth. We do not know how many months or years Joseph waited after that before the Lord told him to return to the land of Israel.

Matthew reminds his readers that Joseph's response to the divine direction makes the exodus of the children of Israel a "type" of this event: "I . . . called my son out of Egypt" (Hosea 11:1). The deliverance from bondage in Egypt through the leadership of Moses over fourteen centuries previously will be overshadowed by the deliverance for the Christ child, and, more significantly, the deliverance from eternal death through the Christ as Savior from sin.

B. Third Divine Direction (vv. 19, 20)

19. But when Herod was dead, behold, an angel of the Lord appeareth in a dream to Joseph in Egypt.

This is now the fourth *dream* mentioned in Matthew (see 1:20; 2:12, 13), and the third dream noting an *angel of the Lord* (see 1:20; 2:13). Even though *Herod* the Great is *dead,* Herod Archelaus, the worst of his sons, is now ruling in Judea (2:22). Returning to Bethlehem would not be the safest thing to do. But whatever the direction God has for *Joseph,* we will see him ready to obey.

20. Saying, Arise, and take the young child and his mother, and go into the land of Israel: for they are dead which sought the young child's life.

Exactly who *are dead* (other than Herod himself) is hard to determine. The plural *they* may be a tie-in to Exodus 4:19 where we see Moses being directed to return *to* Egypt after threats against his life disappear. On the other hand, "they" may include Herod's oldest son Antipater, whom Herod had executed shortly before his own death. (A saying that circulated stated that it was better to be one of Herod's pigs than one of his sons.) In any case, we will continue to see Joseph trusting God's direction.

C. Parental Response and Divine Confirmation (vv. 21, 23)

21. And he arose, and took the young child and his mother, and came into the land of Israel.

Again, we are not given the details connected with this journey. The main point that presents itself is Joseph's responsible reaction. He trusts the all-knowing God. God has directed him in the past, and he knows that God will not fail him in whatever tests are ahead as he fulfills his parental role. Verse 22 informs us that God further warns

---

How to Say It

ANTIPATER. An-*tih*-puh-ter.
ARCHELAUS. Are-kuh-*lay*-us.
BETHLEHEM. *Beth*-lih-hem.
GALILEE. *Gal*-uh-lee.
GIDEON. *Gid*-e-un.
HEROD. *Hair*-ud.
ISAIAH. Eye-*zay*-uh.
JEREMIAH. Jair-uh-*my*-uh.
JUDEA. Joo-*dee*-uh.
MAGI. *May*-jye or *Madge*-eye.
MESSIAH. Meh-*sigh*-uh.
MESSIANIC. Mess-ee-*an*-ick.
NAZARENE. *Naz*-uh-reen.
NAZARETH. *Naz*-uh-reth.
PRIVILY. *prih*-vuh-lee.

Joseph of the continuing danger in Judea, and as a result the young family ends up in Galilee.

23. And he came and dwelt in a city called Nazareth: that it might be fulfilled which was spoken by the prophets, He shall be called a Nazarene.

Nazareth, about seventy miles north of Bethlehem, is a safe place for Joseph to take Jesus and Mary to live. Nazareth is Joseph and Mary's former home (Luke 1:26, 27; 2:4, 39). With family ties and familiar surroundings, Joseph will support his family there by working as a carpenter.

Nazareth may seem to be an unlikely place as the home of the one to be the Messiah. Being *called a Nazarene* is not a compliment (see John 1:46). There may be a reference here to various Old Testament prophecies that allude to the Messiah as being despised (cf. Isaiah 53:3; Psalm 22:6; Daniel 9:26). The word *Nazarene* also sounds like the Hebrew word that is translated as "branch" in Isaiah 11:1.

Conclusion

A. Joseph, a Model

From Matthew's narrative we catch a welcome portrait of Joseph in his role as the earthly stepfather to Jesus of Nazareth. We have examined with interest those occasions where Joseph receives divine direction when crucial decisions have to be made with regard to the Child and His mother, Mary. Joseph accepts with faith and obedience his parental role and all directions from God.

It can be interesting to let our "sanctified imaginations" ponder what the home in Nazareth might have been like. The house probably was one story with a center room and other rooms adjoining. There would have been simple furniture, beds rolled up during the day, an

oven, and water pots in place. Jesus, with His brothers and sisters, would have shared household duties. They would have attended the synagogue school, and they would have been taught the Law of Moses at home. Joseph may even have owned a copy of some portions of the Old Testament. They speak Aramaic and Greek, and they probably can read Hebrew. In the home Joseph is an upright man and Mary is one of the rarest of all women. Such a home would be a type of "greenhouse" for the Child who will have an impact upon generations to come—indeed, upon all of history. [See question #5, page 144.]

The life of Joseph invites us to view his decisions against an Old Testament backdrop. Joseph's reaction to divine direction can result in judgment or blessing—it all depends on the responses that follow the messages. If there is obedience to the divine direction, then there can be blessing. But if disobedience, there is penalty and due judgment. Righteousness results from obedience, and unrighteousness is the alternative—doom, separation from God. God provides the opportunity. We make the choices.

We all are (or should be) continually concerned about doing God's will. Each new day brings life situations that call for choices. We as Christians want to make the right choices, to do what is pleasing to God. It would be easy, we think, if God would give us direct revelation as He did Joseph in this context. Or perhaps Gideon's request regarding the fleece in Judges 6:36-40 is our reason for expecting God to do the same thing for us. But remember that all do not have the same roles before God. Gideon's role as judge is one thing, and Joseph's role in caring for Jesus and Mary is another. Although none of us have such roles today, we do have the direction provided by God's Word, as well as the guiding presence of His Spirit in our lives. As we study His Word and submit our will to His, we will have the guidance we need in all choices. May Joseph serve as a model and example of obedience and righteousness to us all!

B. Prayer

Almighty God, may we have that willingness of Joseph to respond to Your revealed Word as we seek direction in making decisions in our lives. Help us to comprehend the importance of our examples of proper lifestyles for those who look to us to see the gospel at work. How thankful we are that Jesus has given real meaning to life. In Jesus' name, amen.

C. Thought to Remember

Emulate your godly role models so others will emulate you!

Home Daily Bible Readings

Monday, Dec. 9—You Have Found Favor (Luke 1:26-33)

Tuesday, Dec. 10—I Am the Lord's Servant (Luke 1:34-38)

Wednesday, Dec. 11—Elisabeth Greets Mary (Luke 1:39-45)

Thursday, Dec. 12—Mary's Song of Praise (Luke 1:46-56)

Friday, Dec. 13—I Praise God's Mighty Deeds (Psalm 71:15-21)

Saturday, Dec. 14—Great Are God's Works (Psalm 111:1-6)

Sunday, Dec. 15—Magnify the Lord With Me (Psalm 34:1-5)

Learning by Doing

This page contains an alternative lesson plan emphasizing learning activities.
Classes desiring such student involvement will find these suggestions helpful.

Learning Goals

After this lesson each student will be able to:

1. Recall the details of God's call to Joseph and his significant response.

2. Tell how the responses Joseph made to divine direction typify how modern believers should respond to the will of God.

3. State one way he or she can view the challenge to one's faith to follow the model of Joseph.

Into the Lesson

This lesson will emphasize making godly choices. As class members arrive, offer them two choices of snacks, healthful fruit (bananas, apples, oranges) and tasty (but not-so-good-for-you) pastries. Coffee and juice also will be appropriate. Do not comment on their choice of snack.

As you begin the lesson, write or post the word *Choices* at the front of the room. Ask class members to share choices they had to make recently. These may be tough choices and significant decisions or the choices may be simple, everyday choices such as whether to work late *vs.* eating dinner with the family or whether or not to break a diet. Allow several minutes.

Make the transition to Bible study by reminding them that life is filled with choices. Some seem small and insignificant, like whether to choose healthful fruit for breakfast or tasty but fattening pastries. Other choices are tough. One thing is certain, we are all called upon to make choices that may or may not reflect a healthy relationship with God. For those choices, however, we do have some help. Today, our help is in the form of a model. Our model could have said, "No! I won't do it!" Instead, he chose to obey and became an encouraging model of righteousness.

Into the Word

Give each student a printed copy of Matthew 1:18-21, 24, 25; 2:13-15, 19-21, 23. Leave a margin on one side of the text for the student to make notes. Use the following exercises to explore the Word.

Background on Joseph. Use the Lesson Background to prepare remarks about the setting for Joseph's adventure. Include comments about Matthew's choice to emphasize the qualities of Joseph's character and his obedience. Also remind the class of the process of betrothal and marriage in first-century Israel. (See last week's

lesson.) Explain that Joseph is called upon to make several tough choices critical to God's plan.

Clues to Joseph's Character. Ask class members (in teams or small groups) to read Matthew 1:18-21, 24, 25 and circle phrases or sentences that give clues to Joseph's character. Answers may include "being a just man," "not willing to make her a public example," "was minded to put her away privily," "while he thought on these things," "and took unto him his wife." Ask what character trait each phrase exemplifies (e.g., considerate, merciful, intelligent, obedient).

Tough Choices. Ask the groups to number the choices Joseph had to make as they read the text. Then in the margin they are to write a note on what the issue or choice was that he had to make. These will include verse 19 (whether or not to humiliate Mary), verse 20 (whether or not to obey the angel and take Mary as his wife), verse 21 (whether to name the baby as instructed), verse 25 (whether to have sexual intercourse with her), 2:13 (whether or not to flee to Egypt), 2:20 (whether or not to go back to Israel).

Discussion. As groups report, list these decisions on the board. Highlight the more difficult choices Joseph made by asking these questions:

Matthew 1:24: Why would this be a particularly tough choice? What are some of the issues Joseph had to face in order to make this choice?

Matthew 1:25: Why do you suppose Joseph chose not to have sexual contact with Mary until Jesus was born? Did they have intimate relations after Jesus was born? Did they have other children? (See Matthew 13:55, 56.)

Matthew 2:13: How is this a particularly tough choice? *(Economics, travel safety, home.)*

Matthew 2:21: Was this one of the easier choices for Joseph? Why or why not?

Into Life

Display four posters. Each is to have one of the following headings: "Parents," "Work/Career," "Husband and Wife," and "Personal." Tell the class, "We are called upon to make tough choices that affect our spiritual health or the spiritual health of those around us. Brainstorm the tough choices that have an impact on our relationship with the Lord." Note the responses on the appropriate posters. Following the exercise, ask for a prayer that Joseph's model will guide our choices and that we will be found righteous in God's eyes.

Let's Talk It Over

The questions on this page are designed to promote discussion of the lesson by the class and to encourage application of the lesson Scriptures. The answers provided are only discussion starters. Let your class talk it over from there.

1. In our day, pregnancy outside of marriage is all too common. Often there is little disgrace or stigma with the situation. How should the church deal with this situation today? How can we, like Joseph, blend compassion with taking a stand for morality?

In denouncing the immorality of casual sex, the church could ostracize those who commit such acts. But that will not help them. On the other hand, in trying to show love to immoral people, the church could lose its voice against their immoral behavior. The Biblical position is between these two extremes. See Acts 15:20; 1 Corinthians 6:9-20; Galatians 5:19 and compare with 1 Corinthians 5:1-11; 2 Corinthians 2:6-11.

Years ago, churches supported homes for unwed mothers, to aid them spiritually, emotionally, and financially. Today, the social stigma of single motherhood is largely gone, but the spiritual and financial problems are as great as ever, and so is the need for the church to provide spiritual counseling, financial help, moral training, and loving concern.

2. How many names and titles of Jesus can you recall? What is significant about each name?

In the New Testament, Jesus is identified by nearly ninety different names and titles, including *Immanuel* (Matthew 1:23), *Son of David* (Matthew 1:1), and *Christ.* Each name or title has special significance in relation to His ministry. *Immanuel* means God with us. It indicates that Jesus was the Incarnation, God in the flesh. The title *Son of David* indicates that Jesus was the descendent of David Who would be the Messiah or Christ, the "anointed one" of God who would deliver His people from bondage. Even the name *Jesus* has special significance. It is the Greek form of the Hebrew name *Joshua,* meaning Savior. It indicates that the one bearing the name would save His people. As Joshua repeatedly saved Old Testament Israel from annihilation during the conquest of the promised land, so Jesus came to save mankind from sin (Acts 4:12).

3. Have you ever had to choose between obedience and "common sense"? How did you handle the situation? What did you learn from it?

Perhaps your students will remember times when parents or teachers gave directions that seemed foolish or contrary to their own desires. Some may even tell of times, before they were Christians, when doing God's will seemed foolish. In each case, the older and/or wiser person no doubt was proved right by later circumstances. As Christians, we need to learn that God, not we, has the answers.

4. When have you looked back on a situation and believed God's providence had been at work—even if you did not recognize it at the time?

Of course, it would require divine inspiration to be absolutely certain of God's acts. We do have his Word, however, that He does in fact act for our benefit. (See Romans 8:28.) And there are many Biblical examples of God's protecting His people so that they can carry out His plans. The angelic rescue of Peter from prison (Acts 12) is one. We can trust that God will providentially protect His people today so that they, too, can continue to carry out His plans. Probably many of your students can recall times when things just seemed to "work out," and we believe God has been at work to make it so. At other times we feel like things are out of control. Later, perhaps, we see how some good came out of the situation. Again, we feel confident God has guided events. Ask the students to be specific about such cases. What did they learn from the events? And be sure to affirm that God's providence is at work even when we haven't the vaguest notion about what He is doing or how He is doing it!

5. The lesson writer says Joseph's home was a type of "greenhouse" for the kind of Child who would have an impact on the world. What characterizes a home today that is a "greenhouse" for people destined to have an impact on the world for the sake of Christ?

Certainly such a home will value the Word of God. Scripture readings and devotional times will be frequent. Talk in such a home will often turn to the Lord and His church, to ministry, to what God can and will do in the lives of those who reside there. The gifts and abilities that God has given each child will be affirmed and nurtured. Ask parents in your class to tell what specifically they do to nurture their children to have an impact for the gospel.

Mary: Mother of the Messiah

DEVOTIONAL READING: Isaiah 9:1-7.

BACKGROUND SCRIPTURE: Luke 2:1-20.

PRINTED TEXT: Luke 2:1, 4-20.

Luke 2:1, 4-20

1 And it came to pass in those days, that there went out a decree from Caesar Augustus, that all the world should be taxed.

. . . .

4 And Joseph also went up from Galilee, out of the city of Nazareth, into Judea, unto the city of David, which is called Bethlehem, (because he was of the house and lineage of David,)

5 To be taxed with Mary his espoused wife, being great with child.

6 And so it was, that, while they were there, the days were accomplished that she should be delivered.

7 And she brought forth her firstborn son, and wrapped him in swaddling clothes, and laid him in a manger; because there was no room for them in the inn.

8 And there were in the same country shepherds abiding in the field, keeping watch over their flock by night.

9 And, lo, the angel of the Lord came upon them, and the glory of the Lord shone round about them; and they were sore afraid.

10 And the angel said unto them, Fear not: for, behold, I bring you good tidings of great joy, which shall be to all people.

11 For unto you is born this day in the city of David a Saviour, which is Christ the Lord.

12 And this shall be a sign unto you; Ye shall find the babe wrapped in swaddling clothes, lying in a manger.

13 And suddenly there was with the angel a multitude of the heavenly host praising God, and saying,

14 Glory to God in the highest, and on earth peace, good will toward men.

15 And it came to pass, as the angels were gone away from them into heaven, the shepherds said one to another, Let us now go even unto Bethlehem, and see this thing which is come to pass, which the Lord hath made known unto us.

16 And they came with haste, and found Mary and Joseph, and the babe lying in a manger.

17 And when they had seen it, they made known abroad the saying which was told them concerning this child.

18 And all they that heard it wondered at those things which were told them by the shepherds.

19 But Mary kept all these things, and pondered them in her heart.

20 And the shepherds returned, glorifying and praising God for all the things that they had heard and seen, as it was told unto them.

GOLDEN TEXT: [Mary] brought forth her firstborn son, and wrapped him in swaddling clothes, and laid him in a manger; because there was no room for them in the inn.—Luke 2:7.

Portraits of Faith
Unit 1: Personalities Involved in the Messiah's Coming
(Lessons 1-5)

Lesson Aims

After participating in this lesson, students will be able to:

1. Tell how Mary—and the shepherds—acted in faith to fulfill God's plan at the birth of Jesus.

2. Describe the way God's providence was at work in the decree of Caesar and the routine work of the shepherds.

3. Express confidence that God has a work for them.

Lesson Outline

INTRODUCTION
   A. Portrait of Messianic Motherhood
   B. Lesson Background
I. GOING TO BETHLEHEM (Luke 2:1, 4, 5)
   A. Taxation Decree (v. 1)
   B. Bethlehem Registration (vv. 4, 5)
II. GIVING BIRTH TO THE SAVIOR (Luke 2:6-17)
   A. In the Fullness of Time (vv. 6, 7)
   B. Announced by Angels (vv. 8-14)
      Freedom From Fear
   C. Visited by Shepherds (vv. 15-17)
III. REACTIONS TO THE BIRTH (Luke 2:18-20)
   A. By Those Around (v. 18)
   B. By Mary (v. 19)
   C. By the Shepherds (v. 20)
CONCLUSION
   A. The Significance of Mary's Motherhood
   B. Prayer
   C. Thought to Remember

Introduction

A. Portrait of Messianic Motherhood

If you were to enter our country home, built in 1969, from the entry hall you might be ushered straight ahead into the parlor or to the left to the family living area. *Parlor* may sound a bit old-fashioned to some, but I designed it to be a very functional room. At the time the house was built, I was preaching in a local church and teaching at a Bible college. There were various times when we needed that separated room for counseling, meetings, or marriage planning. Our home was always very much alive with six children and their activities; but the parlor was always in good array, ready to receive visitors.

In the center of that room is the library table, and a part of the display on it is an antique photo album, keeping with the old-time decor of the whole room. In the album are pictures of family members of generations past. Life stories can accompany those portraits. In this lesson from Luke 2, we are invited into "Luke's parlor" and given the opportunity again to see the portraits on display. This one is a favorite—Mary: Mother of the Messiah. No other woman in all history has had such a ministry in motherhood.

B. Lesson Background

The portraits we have been examining in Luke 1 and Matthew 1 and 2 have given us opportunities to reexamine the lives of those chosen by God to fill certain roles in the advent of the Messiah. The common element that brings them together is the "fullness of the time" in God's plan to provide salvation (Galatians 4:4, 5). We note the places both men and women had. Our purpose in viewing each one has not been to take the spotlight off the Messiah, but rather to see the ways these people and their ministries are necessary in God's plan. We want to see how these complement the ministry of the Messiah, God's anointed. Each has his or her particular importance in the overall picture. These people bring life to geographical settings. Whether it is Jerusalem, Bethlehem, Nazareth, the hill country of Judah, or even some place in Egypt, the places become very real as we recall the events and their characters.

All of these take on fuller dimensions when we awaken to their connections with us and to God's meeting our need in the Messiah. The coming of the Messiah was a turning point in history, as our calendars remind us. Thus, this lesson presents a climax as we view the portrait of Mary: mother of the Messiah. The prophets predicted His coming, the world awaited it, and Mary gave birth! The angels and the shepherds worshiped. All meditated on its meaning, and many became evangels. Their examples are for us to emulate.

I. Going to Bethlehem
(Luke 2:1, 4, 5)

A. Taxation Decree (v. 1)

1. And it came to pass in those days, that there went out a decree from Caesar Augustus, that all the world should be taxed.

Luke is the only Gospel writer who dates his account by this taxation. The registration or census for the taxation was done every fourteen years by *Caesar Augustus*, who lived from 63 B.C. to A.D. 14. [See question #1, page 152.] For this census each man was required to go back to the city of his ancestors.

B. Bethlehem Registration (vv. 4, 5)

4. And Joseph also went up from Galilee, out of the city of Nazareth, into Judea, unto the city of David, which is called Bethlehem, (because he was of the house and lineage of David,).

Galilee is the region around the Sea of Galilee. *Nazareth* in this area is located on the trade route that connects the coastal plain to Damascus and other points east. South of Galilee is Samaria, and south of that, bounded on the west by the Mediterranean Sea and on the east by the Jordan River and the Dead Sea, is *Judea*.

Bethlehem, located five miles south of Jerusalem, is the original home of King *David*. It was here that young David kept sheep and received Samuel's anointing about a thousand years before the birth of Christ (1 Samuel 16:4, 13). Joseph is a descendant of David, so he must return to Bethlehem to register. (Locate these sites on the map on page 117.)

This verse brings to mind two passages from the Old Testament prophets. One is Isaiah 9:1, 2. Light to dispel the darkness of the land is brought from "Galilee of the nations." The other is Micah 5:2, which foretells a "ruler in Israel" to come from Bethlehem. The events we are considering in our text are reminders that these did not just happen to fulfill prophecy; but when they happened, prophecy was fulfilled.

5. To be taxed with Mary his espoused wife, being great with child.

That Mary is *great with child* suggests she is nearing the time of delivery. We might think, then, that such a trip would be too strenuous for her. She is not legally required to go along, so there must be other considerations. No doubt Joseph is acting as a protective husband by keeping Mary with him, even under these circumstances. Jewish law permits midwives to travel long distances, even on the Sabbath Day, to assist delivery. So even though none is mentioned in the text, it is possible that Mary and Joseph have a midwife with them. Whatever preparations they make, Joseph and Mary cannot anticipate all that is ahead for them. We know they are not alone, for the Heavenly Father is present and ready to supply.

II. Giving Birth to the Savior (Luke 2:6-17)

A. In the Fullness of Time (vv. 6, 7)

6. And so it was, that, while they were there, the days were accomplished that she should be delivered.

It was the "fullness of time" for the birth of the Messiah. What the Holy Spirit had equipped Mary to do was greater than the skills provided the artisans in the building of the tabernacle and all the articles of furniture for it. Yet, this is the same Holy Spirit that indwells each Christian today. The same Spirit is there but not the same manifestation because the role is different.

7. And she brought forth her firstborn son, and wrapped him in swaddling clothes, and laid him in a manger; because there was no room for them in the inn.

We do not know the actual date of Jesus' birth. The traditional observance of December 25 cannot be traced back earlier than the fourth century A.D. However, this issue is not nearly as important as other concerns. [See question #2, page 152.]

One important issue is that of being *firstborn*. Other children will be born to Mary, with Joseph as their natural father (cf. Matthew 13:55, 56; Galatians 1:19). James and Jude will be two of these, and they will write the two New Testament books that bear their names.

There is another factor to bear in mind with regard to the Son of Mary as *firstborn*. Not only does He have the role of firstborn in the family with the responsibilities therein, but He also is "firstborn" among many. He is the "firstborn from the dead" never to die again! As Adam headed up the human family, so does Christ head up the spiritual family as the "second Adam." (See Romans 5 and 1 Corinthians 15.) The hour of anguish for Mary in childbirth is also her hour of glory as mother of the Messiah.

The baby is cared for properly. The expression *wrapped . . . in swaddling clothes* is just one word in Greek, the original language of the text. This denotes the action of giving proper care for a newborn child. From the poor to the palace the same word can be used. The baby's crib is unusual since it is a feeding *manger* for animals, as well as the place—likely some kind of stable behind *the inn*. As early as the second century A.D. tradition designated it a cave. But again, such a detail is unimportant. Since so many have come to Bethlehem for the registration, the city is crowded; sleeping rooms are occupied. Mary and Joseph content themselves with the protection of the stable and the comfort of a manger. And all the while God is watching over them.

B. Announced by Angels (vv. 8-14)

8. And there were in the same country shepherds abiding in the field, keeping watch over their flock by night.

This is the time of year that *shepherds* watch their flocks day and *night*. In this situation, there is not the security of a sheepfold, a protected walled area. Being a shepherd is a common occupation. Shepherds are despised by many religious

"Mary, you have found favor with God."

"Mary treasured up all these things and pondered them in her heart." —Luke 1:30; 2:19, NIV

Visual for lesson 2. *Display this visual at the beginning of your session. Leave it on display until after lesson 4.*

people at the time, since they are considered ceremonially unclean, and thus are not permitted to participate in the religious activities of the community. However, God does not judge by outward appearances, but by what is in the heart (1 Samuel 16:7). [See question #3, page 152.]

9. And, lo, the angel of the Lord came upon them, and the glory of the Lord shone round about them; and they were sore afraid.

The shepherds are familiar with the usual scenes in the sky at night, but the appearance of an *angel* is too great for them. It is not only the appearance of the angel that causes their fear, but also *the glory of the Lord.* In being privileged to view this glory, the shepherds are seeing something not revealed to either Zechariah or Mary when an angel appeared to them. In their fright, the shepherds must be wondering if this appearance means blessing or judgment. They get their answer quickly.

10. And the angel said unto them, Fear not: for, behold, I bring you good tidings of great joy, which shall be to all people.

It is a blessing! Though they are inexperienced in such a glorious event, they know God is acting at this time, as at other times in history, in a special way. The greeting calms their spirits, yet they have had no idea that they are the first people on earth to receive this news. They know now it is *good* news, but all the dimensions of this goodness cannot dawn on them so soon. The fear in their hearts (v. 9) is giving way to *joy.* But what this joy will mean for *all people* is still unknown to them.

How wonderful it is that God can take the commonplace and make it an occasion for awakening people to who He is, what His purposes are, and how those purposes include us! If we will let it, such a scene as this with the shepherds becomes personal for us. Even "nobodies" are important to God, and through them He may reach out to others.

FREEDOM FROM FEAR

Several years ago in central Florida, a man was charged with the crime of frightening another man to death. A young man broke into the trailer home of sixty-seven-year-old Walter Schultz. He was armed with a knife and, according to the indictment, caused such fear as to result in the death of Schultz. He died of a heart attack that was brought on by the assault.

Fear is commonplace, though it is seldom deadly. The fear the shepherds experienced was more awe and reverence than it was terror. Still, the appearance of an angel in the Bible often causes fear. And yet Christ came to take away our fears! When U.S. President Franklin D. Roosevelt listed the four freedoms, one of them was freedom from fear. But no government on earth can give you freedom from fear. Only the Lord Jesus Christ can do that. He does it by forgiving our sins. He does it by comforting our hearts. He does it by assuring us of His presence.

While there are many legitimate fears in the world, most of our fears are phantom fears with no basis in reality. But faith drives out fear, whether real or imaginary. Certainly we still view God with awe and come into His presence with reverence. Certainly we fear sin enough to respect it and avoid it. But the fears that paralyze people, the fears that keep them awake at night and distracted by day, are taken away when faith comes in. The phrase *fear not* appears over sixty times in the *King James Version* of the Bible—that's more than once for every week of the year!

—R. C. S.

11. For unto you is born this day in the city of David a Saviour, which is Christ the Lord.

Angels are the first to know of Jesus' birth, and they are privileged to share it first with the shepherds. Identifying specifics are given. The place of the birth is *the city of David,* which the shepherds know to be Bethlehem. The Child is *Savior.* The shepherds are aware that the Roman emperors are hailed as "Savior" and "Lord." However, another title links these terms for the shepherds: *Christ* or "Messiah"—God's anointed, promised Deliverer (cf. John 1:41; 4:25). He is the hope of all Israel! The shepherds understand this good news is not about a Roman ruler, for it means real deity—Almighty God!

12. And this shall be a sign unto you; Ye shall find the babe wrapped in swaddling clothes, lying in a manger.

Proof for the shepherds is awaiting them at the *manger*. The *sign* is the evidence of the reality of what has been said concerning this birth. The lowly manger will distinguish this One from a Roman emperor. Their hearts undoubtedly are open to learn even more!

13. And suddenly there was with the angel a multitude of the heavenly host praising God, and saying.

This *heavenly* choir is in contrast with Roman choirs that were used in the worship of the emperor. This *heavenly host* is the Greek word for "army." How many angels are present? Immediately the shepherds are made aware that this is an occasion for *praising God*. The presence of God calls forth worship! Therefore, if there are occasions when we have difficulty in worshiping or in serving, we need to get a real sense of the presence of God. Then we won't have to be told to worship and to serve. We can do nothing else!

14. Glory to God in the highest, and on earth peace, good will toward men.

The angels conclude their message to the shepherds with a doxology (a praise). Hebrews 1:14 tells us that angels are "ministering spirits," sent on our behalf. In ministering to these shepherds, the message is one of *peace*. Undoubtedly, the shepherds relate that to the Old Testament concept that God saves His people from their earthly enemies. But in Christ this message is superseded by the idea that God saves His people from the "sin enemy." This is the type of salvation that results in peace between God and people, and it is Christ who will bring this peace about by dying to pay sin's penalty.

Some today have challenged the angel's message. Where is this peace *on earth* and *good will toward men*? Of course, the whole context of the New Testament shows this peace is not for all men, but only those who accept God's grace or good will. Some of the newer translations show that this concept is present in this verse as well. The *New International Version*, for example, has "on earth peace to men on whom his favor rests." Though the reading is quite different, the message—when kept in context—is actually the same, for God's favor rests on those who accept His grace.

C. Visited by Shepherds (vv. 15-17)

15. And it came to pass, as the angels were gone away from them into heaven, the shepherds said one to another, Let us now go even unto Bethlehem, and see this thing which is come to pass, which the Lord hath made known unto us.

How much checking will be necessary for *the shepherds* to find the right stable behind a dwelling or an inn? Fortunately, *Bethlehem* is not a large city. Whatever the challenge, they handle it with confidence, knowing the source of their information concerning the child's birth. The response of these devoted shepherds is a model for us all: every message from the Lord—messages that today come through the pages of Scripture—requires our response and action.

16. And they came with haste, and found Mary and Joseph, and the babe lying in a manger.

The scene is just as the Lord had said it would be. The dominant figures, of course, are the Messiah's mother, *Mary,* the protective *Joseph,* and the baby, properly cared for and lying in the feed *manger*. The lowly shepherds have accepted the message at face value and have acted on it. In so doing, they show more faith than the well-educated priest Zechariah! (See Luke 1:18.) [See question #4, page 152.]

17. And when they had seen it, they made known abroad the saying which was told them concerning this child.

The shepherds become the world's first evangelists of this good news. Luke leaves to our imagination the direction and the destiny of their ministry. Shepherding remains their livelihood, but sharing this thrilling message sets their feet on fire and their hearts ablaze. As Billy Sunday, the preacher of a couple of generations past, said of his own ministry: "It is surprising what a straight blow God can strike with a crooked stick."

III. Reactions to the Birth
(Luke 2:18-20)
A. By Those Around (v. 18)

18. And all they that heard it wondered at those things which were told them by the shepherds.

Home Daily Bible Readings

Monday, Dec. 16—Jesus Is Born (Luke 2:1-7)

Tuesday, Dec. 17—Shepherds Hear the Good News (Luke 2:8-14)

Wednesday, Dec. 18—Mary Ponders the Shepherds' Words (Luke 2:15-20)

Thursday, Dec. 19—A Sword Will Pierce Your Soul (Luke 2:21-35)

Friday, Dec. 20—Anna Sees and Believes (Luke 2:36-40)

Saturday, Dec. 21—Mary Treasures All These Things (Luke 2:41-51)

Sunday, Dec. 22—A Child Has Been Born (Isaiah 9:1-7)

Now the ball is in other people's courts. What will they do with the message? Wonder or amazement can work in one of two ways. Either there will be acceptance of the divine nature of it all that calls for obedient response, or one may be hardened in unbelief. Preaching and teaching the gospel work that way. All is not done by the speaker. People must respond.

B. By Mary (v. 19)

19. But Mary kept all these things, and pondered them in her heart.

Mary is a new mother. Motherhood in itself is a grand blessing of God. But then there are all the other factors: the astounding pronouncement from her relative Elisabeth, the message of the angel to Joseph, Joseph's own caring response, and then the coming of the shepherds with their news. God is so great! And what will be next? Mary's faith grows as she continues to be the Lord's trusting servant. She will defer to her son at His first miracle (John 2:5). She will meet with others in prayer after Jesus ascends into Heaven (Acts 1:14). May our own faith demonstrate a similar commitment and growth.

C. By the Shepherds (v. 20)

20. And the shepherds returned, glorifying and praising God for all the things that they had heard and seen, as it was told unto them.

It is good when the pieces of a puzzle fit together, and the desired picture is complete. The result is worth the effort. What a night this has been for *the shepherds!* When they return to their flocks, they are not the same people they were before. When confronted with the presence and power of God, praise is the proper response (Luke 5:25, 26; 7:16; 13:13; etc.), and praise indeed fills their being. [See question #5, page 152.]

How to Say It

BETHLEHEM. *Beth*-lih-hem.
CAESAR AUGUSTUS. *See*-zer Aw-*gus*-tus.
DAMASCUS. Duh-*mass*-kus.
ELISABETH. Ih-*lih*-suh-beth.
GALATIANS. Guh-*lay*-shunz.
GALILEE. *Gal*-uh-lee.
JUDEA. Joo-*dee*-uh.
MEDITERRANEAN. *Med*-uh-tuh-*ray*-nee-un
    (strong accent on *ray*).
MESSIAH. Meh-*sigh*-uh.
MESSIANIC. Mess-ee-*an*-ick.
NAZARETH. *Naz*-uh-reth.
SAMARIA. Suh-*mare*-ee-uh.
ZECHARIAH. *Zek*-uh-*rye*-uh (strong accent
    on *rye*).

The response of the shepherds is based on satisfactory evidence of the truth of the good news of the Messiah. As with Mary, what the future holds for them they do not know. But they know the meaning of believing God. They know what it means to be instruments in God's hand. Again, submission and commitment are key in our being shepherds ready to serve. Being in the presence of the glory of God brings one first to praise, and then to service.

Conclusion

A. The Significance of Mary's Motherhood

Mary surrenders her whole being to God's will. The promise, the conception, the nine months' waiting, and the birth—but it is more than even all that. Mary knows that the One born of her is the promised Messiah. He is hers and He is God's. The miracle of the virgin birth is a part of the divine framework of God's redemption of sinful man. Each new aspect of life with Jesus and Joseph will bring more occasions for pondering the meaning of it all (cf. Luke 2:25-33, 41-52, etc.).

God does not reveal His entire plan to Mary all at once. She must have faith that whatever plan God has in mind, He is the One who is in charge, and He is the One who will bring that plan to fruition. Mary's mission of being the earthly mother of the Son of God never falters from the manger to the cross. There are times she is tested, but we see no regrets for submitting herself as she does.

Mary's mission does not end with the resurrection of Christ, nor should ours. The last mention of Mary is the time when she is gathered in the upper room with other believers after the ascension of Christ. The group is praying with the apostles and anticipating what will be next (cf. Acts 1:14). Mary typifies the noble qualities of both motherhood and servanthood; thus, we too say, "Blessed art thou among women."

B. Prayer

Our loving Father, thank You for the wisdom in Your plans as You have made forgiveness of sin a reality for us through Your Son, the Messiah. We thank You today for the witness of Joseph and the shepherds, but especially for the portrait of Mary, the earthly mother of the Messiah, and the faith she models to us. In Jesus' name, amen.

C. Thought to Remember

With the evidence we have, there is no substitute for faith, submission, and commitment to Jesus.

Learning by Doing

This page contains an alternative lesson plan emphasizing learning activities.
Classes desiring such student involvement will find these suggestions helpful.

Learning Goals

After participating in this lesson, students will be able to:

1. Tell how Mary—and the shepherds—acted in faith to fulfill God's plan at the birth of Jesus.

2. Describe the way God's providence was at work in the unusual decree of Caesar and the routine work of the shepherds.

3. Express confidence that God has a work for them.

Into the Lesson

"Precious Memories!" Ask class members to pull out their imaginary videos of Christmases past and briefly share a favorite Christmas memory with the class or a small group.

Make the transition to Bible study by telling the class that Mary's favorite imaginary video shot may be of some of the traditional manger scenes: baby Jesus in the manger, shepherds crowding into the small stable, or the like. However, there is another wonderful scene in which she realizes she is being asked to do an extraordinary task by the Lord. She was an ordinary Jewish girl with an extraordinary faith. And she was asked to be a part of something supernatural.

Into the Word

Read aloud today's printed text from Luke 2:1, 4-20. Then divide the class into groups of four to six people. Each group is to work on one of the three following tasks or assignments. Give each group a written copy of their task, a large piece of poster board, and a marker. If you have more than eighteen in your class, you will have more than one group working on the same assignment.

Task #1: Make two columns on your poster board. Head the first column with "Sweet Memories" and the second column with "Sweet Songs." After reading today's text, in the first column list all the words or phrases that may become the foundation of a "sweet memory" for this new mother. In the second column list a line or a phrase of a Christmas carol (or other song) that has helped to preserve these sweet memories. Not all of these memories, of course, have been captured in song.

Task #2: Please read today's text. Then on the poster board provided summarize your understandings and feelings about each of the following questions.

1. Describe how you see God's providence at work in the unusual decree from Caesar. Tell how the occupational routine of the shepherds made them available to be used by God.

2. How was it special that the shepherds were among the first to visit Mary?

Task #3: Please read today's text. Focus on Luke 2:19. Use your imagination and put yourself in Mary's place. Think how God has worked through the life of an unknown girl. On the poster board make a detailed list of all the exciting, marvelous, wonderful, and frightening things Mary may have chosen to note in her mental diary. You may choose to list them as questions. For example, did Mary think about God's use of a far-off Roman emperor's decree to accomplish His will in her life?

Into Life

Use any or all of these discussion questions to apply the lesson to life today.

1. Mary was both an ordinary girl and an extraordinary girl. In what way would you say she was ordinary? In what way would you say she was extraordinary?

2. Let's talk about whom God chooses to use to accomplish His tasks. Who are some other "ordinary" people in Scripture whom God has called? Or even some unlikely people He has used for His purpose? As you make the list, ask, "Why do I consider this person to be ordinary, unlikely?" You may want to ask, "What do I have in common with these ordinary, unlikely people?"

3. Cite examples of persons you know who are in ordinary walks of life but whom you think God is working through in an extraordinary way to accomplish the purposes of His church. What sets these Christian servants apart—what makes them special? What lessons do you learn from them?

Close by asking the class to repeat the lines of this prayer as you read it sentence by sentence: "Dear Lord, thank You for Mary. Thank You for her submissive and adventurous spirit. I know You will give me opportunities to be Your servant. Teach me to watch and listen for these opportunities. And I make this promise—I will use these opportunities and will look for at least one special skill I can develop for You. Amen."

Have someone lead the class in singing the chorus of "I Surrender All."

Let's Talk It Over

The questions on this page are designed to promote discussion of the lesson by the class and to encourage application of the lesson Scriptures. The answers provided are only discussion starters. Let your class talk it over from there.

1. Most of the world's religions, such as Hinduism, make no pretense of being "historical." That is, they do not try to tie their doctrines to historical events. What significance do you see in the fact that Luke mentions the historical background of the birth of Christ? What other key historical events help to confirm your faith?

By including the historical background of Christ's birth, the Gospels are saying, "Check it out for yourself, and you'll see that what we're telling you is true." Luke's mention of names and places and times helps us know that his story is fact, not fiction. Historical facts surrounding Jesus' birth, ministry, and death and resurrection help to confirm their reality. The same is true of other historical details in the Bible. Old Testament kings, for example, are named in historical sources other than the Bible, and the records are consistent. Time and again liberal scholars have alleged historical error in the Bible only to have some new archaeological evidence turn up to confirm the Biblical record after all!

2. Does it bother you that we cannot confirm December 25—or some other specific date—as the day Jesus was born? Why or why not? What do you find significant about the date of Christ's birth?

Anniversaries are important to us, and knowing the right date is critical. Even so, we sometimes celebrate a birthday or wedding anniversary on another date, a date close to the actual anniversary date but more convenient for calling together a large crowd. The same is true of some holidays, at least in the U.S. Many holidays are celebrated on the Monday closest to the anniversary of the historical event they observe. The important thing in each observance is recognizing the historical reality of the event and its lasting significance on people today. The same is true of Jesus' birth. The exact date is not so important when compared with the reality that He did come, and in coming brought salvation.

3. What group in our community is shunned or despised because of some "outward appearance"? How can the church demonstrate God's love for such people?

You and your class will know who these groups are. Are race relations strained in your area? Perhaps the church needs to do more to reach people of a different skin color than yours. Has your church "marketed" itself to a particular demographic unit? Maybe you need also to do something to reach out to people who don't "fit the mold."

4. Many preachers, teachers, and other such leaders have been role models for us. Who, like the shepherds, has been a role model for you even though he or she was not a religious leader by profession? How can you be such a model to someone else?

The church thrives on the involvement of volunteers. These precious saints may work in the secular marketplace, but their passion is ministry. They serve the Lord by teaching, working in the nursery, driving the church bus, acting as chaperones at youth events, coordinating special events, or something else in keeping with their gifts. Some are leaders, and others step in to follow. But their love for the Lord is obvious.

Encourage your class to name those saints who have been role models for them. Try to ascertain what drives these people so you can imitate their faith. (See 1 Corinthians 11:1.)

5. When have you had an experience of being confronted with the presence and power of God? What change did it make in your life?

Some of your class members may tell of attending a retreat or other special program that had a life-changing impact on them. These events sometimes bring together just the right mix of fellowship, separation from the world, and godly leaders to be more than just a "mountain-top" experience. The impact of those events seem to wear off shortly after the person returns to "the valley." But a truly life-changing event has an influence that lasts. It may have been something the student attended as a teen, or a marriage enrichment retreat, or something else.

Some others may have stories of less formal experiences. Perhaps they read something that challenged their belief system and made them dig in and study more fervently. As a result, they have a much firmer grasp of their faith. Maybe another student met someone who had a passionate love for Christ and the Word. Such people will infect others with a similar love.

John the Baptist: Messiah's Forerunner

DEVOTIONAL READING: John 1:1-15.

BACKGROUND SCRIPTURE: Matthew 3; 11:2-19; 14:1-12.

PRINTED TEXT: Matthew 3:1-11; 11:7-10.

Matthew 3:1-11

1 In those days came John the Baptist, preaching in the wilderness of Judea,

2 And saying, Repent ye: for the kingdom of heaven is at hand.

3 For this is he that was spoken of by the prophet Isaiah, saying, The voice of one crying in the wilderness, Prepare ye the way of the Lord, make his paths straight.

4 And the same John had his raiment of camel's hair, and a leathern girdle about his loins; and his meat was locusts and wild honey.

5 Then went out to him Jerusalem, and all Judea, and all the region round about Jordan,

6 And were baptized of him in Jordan, confessing their sins.

7 But when he saw many of the Pharisees and Sadducees come to his baptism, he said unto them, O generation of vipers, who hath warned you to flee from the wrath to come?

8 Bring forth therefore fruits meet for repentance:

9 And think not to say within yourselves, We have Abraham to our father: for I say unto you, that God is able of these stones to raise up children unto Abraham.

10 And now also the axe is laid unto the root of the trees: therefore every tree which bringeth not forth good fruit is hewn down, and cast into the fire.

11 I indeed baptize you with water unto repentance: but he that cometh after me is mightier than I, whose shoes I am not worthy to bear: he shall baptize you with the Holy Ghost, and with fire.

Matthew 11:7-10

7 And as they departed, Jesus began to say unto the multitudes concerning John, What went ye out into the wilderness to see? A reed shaken with the wind?

8 But what went ye out for to see? A man clothed in soft raiment? behold, they that wear soft clothing are in kings' houses.

9 But what went ye out for to see? A prophet? yea, I say unto you, and more than a prophet.

10 For this is he, of whom it is written, Behold, I send my messenger before thy face, which shall prepare thy way before thee.

GOLDEN TEXT: This is he, of whom it is written, Behold, I send my messenger before thy face, which shall prepare thy way before thee.—Matthew 11:10.

Portraits of Faith
Unit 1: Personalities Involved in the Messiah's Coming
(Lessons 1-5)

Lesson Aims

After participating in this lesson, each student will be able to:

1. List features that characterized the lifestyle and ministry of John the Baptist.

2. Compare the nature of John's ministry as forerunner of Jesus with the church's ministry of telling people of Jesus.

3. Suggest a specific way the student or church can perform this ministry.

Lesson Outline

INTRODUCTION
  A. Portrait of John, Preacher and Baptizer
  B. Lesson Background
I. JOHN'S MINISTRY (Matthew 3:1-11)
  A. His Beginning (v. 1)
  B. His Theme (v. 2)
    Rating the Sermon
  C. His Person (vv. 3, 4)
  D. His Audience (vv. 5, 6)
  E. His Challenge (vv. 7-11)
    The Coming Judgment
II. JESUS' EVALUATION OF JOHN (Matthew 11:7-10)
  A. Strength and Courage (v. 7)
  B. Outward *vs.* Inward (v. 8)
  C. Prophet and More (vv. 9, 10)
CONCLUSION
  A. The Impact of John's Ministry
  B. Prayer
  C. Thought to Remember

Introduction

A. Portrait of John, Preacher and Baptizer

There has been a trend among people today to want to get back to nature, back to basics. Natural food products sound the note for those who want to have a healthy diet—low cholesterol and low fat. They want dietary supplements that are "natural." That word *natural* sells. People want quality lives, disease free. "Free" is another buzzword. Many like to be free to do their own thing, free from obligations to others. Sometimes being free is good and sometimes it is not.

At first glance John the Baptist, the Messiah's forerunner, may appear to be "natural and free." He makes his living in a wilderness environment

and eats a Spartan, but completely natural, diet. But when we study his portrait carefully, we find the divine artist sets forth a personality that has greater and more meaningful dimensions. The Bible introduces John the Baptist in all four Gospels. (John the Baptist is not to be confused, of course, with the apostle John.) Bringing the details of those gospels accounts together gives us our portrait. Part of that portrait is the godliness of his parents, Zechariah and Elisabeth, whose portraits we viewed in the first lesson of this series.

Beyond the miraculous nature of his conception, we know nothing of John's childhood. Then suddenly he appears on the scene as a bold preacher of repentance and a baptizer of the penitent. His appearance is rugged—characteristic of one living in the wilderness. He is important enough to be the one sought out by Jesus for His own baptism (Matthew 3:13-15). John is the one who introduces Jesus as the Messiah, directing his disciples to follow Jesus instead, noting that, "He must increase, but I must decrease" (John 3:30).

B. Lesson Background

Since John's parents were of the priestly line of Aaron (Luke 1:5), so was he—though he himself did not become a priest. Instead, he became much more! Undoubtedly, his parents helped to mold him to be the unique person he became. Dedicated to God's service from birth, he was to drink no wine or strong drink. He would be filled with the Holy Spirit from birth (Luke 1:15). The parents were promised that John would be called "the prophet of the Highest" and that he would "go before the face of the Lord to prepare his ways" (Luke 1:76).

John lived in the wilderness area of Judea until he appeared in his special role to prepare the hearts of the people for the Messiah and His kingdom. John's whole personality and his vocabulary reflected the desert lifestyle. He was fully equipped for his ministry and drew many of his preaching illustrations from desert experience.

I. John's Ministry (Matthew 3:1-11)

The ministry of John the Baptist prefaces the public ministry of Jesus. It is fair to refer to John's ministry as the "beginning" of the gospel (cf. Mark 1:1; Acts 1:22).

A. His Beginning (v. 1)

1. In those days came John the Baptist, preaching in the wilderness of Judea.

Luke is more specific than Matthew in designating *in those days* to be "in the fifteenth year of the reign of Tiberius Caesar" (Luke 3:1). This would be late A.D. 26 or early A.D. 27. John's parents, Zechariah and Elisabeth, had lived in the hills of *Judea,* perhaps at Hebron. *John* probably spent his youth in this same area. John is very familiar with this *wilderness* area, which constitutes about one-third of Judea proper. This area is mostly uninhabited, and is arid and hot except for the Jordan Valley just north of the Dead Sea. But here is where John lives "till the day of his showing unto Israel" (Luke 1:80).

What was life like for John here? What did he do? Did he have any portions of the Old Testament prophets? We do not know the day-by-day details, but he could have spent time reflecting on Old Testament prophecies he had learned from his parents. He could meditate and commune with God even as he took care of his daily needs.

B. His Theme (v. 2)

2. And saying, Repent ye: for the kingdom of heaven is at hand.

As he begins his public ministry, this thirty-something preacher has a ready message that seems to dovetail with the message of Old Testament prophets (see Ezekiel 18:30-32; Matthew 11:13). Those prophets had a message of judgment. But if there is repentance, then there can be blessing. If we had been in the audience, we may have heard John begin with the prophet Malachi (see especially Malachi 3:2; 4:1).

John's theme included a call to repentance from sin and an announcement that *the kingdom of heaven* is near. He urged them to repent—to prepare their hearts for the coming Messiah and His kingdom. They wanted change, and that change must begin with their change of heart.

RATING THE SERMON

The British statesman William Lamb, Lord Melbourne who lived from 1779 until 1848, once remarked, "Things have come to a pretty pass when religion is allowed to invade the sphere of private life!" Was he serious or was he joking? True religion always invades the sphere of private life. And good sermons are the means by which it does so. In fact, Lord Melbourne made that remark after listening to an evangelical sermon!

Someone has said that we ought to devise a rating system for sermons like the rating system for movies and television. Some sermons could be rated G. They are generally acceptable. There is nothing disturbing in them. They do not invade our private lives!

Sermons for the spiritually mature would get different ratings. Some could be rated R. These sermons need to be restricted to those who are not upset by the truth and who recognize that sometimes preaching must be controversial. And some sermons could be rated X. This is not because of offensive language but because they contain explosive ideas.

That is the rating we would have to give to John the Baptist—and to many who went before him. This kind of preaching caused Jeremiah to be dropped into a well, Amos to be run out of town, and Stephen to be stoned. Certainly no preacher needs to be unkind, but every sermon should invade the sphere of private life. —R. C. S.

C. His Person (vv. 3, 4)

3. For this is he that was spoken of by the prophet Isaiah, saying, The voice of one crying in the wilderness, Prepare ye the way of the Lord, make his paths straight.

Matthew quotes Isaiah 40:3 to describe John as *the voice.* But the voice needs an audience. John attracts an audience in the desert because his message ties in to the expectations of the day, and word spreads. The simplicity of his personal dress and lifestyle undoubtedly become part of the message that attracts (see vv. 4, 5, below). There has not been preaching (or a preacher) like this since the Old Testament prophets!

John's preaching has as its goal the removal of obstacles that might impede the Messiah and His message. This is what is meant by *make his paths straight.* It is like clearing the way with "God's bulldozer." The biggest obstacle is hardness of heart. When that is removed, people are prepared to accept Jesus when He begins His own ministry (see John 10:40-42).

4. And the same John had his raiment of camel's hair, and a leathern girdle about his loins; and his meat was locusts and wild honey.

John's appearance and lifestyle reflects the desert area where he lives. Rough clothing made from *camel's hair* and held in place by a heavy leather belt covers his strong frame. This is the clothing of a poor person, and surely is not comfortable by any standard. His garb is similar to that of the prophets, like Elijah (2 Kings 1:8; cf. Malachi 4:5; Matthew 17:10-13). His diet is simple and sufficient, but few of us would want to try to survive on *locusts* (large grasshoppers) and *honey,* especially if we had to gather them ourselves! The severity of both his message and his lifestyle work together to witness against the spiritual and physical indolence of the time. [See question #1, page 160.]

D. His Audience (vv. 5, 6)

5. Then went out to him Jerusalem, and all Judea, and all the region round about Jordan.

Here we have a figure of speech called metonymy—the "container" (Jerusalem, Judea, etc.) for the "contained" (the people who live in those places). It captures the atmosphere of John's pulpit, which is surcharged with Messianic expectation. Many like that and respond. John's message and manner are not those of a pretender. It does not make any difference whether the hearers were Jews or non-Jews. The people were excited and enthusiastic, ready to respond (see also John 3:23).

6. And were baptized of him in Jordan, confessing their sins.

John is the one who introduces baptism to the New Testament era. In John's baptism, both Jew and non-Jew are yielding to God's will in *confessing their sins.* John's baptism differs from Christian baptism, which does not come until the Day of Pentecost after Christ's resurrection (Acts 2:38). (Those who receive John's baptism will later need to be rebaptized; see Acts 19:1-5.)

E. His Challenge (vv. 7-11)

7. But when he saw many of the Pharisees and Sadducees come to his baptism, he said unto them, O generation of vipers, who hath warned you to flee from the wrath to come?

The *Pharisees* are a strict religious party of the Jews, priding themselves in their fastidious adherence to the law of Moses. The *Sadducees,* on the other hand, are a liberal party, who do not believe in angels or resurrection (Acts 23:8). It is said that "nothing makes better friends than a common enemy," and for these two groups to join forces like this to investigate what John is doing is quite remarkable!

The fact that these two groups *come to his baptism* does not mean they are coming to *be* baptized (see Luke 7:29, 30). As they approach, John denounces them for their hypocrisy for not showing signs of true repentance. They do not want the wrath or judgment of God, but are not willing to have the change of heart necessary to be ready for the Messiah and His spiritual kingdom.

John is unafraid and unthreatened by those in high stations. [See question #2, page 160.] He is a faithful forerunner, not afraid to use his wilderness vocabulary in calling deceitful people *vipers* (cf. Isaiah 14:29). Vipers are known for eating their parents and escaping fires. What snakes they are, wanting to *flee* the fire of judgment in their own way!

8. Bring forth therefore fruits meet for repentance.

John is separate from the mainline religious system. He calls for people to come away from empty religion. *Fruits* is a good agricultural concept for them to understand. The kind of plant or tree is seen by the fruit borne. If they are going to do God's will, their penitent hearts will be evident in their lifestyles. The religious leaders who

How to Say It

AARON. *Air*-un.
ABRAHAM. *Ay*-bruh-ham.
ANTIPAS. *An*-tih-pus.
ELIJAH. Ee-*lye*-juh.
ELISABETH. Ih-*lih*-suh-beth.
EZEKIEL. Ee-*zeek*-ee-ul or Ee-*zeek*-yul.
HEBRON. *Hee*-brun or *Heb*-run.
HEROD. *Hair*-ud.
ISAIAH. Eye-*zay*-uh.
JUDEA. Joo-*dee*-uh.
LEVITICUS. Leh-*vit*-ih-kus.
MACHAERUS. Muh-*key*-rus or Muh-*kye*-rus.
MALACHI. *Mal*-uh-kye.
MESSIAH. Meh-*sye*-uh.
MESSIANIC. Mess-ee-*an*-ick.
PHARISEES. *Fair*-ih-seez.
SADDUCEES. *Sad*-you-seez.
TIBERIUS CAESAR. Tie-*beer*-ee-us *See*-zur.
ZECHARIAH. Zek-*uh*-rye-*uh*.

come forth make a display, but there is no spiritual change. [See question #3, page 160.]

9. And think not to say within yourselves, We have Abraham to our father: for I say unto you, that God is able of these stones to raise up children unto Abraham.

The Jews of John's era often grab hold of their biological descent from *Abraham* as their security blanket. They feel their heritage insures them against judgment. They fail to see that God has no obligation to them as a nation because of their biological connection. When John looks at the common *stones* around his feet, he emphasizes his point by saying that if God wanted to He could make His *children* from them. To do so, it would be no more difficult than when God created Adam from dust. As Jesus and Paul will stress later, the true children of Abraham are those who have Abraham's deeds and faith (John 8:31-41; Romans 4:16). [See question #4, page 160.]

10. And now also the axe is laid unto the root of the trees: therefore every tree which bringeth not forth good fruit is hewn down, and cast into the fire.

John uses a dramatic analogy to strike home his point. The *trees* have been marked. The tree cutter has his *axe* ready to come down with a mighty blow. Unless there is a change of heart soon, destruction is ahead. They will become firewood. There is not a moment to spare.

It is too easy to have a false sense of security, thinking nothing so bad can happen. Many people put off making a decision, thinking they have plenty of time. But it may be later than they think. God is patient and long-suffering, not wanting any to perish. But if that is the course they choose, he can do nothing except bring due penalty.

THE COMING JUDGMENT

Charlemagne (A.D. 742–814) was the first European ruler known as the Holy Roman Emperor. He was crowned by the Pope himself on Christmas Day of the year 800. Charlemagne subdued various invaders and imposed order on the quarreling princes and wild tribes of central Europe. When he died, his body was embalmed in a sitting position—sitting on a golden chair, with a golden sword at his side, a gold chain about his neck, and a golden volume of the four Gospels on his knees.

But all that will mean nothing when Charlemagne comes to the final judgment. He will not go to the head of the line. When small and great stand before God, he will stand alongside the poorest peasant from an unmarked grave in potter's field. "God is no respecter of persons."

No one will escape that judgment. We don't often hear that these days. But it is a theme we need to hear, and it is a theme that always has been needed. So you find it in the Psalms (see 58:11 and 62:12). You find it in the prophets (e.g., Jeremiah 17:10). It was a part of the preaching of the apostles (Acts 10:42; 17:31). It was a part of the preaching of Jesus (Matthew 11:22; 25:32; Luke 12:48). God is described as the judge of all in the first book of the Bible (Genesis 18:25) and in the last (Revelation 20:12).

The warning John the Baptist gave so long ago is as relevant today as it ever was. We would be wise to heed that warning.   —R. C. S.

11. I indeed baptize you with water unto repentance: but he that cometh after me is mightier than I, whose shoes I am not worthy to bear:

Home Daily Bible Readings

Monday, Dec. 23—John Proclaims Repentance (Matthew 3:1-10)

Tuesday, Dec. 24—John Baptizes Jesus (Matthew 3:11-17)

Wednesday, Dec. 25—John Testifies to the Light (John 1:1-15)

Thursday, Dec. 26—I Am Not the Messiah (John 1:19-28)

Friday, Dec. 27—No One Greater Than John (Matthew 11:2-15)

Saturday, Dec. 28—John's Death (Matthew 14:1-12)

Sunday, Dec. 29—John Came in Righteousness (Matthew 21:23-32)

he shall baptize you with the Holy Ghost, and with fire.

John's baptism is not an end in itself, but it looks to the future. He is the Messiah's forerunner. Greater things are coming. John's baptism will be followed by Jesus' baptism (i.e. Christian baptism). John does not have revelation of all the details; so he preaches his sermon as an Old Testament prophet would.

There are two aspects ahead. There is blessing. That blessing will come on the Day of Pentecost after Jesus' resurrection, when Peter and the other apostles will preach the first gospel messages: "Repent, and be baptized every one of you in the name of Jesus Christ for the remission of sins, and ye shall receive the gift of the Holy Ghost" (Acts 2:38). The other half of the message presents the alternative: *fire.* This is judgment. For the obedient there is blessing; for the disobedient, judgment. It's the individual's choice.

The one who will make such a blessing possible is the Messiah. John, as a lowly servant, says he is not worthy to *bear* His *shoes* (cf. Matthew 3:13-15 and John 1:29, 30). Jesus' ministry will be greater than John's. We today can testify to that fact since we are on this side of the cross and the empty tomb. We know forgiveness of sin and the abiding presence of the Holy Spirit. As Paul reassures in Romans 8:1, "There is therefore now no condemnation to them which are in Christ Jesus, who walk not after the flesh, but after the Spirit."

II. Jesus' Evaluation of John (Matthew 11:7-10)

Early in Jesus' public ministry, Herod Antipas (a son of Herod the Great) threw John into prison (Matthew 4:12; 14:3, 4). John had denounced Herod for taking Herodias, his brother's wife, to be his wife. Of course, Herodias was the power behind the throne that brought about this situation for John—and later his beheading. Dark, dank Machaerus prison was in stark contrast with the fresh air and sunlight of the Judean hills and the Jordan River. But more than the prison, John was struggling to put all the things together about the Messiah and His kingdom. "If Jesus is setting up His kingdom, I should not be here," John could have thought. In fact, John sent word to Jesus and asked, "Art thou he that should come, or do we look for another?" (11:3). He said this even though he had introduced Jesus as the Lamb of God that takes away the sin of the world. Jesus sent back word to John to remind him of the miracles He was doing and the good news He was preaching. In other words, "John, don't forget; it is a spiritual kingdom I am setting up. Don't stumble." [See question #5, page 160.]

A. Strength and Courage (v. 7)

7. And as they departed, Jesus began to say unto the multitudes concerning John, What went ye out into the wilderness to see? A reed shaken with the wind?

They are the disciples *John* has sent to *Jesus* (Matthew 11:2). Their arrival and departure provides Jesus with an opportunity to deliver a ringing declaration of John's greatness. John's question (11:2, 3) did not arise out of a lack of faith, because Jesus' role is still veiled at this point in time. John has served his Lord with daring courage and self-effacing commitment. He is no spindly *reed* of grass!

B. Outward *vs.* Inward (v. 8)

8. But what went ye out for to see? A man clothed in soft raiment? behold, they that wear soft clothing are in kings' houses.

What John's outward appearance suggests is not the full story or the complete portrait of the man. His rough, wilderness garb does not make him come across as being important, unless we think that is the way an Old Testament prophet would be. John introduces the King of kings, but he does not wear royal attire to do so. Clothes don't really "make the man"! What matters is Lord's commendation. In fact, those people *in kings' houses*, wearing their *soft clothing*, are the very ones who now hold John prisoner unjustly!

C. Prophet and More (vv. 9, 10)

9. But what went ye out for to see? A prophet? yea, I say unto you, and more than a prophet.

In a way John is the last of the Old Testament prophets. But what makes him more *than a prophet* is the fact that he was the Messiah's immediate forerunner. John ties together the thread

Visual for
lesson 5

Use this visual to illustrate the Golden Text. Discuss how we, too, can be the Lord's messengers.

of hope in the messages of the prophets with the Messiah, who makes righteousness a reality. John brings the role of a *prophet* to a climax.

10. For this is he, of whom it is written, Behold, I send my messenger before thy face, which shall prepare thy way before thee.

John is the direct announcer of the Messiah. In this he fulfills the anticipation of the message in Malachi 3:1. Jesus gives direct affirmation of this fact. John came in the spirit and power of Elijah, and Jesus further affirms this in verse 14 of Matthew's context. (See also Matthew 17:10-13; Mark 9:11-13; Luke 1:17.) John's whole ministry has been a flaming prediction and testimony concerning the Christ who was coming to take away the sins of the world. Many have misunderstood the God-designed nature of the Messiah's kingdom and have tried to make it something different. Their forceful efforts will not change its spiritual design.

John does not become a part of that kingdom; he died before its beginning. Thus Jesus said, "He that is least in the kingdom of heaven is greater than he" (Matthew 11:11). We have the privilege of serving in the kingdom that John could not. Let us be as faithful to our opportunity as John was to his.

Conclusion

A. The Impact of John's Ministry

John plows and prepares the soil for Jesus to sow the seed of the kingdom of Heaven. John announces a new era even before he knows the Messiah. He has faith in God's messages to him and acts accordingly.

John is a solitary figure. No person pictured in the Bible is alone more than he, but he is not lonely, knowing Whom he serves. John heralds the Dayspring, the Sun of Righteousness, with healing in His wings (Malachi 4:2)—healing for sin sickness. John revives people's faith in the ancient promises. John is great in the message he preaches, and great in his courage in preaching it. John is the Messiah's forerunner. Yet John does not promote himself, for he says of Jesus, "He must increase, but I must decrease" (John 3:30).

B. Prayer

Almighty God, today we have learned how You have been able to work through people like John, people yielded to Your will. Give us courage to introduce others to the Lamb of God, Who alone can forgive sin and provide the Holy Spirit. In Jesus' name, amen.

C. Thought to Remember

Have the courage of your convictions.

Learning by Doing

This page contains an alternative lesson plan emphasizing learning activities.
Classes desiring such student involvement will find these suggestions helpful.

Learning Goals

After participating in this lesson, each student will be able to:

1. List features that characterized the lifestyle and ministry of John the Baptist.

2. Compare the nature of John's ministry as forerunner of Jesus with the church's ministry of telling people of Jesus.

3. Suggest a specific way the student or church can perform this ministry.

Into the Lesson

Option 1: Ask the class to focus on jobs and salaries. Ask the class to cite some of the highest-paying careers today. List these on a board. Then ask for a list of some of the lower-paying careers. Write these on the board, also.

Then ask, "Do salaries necessarily reflect how much good a career contributes to mankind?" Make the transition to Bible study by stating: "Today a very poorly paid prophet calls to the rich and the poor alike to make a difference—to bear fruit. The theme of God's followers' bearing fruit laces the Old and New Testaments. This is an important theme for our Master—and an important lesson for His followers. Today, we will hear that theme again from one of the Bible's most colorful characters."

Option 2: Make an acrostic of the word *"Fruitful."* Print the letters of the word vertically on a sheet of poster board. Ask students to volunteer words that describe a believer's fruitful life that begin with the letter or end with the letter on that line. Make the transition to Bible study by telling the class today's study will give encouragement and ideas on how to honor God by being fruitful.

Into the Word

State: "Today we are going to share the teaching responsibilities. We will work in small teams, make our preparations, and share our findings or conclusions with each other."

Divide the class into groups of four to six and assign each group one of the following tasks. Give group 1 a photocopy of an article about John the Baptist from a Bible dictionary and a copy of the the Lesson Introduction and Lesson Background from the lesson commentary.

Group 2 will need a copy of the lesson commentary on Matthew 3:6, 11, also a Bible dictionary article on John's baptism (often found under

"baptism"). Group 3 should be given a copy of the lesson commentary on Matthew 11:7-10. Group 4 will need a concordance.

Distribute the following written instructions to the appropriate groups.

Group 1. Use the attached article and notes on today's text to gather information about John and his ministry. One person should report on John's unusual birth story and childhood years. Another team member should report on his personal life and the purpose of his ministry. A third person should report on the circumstances of John's imprisonment and terrible death.

Group 2. Read the attached article and lesson commentary on Matthew 3:6, 11. Report on the purpose of John's baptism and its similarities or distinctions from Jewish and Christian baptism.

Group 3. Reread Jesus' evaluation of John in Matthew 11:7-10. After reading notes in the lesson commentary, write a paraphrase of Jesus' remarks, so today's listener can understand.

Group 4. Look up the word *fruit* in the Bible concordance. Find at least four prophetic calls to bear good fruit in the Old Testament. Psalm 1 and Psalm 92 may be helpful. Find definitions or descriptions of good fruit and bad fruit in the New Testament. The words *fruit of the Spirit* are a clue.

Encourage groups to work quickly (about ten minutes). Allow groups to report their findings and summations to the class.

Into Life

Use the commentary on Matthew 11:7, 8 to remind the class of the heart of today's lesson: John's comments on bearing fruit. Use the following questions to stimulate application.

1. The idea of bearing good fruit was a frequent illustration by Bible speakers. Why do you think they used this terminology so often? If you were going to use a similar analogy in today's urban life, what would be an appropriate illustration? *(Dividends, yields, productivity.)*

2. Point out words in the opening activity that deal with bearing fruit in the various stages of life. Ask, "What are practical ways people can bear fruit in these different seasons of life? During youth? Parenting years? Old age?"

Stress that bearing good fruit is an important concept in the Bible. It is repeated over and over. Ask for a volunteer to lead in a prayer of commitment to bear good fruit.

Let's Talk It Over

The questions on this page are designed to promote discussion of the lesson by the class and to encourage application of the lesson Scriptures. The answers provided are only discussion starters. Let your class talk it over from there.

1. What effect do you think John's lifestyle and appearance had on the way his message was received? How would a character like John be received today? What kind of preacher might have an impact today similar to John's impact on his hearers?

John's appearance obviously attracted attention. Some of your students might observe also that it set him apart from the establishment: his message, like his lifestyle, was different. Perhaps someone will suggest his austere lifestyle removed any possibility that he had ulterior motives. He made no profit from his message.

All of these are worthy goals for communicating the gospel today. We need to attract people's attention; how can we do that? The "establishment" in John's day was comprised of religious leaders who were eager for political power and prestige. We certainly want to set ourselves apart from every hint of that kind of motivation. Our motives must be seen as pure. Have the class members get as specific as they are able in suggesting ways of accomplishing these goals.

2. Who are the powerful people today that some are afraid to offend? How should we address such people?

Let your class brainstorm a little and come up with a list of powerful people—perhaps by role rather than by name. This list might include the media, politicians, judges, and the like, but make sure it gets down to the local level. How about wealthy church members, whose "generosity" we are afraid of losing if we offend them? How about the teens, who might not come to our events if they are too challenging and not "fun"? Your class can think of others, but be careful it doesn't turn personal, especially to the point of talking behind someone's back.

Obviously, we need to address each of these "powerful" people in love and with truth (Ephesians 4:15). Our goal must be their salvation, so we will use extreme measures to reach them (1 Corinthians 9:19-22). Again, try to have the class get specific on methods.

3. Today, what constitutes good "fruit" for the Christian?

John challenged the Pharisees and Sadducees to prove the sincerity of their repentance by their actions. Similarly, Jesus said that we would recognize false prophets "by their fruits," or *works* (Matthew 7:20). For the Christian, good fruit is the product of the Holy Spirit, who dwells within us (Galatians 5:22-25). This fruit includes love, joy, peace, patience, kindness, goodness, faithfulness, gentleness, and self-control. Paul also says that we should "walk worthy of the Lord unto all pleasing, being fruitful in every good work" (Colossians 1:10). So, when the Spirit produces fruit within us, these character changes produce good works toward others, which, in turn, lead to more positive character development within.

4. The Jews were proud to include Abraham in their heritage. What is it about our own heritage that may keep us from embracing the future God has for us?

This discussion may go one of several ways. American Christians, among others, may take such pride in the faith of the "founding fathers" that they fail to address the issues of the present. This focus on national heritage may yield some useful conclusions. But others may look at the church's own heritage. Many churches can recall a time past when attendance was greater, the leaders more attentive, and the membership more active. It is tempting to return to the methods of the past. But doing so may ignore the reasons the past leaders chose those methods, matching means to opportunity. If the same opportunities do not exist today, yesterday's methods are not likely to succeed. Finally, there may be some with a personal heritage that holds them back. A parent's desire for a son or daughter to follow a family tradition might interfere with that son or daughter's own perception of God's call. Your class may think of other examples.

5. Jesus, in essence, told John not to lose sight of the spiritual nature of the kingdom and thus to stumble. What causes us to lose sight of the spiritual nature of the kingdom and to stumble?

Materialism comes in many forms, and each one will lead us to focus on the temporal instead of the eternal. If you can share what may cause you to stumble, your students may be more open to revealing their own struggles. As a result, your class together may be able to offer specific helps and encouragement to stay focused on God.

The Rich Man: Wrong Priorities

DEVOTIONAL READING: 1 Timothy 6:6-19.

BACKGROUND SCRIPTURE: Mark 10:17-27.

PRINTED TEXT: Mark 10:17-27.

Mark 10:17-27

17 And when he was gone forth into the way, there came one running, and kneeled to him, and asked him, Good Master, what shall I do that I may inherit eternal life?

18 And Jesus said unto him, Why callest thou me good? there is none good but one, that is, God.

19 Thou knowest the commandments, Do not commit adultery, Do not kill, Do not steal, Do not bear false witness, Defraud not, Honor thy father and mother.

20 And he answered and said unto him, Master, all these have I observed from my youth.

21 Then Jesus beholding him loved him, and said unto him, One thing thou lackest: go thy way, sell whatsoever thou hast, and give to the poor, and thou shalt have treasure in heaven: and come, take up the cross, and follow me.

22 And he was sad at that saying, and went away grieved: for he had great possessions.

23 And Jesus looked round about, and saith unto his disciples, How hardly shall they that have riches enter into the kingdom of God!

24 And the disciples were astonished at his words. But Jesus answereth again, and saith unto them, Children, how hard is it for them that trust in riches to enter into the kingdom of God!

25 It is easier for a camel to go through the eye of a needle, than for a rich man to enter into the kingdom of God.

26 And they were astonished out of measure, saying among themselves, Who then can be saved?

27 And Jesus looking upon them saith, With men it is impossible, but not with God: for with God all things are possible.

GOLDEN TEXT: Jesus beholding him loved him, and said unto him, One thing thou lackest: go thy way, sell whatsoever thou hast, and give to the poor, and thou shalt have treasure in heaven: and come, take up the cross, and follow me.—Mark 10:21.

Lesson Aims

After this lesson each student will be able to:

1. Recount the details of the encounter between Jesus and the rich man.

2. Express the difference between morality and a commitment to giving God first place in one's life.

3. Examine his or her priorities, and yield to God if there is anything that he or she has been unwilling to surrender in order to please and honor God.

Lesson Outline

INTRODUCTION
  A. You Ask Too Much
  B. Lesson Background
 I. AN IMPORTANT QUESTION (Mark 10:17, 18)
  A. "What Shall I Do?" (v. 17)
  B. Asking the Right Person (v. 18)
 II. AN IMPRESSIVE RESPONSE (Mark 10:19, 20)
  A. The Easy Answer (v. 19)
    Tablets of Stone
  B. The Arrogant Answer (v. 20)
III. A LOVING REQUIREMENT (Mark 10:21, 22)
  A. Seeing the Heart (v. 21)
    Sell and Give
  B. Rejecting the Command (v. 22)
IV. AN ASTONISHING LESSON (Mark 10:23-27)
  A. It Isn't Easy! (vv. 23-25)
  B. It's Impossible! (v. 26)
  C. God's Specialty (v. 27)
CONCLUSION
  A. Don't Get Caught in the Eye of the Needle
  B. Prayer
  C. Thought to Remember

Introduction

A. You Ask Too Much

When you get ready to step onto the lot of your local new car dealer, be ready for what some folks call "sticker shock." Many people of retirement age spend far more for cars today than they paid for their first homes! The price of almost everything seems ridiculously high. Candy bars cost a dollar, and a day in the hospital may cost a thousand. Professional ballplayers are paid millions of dollars per year. Perhaps the fans need to go to the

ticket window at their favorite team's stadium and simply say, "You ask too much!" Do you think that would get anyone's attention? Probably not. Boycotts have a very poor track record.

With this week's lesson, we begin a new unit of study that focuses on some of the personalities in Jesus' life and ministry. Jesus' encounter with the rich man is probably one of the saddest moments in that ministry. Jesus had much to offer, but the rich man was unwilling to rearrange his priorities in order to gain that which he said he wanted. We do not read of him again in the New Testament. Did he ever change his mind, return to Jesus, and do what Jesus asked? We simply do not know. In essence, this man said to Jesus, "You ask too much." May his rejection of the Lord's instruction remind us that Jesus knows our hearts, and demands that nothing and no one take His position in our lives.

B. Lesson Background

Parallel accounts of this incident are found in Matthew 19 and Luke 18. Those accounts give us a few more details about the rich man. Matthew tells that he was "young" (19:20), while Luke adds that he was a "ruler" (18:18). From all three Gospels together we have come to call this the account of "the rich, young ruler." There is no elaboration on the title "ruler," so we do not know whether the man was a local official or part of the Jewish aristocracy.

In any case, he found Jesus and asked Him the right question. Before you can get the right answer, you have to know what question to ask! But right questions also must be asked with right motives and attitudes. Jesus, who knows us better than we know ourselves, went right to the heart of the young man's problem.

I. An Important Question (Mark 10:17, 18)

As the tenth chapter of Mark opens, Jesus is on "the farther side of Jordan" (v. 1). This is the east side of the Jordan River, labeled "Perea" on most Bible maps and part of the modern nation of Jordan. There He is thronged by eager crowds, crafty religious leaders, and little children (vv. 1-16).

A. "What Shall I Do?" (v. 17)

17. And when he was gone forth into the way, there came one running, and kneeled to him, and asked him, Good Master, what shall I do that I may inherit eternal life?

After blessing the children, Jesus resumes His journey to Jerusalem (Mark 10:32). Along the way a certain man interrupts the journey. What does he actually know of Jesus? The fact that the man kneels indicates that he has some sense of respect for Jesus. Jesus certainly has no financial superiority over this man (cf. Luke 9:58). And Jesus is not a "ruler" in any earthly sense (cf. John 6:15). Perhaps the rich man has heard of Jesus as a miracle-worker or a great teacher. In any case, something he has heard compels him to kneel before Jesus and ask a very important question about obtaining *eternal life.*

The rich man calls Jesus *Master;* apparently the man has heard that Jesus is a great teacher. (The word translated "Master" here comes from a verb meaning to teach.) Whatever the rich man means when he addresses Jesus in the way he does, it is obvious that he believes there is something extraordinary about Jesus. The man seems to believe that Jesus, above all other Jewish rabbis, can tell him how to have eternal life. [See question #1, page 168.]

B. Asking the Right Person (v. 18)

18. And Jesus said unto him, Why callest thou me good? there is none good but one, that is, God.

Even though the rich man's final response to *Jesus* will be disappointing, as we shall see, we have to give him credit for addressing that important question to the right person. Jesus seems to want to know more about what the rich man believes about Him, so He asks him why he calls Him *good.* A Jewish man would be reluctant to call any human being "good." Only *God* is good! (See Psalms 106:1; 118:1; 1 Chronicles 16:34; 2 Chronicles 5:13.) Is the rich man acknowledging that Jesus is God? That seems to be what Jesus is asking. Whatever the rich man thought about Jesus, he clearly felt that Jesus alone could answer the question that plagued his mind.

II. An Impressive Response (Mark 10:19, 20)

A. The Easy Answer (v. 19)

19. Thou knowest the commandments, Do not commit adultery, Do not kill, Do not steal, Do not bear false witness, Defraud not, Honor thy father and mother.

Mark records no answer to Jesus' question, "Why callest thou me good?" (v. 18). Was it a rhetorical question, posed to make the rich man think but not to be answered? Or did Jesus pause until the silence became awkward, but the rich man could voice no answer? We can only speculate, but it's easy to imagine the rich man's relief when Jesus resumes speaking.

Jesus' preliminary response to the rich man's question seems too simple. The man obviously knows the tenets of the law of Moses, especially the Ten Commandments (see the next verse).

Jesus refers here to the last six of these *commandments.* These are God's instructions concerning how people are to deal with one another. (The first four Commandments, not cited by Jesus, contain God's instructions for man's relationship with Him.) The command to *defraud not* may be a synopsis of the Tenth Commandment. Probably, however, it also refers to the teaching of Deuteronomy 24:14, 15. This is particularly appropriate to remind a rich man that his wealth should not come at the expense of the poor. Jesus will eventually confront the rich man with the heart of his problem, which is his relationship with God. Although Jesus begins with the easy answer, He will not stop there.

TABLETS OF STONE

The Ten Commandments were not written on papyrus, which was in common use but only about as durable as paper. They were not written on clay tablets, also in common use then. Clay tablets could break or crack easily. They were written in stone! Surely there is a lesson in that. These Commandments were meant to endure. Every one of the Ten Commandments of the Old Testament is repeated in some form in the New, except for the one governing the Sabbath Day. You can find a parallel to the other nine in the teachings of Jesus and the apostles. These basic laws are the enduring foundation of a moral and civil society.

It is surprising, and alarming, that in many places people are objecting to the display of the Ten Commandments in public buildings such as courthouses and schools. What is there in those Commandments that is offensive? Nothing. Even more troublesome than removing them is the fact that there are organized groups so zealously devoted to removing them. There can be no civil or moral society that ignores the principles behind them. They are basic to civilization as we know it.

In Babylon three or four centuries before Moses, the ruler Hammurabi developed a code of laws. They do not compare to the Ten Commandments. The Ten Commandments are sharper in focus, briefer yet more comprehensive. They will never be out of date. If we fail to keep them, we make a very large mistake.   —R. C. S.

B. The Arrogant Answer (v. 20)

20. And he answered and said unto him, Master, all these have I observed from my youth.

Does the rich man really believe that he has kept the law perfectly? This answer reminds us of Paul's description of himself prior to his conversion (see Philippians 3:6). Maybe this man, like Paul, claims only to be blameless according to the law—even if not actually perfect. Either way, however, in the presence of the "Good Master" his answer is quite arrogant!

Many people are like the rich man—they think their morality is enough. As long as you don't kick your dog or bother anyone, what's to worry about? The rich man views himself as perfect in the sight of the law. In other words, he is as moral as moral can get. Yet he has the wisdom to know there is more than that to gain eternal life.

Most people today do not have that wisdom. If they think about judgment at all, they view it as a review of life in which they will be found to have been "nice" enough to get into Heaven. The rich man has in his favor a gnawing suspicion that "nice" is not going to be enough.

III. A Loving Requirement
(Mark 10:21, 22)
A. Seeing the Heart (v. 21)

21. Then Jesus beholding him loved him, and said unto him, One thing thou lackest: go thy way, sell whatsoever thou hast, and give to the poor, and thou shalt have treasure in heaven: and come, take up the cross, and follow me.

Jesus looks beyond the rich man's appraisal of himself and sees his heart. Of course, Jesus loves everyone, so Mark's notation that Jesus *loved him* must indicate a special feeling for this man. Perhaps it is love like that of a parent when a child has said something exceedingly immature. The immaturity is an indicator of a continuing need for parental love. [See question #2, page 168.]

Jesus sees the rich man's heart and knows that a barrier exists between him and God. He has another god—his wealth. Jesus loves him and does not want him to be alienated from the Father because of his wealth. The solution to the problem

Visual for lesson 6

Use this visual to call attention to the rich man's expression of grief at Jesus' words (verses 21, 22).

is radical: *sell* all he has and *give* the proceeds *to the poor*. Is Jesus serious? Apparently so!

Does divesting one's earthly wealth and assisting the poor gain eternal life for anyone willing to take such a radical step? No. Altruism is fine, but it does not save us—no good work can do that (Ephesians 2:8-10). In this instance, Jesus senses that the rich man's desire for God is genuine, but it is superseded by his desire for wealth. God does not have first place in the man's heart. His first love is his money! That is the problem. Jesus' solution is painfully honest.

Jesus does not leave the rich man reeling in his thoughts about the proposed solution. Jesus immediately goes on to assure the rich man that he will be making a better investment by having *treasure in heaven*. This call is not exclusive to the rich man. Jesus calls on all who *follow* Him to divest themselves of earthly restraints in seeking God's kingdom (Luke 12:29-34).

Consider what it would mean if we really believe what Jesus said. Obviously, we are not to give away all we have and then become a burden for others to care for (cf. 2 Thessalonians 3:7-10). Jesus challenges us, rather, to consider where our hearts truly are (Matthew 6:19-21; 1 Timothy 6:17-19). Anything we put before God in our heart is an idol (Ezekiel 14:3, 4; Ephesians 5:5; Colossians 3:5). [See question #3, page 168.]

SELL AND GIVE

Francis of Assisi (c. 1181–1226) was the son of a wealthy Italian cloth merchant. He took literally what Jesus said to the twelve whom He sent out as recorded in Matthew 10:7-10. The instruction was similar to that given to the young man in today's lesson. Francis thought all the family wealth should be given to the poor. His father was angry over this application of the words of Jesus, so Francis left home wearing a ragged cloak and a belt taken from the rope around the waist of a scarecrow. He begged from the rich. He gave to the poor. And he preached. His followers became known as the Franciscans and history knows him as Francis of Assisi.

In 1173, Peter Waldo, a wealthy merchant in Lyons, France, had the same idea, so he gave away all his worldly goods and led a life of poverty and preaching. His followers became known as Waldensians. Though fiercely persecuted, they survive to this day, and their views of a simpler Christianity have affected many streams of Christian thought.

These are only two of many who through the centuries have taken the words of today's lesson literally. Certainly we applaud such sacrifice, even though we understand the command to be specific to the young ruler's personal problem, not general instruction for everyone's life. Whatever it is that comes between you and Christ must be given up. Perhaps only you and Christ know what that is. Whether it is wealth or power or pleasure or some other thing, if it keeps you from Christ, it must be sacrificed.   —R. C. S.

B. Rejecting the Command (v. 22)

22. And he was sad at that saying, and went away grieved: for he had great possessions.

Mark records no words from the rich man. (Neither do Matthew or Luke, who also write of this event.) The man just walks away, *sad* and *grieved*. His desire for eternal life is genuine, and he thought he had come to the right person to answer his question. But Jesus simply asked too much. It is in this verse that we first learn that the man is rich—*he had great possessions*. The greater sadness, however, is in the heart of Jesus.

The rich man had the right desire, but was unwilling to make the right investment. Ultimately, his problem is traced to an unwillingness to become a disciple of Jesus. That is where salvation lies. The rich man is unwilling to carry his cross and follow Jesus.

Even though Jesus loves this man, He does not chase after him. He does not offer to change the terms of His command. Jesus could have called out, "Okay, how about half?" This man could have financed much of Jesus' ministry. Is it prudent to offend him? How many preachers have avoided specific topics in sermons fearing that they would alienate some of their more generous contributors?

So the rich man leaves, and Jesus lets him go. We do not hear of this man again in the New Testament. Even so, the question remains, "What does God require of us?" The answer is given by the apostle Paul, who notes that we have only one thing that matters to God. If we put Him first, and offer our lives as "living" sacrifices to Him in becoming His disciples, we will gain what the rich man was looking for (Romans 12:1, 2).

IV. An Astonishing Lesson (Mark 10:23-27)

A. It Isn't Easy! (vv. 23-25)

23. And Jesus looked round about, and saith unto his disciples, How hardly shall they that have riches enter into the kingdom of God!

We can only imagine the reactions of Jesus' *disciples* at this turn of events. They are probably ashen-faced and speechless. How could Jesus ask so much? How could He have let the rich man just walk away? Have they given all their assets to the poor in order to follow Jesus? Will He ask that of them at some point?

How to Say It

ABRAHAM. *Ay*-bruh-ham.
ASSISI. Uh-*see*-see.
DEUTERONOMY. Due-ter-*ahn*-uh-me.
EZEKIEL. Ee-*zeek*-ee-ul or Ee-*zeek*-yul.
HAMMURABI. *Ham*-muh-*rah*-bee (strong accent on *rah*).
LYONS (France). Lee-*own*.
PEREA. Peh-*ree*-uh.
PHILIPPIANS. Fih-*lip*-ee-unz.
RABBI. *rab*-eye.
RABBINICAL. ruh-*bin*-ih-kul.
THESSALONIANS. *Thess*-uh-*lo*-nee-unz (strong accent on *lo*; *th* as in *thin*).

Jesus recognized their lack of understanding. He summarized the whole incident in very simple terms. It isn't easy for rich people to *enter* His *kingdom*. [See question #4, page 168.]

24. And the disciples were astonished at his words. But Jesus answereth again, and saith unto them, Children, how hard is it for them that trust in riches to enter into the kingdom of God!

Jesus' words further astonish His followers. Is this some new teaching? Many of the great figures in Israel's history were men of great wealth—Abraham, David, and Solomon, for example. Have things changed? Is it now wrong to be wealthy?

There is nothing wrong with wealth in and of itself. The problem is that riches often keep people from following God's instruction to trust in Him and follow Jesus. This goes to the heart of the rich man's misunderstanding. It isn't easy to let go of self-sufficiency and learn to trust in God. It is easier to *trust in riches*. (See 1 Timothy 6:10.)

25. It is easier for a camel to go through the eye of a needle, than for a rich man to enter into the kingdom of God.

Jesus now illustrates the difficulty of rich people entering His kingdom with an analogy that seems ridiculous. He uses what is called "hyperbole"—extreme exaggeration to achieve a certain teaching effect.

You may have heard a lesson or sermon from this text that claimed that there was a small gate in the wall around Jerusalem known as *the eye of the needle*. This gate supposedly was so low that no *camel* could pass through it loaded with cargo. The camel first had to be unloaded and then forced to kneel in order to crawl through the gate. Under this theory, Jesus is saying that in order to be a part of His kingdom, we have to unload our earthly "cargo" and humble ourselves. The problem is that there is no evidence that such gate ever actually existed!

B. It's Impossible! (v. 26)

26. And they were astonished out of measure, saying among themselves, Who then can be saved?

The disciples' response is the key to understanding that there was no gate in the wall called "the eye of the needle." If they were familiar with such a gate, they would understand Jesus to be saying that it is difficult to get into the kingdom. They would understand the implicit illustrations of unloading earthly "cargo" and humbling oneself. These thoughts apparently never occur to them. They are incredulous! They know that what Jesus is talking about is impossible.

In response, Jesus' disciples pose an interesting question: *Who then can be saved?* Why do they ask that? Everyone isn't rich. Jesus has not said anything about the poor. Why do the disciples view Jesus' statement about rich people as applying to all people? There are many who live in Jesus' time who consider wealth to be a sign of God's blessing. Logically, then, poverty is a sign of God's disapproval and disdain. If the rich can't get into Heaven, then who can?

The disciples' astonishment might also be the response of people who understand human nature. Rich or poor, everyone can get attached to his or her possessions! Even if our earthly possessions are of little value to others, they may well be of great value to us. Bill Gates might not want my house, but I'm sure glad I have it!

The disciples are having great difficulty accepting the interaction Jesus has just had with the rich man and His subsequent teachings about earthly riches. It seems as though Jesus is saying that true discipleship must be characterized by abject poverty. Such a connection reveals that the disciples have missed Jesus' point.

C. God's Specialty (v. 27)

27. And Jesus looking upon them saith, With men it is impossible, but not with God: for with God all things are possible.

Jesus has to remind His followers that God specializes in the *impossible!* (See Genesis 18:14; Job 42:2; and Luke 1:37.) Making a camel go through the eye of a needle is no more difficult than dividing the Red Sea or causing fire to consume Elijah's offering on Mount Carmel. Jesus—the one who can calm the wind and waves; the one who can walk on water; the one who can feed thousands with a little boy's lunch; the one who can make the blind see and the lame walk; the one who can stop a funeral procession to bring a son back to life and restore him to his mother—can put a camel through the eye of a needle and save a rich man. Jesus' very presence before them is a reminder that God can do things we cannot comprehend, imagine, or duplicate. Jesus is reminding His followers that He is there to do things humans cannot do, and no one, rich or poor, can save himself and gain eternal life.

Conclusion

A. Don't Get Caught in the Eye of the Needle

Peter's follow-up response in verse 28 (not in our text) shows that the disciples still didn't understand that God's favor is not to be earned or deserved. Jesus' conversation with the rich man concerning that man's expectations and ultimate loyalty should have been getting through to the disciples, but it wasn't. Is it getting through to you? If not, you might be caught in the eye of the needle. Placing first loyalty or trust in your own effort or wealth puts you in an impossible situation with God. He cannot save you any more than you yourself can shove a camel through the eye of a sewing needle. God, however, offers the solution to your dilemma: make Him your first priority! Put Him in first place in your heart. Jesus talked about the cost and conditions of discipleship in other places (e.g., Luke 14:25-27). In the end, though, the cost will be worth it (Mark 10:29-31). [See question #5, page 168.]

B. Prayer

Heavenly Father, help us be honest in assessing our priorities. If some idol exists in our hearts, help us remove it and place You on the throne as King of kings in our lives. Help us offer ourselves to You as living sacrifices. Grant us Your peace and blessing. In Jesus' powerful name, amen.

C. Thought to Remember

In light of what Jesus has done *for* us, is it possible for Him to ask too much *of* us?

Home Daily Bible Readings

Monday, Dec. 30—The Rich Man Goes Away Sorry (Mark 10:17-22)

Tuesday, Dec. 31—Hard for the Rich to Enter (Mark 10:23-31)

Wednesday, Jan. 1—Simon Wants to Buy Power (Acts 8:14-24)

Thursday, Jan. 2—I Will Follow You, But . . . (Luke 9:57-62)

Friday, Jan. 3—You Are Lukewarm (Revelation 3:14-20)

Saturday, Jan. 4—What Tomorrow Will Bring (James 4:13-17)

Sunday, Jan. 5—Save Your Life and Lose It (Matthew 16:24-28)

Learning by Doing

This page contains an alternative lesson plan emphasizing learning activities.
Classes desiring such student involvement will find these suggestions helpful.

Learning Goals

After participating in this lesson, each student will be able to:

1. Recount the details of the encounter between Jesus and the rich man.

2. Express the difference between morality and a commitment to giving God first place in one's life.

3. Examine his or her priorities, and yield to God if there is anything that he or she has been unwilling to surrender in order to please and honor God.

Into the Lesson

Give students a piece of paper and ask them to consider and write down what they would like to accomplish financially in the next one to three years. Allow three to five minutes. Then ask people to hold up their hands if their goals include each of the following:

1. Paying off or reducing a debt, such as a credit card.

2. Saving for or purchasing a car or house.

3. Investing for children's college education.

4. Providing financial help for someone else (parents, friend, needy family, or other).

5. Increasing one's level of financial support for the Lord's work.

Make the transition to Bible study by reminding the class that our attitude toward and use of money give hints about our priorities in life.

Into the Word

Give a brief lecture on the background for this study by using the Introduction in the commentary section (page 162).

Divide the class into three groups. Give the students a handout with the following outline and questions. Assign one point to each group. (This activity is also in the student book, *Adult Bible Class.*)

A. The Request.

1. What words in Mark 10:17, 18 indicate the rich man's respect for Jesus? How or why does this indicate respect? *("kneeled to him," v. 17)*

2. What words indicate he knew or suspected that Jesus was deity? *("Good Master, what shall I do that I may inherit eternal life?" v. 17)*

3. Why did Jesus reminded the ruler, "There is none good but one, that is, God"? *(v. 18)*

B. The Response.

1. Read Mark 10:19. Why did Jesus quote the last six of the Ten Commandments and not the first four? See also Exodus 20:1-7.

2. Was the rich man's response in verse 20 honest, arrogant, or self-deceiving? Why?

3. The rich man obviously thought that "nice" was not good enough to get one into Heaven. Yet when told what to do, he didn't do it. What does his experience say about God's expectations?

C. The Requirements.

1. Is Jesus saying (Mark 10:21) that using all of one's earthly wealth and assisting the poor will assure us of Heaven? If not, what is He saying?

2. What lessons do you learn from this event about personal priorities? wealth? trusting God?

Allow the groups to work for about ten minutes. Then ask for persons from Groups A and B to share their findings. Use the lesson commentary to supplement and summarize the answers.

Into Life

Make the transition to application by saying, "Group C has been wrestling with how to apply these teachings of Jesus to our lives today." Invite Group C to report their conclusions.

Display a poster with the heading, "Where your treasure is, there will your heart be also" (Matthew 6:21). State: "Jesus spoke this principle during His famous 'Sermon on the Mount.' His teaching then, as in today's text, was that our view and use of possessions affects and reflects our relationship with Him."

Ask the class to cite different ways we can use our material goods to honor Christ. Ask for a volunteer to list these suggestions on the poster. You may need to stimulate ideas by asking how we can honor Christ in the following areas:

1. Fulfilling family financial responsibilities.

2. Acts of kindness or benevolence.

3. Our gifts or tithes to the Lord's work.

4. Accumulating wealth.

5. Saving for retirement or financial crisis.

6. Our spending habits.

Then ask, "Where would God like to be honored more in *your* material wealth?" Like the rich man, we must make a choice about what we are going to do. Close with prayer, asking for help as we grow in this area of our spiritual lives.

Let's Talk It Over

The questions on this page are designed to promote discussion of the lesson by the class and to encourage application of the lesson Scriptures. The answers provided are only discussion starters. Let your class talk it over from there.

1. What are some things people do to try to earn their way to Heaven? Why does this notion of earning one's salvation by good works persist in the minds of so many? What can we do to change that perception?

Many people believe they are saved because they are "good people." They are law abiding, considerate of others, generally honest, and nice to be around. Others think that salvation depends on some minimal church involvement. For some, like the rich young ruler, eternal life is thought to be gained by doing some special good deed, such as a large bequest to the church.

Many groups through the years have taught that salvation is a matter of doing good deeds. And it makes sense; it seems fair. The Bible does talk of the righteous being saved, but we have to understand that the "righteous," in Biblical terms, are those who have accepted Christ. We have to be sure we do not convey an attitude of being "better" than our non-Christian neighbors. We are saved by grace, and we need to let people know that. If we act like we "deserve" salvation, then others will think they have a right to determine just how good is good enough.

2. Jesus' response to the rich young ruler was based on His love for the man (v. 21). When have you had to issue a strong challenge or even rebuke to another because of your love for him or her? What happened?

Any parent certainly can tell of disciplining children because of love. We want our children to become responsible adults, so we have to rebuke irresponsible behavior and challenge them to reach their potential. Teachers play a similar role. Perhaps a teacher in your class can recall a student who had great potential but had to be pushed to realize his or her potential. Playing a similar role for a peer is not as easy, but it is equally important. If we truly love our brothers and sisters in Christ, we will challenge them to answer the high call of discipleship.

3. What is involved in following Jesus? What does it require us to give up? To do?

Jesus made it clear that following Him means giving Him control of our lives to do with as He sees fit. That means, first, removing from our lives anything that would compete with His authority.

In the ruler's case that meant his wealth. In our case it may be friends, family, a job, or a hobby. After that, following Jesus means being willing to do whatever He desires of us, wherever He wants us to do it. For some that means specialized ministry or missions work. For others that means being willing and able to serve Christ whenever the opportunity arises. Encourage your students to be specific about things they gave up when they decided to follow Jesus. Ask some to tell how they "minister" in Christ's name at work.

4. Why is wealth so often a stumbling block to faith in Christ? How can we use our possessions for God without becoming enslaved by them?

In our society, wealth is the key to many things we desire, such as power, pleasure, security, and comfort. Like a drug, wealth can become addictive and controlling. We must realize that all wealth ultimately belongs to God (Psalm 50:10); therefore, we should treat it as a loan, not as our possession. Second, we need to recognize that all earthly wealth is uncertain and temporary (1 Timothy 6:17). We have no guarantee that we will get it or keep it in this life, and every assurance that we cannot take it with us to the next. Third, we must remember that we will be judged according to how we make use of the riches entrusted to us by God (Luke 16:11). If we are unwilling to use our wealth for God's glory, how can we truly believe we belong to the Lord?

5. How have you found the "cost" of discipleship to be "worth it"?

You may be able to refer to your discussion of question #3 to get this discussion going. Cite some of the things your students said they gave up to follow Jesus (the "cost"). What have they gained in its place to make the exchange "worth it"? Perhaps someone gave up a lucrative position in corporate management. That one may tell of having more time to spend with family and in ministry, less stress, and a greater sense of peace. Another may tell of coming to Christ against the wishes of non-Christian parents and essentially being disowned by his or her family. But that one can tell of finding a place in the family of God and of love and support gained.

Certainly Romans 8:18 and 2 Corinthians 4:16-18 will have a place in your discussion.

Mary and Martha: Friends of Jesus

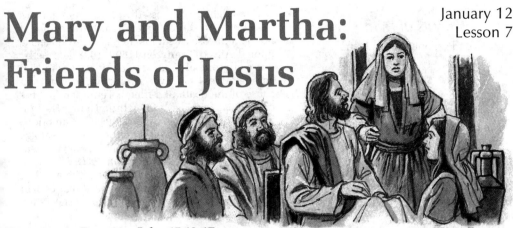

DEVOTIONAL READING: John 15:12-17.

BACKGROUND SCRIPTURE: Luke 10:38-42; John 11:20-32.

PRINTED TEXT: Luke 10:38-42; John 11:20-32.

Luke 10:38-42

38 Now it came to pass, as they went, that he entered into a certain village: and a certain woman named Martha received him into her house.

39 And she had a sister called Mary, which also sat at Jesus' feet, and heard his word.

40 But Martha was cumbered about much serving, and came to him, and said, Lord, dost thou not care that my sister hath left me to serve alone? bid her therefore that she help me.

41 And Jesus answered and said unto her, Martha, Martha, thou art careful and troubled about many things:

42 But one thing is needful; and Mary hath chosen that good part, which shall not be taken away from her.

John 11:20-32

20 Then Martha, as soon as she heard that Jesus was coming, went and met him: but Mary sat still in the house.

21 Then said Martha unto Jesus, Lord, if thou hadst been here, my brother had not died.

22 But I know, that even now, whatsoever thou wilt ask of God, God will give it thee.

23 Jesus saith unto her, Thy brother shall rise again.

24 Martha saith unto him, I know that he shall rise again in the resurrection at the last day.

25 Jesus said unto her, I am the resurrection, and the life: he that believeth in me, though he were dead, yet shall he live:

26 And whosoever liveth and believeth in me shall never die. Believest thou this?

27 She saith unto him, Yea, Lord: I believe that thou art the Christ, the Son of God, which should come into the world.

28 And when she had so said, she went her way, and called Mary her sister secretly, saying, The Master is come, and calleth for thee.

29 As soon as she heard that, she arose quickly, and came unto him.

30 Now Jesus was not yet come into the town, but was in that place where Martha met him.

31 The Jews then which were with her in the house, and comforted her, when they saw Mary, that she rose up hastily and went out, followed her, saying, She goeth unto the grave to weep there.

32 Then when Mary was come where Jesus was, and saw him, she fell down at his feet, saying unto him, Lord, if thou hadst been here, my brother had not died.

Jan 12

GOLDEN TEXT: Jesus answered and said unto her, Martha, Martha, thou art careful and troubled about many things: but one thing is needful; and Mary hath chosen that good part, which shall not be taken away from her.—Luke 10:41, 42.

Portraits of Faith
Unit 2: Personalities in Jesus'
Life and Ministry
(Lessons 6-9)

Lesson Aims

After participating in this lesson, each student will be able to:

1. Tell how Jesus interacted with Martha and her sister Mary on each of two visits to Bethany.

2. Explain the importance of letting Jesus set one's priorities in both the routine and the extreme experiences of life.

3. Tell how his or her faith in Christ has determined at least on significant priority in life.

Lesson Outline

INTRODUCTION
  A. "'Tis Better to Have Loved"
  B. Lesson Background
I. IMPROMPTU VISIT (Luke 10:38-42)
  A. Discerning Disciple (vv. 38, 39)
  B. Distracted Disciple (vv. 40-42)
II. INDIGNANT FAITH (John 11:20-24)
  A. Gentle Confrontation (vv. 20, 21)
    Paying the Debt
  B. Mustard-Seed Moment (v. 22)
  C. Fine-Tuned Faith (vv. 23, 24)
III. INCREDIBLE PROFESSION (John 11:25-27)
  A. Jesus' Teaching (vv. 25, 26)
  B. Martha's Confession (v. 27)
IV. UNALTERED AFFECTION (John 11:28-32)
  A. The Other Sister (vv. 28, 29)
  B. Another Meeting (vv. 30, 31)
  C. Another Broken Heart (v. 32)
    Words and Deeds
CONCLUSION
  A. True Friendship
  B. Prayer
  C. Thought to Remember

Introduction

A. "'Tis Better to Have Loved"

The young man sat forlornly on the front steps of an apartment building. In his hands were a rose, a box of candy, and a Valentine card. The look on his face revealed the disappointment in his heart. The girl he so longed to impress had, alas, been more impressed by another. Expressing both the agony of the heartbroken and the optimism of youth, he said, "'Tis better to have loved and lost than never to have loved at all."

One might be impressed with the young man's handling of a difficult situation, but we should not be impressed with his literary knowledge. He quoted Alfred Tennyson (1809–1892) correctly, but sadly out of context. Tennyson wrote that aching lament not over a romantic loss but because of the death of a friend. Tennyson had become best friends with Arthur Henry Hallum when they attended Trinity College at Cambridge University. When Hallum died of a stroke at age twenty-two in 1833, Tennyson was devastated. He wrote the poem *In Memoriam A. H. H.* in tribute to his dear friend. He had loved him and lost him. His heart ached, but he rejoiced that he had shared his friend's life for those few brief years. Such is the nature of true friendship.

B. Lesson Background

We have been taught that God loves all people (John 3:16) and that God doesn't show favoritism (Deuteronomy 10:17; Acts 10:34). It is obvious, however, that while on earth Jesus was personally closer to some people than to others. Among the Twelve, He had an "inner circle" of Peter, James, and John. Even within that small group, John was especially close to Jesus (see John 13:23; 19:26; 20:2; 21:7, 20, 24). Jesus also developed close personal friendships with others. Mary and Martha, as well as their brother Lazarus are examples. This week's lesson reveals the depth of Jesus' friendship with these sisters.

I. Impromptu Visit
(Luke 10:38-42)

A. Discerning Disciple (vv. 38, 39)

38. Now it came to pass, as they went, that he entered into a certain village: and a certain woman named Martha received him into her house.

It is the third year of Jesus ministry. Sometime during the two-month interval between the Feast of Tabernacles (John 7:2) and the Feast of Dedication (John 10:22), Jesus makes an impromptu visit to the home of His friends Mary and *Martha* in the little village of Bethany. It is an easy stopover anytime Jesus is near Jerusalem. Bethany is just about two miles southeast of that major city (cf. John 11:18).

Martha welcomes Jesus. The fact that it is *her house* probably indicates that she is a widow. If the house were an inheritance from parents, it would be referred to as her brother Lazarus's house (cf. Ruth 1:8). Lazarus is not even mentioned in this text, however. He probably has a separate residence. A fuller description of this household is found in John 11:1-44; 12:2 (see below). [See question #1, page 176.]

39. And she had a sister called Mary, which also sat at Jesus' feet, and heard his word.

Mary is probably younger than Martha. When Jesus arrives at their house, she immediately stops whatever she is doing and devotes her complete attention to Jesus. Sitting at His *feet* is the custom for someone who is in the presence of a teacher. Paul, for example, was taught "at the feet of Gamaliel" (Acts 22:3). Even though Mary is a friend of Jesus, He is the teacher, and she takes the customary position of a student.

Mary is a discerning woman. She understands the privilege of being in the presence of Jesus.

B. Distracted Disciple (vv. 40-42)

40. But Martha was cumbered about much serving, and came to him, and said, Lord, dost thou not care that my sister hath left me to serve alone? bid her therefore that she help me.

As soon as company arrives, *Martha* throws herself into all the preparations of appropriate hospitality. Preparing food for guests is the highest priority in any Middle Eastern home of that era (see Genesis 14:17-20; 18:1-8; Judges 13:15; 2 Kings 4:8). Failure to feed a guest would be an unthinkable affront.

One cannot help but visualize Martha scurrying about the house and occasionally shooting a "Why-aren't-you-in-here-helping-me?" glance at her *sister*. Mary, it seems, never gives a thought to hospitality. Instead, she is perfectly content to sit at Jesus' feet and listen or converse with Him. Burdened with unexpected company and a none-too-helpful sister, Martha finally explodes.

Using a tactic familiar to any parent of siblings, Martha does not directly confront Mary. Instead, she tells Jesus to tell Mary what to do. In fact, she almost scolds Jesus. Doesn't He *care* about Martha's being stuck to do all the work *alone?*

41. And Jesus answered and said unto her, Martha, Martha, thou art careful and troubled about many things.

Jesus is not oblivious to Martha's distractions. He knows she is busy, most likely preparing a meal for Him. He calls her by name and repeats it, perhaps indicating a slight annoyance with her immaturity. She is *careful*, or full of cares—she is worrying about relatively inconsequential matters. Jesus had once gone without food for forty days (Matthew 4:2)! Will a couple of hours without a meal really make that much difference? Rather than enjoying Jesus' company and taking advantage of the opportunity to learn from Him, *Martha* is getting upset about household chores. She should know better.

42. But one thing is needful; and Mary hath chosen that good part, which shall not be taken away from her.

There is some disagreement about what *one thing* Jesus means. It may mean that Martha is trying to make many dishes for a full meal, and Jesus is telling her to simplify things and make just one dish. More likely, Jesus is saying that the one thing necessary is what *Mary* is doing: learning from Him. What Martha is doing is not unimportant, but it can wait. A special opportunity is present, and Mary has chosen not to miss it.

Jesus does not rebuke Martha for her kindness. He is not unappreciative of her hospitality. He simply is trying to get her to understand a basic truth about the kingdom of God. "The kingdom of God is not meat and drink; but righteousness, and peace, and joy in the Holy Ghost" (Romans 14:17). Martha just has her priorities mixed up! [See question #2, page 176.]

II. Indignant Faith (John 11:20-24)

A. Gentle Confrontation (vv. 20, 21)

20. Then Martha, as soon as she heard that Jesus was coming, went and met him: but Mary sat still in the house.

We cannot tell how much time elapses between the events of Luke 10:38-42 and John 11:20-24. It may be no more than a few weeks. After the impromptu visit with *Martha* and *Mary* of Luke 10, Jesus attends the Feast of Dedication in late December (John 10:22, 23). That high profile visit results in threats to His life (10:31, 39), so He retreats across the Jordan River to the east, where it is safer (10:40).

But after being there a short time (11:8), Jesus hears that Lazarus is near death. Jesus does not, however, rush right back to Bethany (11:1-6). In His own time, He finally begins His journey back

Visual for lesson 7

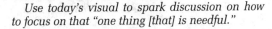

Use today's visual to spark discussion on how to focus on that "one thing [that] is needful."

How to Say It
BETHANY. *Beth*-uh-nee.
DEUTERONOMY. Due-ter-*ahn*-uh-me.
GAMALIEL. Guh-*may*-lih-ul or Guh-*may*-lee-al.
ISAIAH. Eye-*zay*-uh.
JUDEA. Joo-*dee*-uh.
LAZARUS. *Laz*-uh-rus.

into Judea, where His enemies are planning to have Him seized and killed. Jesus probably sends someone ahead to Bethany to let the two sisters know He is nearing the village.

Martha leaves her *house*, which is filled with mourners, to go out and meet Jesus. She probably understands His desire to meet privately instead of in a houseful of people. Mary, meanwhile, stays in the house. This may be her desire, or it may be to keep people from accompanying Martha to meet Jesus.

21. Then said Martha unto Jesus, Lord, if thou hadst been here, my brother had not died.

Martha seems to be scolding Jesus again. Surely greater haste on His part would have spared the life of Lazarus! But we must not be too hard on Martha. Words spoken in grief often seem harsh or indignant. She is emotionally distraught. This is not just a case of distress over a death, however. It is distress over a preventable death.

But notice Martha's belief in Jesus' power to heal. This belief combined with her scolding results in an odd mixture of faith and indignation. Martha does not understand why Jesus has delayed His trip to Bethany. She is hurt and disappointed. Jesus understands her disappointment. He knows our hearts and shares our burdens (Matthew 11:28-30). But, as John 11:40-44 will show (not in our text for today), Jesus has a plan that transcends the desires of the two sisters. Martha will find out that God's ways and thoughts are not the same as ours (Isaiah 55:8, 9). [See question #3, page 176.]

PAYING THE DEBT

Someone asked a Hollywood producer what he thought about death. He replied, "Out here we don't care for it." Except in the most extreme cases, none of us cares for it. Dying used to be called paying the debt of nature. The great English preacher Charles Spurgeon (1834–1892) said that it was more like taking in a paper note and getting gold in exchange. American paper money used to be called "silver certificate." You could actually exchange that piece of paper for silver. That is no longer the case, but the illustration still holds true. When we die we exchange the paper for the real thing.

A man said that once he was walking through a cemetery and saw some distance ahead a stone that said, "DEATH IS ETERNAL." He thought it was an awful epitaph. Then he got closer and saw that one word had been obscured by another stone. It really said, "DEATH IS ETERNAL LIFE."

When the Egyptians decorated their tombs they carved figures of people as they were in death. The English did the same. London's Westminster Abbey is filled with these figures lying, hands folded, as they lay in death. The Greeks, however, memorialized people by carving them as they were in life. The Austrians did even better. On the tomb of the Empress Maria Theresa and her husband, the two figures are carved sitting up—as if just awakening on the morning of the resurrection. We may have to pay the debt of nature, but we will be richly repaid!   —R. C. S.

B. Mustard-Seed Moment (v. 22)

22. But I know, that even now, whatsoever thou wilt ask of God, he will give it thee.

It is difficult to imagine what is in Martha's mind as she speaks these words. Does she regret the tone in her voice of her previous sentence? Is this a "backing off" to express some sort of apology? Or is Martha grasping at straws? It is difficult to believe that Martha has not heard about two previous miracles in which Jesus brought dead people back to life (Luke 7:11-15; 8:41, 42, 49-55). Is Martha hinting to Jesus that perhaps He should resurrect Lazarus? Does she have that much faith? Jesus has taught that it takes only a little faith to prompt God to do miraculous things (Matthew 17:20). Is this a "mustard-seed moment" for Martha? The use of the phrase *even now* suggests that it might well be.

C. Fine-Tuned Faith (vv. 23, 24)

23. Jesus saith unto her, Thy brother shall rise again.

The Jewish people are not unified in what they believe about resurrection. The concept of resurrection is mentioned clearly in only a few places in the Old Testament (e.g., Daniel 12:2, 3). The Sadducees—the "liberal" party of the Jews—do not believe in resurrection, and Jesus addresses their error in Mark 12:18-27. At this point in the text, Jesus' statement to Martha could be taken as a reference to the miracle that is imminent (John 11:43), or it may have been a general reference to the Old Testament concept of resurrection.

24. Martha saith unto him, I know that he shall rise again in the resurrection at the last day.

Martha obviously thinks that Jesus is referring to the *resurrection at the last day* of all who are in the grave. Jesus, however, is interested in fine-tuning her faith. Does she truly believe that the dead *shall rise again?* More importantly, does she truly believe that Jesus has miraculous power over death "even now" (v. 22)? Exactly what does Martha believe? What is the genuine nature of her faith in God? [See question #4, page 176.]

III. Incredible Profession
(John 11:25-27)

A. Jesus' Teaching (vv. 25, 26)

25. Jesus said unto her, I am the resurrection, and the life: he that believeth in me, though he were dead, yet shall he live.

Jesus' profession to be *the resurrection and the life* is astonishing! What does He mean? What is He claiming? We have a clearer understanding of His meaning because of our historical perspective, living after Jesus' own resurrection. What, however, does Martha understand Him to mean? Does she believe that Jesus possesses the power to defeat death—even four days after it happens (see v. 39)?

26. And whosoever liveth and believeth in me shall never die. Believest thou this?

Jesus asks the point-blank question! What does Martha truly believe? What is the nature of her belief in Him? That is life's ultimate question. What do you truly believe about Jesus? How does that belief affect your life? How does it change the way you live? When you stand at the grave of a loved one, do you feel hopeless or hopeful? The words of Jesus echo down the halls of time to whisper to each of us, *Believest thou this?*

B. Martha's Confession (v. 27)

27. She saith unto him, Yea, Lord: I believe that thou art the Christ, the Son of God, which should come into the world.

Martha's confession of faith reminds us of that of Peter (Matthew 16:16). Martha believes that Jesus is the Messiah, God's Anointed One. She believes He is *the Son of God.* But what do those terms mean to Martha? Andrew told Peter that Jesus was the Messiah (*the Christ,* or "Anointed One"), and Nathaniel called Jesus the Son of God (John 1:40-49; cf. 4:25). Was there common acceptance of Jesus as a divine being? We today speak of Jesus as fully human and fully divine. Is that how His contemporaries viewed Him?

Martha's confession of faith, like that of Peter, must be taken at face value. We today can read of Jesus' life and conclude that He was truly God's Son. Surely those who actually saw Him perform miracles also could have held correct beliefs about His identity!

IV. Unaltered Affection
(John 11:28-32)

A. The Other Sister (vv. 28, 29)

28. And when she had so said, she went her way, and called Mary her sister secretly, saying, The Master is come, and calleth for thee.

Jesus apparently asks about *Mary,* so Martha returns home to get her. Martha converses with Mary out of earshot of the mourners gathered at her house so that they will not intrude on Jesus' fellowship with them at this sobering time. But her plan is not successful, as we see from verse 31 below. Martha's designation of Jesus as *the Master* (or Teacher) is a common way to refer to someone who is considered to be a rabbi. (See Mark 10:17 and comments on page 163 above.)

29. As soon as she heard that, she arose quickly, and came unto him.

Filled with the same mixed emotions as Martha, Mary rushes to see Jesus. She is eager to hear His comforting words and experience again the depth of their friendship. Those feelings are probably tinged with disappointment at Jesus' late arrival. Mary is greeting an old friend, but a friend who, in her mind, has let her down.

B. Another Meeting (vv. 30, 31)

30. Now Jesus was not yet come into the town, but was in that place where Martha met him.

Jesus does not accompany *Martha* into Bethany. Perhaps He doesn't want another argument with His enemies to flare up (cf. v. 8). Or Martha may have suggested He remain at their meeting place so that He can avoid the crowd of mourners gathered at their home. In any case, Mary is expected to go to Jesus.

31. The Jews then which were with her in the house, and comforted her, when they saw Mary,

Home Daily Bible Readings

Monday, Jan. 6—Jesus Visits Mary and Martha (Luke 10:38-42)
Tuesday, Jan. 7—The Sisters Send Jesus a Message (John 11:1-6)
Wednesday, Jan. 8—Lazarus Dies (John 11:7-16)
Thursday, Jan. 9—Lord, If You Had Been Here (John 11:17-27)
Friday, Jan. 10—Jesus Weeps (John 11:28-37)
Saturday, Jan. 11—Lazarus, Come Out (John 11:38-44)
Sunday, Jan. 12—Mary Anoints Jesus (John 12:1-8)

that she rose up hastily and went out, followed her, saying, She goeth unto the grave to weep there.

Martha's apparent desire to get *Mary* out of *the house* without being noticed goes unfulfilled. In that time and culture, family tombs were often nearby, and it was customary for families to continue to go to the tomb for days after a person's death. Continuing to visit the tomb was a way of paying homage to the deceased.

Mourners are quick to follow to participate in the wailing and share the grief. Were it not for the pathos of the moment, this scene would be almost comical. Martha tries to get Mary out secretly, and as they are on their way to meet Jesus, they discover they are being followed by a train of wailing mourners! Like many folks, the mourners mean well, but in this instance they were hurting rather than helping. Martha and Mary want to meet their friend Jesus in private. They do not want to be in the midst of a great throng of people.

C. Another Broken Heart (v. 32)

32. Then when Mary was come where Jesus was, and saw him, she fell down at his feet, saying unto him, Lord, if thou hadst been here, my brother had not died.

There is a sweetness to this moment. Despite her disappointment in Jesus' late arrival, *Mary* still falls at His feet. Whenever we read of Mary of Bethany in the New Testament, she is said to be at Jesus' feet (cf. Luke 10:39; John 12:3). We also know that she is weeping (John 11:33). This is a moment of overwhelming emotion. When Mary is finally able to speak, she echoes the words of her sister.

These two women probably have spoken again and again of the "*if* only." It may be that in each hour of Lazarus's deepening illness these sisters had whispered constantly to one another, "If only Jesus were *here*." Just as they had kept a vigil at Lazarus's bedside, they probably also kept a vigil at a window, constantly scanning the horizon to see whether Jesus were finally arriving in Bethany. Mary's disappointment, like that of Martha, is expressed openly. Such is the nature of true friendship. Martha and Mary probably do not think Jesus will bring Lazarus back to life; when Jesus asks for the stone at the entrance to the tomb to be removed, Martha seems hesitant rather than expectant (John 11:39). Despite their disappointment and despair, Martha and Mary appreciate Jesus' presence in their time of grief. He is their friend, and they need His love. And the lesson they will learn about God's greater plan will far outweigh any grief they suffer now (John 11:40-44). [See question #5, page 176.]

WORDS AND DEEDS

Today's printed text stops too soon. That's obvious to anyone familiar with this account. Jesus' words about resurrection are followed by the actual raising of Lazarus. Imagine that you are a preacher and you are preaching on this text. Suddenly you realize that there sits before you a family that has just experienced the death of a loved one. Jesus is not going to come physically to your town as He came to Bethany. He is not going to engage that family in conversation. He is not going to walk with them out to the village cemetery. He is not going to call the name of their loved one and bring that person back to life again. How would you relate the raising of Lazarus to their situation?

There are at least two possibilities. When you read closely today's lesson, you cannot escape the feeling that Martha and Mary found comfort in the presence of Jesus, even though they didn't know He would bring Lazarus back from the dead. You cannot escape the feeling that they found comfort in the *words* of Jesus even though they did not know what He would do. So grieving people in any place and at any time can find comfort in the presence and in the words of Jesus.

But this is also true: if the one who died was a believer, then Jesus *is* going to do for that person what He did for Lazarus. He is not going to do it immediately, but He is going to do it eventually. The only difference is a matter of time! —R. C. S.

Conclusion

A. True Friendship

A true friend will do for us what we *need* in the long run rather than what we *want* in the short run. Such a friend will also lovingly confront us with our blind spots and problem areas. Jesus is just such a friend, as Mary and Martha discovered.

But Jesus, as the Son of God, is unlike any earthly friend we might have because of His death on the cross. Jesus' friendship is expressed not only in His life of love, but also in His death for His friends, while we were still sinners (Romans 5:6-8).

B. Prayer

Father, thank You for loving us and giving us Your Son as our eternal friend. May we draw near to Him, constantly seeking to deepen the bonds of that friendship. May our lives give consistent testimony of that friendship. In name of our Friend—and King—Jesus, amen.

C. Thought to Remember

Jesus is the Friend who never fails us.

Learning by Doing

This page contains an alternative lesson plan emphasizing learning activities.
Classes desiring such student involvement will find these suggestions helpful.

Learning Goals

After participating in this lesson, each student will be able to:

1. Tell how Jesus interacted with Martha and her sister Mary on each of two visits to Bethany.

2. Explain the importance of letting Jesus set one's priorities in both the routine and the extreme experiences of life.

3. Tell how his or her faith in Christ has determined at least one significant priority in life.

Into the Lesson

Before class begins write one of each of the letters of the word *friendship* on ten pieces of light-colored construction paper. Mix up the letters. To begin class, give one of the scrambled letters to each of ten students. Ask them to unscramble the word and stand in the correct order to display it when finished. Note: if your class is smaller, substitute the word *friend*.

State: "Friendships are an important part of our daily lives." Draw three concentric circles on the board. Pointing to the outer circle, tell the class we have some people in our lives we might call "acquaintances." The next circle can represent "friends." The inner circle represents one or two "very close friends." (Write these words in as you identify them.)

Say, "Think of a person you would call a close or intimate friend. Think about what makes this person special to you." Then ask volunteers to tell what traits they thought of.

Make the transition to Bible study by saying, "Today we will glimpse the wonderful friendships of Mary and Martha with Jesus. From them we will learn how to appreciate, understand, and encourage our friendships."

Into the Word

Using the Lesson Background and the circle of friends' illustration from above, remind the class that Mary and Martha (and Lazarus) fall into the very close friendship category. Read aloud Luke 10:38-42 and John 11:20-32, telling the class that these are two very different incidents in the lives of these friends. One has a touch of humor; the other is a sharing of grief.

Ask class members to review the first incident and look for hints to qualities of healthy friendships. What characteristics of friends are demonstrated here? Ask one class member to be a "scribe" and write answers or observations on the chalkboard. *(Answers may include hospitality, listening, enjoying the company of the other person, openness, kindness, and others.)*

Then do the same thing with the second incident. *(Answers may include sympathy, compassion, empathy, honesty, understanding.)*

Display a poster with the words "Jesus did something for Lazarus that no other friend could do." Mention to the class that we cannot overlook the supernatural side to this event. Jesus raised his friend Lazarus from the dead (v. 44). Ask, "What did Jesus do for you that no other friend could do?" *(He died for me!)* Ask, "Is it presumptuous to consider Jesus, the Son of God, our friend? Is there Scriptural foundation for considering Him our friend?" *(See John 15:13-15.)*

Into Life

Ask the class to re-focus on the qualities that make good friendships. We already have discovered and listed some of those. Ask for other qualities that have made their friendships strong. List these with the others already posted.

Then tell the class you are going to provide an opportunity to prepare a note to send to a friend expressing appreciation or offering encouragement. Give each person a piece of paper with three columns. The heading of the first column is to be "Precious Memories"; the second, "Treasured Items"; the third, "Special Qualities." Ask each learner to write the name of a friend at the top of the paper. Give the following instructions: "Think of special experiences you have had with your friend. Note these in the first column. In the second column list possessions that have come from that relationship. These may include photographs, gifts, or some other special item from your experiences together. Use the third column to list some special qualities of your friend. You may mention your friend's persistence, faith, laughter, sensitivity, and/or other traits."

Pause after the instructions for each column to allow the students to write. If time permits, allow a few people to report what they wrote before going on.

Ask the class that they use these notes as a foundation for a letter of appreciation or affirmation to their friend. Ask them to write that letter within the next two days. Close with prayer, thanking God for friends and for our Best Friend!

Let's Talk It Over

The questions on this page are designed to promote discussion of the lesson
by the class and to encourage application of the lesson Scriptures. The answers
provided are only discussion starters. Let your class talk it over from there.

1. "Martha received [Jesus] into her house" (Luke 10:38). How important do you think Christian hospitality is to the church? Why?

Hospitality is commended by several New Testament writers (Romans 12:13; Hebrews 13:2; 3 John 5-8). Paul even listed it as a qualification for widows who wished to receive support from the church (1 Timothy 5:10). This was more than inviting friends over for dinner. Traveling evangelists depended on the hospitality of fellow Christians to house them as they preached the gospel. Roadside inns were rare and often nearly as dangerous as the highways they served. Christian preachers were much safer in the homes of fellow believers.

Today, hospitality may not be a matter of life and death, but it is still important. By hosting new Christians, we encourage them to grow in the faith. By hosting home Bible studies, we encourage the church to grow spiritually and numerically. And by showing hospitality to visiting evangelists and missionaries, we participate in their ministries.

2. Martha was "troubled about many things." We, too, have many things calling for our attention. How can we balance these and still choose "that good part" that Mary chose?

Mixing up priorities is easy in our busy world. Making a living, raising a family, maintaining a house, keeping the cars running, mowing the lawn—the list is endless. But what about Jesus? Is our relationship with Him the first priority in our lives? We, like Martha, can busy ourselves with lots of good and important matters. Jesus asks us not to settle for the good, but to seek Him—the best!

Ask volunteers to tell how they keep "first things first." Perhaps some rise early to have a quiet time with the Lord before the day gets busy. Others may tell of how the family has devotions each day. Still others may tell of how they prepare for the Lord's Day even during the week to be sure their participation in Bible study and worship is not just a matter of habit.

3. The lesson writer notes Martha's "odd mixture of faith and indignation." How can we be sensitive to the conflicting emotions of those who grieve? How can we minister to them?

Anyone who has grieved the loss of a spouse or parent or other loved one knows the tangle of emotions the experience generates. They can help others in the class know a little of what to expect. Nothing is as simple as it seems. What appears to be anger may really be sorrow. What seems to be doubt may be fatigue. We need to be understanding and patient. The most important thing may be simply to be there, to listen, to encourage them to get rest and to eat. We can share our hope with them, too, but not in a preachy or condescending manner. Those who have had similar experiences can tell how they coped.

4. Why should Christians mourn the dead if we know they will be raised in the last day?

Jesus never rebuked Mary and Martha for grieving over Lazarus. Their problem was a failure to trust in Christ to conquer death. We need that same trust today. Grieving for a lost friend or loved one is a natural and therapeutic thing to do. Those who try to repress their grief usually cause themselves greater psychological and spiritual anguish in the future. We should mourn the loss of our Christian brothers and sisters, for the loss of their fellowship, support, and encouragement is significant. At the same time we can rejoice that they will live again because of Christ.

5. Martha and Mary both commented on what would have been if only Jesus had been there. Of course, when Jesus did arrive, things turned out even better than the sisters could have imagined. How can that help us when we start thinking "if only"? How can you use this text to help someone else who is thinking "if only"?

Romans 8:28 comes to mind in situations such as this. We know that God is at work in our situation even if we can't understand what He is doing. In the end, it will be for our benefit. Of course, we do not know whether we will see that benefit in this life or only in the one to come, but we know it will be there.

Martha and Mary both "knew" what Jesus should have done. He should have come and healed Lazarus. But God's purposes for Lazarus, his sisters, and the kingdom were better served by Jesus' following the course He chose. We need to remember that God knows what is best and trust Him to do it.

Pilate: Judge on Trial

DEVOTIONAL READING: 1 Timothy 6:11-16.

BACKGROUND SCRIPTURE: John 18:28–19:16.

PRINTED TEXT: John 18:31-38; 19:12-16.

John 18:31-38

31 Then said Pilate unto them, Take ye him, and judge him according to your law. The Jews therefore said unto him, It is not lawful for us to put any man to death:

32 That the saying of Jesus might be fulfilled, which he spake, signifying what death he should die.

33 Then Pilate entered into the judgment hall again, and called Jesus, and said unto him, Art thou the King of the Jews?

34 Jesus answered him, Sayest thou this thing of thyself, or did others tell it thee of me?

35 Pilate answered, Am I a Jew? Thine own nation and the chief priests have delivered thee unto me: what hast thou done?

36 Jesus answered, My kingdom is not of this world: if my kingdom were of this world, then would my servants fight, that I should not be delivered to the Jews: but now is my kingdom not from hence.

37 Pilate therefore said unto him, Art thou a king then? Jesus answered, Thou sayest that I am a king. To this end was I born, and for this cause came I into the world, that I should bear witness unto the truth. Every one that is of the truth heareth my voice.

38 Pilate saith unto him, What is truth? And when he had said this, he went out again unto the Jews, and saith unto them, I find in him no fault at all.

John 19:12-16

12 And from thenceforth Pilate sought to release him: but the Jews cried out, saying, If thou let this man go, thou art not Caesar's friend: whosoever maketh himself a king speaketh against Caesar.

13 When Pilate therefore heard that saying, he brought Jesus forth, and sat down in the judgment seat in a place that is called the Pavement, but in the Hebrew, Gabbatha.

14 And it was the preparation of the passover, and about the sixth hour: and he saith unto the Jews, Behold your King!

15 But they cried out, Away with him, away with him, crucify him. Pilate saith unto them, Shall I crucify your King? The chief priests answered, We have no king but Caesar.

16 Then delivered he him therefore unto them to be crucified. And they took Jesus, and led him away.

Jan
19

GOLDEN TEXT: [Jesus said,] Every one that is of the truth heareth my voice. Pilate saith unto him, What is truth?—John 18:37, 38.

Lesson Aims

After this lesson each student will be able to:

1. Tell how Pilate was pressured into convicting and sentencing Jesus against his better judgment.

2. Compare Pilate's predicament with the situation of people today who are pressured to compromise principles.

3. Suggest a specific means of reaffirming one's commitment to Christ and resisting pressure to compromise.

Lesson Outline

INTRODUCTION
    A. Getting a Bad Rap
    B. Lesson Background
  I. PROTECTING A KINGDOM (John 18:31-35)
    A. An Unwanted Situation (vv. 31, 32)
    B. A Tricky Question (v. 33)
      The Great One
    C. A Stinging Response (vv. 34, 35)
 II. PROCLAIMING THE KINGDOM (John 18:36-38)
    A. The Right Method (v. 36)
      The Wizard of Ahs
    B. The Right Conclusion (v. 37)
    C. The Right Question (v. 38)
III. PLACATING THE CROWD (John 19:12-16)
    A. The Rejection (vv. 12, 13)
    B. The Repudiation (vv. 14, 15)
    C. The Result (v. 16)
CONCLUSION
    A. An Ironic Judgment
    B. Prayer
    C. Thought to Remember

Introduction

A. Getting a Bad Rap

In the early morning hours of April 15, 1865, a man with a broken leg knocked on the door of Dr. Samuel A. Mudd. The doctor set the man's leg, put a splint on it, and let him stay in his house for a few hours to recuperate. The man with the broken leg was John Wilkes Booth, who had just assassinated U.S. President Abraham Lincoln. Dr. Mudd was accused of complicity in that crime and sentenced to life in prison. President Andrew Johnson pardoned Dr. Mudd in 1869.

Some historians are convinced that Dr. Mudd was one of the conspirators in the Lincoln assassination. Others believe that Dr. Mudd got a "bad rap"—that he had no idea who Booth was or what he had done. Whatever the case, almost everyone knows the saying, "His name is Mudd." Long after his death, Dr. Mudd's name is still an epithet—fairly or unfairly.

Pontius Pilate is an enigmatic figure. People automatically associate him with history's greatest injustice. Pilate, not a particularly sympathetic character, was a man caught in the midst of political intrigue. Several times he tried to do what was right regarding Jesus. In the end, however, he capitulated to pressure from the Jews and had Jesus executed. Did Pilate get a bad rap? Ask yourself that question at the end of this week's lesson.

B. Lesson Background

Palestine was, at the time of Jesus' life, an imperial province of Rome. The Jews had a figurehead king on the throne, but the true power in Palestine was in the hands of the Roman governor. He was considered a personal servant of the emperor. Pilate had control over all civil, military, and criminal matters.

Pilate governed Palestine from A.D. 26 or 27 to 37. Historians of his time have little to say about him. The Roman historian Tacitus barely mentions Pilate. Jewish historians Josephus and Philo of Alexandria give more information, but even their descriptions are sketchy. The most revealing source of information about Pilate is the New Testament. The reference in Luke 13:1 to Pilate's brutality poses many questions, all of which remain unanswered.

Pilate's place in history is marked by his dealings with one man. His record as governor is undistinguished. Pilate could easily have been totally unrecognized in the annals of history—a petty ruler of an obscure province. His name, however, always will be associated with one cowardly act of capitulation. He is the judge whom history, in turn, has put on trial. [See question #1, page 184.]

I. Protecting a Kingdom (John 18:31-35)

A. An Unwanted Situation (vv. 31, 32)

31. Then said Pilate unto them, Take ye him, and judge him according to your law. The Jews therefore said unto him, It is not lawful for us to put any man to death.

After His arrest in Gethsemane, Jesus is subjected to a series of "interviews" with the Jewish high priest Caiaphas and his father-in-law, Annas. Without doubt, Caiaphas wants Jesus to be executed. But Caiaphas knows that the Jewish Sanhedrin no longer has the power to carry out a *death* sentence. It lost that power when Rome changed the nature of its rule over the area in A.D. 6. So Caiaphas follows the proper political channels and sends Jesus to *Pilate*.

Jesus appears before Pilate in the very early hours of Friday morning. It seems that Pilate is not eager to deal with Jesus (John 18:28-30). Pilate, like most governors in the Roman Empire, wants to stay off Rome's radar screen, but the political infighting in Palestine makes that difficult. He may have heard some of the rumors about Jesus, but we can be sure Pilate wants to avoid political intrigue. It is not surprising, then, that Pilate tells the *Jews* to deal with the problem internally. He wants no part of the matter! The proconsul Gallio will take much the same attitude a few years later when dealing with the apostle Paul (Acts 18:12-15).

32. That the saying of Jesus might be fulfilled, which he spake, signifying what death he should die.

Jesus has prophesied that He will be crucified (Matthew 20:19; John 3:14; 12:32, 33). But the Jews do not execute by crucifixion. They normally execute by stoning (Deuteronomy 21:18-23), but even that cannot be done without the Romans' permission. The stoning of Stephen in Acts 7 is not sanctioned by the Romans, but that is not a formal, court-ordered execution. Stephen's death is the impulsive act of an angry mob.

B. A Tricky Question (v. 33)

33. Then Pilate entered into the judgment hall again, and called Jesus, and said unto him, Art thou the King of the Jews?

Despite his desire to be left out of this matter, *Pilate* knows that he has a kingdom to protect. Rome will not tolerate insurrection in any of its provinces, and will deal harshly with any governor who does not investigate quickly rumors of sedition. So protecting Rome's interests is a way of protecting Pilate's own job!

Pilate undoubtedly has heard rumors of the man from Nazareth who some claim to be a *king*. (After meeting Jesus once, Nathanael had declared Him to be "the Son of God" and "the King of Israel"; John 1:49. And in Jesus' appearance before Caiaphas, the high priest had pointedly asked Jesus if He was the Christ—the Messiah— and Jesus had answered, "I am"; Mark 14:61, 62. To the Jewish people, the promised Messiah is to be *the King of the Jews*.) Pilate may have chosen to ignore it, but Jesus' triumphal entry into Jerusalem probably piqued his interest. He may desire to stay out of Jewish inner-circle politics, but he also does not want Rome breathing down his neck. So when the Sanhedrin brings Jesus before him, he knows he has no choice but to examine the case.

Pilate asks what at first glance seems to be a simple question. It is, however, a very tricky question. Is Jesus the king of the Jews? A "yes" answer will take the proceedings down one path, while a "no" answer would take it down another. Jesus eventually will answer "yes," but not just yet.

THE GREAT ONE

The Honeymooners became one of the most popular television "situation comedies" in the 1950s. All America became well acquainted with the antics of blustery Ralph Cramden (played by the rotund one, Jackie Gleason), his patient and long-suffering wife (played by Audrey Meadows), and their upstairs neighbors—a zany free spirit who worked in the sewers of Brooklyn (Art Carney) and his equally long-suffering wife (Joyce Randolph).

Nearly every episode featured two famous lines by Gleason: "One of these days, Alice!" and "Baby, you're the greatest!" But the greatest, at least in Gleason's mind, was Gleason himself. Actors have egos and Gleason was no exception. He went on in show business to be billed as "The Great One." Jackie Gleason was the undisputed king of comedy at a time when black and white television ruled the night.

History establishes that Jesus Christ was indeed the King of the Jews, the King of Israel. More than that, the book of Revelation calls Jesus "King of kings and Lord of lords." All kings have egos, but Jesus had none. He did not have to bluster His way through life as did "The Great One."

How to Say It

ALEXANDRIA. Al-iks-*an*-dree-uh.
ANNAS. *An*-nus.
ANTONIA. An-*toe*-nee-uh or An-*toe*-nyuh.
CAESAR. *See*-zur.
CAIAPHAS. *Kay*-uh-fus or *Kye*-uh-fus.
CORINTHIANS. Kor-*in*-thee-unz *(th as in thin)*.
DEUTERONOMY. Due-ter-*ahn*-uh-me.
GABBATHA (Hebrew). *Gab*-buh-thuh.
GALILEE. *Gal*-uh-lee.
GALLIO. *Gal*-ee-o.
GETHSEMANE. Geth-*sem*-uh-nee.
JOSEPHUS. Jo-*see*-fus.
NATHANAEL. Nuh-*than*-yull *(th as in thin)*.
NAZARETH. *Naz*-uh-reth.
PHILO. *Fie*-low.
PONTIUS PILATE. *Pon*-shus or *Pon*-ti-us *Pie*-lut.
SANHEDRIN. *San*-huh-drun or San-*heed*-run.
TACITUS. *Tass*-ih-tus.

He did not have to climb up on the prow of a ship, as did Leonardo DiCaprio in *Titanic,* and shout into the wind, "I'm the king of the world!"

Was Jesus a king—*the* King? Oh, yes, He was (and is) the King. But He lived like a servant. He was God, but He died as a man. Part of His greatness is in His humility.   —V. K.

C. A Stinging Response (vv. 34, 35)

34. Jesus answered him, Sayest thou this thing of thyself, or did others tell it thee of me?

Pilate certainly does not expect to be questioned by a prisoner, especially this lowly peasant from the hill country of Galilee. But Jesus is not intimidated! He responds with a stinging rebuke. Is Pilate speaking from his own initiative and curiosity, or is he merely parroting the charge of the Sanhedrin? Jesus always cuts to the heart of the matter. There is no pretense with Him. He knows what Pilate is doing and what kingdom Pilate is protecting.

35. Pilate answered, Am I a Jew? Thine own nation and the chief priests have delivered thee unto me: what hast thou done?

What was the tone of Pilate's voice? Was it defensive or contemptuous? No doubt he is caught off-guard by Jesus' question. Some believe he was pleading ignorance: He isn't *a Jew,* so how can he understand what is going on? He did not initiate Jesus' arrest. Jesus' problem is with His own people! They are the ones who are making the accusations against Him.

Others see Pilate as more hostile. Who does Jesus think He is, questioning the Roman governor? Jesus might be able to baffle and outwit those Jewish leaders, but Pilate is not a Jew! Now that the leaders have brought Jesus to him, Jesus had better start answering the charges. What has He *done?*

II. Proclaiming the Kingdom (John 18:36-38)

A. The Right Method (v. 36)

36. Jesus answered, My kingdom is not of this world: if my kingdom were of this world, then would my servants fight, that I should not be delivered to the Jews: but now is my kingdom not from hence.

Jesus acknowledges that He has a *kingdom,* but it is not an earthly kingdom. It therefore poses no threat to the Roman Empire. Earthly kings come to power by might. They have great armies, powerful weapons, and military strategy. They conquer, terrorize, and kill without conscience in order to attain land and people. Jesus' kingdom is different. He does not subjugate people by might but by love. He does not conquer by

power of the sword, but by an appeal to the heart. If His were an earthly kingdom, then His followers would have fought to keep Him from being arrested. In fact, Peter had tried to do just that! (See John 18:10.)

Think about what kind of threat Jesus could have posed to His enemies. If Jesus had been interested in an earthly kingdom, what a military leader He would have been! His army would have been invincible! Think of the possibilities. He had the power to calm the wind and the waves (Mark 4:37-41). Power over nature could come in very handy in the midst of a battle. Jesus could feed thousands of people with miniscule amounts of food (Luke 9:12-17). No need to worry about feeding the troops! Jesus could heal the sick. If a man were wounded in battle, Jesus could heal him immediately and have him rejoin the battle. The ultimate power would have been that of resurrection. If a man were killed in battle, Jesus could raise him to fight again and again! The powers at Jesus' disposal are awe-inspiring. No military force on earth could have stopped Him.

Jesus, however, is not interested in an earthly kingdom or in any form of earthly power. The true enemy is not the Roman Empire, but Satan and death (Luke 10:18, 19; 1 Corinthians 15:26). Jesus will have a kingdom, but it will not be attained by the methods used by sinful men or expected by the Jewish leaders. His method is entirely different. He will love His enemies and do good to those who hate Him (Matthew 5:44). He will not merely proclaim these as vaunted principles, He will practice them. He will die to pay sin's price. He will rise again to defeat the true enemies. [See question #2, page 184.]

In the twentieth century, a chancellor came to power in Germany. Accepting the philosophy "might makes right," he began to bully all of Europe. He proclaimed a rule that would last a thousand years. It lasted less than twelve. Hitler's "Third Reich" was responsible for the deaths of millions of innocent people. His method was wrong and his reign was short. Jesus' method is right, and His reign, in the hearts of men and women throughout the world and throughout the ages, is endless!

THE WIZARD OF AHS

In Frank L. Baum's timeless tale, *The Wonderful Wizard of Oz,* Dorothy and her little dog Toto are transported via a furious cyclone from their humble home on the plains of Kansas to the fantastic and sometimes frightening kingdom of Oz. Dorothy's breathtaking adventures and misadventures with the tin man, scarecrow, and cowardly lion regale the reader and lead him or her into a mystifying kingdom that truly is not of this world.

The power behind this eerie kingdom is an anonymous figure who is "pulling the strings," so to speak. He holds sway over everyone by pretending to be someone he is not. "Oohs and ahs" are extracted from those he is fooling. When the curtain is finally pulled back, he is exposed for all to see. The "wonderful wizard of Oz" is nothing more than a crafty charlatan.

How often we are fooled by the ruler of this world! Like Dorothy and her traveling companions, we are taken in by the tantalizing tinsel or tough-talking tactics of the enemy. Scripture depicts Satan as a deceiver (cf. 2 Corinthians 11:14). Christians must be wary of his devious schemes, lest they be drawn into his counterfeit kingdom.

Jesus firmly declared that His kingdom was not of this world—that His kingdom was not from here. His is a *spiritual* kingdom first and foremost. And to that we can say, with a measure of relief, *"Ah*-men!"   —V. K.

B. The Right Conclusion (v. 37)

37. Pilate therefore said unto him, Art thou a king then? Jesus answered, Thou sayest that I am a king. To this end was I born, and for this cause came I into the world, that I should bear witness unto the truth. Every one that is of the truth heareth my voice.

Jesus' response has left *Pilate* reeling. Pilate had not expected a philosophical debate with this itinerant rabbi from Nazareth. What is this talk about a kingdom not of this world? Pilate wants Jesus to get to the point—is He saying that He is *king* or not?

Jesus affirms that He is a king. (*Thou sayest . . .* is an affirmative response, like "It is as you say.") But Jesus needs to offer further clarification: His is a kingdom of *truth*. Only those on the side of truth will be able to hear His *voice* and listen (cf. 10:3, 16, 27). [See question #3, page 184.]

C. The Right Question (v. 38)

38. Pilate saith unto him, What is truth? And when he had said this, he went out again unto the Jews, and saith unto them, I find in him no fault at all.

Pilate has no idea what Jesus is talking about. Nor does he care! To the pragmatic politician, truth is whatever he needs it to be at the moment. Like many today, Pilate has abandoned the idea of absolute *truth*. He walks away before Jesus can answer his question.

Yet, there standing before Pilate was TRUTH! Jesus is not a man who merely tells the truth; He is the living truth (John 14:6). Knowing Him means knowing truth and freedom (8:32). Jesus makes freedom available to us by the power of His own life, death, and resurrection. And the

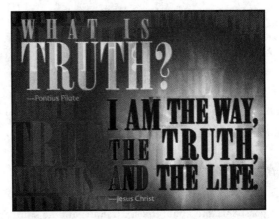

Visual for lesson 8. *Display this poster as you discuss verse 38. Note the irony of Pilate's question, asked in the presence of the One who is Truth.*

One who is the truth also teaches truth. Despite what men may say, there are absolute truths that are immutable. And there is the absolute TRUTH, who lives and reigns in the hearts of His followers. Jesus came to proclaim a kingdom and to proclaim Himself as the King!

Pilate has indeed asked the right questions. Even though he does not acknowledge Jesus as any kind of king except sarcastically (19:14, 15, 19), Pilate at least recognizes that Jesus is no criminal. He can find *no fault* in Him.

III. Placating the Crowd (John 19:12-16)

A. The Rejection (vv. 12, 13)

12. And from thenceforth Pilate sought to release him: but the Jews cried out, saying, If thou let this man go, thou art not Caesar's friend: whosoever maketh himself a king speaketh against Caesar.

Much has happened in the intervening text not included in our lesson (John 18:39–19:11). *Pilate* has squirmed this way and that, trying to get Jesus released. He knows the charge against Jesus is without legal foundation, but that the Jewish leaders have brought Jesus to him out of envy (Matthew 27:18). He knows Jesus poses no threat to Rome, so he wants to *release* Jesus.

The leaders of the *Jews* are livid. They are also cunning politicians. They know the power of rumor and innuendo. Their threat is not veiled as they switch their argument from theology (John 19:7) to politics: *Caesar* will not be pleased to hear that his governor in Palestine has failed to deal with one who claims to be a *king*. As is often the case, hardball politics wins the day. [See question #4, page 184.]

13. When Pilate therefore heard that saying, he brought Jesus forth, and sat down in the judgment seat in a place that is called the Pavement, but in the Hebrew, Gabbatha.

There is some debate among scholars about the location John describes. It may be part of the Roman fortress, the Antonia, which is adjacent to the northwest corner of the temple grounds. In any case, Pilate brings Jesus to a public *place* to pronounce his *judgment* and dispatch the matter. The one to whom all judgment ultimately is trusted (John 5:22) is now to be judged Himself.

B. The Repudiation (vv. 14, 15)

14. And it was the preparation of the passover, and about the sixth hour: and he saith unto the Jews, Behold your King!

Although some have argued that these events took place on Thursday, or even Wednesday, most Bible scholars agree that John spoke of the sixth day of the week, Friday. There also has been some controversy about John's notation of time. If the trial was still in progress at *the sixth hour*, then how could Jesus have been crucified at the third hour, as Mark 15:25 records? The simple solution is that John was using Roman time, which places these events at about 6 A.M. (Other time references in John's Gospel are consistent with a use of Roman time.) Mark used Jewish time, which would place the crucifixion at 9 A.M., three hours after these events.

Pilate's sarcasm and taunting of his Jewish opponents is revealed in his statement, *Behold your King!* Even though Pilate rejects their charge against Jesus, he bows to their wishes and gives in to their threats. The great irony is that the King of the universe is indeed standing in their midst, and no one recognizes it. The blindness noted in John 12:37-41 is complete.

Home Daily Bible Readings

Monday, Jan. 13—When You Have Turned Back (Luke 22:24-34)

Tuesday, Jan. 14—Peter Denies Jesus (Luke 22:54-62)

Wednesday, Jan. 15—Peter Goes Fishing (John 21:1-6)

Thursday, Jan. 16—It Is the Lord (John 21:7-14)

Friday, Jan. 17—Simon, Do You Love Me? (John 21:15-19)

Saturday, Jan. 18—Repent and Be Baptized (Acts 2:37-42)

Sunday, Jan. 19—In Jesus' Name, Walk (Acts 3:1-7)

---

15. But they cried out, Away with him, away with him, crucify him. Pilate saith unto them, Shall I crucify your King? The chief priests answered, We have no king but Caesar.

The Jewish authorities lead the charge to have Jesus crucified. Victory is within their grasp. Again, *Pilate* sarcastically refers to Jesus as their *King.* The reply, *We have no king but Caesar* is blasphemous (cf. Judges 8:23; 1 Samuel 8:7). God has sent His own dear Son to reign over them, but they reject Him and claim allegiance to the pagan in Rome instead. Even that claim is drenched in hypocrisy because they hate Caesar—they just hate Jesus more. [See question #5, page 184.]

C. The Result (v. 16)

16. Then delivered he him therefore unto them to be crucified. And they took Jesus, and led him away.

This pathetic drama moves toward its final act as Pilate gives in to political extortion. Rome will hardly note the crucifixion of a peasant from Galilee who has no friends in high places. The Jewish leaders, on the other hand, could create a political firestorm. Pilate does not need that kind of complication. Pilate wants to do the right thing, but he is a pragmatic governor. History has judged Pilate an evil man. In reality, he is a coward and a political opportunist.

So the King of kings is *led* down the dusty streets of Jerusalem to be nailed to a cross. The Son of God will hang suspended between Heaven and earth to pay the penalty for our sin, to be God's sacrificial Lamb.

Conclusion

A. An Ironic Judgment

God sent His Son to earth. The people who had waited for the Messiah for centuries did not understand the nature of His kingdom and rejected Jesus. Pilate deserves our disdain for his cowardice. The Jews deserve our disdain for they, in one of history's most ironic judgments, rejected Jesus and claimed Caesar as their king. But we must reserve some disdain for ourselves because our sin made Jesus' crucifixion necessary. But today God still gives us the opportunity to make Jesus our King.

B. Prayer

Father, give us wisdom and courage. May we make Jesus our King. May He reign in our hearts with supreme authority. In His holy and majestic name we pray, amen.

C. Thought to Remember

Jesus is the King. Let Him reign in your heart.

Learning by Doing

This page contains an alternative lesson plan emphasizing learning activities.
Classes desiring such student involvement will find these suggestions helpful.

Learning Goals

After participating in this lesson, each student will be able to:

1. Tell how Pilate was pressured into convicting and sentencing Jesus against his better judgment.

2. Compare Pilate's predicament with the situation of people today who are pressured to compromise principles.

3. Suggest a specific means of reaffirming one's commitment to Christ and resisting pressure to compromise.

Into the Lesson

Before class write "His name is mud" on the chalkboard. Also prepare two pieces of paper with one of these names on each, *Mudd* and *Pilate.*

Begin by asking what the saying means. Then ask if any one knows the source of the saying. Use the lesson Introduction (page 178) to tell the story. Do not use Dr. Mudd's name until the end when you attach the paper with his name on it over the word *mud.*

Make the transition to Bible study by saying, "Fairly or unfairly, long after his death, Dr. Mudd's name is still an epithet. In today's study, we glimpse another figure whose name, fairly or unfairly, has been associated with history's greatest injustice. His name is Pilate." At this time place Pilate's name over Mudd's.

Into the Word

Prepare a handout for the class. On one side include the printed Scripture from John 18:28-38, 19:1-16. (The back side is described in the group discussion activity.) Highlight each of seven copies with the reading part for one of the following: a narrator, Pilate, Jesus, two chief priests, and two soldiers. Ask the narrator, "Pilate," and "Jesus" to stand at the front of the class for the reading. The others will read their parts from where they are seated.

Use the Lesson Background to prepare a brief lecture and picture of the setting for this occasion. Focus on the letter "P" during this lecture. Prepare visual cards you can attach to the wall as an outline during this brief lecture. Each card should have one of the following words on it: Palestine, Province, Power, Procurator, and Pilate.

The following activities may be done in small groups or by the entire class. Both tasks should be printed on the back side of the handout.

First Activity. "Pilate was a man caught in political intrigue. He appears to try to do what was right. But in the end he capitulated to pressure and had Jesus executed. Does Pilate get a 'bad rap'? Read the following texts for a closer look. Beside each text, write a phrase that describes his character or actions."

Below that paragraph list the following texts vertically: John 18:28, 29; 18:31-33; 18:33-38; 19:1; 19:4, 5; 19:8; 19:9-12; 19:16; Luke 13:1. Then write, "What conclusions do you draw about Pilate's character and circumstance? How does Pilate's dilemma compare to what we today feel in situations that tempt us to compromise?"

After allowing class members to report their answers, say, "Jesus shares something wonderful with Pilate that helps us understand our future." The next activity will focus on Jesus' teachings about the kingdom of God.

Second Activity. "Reread Jesus' interview with Pilate (John 18:33-38). Answer these questions:

"1. Why did Pilate have to know if Jesus was King of the Jews?

"2. Why—if His kingdom were of this world—did Jesus' say His servants would fight (v. 36)? What is Jesus teaching about His kingdom here?

"3. Jesus gave a reason for His coming to this world (v. 37). What does He mean 'that I should bear witness unto the truth'?

"4. Jesus said, 'I am the way, the truth, and the life' (John 14:6). He didn't say He 'told the truth.' He said, 'I am the . . . truth!' What is the difference?"

After a time, allow the groups to respond.

Into Life

Prepare copies of a sheet with the words "Bring me safely to His Heavenly kingdom." Ask each class member to draw the outline of a crown on the bottom. Tell the class, "We will call this the crown of life. When the apostle Paul wrote his concluding remarks to Timothy, he testified, 'The Lord shall deliver me from every evil work, and will preserve me unto his heavenly kingdom' (2 Timothy 4:18)." Display your poster.

Ask class members to think about what they are looking forward to most in the Heavenly kingdom. Ask them to write just a couple of those things in their crowns. Ask the class to share their hopes in groups of two or three people. Those small groups then can pray together, thanking God for their hope.

Let's Talk It Over

The questions on this page are designed to promote discussion of the lesson by the class and to encourage application of the lesson Scriptures. The answers provided are only discussion starters. Let your class talk it over from there.

1. What marks Pilate's place in history is the way he handled one singular situation: the trial of Jesus. What kind of situations have the potential for becoming the defining moments of our lives? How can we meet these with courage and faith?

Crisis times have great power to shape us. For better or for worse, our response to a crisis can have long-lasting impact. These may include accidents, illness, financial problems, and others. For Pilate, it was a moment of decision. We, too, may face such moments when our sense of what's right collides with our desire for security. Encourage class members to tell how specific events shaped them. Try to draw details from those who faced their crises in faith—how did they maintain faith, who or what encouraged them, and who else was affected by their actions?

Other events also may have great impact. Studying under an inspiring teacher may be one. Taking on a significant responsibility is another. Your learners will think of more. Explore with them how to deal with these situations faithfully.

2. Jesus was not interested in earthly power. To what extent, if at all, is it proper for Christians to seek earthly power?

Jesus had a very specific agenda, and He would not be deterred from it. Building an earthly kingdom would not have furthered that agenda. There are believers who think that Christians should take no part in politics—not holding office or even voting. Most Christians, however, see voting and other political involvement as ways to spread Christian influence into the governing of the nation. Certainly we do not put ultimate confidence in political processes or leaders. And we cannot let matters that pertain only to this life become our priority. But seeking first His kingdom and His righteousness, we may still have some involvement in earthly politics. Government is ordained by God, and the wise steward can balance involvement in it with his or her service for the Lord.

3. How important is the belief in absolute truth to the Christian faith? Why?

In our "postmodern" culture today, many people believe that all truth and all moral values are relative. That is, two people or societies may have different views of truth or morality and both

be right. One person might believe in God and another person may be an atheist, and both are right. One society might practice polygamy and another not, and both are considered moral. If relativism is correct, then Christianity is no more true or false, right or wrong, than any other religion. Clearly, this is unacceptable. Jesus never said He was *a* truth or *a* way to God, He said He is *the* Way and *the* Truth, and "no man cometh unto the Father, but by me" (John 14:6).

4. The Jews pressured Pilate into doing what he did not really want to do by invoking the name of Caesar. How do people today pressure Christians into doing what they know they shouldn't? How can we resist such pressure?

Fear is a powerful motivator. Pilate was afraid he would lose his job—and possibly his life. Unscrupulous employers and supervisors can make believers feel their jobs are in jeopardy if they do not go along with unethical business practices or even immoral personal behaviors. Peer pressure is another powerful tool. Friends and neighbors can make doing the right thing seem like a wrong thing when it exposes their own sinfulness. Name-calling and threats of isolation become powerful weapons in such cases.

Of course, we resist by putting Christ first. But that's easier said than done. Perhaps some real-life stories from your students would help.

5. The Jewish leaders committed blasphemy even as they pushed to have Jesus executed for "blasphemy." Have you ever been condemned by someone for something you knew your accuser to be guilty of? Have you ever found yourself guilty of the very thing you condemned in another? How do you deal with such situations?

We all can be guilty of this very sin. That is the reason Jesus urged us to be careful about judging others (Matthew 7:1). We are not the ones to pronounce judgment. Rather, we ought to rebuke another gently and with the intent of restoring the person (Galatians 6:1, 2).

It is particularly vexing, of course, to be publicly criticized for something when you know the accuser is guilty of the same sin (and you may be innocent). How do we turn the other cheek in such cases? If you have students who have done so, encourage them to tell their stories.

Peter: Restored Leader

January 26
Lesson 9

DEVOTIONAL READING: Acts 4:1-13.

BACKGROUND SCRIPTURE: Luke 22:31-34, 54-62; John 21.

PRINTED TEXT: Luke 22:31-34, 54-62; John 21:17.

Luke 22:31-34, 54-62

31 And the Lord said, Simon, Simon, behold, Satan hath desired to have you, that he may sift you as wheat:

32 But I have prayed for thee, that thy faith fail not: and when thou art converted, strengthen thy brethren.

33 And he said unto him, Lord, I am ready to go with thee, both into prison, and to death.

34 And he said, I tell thee, Peter, the cock shall not crow this day, before that thou shalt thrice deny that thou knowest me.

. . . .

54 Then took they him, and led him, and brought him into the high priest's house. And Peter followed afar off.

55 And when they had kindled a fire in the midst of the hall, and were set down together, Peter sat down among them.

56 But a certain maid beheld him as he sat by the fire, and earnestly looked upon him, and said, This man was also with him.

57 And he denied him, saying, Woman, I know him not.

58 And after a little while another saw him, and said, Thou art also of them. And Peter said, Man, I am not.

59 And about the space of one hour after another confidently affirmed, saying, Of a truth this fellow also was with him; for he is a Galilean.

60 And Peter said, Man, I know not what thou sayest. And immediately, while he yet spake, the cock crew.

61 And the Lord turned, and looked upon Peter. And Peter remembered the word of the Lord, how he had said unto him, Before the cock crow, thou shalt deny me thrice.

62 And Peter went out, and wept bitterly.

John 21:17

17 He saith unto him the third time, Simon, son of Jona, lovest thou me? Peter was grieved because he said unto him the third time, Lovest thou me? And he said unto him, Lord, thou knowest all things; thou knowest that I love thee. Jesus saith unto him, Feed my sheep.

Jan 26

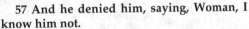

GOLDEN TEXT: Jesus saith to Simon Peter, Simon, son of Jona, lovest thou me more than these? He saith unto him, Yea, Lord; thou knowest that I love thee. He saith unto him, Feed my lambs.—John 21:15.

> ## Portraits of Faith
> Unit 2: Personalities in Jesus'
> Life and Ministry
> (Lessons 6-9)

Lesson Aims

After participating in this lesson, each student will be able to:

1. Cite the events surrounding Peter's denial of Jesus and his eventual restoration.

2. Explain why one who confidently asserts devotion can yield to denial in the heat of opposition.

3. Recall a time when he or she has denied (in word or in deed) the Lord, and express repentance and renewed love for Him.

Lesson Outline

INTRODUCTION
    A. Flawed People
    B. Lesson Background
  I. THE DECLARATION (Luke 22:31-34)
    A. The Enemy's Request (v. 31)
    B. The Savior's Prayer (v. 32)
    C. An Apostle's Affirmation (v. 33)
      Into Prison, and to Death
    D. The Master's Reply (v. 34)
 II. THE DENIALS (Luke 22:54-62)
    A. Interested Party (v. 54)
    B. Three Denials (vv. 55-60)
    C. Jesus' Eyes (v. 61)
    D. Peter's Sorrow (v. 62)
      Recanting a Recantation
III. THE DUTY (John 21:17)
    A. Piercing Question (v. 17a)
    B. Complete Restoration (v. 17b)
CONCLUSION
    A. The Imperfect Man for the Job
    B. Prayer
    C. Thought to Remember

Introduction

A. Flawed People

Occasionally you will hear someone use the phrase "revisionist history." That expression refers to a retelling of history with a different slant on things. Sometimes revisionist history makes things sound a little better than they really were, and sometimes it makes things sound a little worse. It depends on the way a person wants to slant things!

One of the great strengths of the Bible is that it is not "revisionist history." If the Bible were, as

some claim, a collection of myths or fables, why would we so consistently see the foibles and failures of its heroic figures?

Abraham was a great man of God, but his faith sometimes wavered in the face of danger, leading him to lie to protect himself. Moses was God's chosen servant to deliver His people out of bondage and to deliver to those people the law of God. But Moses was also a man with a temper—a temper that once erupted so violently that he killed someone!

Elijah was the great Old Testament prophet who called down fire from Heaven to defeat the prophets of Baal on Mount Carmel. He appeared on the Mount of Transfiguration with Moses and Jesus. Yet Elijah had such severe moments of doubt that he once wished he were dead.

David is the only person in Scripture who is characterized as a man after God's own heart (1 Samuel 13:14; Acts 13:22). But we know also that David was a man guilty of lust, deception, and murder.

In the New Testament, the two most prominent Christian leaders are Paul and Peter. But remember that Paul had been an ardent persecutor of the church. He was responsible for the imprisonment and death of many believers. Peter, the focus of this week's lesson, was also a man deeply flawed.

The Bible's honesty about its heroes adds to its credibility. No revisionist history here! The Bible does not hedge about the flaws of its main characters. The Bible never flinches at the truth.

B. Lesson Background

This week's lesson begins at the Passover meal on Thursday evening. After Jesus instituted the Lord's Supper, He sat talking with His disciples. He had a lot to say. He knew what would happen the next day. Imagine that you knew you had only a few hours to live. Wouldn't you have a lot to say to the people you love? That's probably how Jesus felt. He talked to the disciples about the nature of greatness in God's eyes and about their place in His glorious kingdom. Then He turned to Peter.

I. The Declaration (Luke 22:31-34)

Imagine what might be in Peter's heart when Jesus turns to him. Jesus has been talking about being great and about ruling in His kingdom. Peter has been waiting for this moment for almost three years. He is the one who had proclaimed Jesus to be the Christ, the Son of God (Matthew 16:16). He is the bold one, the fearless leader of the band of disciples. Surely his moment has come!

A. The Enemy's Request (v. 31)

31. And the Lord said, Simon, Simon, behold, Satan hath desired to have you, that he may sift you as wheat.

Simon Peter might not be surprised to hear Jesus say, "The Father and I have been talking about you." Instead, imagine Peter's confusion when he hears Jesus tell him that He and *Satan* have been talking about him!

But Peter is not alone, since the Greek pronoun translated *you* is plural. Jesus is addressing Peter, but speaking of the entire group of disciples. Satan wants to test all of them! Winnowing or sifting of *wheat* is a common event in agricultural Palestine. The disciples understand what Jesus is talking about, but they must wonder why. At the last supper, they undoubtedly are thinking about Jesus' being recognized as the Ruler of Israel and setting up His kingdom. But He is talking about Satan's testing them. Peter is not the only one who is confused! [See question #1, page 192.]

B. The Savior's Prayer (v. 32)

32. But I have prayed for thee, that thy faith fail not: and when thou art converted, strengthen thy brethren.

Jesus addresses Peter personally in this verse (the word translated *thee* is singular). Jesus has asked the Father to bind them together so that Peter will not feel alone and his *faith* will not waver.

But Jesus knows what is about to happen. He knows that Peter will experience a moment of utter failure. But when Peter recovers from this failure—is *converted*—the darkness of his denials will be transformed into a light that burns brightly for Christ. Jesus knows that Peter's post-resurrection boldness can invigorate his fellow apostles in their mission of proclamation. [See question #2, page 192.]

C. An Apostle's Affirmation (v. 33)

33. And he said unto him, Lord, I am ready to go with thee, both into prison, and to death.

We often think of Peter as having "foot in mouth" disease because of his apparent tendency to pop off at times. Not this time! Peter means what he says. At this moment, he truly counts himself as *ready* to die for Jesus. And when the mob comes for Jesus in the garden, Peter will draw his sword and prepare to kill or be killed! It is easy to criticize Peter for his failures, but do not characterize him as a coward.

INTO PRISON, AND TO DEATH

Ivan S. Prokhanoff (1869–1935) was the dynamic leader of the evangelical Christian movement in Russia before and after the Bolshevik Revolution of 1917. Twice he was put in prison for his faith. Arrested by the Cheka, the political police of the revolution, Prokhanoff and his followers (known simply as "Gospel Christians") joyfully witnessed in their cells. "We sang, read the Word of God, and prayed. The red soldiers, militiamen, and even the Cheka came and listened to us. . . . Many people gathered in the street outside to listen to our singing. Was there ever such a testimony?" (*In the Cauldron of Russia*, 1933).

Richard Wurmbrand was a Romanian Jew who converted to Christianity. He spent fourteen years in prison for leading an underground church and smuggling Bibles into Russia. After his release he wrote a best-selling book *Tortured for Christ* (Spire, 1962; reprinted 1998) and in 1966 testified in Washington, D.C. before the Senate Internal Security Subcommittee about what believers like himself were enduring in prisons behind the Iron Curtain. He stripped to the waist to convince skeptical politicians with his "scars and stripes" that torture in Communist prisons was real. But many of his fellow prisoners never came out of the prisons alive. They were terribly "tortured, not accepting deliverance; that they might obtain a better resurrection" (Hebrews 11:35).

> Must I be carried to the skies
>   On flow'ry beds of ease,
> While others fought to win the prize
>   And sailed through bloody seas? —Isaac Watts
>   —V. K.

D. The Master's Reply (v. 34)

34. And he said, I tell thee, Peter, the cock shall not crow this day, before that thou shalt thrice deny that thou knowest me.

If words can pierce the human heart, *Peter* is wounded. What is Jesus saying? Has Peter not just declared his loyalty to the point of imprisonment and death? How, then, can Jesus be saying that Peter will shrink back at simply being accused of knowing Jesus?

In Peter's mind, there is no conceivable scenario in which he will *deny* knowing Jesus. That simply is never going to happen. And to think it will happen three times before the dawn of the next morning is absurd. In his heart, Peter knows that he would rather die than deny!

II. The Denials (Luke 22:54-62)

In order to understand the subsequent denials of Peter, certain events must be placed in context. Jesus and His followers have gone to Gethsemane after celebrating the Passover and instituting the Lord's Supper. There Jesus prayed. His weary disciples succumbed to their exhaustion and slept.

How to Say It

ABRAHAM. *Ay*-bruh-ham.
ANNAS. *An*-nus.
BAAL. *Bay*-ul.
CAIAPHAS. *Kay*-uh-fus or *Kye*-uh-fus.
ELIJAH. Ee-*lye*-juh.
GALILEAN. Gal-uh-*lee*-un.
GALILEE. *Gal*-uh-lee.
GETHSEMANE. *Geth*-sem-uh-nee.
JONA. *Jo*-nuh.
JUDAS. *Joo*-dus.
MALCHUS. *Mal*-kus.

Sometime during the early morning hours on Friday, Judas and the members of the temple guard came to Gethsemane to get Jesus. Jesus accepted the ironic kiss from the traitorous Judas. Then, when the members of the temple guard stepped forward to seize Jesus, Peter drew his sword and tried to defend Jesus by attacking the high priest's servant (John 18:10), slicing off the man's ear. Let's give Peter credit for his courage. He was ready to defend Jesus with his life! How many of us have such courage?

But with adrenaline pumping and muscles tensed for further battle, Peter sees Jesus reach for something on the ground. It is the severed ear of Malchus. Jesus turns to Peter and tells him to put away his sword (John 18:11). Then Jesus miraculously restores Malchus's ear to its proper place on the side of his head (Luke 22:51). Imagine the confusion in Peter's mind! Jesus had just said, in effect, "Peter, that just isn't the way we do things!"

Peter does not understand just how God is going to do things. He is no coward, but he is very confused. He is also embarrassed and hurt. Jesus' healing of Malchus probably humiliated Peter. He is probably asking himself, "What am I supposed to do?" He stands there perplexed as the soldiers lead Jesus away.

A. Interested Party (v. 54)

54. Then took they him, and led him, and brought him into the high priest's house. And Peter followed afar off.

Perhaps because of the early hour, Jesus is taken to *the high priest's* home rather than to any official site. Annas, the father-in-law of the high priest, will interrogate Jesus. Caiaphas, the high priest himself, also will ask questions (John 18:12, 13). Luke's focus at this point, however, is upon *Peter.* When Jesus is taken from the garden, Peter probably does not move for a moment. When he does move, he does not run off and hide in a cave. He follows the mob—from a safe distance.

The stunning sequence of events in Gethsemane has unnerved a very confused Peter. He does not walk away from the situation because He wants to know how events will unfold from that point on. Perhaps Gethsemane was the wrong place, and Jesus is waiting to get inside the walls of Jerusalem before effecting some miraculous escape. Perhaps Peter will have an even better opportunity for heroic action in defense of Jesus. Peter does not know what is going to happen, but he is an interested party. Whatever is about to happen, Peter apparently wants to be close by.

B. Three Denials (vv. 55-60)

55. And when they had kindled a fire in the midst of the hall, and were set down together, Peter sat down among them.

The high priest's house is actually a palace. Like most palaces of the time, it includes open courtyards. Some people in the palace complex know the apostle John. He accompanies *Peter* into the city, and they are allowed onto the palace grounds (John 18:15-17). It is not yet dawn and it is cold, so it is normal to build *a fire.* After first standing beside the fire, Peter sits *down* with others who are warming themselves there (John 18:18).

56. But a certain maid beheld him as he sat by the fire, and earnestly looked upon him, and said, This man was also with him.

The people gathered beside *the fire* obviously are aware of some of the events that have taken place. They know that something is going on between Jesus and someone in the high priest's palace. Such a hubbub at this hour of the morning is unusual. People are curious!

If anyone ever wanted to go unnoticed in a crowd, it is Peter at that moment. But a young woman staring at Peter recognizes him as an associate of Jesus.

57. And he denied him, saying, Woman, I know him not.

Peter suddenly hears himself saying that he does not even *know* Jesus. This is not a reasoned response—it is an adrenaline rush into self-preservation. Peter is in the wrong place, at the wrong time, associated with the wrong person. He does not have time to think about the past or the future. He lives only in that moment, and in that moment he does something he never dreamed he would do.

58. And after a little while another saw him, and said, Thou art also of them. And Peter said, Man, I am not.

Peter's first denial has bought him a *little* time, but it also causes people to look at him more closely. Then someone else speaks up and claims that Peter is a part of the group that followed

Jesus. We must remember that Jesus often has been the center of attention in Jerusalem, and Peter is no shrinking violet. So it is not unreasonable to think people would recognize him. But Peter again denies that association.

Peter is like an animal caught in a trap. He is acting out of fear and not from logic. It is not just that Peter fears for his life—he is confused about why Jesus is acting the way He is. All the solid ground has fallen away from under Peter, and he isn't sure of anything except his own desire to survive.

59. And about the space of one hour after another confidently affirmed, saying, Of a truth this fellow also was with him; for he is a Galilean.

Peter's second denial bought him more time, but it also has given someone time to look more closely at him and to listen to him talk. It is Peter's *Galilean* accent that gives him away (Matthew 26:73). Everyone knows that Jesus is from Galilee and most of the men in his band of close associates are also Galileans. The man who spoke was confident that he is correct about Peter. Peter feels he must appear equally confident that the man is wrong.

60. And Peter said, Man, I know not what thou sayest. And immediately, while he yet spake, the cock crew.

Peter vehemently denies any knowledge of what his accuser was talking about—even invoking a curse (an oath; Matthew 26:74; Mark 14:71). His life is at stake. He cannot afford to be ambiguous. He has to be forceful and persuasive. The words fly from his mouth.

Then, with the final syllables of Peter's denial still hanging in midair, the rooster crows to welcome the morning and fulfill Jesus' prophecy. [See question #3, page 192.]

C. Jesus' Eyes (v. 61)

61. And the Lord turned, and looked upon Peter. And Peter remembered the word of the Lord, how he had said unto him, Before the cock crow, thou shalt deny me thrice.

This is surely one of the most poignant moments in the Bible. Perhaps Jesus has been brought into the courtyard or is passing by a window. He is close enough to see and hear *Peter*. Jesus turns just long enough to make direct eye contact with him.

What Peter suddenly feels is more than a lump in the throat. It far transcends embarrassment or humiliation. This is one of those moments when the whole world changes. Having *remembered* the words of Jesus, Peter is abruptly reminded of Jesus' identity. He is the one who can foretell future events. He is God in the flesh. And Peter has

just denied any association, much less loyalty, to Him.

Jesus' look does not merely remind Peter of His identity and power; it is the look of one friend into the eyes of another. It is almost impossible to fathom the sense of betrayal, hurt, and at the same time love in those eyes. If the events of the preceding hours had confused Peter's mind, the eyes of his friend surely break his heart.

D. Peter's Sorrow (v. 62)

62. And Peter went out, and wept bitterly.

With his mind reeling and his heart aching, Peter flees. He doesn't just tear up or get reddened eyes. His weeping is the kind that must have left him unable to catch his breath. Jesus' look has penetrated Peter's soul, and he feels an anguish he has never known before. Peter has promised to die for Jesus, and then, during the span of a very short time, denies even knowing Him. And Jesus has heard those terrible words spew from Peter's mouth. For the rest of Peter's life, will the sound of a rooster crowing bring back those tears again and again? [See question #4, page 192.]

RECANTING A RECANTATION

On a visit to England several years ago, I had the privilege to stand in the very pulpit where Thomas Cranmer (1489–1556) once preached. As I stood in the pulpit, I placed my hands on the very wood where he once had placed his hands. And I recalled his bittersweet story.

Thomas Cranmer was a Cambridge-educated preacher who had come under the influence of Martin Luther during travels on the continent. Cranmer was glad when Henry VIII brought an end to the rule of the Pope over the Church of England. In 1532, Henry VIII appointed Cranmer

Home Daily Bible Readings

Monday, Jan. 20—Jesus Brought Before Pilate (John 18:28-32)
Tuesday, Jan. 21—Pilate Questions Jesus (John 18:33-37)
Wednesday, Jan. 22—Pilate's Wife Dreams (Matthew 27:15-19)
Thursday, Jan. 23—Here Is the Man (John 18:38–19:5)
Friday, Jan. 24—Pilate Tries to Release Jesus (John 19:6-12)
Saturday, Jan. 25—Pilate Washes His Hands (Matthew 27:21-26)
Sunday, Jan. 26—Jesus Handed Over to Be Crucified (John 19:13-22)

Visual for lesson 9. *Display this visual as you set the scene for the last verse of the text. It comes from verse 15, two verses before the printed text.*

as the first Protestant archbishop of Canterbury. After Henry VIII died, Cranmer became the prime "mover and shaker" in the English Reformation. *The Book of Common Prayer,* still used by the Anglican Church today, and the Forty-Two Articles (which was made the official creed of the Anglican Church in 1553) were largely the work of Thomas Cranmer. He was the hero of the day.

But when Edward VI died of tuberculosis in 1553, his sister "Bloody Mary" took the throne and did her best to return England to the fold of Roman Catholicism. By the end of 1556, seventy-five people had been burned at the stake, among them Thomas Cranmer. In a moment of weakness the acknowledged hero of English Protestantism recanted, signing a statement in which he denied the cause for which he had labored. Then, realizing the shock waves that would result from what he had done, he recanted his recantation. On March 21, 1556, at Oxford, by a great act of the will he held his hand that had signed the denial in the flames until the flesh dropped from the bones.

If Peter could have burned out his tongue and thus erased his denial, he would have done it. But no act of the will could undo what Peter had done. There was only one solution. Nothing but the grace of God could take away Peter's shame.

God's grace is greater than our disgrace.—V. K.

III. The Duty (John 21:17)

The final verse of this week's lesson provides what Paul Harvey calls "the rest of the story." After Peter flees the courtyard, Jesus goes through other appearances before officials and is finally crucified. Then, on Sunday morning, He rises from the dead. He appears before His disciples a number of times before His final ascension into Heaven. John 21:17 relates a portion of one of those appearances.

A. Piercing Question (v. 17a)

17a. He saith unto him the third time, Simon, son of Jona, lovest thou me? Peter was grieved because he said unto him the third time, Lovest thou me?

Jesus has a job for *Peter* to do, but the Lord has to ask some questions to be sure Peter is up to the task. The most important question centers on the degree of Peter's devotion to Him. Just as Peter has given voice to three denials, Jesus poses His question three times. Peter is anguished that such a repetition is necessary.

B. Complete Restoration (v. 17b)

17b. And he said unto him, Lord, thou knowest all things; thou knowest that I love thee. Jesus saith unto him, Feed my sheep.

Peter is a changed man. He had been transformed by his own anguish and by seeing *Jesus* alive again. Too much has been made of the different words for *love* (in the Greek) that Jesus and Peter use. Much more important is that Peter's earlier, three-fold denial is now replaced by a three-fold affirmation of love.

Jesus knows that Peter is a changed man, and He knows that Peter is up to the job of proclaiming the gospel and caring for the body of believers who will be the church, as are the other disciples. Jesus' complete restoration of Peter is expressed in the simple words, *Feed my sheep.* [See question #5, page 192.]

Conclusion

A. The Imperfect Man for the Job

God uses imperfect people. Perhaps of all the imperfect people who appear in the pages of the Bible, none is more striking than Peter—the man who denied even knowing Jesus after following Him for over three years. But God is in the restoration business! He is the great Potter, and we are His clay. He takes the shattered pieces of our imperfect lives and not only restores our fellowship with Him, He makes us useful in His kingdom. What a mighty God we serve!

B. Prayer

Father, help us remember that no matter what we have done, we can be restored to fellowship with You and to usefulness in Your kingdom. In Jesus' name, amen.

C. Thought to Remember

God is in the restoration business!

Learning by Doing

This page contains an alternative lesson plan emphasizing learning activities. Classes desiring such student involvement will find these suggestions helpful.

Learning Goals

After participating in this lesson, each student will be able to:

1. Cite the events surrounding Peter's denial of Jesus and his eventual restoration.

2. Explain why one who confidently asserts devotion can yield to denial in the heat of opposition.

3. Recall a time when he or she has denied (in word or in deed) the Lord and express repentance and renewed love for Him.

Into the Lesson

Remind the class that this series of character studies has made the point that God uses imperfect people to accomplish His will. Ask people to identify Old or New Testament heroes of faith who failed God, disappointed God, or resisted God's will. Ask people to stand and identify the person by speaking in the first person. They are to say the name, some action of faith for which the person is noted, and what the person did to hurt, disappoint, or flee from the Lord. Post a visual with the opening and closing lines of their presentation:

Opening: "My name is _____, and. . . ."
Closing: "I blew it, and I'm not proud of that."

Give this example: "My name is Elijah, and God used me on Mount Carmel to call down fire from Heaven and defeat the prophets of Baal. But I confess that there were times I doubted the Lord so much that I actually said, 'I wish I were dead.' I blew it, and I'm not proud of it."

As volunteers do so, write the names they mention on the board. Make the transition to Bible study by either drawing a circle around Peter's name or by adding his name. State: "Peter is another wonderful example of how God can work through people with foibles and failures."

Into the Word

The following clusters of activities may be done in small groups or accomplished by the whole class. If done in small groups, write the instructions below for each group. Give group 1 a piece of poster board and marker pen.

Activity 1. Scan all of Luke 22:31-62. On a piece of poster board titled, "An Exercise in Chronology," make three major headings of the places where events took place in this passage. Under each of the headings, list a summary of the events.

Activity 2. Try to imagine what was in Peter's heart when he went through this life-changing experience. Answer the following questions.

1. Did Peter deny Jesus because he was a coward? Why do you say so?

2. Was Peter simply overconfident with bravado (v. 33)? Why do you say so?

3. Why did he deny Jesus? Why would he do such a thing? What does his action teach us?

Activity 3. Peter has made confident statements of determined faithfulness. But he blew it! He denied Jesus. However, after the resurrection, Peter changed and was restored. After reading John 21:17, answer these questions.

1. Why did Jesus ask Peter the same question three times?

2. What was Jesus asking of Peter by saying, "Feed my sheep"? What would the image of the shepherd mean to Peter? (See also John 10:15.)

Into Life

Remind the class that God uses imperfect people and that He is in the restoration business for those who disappoint Him. Give each student a handout of the following activity. At the top of the page should be the title, "Chapter Titles for My Book." Below that, the page should read as follows:

"If you were writing a book about your walk with Christ, what would you use as chapter titles for the following chapters?

"Chapter 1, a chapter describing how you came to know and accept Jesus. (If you are not yet a Christian, this chapter can describe how God is working in your heart today.)

"Chapter 2, a chapter describing an event(s) when you blew it and disappointed the Lord.

"Chapter 3, a chapter describing the healing of the event(s) described in chapter 2, if such healing has already occurred.

"Chapter 4, a chapter describing what you think God is calling you to do or try right now."

Give students five minutes to write as many chapter titles as they are able. Then, in small groups (or with the whole class), ask them to share their chosen titles for chapter 2. They do not need to share the events of that chapter if they do not want to. Then remind the class that we, like Peter, have blown it—and repeatedly blow it. But God still calls imperfect people like us to serve. Remind them to "complete" chapter 4 by saying "yes" to God's call.

Let's Talk It Over

The questions on this page are designed to promote discussion of the lesson by the class and to encourage application of the lesson Scriptures. The answers provided are only discussion starters. Let your class talk it over from there.

1. Satan wants to enslave every Christian, just as he wanted Peter and the other apostles. (See 2 Timothy 2:26; 1 Peter 5:8; Revelation 2:10.) How does knowing this help you? How can Christians be more sensitive to spiritual forces at work?

The Bible warns the one who thinks he stands to take heed lest he fall (1 Corinthians 10:12; cf. Galatians 6:3). Being ignorant of Satan's schemes leaves the believer vulnerable. The wise Christian will stay away from those things that may present opportunities for temptation. (What are some of those things?) He or she will seek refuge in the Word and in the fellowship of other believers. Let your class suggest means of being aware of the battle between spiritual forces. Have some of them read helpful books on the subject? Maybe someone knows of a Web site that is helpful. Perhaps someone could volunteer to do a concordance search or use a topical Bible to further research the subject. He or she could report next week or E-mail the results to class members.

2. How do experiences of testing equip us to strengthen the faith of other Christians? How can we encourage other people to do that?

Paul says God comforts us in our trials so that we, in turn, can comfort others with the comfort we have received (2 Corinthians 1:4). The word for *comfort* in that passage is broad; it is often translated as "encouragement." Surely the faithful example of a victorious saint will help another believer to resist temptation. Perhaps some of your students can tell of faithful examples who have encouraged them along the way.

But notice the case of Peter. Peter would falter; his faith would fail and he would be guilty of a heinous sin. But Jesus said he, when he was "converted," would be able to strengthen his brothers. What lessons have we learned from failure? Discuss how the church can cultivate an environment in which people are not afraid to admit their failings so that they and others can grow from them.

3. How was it possible for Peter to deny Christ? What factors contributed to his failing? What danger signs can we see in his experience that we should watch for in our own lives?

Part of Peter's problem was that he completely misunderstood the nature of Jesus' mission, not realizing that Christ had to go to the cross (Matthew 16:21-23). We need to be careful that we do not misunderstand the mission of the church. We need to continue to explore the Scripture and to take every opportunity to understand it better.

Peter also made rash promises he could not keep. He had not really thought through the issue, so when the time came to test his resolve, he folded under pressure. We need to be careful about making promises that we have not counted the cost of keeping.

4. Peter had promised to die for Jesus, but he was not willing even to admit he knew Him. How can Christians avoid committing Peter's sin of denial when their faith is severely tested?

First, the Christian must have a positive attitude about testing. James says we should rejoice when we are tempted because the testing of our faith produces endurance (James 1:2, 3). That endurance can see us through even worse trials in the future. We must not allow trials to discourage us. Second, the Christian should focus on Jesus and eternal life, not on the temporary tribulations of this life (Hebrews 12:1, 2). Third, the Christian must rely on God's power. Paul said that no temptation is inescapable (1 Corinthians 10:13). We may not be able to avoid persecution, but we can resist the temptation to deny Christ to save our lives. History is full of stories of brave Christians who died rather than renounce their faith. If they endured, we can, too.

5. What comfort can we take from the fact that Jesus forgave Peter for his earlier denials?

The Scriptures teach that, if we confess our sins, God is faithful to forgive us our sins, and to cleanse us from all unrighteousness, because the blood of Jesus cleanses us from all sin (1 John 1:7, 9). Unfortunately, some Christians who have fallen are convinced that their sins are so bad that God could never forgive them. This is not only contrary to Biblical teaching, it is contrary to history. If Jesus could forgive Peter for his denials, then He can forgive us when we fall, too. Even today, testimonies from repentant criminals and other "hard-core" sinners are among the most uplifting of messages. Again, we need to cultivate an atmosphere that allows us to share our failings as well as our successes, and to let the body grow through these experiences.

Barnabas: Encourager and Enabler

DEVOTIONAL READING: Hebrews 10:19-25.

BACKGROUND SCRIPTURE: Acts 4:32-37; 9:26, 27; 11:19-30; 15:36-41.

PRINTED TEXT: Acts 4:36, 37; 9:26, 27; 11:22-26; 15:36-41.

Acts 4:36, 37

36 And Joses, who by the apostles was surnamed Barnabas, (which is, being interpreted, The son of consolation,) a Levite, and of the country of Cyprus,

37 Having land, sold it, and brought the money, and laid it at the apostles' feet.

Acts 9:26, 27

26 And when Saul was come to Jerusalem, he assayed to join himself to the disciples: but they were all afraid of him, and believed not that he was a disciple.

27 But Barnabas took him, and brought him to the apostles, and declared unto them how he had seen the Lord in the way, and that he had spoken to him, and how he had preached boldly at Damascus in the name of Jesus.

Acts 11:22-26

22 Then tidings of these things came unto the ears of the church which was in Jerusalem: and they sent forth Barnabas, that he should go as far as Antioch.

23 Who, when he came, and had seen the grace of God, was glad, and exhorted them all, that with purpose of heart they would cleave unto the Lord.

24 For he was a good man, and full of the Holy Ghost and of faith: and much people was added unto the Lord.

25 Then departed Barnabas to Tarsus, for to seek Saul:

26 And when he had found him, he brought him unto Antioch. And it came to pass, that a whole year they assembled themselves with the church, and taught much people. And the disciples were called Christians first in Antioch.

Acts 15:36-41

36 And some days after, Paul said unto Barnabas, Let us go again and visit our brethren in every city where we have preached the word of the Lord, and see how they do.

37 And Barnabas determined to take with them John, whose surname was Mark.

38 But Paul thought not good to take him with them, who departed from them from Pamphylia, and went not with them to the work.

39 And the contention was so sharp between them, that they departed asunder one from the other: and so Barnabas took Mark, and sailed unto Cyprus;

40 And Paul chose Silas, and departed, being recommended by the brethren unto the grace of God.

41 And he went through Syria and Cilicia, confirming the churches.

GOLDEN TEXT: When he [Barnabas] came, and had seen the grace of God, [he] was glad. . . . For he was a good man, and full of the Holy Ghost and of faith.
—Acts 11:23, 24.

Lesson Aims

After participating in this lesson, each student will be able to:

1. Tell how Barnabas lived up to his name as an encourager to the early church, to Saul of Tarsus, and to John Mark.

2. Explain why encouragement is so needed in ministry.

3. Suggest a specific means of encouraging a Christian worker.

Lesson Outline

Introduction

A. "I Believe in You"

Was there a person who changed your life because he or she believed in you? Perhaps it was a coach or a teacher. There are millions who can see our flaws, but how many will notice our potential? It is only natural that you would be drawn to people like those.

The problem is there are not enough such people. Add up the criticism others give us and the criticism we give ourselves, and it is a heavy burden. What a treasure are those who see our best qualities and spur us on to become even more

than we are! The man who occupies our attention in this lesson was clearly a person who believed in people.

B. Lesson Background

Today's lesson is drawn from several passages in the book of Acts. These passages form a series of snapshots of a man called Barnabas, also known as Joseph or Joses. Admittedly he is not as well known as some of the other characters in the New Testament. He is surely at the top of the list of the second rank.

Barnabas is best known as the supporter, mentor, and traveling companion of the apostle Paul. F. F. Bruce notes that one might question "whether Barnabas belonged to the Pauline circle or . . . Paul belonged rather to the circle of Barnabas." In his early work with Saul (Paul's previous name), Barnabas is clearly preeminent. The book of Acts initially refers to this team as Barnabas and Saul (11:25; 12:25). Later, it becomes Paul and Barnabas (13:42, 43), but there is no hint that there was ever any jealousy about this.

We know nothing factual of Barnabas's physical qualities, although we have one tantalizing clue. On one occasion, some villagers who saw Barnabas and Paul do miracles called Barnabas "Jupiter" and Paul "Mercurius" (Acts 14:12). Jupiter (or Zeus) was the king of the gods of the mythical Greek pantheon, and Mercurius (or Mercury or Hermes) was his messenger. We might infer by their identification that Barnabas was the more physically impressive while Paul, "the chief speaker," was the more talkative.

We do not know when Barnabas became a Christian. The historian Eusebius claims that he was one of the seventy disciples Jesus commissioned to preach in Luke 10:1, but we have no reliable evidence of this.

Let us proceed now to the events that give us insight into Barnabas and his positive character qualities.

I. Generosity (Acts 4:36, 37)

In our lesson today, we'll be jumping around through the text in Acts to sketch our portrait of Barnabas. As we begin, the events of the Day of Pentecost are still fresh in people's minds.

A. Barnabas's Background (v. 36)

36. And Joses, who by the apostles was surnamed Barnabas, (which is, being interpreted, The son of consolation,) a Levite, and of the country of Cyprus.

Although Barnabas's proper name is *Joses* (or Joseph), he comes to be known almost exclusively by his nickname, which means *"son of con-*

solation," "son of encouragement," or "son of ex-hortation." Many people in the Bible take on new names or become known by some nickname. In the Old Testament the list includes Abraham and Jacob. In the New Testament it includes Simon Peter and Paul. [See question #1, page 200.]

Barnabas, as *a Levite*, is of the ancient priestly tribe of Israel. *Cyprus*, his home, is a large island about one hundred miles off the coast. John Mark, whom we will meet later, is a relative (Colossians 4:10).

B. Barnabas's Gift (v. 37)

37. Having land, sold it, and brought the money, and laid it at the apostles' feet.

The early church is noted for its extraordinary generosity—in its willingness to have a common treasury through which to care for the needs of its members. Barnabas serves as an illustration of that generosity. He also serves as a backdrop for the mistaken and tragic decision of Ananias and Sapphira (Acts 5:1-11).

Some have compared this shared treasury to modern Communism. This comparison is not warranted, since this generosity is always volun-tary. The purpose of relating this account is not to develop an economic model, but to illustrate a spiritual dynamic of the early church.

Levites, descendants of Levi, had no tribal land in Israel except for the forty-eight Levitical cities designated in Joshua 21. Was this *land* that Bar-nabas owned near one of those? Was it in his na-tive land of Cyprus? We simply don't know. Wherever it was, selling the land and giving all *the money* is a significant sacrifice. Laying the money *at the apostles' feet* is the method of shar-ing this offering. [See question #2, page 200.]

II. Discipling (Acts 9:26, 27)

As we move from Acts 4 to Acts 9, at least three years have passed. Stephen has been stoned, and Saul of Tarsus stood by holding the coats of those who stoned him (Acts 7:58). The gospel is spreading as the church is persecuted and scattered. But then Saul, the chief persecu-tor, is converted. Later he returns to Jerusalem.

A. An Unlikely Disciple (v. 26)

26. And when Saul was come to Jerusalem, he assayed to join himself to the disciples: but they were all afraid of him, and believed not that he was a disciple.

Galatians 1:18 tells us that Saul's arrival is about three years after his conversion. The disci-ples' suspicion, given Saul's record, is under-standable (cf. Acts 8:3). We have the benefit of hindsight to know that his conversion is genuine.

The church in *Jerusalem* will not soon forget the image of *Saul* holding the coats of those who stoned Stephen to death. This puts Saul in an awkward situation. He cannot go back to his old friends, for they will not embrace his conversion. The church is not yet ready to accept him, either. This must be a lonely time for him.

Into that void of loneliness steps Barnabas. Vouching for someone always involves risk. Peo-ple frequently let us down. Vouching for a per-son like Saul, with his history, is a great risk, indeed.

B. A Risky Endorsement (v. 27)

27. But Barnabas took him, and brought him to the apostles, and declared unto them how he had seen the Lord in the way, and that he had spoken to him, and how he had preached boldly at Damascus in the name of Jesus.

Barnabas is the one willing to take this former enemy of the church and introduce him to the leaders and *apostles*. What is most problematic about Saul is that there undoubtedly is some lin-gering resentment and suspicion. When the church's chief persecutor becomes a convert, there are bound to be some who doubt the sincer-ity of the conversion. That is only human nature.

The apostles mentioned here do not include all (or only) the Twelve. Paul notes in Galatians 1:18, 19 that he visited only Peter and James the Lord's brother. Barnabas tells them about Saul's vision and courageous preaching in the days after his conversion. Mentioning Saul's boldness is perhaps a way to underscore to the apostles that Saul has put his own life at risk. Indeed, Saul only recently had escaped death in Damas-cus (Acts 9:22-25). Anyone risking life and limb for the gospel would not be some kind of spy.

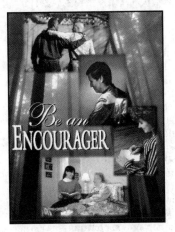

Visual for lesson 10

Post this visual at the beginning of the session. It sets the stage for application of this lesson.

STANDING SPONSOR

I am convinced that Acts 9:27 is the pivotal passage in the book of Acts. Were it not for that single adversative conjunction *but* at the beginning of verse 27, the book of Acts might well have ended with verse 26 on an extremely negative note. Here is the Jerusalem church, "the mother of us all," about to reject one of her sons—a son who, if given a chance, will do more for her and the world than any other of her illustrious children in all history.

Don DeWelt said of Barnabas, "He believed when others doubted; he loved while others were suspicious." Do we really believe that God's grace is greater than man's disgrace?

On May 10, 1993, convicted serial killer Jeffrey Dahmer repented and was baptized in a maximum-security prison in Portage, Wisconsin. A personal friend of mine, Roy Ratcliff, a minister with a Church of Christ in nearby Madison, made the initial contact, did the teaching, baptizing, and follow-up work with Dahmer until he was brutally bludgeoned to death by a fellow inmate on November 28, 1994. *Newsweek* magazine, December 12, 1994, later reported that Ratcliff was Dahmer's only regular visitor.

Roy testified, "Since the baptism, the most frequent question I have been asked is if I believe that all of Jeffrey Dahmer's sins have been forgiven. . . . 'Aren't there some sins too evil to be forgiven?' All such questions reflect a poor understanding of the grace of God and the complete forgiveness that is available in Christ Jesus" (*One Body*, Autumn 1994).

Thank God for brave souls who dare to stand sponsor for those converted from a life of sin and shame!

—V. K.

III. Mentoring (Acts 11:22-26)

Barnabas's efforts on Saul's behalf were successful. Saul was accepted by the church, "and he was with them coming in and going out at Jerusalem" (Acts 9:28). His bold preaching soon got him in trouble with some enemies of the church, however, so he was sent to his hometown of Tarsus for safety (Acts 9:29, 30). When we next hear of him, it is Barnabas once again who is encouraging his ministry.

A. A Ministry (vv. 22-24)

22. Then tidings of these things came unto the ears of the church which was in Jerusalem: and they sent forth Barnabas, that he should go as far as Antioch.

Antioch in Syria is a major commercial center, the third largest city in the Roman Empire. And something wonderful is happening there: *the church* is growing! (See Acts 11:19-21.) This growth is coming in part from Gentile converts (v. 20). The mother church *in Jerusalem* is understandably concerned about the ramifications. It is a tribute to his character that *Barnabas* is selected to investigate. Being from Cyprus, Barnabas understands the Gentiles. (Some men from Cyprus are in Antioch preaching; see 11:20.) Being a Levite, Barnabas is trusted by the Jewish believers.

23. Who, when he came, and had seen the grace of God, was glad, and exhorted them all, that with purpose of heart they would cleave unto the Lord.

The encouragement Barnabas receives in Antioch leads him to encourage others there in turn. He is certain that these conversions are genuine, and evidently he does much preaching and teaching for this church. He encourages them to build on the great beginning they have made and to continue to *cleave unto the Lord.*

24. For he was a good man, and full of the Holy Ghost and of faith: and much people was added unto the Lord.

What a summary of a man's character! Every Christian would be glad to be considered *full of the Holy* Spirit and full *of faith.* In addition, it is no small thing to be labeled *a good man.* Being called "good" does not mean perfect. It is not an exaltation of human goodness, but rather a description of how the goodness of *the Lord* is exemplified in Barnabas. The result of his ministry is more converts to the Lord. [See question #3, page 200.]

B. An Assistant (vv. 25, 26)

25. Then departed Barnabas to Tarsus, for to seek Saul.

The success of the endeavor prompts *Barnabas* to look for an associate in ministry. The particular nature of the church in Antioch somehow makes Barnabas think of Saul. Perhaps it is the Gentile involvement. Even though Saul is Jewish and thoroughly trained in the law, he has grown up in the Gentile world and understands Gentiles. As his Greek name Paul becomes more dominant (Acts 13:9), he will become known as the apostle to the Gentiles (18:6).

What Saul has been doing in *Tarsus,* his hometown (21:39), is not known. He may well have been there for several years. But those years were not wasted; they are undoubtedly a period of preparation.

26. And when he had found him, he brought him unto Antioch. And it came to pass, that a whole year they assembled themselves with the church, and taught much people. And the disciples were called Christians first in Antioch.

The work of Barnabas and Saul continues for a *year* with great success. This verse also gives us an interesting detail in that it is in *Antioch* that the followers of Jesus are first *called Christians*. The Greek word used here has been understood in various ways. Some say it signifies "follower of Christ." Others favor "member of the household of Christ."

We do not know who coins the term *Christians*. Some argue that it is God Himself, but there is no strong evidence for that. Others propose that it is the citizens of Antioch—perhaps in some kind of derogatory sense. In any case, it has become the term of choice for disciples of Jesus, even in our own time. Previously, Christians were simply known as disciples (6:1), brothers (9:30), or members of the "way" (9:2).

IV. Conflict Management (Acts 15:36-41)

Much has happened between chapters 11 and 15 of Acts. Barnabas and Saul have completed a missionary journey and returned to Antioch (13:1–14:28). From there they traveled to Jerusalem to participate in the Jerusalem Conference (15:1-29). Saul, now known as Paul, returns with Barnabas, Silas, and some others to resume the ministry in Antioch—for a while (15:30-35).

A. A Problem (vv. 36-38)

36. And some days after, Paul said unto Barnabas, Let us go again and visit our brethren in every city where we have preached the word of the Lord, and see how they do.

We don't know exactly how long *some days after* signifies, but the year is now about A.D. 50. *Paul* wants to go back to the churches he and *Barnabas* had planted on their first missionary journey and to encourage them. This is a sensible plan, and Barnabas is eager to go along. But the agreement between them ends there.

37, 38. And Barnabas determined to take with them John, whose surname was Mark. But Paul thought not good to take him with them, who departed from them from Pamphylia, and went not with them to the work.

Barnabas wants to take along his relative *John Mark*, who had accompanied them part-way on the first missionary journey (Acts 12:25; 13:5). John Mark is most likely the author of the book of Mark. Many believe he also was the young man whose presence in the Garden of Gethsemane is reported only by Mark (Mark 14:51, 52). We don't know why, but Mark had left them during that journey (13:13). Paul sees this as a desertion and believes that this disqualifies him for this trip. [See question #4, page 200.]

B. A Solution (vv. 39-41)

39. And the contention was so sharp between them, that they departed asunder one from the other: and so Barnabas took Mark, and sailed unto Cyprus.

Fresh from a great victory at Jerusalem where they had stood together for including the Gentiles in the church (15:2), these two giants of the faith now split over an issue of procedure! They are great men, but men nonetheless. The Bible does not gloss over their weaknesses. We sometimes live under the illusion that the great heroes of the faith never had disagreements. This text dismisses that notion. Some see a subtext here because Paul and Barnabas have had a previous disagreement. (See Galatians 2:13.) However, while we do not minimize the incident, we dare not make too much of it, either.

Nothing more is ever said about this trip without Paul to *Cyprus*. Barnabas and Mark are, however, mentioned in complimentary terms in Paul's letters (1 Corinthians 9:6; Colossians 4:10; 2 Timothy 4:11; Philemon 24), so there must have been some kind of reconciliation. In his decision to part company, Barnabas is actually doing what he once did for Paul: he is being a sponsor and mentor for a promising servant of the Lord.

Some have asked, "Who was right—Paul or Barnabas?" Evidence can be presented on both sides, and it probably doesn't matter. Some think the fact that Mark later proved himself (Paul

---

How to Say It

ANANIAS. An-uh-*nye*-us.
ANTIOCH. *An*-tee-ock.
BARNABAS. *Bar*-nuh-bus.
CILICIA. Sih-*lish*-i-uh.
CYPRUS. *Sigh*-prus.
EUSEBIUS. You-*see*-be-us.
GALATIANS. Guh-*lay*-shunz.
GETHSEMANE. *Geth*-sem-uh-nee.
HERMES. *Her*-meez.
JOSES. *Jo*-sez.
JUPITER. *Joo*-puh-ter.
LEVI. *Lee*-vye.
LEVITE. *Lee*-vite.
LEVITICAL. Leh-*vit*-ih-kul.
MERCURIUS. Mur-*koo*-ri-us.
MERCURY. *Mur*-kyuh-ree.
PAMPHYLIA. Pam-*fill*-ee-uh.
SAPPHIRA. Suh-*fye*-ruh.
SILAS. *Sigh*-luss.
SILVANUS. Sil-*vay*-nus.
TARSUS. *Tar*-sus.
ZEUS. Zoose.

even asked for John Mark to come to him) proves that Barnabas was right. Perhaps, however, it was the combination of Paul's toughness and Barnabas's gentleness that helped develop Mark into the helpful servant he became.

CONTENDING WITHOUT CONTENTION

A Christian minister once wrote a wonderful little tract called "Come to Jesus." The piece was instrumental in bringing many lost people to the Lord. But some years later the author had a falling out with a Christian brother. He became a merchant of venom and wrote a bitter broadside, consigning to Hell the man with whom he disagreed. When he asked another Christian friend what title he should give to his new tract he was told, "Why don't you call it 'Go to the Devil' by the author of 'Come to Jesus'?"

General Stonewall Jackson once overheard some of his troops arguing with each other over which strategy should be used in battle. In the heat of discussion some of them began making personal attacks on each other. Jackson, pointing to the battlefield, wisely reminded them, "Remember, gentlemen, the enemy is over there."

We do not have the luxury of fighting with each other. We do not wrestle against flesh and blood but against spiritual powers. Satan is our real enemy. Each of us must make every effort to keep the unity of the Spirit in the bond of peace. God wants us to contend for the faith without being contentious with one another. A house divided against itself cannot win the war. —V. K.

40, 41. And Paul chose Silas, and departed, being recommended by the brethren unto the grace of God. And he went through Syria and Cilicia, confirming the churches.

Home Daily Bible Readings

Monday, Jan. 27—Barnabas, Son of Encouragement (Acts 4:32-37)
Tuesday, Jan. 28—Barnabas Speaks Up for Saul (Acts 9:23-30)
Wednesday, Jan. 29—Barnabas Exhorts Antioch Believers (Acts 11:19-24)
Thursday, Jan. 30—Barnabas Brings Saul to Antioch (Acts 11:25-30)
Friday, Jan. 31—Barnabas and Saul Are Set Apart (Acts 13:1-5)
Saturday, Feb. 1—They Relate All God Has Done (Acts 14:21-28)
Sunday, Feb. 2—Barnabas Chooses Mark (Acts 15:36-41)

Silas, also known as Silvanus, takes Barnabas's place as Paul's traveling companion. We don't know where *Paul* first met Silas. But we do know that when the Jerusalem church council decided that Gentiles did not have to become Jews before they could be Christians, Silas was one of the men who accompanied Paul and Barnabas to Antioch to deliver the report and encourage the new believers (Acts 15:22).

Was it God's intention that Paul and Barnabas split up? Probably not. But God in His grace makes good come from bad, and this parting of ways is no different. Perhaps without this opportunity Silas never would have become as involved in missionary work as he did. Without Barnabas's continued mentoring, perhaps John Mark would have been "lost" to continued work for the kingdom of God. [See question #5, page 200.]

Conclusion

A. Good Shot

Perhaps you have heard the story of the little boy who said to his dad, "Let's play darts. I'll throw the darts, and you stand there and say, 'Good shot.'" This little story illustrates how even at an early age we need encouragers in our lives. One Bible teacher says that we should institute a new office in the church. He says that we need "cheerleaders," people who have the spiritual gift of encouragement.

Leslie Flynn notes that even though Barnabas left no epistle or gospel, he did influence much of our New Testament because of his significant impact on both Paul and John Mark. Adding Barnabas's indirect influence on Luke, through Paul, the impact becomes staggering.

As to what becomes of Barnabas, we have no reliable information. One ancient tradition says he was stoned to death, and another says he moved to Cyprus, served the Lord for many years, died, and was buried there. While we may be curious, it doesn't really matter. We have enough information about "the encourager" that can inspire us to be encouragers as well.

B. Prayer

Dear Father, help me to find ways to encourage those with whom I come in contact. Help me to see the best in people, and help me to bring out the best in people. In doing so, I hope to bring glory to Your name and success to Your cause. In the name of Jesus I pray, amen.

C. Thought to Remember

People who encourage others are the most blessed people in the world.

Learning by Doing

This page contains an alternative lesson plan emphasizing learning activities. Classes desiring such student involvement will find these suggestions helpful.

Learning Goals

After participating in this lesson, each student will be able to:

1. Tell how Barnabas lived up to his name as an encourager to the early church, to Saul of Tarsus, and to John Mark.

2. Explain why encouragement is so needed in ministry.

3. Suggest a specific means of encouraging a Christian worker.

Into the Lesson

Remind the class that we have been discovering models for living as Christians. Today's model is a man named Joseph. He is better known, however, by his nickname, Barnabas (see the notes on Acts 4:36). "Barnabas" means "son of consolation," "son of encouragement," or "son of exhortation." Ask, "If people were to give you a nickname about your service to Christ, what might it be? You may be known as 'Mr. Sunday School,' 'church handyman,' 'the elder's elder,' 'model mom,' 'Mr. Sound Man,' 'the nursery specialist,' or some other." Then have groups of about four people assign positive "nicknames" to each other that the group believes would be appropriate to each person's service to Christ. Allow a representative from each group to introduce the nicknames to the class. Make the transition to Bible study by saying, "It is good to be recognized for what you do. One quality we need so much in the church is the one Barnabas will teach us: the ability to encourage one another."

Into the Word

During the week before class, recruit four people to give a brief "eyewitness report" on Barnabas's activities. Each person will be given (1) one of the Scripture texts for today's lesson, (2) a copy of the lesson commentary for the text assigned, and (3) this note: "Imagine you were a witness to the events described in this Scripture text. Read the lesson commentary. Then plan a brief testimony to share with the class about what you witnessed, the circumstances shaping the event, and how Barnabas fulfilled his nickname 'son of encouragement.' Also, tell how this event touched or impressed you." Bring to class a staff, a prayer shawl, or a scroll to give as a way to identify the person giving the testimony.

Follow this procedure for each witness. First, give the person the staff, shawl, or scroll to identify who will speak. After this witness tells his or her story, read the text (see below) and discuss it, using the questions found below. Also, write the heading "Encourager" on the chalkboard. List the means used by Barnabas to encourage another as the class discusses the questions.

First Witness (Acts 4:36, 37). What way did Barnabas use to be an encourager in this incident? *(Generosity.)* Some say the way the early church shared their possessions was a form of Communism. What is the difference between the church's sharing and Communism?

Second Witness (Acts 9:26, 27). What way did Barnabas use to become an encourager in this text? *(He was an enabler of Saul's ministry.)* Who was encouraged? Why might this attempt to enable Saul (Paul) be risky for Barnabas?

Third Witness (Acts 11:22-26). What ways did Barnabas use to encourage the Antioch church? *(Exhortation, mentoring, teamwork.)* What clues to his character do you see in this text?

Give the staff, shawl, or scroll to the final witness. Read Acts 15:36-41; then observe that this part of the story shows a human side to Barnabas in a conflict. Ask, "Do you see qualities here that serve as models, either good or bad?" *(Conflict management.)*

Into Life

Make the transition by reminding the class that *Barnabas* was a nickname describing a quality of his life. And we have seen that we can be encouragers by using many different approaches. Ask the class to suggest other ways to encourage, and add these ideas to the list on the chalkboard.

Remind the class that Barnabas was especially encouraging to church leaders. He laid a generous offering at the apostles' feet, endorsed and encouraged Paul when he was a new disciple, and more. Let's focus on how we may be encouragers to church leaders, such as teachers, ministers, elders, and youth leaders. Give each person a handout with three statements to complete.

I will encourage_____.
(Name of a church leader.)

I appreciate this person because _____.

I will do the following to encourage this person: _____.

(Remind them to use the list on the board.)

Let's Talk It Over

The questions on this page are designed to promote discussion of the lesson by the class and to encourage application of the lesson Scriptures. The answers provided are only discussion starters. Let your class talk it over from there.

1. If someone were to give you a nickname based on what you do in the church, what would it be? Why? What would you like it to be? How can you make that more likely?

Look at the "Into the Lesson" activity on page 199 for some ideas on this. But note also that some of us might be known by more negative names: "Sam Snores-a-lot," "Mr. Complainer," "Miss Never-did-it-that-way," "Gary Gossip," or "Whining Wilma." Don't pressure anyone to reveal what negative nickname might be attached to him or her, but spend more time seeking ways to be known by positive ones. Perhaps Whining Wilma can make a special effort to say something positive about the service or someone present each week. Maybe Sam Snores-a-lot can work on getting more rest on Saturday night.

2. Note how the money was given in the early church. They laid it at the apostles' feet—with no strings attached. Nothing is said of designated offerings ("Use this for this purpose.") Do you think this suggests the church should not accept designated offerings today? Why or why not?

Designated offerings are commonplace in most churches. They are especially appropriate when the leadership establishes several "funds" to which the membership is invited to contribute. This allows the members to have some influence in establishing priorities in the church. When such funds have not been established, however, this may present a problem. Givers interested in taking a tax deduction for their contributions should know that these may be disallowed if the giver maintains "control" of the gift. And designated gifts are sometimes used to undermine the priorities established by the church leadership. Some people are also concerned about a member designating a gift to a group or individual that espouses anti-Christian ideals or practices. Does the church want to be party to that?

3. Acts 11:24 summarizes the character of Barnabas. What characteristics (from this verse or others) do you especially appreciate about him as a good role model for Christians today?

Barnabas set the tone for sacrificial giving in the early church by his generosity in selling his land and giving the proceeds to the apostles. He exhibited courage in befriending Paul when everyone else was afraid to. Barnabas was also known as a good man, full of the Holy Spirit and of faith. He set a high moral and spiritual tone for the church. He was also a model of Christian service. He left behind whatever profession he followed to participate in at least two missionary journeys. He also showed great humility, surrendering his leadership role to Paul when Paul's natural dominance emerged. Finally, Barnabas was a model of encouragement, exhorting his fellow Christians to spiritual growth, earning him his nickname, Barnabas, "son of consolation."

4. Paul and Barnabas disagreed over the issue of John Mark's failure. How should the church deal with those who fail in some ministry and then want to participate again?

In the New Testament there are several examples of people who failed in more significant ways than John Mark. Peter denied Christ, but he returned to his faith after the resurrection. Paul commanded the Corinthians to put a blatant sinner out of the church (1 Corinthians 5), and to take him back after he had repented (2 Corinthians 2). The church must always pursue a course that assists in the restoration of members who fail in some way or another.

This does not always mean, however, that they should be accepted without probation. Paul speaks of deacons being "proved" before serving. An elder is not to be a "novice" or recent convert. The same principle might suggest that one who failed in some ministry should receive additional training or limited, supervised responsibilities for a time. This, too, attempts to restore the person.

5. How should Christians handle serious disagreements between themselves?

In resolving such conflicts, we are concerned for the persons involved and for the church and its reputation. Paul was concerned for the success of the work, so he would not risk taking John along. Barnabas was concerned for the welfare of John Mark. Making two teams addressed both concerns. Apparently they came to this solution without resorting to personal attacks or bitter words. They stuck to the issues. Paul was able to be complimentary to both Barnabas and John Mark later (1 Corinthians 9:6; Colossians 4:10; 2 Timothy 4:11; Philemon 24).

Paul: Obedient Messenger

DEVOTIONAL READING: Ephesians 3:1-13.

BACKGROUND SCRIPTURE: Acts 25:23–26:32.

PRINTED TEXT: Acts 26:12-23, 27-29.

Acts 26:12-23, 27-29

12 Whereupon as I went to Damascus with authority and commission from the chief priests,

13 At midday, O king, I saw in the way a light from heaven, above the brightness of the sun, shining round about me and them which journeyed with me.

14 And when we were all fallen to the earth, I heard a voice speaking unto me, and saying in the Hebrew tongue, Saul, Saul, why persecutest thou me? it is hard for thee to kick against the pricks.

15 And I said, Who art thou, Lord? And he said, I am Jesus whom thou persecutest.

16 But rise, and stand upon thy feet: for I have appeared unto thee for this purpose, to make thee a minister and a witness both of these things which thou hast seen, and of those things in the which I will appear unto thee;

17 Delivering thee from the people, and from the Gentiles, unto whom now I send thee,

18 To open their eyes, and to turn them from darkness to light, and from the power of Satan unto God, that they may receive forgiveness of sins, and inheritance among them which are sanctified by faith that is in me.

19 Whereupon, O king Agrippa, I was not disobedient unto the heavenly vision:

20 But showed first unto them of Damascus, and at Jerusalem, and throughout all the coasts of Judea, and then to the Gentiles, that they should repent and turn to God, and do works meet for repentance.

21 For these causes the Jews caught me in the temple, and went about to kill me.

22 Having therefore obtained help of God, I continue unto this day, witnessing both to small and great, saying none other things than those which the prophets and Moses did say should come:

23 That Christ should suffer, and that he should be the first that should rise from the dead, and should show light unto the people, and to the Gentiles.

. . . .

27 King Agrippa, believest thou the prophets? I know that thou believest.

28 Then Agrippa said unto Paul, Almost thou persuadest me to be a Christian.

29 And Paul said, I would to God, that not only thou, but also all that hear me this day, were both almost, and altogether such as I am, except these bonds.

Feb 9

GOLDEN TEXT: Whereupon, O king Agrippa, I was not disobedient unto the heavenly vision.—Acts 26:19.

Lesson Aims

After participating in this lesson, each student will be able to:

1. Recite the details of Paul's experience on the road to Damascus and his response to it.

2. Explain why Paul's conversion and call are significant to the spread of the gospel.

3. Assess his or her own response to God's call and determine to take one specific step to conform to God's call more closely.

Lesson Outline

Introduction

A. Where Would We Be Without Him?

Who can understand Christianity without understanding Paul? In modern times he has frequently been criticized, yet where would the church be without his influence? Of course, Jesus was the founder of Christianity, but it was Paul who became its intellectual center and its pre-eminent missionary and church planter. And ultimately we can understand Paul only if we first understand his conversion. This lesson centers on one of Paul's explanations of that conversion.

The book of Acts tells us much about Paul's life, and his epistles reveal much of his thinking.

We know little to nothing, however, about his physical appearance. Second Corinthians 10:10 suggests that people thought him to be physically unimpressive. An ancient tradition says Paul was bald-headed, bowlegged, small but muscular, with eyebrows that met in the middle, and a prominent nose. He may have had some persistent physical problem, which is what many assume to be the "thorn in the flesh" he wrote of in 2 Corinthians 12:7. Some believe his thorn in the flesh involved some kind of eye problem that may have made it difficult to look him in the face.

We know a lot about Paul's hometown of Tarsus. Tarsus was a river city near the northeast corner of the Mediterranean Sea, and it saw many name changes through the years. The Roman general Mark Antony (c. 83–31 B.C.) became quite fond of the city during his military campaigns. It was at Tarsus that he first met Queen Cleopatra of Egypt. Paul was right when he said it was "no mean city" (Acts 21:39).

Still, there is much we don't know and we will never know about Paul (at least in this life). But what we do know is enough to develop an appreciation of the man and his influence. Some have said that as Shakespeare is to literature, Paul is to theology. Frederick Buechner calls him the "Johnny Appleseed" of church planting.

B. Lesson Background

The incident we examine today is Paul's defense before King Agrippa in about A.D. 60. Officially named Marcus Julius Agrippa II, this ruler is known more simply as Herod Agrippa II. He was the great-grandson of Herod the Great, who was the ruler when Jesus was born. Since Herod was a family name, there were several in the dynasty who bore that designation, so some confusion concerning identity is natural.

Agrippa had been reared in Rome and was a court favorite during the reign of Emperor Claudius, who ruled A.D. 41–54. Agrippa oversaw a small piece of his family's original kingdom. He was frequently in the company of his sister Bernice, as he was in this incident. Rumors abounded that their relationship had become incestuous. Bernice later became the mistress of General (later Emperor) Titus, who was immortalized by an arch in Rome and a play by Shakespeare. As the mistress of the general, Bernice eventually moved with him to Rome. Later, however, he sent her away because she was not accepted by Roman society. Herod Agrippa II was the last king descended from Herod the Great.

Paul's defense before Agrippa takes place in the city of Caesarea, a port city by the Mediterranean Sea. (This is not Caesarea Philippi, where Peter made the Good Confession—Matthew 16:13-20.

That city is located some seventy miles to the northeast.) The city in our lesson is often called Caesarea by the sea. It was considered a more hospitable town for the Romans than Jerusalem, so Roman governors spent most of their time there. It was built by Herod the Great (reigned 37–4 B.C.) and was named in honor of Caesar Augustus (reigned 27 B.C.–A.D. 14). It was here that Peter first preached to the Gentiles (Acts 10).

Festus, the Roman provincial governor, set up the meeting between Paul and Agrippa. New in his position, Festus evidently wanted to dispose of the troublesome cases and was determined to come to some kind of resolution about Paul. After all, Paul had been in prison for two years. We know much less about Festus than we do about his predecessor. The Jewish historian Josephus mentions Festus, and we can suppose from what is recorded that the rule of Festus was fairly brief. It was also a stormy period. All indications are that during the entire reign, Festus sided with Herod Agrippa and they became good friends.

I. Paul's Compelling Vision
(Acts 26:12-18)

A. The "Where" of the Vision (v. 12)

12. Whereupon as I went to Damascus with authority and commission from the chief priests.

The account Paul relates to Agrippa appears three times in the book of Acts: here and in chapters 9 and 22. This repetition illustrates how crucial the account is, not only to Paul, but also to the church as a whole. There are variations in the three accounts, depending on what needs to be emphasized.

Damascus was a Gentile city, but it had a strong Jewish population. Some have claimed Damascus to be the oldest continuously inhabited city in the history of the world. Indeed, its more than fifty references in the Bible go back as early as the days of Abraham (Genesis 14:15).

The two previous accounts of Paul's conversion in Acts tell that he carried letters (9:2; 22:5). No doubt these "letters" spelled out Paul's *authority and commission from the chief priests.*

B. The "What" of the Vision (vv. 13-15)

13. At midday, O king, I saw in the way a light from heaven, above the brightness of the sun, shining round about me and them which journeyed with me.

Here, Paul adds a bit more detail than that found in the earlier two accounts. *Midday* indicates this event happened at approximately noontime. The reason this detail is significant is that the *light* that surrounded him was even

brighter than the noonday *sun.* The light could not be lightning, for there was no indication of storm conditions. Acts 9:8 and 22:11 mention Paul's being blinded by this light. Clearly, this was a supernatural occurrence; there is no natural explanation for it.

14. And when we were all fallen to the earth, I heard a voice speaking unto me, and saying in the Hebrew tongue, Saul, Saul, why persecutest thou me? it is hard for thee to kick against the pricks.

God is conversant in all human languages, and he chose *Hebrew* to make an impact on Paul. Whether this was what we might call "classic Hebrew" or Aramaic (which was at that time the language of the Hebrews), is hard to say. The terms used could refer to either. If it was the former, the impact on Paul would be that of quoting the ancient tongue of his ancestors, the language of the Scriptures—seldom heard except in the synagogue in Paul's day. If it was Aramaic, then the impact would be that of speaking in his native language. Paul probably heard and spoke Greek, the common trade language of the day, more than his native language (cf. Acts 21:37).

This is the only place where Paul quotes Jesus as saying, *"It is hard for thee to kick against the pricks."* Scholars point out that this was a common expression that described being in opposition to a deity or perhaps being in opposition to one's destiny. A "prick" is a goad or cattle prod. It is used to get an animal to go in a certain direction. A compliant animal will feel the pricking of the goad and turn in the desired direction. A more stubborn one will resist, even kicking at the goad (and the person wielding it). Invariably this just creates more trouble for the animal.

In Paul's case, such "goads" perhaps include the example of Stephen and the courage of those Saul was persecuting at the time. That Paul was kicking against this prompting suggests he was troubled by them. They had caused him to doubt his own position and consider that of the "Way." [See question #1, page 208.]

15. And I said, Who art thou, Lord? And he said, I am Jesus whom thou persecutest.

Even though Paul referred to the person who appeared to him as *Lord,* he may not have had anything particularly religious in mind at this point (cf. Acts 9:5; 22:8). The Greek behind this word could be used in the sense of calling someone "sir," but Paul most certainly did accept the lordship of Christ in short order.

There is a word of encouragement to the church in Jesus' words. Notice that Jesus regards persecution against the church as something personal. It is persecution against Him. He does not take it lightly.

THE FORTY MARTYRS OF SEBASTE

Persecution of the church (which, in reality, is persecution against Christ) has continued without ceasing since the establishment of the church. Those who wear the name of Christ must be prepared to bear the sufferings of Christ. One of the most stirring and enduring stories of persecution is that of the forty martyrs of Sebaste.

The account of their heroic martyrdom, according to Basil of Caesarea, goes something like this. Forty men, all Roman soldiers of the Twelfth "Thundering" Legion, serving during the reign of Licinius, were stationed near Sebaste in Lesser Armenia. The year was about A.D. 320. Refusing orders to sacrifice to the gods and renounce Christ, they were condemned to a cruel death.

The forty soldiers were stripped of their clothing and were forced to stand on the ice of a frozen lake until they either recanted or died. Bonfires, warm baths, and hot food tempted them on the shores of the frozen lake. One soldier, in a moment of weakness, broke ranks and left his companions. The remaining thirty-nine soldiers held fast.

Then something wonderful happened. One of the soldiers standing guard, who was not a believer, was deeply affected by the witness of the persecuted Christian soldiers. He threw off his clothing and joined his comrades on the lake. The next morning there were forty frozen bodies. They died as one, the tortured but triumphant body of Christ.   —V. K.

C. The "Why" of the Vision (vv. 16-18)

16. But rise, and stand upon thy feet: for I have appeared unto thee for this purpose, to make thee a minister and a witness both of these things which thou hast seen, and of those things in the which I will appear unto thee.

This is a brief summary of what Jesus communicated to Paul personally some twenty-five years previously. It also summarizes what Jesus communicated to Paul through God's messenger, a man named Ananias (see Acts 22:14, 15). This vision was not just for Paul's conversion, but also for receiving his divine orders of apostleship. [See question #2, page 208.]

17. Delivering thee from the people, and from the Gentiles, unto whom now I send thee.

Paul now relates the commission he received for his lifework: he was to be a special envoy to the Gentile world. This meant double trouble for him since he would then face opposition from both Jews and *Gentiles*. But Jesus promised to see him through those trials.

18. To open their eyes, and to turn them from darkness to light, and from the power of Satan unto God, that they may receive forgiveness of sins, and inheritance among them which are sanctified by faith that is in me.

Paul's mission is dramatic. He will *open* spiritually blinded *eyes*, take people to the *light*, turn them away from *Satan*, help them find *forgiveness*, and prepare them for the *inheritance* in Heaven. (The church's ongoing commission is the same as Paul's, although worded a bit differently; Matthew 28:19, 20.)

Much of the gospel is summarized in these brief words. Many of these concepts also appear in the preaching of Jesus. Jesus compared sinfulness to spiritual blindness (e.g., Matthew 23:16-19). The Gospels frequently make use of the imagery of light and *darkness* (e.g., Matthew 4:16). Jesus also warned us about the strategy of the evil one (Mark 4:15).

Parenthetically, the word *satan* means "adversary." Sometimes the word *satan* is used for any kind of adversary. When it is used as a proper name, *Satan*, it refers to the ultimate adversary, the devil. [See question #3, page 208.]

FROM DARKNESS TO LIGHT

Perhaps no world is darker than the world that imitates light. Ben Alexander was born a Jew on Christmas Day, 1920, in London's notorious East End. He went to Hebrew school and learned the Ten Commandments, but that was about the extent of his spiritual upbringing. Young Ben was terrified when his father died screaming one dark night. From that time forward, nights became micro-eternities.

Ben came to seek solace in the practice of spiritualism, which involves communicating with the spirit world. He attended séances. He became a practicing "medium." His unholy fascination with the occult world grew deeper and darker year by year.

Home Daily Bible Readings

Monday, Feb. 3—Paul Stands Before Festus (Acts 25:1-12)

Tuesday, Feb. 4—Festus Explains Paul's Case (Acts 25:13-22)

Wednesday, Feb. 5—Paul Comes Before Agrippa (Acts 25:23-27)

Thursday, Feb. 6—Paul Begins His Defense (Acts 26:1-8)

Friday, Feb. 7—Paul Tells of His Conversion (Acts 26:9-18)

Saturday, Feb. 8—I Was Not Disobedient (Acts 26:19-23)

Sunday, Feb. 9—Paul's Appeal to Agrippa (Acts 26:24-32)

Visual for
lesson 11

"*Whereupon, O king Agrippa,
I was not disobedient unto the heavenly vision.*"
Acts 26:19

*Today's visual pictures Paul before Agrippa.
The quotation is from verse 19.*

Eventually Ben set sail for America to found a spiritualist society. Instead, in God's providence, he found Christ. Someone loved him enough to introduce him to Jesus Christ, "the light of the world." Ben's night turned to day. All the answers he had been desperately seeking for he found in Christ. He had been turned from darkness to light, from the power of Satan to God.

Not long after his conversion, Ben began a special ministry called *ESP Ministries.* ESP stands for "Exposing Satan's Powers." Ben's unique ministry, headquartered in St. Petersburg, Florida, has helped untold thousands of people worldwide to escape the darkness of Satan's kingdom and come into the glorious kingdom of Christ's light.   —V. K.

II. Paul's Complete Obedience
(Acts 26:19-21)

A. Immediate Obedience (vv. 19, 20)

19. Whereupon, O king Agrippa, I was not disobedient unto the heavenly vision.

Even before Paul became a Christian, he was zealous for God. Whatever else one might say about him, he always obeyed what he thought God wanted him to do. When Paul received orders from Jesus, he carried them out. This is what Paul wants *king Agrippa* to know: he is under authority and is following orders.

20. But showed first unto them of Damascus, and at Jerusalem, and throughout all the coasts of Judea, and then to the Gentiles, that they should repent and turn to God, and do works meet for repentance.

Paul gives a general summary of the territory he has covered in his ministry up to this point. This is not a chronological list, but more of a

spatial list. (See Acts 1:8; Romans 15:19.) [See question #4, page 208.]

Paul stresses the substance of his message by informing the king that he told his listeners to *repent and turn to God*—ideas that are virtually synonymous. He also mentions that he has urged them to do deeds that are consistent with their *repentance.* There is no incompatibility between faith and works in the Bible as long as one doesn't try to "earn" salvation by those works (cf. Romans 3:28; 4:1-25; Ephesians 2:8, 9; James 2:14-26).

B. Costly Obedience (v. 21)

21. For these causes the Jews caught me in the temple, and went about to kill me.

At the end of his third missionary journey, Paul had returned to Jerusalem and *the temple* (Acts 21:17-26). The Roman authorities had stepped in and saved Paul's life when a lynch mob tried to seize him (21:27-36). When a plot to kill Paul was uncovered in Jerusalem, Paul was transferred to Caesarea (23:12-35). When Governor Festus tried to transfer Paul's case back to Jerusalem to appease the Jews, Paul felt compelled to appeal to Caesar (25:9-12), and that appeal eventually brought him to this point before Agrippa. The appeal to Caesar is the right of a Roman citizen, and the book of Acts makes clear that Paul is indeed such a citizen (22:25-29). This fact gives him more civil rights than *Jews* would ordinarily have.

III. Paul's Challenging Mission
(Acts 26:22, 23, 27-29)

A. The Gospel Made Accessible (vv. 22, 23)

22. Having therefore obtained help of God, I continue unto this day, witnessing both to small and great, saying none other things than those which the prophets and Moses did say should come.

Paul is comfortable in all kinds of settings and with all kinds of people. When he says he witnessed *both to small and great,* he means those who are considered as such by society. Paul preaches to whoever will listen, regardless of social class. (See Romans 12:16; James 2:1-7.)

Paul defends his message as being completely consistent with what was taught by *the prophets and Moses.* This is first a legal defense, since the Jews have accused him of violating Jewish law. But Paul has more in mind than a legal defense. He is laying the foundation to preach the resurrection, as we see in the next verse.

23. That Christ should suffer, and that he should be the first that should rise from the dead, and should show light unto the people, and to the Gentiles.

When a Christian presents the gospel to an unbeliever, the point can come when the listener refuses to hear any more (cf. Acts 17:32; 22:22). For the Roman governor Festus, this is that point, as verse 24 shows. The idea of a suffering Messiah is somewhat of a stumbling block to those who first hear the gospel. Paul mentions it here as part of the substance of his preaching, and he is well aware that this concept was prophesied by the prophet Isaiah (chapter 53) over seven hundred years before. [See question #5, page 208.]

Not only is the Messiah's suffering a major theme for Paul, but so is the Lord's resurrection. Paul further stresses that the message is not just for Jews, but also for *the Gentiles*. This is consistent with his teaching in many other places.

B. The Gospel Made Personal (vv. 27-29)

27. King Agrippa, believest thou the prophets? I know that thou believest.

After responding to Festus's interruption (vv. 24-26), Paul turns his attention back to *King Agrippa*. Paul gives him the benefit of the doubt in noting the king's belief in *the prophets*. Agrippa has a reputation for being knowledgeable about the Scriptures and the customs of Judaism (Acts 26:3).

28. Then Agrippa said unto Paul, Almost thou persuadest me to be a Christian.

Agrippa's response might literally be rendered, "In a little you persuade me to be a Christian." If

---

How to Say It

AGRIPPA. Uh-*grip*-puh.
ANANIAS. An-uh-*nye*-us.
ARAMAIC. *Air*-uh-*may*-ik (strong accent on *may*).
ARMENIA. Ar-*mee*-nee-uh.
AUGUSTUS. Aw-*gus*-tus.
BASIL. *Bay*-zul.
BERNICE. Ber-*nye*-see.
BUECHNER. *Beek*-ner.
CAESAREA. Sess-uh-*ree*-uh.
CLAUDIUS. *Claw*-dee-us.
CLEOPATRA. Clee-oh-*pat*-ruh.
DAMASCUS. Duh-*mass*-kus.
FESTUS. *Fes*-tus.
HEROD. *Hair*-ud.
ISAIAH. Eye-*zay*-uh.
JOSEPHUS. Jo-*see*-fus.
LICINIUS. Luh-*sih*-nee-us.
MEDITERRANEAN. *Med*-uh-tuh-*ray*-nee-un (strong accent on *ray*).
SEBASTE. Seh-*bas*-tee.
TARSUS. *Tar*-sus.

---

the king said this matter-of-factly or pensively, then the *King James Version* accurately captures the message. The king is on the verge of accepting Paul's message and, thus, accepting Christ. This wording has given us the old gospel invitation song, "Almost Persuaded." However, if Agrippa spoke sarcastically, then his intent might better be reflected in something like, "Do you think that in such a short time you can persuade me to be a Christian?" *(New International Version)*.

29. And Paul said, I would to God, that not only thou, but also all that hear me this day, were both almost, and altogether such as I am, except these bonds.

If Agrippa is sarcastic, Paul is undaunted. He presses the invitation. No doubt, Paul expresses this sentiment while gesturing to his *bonds*, or chains. Paul certainly doesn't like being a prisoner, but he could wish that other than that, Agrippa would be as he is. It is his desire that all who listen to him will become Christians.

Conclusion

A. From Persecutor to Persecuted

Paul eventually went to Rome, which had been his dream for some time (Acts 19:21). But it was not in the manner he had originally planned. The book of Acts ends with the apostle Paul under house arrest there, evidently waiting for his appeal to be heard. Even so, he is relatively free to share the gospel from his place of detainment.

We know Paul still had other hopes for the gospel. Among them was his dream to visit Spain (Romans 15:24). While we don't have any Biblical accounts about this period in his life, a persistent legend holds that Paul was released from prison, did go to Spain, was arrested again, and beheaded about A.D. 66 or 67.

Paul, who once had caused persecution, became a victim of it himself through much of his ministry. He who once watched with approval as Stephen was stoned to death ultimately faced his own martyrdom (2 Timothy 4:6). Whatever the circumstances of that martyrdom, there is no doubt that he considered it a great honor.

B. Prayer

Dearest Father, I may not have the intellect or the determination of an apostle Paul, but I can still be obedient. Just as You found the right place for Paul to exercise his ministry, help me find the right place to exercise mine. Through our Lord Jesus we pray, amen.

C. Thought to Remember

If the Lord changes you,
you may well change your world.

Learning by Doing

This page contains an alternative lesson plan emphasizing learning activities.
Classes desiring such student involvement will find these suggestions helpful.

Learning Goals

After participating in this lesson, each student will be able to:

1. Recite the details of Paul's experience on the road to Damascus and his response to it.

2. Explain why Paul's conversion and call are significant to the spread of the gospel.

3. Assess his or her own response to God's call and determine to take one specific step to conform to God's call more closely.

Into the Lesson

Before class hang three signs from the ceiling in different areas of the room. One sign is to read "Big Mistakes: Social." Another will read "Big Mistakes: Spiritual." The third will read "Big Mistakes: Financial." Have five to seven chairs under each sign. For larger classes, add additional signs with the same headings.

As people enter, tell them to be seated under a sign that represents a big mistake they have made in life. (Reassure them they won't have to tell what the mistake was unless they choose to.)

Introduce the lesson by saying, "Everyone makes mistakes—and most of us at some time make big mistakes. We make mistakes in relationships, personal behavior, finances, and in religious decisions or activities."

Ask those willing to share with the small group a brief summary of a big mistake he or she has made. After ten minutes or less, ask one from each group to share his or her mistake with the entire class. This may be a good time to allow persons who may not have had time to share their mistakes with the small groups to speak.

Make the transition to Bible study by reminding them that we all make mistakes—and sometimes they are truly significant. Saul (Paul) also made mistakes. He made a major mistake in his religious life. His error and how he changed will teach us much.

Into the Word

"Teamwork!" Ask each person to select a partner to answer the following questions on a handout. Before they begin, however, give a brief lecture on the setting for this study by using the lesson Introduction and Background from the lesson commentary (page 202). Prepare small posters with the following outline points to attach to the wall during your lecture: "Paul's

Physical Appearance," "Tarsus," "Johnny Appleseed of Church Planting," "King Agrippa and Bernice," "Caesarea," and "Festus."

Then ask the teams to read the printed text and answer the following questions on the handout that you have prepared and distributed:

1. What does verse 12 reveal about Saul's commitment to the Lord before his conversion?

2. What clues do you find in verse 13 that this was a supernatural event?

3. Why did God speak in Hebrew to Saul?

4. What did Jesus mean when He said, "It is hard for thee to kick against the pricks" (v. 14)?

5. What is the purpose of Saul's vision? What did the Lord want of Saul?

6. What was the cost of Paul's obedience to his commission (v. 21)?

7. What was the focus or heart of Paul's message throughout his ministry (v. 23)?

8. "What if . . . ?" Suppose Saul had refused to accept Jesus. Recall some of Saul's experiences and the lives that he touched. Note some of the consequences if he had failed to accept his task.

Allow about fifteen minutes for this project. Then allow people to report conclusions or answers to each question. Use your lesson commentary to supplement answers. List answers to question 8 on a visual.

Into Life

"Lessons Learned!" Make the transition to application by reminding the class that believers today, like Paul, have been called to share the gospel. If we do not do our job, there will be negative consequences. First, ask class members to suggest categories or groups of people with whom most Christians have opportunity to share the gospel (children, grandchildren, spouse, neighbors, work associates). List these on the chalkboard or a poster.

Second, ask, "What are the potentially negative consequences of not completing our mission?" Again, list answers.

Third, give each person an index card. Ask everyone to write on the card the name of one person with whom he or she will share the gospel this week. Each student is to carry the card until he or she has completed the commission.

Finally, ask the teams created in the Bible study portion of the lesson to pray together, asking for help in completing this commitment.

Let's Talk It Over

The questions on this page are designed to promote discussion of the lesson by the class and to encourage application of the lesson Scriptures. The answers provided are only discussion starters. Let your class talk it over from there.

1. Why do some people, like Saul, resist the gospel so strenuously? What "pricks" or "goads" point people to Christ today, even if they "kick against" such prodding?

Some people resist because they are skeptical about the claims of Christianity. They don't believe in God, or miracles, or life after death. But almost all of them know someone whose life has been changed by the gospel. They are prodded by the recognition that some things in life are beyond their control—Someone else must be in charge. Other people resist the gospel because they are comfortable with their own moral code, or lack of one, and don't want to have to change. Christianity demands "too much" of them, ethically, and makes them feel guilty. But that very guilt is a goad that keeps pointing them in the right direction.

2. Jesus said He would make Saul a "minister." What can congregations do to channel young people into ministry today?

First, we must talk about ministry and ministers in a positive way. Why would a young person be interested in ministry if he hears his parents continually criticizing their preachers? Second, we must help our young people experience ministry. Send them on short-term mission trips to experience the fields firsthand. Organize the youth groups to do service projects, not just to have fun. Third, we must help them get the training they need. Support Bible colleges and Bible college students to make ministry training affordable. Provide openings for student interns, so they can learn on the job. If the church wants to have qualified ministers in the future, we have to do the recruiting and training today.

3. Why is it important to realize that our real enemy is Satan, not the people under his power?

When Jesus rose from the dead, He began the final destruction of Satan by making it possible for mankind to be freed from the snare of death (Luke 4:18; 1 Corinthians 15:50-57; Ephesians 4:8). This is what the Bible means when it speaks of Jesus' destroying the works of the devil (1 John 3:8). The purpose of preaching the gospel, as the Lord told Saul, was to rescue those who are in Satan's power. To do that, we have to realize that the world is being deceived by Satan

(Revelation 12:9), as we were before we obeyed the gospel. If we could escape by learning the truth, so can they. However, if we view the lost as the enemy, we will never be motivated to confront Satan to rescue them. Our fight, Paul said, is not with flesh and blood, but the rulers of darkness of this world (Ephesians 6:12).

4. What can we learn from Paul's pattern of evangelism? How can we follow his example?

Paul's pattern of ministry is outlined in verse 20 (cf. Acts 1:8). Paul began preaching in his backyard, to the people closest to him, whom he knew best. Then he began to branch out farther and farther, finally reaching out to those who were quite different from him, ethnically, religiously, and culturally. There are two lessons to be learned from Paul's approach. One is to begin close to home, with people who share a common language and culture, to make evangelism as uncomplicated as possible. The other lesson is not to restrict the gospel to those who are close to home. The Great Commission says to go into all the world. At some point, the church has to reach out beyond its own neighborhood. This can be done both through missions and through cross-cultural work in our own communities, as opportunities present themselves.

5. What stumbling blocks inhibit people from accepting Christ today?

The most important stumbling block is sin. If someone cannot see a need for salvation, or if he has no desire to deal with the sin in his life, he is unlikely to turn to Christ for help. Beyond that, people may stumble over friends and family who are not interested in Christianity themselves, or who present such a poor picture of Christianity in their lives that they discourage others from the faith. A host of worldly things, which a person might pursue in place of salvation, also become stumbling blocks. As Jesus said, "Ye cannot serve God and mammon" (Luke 16:13). Many people realize this and choose things over God. Finally, the belief that there are no absolutes is a major stumbling block to many today. If nothing is absolutely true or false, then the notions of sin and salvation are irrelevant. As your class thinks of other stumbling blocks, discuss also some means of helping people to get over these blocks.

Timothy: Valued Helper

Devotional Reading: 2 Timothy 2:1-7.

Background Scripture: Acts 16:1-5; 17:13-15; 18:5; Philippians 2:19-24; 1, 2 Timothy.

Printed Text: Acts 16:1-5; Philippians 2:19-24; 1 Timothy 1:1-3; 2 Timothy 1:3-6.

Acts 16:1-5

1 Then came he to Derbe and Lystra: and, behold, a certain disciple was there, named Timothy, the son of a certain woman, which was a Jewess, and believed; but his father was a Greek:

2 Which was well reported of by the brethren that were at Lystra and Iconium.

3 Him would Paul have to go forth with him; and took and circumcised him because of the Jews which were in those quarters: for they knew all that his father was a Greek.

4 And as they went through the cities, they delivered them the decrees for to keep, that were ordained of the apostles and elders which were at Jerusalem.

5 And so were the churches established in the faith, and increased in number daily.

Philippians 2:19-24

19 But I trust in the Lord Jesus to send Timothy shortly unto you, that I also may be of good comfort, when I know your state.

20 For I have no man likeminded, who will naturally care for your state.

21 For all seek their own, not the things which are Jesus Christ's.

22 But ye know the proof of him, that, as a son with the father, he hath served with me in the gospel.

23 Him therefore I hope to send presently, so soon as I shall see how it will go with me.

24 But I trust in the Lord that I also myself shall come shortly.

1 Timothy 1:1-3

1 Paul, an apostle of Jesus Christ by the commandment of God our Saviour, and Lord Jesus Christ, which is our hope;

2 Unto Timothy, my own son in the faith: Grace, mercy, and peace, from God our Father, and Jesus Christ our Lord.

3 As I besought thee to abide still at Ephesus, when I went into Macedonia, that thou mightest charge some that they teach no other doctrine.

2 Timothy 1:3-6

3 I thank God, whom I serve from my fore-fathers with pure conscience, that without ceasing I have remembrance of thee in my prayers night and day;

4 Greatly desiring to see thee, being mindful of thy tears, that I may be filled with joy;

5 When I call to remembrance the unfeigned faith that is in thee, which dwelt first in thy grandmother Lois, and thy mother Eunice; and I am persuaded that in thee also.

6 Wherefore I put thee in remembrance, that thou stir up the gift of God, which is in thee by the putting on of my hands.

Feb 16

Golden Text: Ye know the proof of him, that, as a son with the father, he hath served with me in the gospel.—Philippians 2:22.

Portraits of Faith
Unit 3: Personalities in the Early Church
(Lessons 10-13)

Lesson Aims

After this lesson each student will be able to:

1. Describe Timothy's background and character as seen in the lesson texts under consideration.

2. Tell why a supporting role in ministry is vital to the ministry's success.

3. Identify a young person whom he or she can encourage to get involved in ministry in the church.

Lesson Outline

INTRODUCTION
    A. Best Supporting Actor
    B. Lesson Background
 I. TIMOTHY, THE TEAMMATE (Acts 16:1-5)
    A. Family Background (vv. 1, 2)
    B. Religious Background (v. 3)
    C. Early Labors (vv. 4, 5)
 II. TIMOTHY, THE SERVANT (Philippians 2:19-24)
    A. Affinity With Paul (vv. 19, 20)
    B. Concern for the Church (vv. 21-24)
III. TIMOTHY, THE TEACHER (1 Timothy 1:1-3)
    A. Taught by Paul (vv. 1, 2)
       Hope Never Dies
    B. Trusted by Paul (v. 3)
IV. TIMOTHY, THE LEADER (2 Timothy 1:3-6)
    A. Prayer for Leadership (vv. 3, 4)
    B. Preparation for Leadership (v. 5)
    C. Empowerment for Leadership (v. 6)
CONCLUSION
    A. A First-rate Second-rater
    B. Prayer
    C. Thought to Remember

Introduction

A. Best Supporting Actor

Would an actor prefer to be nominated for an Oscar for "Best Actor" or for "Best Supporting Actor"? From all the publicity, the "Best Supporting" Oscar is seen as less prestigious.

But every great endeavor needs people who can serve in supporting roles. Young actors are frequently told, "There are no small parts—only small actors." Plays, movies, and television programs are greatly enhanced by the work of supporting actors and actresses. No great story can be told without them.

Timothy had no problem with playing a supporting role in the work of the kingdom. As often happens with actors who play the supporting role well, Timothy later moved into a leading role.

B. Lesson Background

In some respects they may have seemed like the odd couple. Paul was probably middle-aged, and Timothy likely was a teenager. While Timothy knew the Scriptures (2 Timothy 3:15), he probably was not formally schooled in religion. Paul, on the other hand, possessed the best theological education available in his day (Acts 22:3). Paul was bold, but Timothy may have been somewhat timid (1 Corinthians 16:10). Nevertheless, they became inseparable—in spirit even if often separated by space.

Timothy's name is mentioned in ten of Paul's letters, and Timothy may have played a small role in the writing of some of those. Paul addresses two letters directly to him, and we will look at some references from those epistles as part of this lesson.

I. Timothy, the Teammate
(Acts 16:1-5)

The year is about A.D. 50 or 51, and Paul is in the early stages of his second missionary journey. Paul and Silas are revisiting the cities in Galatia where Paul and Barnabas had planted churches earlier. Paul's first visit to this area had not been pleasant; it was stressful and unusual. While in Lystra, he and Barnabas had been taken to be Greek gods by the local populace (Acts 14:11-13). But then the crowd was swayed and Paul barely escaped with his life, having been stoned and left for dead (14:19). Still, it is obvious that good things had happened in the ministry when they were there the first time. Sometime during this visit, Paul must have come into contact with Timothy's family and led them to conversion.

A. Family Background (vv. 1, 2)

1, 2. Then came he to Derbe and Lystra: and, behold, a certain disciple was there, named Timothy, the son of a certain woman, which was a Jewess, and believed; but his father was a Greek: which was well reported of by the brethren that were at Lystra and Iconium.

This is the first of six references to *Timothy* in the book of Acts. (Some editions of the *King James Version* spell his name "Timotheus.") Timothy is already a *disciple*. No doubt Timothy was converted, or at least his mother and/or grandmother were (2 Timothy 1:5), during Paul's first visit.

(Paul's reference to Timothy as his "son" in 1 Corinthians 4:17 implies that he is a convert of Paul.) In time he will become invaluable to the apostle. He knows both the Greek world and the Jewish world. He understands both worlds and is comfortable in either one.

The Jewish population around *Derbe, Lystra,* and *Iconium* is very small at the time, so mixed marriages are more common here than in Judea. It also appears from the way this is worded that Timothy's *father* is probably dead.

The fact that Timothy is *well reported* indicates that he is already involved in church work in servant roles. Perhaps he is involved even in preaching and teaching roles.

B. Religious Background (v. 3)

3. Him would Paul have to go forth with him; and took and circumcised him because of the Jews which were in those quarters: for they knew all that his father was a Greek.

In passages such as Acts 15:1, 2; Romans 2:25-29; and 1 Corinthians 7:18, *Paul* makes it clear that circumcision is no longer necessary now that the New Covenant has come. Some students find it startling, then, to read here that he had Timothy *circumcised.*

But the issue at hand is not one of doctrinal necessity, but practical expediency. Paul realizes that for Timothy to remain uncircumcised will be a hindrance to bringing the gospel message to *the Jews* in that area. As F. F. Bruce notes, the Jews in that area would consider Timothy to be a Gentile, and the Gentiles would consider him to be a Jew.

Some question Paul's judgment here. They say it seems inconsistent with his views on circumcision. They point out that, in another case, Paul had decided not to circumcise Titus (Galatians 2:1-5). But these critics forget that while Paul thought circumcision unnecessary for Gentiles, Jewish practices were still appropriate for Jews. Paul continued to practice those customs the rest of his life. Titus was in no way considered to be Jewish, and Paul did not want to appear to be demanding obedience to the law as a condition of salvation (Acts 15:1-11). Attempting to be justified by law-keeping was a major problem with certain churches, and circumcision had become a flashpoint in this doctrinal struggle (Galatians 5:1-6). So Paul's differing treatments of Timothy and Titus is completely consistent with his stated views on the issue. [See question #1, page 216.]

C. Early Labors (vv. 4, 5)

4. And as they went through the cities, they delivered them the decrees for to keep, that were ordained of the apostles and elders which were at Jerusalem.

Paul, Silas, and Timothy undertake a trip to *the cities* that Paul had visited on Paul's first missionary journey with Barnabas. *They* take with them the letter written by the leaders in *Jerusalem* concerned with allowing Gentiles to become Christians with few restrictions (Acts 15:22-29). The so-called "Jerusalem Conference" had been made up primarily of *the apostles and elders* of the Jerusalem church (Acts 15:6), which could now be regarded as the "mother" church. It is impossible to overestimate the importance of this conference's decision for the Gentile believers and the church at large. There is no question that the church already had made inroads into predominantly Gentile areas, but would the Gentiles be accepted, and on what basis?

James the brother of Jesus, who had become a prominent leader in the Jerusalem church, apparently chaired this conference (Acts 15:13-21). Interestingly, Peter was the most vocal advocate for the Gentiles (Acts 15:7-11). Barnabas and Paul also made a report. After all the debate and discussion, little was asked of the Gentiles in terms of adherence to Jewish custom. They were asked to abstain from idolatry, the drinking of blood, meat from strangled animals, and sexual immorality. This letter was seen as an official welcome to the Gentiles. Interestingly, just as Silas replaces Barnabas, it seems that Timothy replaces John Mark in Paul's heart and strategies.

5. And so were the churches established in the faith, and increased in number daily.

This verse provides a summary statement of all the progress on this part of the journey through the territory of Galatia. The mention of both spiritual growth and numerical growth recognizes the importance of each. [See question #2, page 216.]

II. Timothy, the Servant (Philippians 2:19-24)

Probably ten years have now passed. After Paul's trial before Agrippa (see last week's lesson) he was sent to Rome. There he was incarcerated for two years (Acts 28:30). During this time he wrote several of his epistles, including the one to the Philippians (Philippians 1:13, 14).

A. Affinity With Paul (vv. 19, 20)

19. But I trust in the Lord Jesus to send Timothy shortly unto you, that I also may be of good comfort, when I know your state.

Paul wants to know how things are going with the church at Philippi, a church that Paul and his companions had established on the second missionary journey (Acts 16:11-40). To find out, he will have to send a personal representative to gain the information he desires.

Visual for lesson 12. *John Wilson preached for many years in Springfield, Ohio, and encouraged many "Timothys" to join him in ministry.*

We do not know when *Timothy* went to Rome or why. Perhaps Paul summoned him for this very mission.

20. For I have no man likeminded, who will naturally care for your state.

There is *no* one else Paul can think of who is as ready for this task as is Timothy. The Philippians do not need an introduction to Timothy, for they already know him. Still, Paul wants them to appreciate how in tune Timothy is with the mind of Paul. The word *likeminded* can be translated literally as "equal soul." Not only is Timothy in tune with Paul, but he also has a genuine concern for the church.

B. Concern for the Church (vv. 21-24)

21, 22. For all seek their own, not the things which are Jesus Christ's. But ye know the proof of him, that, as a son with the father, he hath served with me in the gospel.

Unfortunately, some who preach *the gospel* do so from wrong motives (Philippians 1:15, 16). Not Timothy! He stands as an example of a person who clearly and unambiguously seeks *the things which are Jesus Christ's.* Paul, we presume, has no *son* in the flesh, but Timothy is his son in the faith. It is certainly true that some people who labor together in the gospel are as close or closer than blood relatives. [See question #3, page 216.]

23. Him therefore I hope to send presently, so soon as I shall see how it will go with me.

Paul urges patience on the Philippian church. He does not want to let Timothy go until his own fate is determined. Paul may have had some upcoming legal decision in mind. He not only needs Timothy with him at this crucial time, but if he waits Timothy will have some fresh news to pass on.

24. But I trust in the Lord that I also myself shall come shortly.

Paul decides to be content no matter what the outcome for himself. He has no special revelation, but he is optimistic that he will be released from this particular imprisonment. The book of Acts ends with Paul still incarcerated, but church tradition indicates that he was released.

III. Timothy, the Teacher (1 Timothy 1:1-3)

This part of our lesson comes from one of the two letters that bear Timothy's name. It is now about A.D. 65, and Paul and Timothy have known each other for fifteen years or so.

A. Taught by Paul (vv. 1, 2)

1. Paul, an apostle of Jesus Christ by the commandment of God our Saviour, and Lord Jesus Christ, which is our hope.

The conventional way to begin a letter in the ancient world is to affix the signature first. In the opening of the letter, *Paul* identifies himself as *an apostle . . . by the commandment of God.* In a general sense, all of the apostles served at the commandment of God. Paul may be referring specifically to his commission on the road to Damascus. He may also be responding to critics who think that he is not a genuine apostle. Paul feels the need to affirm and defend his apostleship in other places as well (1 Corinthians 9:1, 2; 2 Corinthians 12:11, 12; Galatians 1:1).

He mentions *Jesus* as *Lord* here also. Jewish Christians understand Jesus to be the Messiah. As the gospel spreads to the Gentile world, the concept of Messiah is not as significant. Gentiles have little understanding of what a messiah is. As the gospel proceeds, *Lord* becomes a more significant title, since both Jew and Gentile can understand it.

HOPE NEVER DIES

The 1994 movie *The Shawshank Redemption* is a story about hope. The two central characters, Andy and "Red," are serving time in a prison notorious for corruption. Both men are in for murder: Andy, for a murder he did not commit; "Red," for one he did commit when he was young.

The warden is nothing more than a bully and a thief. He and many of the crooked prison guards use Andy's banking skills to salt away laundered money. But Andy outsmarts them all. For twenty years he piles up evidence. Then he uses a small rock hammer to tunnel his way to freedom.

After Andy's daring escape, shocking exposure of the evils at Shawshank, and the warden's suicide, Red is finally paroled. He has spent forty years at Shawshank. In a previously agreed upon place, Red finds a note from Andy. It is in a tin box along with some money to help Red on his way. The note reads: "Hope is a good thing . . . and no good thing ever dies."

The Christmas hymn, "O Little Town of Bethlehem" tells us that Jesus Christ personifies "the hopes and fears of all the years." Indeed, He is our hope—"a living hope," "the hope of glory," "the blessed hope." And that is a hope rooted in more than the clever scheming of a movie character; it is based on the infinite power of God Himself.

> My hope is built on nothing less
>   Than Jesus' blood and righteousness;
> I dare not trust the sweetest frame,
>   But wholly lean on Jesus' name.
>   —Edward Mote (1797–1874)

—V. K.

2. Unto Timothy, my own son in the faith: Grace, mercy, and peace, from God our Father, and Jesus Christ our Lord.

Interestingly, the two letters addressed to *Timothy*, along with the letter to Titus, have come to be known as "the Pastoral Epistles." Timothy certainly has a pastoral concern for the churches, as we saw hinted at in Philippians 2:20 above. But the phrase "Pastoral Epistles" deals more with the concerns of Paul as the author of these works rather than Timothy as the recipient.

As we have already noted, Paul sees Timothy as a *son*—not a son of the flesh, but a son *in the faith*. As the years have passed, there has been no lessening of Paul's appreciation for Timothy in this regard (cf. 1 Corinthians 4:17). [See question #4, page 216.]

The greeting we see here is typical of Paul in that *grace* and *peace* appear in the salutation of all thirteen of his letters. Many commentators note that in this greeting is a hint of the union between Jew and Gentile since "grace" (the Greek word *charis*) is a typical Gentile greeting while "peace" (the Hebrew word *shalom*) is a typical Jewish greeting. Added to Paul's traditional greeting is the word *mercy*. Since there is a special personal dimension to this letter, Paul adds a personal blessing.

B. Trusted by Paul (v. 3)

3. As I besought thee to abide still at Ephesus, when I went into Macedonia, that thou mightest charge some that they teach no other doctrine.

In Philippians 2 (above), it is Paul who "stays put" while Timothy travels. Now the reverse is true. *Ephesus* (which means "desirable") is one of the most fascinating cities of its time, and its ruins are a worthwhile visit even today. Ephesus is the location of one of the seven wonders of the ancient word, the temple of Artemis. Paul had set off a riot in this city in the process of establishing one of the most noteworthy churches in Biblical times (Acts 19).

The primary thing Timothy is to do at Ephesus is *teach*. One of the most difficult challenges for a Christian teacher is to deal with matters of *doctrine*. Doctrinal disputes can produce very sharp disagreements. Teaching doctrine is always a challenge, particularly when false doctrine is making its way around. Paul entrusts to Timothy the challenging task of helping the fledgling church sort out true from false doctrine, and silence those teaching falsehood. (See also 1 Timothy 6:3-5.)

What doctrinal problems does the church at Ephesus face? If you continue reading through verse 7, you get a hint. In verse 4, Paul refers to people's devoting themselves to fables (or myths) and genealogies. (Paul repeats this concern, in part, in Titus 1:14.) This statement probably refers to one of two possibilities. It may refer to Jewish myths and Old Testament genealogies.

Another possibility is that it refers to what will later become known as Gnosticism. One of the Gnostic beliefs was that there were a good god and an evil god. The evil god, who they believed created the world, was the result of countless emanations from the good god. (These emanations could be considered a *genealogy* of the evil god.) Either of these concepts would have been damaging to the church and needed correction.

How to Say It

AGRIPPA. Uh-*grip*-puh.
ARTEMIS. *Ar*-teh-miss.
BARNABAS. *Bar*-nuh-bus.
CHARIS (Greek). *kah*-riss.
CORINTHIANS. Kor-*in*-thee-unz *(th* as in *thin).*
DERBE. *Der*-be.
EPHESUS. *Ef*-uh-sus.
EUNICE. U-*nye*-see or *U*-nis.
GALATIA. Guh-*lay*-shuh.
GALATIANS. Guh-*lay*-shunz.
GENTILES. *Jen*-tyles.
GNOSTICISM. *Nahss*-tih-*sizz*-um (strong accent on *Nahss*).
ICONIUM. Eye-*ko*-nee-um.
LYSTRA. *Liss*-truh.
PHILIPPI. Fih-*lip*-pie or *Fil*-ih-pie.
SHALOM (Hebrew). shah-*lome*.
SILAS. *Sigh*-luss.
TIMOTHEUS. Ti-*mo*-the-us *(th* as in *thin).*
TITUS. *Tie*-tus.
WELSHIMER. *Wel*-shuh-mer.

IV. Timothy, the Leader
(2 Timothy 1:3-6)

We now move to Paul's second letter to Timothy, probably written just before Paul's execution in A.D. 66 or 67.

A. Prayer for Leadership (vv. 3, 4)

3. I thank God, whom I serve from my forefathers with pure conscience, that without ceasing I have remembrance of thee in my prayers night and day;

In mentioning his *forefathers,* Paul reflects on his religious heritage. Even though he is the apostle to the Gentiles, Paul appreciates his Jewish heritage. It is as important to him now in the waning days of his life as it had been earlier (Acts 22:3; 24:14).

Paul's claim of a *pure conscience* does not mean that he is perfect, but that he is satisfied with the sincerity of his service (cf. Acts 23:1). Perhaps these references to his heritage and his conscience are both hints to Timothy as a church leader that he, too, should embrace and pass on a sound heritage while maintaining a good conscience. Timothy may be encouraged to do both as he experiences the reality of Paul's continual *prayers.* [See question #5, page 216.]

4. Greatly desiring to see thee, being mindful of thy tears, that I may be filled with joy.

Paul probably recalls the last time he and Timothy parted, when probably they both shed *tears.* (See the tearful parting of Paul and the Ephesian elders in Acts 20:36-38.) We do not know when this parting was, but Paul certainly desires to see Timothy one last time (2 Timothy 4:9, 21).

B. Preparation for Leadership (v. 5)

5. When I call to remembrance the unfeigned faith that is in thee, which dwelt first in thy grandmother Lois, and thy mother Eunice; and I am persuaded that in thee also.

After recalling his own religious heritage in verse 3, Paul now reminds Timothy of his. Timothy is an example of what can happen when the faith is passed down in a family. Both his mother and grandmother were well versed in the Scriptures and shared that knowledge with Timothy.

Even though *Eunice* and *Lois* are Jewish, their names are distinctly Greek. Since they live in the Greek world, this is not very unusual. The name Eunice means "good victory." Timothy's name, interestingly, means "friend of God."

C. Empowerment for Leadership (v. 6)

6. Wherefore I put thee in remembrance, that thou stir up the gift of God, which is in thee by the putting on of my hands.

Our ability to fulfill the call of God in our lives comes from the Holy Sprit. Paul undoubtedly has in mind a particular spiritual *gift* that was given, in Timothy's case, by a prophecy and the laying on of *hands* of Paul and a body of elders (1 Timothy 4:14). Even spiritual gifts given by an apostle must be put to use if they are to be effective. That is the reason Timothy is told to *stir up* this gift.

Conclusion

A. First-rate Second-rater

P. H. Welshimer (1873–1957) advised preachers, "If you have to be a second-rater, then be a first-rate second-rater." Surely Timothy is at least a first-rate second-rater!

What ultimately becomes of Timothy, we do not know. We do know that he was imprisoned later, but eventually released (Hebrews 13:23). There are very few reliable traditions that give us any hint about how Timothy lived the rest of his life or about his death.

But what we do know of Timothy's life is enough to encourage us to follow his example. A famous conductor purportedly was asked what was the most difficult instrument in the orchestra to play. With a twinkle in his eye he is said to have replied, "Second fiddle!" Someone has to play it, and Timothy played it like a virtuoso.

B. Prayer

Help us, Father, to value those who mentor us. Help us to be willing to mentor others that Your Word may go forth from generation to generation. In the name of our Redeemer we pray, amen.

C. Thought to Remember

Everyone needs both a Paul and a Timothy in his or her life.

Home Daily Bible Readings

Monday, Feb. 10—Paul Takes Timothy With Him (Acts 16:1-5)

Tuesday, Feb. 11—I Have No One Like Him (Philippians 2:19-24)

Wednesday, Feb. 12—A Loyal Child in the Faith (1 Timothy 1:1-5)

Thursday, Feb. 13—A Man of Sincere Faith (2 Timothy 1:1-7)

Friday, Feb. 14—Timothy and Silas Stay in Berea (Acts 17:10-15)

Saturday, Feb. 15—Paul Sends Timothy to Encourage (1 Thessalonians 3:1-6)

Sunday, Feb. 16—Come to Me Soon (2 Timothy 4:9-15)

Learning by Doing

This page contains an alternative lesson plan emphasizing learning activities.
Classes desiring such student involvement will find these suggestions helpful.

Learning Goals

After participating in this lesson, each student will be able to:

1. Describe Timothy's background and character as seen in the lesson texts under consideration.

2. Tell why a supporting role in ministry is vital to the ministry's success.

3. Identify a young person whom he or she can encourage to get involved in ministry in the church.

Into the Lesson

Before class prepare and display a poster that says "Best Supporting Actor." Begin this session by asking class members to identify ministry teams in your church. "Teams" may be groups such as financial teams, care-building teams, elders, church staff, teaching teams, or others. If possible, include the names of people of the smaller teams (fewer than six or seven). List these team categories on the chalkboard or on a poster. This list may be long.

Next, ask class members to identify the leaders of these teams. Write their names or place an asterisk by names already listed.

Make the transition to Bible study by using the lesson Introduction on page 210 to emphasize the value of talented people who play supporting roles in the church's ministry teams.

Into the Word

Interview With Paul. Play the part of Paul for an interview (or recruit a class member). Put on one piece of clothing, or use a prop (staff, beard, robe, shawl) that identifies you as an actor in this role. Prepare the following list of questions to be asked of you by class members. Also ask different people to read today's printed text at the appropriate times. Use your lesson commentary to prepare your responses. As you put on your clothing or prop, explain to the class what you are staging and that the focus of this interview is about your young assistant, Timothy.

Sample questions for the interview include the following:

1. (Have a class member read Acts 16:1-5.) "Paul, before you came to this area and met Timothy, you had been here before. I know your first trip was not pleasant. Tell us what happened."

2. "One of the great results of that visit, of course, is that you eventually got acquainted with Timothy. Tell us a little bit about his background and what drew you to him."

3. "Paul, the record says that you circumcised Timothy. Why did you do that?"

4. "When you, Timothy, and Silas made your trip back through cities you had visited before, the record says you gave them decrees to keep that were from the apostles and elders and Jerusalem. Explain what this was all about."

5. (Have someone read Philippians 2:19-24.) "Explain this record to us, Paul."

6. (Have 1 Timothy 1:1-3 read.) "I notice, Paul, that you are giving more and more responsibility to Timothy. When you went to Macedonia, you asked Timothy to stay in Ephesus. Why was it important for him to be there?"

7. "There is one more text I'd like to ask about." (Have someone read 2 Timothy 1:3-6.) "I notice you pay tribute to Timothy's home life. How do you think his background shaped him into such a valuable teammate?"

Into Life

As you discard your stage props or slip out of your garb, explain that Timothy was a great teammate or "supporting actor." Ask the following discussion questions to encourage application.

1. What qualities or characteristics help to make great support persons in ministry teams? (List answers on the board or poster.)

2. Why are supporting roles valuable in ministry today? (Ask people to illustrate their answers.)

3. Paul encouraged Timothy to "stir up the gift of God" (2 Timothy 1:6). Even Timothy needed to be encouraged to develop and use gifts God had given him. What are some ways we can encourage young people in our church to develop their leadership skills and their spiritual lives? (List these ideas on a poster or chalkboard.)

Give each class member an index card. Ask each to write the name of one teenager or young adult in the church he or she will encourage to be more involved in the church's ministry.

Then, if possible, try to find a way to allow the skill or gift of that young person to be used. Call attention to the list from discussion question 3 above for ideas on how to encourage that young person. Class members may even need to contact a church leader, asking him to help find a way to use that young person in ministry or service.

Let's Talk It Over

The questions on this page are designed to promote discussion of the lesson by the class and to encourage application of the lesson Scriptures. The answers provided are only discussion starters. Let your class talk it over from there.

1. Paul had Timothy circumcised to be accepted by the Jews. What limits should we put on accommodating our hearers? How far can we go in being "all things to all men"?

"All things to all men" comes from 1 Corinthians 9:22. The issue there is Christian liberty. Paul says he limits his own freedom in Christ in order to help others come to know the Lord. So the first principle on accommodating people might be that we do it for their good, not our own. Some people will accommodate others just to avoid confrontation. This was not Paul's motive.

Have the class read the rest of 1 Corinthians 9 for other ideas. Notice the goal: "that I might by all means save some." Notice some of the limits Paul himself expresses, as in verse 21.

Finally, be sure to get practical on how to accommodate people in your own community to help them hear the gospel. Would a different starting time for your worship hour help? Would some home Bible studies help you to go where they are instead of expecting them to come to you? Would a day care service be practical? Or how about a car care clinic for single moms?

2. We note in the lesson that both spiritual and numerical growth are important in the church. What emphasis should we put on each? How should we balance the two?

Luke mentions that, where Paul, Silas, and Timothy visited, the churches were "established in the *faith*, and increased in *number* daily" (Acts 16:5). As the believers grew spiritually, they would have been more concerned about evangelizing the lost. They also would have been bolder to share their faith despite possible persecution. Most importantly, they would have learned to depend on God for numerical growth, not on themselves, which would have opened the door for His blessings. Perhaps we should see numbers as something of a barometer of spiritual growth. If the numbers aren't there, it may suggest we are not providing adequate spiritual nurture. But we dare not do things just to increase the numbers without having a solid spiritual foundation.

3. How can you tell when people "seek their own" and when they will "care for your state"?

Some people are clever about hiding their real intentions, but usually it is obvious when a person is serving out of love—and when he or she isn't. Many Sunday school teachers, for the love of the children they teach, invest considerable sums into the purchase of teaching supplies. Missionaries and other Christian workers forego the potential for lucrative salaries in secular positions to spread the gospel. Many elders give up time at home in order to attend meetings, visit with sick and shut-in church members, or lead Bible studies or support groups.

4. Who might refer to you as a son or daughter in the faith? Why? How do you show your appreciation to this person? And whom might you call a son or daughter in the faith? Why? (If no one, why not?)

This is a wonderful opportunity to affirm those who have led by word and lifestyle. Is there an older member in your church that used to teach Sunday school, and many of your students remember her class? Is there a former (or current) minister who led many of your students to the Lord? Encourage the students to talk about those who have had the greatest impact on their spiritual lives. Plan specific ways to thank these people. (If some are deceased, perhaps a note to a surviving spouse or child would be appropriate.)

5. What do you think Paul prayed about in Timothy's behalf? Why?

Of course, we do not know specifically, but there are some hints. The very qualities he encouraged Timothy to display and the tasks he urged Timothy to complete must have been the object of some of his prayers. These include his ability to refute false teaching (1 Timothy 1:3, 18), to have orderliness in the church (3:15), to remind the brethren of truth (4:6), to keep his own lifestyle pure and exemplary (4:12), etc. Have your students look for other commands in 1 and 2 Timothy that may well be the object of Paul's prayers.

Consider how we can follow Paul's example. Have the students suggest who needs us to pray like this. Perhaps you can think of specific ways to pray for your minister(s), for the elders and deacons, for Sunday school teachers. How about the young people? The more we commit the work of our churches to God, the more He will accomplish through us!

Priscilla and Aquila

DEVOTIONAL READING: Ephesians 4:1-13.

BACKGROUND SCRIPTURE: Acts 18:1-4, 18-26;
Romans 16:3-5a; 1 Corinthians 16:19; 2
Timothy 4:19.

PRINTED TEXT: Acts 18:1-4, 18, 19a, 24-26;
Romans 16:3-5a; 1 Corinthians 16:19; 2
Timothy 4:19.

Acts 18:1-4, 18, 19a, 24-26

1 After these things Paul departed from
Athens, and came to Corinth;

2 And found a certain Jew named Aquila,
born in Pontus, lately come from Italy, with
his wife Priscilla, (because that Claudius had
commanded all Jews to depart from Rome,)
and came unto them.

3 And because he was of the same craft, he
abode with them, and wrought: (for by their
occupation they were tentmakers.)

4 And he reasoned in the synagogue every
sabbath, and persuaded the Jews and the
Greeks.

. . . .

18 And Paul after this tarried there yet a
good while, and then took his leave of the
brethren, and sailed thence into Syria, and
with him Priscilla and Aquila; having shorn
his head in Cenchreae: for he had a vow.

19a And he came to Ephesus, and left them
there.

. . . .

24 And a certain Jew named Apollos, born
at Alexandria, an eloquent man, and mighty
in the Scriptures, came to Ephesus.

25 This man was instructed in the way of
the Lord; and being fervent in the spirit, he
spake and taught diligently the things of the
Lord, knowing only the baptism of John.

26 And he began to speak boldly in the synagogue: whom when Aquila and Priscilla had
heard, they took him unto them, and expounded unto him the way of God more perfectly.

Romans 16:3-5a

3 Greet Priscilla and Aquila, my helpers in
Christ Jesus:

4 Who have for my life laid down their own
necks: unto whom not only I give thanks, but
also all the churches of the Gentiles.

5a Likewise greet the church that is in their
house.

1 Corinthians 16:19

19 The churches of Asia salute you. Aquila
and Priscilla salute you much in the Lord,
with the church that is in their house.

2 Timothy 4:19

19 Salute Prisca and Aquila, and the
household of Onesiphorus.

GOLDEN TEXT: Greet Priscilla and Aquila, my helpers in Christ Jesus: who have for
my life laid down their own necks: unto whom not only I give thanks,
but also all the churches of the Gentiles.—Romans 16:3, 4.

Feb
23

Portraits of Faith
Unit 3: Personalities in the Early Church
(Lessons 10-13)

Lesson Aims

After this lesson students will be able to:

1. List three cities where Priscilla and Aquila labored for the Lord, and note something of their work in each.

2. Explain how Priscilla and Aquila's style of hospitality and teaching can be used to help the church today.

3. Express appreciation to people who help to facilitate the ministry in their church.

Lesson Outline

Introduction

A. Great Teams

Some names are always thought of together. Names like Fred and Ginger, Lucy and Desi, and George and Gracie. In the Bible one particular couple stands out, for they are always mentioned together. They are Priscilla and Aquila.

Priscilla and Aquila are mentioned six times in the New Testament. In four of those references Priscilla is named first, an indication of her importance among Christians. Sometimes the Greek text refers to Priscilla by her more formal name, Prisca.

B. Lesson Background

While the Bible exalts marriage, we find few detailed examples of solid marriages in its pages. No doubt there were many such marriages among God's people, but we just don't have the details necessary to examine them closely. We know, for instance, that Peter had a wife and that she traveled with him on at least some of his journeys, but we know nothing else about that marriage (see Matthew 8:14; 1 Corinthians 9:5). Today we learn about a wonderful Christian couple by the name of Priscilla and Aquila.

This lesson also highlights the important part that both men and women played in the church of the first century. Today, some Bible passages are hotly debated in how they do or do not speak to the issue of gender roles in the church. This lesson does not address those issues. Instead, we will adopt a focused look at a particular man and woman—a married couple—who played a crucial part in growth of the infant church.

I. The Team Introduced
(Acts 18:1-4, 18, 19a)

As we pick up the narrative here, the year is about A.D. 51. Paul is on his second missionary journey. Having traveled through Galatia, he had hoped to visit Asia Minor, but that would have to wait (Acts 16:6). Instead, he and his party arrive in Troas, where Paul receives a vision compelling him to minister in Macedonia (vv. 7-10). The remainder of Acts 16 and chapter 17 tell of what happened in Macedonia and in Athens, Greece. During this part of the trip Paul sometimes sends his coworkers on separate missions while he continues on his own (Acts 17:14; 1 Thessalonians 3:1-5). So as our text begins, Paul is traveling alone from Athens to Corinth.

A. Meeting Paul (vv. 1-4)

1. After these things Paul departed from Athens, and came to Corinth.

Paul's association with Priscilla and Aquila begins when *Paul* travels from *Athens* to *Corinth*, a distance of about forty miles. Athens is named in honor of the mythical Greek goddess Athena, and at the time it is a city of great philosophical ferment. Perhaps a bit discouraged from the lukewarm response to his preaching in that city (Acts 17:16-34), Paul has decided to move on.

As Paul enters Corinth in southern Greece, he finds a military outpost and a crossroads for commerce. This city has all the advantages and disadvantages that such a setting brings. Corinthians are particularly fond of the Greek god Apollo and the goddess Aphrodite, and the city is known for its immorality.

2. And found a certain Jew named Aquila, born in Pontus, lately come from Italy, with his wife Priscilla, (because that Claudius had commanded all Jews to depart from Rome,) and came unto them.

Aquila is specifically called a *Jew* even though he has a distinctly Roman name, a name that means "eagle." He is originally from the territory of *Pontus,* near the Black Sea. Pontus is adjacent to Bithynia, a territory the Holy Spirit did not allow Paul to enter (Acts 16:7). There must have been a strong Jewish presence in Pontus since residents of that area are mentioned as being in Jerusalem on the Day of Pentecost (Acts 2:9).

Aquila and *Priscilla* probably had made their home in *Rome.* No doubt they had conducted business in that city just as they are doing in Corinth when Paul meets them. Since Priscilla is not specifically called a Jew, some believe that she is a Gentile who married into the Jewish faith. Whether she was from Pontus or Rome or some other place is unknown.

Since nothing is said of Paul's converting Priscilla and Aquila, it is generally assumed that they already had become Christians before meeting Paul in Corinth. Was Aquila one of the Jews from Pontus in Jerusalem at that momentous Pentecost? (See Acts 2:8, 9.)

Claudius ruled the Roman Empire from A.D. 41 to 54. Because of an edict by that emperor in A.D. 49 or 50, Aquila and Priscilla had to leave Rome. (Historical references outside the Bible also mention this edict.) The historian Suetonius discusses the eviction and even mentions a leader named "Chrestus." Probably Suetonius had the name slightly wrong—it should be "Christus" or "Christ." If so, then the unrest in Rome that prompted the eviction probably was related to tensions within Judaism regarding Jesus. To the Roman authorities, Christianity is just a sect of Judaism. So even if Aquila and Priscilla were Christians in Rome, they would still be evicted because of Aquila's Jewish heritage.

All this suggests that the first group of Christians in Rome may have been a predominantly Jewish group rather than a Gentile group. With the Jews evicted, those of Gentile background began to be the majority of Christians in Rome (Romans 1:5, 6). We know that when Paul wrote the book of Romans in about A.D. 57, he had not yet had an opportunity to visit this church. By that time, however, the edict of Claudius was no longer in force and Aquila and Priscilla had returned to their home in the capital city (Romans 16:3, below).

3. And because he was of the same craft, he abode with them, and wrought: (for by their occupation they were tentmakers.)

Paul, in a strange pagan city, is no doubt glad to meet this hospitable couple as he looks for a place to ply his trade or *craft.* All Jewish boys are expected to learn some kind of trade, and Paul's is tent-making. (The term probably refers to something that includes more than making tents; we might call such a one a "leather worker.") It seems that Paul frequently uses his trade skills to support himself on his missionary journeys rather than accept support from churches (cf. Acts 20:34; 1 Corinthians 9:3-5; 1 Thessalonians 2:6-9; 2 Thessalonians 3:6-10; however, also see 2 Corinthians 11:7-9). What a joy it must have been to Paul to find that this couple, with whom he shared job skills, also shared his faith in Jesus.

Paul, Aquila, and Priscilla have given us a name for a certain kind of missionary or preacher. We use the term *tentmakers* to refer to Christian workers who earn their livelihood in a secular occupation while also preaching and teaching the gospel. [See question #1, page 224.]

4. And he reasoned in the synagogue every sabbath, and persuaded the Jews and the Greeks.

With the help of this hospitable couple, Paul begins preaching in the local *synagogue,* trying to

---

How to Say It

ANTIOCH. *An*-tee-ock.
APHRODITE. Af-ruh-*dite*-ee.
APOLLO. Uh-*pah*-low.
APOLLOS. Uh-*pahl*-us.
AQUILA. *Ack*-wih-luh.
ATHENS. *Ath*-unz.
BITHYNIA. Bih-*thin*-ee-uh.
CENCHREAE (CENCHREA). *Sen*-kree-uh.
CLAUDIUS. *Claw*-dee-us.
CORINTH. *Kor*-inth.
CORINTHIANS. Kor-*in*-thee-unz *(th* as in *thin).*
CHRESTUS. *Crest*-us.
CHRISTUS. *Criss*-tus.
EPHESIANS. Ee-*fee*-zhunz.
EPHESUS. *Ef*-uh-sus.
JUDAISM. *Joo*-duh-izz-um or *Joo*-day-izz-um.
MESSIAH. Meh-*sigh*-uh.
NAZARITE. *Naz*-uh-rite.
NAZIRITE. *Naz*-ih-rite.
ONESIPHORUS. *Ahn*-uh-*sif*-oh-ruhs (strong accent on *sif).*
PONTUS. *Pon*-tuss.
PRISCA. *Pris*-kuh.
PRISCILLA. Prih-*sil*-uh.
SEPTUAGINT. Sep-*too*-ih-jent.
SUETONIUS. Soo-*toe*-nee-us.
SYNAGOGUE. *sin*-uh-gog.
SYRIA. *Sear*-ee-uh.
TROAS. *Tro*-az.

convince his fellow *Jews* about Christ. It was customary in the ancient world to ask a visiting rabbi to address the assembly on the *sabbath* (cf. Luke 4:16). If there were ten male Jews in a community, they could have a synagogue.

Paul normally begins his evangelistic efforts in such gatherings. This practice makes sense given the fact that Christianity has Old Testament Judaism as its foundation (John 4:22). The worshipers are familiar with the Old Testament and its prophecies of the Messiah. Thus it is a good, practical place to find a ready-made audience. Apparently some *Greeks* (Gentiles) attend these Sabbath assemblies as well. [See question #2, page 224.]

B. Entrusted by Paul (v. 18, 19a)

18. And Paul after this tarried there yet a good while, and then took his leave of the brethren, and sailed thence into Syria, and with him Priscilla and Aquila; having shorn his head in Cenchreae: for he had a vow.

The ministry in Corinth is very fruitful, but *Paul* decides to travel back to *Syria* where his home base of Antioch is located. Paul now has been in Corinth at least eighteen months (Acts 18:11), and it's time to move on. When he goes, *Priscilla and Aquila* begin the journey *with him*. Theirs is the kind of business that easily moves from place to place. It is possible that they turn over their Corinth operation to someone else and prepare to open a new business elsewhere.

Priscilla and Aquila's willingness to uproot and accompany Paul for an uncertain future speaks to their devotion and faith. Did they volunteer, or did Paul ask them to accompany him? There is no way to know, but one easily imagines the idea springing almost spontaneously as the three discussed Paul's future labors.

Luke reveals an interesting detail about Paul here. He has finished—or initiated—a *vow*. It seems to be what was called the Nazarite (or Nazirite) vow or something akin to it (Numbers 6:1-21). Such a vow includes letting one's hair grow. We remember that Samson was a Nazarite, and he let his hair grow by decree of an angel of the Lord (Judges 13:5). Now that Paul's vow is completed, he cuts his hair. (Some students believe the hair was shaved at the initiation of the vow as well as at the completion—so this may be the beginning of a vow.)

Even though Paul is increasingly comfortable in the Gentile world, he is still a Jew and takes his Jewish obligations seriously. Eventually he will go to Jerusalem, where he will be asked to sponsor four others who have completed vows (Acts 21:17-26). Many believe it is at that time that Paul completes the terms of his own vow mentioned here.

19a. And he came to Ephesus, and left them there.

Now the travelers spend some time in the great city of *Ephesus*. When Paul leaves this place, he turns over the ministry there to Priscilla and Aquila. This was probably Paul's intent from the time they left Corinth.

As was mentioned in last week's lesson, Ephesus is a significant city in the Roman Empire. It is significant in church history as well. On his third missionary journey, Paul will spend the better part of three years here (Acts 20:31). The church in Ephesus was one of seven to receive a special message from Christ (Revelation 2:1-7). There is also a book to the Ephesians in the New Testament. These facts speak highly of Priscilla and Aquila's ministry there. [See question #3, page 224.]

II. The Team Instructs (Acts 18:24-26)

As we move to our next section of text, Paul has said farewell to Priscilla and Aquila (Acts 18:21), has completed his second missionary journey (18:22), and has begun his third (18:23). Priscilla and Aquila are prominent in the ministry at Ephesus while Paul is away.

A. Whom They Teach (vv. 24, 25)

24. And a certain Jew named Apollos, born at Alexandria, an eloquent man, and mighty in the Scriptures, came to Ephesus.

While in *Ephesus*, Priscilla and Aquila meet a Jewish scholar and orator *named Apollos*. The fact that he is *mighty in the Scriptures* is what tells us that he is a scholar. He is also described as *eloquent*, indicating skill in public speaking.

Apollos's scholarly abilities undoubtedly have been honed in his hometown of *Alexandria* in northern Egypt. This city was founded by, and named for, Alexander the Great in 332 B.C. It is an important seat of learning at the time. The scholars of the large Jewish colony in that city had produced the Septuagint (the Greek version of the Old Testament) about 250 years before Christ.

Apollos becomes very prominent in early Christianity. One of the factions that eventually develops in the church at Corinth even claims to follow him (1 Corinthians 3:4), although Apollos himself is surely not to blame for that problem. Other passages that establish his prominence are Acts 18:27, 28; 19:1; 1 Corinthians 3:22; 4:6; 16:12; and Titus 3:13.

25. This man was instructed in the way of the Lord; and being fervent in the spirit, he spake and taught diligently the things of the Lord, knowing only the baptism of John.

We don't know exactly how Apollos received his first instruction *in the way of the Lord.* Since he knows *only the baptism of John,* his incomplete information about Jesus likely comes from disciples of John the Baptist.

B. How and What They Teach (v. 26)

26. And he began to speak boldly in the synagogue: whom when Aquila and Priscilla had heard, they took him unto them, and expounded unto him the way of God more perfectly.

To encourage this great preacher, this gentle couple does not confront him publicly but invites him to their home instead. There they privately point out to him where his knowledge of *the way of God* is incomplete. To his credit, Apollos accepts this instruction readily and becomes one of the most influential preachers of the apostolic age. The prominence of Apollos in the writings of Luke and Paul speaks also of the importance of Apollos's instruction by Aquila and Priscilla.

Aquila and Priscilla serve as a model of Christian hospitality for us today. Not only do they open their home to an itinerant preacher, later they also will allow the church to meet in their house. We will see this in the next section. [See question #4, page 224.]

HOW TO REACH A ROCKER

In their book *When God Builds a Church*, authors Bob and Rusty Russell tell the remarkable story of the Southeast Christian Church in Louisville, Kentucky. Evangelism is the primary mission at Southeast, one of America's largest and fastest growing congregations.

Before she moved to Louisville, Liz Curtis was billed as "Detroit's number one lady of rock 'n' roll." Her lifestyle was so bad that even shock jock Howard Stern told her, "Liz, you've got to clean up your act!"

In Louisville, Liz ran into Evelyn and Tim Kelly, new Christians at Southeast, who hosted a morning talk show at her new radio station. They invited her to church. Bob Russell was preaching from Ephesians 5 on how husbands should be like Christ in being willing to die for their wives. Liz whispered to Evelyn, "If I ever met a man who'd die for me, I'd marry him in a minute!"

Evelyn whispered back, "Liz, a Man has already died for you."

Several Sundays later, Liz gave her life to Christ. "I was delivered, body and soul, from one location to another—from the gates of Hell to the gates of Heaven."

Today Liz Curtis Higgs is one of the most popular speakers in America. She is a member of the National Speakers Association's Hall of Fame. Her books include *Bad Girls of the Bible.* She, like Apollos, is reaching many for Christ because Evelyn and Tim Kelly, like Priscilla and Aquila, reached out to her.   —V. K.

III. The Team Remembered (Romans 16:3-5a; 1 Corinthians 16:19; 2 Timothy 4:19)

As Paul moves into the latter stages of his missionary journeys, eventually to face execution, he remembers Priscilla and Aquila with fondness.

A. Roman Connection (Romans 16:3-5a)

3. Greet Priscilla and Aquila, my helpers in Christ Jesus:

As he writes to the church at Rome, Paul is probably back in Corinth, and the year is about

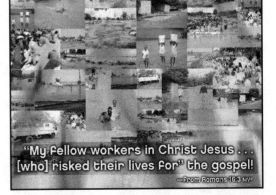

Visual for lesson 13. *These photos are from actual mission fields showing some of the risks that must be endured for the spread of the gospel.*

A.D. 57. With the death of Emperor Claudius in 54 his edict (see Acts 18:2) had expired. *Priscilla and Aquila* eventually, then, moved back to Rome. Paul mention both as his *helpers,* indicating that women as well as men played an important part in the life and work of the early church.

4. Who have for my life laid down their own necks: unto whom not only I give thanks, but also all the churches of the Gentiles.

Paul indicates that this noble couple risked their lives for him. We don't know any specific incident Paul had in mind. Perhaps the riot in Ephesus (probably A.D. 53; cf. Acts 19:23-41) was the occasion. Some believe the phrase *laid down their own necks* to be more than a figure of speech. They suggest the couple was in danger of suffering a beheading!

RISKING YOUR NECK FOR OTHERS

Would you put your own life on the line for someone else? Would you risk the life of your mate or your children to save someone who is not even a member of your family? That was the choice that many Gentiles made in Nazi-occupied Europe during World War II. Some, without even thinking twice, put all at risk to hide Jewish people from those who were seeking them.

In her best-selling book *The Hiding Place,* Corrie ten Boom relates how her parents took compassion on Jews and hid them in a secret room above their tiny clock shop in Haarlem, Holland. Father ten Boom would tell them, "In this household God's children are always welcome."

But the ten Boom family paid a high price for caring. On February 28, 1944, the dreaded Gestapo raided their home. The hiding place went undiscovered, but the ten Booms were arrested anyway. Father ten Boom died in The Hague and Corrie's sister, Betsie, died in the notorious Ravensbrück concentration camp. In God's providence, Corrie was released due to a clerical error. One week later, all women her age who were still at the camp were marched to the gas chambers. Ninety-six thousand women perished at Ravensbrück.

Although we do not know how Priscilla and Aquila risked their necks for Paul, we know that compassion for others is always the right thing to do.   —V. K.

5a. Likewise greet the church that is in their house.

Many of the congregations in the first century meet in private homes. Evidently Priscilla and Aquila open their home to *the church* in Rome as a place of worship. For this couple to have a home large enough for this purpose indicates that they are somewhat wealthy.

B. Corinthian Connection (1 Corinthians 16:19)

19. The churches of Asia salute you. Aquila and Priscilla salute you much in the Lord, with the church that is in their house.

This passage comes after Romans in the New Testament, but was written earlier. Paul is back in Ephesus on his third missionary journey as he writes (1 Corinthians 16:8, 9). The year is probably early A.D. 56. Naturally, the Corinthians to whom Paul writes still remember *Aquila and Priscilla* with great fondness from their previous time there (Acts 18:1-3). Again *their house* is open to the church. This is obviously a pattern in the lives of this couple. [See question #5, page 224.]

C. Ephesian Connection (2 Timothy 4:19)

19. Salute Prisca and Aquila, and the household of Onesiphorus.

This writing comes much later, from what is probably Paul's final correspondence. Paul is now a prisoner in Rome, and the year is about A.D. 65. As he writes to Timothy, that young preacher is laboring back in the great city of Ephesus. Evidently, Priscilla and *Aquila* have left Rome to return once again to Ephesus, and are in some way assisting Timothy in his ministry there. This is one instance where Paul refers to Priscilla by her more formal name, *Prisca.*

We know little about *Onesiphorus.* We know he risked much trying to find Paul in Rome (2 Timothy 1:16-18). He probably gave Paul some financial support. Some deduce that since Paul speaks only of his *household* that Onesiphorus is either absent or has passed away.

Conclusion

A. Together Forever

In our wedding ceremonies, we speak of two becoming one. If any couple is a model for that relationship, it is Aquila and Priscilla. Their unity is not, however, a unity of flesh only. These two are so connected spiritually that for the rest of history Christians cannot think of one without the other. What a model for Christian husbands and wives today!

B. Prayer

Thank You, Lord, for Christian homes, Christian couples, and Christian hospitality. We thank You for those who can stand for truth without sacrificing kindness and civility. Help us to learn from their example. In Jesus' name we pray, amen.

C. Thought to Remember

Two can make a big difference in the work of the Lord if they are one in spirit.

Learning by Doing

This page contains an alternative lesson plan emphasizing learning activities.
Classes desiring such student involvement will find these suggestions helpful.

Learning Goals

After this lesson each student will be able to:

1. List three cities where Priscilla and Aquila labored for the Lord, and note something of their work in each.

2. Explain how Priscilla and Aquila's style of hospitality and teaching can be used to help the church today.

3. Express appreciation to a person or couple who helps to facilitate the ministry in your church.

Into the Lesson

Mount two large pieces of poster board on the wall. One should have the heading "House Church: Blessings." The other should read "House Church: Challenges." Explain that house churches were very common in the New Testament culture, even as they are in some countries today. House churches offer some wonderful opportunities and blessings. But they also have unique problems. Ask the class to cite what they think would be blessings or challenges unique to these churches. Ask "scribes" to note these suggestions on the posters.

Make the transition to Bible study by saying, "Our focus today is not so much on the house church as it is upon the kind of person who could host or start this kind of church. In the lives of these people we will find qualities that should be attractive to believers today."

Into the Word

Using the lesson commentary Introduction and Background (page 218), prepare a brief lecture to introduce Priscilla and Aquila. Have a map available to locate Pontus, Corinth, Ephesus, and Rome.

Also, tell the class two familiar phrases used in today's culture that have their roots in today's text: "Tent-making Preachers (or Missionaries)" and "risked their necks."

Before class mount three pieces of poster board around the room. One should be labeled "Rome," one, "Corinth," and one, "Ephesus." Ask class members to cluster in three groups, each near a poster. Give the groups these written assignments, along with photocopies of the lesson commentary on their assigned texts.

Corinth: Read Acts 18:1-4 and 1 Corinthians 16:19. Then answer the following and put notes on the poster board that will help the rest of the class understand what happened in that city.

1. What was the city of Corinth like?

2. Tell about the national roots of Priscilla and Aquila and why they had come to Corinth.

3. What was the occupation of this couple— and of Paul? Explain the term *tent-making preachers*. Describe the religious leadership of this couple in Corinth.

Ephesus: Read Acts 18:18, 19, 24-26 and 2 Timothy 4:19. Answer the following questions and put notes on the poster that will help the class identify what happened in Ephesus.

1. What was Priscilla's more formal name, as used in 2 Timothy 4:19?

2. Tell what happened through the ministry of Priscilla and Aquila in Ephesus. Lesson commentary notes (vv. 24-26) will be especially helpful. Note the remarks about a house church.

3. Explain why Paul cut his hair.

Rome: Read Acts 18:2 and Romans 16:3-5a. Answer the following questions and write notes on the poster that will help the class understand what happened in Rome.

1. Explain the risks this couple took for Paul, as well as the phrase "laid down their necks."

2. What service to Christ did this couple give in Rome?

3. This text compliments the ministry of a woman in the New Testament church. Who were some other women noted for their leadership and service to the early church? (Acts 16:14, 15 and Romans 16:1, 2 will be helpful.)

Into Life

Say, "While not many churches meet in homes today, there are many lessons about how to live life as we observe this couple." Write the following headings at the top of the board: "Christian Marriage," "Christian Hospitality," and "Christian Teaching." Ask the class to brainstorm lessons we learn from this couple for these. After this exercise, tell the class, "There is one more very important lesson to learn from this study. But this lesson comes from Paul. Notice how often and how lavishly he encourages the ministry of Priscilla and Aquila." Distribute "thank you" cards and ask class members to write a note to a "tent-making" minister (volunteer), encouraging and thanking that person for the ministry and service given.

Let's Talk It Over

*The questions on this page are designed to promote discussion of the lesson
by the class and to encourage application of the lesson Scriptures. The answers
provided are only discussion starters. Let your class talk it over from there.*

**1. Suppose another member of your church
says, "I think preachers should work secular jobs
as Paul did—and not be paid by the church."
How would you respond?**

It would be important to know what prompted
such a claim. Is the church struggling financially, and the preacher's salary is hard to come
by? Or is the church member stingy and unwilling to practice good stewardship?

There are times and places where tent-making
ministries are helpful—especially in mission
work. One advantage of such a ministry is that it
is self-supporting. Another advantage is that such
missionaries often can gain entrance to countries
that do not allow traditional missionaries.

On the other hand, there are also disadvantages to the tent-making approach. Even part-
time secular jobs take precious time away from
ministry. Consequently, Paul discontinued his
tent-making in Corinth after Silas and Timothy
arrived, and devoted himself completely to ministry (Acts 18:5). Paul defends the practice of
paying an evangelist in 1 Corinthians 9:7-11, 14.
(See also 1 Timothy 5:17, 18.)

**2. Paul regularly went into synagogues to find
an audience for his preaching. Where can we go
or what can we do to get a hearing for the gospel?**

The logic of Paul's approach is obvious: the
Jews presented the apostles with a ready-made
audience of people who were already familiar
with the Bible and with God's plan to send His
Messiah into the world. Today, evangelists and
church planters often use a similar approach.
First, they look for people who have some kind of
Christian background. Then, from that nucleus
they branch out to people who have never heard
the gospel, but are looking for spiritual meaning
in life. We can locate both groups of people
through surveys, home Bible studies, and newspaper and radio ads, to name a few methods. See
how many more methods your students can list.

**3. Paul left Priscilla and Aquila in Ephesus to
prepare for planting a church in that city. How
can Christians today determine the best places
to plant new congregations?**

Paul's method was to plant churches in large,
strategically located cities—centers of trade, religion, and education. He went to cities located on
important highways and shipping lanes.
Churches founded there could easily spread the
gospel to surrounding towns and villages and beyond. Today's church can follow Paul's example.
We can plant congregations in highly visible locations, on main thoroughfares, in rapidly growing
population centers. These congregations can then
reach out to surrounding locales. As the world
becomes increasing urbanized, the church must
penetrate those urban areas, where the majority
of lost souls can be found. Discuss what your
church (whether it is located in such an area or
not) can do to reach these strategic urban centers.

**4. What if an eloquent speaker visited your
church but taught error? Who should correct
him? How? What would *you* do?**

Priscilla and Aquila did not wait for someone
else to help Apollos; they did it themselves. However, their situation was much different from
ours. They were not in an established church.
There was no evangelist; there were no elders.
They had worked with Paul, so they probably
were the most knowledgeable people in town.

As you discuss this, note the following. Elders
are charged to teach the truth and refute error
(Titus 1:9) and to take heed to the flock (Acts
20:28-31). Timothy and Titus were also charged to
preserve sound doctrine. All believers are charged
to restore those who stumble (Galatians 6:1, 2).

**5. Some people believe the New Testament
allows only for "house churches" and that erect-
ing church buildings is wrong. How would you
answer such a claim?**

The early church used both homes and public
facilities. In areas where there were no synagogues or where the synagogues were closed to
the church, private homes would have been the
logical place to meet. In times of persecution,
private worship in homes offered safety.

House churches offer a significant financial
advantage. They also offer an informal atmosphere and closeness of fellowship. On the other
hand, their lack of space, facilities, and parking
can severely limit a growing congregation. They
may also suffer from poor location and lack of
visibility to the surrounding community. The
early church did what it had to do to spread the
gospel, and so must we!

Spring Quarter, 2003

Jesus: God's Power in Action
(Mark)

Special Features

Lessons

Unit 1: Jesus' Early Ministry

Unit 2: Jesus' Crucifixion and Resurrection

Unit 3: Jesus' Responses to Faith

About These Lessons

As Christians, we wear the name of Christ. He is the Head of the church. His teachings and His actions comprise the foundation of our faith. Therefore, it is important to study the life of Christ with some regularity. This quarter's study comes from the Gospel of Mark, a fast-paced account of the life of Jesus well-suited to Mark's readers of the first century—and the twenty-first!

Mar
2

Mar
9

Mar
16

Mar
23

Mar
30

Apr
6

Apr
13

Apr
20

Apr
27

May
4

May
11

May
18

May
25

Quarterly Quiz

The questions on this page may be used in several ways: as a pretest at the beginning of the quarter; as a review at the end of the quarter; or as a review after each lesson. The questions are based on the Scripture text of each lesson (King James Version). ***The answers are on page 228.***

Lesson 1

1. The same One who descended on Jesus at His baptism also drove Him into the wilderness to be tempted. Who was it? *Mark 1:10, 12*

2. Jesus called two sets of brothers to be His disciples: Simon and _____, James and ____. *Mark 1:16, 19*

Lesson 2

1. What were Jesus' first words to the man who was sick of the palsy? *Mark 2:5*

2. When the man with the palsy took up his bed and walked, what was the reaction of the crowd? (apathy, disbelief, amazement?) *Mark 2:12*

3. Whom did Jesus come to call to repentance? *Mark 2:17*

Lesson 3

1. When Jesus calmed the storm, His disciples feared exceedingly. T/F *Mark 4:41*

2. Where did the man with the unclean spirit live? *Mark 5:3*

3. After Jesus cast them out, the devils went into a herd of _____. *Mark 5:11-13*

Lesson 4

1. When Jesus visited His hometown, what caused Him to marvel? *Mark 6:6*

2. What was the only extra item the disciples were allowed to take on their preaching trip? *Mark 6:8*

3. The message that the disciples preached was that Jesus was the Messiah. T/F *Mark 6:12*

Lesson 5

1. For what reason did the scribes and Pharisees criticize Jesus' disciples? *Mark 7:2*

2. Which of the Ten Commandments did Jesus accuse the Pharisees and scribes of rejecting by means of their tradition? *Mark 7:10*

3. Jesus said that only the things which enter into a man defile him. T/F *Mark 7:15*

Lesson 6

1. What did Jesus send two of His disciples to find? (a colt, a loaf of bread, a place to stay?) *Mark 11:2*

2. Jesus said the Lord's house should be called the house of _____, but the merchants in the temple had made it a den of _____. *Mark 11:17*

Lesson 7

1. Jesus celebrated the passover with the Twelve in a large upper room. T/F *Mark 14:15-17*

2. During the meal Jesus told His disciples that one of them would _____ Him. *Mark 14:18*

Lesson 8

1. What happened to Jesus' garments when He was crucified? *Mark 15:24*

2. Between the sixth and the ninth hour of the day of the crucifixion, what unusual phenomenon occurred? *Mark 15:33*

3. When the women came to the sepulchre, where did they see the young man? (sitting inside, standing outside, sitting on the stone?) *Mark 16:5*

Lesson 9

1. When Jairus saw Jesus, what did he do? *Mark 5:22*

2. The woman who touched Jesus had spent all her money on what? (wine, clothes, physicians?) *Mark 5:26*

3. The young girl whom Jesus raised from the dead was ____ years old. *Mark 5:42*

Lesson 10

1. What was wrong with the Syrophoenician woman's daughter? *Mark 7:25, 26*

2. When Jesus healed the man who was deaf and had a speech impediment, He put His fingers in his ears and touched his tongue. T/F *Mark 7:33*

Lesson 11

1. What was the name Jesus called Peter when he rebuked Jesus for saying He would be killed? (Simon, Satan, Sinner) *Mark 8:33*

2. The two who appeared with Jesus when He was transfigured were ____ and ____. *Mark 9:4*

Lesson 12

1. In what ways had the dumb spirit tried to destroy the man's son? *Mark 9:22*

2. The afflicted boy's father cried out, "Lord, I believe; help thou mine ____." *Mark 9:24*

Lesson 13

1. What honor did James and John ask Jesus to give them? *Mark 10:37*

2. Blind Bartimeus had to be encouraged to ask Jesus to heal him. T/F *Mark 10:47, 48*

Jesus and Unchanging Truth

by Ronald L. Nickelson

THE WORLD AROUND US KEEPS CHANGING! Some changes are so monumental and sudden that they are simply impossible to miss. Other changes are more subtle. They come about over longer periods of time. Because they happen so slowly, they are easy to miss. Even people living through the changes can miss them. Such changes can come in such small increments that our resistance to them is very low.

One example is the concept of "truth." For most of human history truth was understood to be something that was *revealed* by God. We found meaning in the truth by listening to it. Our duty after listening to the truth was to obey.

But this understanding of truth changed in the 1780s with the birth of the "scientific method." After that time, truth was not something revealed by God, but something *discovered* by science. Humans found meaning in the truth by observing things around them. Our duty after observing and discovering was not to obey, but to learn more.

In the latter part of the twentieth century, truth for many people became something to be *experienced* by each individual. No longer was there one path to truth, whether revealed by God or discovered by science. Each person was to figure out "what works for me." With such an understanding, the duty of humanity is not obedience or learning, but survival.

What a challenge it is for Christians to break through such a mind-set! But despite these sobering changes, the message of Christianity is unbending: God has acted and spoken through His Son, Jesus Christ, and those actions and words *reveal* truth. This truth is objective fact.

This quarter's lessons present truth about God's power at work in Jesus to change people's lives. The truth of those changes is a truth that leads us to faith in Him. The theme for the quarter is "Jesus: God's Power in Action." This study is divided into three units. In the first unit, we will explore the beginning of Jesus' ministry and the conflict that He encountered almost immediately—many people were not ready for the truth that He brought. The second unit looks at Jesus' final week on earth before His crucifixion—here, even the disciples themselves will continue to misunderstand the truth about Jesus. The third unit emphasizes the importance Jesus placed on people's faithful response to Him—not a blind, unreasoning faith, but a faith based on the truth of Jesus' words and actions.

Unit 1: Jesus' Earthly Ministry

Lesson 1: Jesus Begins His Ministry. "Well begun is half done," as the old saying goes. And what a startling beginning this is to Jesus' ministry! Following His Heavenly Father's personal affirmation at His baptism, Jesus chooses some rather unlikely men to be His first disciples. But God would work through those men to change the course of human history. This is truth!

Lesson 2: The Conflict Begins. The truth of Jesus' miracles are designed to lead us to faith (see John 20:30, 31). Jesus' healing of the paralyzed man became an occasion to demonstrate His ability to forgive sin (Mark 2:9). But some refused to believe. Jesus' miracles still challenge us. We must place our faith in Jesus or become His enemy. There is no "in between." That was truth in Jesus' day, and is still truth now.

Lesson 3: Jesus Displays His Authority. Even after placing faith in Jesus, doubts can still arise. The disciples who walked with Jesus had their doubts addressed right before their very eyes, as in the stilling of the storm. And while we today do not walk side-by-side with Jesus in a physical sense, we can have the same assurance as they. The facts of history have firmly established Jesus' power and authority. When doubts arise in our own lives, we can look back to those truths and have our faith strengthened anew.

Lesson 4: Rejection and Mission. When you face a mountain in life you can allow it to stop you or you can resolve to go over it, around it, or through it no matter the cost. Jesus faced much opposition during His earthly sojourn—opposition that eventually led to His death. One of the saddest cases of rejection was by those who knew Him best: His hometown folk. But that rejection didn't stop Him. Jesus put His mission ahead of His own well-being. He expects us to do so as well. This, too, is truth.

Lesson 5: What Really Defiles. The idea of "truth" means that there are things that are "untrue"—things that are false. Unless we know the difference, we can get into big trouble! The Pharisees and scribes of Jesus' day stumbled at this point. They had the false idea that impurity came from failure to observe traditions that they had established. When Jesus pointed out their wrong beliefs, they could not accept it. Jesus' words still point out wrong beliefs today. When we read His words, will we accept them as truth for the twenty-first century?

Unit 2: Jesus' Crucifixion and Resurrection

Lesson 6: The Messiah Challenges the Corrupt. Sometimes Jesus uses only words to speak truth. At other times He adds actions to His words. His cleansing of the temple shortly before His death is one example. Religious leaders who should have been protecting the people were the very ones who were "fleecing the flock." Jesus' action foreshadowed the awful judgment that awaits such corrupt leaders! (See Jude 12, 13.)

Lesson 7: Jesus Gives Passover New Meaning. Traditions can be useful to us. As long as they don't become empty ritual, they allow us to connect with and remember the past. This was the case with the Israelite's annual Passover celebration. Each celebration called to mind the actions God took to deliver His people from Egyptian bondage. But after more than fourteen centuries, Jesus brought a much more important meaning to this observance: remembrance of the actions God was taking to deliver His people from the bondage of sin. The Passover celebration became the Lord's Supper until Jesus returns. This, too, is a truth of history.

Lesson 8: Jesus Dies and Lives Again. Jesus Christ is the focal point of all history, and the focal point of His earthly ministry is His own death and resurrection. Until it happened, the disciples did not understand how that could be true. When it happened, even with eyewitness testimony, they couldn't grasp the truth of the resurrection (Luke 24:11; John 20:24, 25). But finally they did. And on the last day, "every eye shall see him" (Revelation 1:7), and every person will finally know the truth.

Unit 3: Jesus' Responses to Faith

Lesson 9: Faith Conquers Fear. When challenges beyond human control come along, what does the unbeliever have except fear? But a person who has faith in the power of God does not fear. He or she believes that God will handle all problems in His own way, on His own time schedule. Long-term illness and death challenged the subjects of our study in today's lesson. But these were no match for Jesus. These and every other fearful condition remain no match for Him today. On this certainty the Christian's faith stands.

Lesson 10: Jesus Honors Bold Faith. This lesson shows us the great things that are possible when people approach God with boldness combined with right motives. The Syrophoenician woman would not be put off—her faith in Jesus was too great to allow her to back down. God still desires His people to approach His throne of grace with boldness and confidence (Hebrews 4:16).

Lesson 11: Putting Faith in Jesus Alone. Today people put small degrees of faith in many things: the elevators they use, the cars they drive, the airplanes on which they fly. But when it comes to a person's eternal destiny, one must put faith in Jesus alone! On a high mountain in the land of Israel, God made this point clear when He said of Jesus, "This is my beloved Son: hear him" (Mark 9:7).

Lesson 12: Expressing Honest Faith. Although our faith is to be fearless (lesson 9), bold (lesson 10), and exclusively in Jesus (lesson 11), sometimes we all have doubts. The father who brought his troubled son to Jesus had faith, but he still wrestled with "unbelief" (Mark 9:24). If we admit the truth, so do we all.

Lesson 13: Faith Becomes Sight. Jesus, during His earthly ministry, granted eyesight to blind men because of their faith. This lesson provides one example. But the more important point is that Jesus can heal spiritual blindness! Those of us who always have had physical eyesight must make sure that we are walking by faith, and not placing our trust in only that which is "by sight" (2 Corinthians 5:7). We have a confident expectation that our faith will eventually result in the type of sight that results in all our questions being answered. In eternity, we will have a type of sight that none of us now possesses (cf. 1 John 3:2).

The Gospel of Mark is sometimes called the "Gospel of Action." But your study will not be complete until this Gospel *of* action is translated into the gospel *in* action—as you and your students put into practice the bold faith that Jesus inspires.

Answers to Quarterly Quiz on page 226

Lesson 1—1. the Spirit. 2. Andrew, John. **Lesson 2**—1. "Son, thy sins be forgiven thee." 2. amazement. 3. sinners. **Lesson 3**—1. true. 2. among the tombs. 3. swine. **Lesson 4**—1. their unbelief. 2. a staff. 3. false (men should repent). **Lesson 5**—1. they ate with unwashed hands. 2. honor thy father and thy mother. 3. false. **Lesson 6**—1. a colt. 2. prayer, thieves. **Lesson 7**—1. true. 2. betray. **Lesson 8**—1. those in charge cast lots for them. 2. darkness over the whole land. 3. sitting inside. **Lesson 9**—1. fell at His feet. 2. physicians. 3. twelve. **Lesson 10**—1. she had an unclean spirit. 2. true. **Lesson 11**—1. Satan. 2. Elijah, Moses. **Lesson 12**—1. cast him into the fire and into the waters. 2. unbelief. **Lesson 13**—1. to sit on His right and left hand in glory. 2. false (he kept crying out to Jesus).

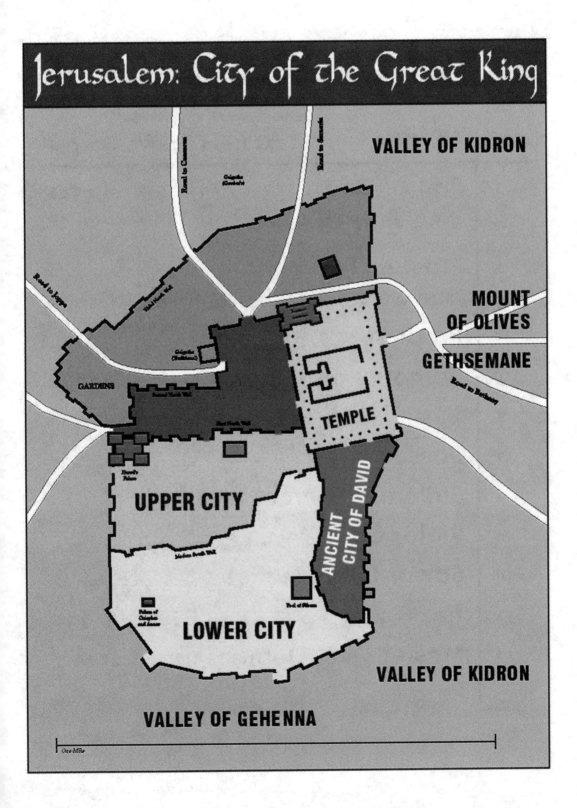

Who Is Jesus?

Lesson	**He is**	Text from Mark's Gospel
1	Son of God	1:9-26
2	Friend of Sinners	2:3-17
3	Master Over Wind and Sea	4:36-41; 5:2-13
4	Prophet	6:1-13
5	Authority on the Law	7:1-15
6	Messiah	11:1-9, 15-18
7	Passover Lamb	14:12-25
8	Suffering Servant	15:21-25, 33-37; 16:1-8
9	Victor Over Death	5:22-36, 41, 42
10	Savior for All Nations	7:24-37
11	The Christ	8:27-36; 9:2-8
12	Master Over Demons	9:14-29
13	King	10:35-52

Going About Doing Good

Teaching With Projects

by Ronald G. Davis

LEARNING BIBLE CONTENT is never intended to be an end in itself. Notable atheists and agnostics have shown skill in quoting Scripture, but their knowledge of God's Word has not accomplished what it can do and is designed to do. In Paul's Spirit-driven words of Ephesians 4:11, 12, when the apostles, prophets, evangelists, pastors and teachers have fulfilled their ministries, the disciples should be prepared for works of ministry (or service). Each one should closely resemble the Master, who is characterized as One who "went about doing good" (Acts 10:38).

The studies in this unit are pictures of "Jesus: God's Power in Action." Though there is an emphasis on the divine power in Jesus' deeds, we must note also the motive. The Lord's deeds are done out of a heart of compassionate service. From calming the disciples' terror on the sea to rolling back the depressing weight of parental anxiety of Jairus for his dying daughter, Jesus acted because He loves. From a resurrected appearance to the sorrowing women in the garden to the release of the demon-possessed boy in Galilee, Jesus acted to wipe away the tears of anguish. He went about doing good because He is good. So must be His disciples.

In addition to the knowledge and belief objectives every adult teacher has in such a study as this, he certainly will have basic behavior objectives. What good is knowledge unless it builds faith? What good is faith if it does not issue forth in good deeds of service?

Plans and Projects

Teachers want results. Teaching by projects is a logical culmination of wanting results. Without results, a teacher must wonder whether he has actually taught.

Projects can be designed for learning groups (the whole class or small groups within the class) or individuals. Some can be accomplished in the classroom; some require learners to leave the classroom with intentions, intentions to do good. Some require presents, tangible evidence of loving grace; some require presence, simply "being there." Some are long-term and time-consuming; some are "along-the-way" interludes.

In any lesson series, the perceptive teacher will ask, "What can I have my learners do—or at least recommend they do—that will demonstrate they are learning the truths of our texts?"

Fear and Faith

A number of the lessons in this series picture Jesus at work allaying the fears and anxieties of people in physical and emotional distress. Consider lesson 9 and the healing of the synagogue ruler's daughter. Consider Jesus' dealing with the desperate Syrophoenician mother in lesson 10. What deeds of kindness can be done for parents who are struggling with the panic and disruption of an ailing child? Will something as simple as addressing a "Thinking of You" card from the whole class be of value? Will such occasions demand that the class consider a system of once-a-week child-care provision to enable parents a time of personal freedom? Will a monetary gift from the class (or simply a wholesome game or toy for a child) prove to be the one encouraging act of worth? Does the whole church need a support group for parents in such circumstances, and how can an adult class give impetus to such a ministry? The teacher's role in all such activity may be nothing more than catalyst. Or the teacher may need to become "Project Manager," seeing to all the small details necessary to maintain the service.

Doubt and Encouragement

Lesson 12 is an intriguing picture of one caught "in the middle of faith," believing and yet doubting, doubting and yet believing. Many adults have daily interaction with those similarly caught. Some of their friends and associates could easily express the same "If you can" (Mark 9:22) to Jesus. How can the adult class step into the lives of such individuals and build their faith in the power of Jesus?

Testimony is a key to faith development. All through the Gospels men and women build faith in others by simply affirming "What Jesus Has Done for Me." A simple card and note from a friend who has experienced the loss of a loved one and felt the comforting hand of God's Spirit may be just what a struggling believer needs at a time of personal loss. Sending an impersonal sympathy card—even if it carries a personal signature but no other mark of personal attention—will probably leave the same sense of isolation and loneliness it finds. But a personal "I-know-what-He-did-for-me" card brings both association and fellowship. The teacher may need to do nothing more than begin the practice of modeling such an approach in his own sympathy cards to class members, but the model set before a whole class in a setting such as lesson 12 has potential for a quicker, broader change.

Awe and Anticipation

In lesson 3, Jesus' power demonstrates itself in an altogether different realm: the order in the natural sciences. His total ability to intervene in the laws of nature that He imposed at creation is always awe inspiring. "What manner of man is this, that even the wind and the sea obey him?" (Mark 4:41). Living in the twenty-first century has taken away some of the marvel from the marvelous. A class project to remind friends and families of God's power in nature could be faith enhancing.

Discuss with your class "tag lines" that could be added to E-mails, faxes, magnetic disks, telephone voice mail, and the like. Such tags can declare the glory of God in electronics science. For example, "Isn't God good? He created magnetism and allowed us to discover its values!" Or, "Created in God's image, we get to communicate with one another as He has communicated with us!" Or, "Thanking God for His gift of insight to Bill Gates." Or "It took ancient scribes months to copy long documents. We can do it with a 'Control/C.' Praise the Lord!"

A study display board in the classroom, with a theme such as "By God's Design," can remind adult learners of the grand intricacy and interrelatedness of His creation. Those in the class with scientific or medical expertise probably could create such a display for the class to enjoy. A presentation and/or discussion of the "fearful and wonderful" elements involved would be most worthwhile. Lesson 5 could be enhanced by a display on nutrition; lesson 9 would profit from a display on blood; lesson 10 begs for an information board on hearing and deafness; lesson 13 lends itself to a display on sight and blindness. A teacher who has class members with training and/or personal experience in any of these subjects would bless the class member and the class by asking for that person's help. Professional classroom teachers could offer some graphics advice and may have access to display materials in a variety of subject matters.

For those who like big plans: an adult class could sponsor a children's science fair in the church with a theme such as "God Puts the Marvel in Marvelous," or " . . . the Awe in Awesome," or "God Is There in Little and Big" (emphasizing design in creation). A class-endowed cash prize

and/or gifts of children's books on creation science may well encourage participation. Working with the church's children's leadership would have the happy benefit of establishing a sense of unity and fellowship often missing between adult classes and the programs and leaders of children. And the resulting learner projects can offer a potential learning activity for any who visit the resultant displays. Most church facilities have a fellowship space that could be "adorned" with such projects for at least one weekend for interested worshipers.

Arts and Crafts

Many adults spend leisure time in pursuing arts and crafts. The perceptive teacher will look for ways the avocational interests of his charges can be applied to group studies. Whether in the visual arts, graphic arts, musical arts, or construction arts, interested group members could produce a variety of useful and aesthetic items in relationship to truths being studied.

Badge and button makers could produce something as simple as a pin with a stethoscope design to be given to class members at the end of lesson 2, as a reminder (and conversation starter) of the Golden Text: "They that are whole have no need of the physician, but they that are sick: I came not to call the righteous, but sinners to repentance" (Mark 2:17). A heart pin could be effective reinforcement for lesson 5 on "What Really Defiles."

A musically talented learner could write a simple chorus on a key verse, such as lesson 9's "Be not afraid, only believe." Teaching it to the class would add the double blessing, first to the composer, and then to the class.

A model-building enthusiast could provide a replica of a first-century fishing boat for illustration in lesson 3.

A person who enjoys graphic design on the computer could prepare a number of items for group distribution in relation to Bible texts studied. A decorative and laminated bookmark with a Golden Text could encourage Bible memorization and use. A sheet with a border of human eyes could become a "Thank You, God" log of things a person sees for a week for which he or she is most thankful. This could be used for a follow-up on lesson 13 of the blind man healed.

A skilled photographer could provide images of people being baptized for use in lesson 1, which includes the baptism of Jesus.

Going About Doing Good

Give your learners something to do. Give them something good to do. You may be surprised at the learning that comes, at the growth that occurs.

Jesus Begins His Ministry

March 2
Lesson 1

DEVOTIONAL READING: Luke 4:14-21.

BACKGROUND SCRIPTURE: Mark 1:1-45.

PRINTED TEXT: Mark 1:9-26.

Mark 1:9-26

9 And it came to pass in those days, that Jesus came from Nazareth of Galilee, and was baptized of John in Jordan.

10 And straightway coming up out of the water, he saw the heavens opened, and the Spirit like a dove descending upon him:

11 And there came a voice from heaven, saying, Thou art my beloved Son, in whom I am well pleased.

12 And immediately the Spirit driveth him into the wilderness.

13 And he was there in the wilderness forty days tempted of Satan; and was with the wild beasts; and the angels ministered unto him.

14 Now after that John was put in prison, Jesus came into Galilee, preaching the gospel of the kingdom of God,

15 And saying, The time is fulfilled, and the kingdom of God is at hand: repent ye, and believe the gospel.

16 Now as he walked by the sea of Galilee, he saw Simon and Andrew his brother casting a net into the sea: for they were fishers.

17 And Jesus said unto them, Come ye after me, and I will make you to become fishers of men.

18 And straightway they forsook their nets, and followed him.

19 And when he had gone a little further thence, he saw James the son of Zebedee, and John his brother, who also were in the ship mending their nets.

20 And straightway he called them: and they left their father Zebedee in the ship with the hired servants, and went after him.

21 And they went into Capernaum; and straightway on the sabbath day he entered into the synagogue, and taught.

22 And they were astonished at his doctrine: for he taught them as one that had authority, and not as the scribes.

23 And there was in their synagogue a man with an unclean spirit; and he cried out,

24 Saying, Let us alone; what have we to do with thee, thou Jesus of Nazareth? art thou come to destroy us? I know thee who thou art, the Holy One of God.

25 And Jesus rebuked him, saying, Hold thy peace, and come out of him.

26 And when the unclean spirit had torn him, and cried with a loud voice, he came out of him.

GOLDEN TEXT: There came a voice from heaven, saying, Thou art my beloved Son, in whom I am well pleased.—Mark 1:11.

Jesus: God's Power in Action
Unit 1: Jesus' Early Ministry
(Lessons 1-5)

Lesson Aims

After participating in this lesson, each student will be able to:

1. Cite the significant details of Jesus' early ministry, including His baptism and teaching.

2. Explain the urgency of Jesus' ministry, both in His day and in ours.

3. Express a commitment to speak the good news of God's kingdom with boldness, knowing that Christ's own authority empowers us.

Lesson Outline

INTRODUCTION
 A. Urgent Mission
 B. Lesson Background
I. THE BAPTISM OF JESUS (Mark 1:9-11)
 A. Submission (v. 9)
 B. Affirmation (vv. 10, 11)
II. THE TEMPTATION OF JESUS (Mark 1:12, 13)
 A. Action of the Holy Spirit (v. 12)
 B. Action of Satan (v. 13)
  Survivor
III. THE MESSAGE OF JESUS (Mark 1:14-20)
 A. The Reality (vv. 14, 15)
 B. The Necessity (vv. 16-20)
  When Celebrities Call
IV. THE AUTHORITY AND POWER OF JESUS (Mark 1:21-26)
 A. Authority to Teach (vv. 21, 22)
 B. Power to Heal (vv. 23-26)
CONCLUSION
 A. Early Indications
 B. Prayer
 C. Thought to Remember

Introduction

A. Urgent Mission

Leighton Ford knows what it means to be frightened when a child wanders off. He describes the day his daughter came up lost: "During the nearly two hours that Debbie Jean was missing, nothing else mattered. In my study were books to read, letters to be answered, articles to be written, planning to be done—but it all was forgotten. I could think of only one thing: my little girl was lost. I had only one prayer, and I prayed it a thousand times. 'Oh, God, help me to

find her.' How often, I asked myself later, had I felt such a terrible urgency about people who were lost from God?"

Mark begins his Gospel with a record of how Jesus began His ministry. The word *urgent* marks everything Jesus did. Time was short. The moments could not be wasted. The kingdom of God could not wait for trivial concerns.

B. Lesson Background

The Gospel of Mark is second in order among the Gospels of the New Testament. The shortest of the four Gospels, Mark presents a compact but powerful account of Jesus' words and, especially, His actions. Readers notice from the first lines some of the obvious differences between this Gospel and the other three. The Gospel of John begins with a reflection on the existence of Christ before the creation of the world. Matthew and Luke begin with details of Jesus' birth. Mark skips past this information to go directly to Jesus' baptism as the beginning point of his presentation.

This difference should not be misunderstood. Mark does not imply that the origin of Jesus is unimportant. As a matter of fact, Mark's Gospel opens with an identification of Jesus as "Jesus Christ, the Son of God" (1:1). In this way Mark emphasizes that Jesus came from God in order to announce God's kingdom. Mark establishes that this Jesus began His ministry by submitting to the baptism of another servant sent by God, John the Baptist (1:1-9).

After describing Jesus' baptism, Mark focuses (from 1:14 to 3:6) on the early stages of Jesus' Galilean ministry. There Jesus calls His first disciples (1:16-20) and establishes His authority in His teaching. He also demonstrates His power to drive out demons (1:21-28).

I. The Baptism of Jesus
(Mark 1:9-11)

A. Submission (v. 9)

9. And it came to pass in those days, that Jesus came from Nazareth of Galilee, and was baptized of John in Jordan.

In those days refers to the time of John the Baptist's ministry around the *Jordan* River. This is an area remote enough from Jerusalem and Jericho that Mark can refer to it in verse 4 as "the wilderness." To the north is the territory *of Galilee*, some fifty miles distant. Jesus comes from the village of *Nazareth*, located in the hills of lower Galilee. The time is about A.D. 27, and Jesus is about thirty years old (Luke 3:23).

Mark reports in a matter-of-fact way that Jesus is *baptized* by *John* the Baptist. He does not report any of the conversation that Matthew includes—

an exchange related to why Jesus would consent to baptism by a preacher who is proclaiming the need for repentance from sin. Matthew's expanded account explains that Jesus submits to this baptism, not because He is in need of forgiveness, but because He is determined to "fulfil all righteousness" (Matthew 3:15). [See question #1, page 240.]

B. Affirmation (vv. 10, 11)

10. And straightway coming up out of the water, he saw the heavens opened, and the Spirit like a dove descending upon him.

There is no other example in the Bible of someone's baptism being accompanied by these signs from Heaven. Some suggest that the words *he saw* indicate that only Jesus saw the opening of the heavens and the Spirit's descent. John, however, makes it clear that John the Baptist also "saw the Spirit descending from heaven" (John 1:32). Mark's word for *opened* is a vivid term meaning "to rip open," as if it were some cosmic event (cf. Isaiah 64:1). Mark's description of the descent of *the Spirit* can be taken to mean either that the Spirit took the form of *a dove* and descended or that the Spirit's descending resembled the way a dove descends. Once again, a look at another Gospel account clears up the matter. This time it is Luke who helps us. He says specifically that "the Holy Ghost descended in a bodily shape like a dove" (Luke 3:22). Thus, these signs confirming the uniqueness of Jesus' baptism could be verified by objective witnesses.

The words *coming up out of the water* can hardly be understood without thinking of baptism by immersion. Nothing about other modes of baptism requires one to step down into the water. Jesus is immersed in the water just as other believers later in the New Testament record (see Acts 8:38; Romans 6:4).

The word *straightway* ("at once" or "immediately") is an early indication of the urgency Mark sees in Jesus' actions. Mark uses this term more than forty times in his Gospel. Thus he presents an image of Jesus hurrying about the business of the kingdom. The time is short!

11. And there came a voice from heaven, saying, Thou art my beloved Son, in whom I am well pleased.

With the *voice from heaven* it is clear that all three personalities of the Trinity—Father, *Son*, and Holy Spirit—are involved in this event. While the word *Trinity* is not found in the Bible, passages like this one imply the truth of the concept. The phrases *beloved Son* and *well pleased* represent the Father's confirmation of Jesus. They also express His confidence in the work He sends Jesus to do (cf. Psalm 2:7; Isaiah 42:1).

II. The Temptation of Jesus (Mark 1:12, 13)

A. Action of the Holy Spirit (v. 12)

12. And immediately the Spirit driveth him into the wilderness.

No sooner has Jesus come up from the waters of baptism than the Holy *Spirit* forces Him *into the wilderness*. The word *driveth* is just as strong in the original language of Mark's Gospel as it sounds to us in English. Jesus is now in the arena of temptation. He has moved without delay from a moment of exaltation to an experience of testing.

Perhaps the connection between these events is not so unusual. In our own lives, do occasions of high achievement sometimes lead us to our times of greatest vulnerability? Does praise open us up to temptation? Does hearing the expressions of congratulations bring us closer than at any other time to the devil's schemes? [See question #2, page 240.]

B. Action of Satan (v. 13)

13. And he was there in the wilderness forty days tempted of Satan; and was with the wild beasts; and the angels ministered unto him.

As much as Jesus' baptism represents the initiation of His ministry, so does this period of testing. Jesus does not present Himself as God's Son without facing the temptations of *Satan*. Although Mark's account of Jesus' testing *in the wilderness* (or "desert") does not include details provided by the other gospel accounts, Hebrews 5:8 states that Jesus learned obedience by the things He suffered. In some sense this experience contributes to Jesus' right to carry the title of high priest appointed by God for every sinner in need of God's grace (Hebrews 4:15).

"Thou art my beloved Son . . .

in whom I am well pleased."
—Mark 1:11

Visual for lesson 1

Post today's visual, shown above, as you begin to discuss the lesson text (verse 9).

These *forty days* in the wilderness remind us of Moses who was with the Lord for forty days and nights without bread or water at the time of the giving of the law (Exodus 34:28). And as God sent an angel to minister to Old Testament Israel in the wilderness (Exodus 23:20, 23; 32:34), so He also puts *angels* at Jesus' disposal in this period of testing.

SURVIVOR

Just a few years ago, so-called "reality TV" was the hottest gimmick in TV programming. Complete strangers were forced into contrived circumstances that were exhaustively videotaped, then edited for the most sensational scenes. The archetype of these series was "Survivor," set on a deserted island. The contestants were divided into "tribes" that engaged in contests of strength, skill, or cunning and faced other challenges such as eating live earthworms or cooked rats.

The participants voted each other off the island one by one until only one remained to collect the $1 million prize—a scenario designed to bring out the worst in human nature. In the final episode, one of the last contestants said to another, who voted against her, "If I were ever to pass you along in life again and you were laying [sic] there dying of thirst, I would not get you a drink of water. I would let the vultures take you—with no ill regrets."

What a striking difference from Jesus' "survival" experience in our text! That was not "reality TV"; it *was* reality! Our Lord fought an enemy with a diabolical agenda, not just someone scheming to win a million dollars. If testing proves the worth of our character, Jesus set our example. Real "survivors" find their role model in Jesus, not in greedy television contestants!

—C. R. B.

III. The Message of Jesus (Mark 1:14-20)

A. The Reality (vv. 14, 15)

14. Now after that John was put in prison, Jesus came into Galilee, preaching the gospel of the kingdom of God.

John the Baptist's ministry ends sometime after Jesus' baptism. This end comes about because of John's imprisonment, an event mentioned by both Matthew (4:12) and Luke (3:19, 20).

But Jesus is not deterred from preaching about the kingdom, whatever the threat. Herod Antipas, who has imprisoned John, reigns in *Galilee*. But this is where Jesus goes in order to preach *the gospel of the kingdom of God.*

Although the exact phrase "the kingdom of God" cannot be found in the Old Testament, the

---

concept is found in many places. Passages such as Exodus 15:18; Psalms 29:10; 145:13; Daniel 2:44; 4:3, 34; and 7:27 form the basis for Jesus' announcement of this kingdom. Many Jews of the first century hope for the arrival of this kingdom (see Acts 1:6). It is good news ("gospel") because God will establish this kingdom in righteousness. It will stand in contrast to the kingdoms founded by rulers like Herod Antipas where preachers of righteousness can be murdered (Matthew 14:1-12).

15. And saying, The time is fulfilled, and the kingdom of God is at hand: repent ye, and believe the gospel.

Now Mark notes specifically the core of Jesus' message about *the kingdom:* He is preaching that *the time* is now. The kingdom is very close—it *is* at hand. Jesus' message is that God's "time" has come. God's plans to usher in the kingdom are reaching their fulfillment. The message is urgent. There is no time for delay.

B. The Necessity (vv. 16-20)

16, 17. Now as he walked by the sea of Galilee, he saw Simon and Andrew his brother casting a net into the sea: for they were fishers. And Jesus said unto them, Come ye after me, and I will make you to become fishers of men.

The sea of Galilee is the beautiful fresh-water lake about seventy miles north of Jerusalem. Lying about seven hundred feet below sea level, it stretches some fourteen miles north to south and six miles east to west. Fishing is a primary industry of the region.

To make disciples, *Jesus* goes to places where people live their everyday lives. Mark does not pause to tell us whether *Simon* (Peter) and his brother *Andrew* have ever met Jesus (as John 1:35-42 tells us), but emphasizes the direct challenge issued by Jesus regarding discipleship. This challenge demands immediate response. Jesus' call is not to part-time discipleship but to a permanent adventure in the work of proclaiming the kingdom of God that is so close at hand.

The only promise the men have is that which Jesus includes in the call: the promise to make them *fishers of men.* Jesus uses their own experience in fishing to portray what is possible in the preaching of the kingdom. They can be disciples who know how to gather in people for the kingdom of God. [See question #3, page 240.]

WHEN CELEBRITIES CALL

Turning off your telephone so you can enjoy an evening meal in peace no longer lets you escape from telemarketers. Whether the ringer on your phone is off or you are away from home, if you have an answering machine or service for your telephone, you still can get "phone spam." This is a computer-driven phone call in which your number is automatically dialed.

Telemarketers and politicians have found that a message can be sent to two hundred thousand answering machines per hour. They have also found that by using the voices of famous politicians, entertainment personalities, and sports stars, most people will listen to the message. It seems that many of us are happily deluded into thinking a celebrity is actually calling *us!*

But really, how significant is it when celebrities who care not at all about us as individuals send us a recorded phone call? Their only interest is in their political cause or their own pocketbooks! However, when the fishermen by the Sea of Galilee received their call from Jesus, it was a different story. Jesus was offering them a new life—one that would be filled with hardships, to be sure, but a new life, nevertheless—that would give them a key role in a movement that would change the world. It's exciting to think that Jesus offers us a similar call with the same amazing opportunities!   —C. R. B.

18. And straightway they forsook their nets, and followed him.

Mark gives no details about the practical issues of the decision by Simon Peter and Andrew. Nothing is said concerning arrangements that would have to be made for their absence. Mark

---

How to Say It

BABYLONIAN. Bab-ih-*low*-nee-un.
BOANERGES. *Bo*-uh-*nur*-geez (strong accent on *nur*).
CAPERNAUM. Kuh-*per*-nay-um.
GALILEE. *Gal*-uh-lee.
HEROD ANTIPAS. *Hair*-ud *An*-tih-pus.
ISAIAH. Eye-*zay*-uh.
JERICHO. *Jair*-ih-co.
NAZARETH. *Naz*-uh-reth.
NEHEMIAH. *Nee*-huh-*my*-uh (strong accent on *my*).
SYNAGOGUE. *sin*-uh-gog.
ZEBEDEE. *Zeb*-eh-dee.

---

does not even describe a goodbye to their families. The urgency of Jesus' call is met with an instant response. The kingdom of God is too close to be bothered with earthly concerns. The Son of God has spoken.

19. And when he had gone a little further thence, he saw James the son of Zebedee, and John his brother, who also were in the ship mending their nets.

Jesus finds two more men as He walks along the shore of the lake. Jesus will later call *James* and *John* "Boanerges," which means "Sons of Thunder" (Mark 3:17). The four men now mentioned appear at the head of all the lists of the disciples of Jesus (Matthew 10:2-4; Mark 3:16-19; Luke 6:14-16; Acts 1:13).

20. And straightway he called them: and they left their father Zebedee in the ship with the hired servants, and went after him.

James and John answer the urgent summons without hesitation as the authority of Jesus is openly displayed. The picture of *their father Zebedee*, who is *left* alone in the boat, is softened somewhat by the mention of the *hired* hands he still has. When the Son of God calls people to become His followers, they respond in a hurry! (In a later instance, Jesus will not mince words with two men who want to delay their service because of practical concerns; see Luke 9:59-62.) [See question #4, page 240.]

IV. The Authority and Power of Jesus (Mark 1:21-26)

A. Authority to Teach (vv. 21, 22)

21. And they went into Capernaum; and straightway on the sabbath day he entered into the synagogue, and taught.

Capernaum is a fishing town located on the northwest shore of the Sea of Galilee. Today the ruins of a *synagogue* are still visible, though the first-century structure lies underneath the present remains as foundation stones. Also visible are the ruins of a house thought to be that of the apostle Peter. This makes Capernaum a natural base for the ministry of Jesus (cf. Matthew 4:13).

The synagogue is the Jewish institution that grew up during the Babylonian captivity so that Jews would have a place to pray, read Scripture, and worship God while far from their homeland. Jesus and the apostles often begin their preaching efforts by finding the nearest synagogue (Luke 4:15; Acts 14:1; 17:1, 2) because most synagogues welcomed visiting rabbis to teach the lesson on *the sabbath day.*

22. And they were astonished at his doctrine: for he taught them as one that had authority, and not as the scribes.

The astonishment of Jesus' audiences is well documented in Mark's Gospel (see 6:2; 7:37; 10:26; 11:18). Here he contrasts the *authority* in Jesus' teaching with *the scribes* who are the scholars of the day. On virtually any matter of *doctrine* the rabbis of the time fill their teaching with quotations of other rabbis, often indicating where they are at odds with one another.

But Jesus has *authority* as the Son of God. He speaks as the author of truth, proclaiming the very words of God. All Scripture, of course, should be interpreted and explained so that people can understand. (The lessons in this book are examples; see also Nehemiah 8:7, 8.) But when teaching starts to embrace human tradition to the exclusion of God's explicit commands, danger looms (Mark 7:7, 8). [See question #5, page 240.]

B. Power to Heal (vv. 23-26)

23. And there was in their synagogue a man with an unclean spirit; and he cried out.

An unclean spirit is a demon. That this man is *in their synagogue* can either mean that he is a member of the assembly itself or that he is merely in the building that day. This is the first of four exorcisms recorded by Mark. (See 5:1-20; 7:24-30; 9:14-29.)

24. Saying, Let us alone; what have we to do with thee, thou Jesus of Nazareth? art thou come to destroy us? I know thee who thou art, the Holy One of God.

The words of the man are in reality those of the demon crying out, since Jesus responds specifically to the demon in the verse to follow. In referring to *us,* this demon is apparently speaking for all demons. Recognizing in Jesus the authority and power *of God,* they know that His mission is to *destroy* them (cf. 1 John 3:8). They must realize that they have made themselves

enemies of God (see James 2:19). Many scholars see the demons' identification of *Jesus of Nazareth* by name and title to be a reflection of the belief that when demons name an individual it implies gaining some power over that person.

Ironically, though, even the confession of these demons acknowledges the major affirmations of Mark 1. Already truth about Jesus has been confessed by Mark himself, by the Father God, and (by implication) John the Baptist (1:7, 8). Now even the demons confess Him.

25. And Jesus rebuked him, saying, Hold thy peace, and come out of him.

No demon has greater power than *Jesus.* If the demon thinks he has gained some advantage by speaking Jesus' name, he soon learns better. Jesus does not need any of the chants or remedies often connected with driving out (exorcising) demons. All He needs to do is rebuke the demon and command him to leave the man. (For an instance where certain individuals attempt to use Jesus' name as a "magic formula," see Acts 19:13-16.) Christians do not need to fear the devil because the One who is in us is greater than he who is in the world (1 John 4:4).

26. And when the unclean spirit had torn him, and cried with a loud voice, he came out of him.

With a last demonstration of loud demonic power, the *spirit* convulses the man and departs. As the following verse shows, there is no doubt on the part of the onlookers that this is a supernatural event. This opening salvo sets the stage for the battle that will rage between the Son of God and the forces of Satan throughout Jesus' earthly ministry.

Conclusion

A. Early Indications

"As the twig is bent" is an expression we sometimes use to speak about the direction a young life takes and how it shapes the end result. The phrase can be applied to Jesus' early ministry. His words and actions demonstrate the major theme of His entire mission. Our ministry for Jesus should be characterized by this urgency of the kingdom of God that is so obvious in Jesus.

B. Prayer

Lord, help me to go about my service for Christ as if today will be the last day I have before seeing Him face to face. Through Christ and His authority I pray, amen.

C. Thought to Remember

"Only one life, 'Twill soon be past.
Only what's done for Christ will last."

Home Daily Bible Readings

Monday, Feb. 24—Jesus Is Baptized, Tempted (Mark 1:1-13)

Tuesday, Feb. 25—Jesus Calls Four Fishermen (Mark 1:14-20)

Wednesday, Feb. 26—Follow Me (John 1:43-51)

Thursday, Feb. 27—You Will Catch People (Luke 5:1-11)

Friday, Feb. 28—Jesus Casts Out an Unclean Spirit (Mark 1:21-28)

Saturday, Mar. 1—Jesus Heals Many Sick Persons (Mark 1:29-38)

Sunday, Mar. 2—Jesus Preaches Throughout Galilee (Mark 1:39-45)

Learning by Doing

This page contains an alternative lesson plan emphasizing learning activities. Classes desiring such student involvement will find these suggestions helpful.

Learning Goals

After participating in this lesson, each student will be able to:

1. Cite the significant details of Jesus' early ministry, including His baptism and teaching.

2. Explain the urgency of Jesus' ministry, both in His day and in ours.

3. Express a commitment to speak the good news of God's kingdom with boldness, knowing that Christ's own authority empowers us.

Into the Lesson

Before class, arrange chairs so that class members sit in groups of four. On a poster or chalkboard list the following roles: son, daughter, husband, wife, father, mother, brother, sister, employee, employer, tenant, landlord, landowner, church member, student, auto owner, small group member, stepparent, stepchild, other. When everyone is seated, say, "Each of us has many roles in life. Please examine this list and indicate the roles that apply to you and that tell your group members about your life." (This activity is also found in *Adult Bible Class*.)

After about five minutes encourage each group to discuss the roles that they like, that are challenging, that are frustrating, and that give them self-esteem.

After an additional five minutes call the groups together. Then say, "Today as we study Mark's Gospel, we will notice how Jesus fulfilled different roles during His time on earth."

Into the Word

Lecture. Using the Lesson Background (page 234), prepare a five-minute introduction to the book of Mark. Be sure to emphasize the urgency with which Jesus began His ministry.

Story Panels. Create groups of up to six students each and give them the following assignment. (If you have more than eighteen students, create more groups and repeat assignments.) You will need paper, a pencil or pen, markers or art supplies, and a Bible for each student.

Explain that a story panel is a series of "snapshots" of the events described in the text. (A blank one is provided in the student book.) Then assign the groups as follows:

Group 1: Create a story panel of Jesus' baptism that includes all who were there. Depict the events as described in Mark 1:9-13.

Group 2: Create a story panel of the calling of the first disciples. These events are described in Mark 1:14-20.

Group 3: Create a story panel of Jesus driving out the unclean spirit. This event is described in Mark 1:21-28.

Allow fifteen minutes for work; then ask each group to present its storyboard. The exposition section of this commentary will help you to answer students' questions.

Acrostic. Point out to students that there was a sense of urgency in Jesus' ministry. Then write the words "AT ONCE" vertically on a chalkboard or on an overhead transparency. (A similar exercise is in the student book.) Ask students to read Mark 1:9-26 and find words beginning with these letters to describe Jesus' ministry. Words may include *amazing, teaching, obedient, newsworthy, captivating,* and *embracing.* Lead a short discussion using the following questions:

Which verses portray the urgency of Jesus' ministry? *(1:12, 18, 20, 38, 43)*

Why does Jesus have this urgency? *(1:15)*

Why should we have a sense of urgency yet today? *(The kingdom of God is still near and still needs to be announced!)*

Into Life

The urgency of the ministry and rapid response to the message is evident in today's text. Give each student a paper with the following headline: "EXTRA! EXTRA! Good News Proclaimed! Jesus Calls Followers to Proclaim Truth."

Say, "Jesus called His disciples to speak the good news with boldness. Under the headline, add your personal response to proclaim this news to others. Use the verses cited below to make your answer."

Mark 1:15, 17—I will _____ *(follow Him).*

Mark 1:27—I have _____ *(Jesus' authority to speak).*

_____ (Signature)

Each student should be able to commit to proclaiming the good news of God's kingdom on the basis of having Christ's authority.

Pray for the students to have boldness in proclaiming the good news this week.

Let's Talk It Over

The questions on this page are designed to promote discussion of the lesson by the class and to encourage application of the lesson Scriptures. The answers provided are only discussion starters. Let your class talk it over from there.

1. What is significant to you about Jesus' desire to "fulfil all righteousness"? How much does it motivate you to obedience?

If Jesus sensed the need to yield Himself to God's righteous plan, how can any believer deny the same need today? Although we are not baptized for the same reason Jesus was, submitting to baptism is one point in which believers can directly imitate their Savior.

And the issue goes way beyond baptism. Submission is the issue. God's way is the right way. Even though salvation is not attained by obedience to that way, that in no way diminishes the need for submission to the will of God: seeking to fulfill all righteousness as much as we can.

2. Why is a transition from exaltation to temptation so common in the life of a Christian? What can we do about it?

Satan has far more to gain from toppling a committed Christian than he does from attacking one who is presently far from God. While it would seem that one would be weakest when struggling or down, Satan often finds Christians most vulnerable when experiencing a period of exaltation, triumph, or victory in life. Perhaps you or your students can recite specific examples.

This may suggest that we need to pray for one another as much or more when things are "going right" than when things seem to be going wrong. It is easy to become complacent and not realize we are in Satan's sights. Discuss how Christians can more regularly pray for one another and hold each other accountable so as not to fall into Satan's clutches.

3. At least four of Jesus' disciples were fishermen. Matthew was a tax collector. Simon was a political activist (a "zealot"). From what kinds of places do we see Jesus' disciples coming today? What is the significance of that?

Whether Jesus called these men because of the various careers that they were in, or in spite of the various careers that they were in, is unclear. Regardless, it is clear that Jesus was no "respecter of persons." At no point does He show preference to one of the disciples because of his occupational background. Today our churches are filled with "white-collar" businessmen and women and "blue-collar" workers or tradespeople. The Holy Spirit has given each of us gifts that transcend our intelligence, educational backgrounds, and occupational circumstances. God uses people of all kinds.

4. What can we learn from the consistent examples of urgency in Jesus' message, followed by a rapid, wholehearted response from His followers?

Everything that Jesus said in Mark 1 suggested urgency, movement, and action. While it might not be accurate to say that Jesus was "in a hurry," there is an undeniable urgency in His mission and ministry from the beginning. At the same time, there is never an instance in Mark 1 where someone disobeyed His urgent call or command. Each one, even an evil spirit, obeyed Him immediately. The disciples were not slow in their response. Jesus' timeless message is still of urgent importance. We have no excuse for delay when Jesus calls us to become His witnesses. Jesus has not placed upon us the demands faced by Peter, Andrew, James, and John. We can keep our employment. We can go on living with our families. But we never can sit idly by as Jesus summons us to speak out for Him.

5. What was it that made Jesus' teaching so much more authoritative than that of the rabbis? How does it compare with teaching of our day?

The lesson writer indicates that the rabbis were fond of quoting other rabbis. When Jesus spoke, what was it that made His absolute authority so obvious to His hearers? Surely His knowledge of Scripture, His application of Scripture, His honor of Scripture above the rules of men, and His ability to back up that which He taught with miracles and healings were part of it. But there also must have been something of His personal manner that conveyed authority. John tells of an event in Gethsemane when Jesus' authority was so overwhelming even His enemies fell at His feet (John 18:4-6). The lesson writer states, "But Jesus has authority as the Son of God. He speaks as the author of truth." In today's society where "truth" is relative, and where contradicting messages can be considered politically correct and therefore valid, the authority of Jesus still stands out as clearly to those who will listen to Him.

The Conflict Begins

DEVOTIONAL READING: Luke 15:1-7.

BACKGROUND SCRIPTURE: Mark 2:1–3:6.

PRINTED TEXT: Mark 2:3-17.

Mark 2:3-17

3 And they come unto him, bringing one sick of the palsy, which was borne of four.

4 And when they could not come nigh unto him for the press, they uncovered the roof where he was: and when they had broken it up, they let down the bed wherein the sick of the palsy lay.

5 When Jesus saw their faith, he said unto the sick of the palsy, Son, thy sins be forgiven thee.

6 But there were certain of the scribes sitting there, and reasoning in their hearts,

7 Why doth this man thus speak blasphemies? who can forgive sins but God only?

8 And immediately, when Jesus perceived in his spirit that they so reasoned within themselves, he said unto them, Why reason ye these things in your hearts?

9 Whether is it easier to say to the sick of the palsy, Thy sins be forgiven thee; or to say, Arise, and take up thy bed, and walk?

10 But that ye may know that the Son of man hath power on earth to forgive sins, (he saith to the sick of the palsy,)

11 I say unto thee, Arise, and take up thy bed, and go thy way into thine house.

12 And immediately he arose, took up the bed, and went forth before them all; insomuch that they were all amazed, and glorified God, saying, We never saw it on this fashion.

13 And he went forth again by the sea side; and all the multitude resorted unto him, and he taught them.

14 And as he passed by, he saw Levi the son of Alpheus sitting at the receipt of custom, and said unto him, Follow me. And he arose and followed him.

15 And it came to pass, that, as Jesus sat at meat in his house, many publicans and sinners sat also together with Jesus and his disciples; for there were many, and they followed him.

16 And when the scribes and Pharisees saw him eat with publicans and sinners, they said unto his disciples, How is it that he eateth and drinketh with publicans and sinners?

17 When Jesus heard it, he saith unto them, They that are whole have no need of the physician, but they that are sick: I came not to call the righteous, but sinners to repentance.

GOLDEN TEXT: [Jesus] saith unto them, They that are whole have no need of the physician, but they that are sick: I came not to call the righteous, but sinners to repentance.—Mark 2:17.

Jesus: God's Power in Action
Unit 1: Jesus' Early Ministry
(Lessons 1-5)

Lesson Aims

After participating in this lesson, each student will be able to:

1. Tell how today's texts illustrate that the heart of Jesus' mission was bringing the good news of God's grace to sinners.

2. Express appreciation for the grace that God offers and a sense of obligation to share that grace with others.

3. Tell what specific action he or she can take to show forgiveness to someone who is alienated from his or her fellowship.

Lesson Outline

INTRODUCTION
    A. Forgive and Forget
    B. Lesson Background
  I. JESUS HEALS A PARALYZED MAN (Mark 2:3-12)
    A. The Faith of Friends (vv. 3, 4)
      Unwanted Visitors
    B. The Authority of Jesus (v. 5)
    C. The Thoughts of Enemies (vv. 6-8)
    D. The Power of Jesus (vv. 9-12)
 II. JESUS ASSOCIATES WITH SINNERS (Mark 2:13-17)
    A. Invitation to a "Sinner" (vv. 13, 14)
      Befriending the Friendless
    B. Meal With Sinners (vv. 15, 16)
    C. Ministry to Sinners (v. 17)
CONCLUSION
    A. Open Door of Forgiveness
    B. Prayer
    C. Thought to Remember

Introduction

A. Forgive and Forget

Charlie Shedd tells a story about forgiveness in his book *Letters to My Grandchildren*. The evening began when little Philip came storming into the house, mad, mad, mad. To say that the word *angry* is the better choice would not work this time. This boy was mad, and it was all Ronnie's fault, again. Ronnie was Philip's buddy, and he lived across the street. But now things had changed. Ronnie was no longer his buddy. Not this time. Not forever! Whatever it was that Ronnie had done, he could never come into the house again! Never!

So Mom and Dad ate their meal with a certain sadness. They liked Ronnie a lot. Then suddenly the doorbell rang. As usual, Philip jumped up from the table to answer the door and back he came with, guess whom? It was Ronnie. "Hey, Mom, can Ronnie have some ice cream, too?"

"Of course he can, Philip. But what about all of those things you were saying? Did you mean them?"

"I meant them. But me and Ronnie, we got good forgetters!"

In today's lesson, Mark's account puts the emphasis on God's desire to forgive. He has sent His Son into the world for that very purpose. Jesus puts Himself in situations where He will have contact with sinners who need God's grace. He does this deliberately, even though there will be those who criticize Him for doing so. His ministry cannot succeed unless He associates with those who need His help.

B. Lesson Background

For His ministry in Galilee, Jesus chose as His "headquarters" the fishing town of Capernaum, located on the northwest shore of the Sea of Galilee (cf. Mark 1:14, 21; 2:1). The convenience of this base of operations may have been assured by the fact that Capernaum was the home of Simon Peter and his brother Andrew (1:29). The ministry of Jesus already had gained notoriety in the region of Galilee. He had driven out unclean spirits (1:25, 39), healed Peter's mother-in-law (1:31), preached in their synagogues (1:39), and healed a leper (1:41).

In 2:1–3:6, Mark turns his attention to five separate incidents in the vicinity of Capernaum. In each one Jesus' actions caused conflict with the religious leaders. Nothing in Mark's description of these events requires us to understand them as occurring in chronological sequence. They are simply incidents (perhaps typical kinds of incidents) where Jesus' actions resulted in controversy. We consider two of these five incidents today.

I. Jesus Heals a Paralyzed Man (Mark 2:3-12)

The scene to be described takes place in a Palestinian house in Capernaum (2:1). These houses are built with flat roofs, consisting of wooden beams and a mixture of sticks and mud filling in the gaps. Because of the heat, the rooftops are often used as places to relax at the end of the day. Outside steps lead up the side of the house to the roof. In this case, the teaching of Jesus has drawn such a crowd that the single room inside is full of people.

A. The Faith of Friends (vv. 3, 4)

3. And they come unto him, bringing one sick of the palsy, which was borne of four.

Palsy is probably a paralysis of some kind. This disease has taken away the man's ability to walk, and so he is carried by *four* of his friends. We might picture these men carefully transporting the paralyzed man on a mat, which they hold by the four corners as they walk along the dusty street leading to the house where Jesus can be found. Their faith is enabling this man to see Jesus.

4. And when they could not come nigh unto him for the press, they uncovered the roof where he was: and when they had broken it up, they let down the bed wherein the sick of the palsy lay.

Because the people are pressed into the room where Jesus is teaching, the four who carry the paralyzed man are unable to gain access to Jesus (cf. 2:2). But their determination will not allow them to be turned away. So they climb the outside stairway, hauling the paralyzed man on the *bed* (or mat) to the *roof*. There they begin to dig through the hard-packed mud and thatch. The noise of this activity and the falling debris undoubtedly catch the attention of all inside. [See question #1, page 248.]

UNWANTED VISITORS

Year after year, by far the biggest tourist event in the entire state of South Dakota is the weeklong August gathering of "bikers" of every type imaginable in the town of Sturgis. Years ago, it was mostly "outlaw" bikers who came, brawling a bit and doing a lot of macho posturing. Many residents would leave town to avoid the trouble caused by the unwanted visitors. Renting out their houses for $2,500 or so per week made the inconvenience easier to take and also helped pay for repairs after the visitors were gone.

How to Say It

ALPHEUS. Al-*fee*-us.
ANTIPAS. *An*-tih-pus.
BLASPHEMIES. *blas*-fuh-meez.
CAPERNAUM. Kuh-*per*-nay-um.
DECAPOLIS. Dee-*cap*-uh-lis.
GALILEE. *Gal*-uh-lee.
HEROD. *Hair*-ud.
ISAIAH. Eye-*zay*-uh.
LEVI. *Lee*-vye.
MACCABEAN. Mack-uh-*be*-un.
MESSIAH. Meh-*sigh*-uh.
MESSIANIC. mess-ee-*an*-ick.
PALESTINIAN. Pal-uh-*sten*-ee-un.
PHARISEES. *Fair*-ih-seez.
SYNAGOGUE. *sin*-uh-gog.

Nowadays, the "outlaws" are themselves complaining about unwanted visitors. "Rich Urban Bikers" (RUBs), the new breed of motorcyclists, have invaded Sturgis. They are dentists, lawyers, teachers, and other respectable citizens who have fantasies of a more exciting—and perhaps more perverse—lifestyle. They have changed the flavor of the event. There are fewer fights and arrests now that the RUBs have arrived.

The four men who tore up the roof and ceiling to lower their friend to Jesus were, no doubt, unwanted visitors. They upset the agenda of those already there; they messed up the house and got dirt on those sitting below them. But Jesus welcomed them and met their needs. What lesson might the church learn from how Jesus handled these unwanted visitors? Would He welcome those whom we wish would go somewhere else?

—C. R. B.

B. The Authority of Jesus (v. 5)

5. When Jesus saw their faith, he said unto the sick of the palsy, Son, thy sins be forgiven thee.

The *faith* of the paralyzed man and his friends is clear to Jesus. Mark's Gospel frequently notes the faith of the people who come to Jesus for healing (5:34, 36; 9:23-34; 10:52). Jesus Himself often speaks about the role of *faith* in the healings that He performs, though the Gospels also present instances where Jesus heals without any evidence of faith on the part of the afflicted person (Luke 7:11-17; John 11:38-44). In pronouncing forgiveness of the man's *sins*, Jesus' words represent a claim about His own identity.

C. The Thoughts of Enemies (vv. 6-8)

6. But there were certain of the scribes sitting there, and reasoning in their hearts.

The *scribes* are the Bible scholars of the day. Mark already has mentioned them by noting the contrast people see between their teaching and that of Jesus (1:22). The scribes will later become adversaries of Jesus (2:16), coming from all parts of Palestine to observe His teaching (cf. Luke 5:17).

7. Why doth this man thus speak blasphemies? who can forgive sins but God only?

As interpreters of the Scripture, the scribes are certainly correct in thinking that only *God* can *forgive sins* (cf. Exodus 34:6, 7; Isaiah 43:25; 44:22). For any mere mortal to assume the right to extend divine forgiveness of sins is to presume upon God. Thus the scribes conclude that Jesus is guilty of speaking *blasphemies*.

The scribes also know that the law makes blasphemy a capital offense (Leviticus 24:14-16). Since they think Jesus is now committing blasphemy, Jesus will have to pay with His life.

8. And immediately, when Jesus perceived in his spirit that they so reasoned within themselves, he said unto them, Why reason ye these things in your hearts?

Jesus meets their unstated objections with a question. Like so many of Jesus' questions, this one probes the depths of their position (cf. Matthew 6:25, 26; Mark 3:33; 8:36, 37). This question, combined with another in the next verse, will demand that they consider how mistaken they are in their concept of Jesus' identity.

D. The Power of Jesus (vv. 9-12)

9. Whether is it easier to say to the sick of the palsy, Thy sins be forgiven thee; or to say, Arise, and take up thy bed, and walk?

The scribes refuse to believe that Jesus has power to forgive *sins*. Therefore, they reason, Jesus can pronounce forgiveness all He wants to, but it is without effect since only God can forgive sins. Anyone who takes on this divine right is trying to do the impossible and cannot be taken seriously!

But Jesus claims the authority to do both—to grant divine forgiveness of sins as well as to speak the powerful word of healing. Forgiveness can be faked; healing cannot. So if He speaks the word of healing so that His authority can be put to the test, then they must accept His authority to grant what cannot be seen.

In focusing on the sins of the paralyzed man, Jesus gives a powerful demonstration of the core of His preaching. The good news of the kingdom of God is that Jesus can provide forgiveness, that He came into the world not "to condemn the world" but that through Him the world might be saved (John 3:17). [See question #2, page 248.]

10. But that ye may know that the Son of man hath power on earth to forgive sins, (he saith to the sick of the palsy).

Jesus obviously is moved with compassion to heal the ailing man, and He is impressed with the faith of the man and his friends. But Jesus has a more important reason for speaking the word of healing on this occasion. The phrase *that ye may know* corresponds directly to the unspoken objections of His critics. They do not believe that Jesus has authority to grant divine forgiveness of *sins*. Now He will prove that He does have this authority by granting release from a malady that can be removed only by the *power* of God. The scribes will then be able to see the evidence of Jesus' authority and reconsider their opposition to Him, since God obviously will not grant the power to heal to a blasphemer.

Jesus identifies Himself with the title *Son of man* dozens of times in the Gospels. The title seems to come from Daniel 7:13, 14 where the

"Son of man" appears as a Heavenly figure who receives authority, power, and glory from the Lord in the last days.

11. I say unto thee, Arise, and take up thy bed, and go thy way into thine house.

Without any gimmickry Jesus simply gives the command to the paralyzed man. There is no magical formula. There is no chant or potions to drink. In this instance, there is not even a touch (cf. 7:33). Jesus simply speaks the word of healing as the One having full authority to do so. He does not even have to say anything like "by the power of God" or "through the anointing of the Spirit." He orders the man to *arise* as if the man's disease presents no challenge.

12. And immediately he arose, took up the bed, and went forth before them all; insomuch that they were all amazed, and glorified God, saying, We never saw it on this fashion.

In this instance no series of treatments is necessary (cf. Mark 8:22-26). The paralyzed man simply gets up as any healthy man, rolls up his *bed,* and walks out of the room. Jesus has performed a miracle that speaks volumes about His identity. He has performed an act that is visible (physical healing) to prove that He can perform an act that is invisible (forgiveness of sins). The One who possesses the power to do so stands before them. He is the One they were questioning in their hearts.

The stunned crowd undoubtedly understands the connection Jesus is making between the forgiveness of sins and the healing of paralysis. Their amazement is a theme of Mark's Gospel (cf. 1:22; 5:20, 42; 6:2, 51; 7:37; 11:18). [See question #3, page 248.]

II. Jesus Associates With Sinners (Mark 2:13-17)

The next incident in Mark 2:1–3:6 shows the kinds of controversies that swirl around Jesus. This particular incident relates to Jesus' contact with sinners.

A. Invitation to a "Sinner" (vv. 13, 14)

13. And he went forth again by the sea side; and all the multitude resorted unto him, and he taught them.

The mention of the *sea side* locates the event in the area of the Sea of Galilee, probably directly adjacent to Capernaum. Jesus' fame has been mentioned already in Mark 1:28, and we can imagine that at this stage in His ministry Jesus is attracting large audiences wherever He goes. Because He has come to proclaim the arrival of the kingdom of God, Jesus is always prepared to teach whenever a crowd gathers.

14. And as he passed by, he saw Levi the son of Alpheus sitting at the receipt of custom, and said unto him, Follow me. And he arose and followed him.

Levi is the same person identified as Matthew in Matthew 9:9; 10:3. *Levi* could be his given name, while *Matthew* may be a name given to him later, as Jesus gave Simon the name *Peter* (Mark 3:16). As a tax collector, Levi is most likely employed by Herod Antipas. If Capernaum is the location of this incident, Levi may be sitting alongside the international road leading into Capernaum from the territory of Herod Philip or the Decapolis to the east. Levi's role is to collect the toll tax from travelers who might be moving goods for sale along the road.

Tax collectors in the first century are a despised lot. Jews are especially incensed at what they consider treason by their countrymen who collect money for the hated Roman occupational government. Besides that, most tax collectors are assumed to be cheats who extort more money than required by Rome and pocket the difference. Men such as Levi are not looked on with respect.

Nevertheless, Jesus says to Levi *follow me* just the way He had with Simon, Andrew, James, and John (Mark 1:16-20). For these four, responding to the call of Jesus meant leaving an occupation that would still be there if they went back to it. There is no such comfort for Levi, since he will not be welcomed back if he changes his mind later. Even with so much at stake, Levi responds exactly as did the four fishermen: leaving immediately to follow Jesus. [See question #4, page 248.]

BEFRIENDING THE FRIENDLESS

Steven Kent, at age forty-five, was homeless, an alcoholic, and one of society's outcasts. Kent never committed any serious offenses, but he had been arrested seventy-five times for a host of minor ones. He had lived this way for twenty years when a wealthy relative died and left him $300,000. So he got on a bus heading from Long Beach, California, to Ohio to collect his inheritance. But the bus driver kicked him off because of his appearance (and possibly because of the way he smelled).

Then Ron Quarn, a police officer who had known Kent for years, found him. Quarn took him to jail and got him sober and cleaned up. Quarn paid for a haircut, bought Kent some new clothes and shoes, and once again put him on an Ohio-bound bus to collect his fortune and start a new life.

Levi and his friends were the kind of outcasts that "respectable" people thought would never

change. But when Jesus befriended them, His actions said in a powerful, positive way, "You have worth in God's eyes and in mine. Let me help you make something new out of your life." Are we ever, like Jesus, God's agents of change for society's outcasts?   —C. R. B.

B. Meal With Sinners (vv. 15, 16)

15. And it came to pass, that, as Jesus sat at meat in his house, many publicans and sinners sat also together with Jesus and his disciples; for there were many, and they followed him.

The issue that generates the controversy is now developed further. The call of Levi leads to a dinner party that includes *many* other *publicans* (or tax collectors). The use of the word *sinners* here is not intended to suggest those participating in the dinner party are worse in Jesus' eyes than anyone else. Instead, it indicates that they are considered sinners by the religious authorities because they do not follow certain man-made rules of conduct. Tax collectors fall into this category, as do all Gentiles. The dinner at Levi's house is open to many friends of Levi whom the elite scribes and Pharisees think of as unholy people.

Apparently Levi invited Jesus to attend this dinner and He accepted. This brings Jesus into contact with Levi's friends and acquaintances who have been invited as well. Here is the basis of the problem. Does the guest list of sinners include thieves, adulterers, and lawbreakers? Are they the kind of people with whom the Son of God should be sitting for dinner? Jesus' association with such people becomes an issue in other Gospel passages as well (see Matthew 11:19; Luke 15:1, 2).

16. And when the scribes and Pharisees saw him eat with publicans and sinners, they said

Home Daily Bible Readings

Monday, Mar. 3—Your Sins Are Forgiven (Mark 2:1-12)

Tuesday, Mar. 4—Jesus Eats With Tax Collectors (Mark 2:13-17)

Wednesday, Mar. 5—Joy Over a Sinner Who Repents (Luke 15:1-7)

Thursday, Mar. 6—New Wine in Old Wineskins (Mark 2:18-22)

Friday, Mar. 7—Sabbath Was Made for Humankind (Mark 2:23-28)

Saturday, Mar. 8—Jesus Heals on the Sabbath (Mark 3:1-6)

Sunday, Mar. 9—You Are the Son of God! (Mark 3:7-12)

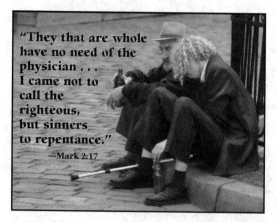

"They that are whole have no need of the physician . . . I came not to call the righteous, but sinners to repentance."

—Mark 2:17

Visual for lesson 2. *Display this visual as you discuss verse 17. Ask, "What are we doing to call sinners to repentance?"*

unto his disciples, How is it that he eateth and drinketh with publicans and sinners?

According to the standards of the *Pharisees,* Jesus is committing a serious offense. To *eat with* people like this is to express personal friendship with them. When added to the messianic claims of Jesus, the Pharisees can point to a theological problem as well. The Messiah is going to institute the Heavenly banquet where Abraham, Isaac, and Jacob will sit down with those who were coming from the east and the west. How can Jesus think that the Messiah will also sit down with *sinners?* (See Matthew 8:11.) In other words, how can sinners be included in the banquet with the Messiah?

This is the first mention of Pharisees in Mark's Gospel. They are one of the major Jewish religious parties of the time, although their origin is shrouded in mystery. They are not found in the Old Testament. Most scholars trace their history to the Maccabean revolt of the second century B.C.

C. Ministry to Sinners (v. 17)

17. When Jesus heard it, he saith unto them, They that are whole have no need of the physician, but they that are sick: I came not to call the righteous, but sinners to repentance.

The Pharisees' attitude shows that they don't understand Jesus' mission at all. The Jewish leaders expect a Messiah who will vindicate the *righteous* and crack down on the *sinners.* Since Jesus isn't meeting that expectation, conflict results.

In responding to the implied criticism of the Pharisees, Jesus declares again the core of His mission. He intends to serve in the same way that a *physician* does. He will bring healing to those who are spiritually *sick.* His message of the

arrival of the kingdom of God (Mark 1:15) is to be understood as a message of God's own initiative to restore those whose lives are ruined because of sin.

Jesus thus argues that He cannot accomplish this mission without coming into contact with those most in need of the truth of God. Of course, we know that there is no one who is truly righteous on his or her own because all are sinners (Romans 3:10, 23). In using the categories "the righteous" *vs.* "sinners," Jesus is arguing from the Pharisees' point of view. If the Pharisees continue to view themselves as "righteous" rather than as "sinners," they will not be included in Jesus' mission.

Jesus also understands that those who think they are *whole* (or healthy) are fooling themselves. They, too, are more sick than they know. Yet they will be the ones in the end who mockingly look upon His suffering and say, "Physician, heal thyself" (Luke 4:23). [See question #5, page 248.]

Conclusion

A. Open Door of Forgiveness

Jesus' early efforts to reach people with the truth of the gospel of forgiveness were met with resistance from those who could not understand His claims about Himself or His habit of mixing with sinners. Nevertheless, He refused to back down. Jesus presented a message that highlighted the open door of God's forgiveness. He kept His guard up so that when criticized for His actions, He could articulate His approach as consistent with the mission of the Messiah.

Modern believers must not be handcuffed in their ministry to unbelievers. We are surrounded by people who need to experience the grace of God's forgiveness. We have in our hands the cure that the physician prescribes! How can we justify any lack of attention to those who need the cure? How can believers refuse to carry the good news of God's forgiveness to people whose lives are ruined by sin? Because Jesus extended divine forgiveness to sinners like us, we have the hope of eternal life. Now, through us, He extends that offer to others. We have the privilege of making sure someone else gets to hear about Jesus.

B. Prayer

Lord, forgive us our trespasses as we forgive those who trespass against us. Then lead us to speak to someone today about God's good news of forgiveness. Because of Christ we pray, amen.

C. Thought to Remember

Jesus never met a sinner He didn't love.

Learning by Doing

This page contains an alternative lesson plan emphasizing learning activities.
Classes desiring such student involvement will find these suggestions helpful.

Learning Goals

After this lesson each student will be able to:

1. Tell how today's texts illustrate that the heart of Jesus' mission was bringing the good news of God's grace to sinners.

2. Express appreciation for the grace that God offers and a sense of obligation to share that grace with others.

3. Tell what specific action he or she can take to show forgiveness to someone who is alienated from his or her fellowship.

Into the Lesson

Getting to know the heart of a person helps us to understand his or her actions. Introduce today's lesson by having students sit in pairs face-to-face. Each pair will then alternate answering the following questions. Have these questions available to each person.

How did you get your name?

Where did you live when you were twelve years old, and what was your favorite springtime activity?

Describe a pet you had as a child (or wish you had).

What has been your favorite job? Why?

Of the things you own, what brings you the most enjoyment?

Describe your most memorable trip or vacation.

Encourage your class to answer these questions quickly. If your class is small (less than fifteen), have each person introduce his or her partner to the class by saying the name and then telling the most interesting thing that he or she learned about the other person. (For a larger class, form groups of six and have the students do the introductions within those groups.)

"Our introductory activity was designed to get a glimpse into the heart of your partner. By asking a few questions and listening to the answers, you got a better idea of who they are and what they care about. In today's text, we will seek to discover what was the heart of Jesus' mission."

Into the Word

Before class recruit individuals to do research for the settings of the two stories presented. One should focus on the building and use of houses in Capernaum. The other is to focus on the role and responsibility of tax collectors in Jesus' day. Each report should take three to four minutes.

Divide your class into groups of four to six. Each group will need a copy of the following questions, as well as a paper heart.

Group 1: Read Mark 2:1-12.

Group 2: Read Mark 2:13-17.

(If you have a large class, you may add groups that will study Mark 2:18-22; 2:23-27; 3:1-6. These groups will answer the same questions.)

Who is present during the event recorded in this account? What action does Jesus take? What do the teachers think of Jesus? What does Jesus say? What does this indicate about Jesus' purpose? *(His purpose was to bring good news of God's grace to sinners.)*

Have the group members write on the heart the following: "The heart of Jesus' mission was _____."

Bring the groups together and discuss their findings. Display a large heart. After all groups have finished, summarize by saying, "We have seen the heart of Jesus' mission. Let's write it on this heart: 'Bring good news of God's grace to sinners.' That is the reason Jesus came. He brings that message to each of us."

Into Life

Say, "Jesus entered the lives of those who were alienated from Jewish fellowship. Each was in need of forgiveness and restoration. As a result of Jesus' actions, people were amazed!

"Today some are alienated from Christ. We are called to reach out to them as Jesus' representatives. Write two or three names of people you know who are alienated. Then write one or two ways you can reach out. Put a time frame for contacting them." (Have the students write on the back of the sheet of questions you used in the "Into the Lesson" activity above.)

After the students have completed the above activity, distribute three-by-five index cards to each. Give the following instructions: "Write a prayer of appreciation to God for the grace you have been offered. Most of you have received that grace and forgiveness. If you have not yet received it, I would love to talk to you after class. As a part of your prayer ask God to give you urgency to share grace with others, as well as the opportunity to do so."

After students have finished, close with prayer. Be prepared to tell and show anyone who comes how to receive God's grace in Christ.

Let's Talk It Over

The questions on this page are designed to promote discussion of the lesson by the class and to encourage application of the lesson Scriptures. The answers provided are only discussion starters. Let your class talk it over from there.

1. Some striking characteristics of the paralytic's friends are their determination, their persistence, their resourcefulness, and their teamwork. How are the same characteristics necessary in our efforts to bring people to Jesus?

We cannot bring people to a flesh-and-blood Jesus today. Through our words and actions, we must bring Jesus to them. Our obstacles, then, are not crowds and physical structures; they are ideas and preconceptions and untruths. How determined are we to get our neighbors to meet Jesus? If we are rebuffed by circumstances, are we willing to try again, or to try something else? What resources do we have at our disposal? How can we get others to join in our efforts? Do we need to offer training? Try to get specific about what obstacles your church must overcome and how these characteristics can help.

2. The lesson writer says that Jesus' focus on forgiving the paralytic's sin shows that forgiveness is the "core" of Jesus' ministry. How can we be sure that we share His concern on a personal level, that we are accepting of those who come to Christ and not condemning?

Paul tells the Corinthian believers to "think of what you were when you were called." By doing this, he asks them to recall the time before they experienced grace, so that they can be reminded that they didn't always "have it all together." In order for us to display grace to new believers, we must be reminded continually that we are—first and foremost—recipients of grace. Only then do we become its ambassadors. In many cases, churchgoers become so isolated from the unsaved that they not only forget what it was like to be unsaved, but they also lose their ability to relate to unsaved people. Ask class members to suggest specific ways to be involved with unbelievers to secure opportunities to extend grace.

3. Those who saw Jesus heal the paralyzed man were "amazed, and glorified God." Are we "amazed" at Jesus' works? Why or why not? How can we "glorify God" because of Jesus?

We have read the reports of Jesus' miracles so often that we may have lost our sense of wonder over them. But the fact that we are no longer surprised by Jesus' miracles should in no way diminish our appreciation of them as awesome deeds worthy of our wonder. Focusing on them should lead us to worship the Lord from the heart. We can and must glorify God with our words and with our actions. We can glorify Him in worship services and in lives of loving service.

4. What is the significance of Jesus' calling a tax collector to Him on the same terms as He had called four fishermen?

To the people of Jesus' day, the profession of "publican," or tax collector, was one of the worst. Never do we read of an instance where Jesus was criticized for mingling with fishermen; yet His association with tax collectors was a constant source of criticism. Yet Jesus told Levi to "follow me" in the way that He had told the fishermen to "follow me." He did not differentiate between the men on the basis of their professions. In the eyes of the people, a tax collector was unfit to be a follower of the Messiah. In the eyes of God, no one is "fit" to be a follower, but He will make us "fit." It is only by God's grace that *any* of us can be with the Lord, and it is important to reflect that truth. If a modern-day equivalent to a publican came to our church, would we welcome him or her as Jesus did? Discuss how such a scenario could play out in your church. What kind of people are the "publicans" of today? How can we welcome them without condoning their sin?

5. Jesus "came not to call the righteous, but sinners to repentance." Does our church reflect that priority? How much of our efforts are directed at the "righteous" (church members) and how much toward calling "sinners" (the unsaved)? How can we be sure we have the right balance?

Of course, much of our "programming" must be directed at church members. We have an obligation to edify and equip the members. But we must be equipping them for the task of winning the lost! Our Sunday school, small groups, and other study and fellowship times must be open to nonmembers. And we must be intentional about bringing people who are not members into those experiences. Have class members suggest specific ways to do that.

But we cannot expect the unbelievers to come to us. The Commission is to "Go." How can we, in our day and time, go to the lost with the message of salvation?

Jesus Displays His Authority

DEVOTIONAL READING: John 5:2-17.

BACKGROUND SCRIPTURE: Mark 4:35–5:20.

PRINTED TEXT: Mark 4:36-41; 5:2-13a.

Mark 4:36-41

36 And when they had sent away the multitude, they took him even as he was in the ship. And there were also with him other little ships.

37 And there arose a great storm of wind, and the waves beat into the ship, so that it was now full.

38 And he was in the hinder part of the ship, asleep on a pillow: and they awake him, and say unto him, Master, carest thou not that we perish?

39 And he arose, and rebuked the wind, and said unto the sea, Peace, be still. And the wind ceased, and there was a great calm.

40 And he said unto them, Why are ye so fearful? how is it that ye have no faith?

41 And they feared exceedingly, and said one to another, What manner of man is this, that even the wind and the sea obey him?

Mark 5:2-13a

2 And when he was come out of the ship, immediately there met him out of the tombs a man with an unclean spirit,

3 Who had his dwelling among the tombs; and no man could bind him, no, not with chains:

4 Because that he had been often bound with fetters and chains, and the chains had been plucked asunder by him, and the fetters broken in pieces: neither could any man tame him.

5 And always, night and day, he was in the mountains, and in the tombs, crying, and cutting himself with stones.

6 But when he saw Jesus afar off, he ran and worshipped him,

7 And cried with a loud voice, and said, What have I to do with thee, Jesus, thou Son of the most high God? I adjure thee by God, that thou torment me not.

8 For he said unto him, Come out of the man, thou unclean spirit.

9 And he asked him, What is thy name? And he answered, saying, My name is Legion: for we are many.

10 And he besought him much that he would not send them away out of the country.

11 Now there was there nigh unto the mountains a great herd of swine feeding.

12 And all the devils besought him, saying, Send us into the swine, that we may enter into them.

13a And forthwith Jesus gave them leave.

GOLDEN TEXT: What manner of man is this, that even the wind and the sea obey him?—Mark 4:41.

> ## *Jesus: God's Power in Action*
> ### Unit 1: Jesus' Early Ministry
> ### (Lessons 1-5)

Lesson Aims

After participating in this lesson, each student will be able to:

1. Recall the basic facts of Jesus' calming the storm and casting the demons out of the Gadarene demoniac.

2. Tell how these events provide evidence that Jesus is the Son of God.

3. Express a confidence that Jesus will help him or her to deal with a situation that previously has caused fear.

Lesson Outline

INTRODUCTION
    A. "Your Father Knows the Way"
    B. Lesson Background
I. JESUS CALMS THE STORM (Mark 4:36-41)
    A. The Storm Erupts (vv. 36, 37)
       When Things Don't Go as Planned
    B. The Disciples Panic (v. 38)
    C. The Lord Rebukes (vv. 39-41)
II. JESUS CASTS OUT DEMONS (Mark 5:2-13a)
    A. Degradation (vv. 2-5)
       Led by What Kind of Spirit?
    B. Dialogue (vv. 6-12)
    C. Deliverance (v. 13a)
CONCLUSION
    A. A Life of Authority and Power
    B. Prayer
    C. Thought to Remember

Introduction

A. "Your Father Knows the Way"

James Hewett describes the fear of a small boy in terms that even adults can understand. He remembers his boyhood years, he says, when he was growing up in Pennsylvania. His family would often visit his grandparents, who lived nine miles away. One night a thick fog settled over the hilly countryside before they had started home. He remembers being terrified and asking if they shouldn't be going even slower than they were. Mother said gently, "Don't worry. Your father knows the way." James's father had walked that road during the war when there was no gasoline. He had ridden that blacktop on his bicycle to court James's mother. And for years he had

made those weekly trips back to visit his own parents. "How often when I can't see the road of life and have felt that familiar panic rising in my heart I have heard the echo of my mother's voice: 'Don't worry. Your father knows the way.'"

Today's lesson speaks powerfully that same comforting reminder. Don't worry. Your Father knows the way. His Son brings us confidence to face our worst fears.

B. Lesson Background

The Gospel of Mark begins with the declaration that Jesus Christ is the Son of God. Then Mark shows that the evidence of this fact is overwhelming. Jesus is proved to be the Son of God by the Heavenly voice that was heard at His baptism (Mark 1:11), by the way He taught with authority (1:22), by His ability to cast out a demon from a man in the synagogue (1:27), and by His authority to grant divine forgiveness (2:10).

In spite of this evidence, opposition grew against Jesus. The scribes thought Jesus to be committing blasphemy against God (2:7). The scribes and Pharisees questioned Jesus' eating with sinners (2:16). The Pharisees and the Herodians looked for ways to destroy Jesus (3:6). With so much controversy swirling around Him, Jesus withdrew once again to the lake (3:7).

At this point Mark begins another section of his Gospel. This section will offer some parables of Jesus (see Mark 4:1-34) along with some of the miracles He performed (4:35–5:43). Bracketing this material on the front side are Jesus' call of the Twelve (3:13-19) and Jesus' rejection by His family (3:19-35), and on the back side Jesus' rejection by His hometown (6:1-6a). Our lesson today focuses on two incidents in the middle portion of this section. In these verses the power and authority of Jesus are on display. But all of this is presented in the context of rejection by those who ought to understand by now that Jesus is the Son of God.

I. Jesus Calms the Storm (Mark 4:36-41)

After teaching the crowds in parables and explaining to His disciples what they meant, Jesus requested that they get into a boat and sail to the other side of the Sea of Galilee (Mark 4:35).

A. The Storm Erupts (vv. 36, 37)

36. And when they had sent away the multitude, they took him even as he was in the ship. And there were also with him other little ships.

While *the multitude* sat on the shore, Jesus had been teaching from a boat (Mark 4:1). Now, for some reason, Jesus wants to leave and go directly to the other side. Is it because of some sense of danger? Is it just to retreat from the crowds for a time? (Later events suggest He was simply exhausted and needed a break. See v. 38.) Whatever the reason, the disciples are ready to grant His desire. *They took Him even as he was* implies that the disciples do not even take time to go ashore before heading on across the lake. At any rate, Jesus and the disciples begin making their way eastward across the Sea of Galilee. (See page 236 for a description of this lake.)

37. And there arose a great storm of wind, and the waves beat into the ship, so that it was now full.

Because of the cooler breezes that blow from the Mediterranean into the basin of the Sea of Galilee, a *wind* vortex can form that creates violent storms and *waves*. Mark's language here describes a furious squall with winds that force the waves into the fishing boat. The boat takes on water. The fear that it could be swamped is sweeping over the disciples. Such an experience would be especially frightening after dark.

WHEN THINGS DON'T GO AS PLANNED

The event, scheduled for July 14, 2000, had been carefully planned: the decommissioned Royal Canadian Navy destroyer *Yukon* had had holes cut into its sides at strategic points, and it had been towed into place and anchored where it would be sunk the following day. It was to be part of an extravagant farewell to the ship. Speeches were planned, fireworks would explode, nearly five hundred people had paid thirty dollars each to watch from a nearby cruise ship, and the whole thing would be covered on live television.

It was all to begin with the detonation of onboard explosives that would send the ship to the bottom. There it would become part of an artificial reef off the coast of San Diego at a favorite spot of sport divers. But things didn't go as planned. About midnight, just hours before the celebration was to begin, the Yukon began taking on water. Within ninety minutes it was gone!

Things weren't going as planned for the disciples on the Sea of Galilee, either. They had no plans for sinking their boat, but the sudden storm made it look as if that was what would happen—and it seemed that Jesus didn't even care about their predicament! But when the right time came, He was there to help. There's an old saying, "God may not come when we call Him, but He always comes on time." That's a good thing to remember when the storms of life threaten to sink our boats.   —C. R. B.

B. The Disciples Panic (v. 38)

38. And he was in the hinder part of the ship, asleep on a pillow: and they awake him, and say unto him, Master, carest thou not that we perish?

The *hinder* (or rear) *part of the ship* is the stern. After the weary day of teaching the crowds, Jesus has found a cushion to use for *a pillow*, and He has fallen *asleep*. Neither the rising winds and waves nor the rising fear of the disciples disturb His sleep.

The picture of the sleeping Jesus in the middle of the storm should not be overlooked. References in the Old Testament present sleep as the answer of a confident believer to the dangers of this world (see Job 11:18, 19; Psalm 3:5; 4:8). Jesus shows no fear because He truly has no reason to fear. His trust in His Father is complete.

To the disciples, however, the rolling boat and the relentless waves mean that they all are going to die a horrible death. For Jesus to be sleeping through the storm is incomprehensible to them. They do not yet seem to realize that Jesus is the Son of God. So in their fear they rebuke the One whose power and authority is limitless! Had they fully understood that Jesus is the Son of God, they would have realized how perfectly safe they were even in the face of danger.

C. The Lord Rebukes (vv. 39-41)

39. And he arose, and rebuked the wind, and said unto the sea, Peace, be still. And the wind ceased, and there was a great calm.

The New Testament makes clear that Jesus is the Creator. That the Creator is able to command His own creation in a miraculous way should not surprise us! (See John 1:1-4; Colossians 1:16.) The word *rebuked* echoes Jesus' earlier rebuke of the unclean spirit (Mark 1:25).

40. And he said unto them, Why are ye so fearful? how is it that ye have no faith?

After the storm calms down, Jesus turns to His disciples with two questions. The obvious

---

How to Say It

DECAPOLIS. Dee-*cap*-uh-lis.
FYODOR. *Feh*-oh-door.
FYODOROVTSY. Feh-oh-door-*ovt*-see.
GADARENE. *Gad*-uh-reen.
GALILEE. *Gal*-uh-lee.
GENTILE. *Jen*-tile.
GERASA. *Gur*-uh-suh.
GERASENES. *Gur*-uh-seenz.
GERGESA. *Gur*-guh-suh.
GERGESENES. *Gur*-guh-seenz.
HERODIANS. Heh-*roe*-dee-unz.
PHARISEES. *Fair*-ih-seez.
RYBALKIN. Reh-*ball*-kin.

contrast is between *faith* and fear. By this point in their experience with Jesus, the disciples should have been able to recognize that such dangers pose no real threat since the Messiah's work is not yet completed. This fact should have allowed them to show more courage when facing situations that bring fear and anxiety. This will not be the last time that Jesus will have to chastise them for a lack of faith (cf. Mark 7:18; 8:17-21). [See question #1, page 256.]

41. And they feared exceedingly, and said one to another, What manner of man is this, that even the wind and the sea obey him?

The disciples had brought their concern about the storm to Jesus, apparently with some kind of hazy idea that He could "do something" (v. 38). But now that Jesus has indeed done something, the disciples *feared exceedingly*. This kind of fear can include the idea of being in awe, for Jesus has just displayed awe-inspiring power. But perhaps their fear is more than that because they have expressed doubt before One who is obviously able to control *the wind and the sea*. [See question #2, page 256.]

So far Mark has selected certain events in the ministry of Jesus that prove that Jesus is the Son of God (1:1) and that He has a mission to perform (1:15). Jesus' calming of the stormy sea makes both points. The next incident does the same.

II. Jesus Casts Out Demons (Mark 5:2-13a)

This incident takes place after Jesus and the disciples have crossed from the western to the eastern shore of the Sea of Galilee (5:1). The western side of this lake is mainly populated by Jews. On the eastern side is the Decapolis ("ten cities"), which is primarily a Gentile area. Mark indicates the location is "the country of the Gadarenes" (5:1), but that designation is too broad for us to know exactly where the boat landed. Some ancient manuscripts give the name as the "Gerasenes," and Matthew's account calls it "the country of the Gergesenes" (Matthew 8:28). Gerasa (or Gergesa) is located some thirty-five miles from the southeast shore of the Sea of Galilee, but this city apparently owned territory that joined the sea. In this area can be seen a fairly steep slope within forty yards of the water's edge.

A. Degradation (vv. 2-5)

2. And when he was come out of the ship, immediately there met him out of the tombs a man with an unclean spirit.

A couple of miles from the site of a steep slope on the southeastern side of the Sea of Galilee is

an area with cavern *tombs*, and this *man* lives among these tombs (v. 3). Only a social outcast would live this way (cf. Isaiah 65:1-7). The man has seen (even in the darkness) the boat moving in his direction (v. 6, below). (Matthew 8:28 notes that there actually were two demon-possessed men, so Mark is likely mentioning only the most prominent or the most vocal of these.) [See question #3, page 256.]

LED BY WHAT KIND OF SPIRIT?

A small, persecuted Christian sect living in semi-exile in central Russia is known as the Fyodorovtsy. They believe Christ returned in the form of a Russian peasant named Fyodor Rybalkin sometime after World War I. According to some reports, Rybalkin went about teaching and performing miracles. Other reports say that he was sent to an asylum for the insane, or that he was arrested by the Communists. But whatever happened to him, the Fyodorovtsy believe he will soon resume his Second Coming and save them from their persecution.

In keeping with Jesus' words that in the kingdom of Heaven there is no marriage, the sect's young people must make a spiritual commitment to be celibate all their lives. The sect has another strange belief: that God forbids them to make proselytes or evangelize. Thus, in their exile from the world, "the Fyodorovtsy" have declined in number from several thousand in the 1920s to only sixty today.

Like the Fyodorovtsy, the demon-possessed man in our text lived in exile. His strange behavior (which was also "spiritual" in its origins) caused others to force him away from them. Without doubting the sincerity of any who claim to follow Christ, we still must observe that various kinds of spirits make people do strange things—and not all of those spirits are the *Holy Spirit*.   —C. R. B.

3, 4. Who had his dwelling among the tombs; and no man could bind him, no, not with chains: because that he had been often bound with fetters and chains, and the chains had been plucked asunder by him, and the fetters broken in pieces: neither could any man tame him.

This man does not suffer from a "mental illness," as some have alleged. This is supernatural demon possession. Because of his wild behavior, the people in the region naturally have looked for ways to control him. Apparently he has been driven away from society because efforts to control him with *chains* and leg irons have failed. His strength, most likely enhanced in a supernatural way by the forces of Satan, has made him impossible to subdue. Such an existence is degrading and is a mockery of the noble image of humanity that God intended in His creation of people.

5. And always, night and day, he was in the mountains, and in the tombs, crying, and cutting himself with stones.

The man is isolated from society and apparently in great torment. With no family or friends to look after him, he spends his time in fearful shrieking among *the tombs*. The likelihood is that no one has enough courage to get close to him. His demonic condition makes every day a misery. Some associate his custom of *cutting himself with stones* with demonic worship (cf. 1 Kings 18:28). Others see it as erratic behavior by one whose mind is tormented beyond rational thought. [See question #4, page 256.]

B. Dialogue (vv. 6-12)

6. But when he saw Jesus afar off, he ran and worshipped him.

The fact that the man *worshipped* Jesus should not be taken to mean that he honors Jesus as the Son of God. The term for *worship* in this verse basically refers to the act of bowing before another. It is used of worshiping God or idols, of doing obeisance before a king, or even welcoming an honored guest.

The respect the demon shows is born of fear. Mark's Gospel already has shown how the demons are inclined to acknowledge the truth of who Jesus is (cf. 1:24 from lesson 1). In 3:11 we read that unclean spirits who saw Jesus "fell down before him." The homage he pays to Jesus in this verse and the words he shrieks in the next certainly lead to this conclusion.

7. And cried with a loud voice, and said, What have I to do with thee, Jesus, thou Son of the most high God? I adjure thee by God, that thou torment me not.

The demon obviously is controlling the words of the man who comes to Jesus. The question about *what* Jesus has *to do with* him is another way of begging Jesus to leave him alone. Interestingly, the question the disciples asked in Mark 4:41 is correctly answered here by the demon! Although it is not true "worship," the demon's confession that Jesus is the *Son of the most high God* is the highest tribute.

Even so, the demon's presumptuous posturing is evident. Claiming to know the identity of Jesus and then shouting His name is considered a means for gaining some control over an adversary (see discussion on page 238). Apparently the demon understands that God's judgment is coming on all unclean spirits, a sentiment reflected in the words of demons elsewhere in the Gospels (e.g., Mark 1:24). The punishment of which this demon speaks is that of the eternal *torment* that

Who Is Jesus?

Lesson	He is	Text from Mark's Gospel
1	Son of God	1:9-26
2	Friend of Sinners	2:3-17
3	Master Over Wind and Sea	4:36-41; 5:2-13
4	Prophet	6:1-13
5	Authority on the Law	7:1-15
6	Messiah	11:1-9, 15-18
7	Passover Lamb	14:12-25
8	Suffering Servant	15:21-25, 33-37; 16:1-8
9	Victor Over Death	5:22-36, 41, 42
10	Savior for All Nations	7:24-37
11	The Christ	8:27-36; 9:2-8
12	Master Over Demons	9:14-29
13	King	10:35-52

Visual for lessons 3 and 11

Display this chart as you begin the lesson. It will be useful for this and other lessons in the quarter.

stands waiting at the final judgment (cf. Matthew 25:41; 2 Peter 2:4; Jude 6; Revelation 20:10). The spirit that torments the man now fears torment himself. [See question #5, page 256.]

8. For he said unto him, Come out of the man, thou unclean spirit.

This verse explains why the demon is so agitated: the bold words shouted by the demon (v. 7) came as a result of Jesus' command that he leave the man. The word *for* ("because") makes clear the cause-and-effect relationship of these words of Jesus and the demon. So mighty is the power of Jesus' position as the Son of God that the command for the demon to leave the man sends this *spirit* into a frenzy of trying to bargain for his survival.

9. And he asked him, What is thy name? And he answered, saying, My name is Legion: for we are many.

This is the first indication of the number of demons involved. The name *Legion* has reference to a Roman military force of six thousand soldiers—though the word was also used of any very large, often unspecific, number. The words of the demon may mean that this demon is speaking for thousands of other demons who are also opposed to God (cf. 1:24), or it may well mean the man is possessed by a very large number of demons.

Some take the Bible's references to demon possession as evidence that the first century was dominated by superstition and ignorance. To them, the idea of demon possession is a relic of an unscientific culture. But the New Testament writers are certainly able to speak about illness without referring to demons as the cause (cf. John 9:1-3; Philippians 2:26, 27). In fact, it distinguishes certain illnesses from demon possession in Matthew 4:23, 24.

Thus the people who hear Jesus teach do not necessarily conclude that every sickness is to be explained by demon possession. The modern scientific method cannot be used to prove or disprove the spiritual realm because these are issues that are established by the evidence of history, and not by repeatable experiments in the laboratory.

What about demon possession today? If it was possible in the day of Jesus, then it cannot be ruled out as a possibility today. We would be foolish to try to explain every abnormality in life as a case of demon possession, but we would also be foolish to think that the devil of the Bible has ceased all of his activities!

10. And he besought him much that he would not send them away out of the country.

Previously Jesus had met and conquered a demon in a Jewish man in the synagogue (Mark 1:25, 26). Now Jesus must deal with not just one demon, but a legion of them—and from a wild-eyed Gentile living in the cavern tombs at that! The request that they not be sent *out of* the area may be a subtle way of asking that they not be thrown into their place of eternal punishment (Luke 8:31; Revelation 20:1-3).

11. Now there was there nigh unto the mountains a great herd of swine feeding.

For Jews, *swine* are just as unclean as tombs and evil spirits (see Leviticus 11:7, 8; Deuteronomy 14:8; Isaiah 65:4; 66:17). The presence of a *herd* of pigs in this location is another indication that Jesus is visiting a Gentile area.

12. And all the devils besought him, saying, Send us into the swine, that we may enter into them.

Since the demons recognize that they are powerless before Jesus, they ask for a lesser punishment. Rather than being thrown into eternal torment, could they not be thrown into (or among) the herd of pigs? With this request the demons perhaps hope also to create antagonism against Jesus—something we see in verse 17. In any case, they have no alternative but to do whatever the Son of God orders.

C. Deliverance (v. 13a)

13a. And forthwith Jesus gave them leave.

Jesus' reason for permitting the demons to enter the herd of pigs is not easy to determine. Their action among the pigs is certainly dramatic (see v. 13b). Perhaps the drowning of the pigs makes clear to the man who was possessed not only the reality of demon possession, but also the power of the One who can throw them out. The need to verify the authority of Jesus is probably the best explanation for His decision.

We should also note, however, that Jesus does not appear eager to deal out the ultimate punishment that even the demons know is coming. The final punishment of the demonic powers seems to be set for a specific time (cf. Revelation 20:10).

This incident also reveals that human opposition to Jesus doesn't come from just His fellow Jews. As the rest of the account unfolds (vv. 13b-17, not in our text today), the inhabitants of the area will show that they value pigs over people.

Conclusion
A. A Life of Authority and Power

Our faith is encouraged by the knowledge that Jesus as the Son of God has authority over every danger of life that we will face. Whether it is the storms of life that come suddenly to frighten us into doubting, or our worst fears rising to confront us about unseen spiritual powers—Jesus has the authority and power to keep us safe.

The power of Jesus is the best evidence of His authority. Not only did He teach with authority different from the scribes (Mark 1:22), but when He spoke miraculous things happened. He spoke to the furious sea, and the waves fell silent. He commanded demons, and they instantly abandoned their operations. With this kind of authority and power, how wonderful to have Jesus as our Creator, Redeemer, and King!

B. Prayer

Oh, Lord, may we remember today that with Jesus as our Creator, Redeemer, and King, we never have to fear our enemies, even if they are more powerful than we are. Through Jesus we pray, amen.

C. Thought to Remember

"Greater is he that is in you, than he that is in the world" (1 John 4:4).

Learning by Doing

This page contains an alternative lesson plan emphasizing learning activities.
Classes desiring such student involvement will find these suggestions helpful.

Learning Goals

After participating in this lesson, each student will be able to:

1. Recall the basic facts of Jesus' calming the storm and casting the demons out of the Gadarene demoniac.

2. Tell how these events provide evidence that Jesus is the Son of God.

3. Express a confidence that Jesus will help him or her to deal with a situation that previously has caused fear.

Into the Lesson

As your students arrive, have the chairs arranged in groups of four. On each chair should be a half-sheet of letter-size paper on which are drawn four squares in a grid pattern. Outside the grid on the left side write "High Anxiety" beside the upper boxes, "Low Anxiety" beside the lower. Below the left boxes write "Can't Control"; below the right boxes "Can Control."

Ask the students to list in the appropriate quadrants several things that could cause anxiety in their lives, such as family, teens, world events, finances, work, marriage, stock market, illness, moving, bills, terrorism, death of a loved one. For instance, finances might fit the "High Anxiety/Can Control" quadrant. A parent of a "prodigal" child might list teens in the "High Anxiety/Can't Control" quadrant. After about three minutes have volunteers tell some of the anxieties they listed and which quadrants they put them in.

Make the transition to the text saying, "Each of us wrote several anxieties we are facing. Our lesson features a time when the disciples were afraid and Jesus calmed their fears. Listen for ways Jesus calms our fears."

Into the Word

Prior to class, recruit a student to prepare a short presentation on the purpose of Mark's Gospel with a chart showing Mark's proofs of Jesus being God's Son and the opposition He faced. Explain our text's place in the book.

After the presentation, divide your class into at least two groups.

Group One will develop a dramatic presentation of Mark 4:36-41 with sound effects and visual effects, as far as the classroom allows. Provide plenty of paper and broad-tip markers for creative scenery. Remind participants that

they have only ten to fifteen minutes to make their preparations.

Group Two will develop an interview of the demon-possessed man, based on Mark 5:1-20. The group should think of ways to communicate clearly the events and the emotion of the passage. The interview can be taped (audio or video) and replayed for the class, or a live interview can be presented. This group will have ten to fifteen minutes to plan and prepare the presentation.

If your class is larger, assign these activities to the extra groups. Group One will need thirteen people; Group Two will need six. If you have extra groups, be sure to have enough materials and a recorder. Choose a representative for each group.

After the presentation ask, "What aspects of these two events show Jesus to be in control?" *(You are looking for such answers as: Jesus rebukes the wind and sea, and they become calm [4:38, 39]; Jesus speaks to the unclean spirit, and the demon-possessed man is set free [5:8].)*

Say, "What about these texts shows Jesus to be God's Son?" Students should respond with answers based on 4:41 and 5:15. You may want to make clarifying comments based on the commentary and your own study.

Into Life

Choose one or more of the following activities to help your students apply this lesson.

Option 1: Personal Testimony. Ask each learner to prepare a two-minute testimony on the topic, "How Jesus helps me deal with fear." Appropriate questions to be answered by the testimony are these: How do you know Jesus is more powerful than your fears? What ways have you tried to answer your fears without Christ? What differences has Jesus made in your life?

Option 2: Reflection on Anxieties. Refer students back to the opening activity. Have each student take his or her grid and briefly discuss one or two more areas with a neighbor. Ask each student to turn to 1 Peter 5:7 (or have it printed for the students). Ask each pair to pray together, asking God to take away the anxiety for things that can't be controlled, wisdom to discern high and low anxieties, help in finding solutions, and peace in situations that can be controlled. As a final indication of surrender, students should write "1 Peter 5:7" across their grids.

Let's Talk It Over

The questions on this page are designed to promote discussion of the lesson by the class and to encourage application of the lesson Scriptures. The answers provided are only discussion starters. Let your class talk it over from there.

1. How does Jesus' authority over nature and circumstances affect the way we view dangerous or fear-filled situations?

In today's world, we face dangerous situations on a daily basis: the threat of a natural disaster, the danger of operating a vehicle at high speeds, the liabilities associated with raising a teenager, the fragility of the stock market, the cholesterol levels in just about everything we eat. It is always good to exercise due caution, but we must not be ruled by our fears. As Christians we serve a Savior who has authority and sovereignty over every situation we face, dangerous or otherwise. Jesus demonstrates in Mark 4 that there really is no situation that He is unable to control, and that sometimes He allows us to experience the storm. We are told many times in Scripture to be careful, but over three hundred times we are told not to be afraid. Even in situations requiring caution, we know that Christ has it all under control.

2. What is the problem with a person who claims to be a Christian, yet is ruled by his or her fears? What can other believers do to help such a one to be more of a person of faith?

As human beings, it is natural for us to fear something—usually, numerous things. Yet a recurring message from God to man throughout the Bible is "Fear not," or "Do not be afraid." Such a response to God is based on a faith that supersedes our senses, our logic, and our experiences. As Christians, one of our biggest journeys of faith will be to leave behind that place where we are paralyzed by fear to go forward courageously into the face of our most dreaded storms. Sometimes what we need is the reassurance of another who has been through a similar storm and found Jesus faithful. This kind of counsel is what we can offer timid believers.

3. Compare and contrast the man in the tombs with Levi (Mark 2). What does Jesus' willingness and ability to deal with these people tell us about Him?

Levi was a reasonable, employed, civilized, ambitious Galilean who became a voluntary follower of Jesus. On "the other side" of the Sea of Galilee Jesus found a deranged, unemployed, uncivilized, useless Gentile man possessed against his will by an evil spirit. Though very different, they have in common the fact that respectable Jewish society would have considered them both outcasts. One was a publican—a collaborator with the enemy and a traitor to his country. The other was a Gentile, and not only that but obviously under the control of Satan. But Jesus was no "respecter of persons." He came to seek and save the lost—all the lost. In our culture, we must be sure that our churches don't "cater" to one type of person or problem. The power of Jesus is seen in His ability to transform people from every kind of lifestyle, and then to utilize their gifts in a diverse body made up of different gifts, temperaments, and backgrounds.

4. Today there are many people whose condition is as pitiable as that of the demon-possessed man. They are not necessarily possessed, but they may be homeless, mentally ill, wracked by guilt, physically disabled, or otherwise affected. What is our church doing to minister to such people, who dwell on the fringe of polite society? What more can we do?

Talk about specific programs (regular or occasional) your church provides for the most desperate of society. Do you have any means of ministering to homeless people? Do you provide them meals, a place to sleep, help in looking for employment? Do you have a counseling ministry or some outlet to which to refer those in need of such a service? How can your class members be more directly involved in order to share the personal touch Jesus had?

5. The demons were afraid of being sent to their eternal torment (i.e., Hell). How much do we talk about Hell today? Is it enough, too much, or too little? What is the value of preaching and teaching about Hell?

People need to know that Hell is real and that all who do not accept God's gracious offer of salvation in Jesus Christ will spend eternity there. Of course, we should not use images of Hell in such a frightening manner as to manipulate people, but we do no one any favor by minimizing Hell's reality. Along with our warnings of Hell, of course, we must place the good news that no one needs to go there. Jesus has paid the price so that we can spend eternity in His presence. Only with these two truths in balance do we tell the whole story.

Rejection and Mission

DEVOTIONAL READING: John 12:44-50.

BACKGROUND SCRIPTURE: Mark 6:1-13.

PRINTED TEXT: Mark 6:1-13.

Mark 6:1-13

1 And he went out from thence, and came into his own country; and his disciples follow him.

2 And when the sabbath day was come, he began to teach in the synagogue: and many hearing him were astonished, saying, From whence hath this man these things? and what wisdom is this which is given unto him, that even such mighty works are wrought by his hands?

3 Is not this the carpenter, the son of Mary, the brother of James, and Joses, and of Judas, and Simon? and are not his sisters here with us? And they were offended at him.

4 But Jesus said unto them, A prophet is not without honor, but in his own country, and among his own kin, and in his own house.

5 And he could there do no mighty work, save that he laid his hands upon a few sick folk, and healed them.

6 And he marveled because of their unbelief. And he went round about the villages, teaching.

7 And he called unto him the twelve, and began to send them forth by two and two; and gave them power over unclean spirits;

8 And commanded them that they should take nothing for their journey, save a staff only; no scrip, no bread, no money in their purse:

9 But be shod with sandals; and not put on two coats.

10 And he said unto them, In what place soever ye enter into a house, there abide till ye depart from that place.

11 And whosoever shall not receive you, nor hear you, when ye depart thence, shake off the dust under your feet for a testimony against them. Verily I say unto you, It shall be more tolerable for Sodom and Gomorrah in the day of judgment, than for that city.

12 And they went out, and preached that men should repent.

13 And they cast out many devils, and anointed with oil many that were sick, and healed them.

GOLDEN TEXT: Jesus said unto them, A prophet is not without honor, but in his own country, and among his own kin, and in his own house.—Mark 6:4.

Jesus: God's Power in Action
Unit 1: Jesus' Early Ministry
(Lessons 1-5)

Lesson Aims

After participating in this lesson, each student will be able to:

1. Tell how Jesus was rejected at Nazareth and how He responded with an expansion of ministry by sending out the Twelve to preach.

2. Compare the rejection of Jesus with the rejection of His messengers today.

3. Suggest at least one specific way to get involved in the effort to preach the gospel at home or around the world.

Lesson Outline

INTRODUCTION
    A. "I Agree With Jesus"
    B. Lesson Background
I. JESUS PREACHES IN HIS HOMETOWN (Mark 6:1-6)
    A. Homecoming (vv. 1, 2)
    B. Rejection (vv. 3, 4)
    C. Unbelief (vv. 5, 6)
    Acknowledging the Power of God
II. JESUS SENDS THE TWELVE TO PREACH (Mark 6:7-13)
    A. A Powerful Mission (v. 7)
    God and Culture
    B. An Urgent Mission (vv. 8-12)
    C. A Preaching Mission (v. 13)
CONCLUSION
    A. Family Rejection
    B. Prayer
    C. Thought to Remember

Introduction

A. "I Agree With Jesus"

In May of 2000, a controversy broke out at a high school in the Columbus, Ohio, suburb of Upper Arlington. Many of the students, and for a while some of the teachers, began wearing bright yellow T-shirts emblazoned with the words, "I agree with Justin." The shirts expressed support for Justin Rule, one of the high school's very outspoken Christians, who had taken a public position regarding his faith. When the *Columbus Dispatch* interviewed some of the seniors about the story, one student expressed concern that too much of the focus would be directed toward Justin. Other students, however, considered wearing the T-shirts a good witnessing tool. One of them said putting "Jesus" in the slogan would have created a "bigger problem" for some people. She called the slogan "a more subtle way of exploring his beliefs."

In today's lesson Jesus demonstrates that sometimes the most difficult place to share one's faith is in the company of our friends and neighbors. Those who know us best are often those who least want to hear our testimony. But the example of Jesus challenges us to make God's message of truth available to every person who will listen to the gospel.

B. Lesson Background

Mark's Gospel shows how Jesus was treated badly by His family and hometown (Mark 6:1-5). But Jesus took no time for self-pity. He moved on to other towns and villages to preach the good news (6:6). Then He prepared His disciples to begin a broader ministry to take in the whole region in an extended preaching tour (6:7-13).

In our previous lessons in Mark we have noted that Jesus' own works prove that He is the Son of God. The parables of Mark 4 tell how God's kingdom was being ushered in by Jesus. The powerful miracles of Jesus' calming the storm, casting out demons, healing the sick, and raising the dead to life all testify to the fact that this Jesus must be God's Son (4:35–5:43). Bracketing this material are statements regarding Jesus' disciples and His family. In Mark 3:13-19, Jesus chose twelve followers who would become like family to Him (cf. 3:31-34), and in 6:1-6 Jesus comments on the rejection He faced by His own hometown. But for all of the evidence that Jesus is God's Son, He still experienced hostility. Those who wanted to destroy Him were finding His teaching objectionable (cf. 3:20-30).

Geographically, the focus of Jesus' ministry to this point in Mark's Gospel has been Galilee. Many of the incidents reported take place in Capernaum, on the northwest shore of the Sea of Galilee. But Jesus has also extended His ministry to Gentiles, as seen in last week's lesson. In Mark 6, the reader is again back in Galilee (cf. 5:21), this time at Nazareth, Jesus' hometown. The time is late in the second or early in the third year of Jesus' three-and-a-half year ministry.

I. Jesus Preaches in His Hometown (Mark 6:1-6)

One might think that returning to His hometown will provide some grand opportunities for Jesus. He can be welcomed back by people who knew Him from childhood. But His old friends from Nazareth are not ready for His message.

A. Homecoming (vv. 1, 2)

1. And he went out from thence, and came into his own country; and his disciples follow him.

The reference to Jesus' departure can be traced back to His raising of Jairus's daughter (reported in Mark 5:21-43), an event that probably took place in Capernaum. Now it is time for Jesus and *his disciples* to leave, so He travels twenty miles southwest, walking up into the hills to Nazareth. The journey takes about a day, and we can only imagine the teaching opportunities presented by this time together on the road.

2. And when the sabbath day was come, he began to teach in the synagogue: and many hearing him were astonished, saying, From whence hath this man these things? and what wisdom is this which is given unto him, that even such mighty works are wrought by his hands?

Mark alerts the reader to the purpose of Jesus' journey to Nazareth: He has come *to teach*. He is not there merely for a personal visit. His concern is for the kingdom of God to be preached and for His disciples to receive the kind of preparation needed to carry this work throughout Galilee.

The Jewish *sabbath day* is Saturday, the seventh day of the week. Jesus remains faithful in His Sabbath Day attendance at *the synagogue*. The custom of the synagogue is to invite guest rabbis to teach the lesson of the day (cf. Mark 1:21, 22; Luke 4:16). Jesus is ready when His opportunity comes. Whether these people had heard Jesus teach before is impossible to know. His fame already has spread far and wide in Galilee (1:28). At any rate they are *astonished* at what they hear.

The amazement of Jesus' audiences is a major theme in Mark's Gospel (cf. 1:22, 27; 2:12; 5:20, 42; 7:37; 11:18; 12:17). These crowds recognize in His teaching a stunning depth of *wisdom*, but they cannot determine the source of this wisdom. They know about the *mighty works* that Jesus has performed, and they wonder where such power and wisdom have come *from*. Their two options are either God or Satan. They are trying to decide between the two (cf. Mark 3:22).

B. Rejection (vv. 3, 4)

3. Is not this the carpenter, the son of Mary, the brother of James, and Joses, and of Judas, and Simon? and are not his sisters here with us? And they were offended at him.

The questions now become more personal. The audience not only expresses difficulty with the origin of Jesus' teaching, but it is also reluctant to take Him seriously.

Though elsewhere Jesus is called the "carpenter's son" (Matthew 13:55), here the occupation is connected with Jesus Himself. A *carpenter* can be a skilled mason or smith, as well as a worker with wood. The term also applies to those who work in building construction, as well as with smaller tools. The questioners seem to express an opinion that Jesus, as a worker with His hands, is in no better position than they to understand the mysteries of God.

Usually, a Jewish man is described in relation to his father, not his mother. Some scholars see the phrase *the son of Mary*, then, as hinting at some scandal regarding Jesus' birth. Perhaps there are some here who remember Joseph's original intention to divorce Mary when her pregnancy became known (Matthew 1:18, 19), and thus they know Jesus is Mary's son but not Joseph's. Other students, however, believe the phrase merely indicates that Joseph has already died.

From these questions it is clear that Jesus will not receive honor as the Son of God, or even as a great prophet, in Nazareth. As the crowd begins asking about Jesus' brothers and *sisters*, it is clear that the purpose of the questions is to argue that Jesus is a "commoner." These friends and neighbors know Jesus' family, His occupation, and His ordinary circumstances. They are *offended at Him* in that they reject His teaching. [See question #1, page 264.]

4. But Jesus said unto them, A prophet is not without honor, but in his own country, and among his own kin, and in his own house.

Jesus is aware of the sentiments in Nazareth, and He puts their attitude into perspective by quoting a familiar proverb (cf. Matthew 13:57; Luke 4:24; John 4:44). Jesus' reference to *his own house* imply that He is not believed even among His own mother, brothers, and sisters (cf. Mark 3:21, 31, 32).

Visual for
lesson 4

Post this visual as you discuss verse 4. Note how rejection did not keep Jesus from His mission.

How to Say It

CAPERNAUM. Kuh-*per*-nay-um.
DEUTERONOMY. Due-ter-*ahn*-uh-me.
EZEKIEL. Ee-*zeek*-ee-ul or Ee-*zeek*-yul.
GALILEE. *Gal*-uh-lee.
GENTILES. *Jen*-tyles.
GOMORRAH. Guh-*more*-uh.
JAIRUS. *Jye*-rus or *Jay*-ih-rus.
JOSES. *Jo*-sez.
NAZARETH. *Naz*-uh-reth.
SHEMA (Hebrew). sheh-*ma*.
SYNAGOGUE. *sin*-uh-gog.

C. Unbelief (vv. 5, 6)

5. And he could there do no mighty work, save that he laid his hands upon a few sick folk, and healed them.

Mark's summary of the situation in Nazareth includes a negative element about the effectiveness of Jesus' *work* there. Their lack of faith creates an environment in which Jesus refuses to perform the kind of miraculous deeds that He has done elsewhere, such as in Capernaum (cf. Mark 1:23-28, 32-34). Nevertheless, He demonstrates that the lack of miracles is not due to His own weakness, since He does heal *a few sick* people. No doubt these few people perceive no limitations to His power. [See question #2, page 264.]

The mention of the laying on of *hands* is also prominent in the healings recorded in Mark's Gospel (5:23; 7:32; 8:22, 25). This action by Jesus seems to set Him apart from Jewish healers, who are not inclined to touch people with any disease.

6. And he marveled because of their unbelief. And he went round about the villages, teaching.

Thus far in Mark's Gospel it is always the crowd that is amazed at Jesus (cf. 1:22, 27; 2:12; 5:42). But now it is Jesus' turn to be amazed. In the case of these friends and neighbors from Nazareth, their stubborn refusal to see the truth is amazing indeed.

But Jesus does not permit this disappointment to keep Him from His work. He continues traveling to *villages* to teach the gospel. Such a response to the disappointment of kingdom work should inspire modern believers not to give up when our witness is rejected.

ACKNOWLEDGING THE POWER OF GOD

Alcoholics Anonymous (or "AA" as it is commonly known) has helped millions of people to overcome alcoholic addiction. A key feature of its program (and undoubtedly its most important) is its insistence that the person seeking recovery turn life over to a "Higher Power." While AA tries to broaden its appeal by saying the higher power can be anything you want it to be—even AA itself—most alcoholics who have gone through the program acknowledge that power to be God.

Non-believers, however, have turned to Secular Organizations for Sobriety, which denies the need for a spiritual component to recovery from alcoholism. Most of us will agree that this dislike for acknowledging God's reign over us is symptomatic of many of the problems our culture faces. Many people find it hard to admit the fact of God's presence in life.

It was much the same in Nazareth when Jesus returned to the village in which He had grown up. The residents could not deny the mighty works He had done elsewhere, but they couldn't bring themselves to admit that He was the Son of God. Hadn't they known Him since He was a child? Their refusal to acknowledge the presence of God in their midst had tragic results: "He could there do no mighty work" (Mark 6:5) because of their lack of faith. None of us should be surprised if a lack of faith prevents God from doing great things in our lives.   —C. R. B.

II. Jesus Sends the Twelve to Preach (Mark 6:7-13)

The ministry of Jesus now has reached a point for a broader proclamation of the good news. Mark's Gospel turns its attention to the way this ministry expands throughout Galilee and beyond its borders (6:7-13, 30–8:13), to the rising pressure from political authorities (6:14-29), and to the blindness of the disciples regarding the person and mission of Jesus (6:52; 8:14-21, 32).

A. A Powerful Mission (v. 7)

7. And he called unto him the twelve, and began to send them forth by two and two; and gave them power over unclean spirits;

After all of the preparation by Jesus of the disciples, it is now time for them to begin the process of calling Israel back to God. He has promised them that He would make them "fishers of men" (Mark 1:17), and they have been with Him both in public and in private (cf. 3:7, 13; 4:10). They have witnessed His power at work in healings and in miracles of nature. From the very first, Jesus has prepared for this day (3:14, 15). The *power* that Jesus already has exercised over demons He now gives to His disciples (cf. 1:25, 39; 5:13). They serve in this capacity under His authority. [See question #3, page 264.]

The significance of the number *twelve* should not be overlooked. Jesus' mission involves preaching the kingdom to the lost sheep of Israel (Matthew 15:24). His ministry involves the restoration of Israel (Acts 1:6, 7). It is natural, then, that this ministry make use of twelve disciples, just as Moses' ministry dealt with Israel's twelve tribes. The fact that they go *two by two* is a reflection of the Jewish priority for truthful witnesses (cf. Deuteronomy 17:6; 19:15; Matthew 18:16; Hebrews 10:28). The practice is still a good one for those church leaders who want to avoid the risks that can occur when one person travels alone in a ministry of visitation.

GOD AND CULTURE

Numerology has long fascinated the human mind. Ancient astrologers combined this fascination and the desire to control one's destiny with their readings of the stars and planets to offer advice that bordered on the fantastic. A trip to any New Age bookstore or a search of the Internet for "numerology" sites will prove that the ancient fascination is still very much alive.

In the middle of all of this is the Bible. Ancient Hebrews also paid attention to the significance of certain numbers. For example, the number *one* was symbolic of God as stated in the *shema*: "Hear, O Israel: The Lord our God is one Lord" (Deuteronomy 6:4). *Twelve* was the number of the sons of Jacob, and thus of the tribes of Israel. We should note that the Bible's use of numbers lacks the trust in the magical qualities of numbers found in other ancient cultures as well as in modern superstitions.

Nevertheless, it would have been significant to the Jewish mind that Jesus sent out the twelve disciples to preach the gospel of the kingdom to Israel, and that He sent them out two-by-two, as the law required for verification of the testimony of witnesses. It is an example of the fact that God, who stands above all human culture, desires that we present His message of salvation in ways that speak to each culture so that all may come to know Him.   —C. R. B.

B. An Urgent Mission (vv. 8-12)

8. And commanded them that they should take nothing for their journey, save a staff only; no scrip, no bread, no money in their purse.

The prohibition of extra provisions makes the point that this preaching tour is urgent because time is short. *Scrip* can describe a bag for money or perhaps the more general idea of a "knapsack." In traveling so lightly the disciples will be demonstrating that they trust in God to provide hospitality from those who believed the good news. It will also set them apart from traveling preachers of the day who move about with *bread* and a bag for collecting *money*.

Matthew 10:9, 10 says that the disciples are not to "provide" (or "procure") *a staff* for this

tour. At first this prohibition seems curious since the verse before us says that they are to *take a staff*. But that verb *provide* in Matthew's account may indicate that the disciples already have at least one walking stick per team, and they are forbidden from getting any more. The walking stick that each team already has is the one Mark's account allows them to take along.

9. But be shod with sandals; and not put on two coats.

The extra coat would be a benefit, because sleeping outside on chilly Galilean nights is easier for travelers if they can use a coat as a blanket. Matthew 10:10 forbids *sandals,* and the difference between the two accounts may be explained in the same way as that of the staff (v. 8, above). That is, they were not to take along an extra pair of sandals.

10. And he said unto them, In what place soever ye enter into a house, there abide till ye depart from that place.

These directions are intended to keep the disciples from moving from *house* to house after arriving at a village. They are to exemplify gratitude by accepting the first offer of hospitality that comes to them, and then remaining in that house even if some better offer comes along. This strategy will prevent needless hard feelings against the mission and keep the disciples focused on the reason they are in any particular village in the first place. [See question #4, page 264.]

11. And whosoever shall not receive you, nor hear you, when ye depart thence, shake off the dust under your feet for a testimony against them. Verily I say unto you, It shall be more tolerable for Sodom and Gomorrah in the day of judgment, than for that city.

Jesus anticipates that the disciples will face rejection. After all, if the Son of God has been

Home Daily Bible Readings

Monday, Mar. 17—A Prophet Without Honor (Mark 6:1-6)

Tuesday, Mar. 18—People Question Jesus as Messiah (John 7:37-44)

Wednesday, Mar. 19—No Prophet Comes From Galilee (John 7:45-52)

Thursday, Mar. 20—The Kingdom of Heaven Is Near (Matthew 10:5-15)

Friday, Mar. 21—Be Wise Serpents, Innocent Doves (Matthew 10:16-26)

Saturday, Mar. 22—Whoever Welcomes You (Matthew 10:37-42)

Sunday, Mar. 23—Jesus Sends Out the Twelve (Mark 6:7-13)

rejected, why would the disciples expect anything less than rejection? The theme of rejection already has grown more prominent in Mark's Gospel. Beginning with the objections of the scribes about Jesus' teaching about divine forgiveness (2:6, 7), the tension has been increasing, even reaching to the point where enemies are looking for ways to destroy Jesus (3:6), and claiming that He is allied with Satan (3:22). He has been rejected even in His own hometown of Nazareth (6:1-6).

When rejection comes, Jesus encourages the disciples to *shake the dust* from themselves. This practice seems to be connected with the Jewish custom of shaking dust that had gathered on their clothing when they returned to the land of Israel from Gentile areas (cf. Acts 13:51; 18:5, 6). The Jews saw themselves as removing contaminated, pagan dust. Jesus turns this custom around, making Jewish dust the contaminant!

Since rejection of the Son of God is equal to the rejection of God, those who refuse to hear the news of the kingdom of God will be placing themselves under the judgment of God. Perhaps the greatest examples of cities that knew firsthand about the judgment of God were *Sodom and Gomorrah* (Genesis 19:23-29). Jesus uses them for comparison of the divine judgment that will fall upon cities that will reject the message the disciples are bringing. The Old Testament uses those two cities as the proverbial "bad example" more than a dozen times. In the New Testament, see Romans 9:29; 2 Peter 2:6; Jude 7; and Revelation 11:8.

(The reference to Sodom and Gomorrah in this verse does not appear in some of the Greek manuscripts discovered since the time the *King James Version* was translated. Thus, it is not included in many of the modern translations. The reference does appear, however, in the parallel account of Matthew 10:15, so it seems evident that Jesus did, indeed, make reference to God's judgment against these cities.)

12. And they went out, and preached that men should repent.

At this point Mark summarizes the ministry carried out by the disciples. This message of repentance was the message of John the Baptist (1:4) and of Jesus Himself (1:15). The preaching of the disciples is an extension of the preaching of Jesus. [See question #5, page 264.]

The idea of repentance involves turning from sin to God. It is a message that was emphasized many times by the prophets of the Old Testament who called Israel back to the Lord (e.g., Ezekiel 14:6; 18:30). Jesus makes the matter of repentance the central theme of His preaching of God's kingdom.

C. A Preaching Mission (v. 13)

13. And they cast out many devils, and anointed with oil many that were sick, and healed them.

As Jesus ministers freely, so do His disciples. Repentance is the first element of their ministry (v. 12), and the exorcism of *devils* is the second. (Mark uses *unclean spirits* and *demons* interchangeably with *devils*.) Jesus has given them power to accomplish these exorcisms (6:7), and they use that power as needed. The third element of the disciples' ministry is healing of the *sick*. The New Testament connects *oil* with healing in Luke 10:34 and James 5:14. In Jesus' day, oil is considered to have medicinal value.

Today, every believer who wants to serve Christ can help to guarantee that the good news is heard in every city and town. Efforts of the church to witness in our communities always need willing believers. Missionary efforts around the globe need enthusiastic believers who hear the command of Jesus to take the good news to every village. As Jesus emphasized to the disciples, we cannot expect that everyone will respond positively. Even so, our duty is to preach and teach. God will give the harvest (1 Corinthians 3:6).

Conclusion

A. Family Rejection

Mark's Gospel presents what we may consider the ultimate rejection of Jesus. To think that our own family—our spouse, our parents, our children—would turn their backs on us is a thought that we find too excruciating to bear.

But for Jesus the mission was too important to let it be stalled. Jesus counted the disciples as His new family (Mark 3:35). They were the ones who would enter into this mission with Him. Their witness would make it possible for the kingdom of God to claim believers from every village. Jesus not only continued the mission in the face of rejection, He expanded it by including twelve missionaries in the effort. All of this should remind us how dedicated Jesus was (and is) to our salvation. His love compelled Him to bypass every rejection so that He could bring it about.

B. Prayer

Oh Lord, fill me with the determination of Jesus. Let me have the drive that it takes to outlast every criticism, every disappointment, and every setback so that Your salvation can be known by everyone. In the name of the Savior who gave His all for me, amen.

C. Thought to Remember

When times get tough, the faithful keep going.

Learning by Doing

This page contains an alternative lesson plan emphasizing learning activities.
Classes desiring such student involvement will find these suggestions helpful.

Learning Goals

After participating in this lesson, each student will be able to:

1. Tell how Jesus was rejected at Nazareth and how He responded with an expansion of ministry by sending out the Twelve to preach.

2. Compare the rejection of Jesus with the rejection of His messengers today.

3. Suggest at least one specific way to get involved in the effort to preach the gospel at home or around the world.

Into the Lesson

As the students arrive, have the classroom as "homey" as you can make it. As people are getting comfortable, say, "Think of an incident from your childhood that no one in this group knows: an accident, adventure, prank, or happy event. Keep your stories 'light,' and tell us about these incidents." Start things by relating a story from your own childhood.

If your class is large, make this a "neighbor-nudge" activity, where students simply turn to someone next to them and tell their stories.

Make the transition to Bible study by saying, "Today's study focuses on a time Jesus was in His hometown. The townspeople knew Him as a boy. Their responses to Him are alarming. We will see how Jesus reacts to their criticism."

Into the Word

Have a volunteer read Mark 6:1-13. Introduce the study by saying, "Throughout Scripture we see people rejecting God's Word and His messengers. Today as we study, we will compare several Biblical incidents with the story in Mark 6."

If you have a large class, use all the group activities. Divide the class into groups of four to six. Each group will write an interview from the assigned story. They are to pose questions and then find the answers in the text. *(Questions may include: What did you see happen here? What were the responses of the other participants? How did you feel while this was happening? What do you believe the outcome of these events will be?)*

If the group writes questions that don't have direct answers in the text, allow them to be creative in their answers. As leader, move between the groups to offer assistance.

Group One: Interview Jesus and other participants in Mark 6:1-13.

Group Two: Read Acts 17:1-15. Interview Paul, members of his party, and the opposition.

Group Three: Read 1 Kings 18:20-40. Interview Elijah, Ahab, the priests of Baal, bystanders, and others.

Allow fifteen minutes to prepare. Group One will present its interview to the whole group. If you used other projects, ask for a brief summary from each.

Lead a brief discussion with these questions:

1. What do these stories have in common? *(Believers have their messages rejected.)*

2. Why do you think this opposition occurs? *(Critics find the teaching objectionable.)*

3. How does each event end? *(People believe God's message. More people speak the message. Jesus calls new messengers!)*

4. What do you conclude from these events and writings? *(We, too, will face opposition but are to remain faithful.)*

Into Life

Display two pieces of poster board. Label the top of one "Nazareth News," the other "Daily Press." Ask the students to name the characteristics of rejection faced by Christ and have someone write them under "Nazareth News." Also ask for types of rejection faced by His followers today, and write these under "Daily Press."

Ask students to identify ways the message of Christ has been rejected when they attempted to convey it to others. Read 1 Peter 4:12-19. Ask another volunteer to read Romans 10:12-15. Ask the class, "What should be our response to opposition?" *(Continue to carry the message!)*

This week, get a list of missionaries and the countries they serve from your church office or treasurer. Bring a map or globe to class to pinpoint locations.

"As we close today, I want us to be aware of those carrying the good news around the globe. What ways can we encourage them in their efforts?" Distribute your list of missionaries.

"Who are some people with whom you are trying to share the gospel? Write their names on your paper. What are some ways you can seek to reach them more effectively?"

"Choose one or two of the suggestions we have made. Share your choices with your neighbor and pray together that you will be faithful in completing your choice."

Let's Talk It Over

The questions on this page are designed to promote discussion of the lesson by the class and to encourage application of the lesson Scriptures. The answers provided are only discussion starters. Let your class talk it over from there.

1. What kinds of doubts, predictions, rejections and questions are likely to come at us from those who know us best, or knew us once? How do we deal with them?

Non-believing family members and friends sometimes question whether one's conversion was real. Consistent, long-term faithfulness is the best demonstration that it is. Memories of past sins and weaknesses always will be present, but little by little they can be erased by continued faithfulness and a loving attitude. The new Christian will need to capitalize on opportunities to demonstrate that he or she is different from what he used to be, and that she doesn't look down on anyone or consider herself better than anyone. In Jesus' case, there was no sin in His past for the neighbors to recall. They just couldn't accept that He was anything "special." Today, any hint that one has chosen a "better" way of life is seen as "offensive" to those who continue in that old way. This cannot be avoided. We must simply demonstrate with love that there are standards of right and wrong, truth and error, and that we have sided with the truth.

2. What is the result for those who hear the gospel message yet refuse to take Jesus seriously?

In Nazareth Jesus' power to do miracles in the lives of the people was severely limited because of their lack of faith. That continues to be true. Those who come to God must believe that He exists and that He rewards those who seek Him (see Hebrews 11:6). And it's not just a belief in God that is required: we must accept Jesus Christ. (See John 14:6; Acts 4:12; Hebrews 10:28, 29.) Those who do not take Jesus seriously do so to their own eternal peril.

Of that there should be no debate. Perhaps your class could, however, discuss some temporal results of faith in Christ. Why are some Christians happier than others? Do Christians live longer than non-Christians? What should we make of clinical studies that show people who are prayed for get well more often than those who are not?

3. What different levels of support and involvement in world missions exist at our church? How can we increase our involvement, both individually and for the church as a whole?

The most basic level of missions involvement is simply to put an offering in the collection plate. How does your church sponsor missions? Is it a percentage of the total offering, or is there a specific missions fund? How can you encourage members to grow in their missions giving?

A higher level of commitment is required to join the missions committee or ministry at one's church, becoming active in making decisions and allocating resources so that the gospel can be preached through the world. Is there a missions committee at your church? Is it open to anyone? If not, how can people get more directly involved in the support of missions?

The highest level of missions involvement, of course, is actually to go to the mission field, whether as a short-term or full-time missionary. How can your church encourage more people to make this commitment?

4. How is the way we use our homes an indication of our stewardship and faith? What hospitality opportunities are available to all of us in the coming month?

It is truly shocking that sometimes the ministry of the church is stalled because of believers who refuse to use their homes for the glory of God. Whether the opportunity involves visiting missionaries, youth groups needing a place to meet for games, couples who need a place for informal counseling or many other needs, believers who will open their homes form the basis of so many mission efforts of the church. God's blessings always bring with them responsibilities. If God has blessed us with a home, then He expects us to use it for the work of the kingdom.

5. How well may our words, or what the church preaches, be considered an extension of the preaching of Jesus? How can that dynamic be improved?

Through our actions and through the stands of the church, the world should get an accurate picture of what Jesus preached and lived. We must renew a commitment to God's Word. The multiplicity of ideas thrown out in casual conversation and in the media is enough to confuse even a long-time committed Christian. We must go back to the Word and rediscover Jesus as the ultimate source of truth!

What Really Defiles

DEVOTIONAL READING: Psalm 51:10-17.

BACKGROUND SCRIPTURE: Mark 7:1-23.

PRINTED TEXT: Mark 7:1-15.

Mark 7:1-15

1 Then came together unto him the Pharisees, and certain of the scribes, which came from Jerusalem.

2 And when they saw some of his disciples eat bread with defiled, that is to say, with unwashen hands, they found fault.

3 For the Pharisees, and all the Jews, except they wash their hands oft, eat not, holding the tradition of the elders.

4 And when they come from the market, except they wash, they eat not. And many other things there be, which they have received to hold, as the washing of cups, and pots, brazen vessels, and of tables.

5 Then the Pharisees and scribes asked him, Why walk not thy disciples according to the tradition of the elders, but eat bread with unwashen hands?

6 He answered and said unto them, Well hath Isaiah prophesied of you hypocrites, as it is written, This people honoreth me with their lips, but their heart is far from me.

7 Howbeit in vain do they worship me, teaching for doctrines the commandments of men.

8 For laying aside the commandment of God, ye hold the tradition of men, as the washing of pots and cups: and many other such like things ye do.

9 And he said unto them, Full well ye reject the commandment of God, that ye may keep your own tradition.

10 For Moses said, Honor thy father and thy mother; and, Whoso curseth father or mother, let him die the death:

11 But ye say, If a man shall say to his father or mother, It is Corban, that is to say, a gift, by whatsoever thou mightest be profited by me; he shall be free.

12 And ye suffer him no more to do aught for his father or his mother;

13 Making the word of God of none effect through your tradition, which ye have delivered: and many such like things do ye.

14 And when he had called all the people unto him, he said unto them, Hearken unto me every one of you, and understand:

15 There is nothing from without a man, that entering into him can defile him: but the things which come out of him, those are they that defile the man.

GOLDEN TEXT: From within, out of the heart of men, proceed evil thoughts, adulteries, fornications, murders.—Mark 7:21.

Jesus: God's Power in Action
Unit 1: Jesus' Early Ministry
(Lessons 1-5)

Lesson Aims

After participating in this lesson, each student will be able to:

1. Recall Jesus' answer to the Pharisees and scribes about what really defiles those who try to live a pure life.

2. Contrast Jesus' method of purity with legalistic plans of achieving purity.

3. Confess specific sins that need to be eliminated from his or her lifestyle and pray to God for victory over them.

Lesson Outline

INTRODUCTION
   A. Better Than Soap
   B. Lesson Background
 I. RITUAL CLEANSING (Mark 7:1-5)
   A. Faultfinding (vv. 1, 2)
   B. Handwashing (vv. 3, 4)
   C. Questioning (v. 5)
II. HUMAN TRADITIONS (Mark 7:6-15)
   A. Lips vs. Heart (v. 6)
   B. Man's Teaching vs. God's Commandments (vv. 7-12)
     Going Beyond What God Has Said
   C. Impotence vs. Power (v. 13)
   D. From Without vs. From Within (vv. 14, 15)
     What Comes From the Inside
CONCLUSION
   A. Deceiving Traditions
   B. Prayer
   C. Thought to Remember

Introduction

A. Better Than Soap

Warren Wiersbe has a story that illustrates how gutter talk has become a substitute for a comedy routine. A Christian woman attended an anniversary dinner in honor of a friend, not knowing that there would be a program of coarse-talking comedy following the meal. The so-called comedian tried to entertain the crowd with dirty jokes and humor that degraded everything that the Christian guest held to be sacred and honorable. At one point in the program, the comedian's throat became dry. "Please bring me a glass of water," he called to a waiter. At that point the Christian

woman added, "And bring a toothbrush and a bar of soap with it!"

It would be nice if soap in the mouth could cure the problem of filthy speech, but unfortunately this cure is not strong enough. Something more is needed—a remedy that goes deeper than the tongue. Christians have the power of God's Word in their hearts (Colossians 3:16). They want their speech seasoned with salt (4:6) so that the words that they speak portray effectively the goodness of the Lord.

Today's lesson focuses on Jesus' instructions about purity. The incident recorded in Mark 7:1-15 offers contrasting views about what we have to do to acquire purity in life. The teachers of the day offered solutions to impurity that only made matters worse. Jesus challenges them and us to consider again whether the purity demanded by God is a high enough priority.

B. Lesson Background

This section of Mark's Gospel highlights the expansion of Jesus' ministry beyond Galilee. While Jesus' ministry was expanding, however, trouble loomed on the horizon. Herod Antipas condemned John the Baptist to the executioner's sword (Mark 6:14-29). In addition, the disciples seemed incapable of understanding who Jesus was (8:14-21) even after He miraculously fed five thousand on the Jewish side of the Sea of Galilee (6:30-44), and the four thousand on the Gentile side (8:1-10). In today's lesson it becomes clear that the scribes and Pharisees do not understand basic truths concerning Jesus' doctrine of pure living. More importantly, they do not understand that the law revolves around Jesus, and not the reverse.

What must have been even more discouraging to Jesus was that even His own disciples could not grasp His message (Mark 7:17-23). If the disciples could not grasp His point about "unclean" foods, how would they ever be able to understand about reaching "unclean" Gentile people? If they could not understand that the gospel should be preached to Gentiles as well as Jews, then the kingdom of God would remain locked up in Palestine. There could be no Great Commission (Matthew 28:19, 20) to preach the gospel around the world. So much depended on Jesus' teaching in Mark 7:1-15! The lesson resulted from a question posed about the habits of Jesus' disciples. Once again, Jesus' enemies provided the perfect opportunity to reveal the truth of God.

I. Ritual Cleansing (Mark 7:1-5)

Jesus' ministry is now attracting the attention of the religious leaders from Jerusalem.

A. Faultfinding (vv. 1, 2)

1. Then came together unto him the Pharisees, and certain of the scribes, which came from Jerusalem.

This isn't the first time that religious officials have come to Galilee *from Jerusalem* to investigate Jesus (cf. Mark 3:22). The temple is located in Jerusalem and that city is considered the holy city of God. Consequently, religious people among the Jews tend to hold the authority of those in Jerusalem in high regard. No doubt these officials are skeptical of Jesus and ready to find fault with His doctrine and activities. The report they will make regarding Jesus undoubtedly will be used to warn synagogues throughout Galilee that He is a dangerous force to be reckoned with.

2. And when they saw some of his disciples eat bread with defiled, that is to say, with unwashen hands, they found fault.

The religious officials have no trouble finding a "problem." Perhaps by attending some banquet where Jesus and the disciples are present, they discover that Jesus' disciples do not practice ceremonial cleansing of the *hands* before eating. The Pharisees' point is not that people should wash their hands to avoid picking up germs. These officials do not know anything about germs in the modern sense of the word. Their contention, rather, is that eating with unwashed hands means that the one eating the food is becoming defiled spiritually, because "unclean" hands contaminate the food in a spiritual way. The Jewish officials draw their concern from the law of Moses, which warns against touching things that are unclean (e.g., Leviticus 5:2; 11:8).

B. Handwashing (vv. 3, 4)

3. For the Pharisees, and all the Jews, except they wash their hands oft, eat not, holding the tradition of the elders.

To prevent uncleanness during a meal, Jewish rabbis had developed a practice of ceremonial handwashing before meals. Jewish literature confirms the accuracy of this stress on ceremonial cleansing.

The Jews, of course, have the written law of Moses. But over the years the Pharisees also have developed their own "oral law." They hold the two to be almost equal in authority. By the year A.D. 200, their oral law becomes written down into a law code called the Mishnah. This code contains detailed instructions about when and how thoroughly the hands need to be washed before eating. Among some Jewish groups the washing of the hands was considered only a minimum. The strict Essenes, for example, took baths before meals.

Since Jesus' disciples are not abiding by the accepted regulations for cleansing their hands, the Pharisees conclude that they are defiled. And if Jesus as a teacher of God's law is not correcting His own disciples, then He must be a false teacher, to be dealt with accordingly.

It seems obvious to modern Bible students that the Pharisees' standard is man-made. Those who know the Old Testament realize that such regulations are given nowhere in the law of Moses. In other words, these Jewish religious officials are trying to hold Jesus and His disciples to a law that is not actually a law from God. It is a *tradition of the elders* that they consider binding. For the first-century resident of Galilee, however, that distinction is not so obvious. Copies of the Scripture are scarce, and most of the knowledge of them is passed on orally. If the religious leaders say this is binding, the average citizen assumes it must be Scriptural.

4. And when they come from the market, except they wash, they eat not. And many other things there be, which they have received to hold, as the washing of cups, and pots, brazen vessels, and of tables.

The Pharisees' concern about defilement extends also to kitchen utensils, which must be washed as well. Their requirements are directed at making these concerns into spiritual issues. Eating from an unwashed cup means that you could lose your standing before God. Eating with unwashed hands makes you no better than the Gentiles, who neither know God nor have a share in His blessing.

Mark's rather lengthy explanation of these Jewish customs leads us to believe that he is addressing a Gentile audience, who would need such an explanation. (Matthew, in his parallel account in chapter 15, does not include any such explanation.) Many scholars believe that Mark sent his Gospel to the church in Rome. [See question #1, page 272.]

C. Questioning (v. 5)

5. Then the Pharisees and scribes asked him, Why walk not thy disciples according to the tradition of the elders, but eat bread with unwashen hands?

The Pharisees and scribes are not asking this question for the purpose of gaining information. The question is designed to accuse Jesus of being careless about His obligation to the will of God in not correcting His disciples.

At this point, it should be apparent that the Pharisees are focused on outward purity rather than inward purity—thinking that the first automatically leads to the second. They do not pause in their criticisms to wonder if Jesus' heart is in the right place. They do not qualify their criticism by noting the actions of Jesus that do conform to the traditions of the elders: His synagogue attendance, His study of the Scriptures, or His prayer life. They do not pause to consider the evidence of the miracles that confirm His status as the Son of God. Rather, they spend their energies finding fault with His practices relating to questions of external cleanness.

II. Human Traditions (Mark 7:6-15)

For Jesus, spiritual purity is a deeper issue than whether the hands are cleansed. His response to the Pharisees is direct and caustic.

A. Lips *vs.* Heart (v. 6)

6. He answered and said unto them, Well hath Isaiah prophesied of you hypocrites, as it is written, This people honoreth me with their lips, but their heart is far from me.

In answer to the Pharisees, Jesus quotes *Isaiah* 29:13. But He prefaces the quotation with a statement to make sure they know that the words of the prophet point directly at their brand of religious hypocrisy. When He says that Isaiah had prophesied about *them,* Jesus does not mean that the prophet Isaiah originally had Pharisees and scribes in mind. Rather, Jesus means that the same hypocrisy that Isaiah found prominent in eighth-century B.C. Israel could be seen among the religious leaders of Jesus' own day.

The condemnation Isaiah spoke about distinguished between the worship of God that is outward versus the inward devotion to God that is essential for true believers. The Pharisees, too, are demonstrating more interest in fulfilling man-made regulations than in honoring God. (See also Jeremiah 12:2.) This is the first time the Gospels record Jesus' use of the term *hypocrites* for these religious officials. It will not be the last. [See question #2, page 272.]

How to Say It

AMORPHOPHALLUS TITANUM. Uh-*mor*-fuh-*fal*-us tie-*tan*-um (strong accent on *fal*).
AUGHT. awt.
CORBAN. *Kor*-bun.
ESSENES. *Eh*-seenz.
GALILEE. *Gal*-uh-lee.
GENTILES. *Jen*-tyles.
HEROD ANTIPAS. *Hair*-ud *An*-tih-pus.
ISAIAH. Eye-*zay*-uh.
JEREMIAH. Jair-uh-*my*-uh.
MISHNAH. *Mish*-nuh.
PHARISEES. *Fair*-ih-seez.

B. Man's Teaching *vs.* God's Commandments (vv. 7-12)

7. Howbeit in vain do they worship me, teaching for doctrines the commandments of men.

Jesus now finishes the quotation from Isaiah. In so doing, He calls attention to the crux of the problem: the Pharisees are substituting human authority for authority that belongs to God alone. They are holding people accountable for traditions that in some cases have no sign of God's approval. They are willing to judge people as unfit spiritually merely on the basis of human tradition.

8. For laying aside the commandment of God, ye hold the tradition of men, as the washing of pots and cups: and many other such like things ye do.

The mistake the religious leaders are making is not in merely adding traditions to the Word *of God* (as bad as that would be). They are creating traditions that actually overrule that Word! Jesus assumes a distinction between the Word of God and the words of the rabbis. Though many Jews apparently miss the distinction, Jesus makes clear that neglecting to separate the two leads to big problems. In Colossians 2:20-22 Paul also warns about keeping this distinction. [See question #3, page 272.]

GOING BEYOND WHAT GOD HAS SAID

Men who have come to the West from other cultures usually dress like Westerners, but women from those cultures often choose to keep their traditional dress styles. However, in some parts of the world, there are very rigid strictures on women's clothing and behavior, usually the result of strict religious rules. Saudi Arabian women, for example, wear several veils so that their eyes are the only parts of their bodies visible to the public. An American envoy has complained that when Saudi women come into the U.S. Embassy to have their pictures taken for visas, all that can be seen is their eyes. All their pictures are, for all practical purposes, identical!

The laws go beyond dress: women are not allowed to socialize with men outside the family or home. One of the few places Saudi women are seen in public is in restaurants, but even there they are seated only with the men of their families in special family sections.

What is it about religion that tempts us to go beyond what God has said and impose our own ideas of spirituality on others? Jesus had no time for legalistic religion. He condemned the Jewish traditions that required more than God had demanded and actually nullified the purpose of God's commands. Do we as Christians have attitudes that parallel those that Jesus repudiated?

—C. R. B.

9. And he said unto them, Full well ye reject the commandment of God, that ye may keep your own tradition.

Not only are the Pharisees willing to prefer a man-made *tradition* over the Scripture, they are also willing to use traditions directly to violate the law of Moses.

10. For Moses said, Honor thy father and thy mother; and, Whoso curseth father or mother, let him die the death.

Jesus assaults their hypocrisy by pointing to the Fifth Commandment (Exodus 20:12). The second reference is Exodus 21:17, which comes after the Ten Commandments but serves as a reinforcement of the Fifth Commandment.

To honor one's parents includes a commitment not to allow aging parents to become destitute. Jesus' concern here is not surprising. Honor of one's parents is basic to the will of God as expressed in the Old Testament.

11, 12. But ye say, If a man shall say to his father or mother, It is Corban, that is to say, a gift, by whatsoever thou mightest be profited by me; he shall be free. And ye suffer him no more to do aught for his father or his mother.

Corban is a Hebrew term that refers to a religious *gift* that is reserved for God. The gift might take the form of an animal for sacrifice (Leviticus 1:2, 3, 10; 3:1; 27:9), a vegetable offering (Leviticus 2:1, 5), or a gift of precious metals (Numbers 7:13; 31:50). To declare any of these items to be "Corban" is to remove it from mundane uses. The Pharisees have supplanted the Fifth Commandment with an improper application of Corban.

Jesus is criticizing the practice of designating certain property as "Corban" in a deliberate attempt to withhold support from aging parents, or to shame parents one is feuding with. Adults could thus use the declaration of "Corban" to keep money from going to their parents until their parents are safely dead. Then they could take advantage of the liberal "Corban" laws that allow for a reversal of their previous declaration. The money that was set aside for God while their parents were living could then be declared no longer set aside for God.

This trick allows Jewish adults to ignore their parents' needs in their old age and to feel justified that they are honoring God's law. Jesus' accusation is that the religious leaders are sponsoring a violation of the law while leaving the worshiper with no sense of wrongdoing. [See question #4, page 272.]

C. Impotence *vs.* Power (v. 13)

13. Making the word of God of none effect through your tradition, which ye have delivered: and many such like things do ye.

Visual for lesson 5. *Post today's visual as you conclude your discussion of verse 15. Discuss how one can receive a "spiritual heart transplant."*

Jesus concludes His criticisms of the practice of the Pharisees and scribes by going to the heart of the danger. Rather than using tradition to help people understand and apply *the word of God*, their tradition actually nullifies that Word. Jesus ends His comments by noting that there are more traditions of this kind that He could list. But this one is sufficient to make the point.

D. From Without *vs.* From Within (vv. 14, 15)

14. And when he had called all the people unto him, he said unto them, Hearken unto me every one of you, and understand:

Jesus has been addressing His words to the Pharisees and scribes. But now He turns to *the people* to make sure that they hear the conclusion of the matter. He calls upon them to hear His words as if they represent the Word of God—words they must *understand* and obey!

15. There is nothing from without a man, that entering into him can defile him: but the things which come out of him, those are they that defile the man.

For Jewish listeners, this declaration is quite a shock. Not only is Jesus slapping down the authoritative traditions of the Pharisees, He is also pronouncing a certain Old Testament distinction to be no longer valid! Old Testament regulations clearly divided foods into clean and unclean categories (cf. Leviticus 11). Surely only God Himself can change these regulations. But that's exactly what Jesus does (see Mark 7:19).

But the disciples do not yet grasp what is going on here (v. 18). It will take church leaders of the first century some time to let go of their food laws. A few years later, Peter will see a vision of a sheet being lowered from heaven with unclean animals on it. He will refuse to obey the command to eat any of the food, arguing that he has never eaten anything impure or unclean (Acts 10:14). Finally the Heavenly voice convinces him not to call unclean anything that God has made clean. While the Christians in Rome are debating this matter of clean and unclean foods, Paul points out that no food is unclean of itself. Instead, it becomes unclean based on the conscience of the person eating it (Romans 14:14).

Today, Christians are not obligated to the dietary regulations of the Old Testament because Jesus declared all foods clean in Mark 7:19. These words of Jesus have changed our lifestyle forever. But more importantly, Jesus also clarified what it is that really defiles a person. The things that come out of a person in terms of attitudes, words, and expressions of thought—whether good or bad—reveal the content of the heart (see 7:20-23). Our words, therefore, serve as a kind of spiritual thermometer, revealing our true "temperature" as far as our devotion to God is concerned. What really defiles us is a sinful heart. The only way to get rid of that kind of defilement is to have our hearts cleansed from sin. The only cleansing agent strong enough to do that is the blood of Jesus Christ. [See question #5, page 272.]

WHAT COMES FROM THE INSIDE

The largest flower blossom in the world is the *Amorphophallus titanum*. Ranging in color from crimson to purple, its grows to six feet in height and features a petal that is three feet wide. It has a striking, even beautiful, blossom that lasts only a couple of days and is rarely seen outside its native habitat, the jungles of Sumatra. The plant first flowered in "captivity" in 1937 at the New York Botanical Gardens and has done so only ten other times since then.

When a specimen blossomed in 1999 at the Huntington Gardens in San Marino, California, a record two-day crowd of twenty-two thousand people came to see this rare event in the world of horticulture. But they came more for another reason than for its beauty: the perfume of the blossom smells like rotting meat. A staff member at the Huntington Gardens described it as smelling like the decaying carcass of an opossum that had died under his house. What is seen on the outside is quite attractive; what emanates from within is loathsome.

This is what Jesus was saying to the people who had listened to His debate with the Pharisees: what comes from within us determines our purity or defilement, not external matters such as hands that are not ceremonially pure. The Pharisee's problem is sometimes ours as well; we so often judge people by external factors, don't we?   —C. R. B.

Conclusion

A. Deceiving Traditions

Today's lesson points to a ploy that comes from Satan himself: getting believers focused on human traditions instead of God's Word. Satan wins when believers assume they are serving God when they are really serving themselves. Satan wins when believers assume they have purified themselves from sin when they are really just ignoring sin. The danger is that human traditions can make Christians feel guiltless at just the wrong time.

Christ wants to remove our sins and cleanse our consciences from guilt so that we have substantial reasons for being right with God. Human traditions deceive us into thinking that we can be right with God before the sin has been removed from our life. This is the reason that Jesus took so seriously this false security of the Pharisees and scribes. It is always better to allow the Word of God to affect us in the fullness of its power. With eternity at stake, it is always dangerous to allow human traditions to dilute this power.

B. Prayer

Lord, give me the wisdom to let Your Word have its way in my heart today. Please make Your Word powerful as it speaks to me, convicting me of every sin, and setting me free. In Christ I pray, amen.

C. Thought to Remember

Let the Word of God judge your traditions, and not the other way around.

Learning by Doing

This page contains an alternative lesson plan emphasizing learning activities.
Classes desiring such student involvement will find these suggestions helpful.

Learning Goals

After participating in this lesson, each student will be able to:

1. Recall Jesus' answer to the Pharisees and scribes about what really defiles those who try to live a pure life.

2. Contrast Jesus' method of purity with legalistic plans of achieving purity.

3. Confess specific sins that need to be eliminated from his or her lifestyle and pray to God for victory over them.

Into the Lesson

"Keeping up appearances" is a saying used by many when they make an effort to look all right on the outside but are falling apart on the inside. Group your students in threes. Each group member is to spend a few moments reflecting on, then responding to, the following: "Many people have joined the 'do-it-yourself' school of home decorating and repairs. Often this involves covering up previous defects or mistakes. Tell your group members of your worst experience with decorating or making repairs." Allow five minutes for the sharing. Call on volunteers to share a story.

Say, "In our text today Jesus encounters the teachers of Jewish law. The conflict is over what makes a person spiritually unclean. The teachers would talk about what happens on the outside of a person. We will see Jesus answer in a way very different from what they were expecting."

Into the Word

Create three groups of six among your class members. Each group will work on one of the following assignments. If you have more than eighteen, create extra groups and repeat assignments. Each group needs at least four members.

Group 1: Research the Old Testament, particularly Leviticus, Numbers, and Deuteronomy to create a quick chart containing some of the rules, regulations, and acts concerning "clean" and "unclean." Provide poster sheets or overhead transparencies and a projector.

Group 2: Write a short debate between Jesus and the Pharisees and scribes. The topic will be Mark 7:15. One side will make points in support, as Jesus. The other side will make points negating the verse, as the Pharisees and scribes.

Group 3: Make a chart contrasting Jesus' method of purity with that of the Pharisees and scribes. Students will need to read Mark 7:1-23 to develop the chart. (This activity is in the student book.)

After fifteen minutes reconvene your groups for their reports.

Into Life

Say, "How easily we can get caught up in the pace of life, trying to achieve spirituality by keeping ourselves 'looking clean.' Jesus teaches the Pharisees to pay attention to the 'inside' for maintaining purity."

Today's Scripture calls for a difficult application. You will be helping your students confess sin. As a teacher, your example will help the students participate more readily.

Say, "There are three ground rules for this application section. First, we will treat everyone here in a loving, gracious manner. No preaching or judging will be allowed. Second, you may pass or keep your confession silent. Third, anything said here is not to be repeated."

Option 1: Ask each member of the class to think quietly about what he or she needs to confess to God. After sixty to ninety seconds lead the class in this prayer: "Father, forgive us for the ways we have sinned against You. In Jesus' name, amen."

Then have three volunteers read the following verses: Psalm 51:10-12; 1 John 1:9; Acts 2:38. Ask each class member to reflect on the verse that applies to him or her. Then close with this prayer: "Heavenly Father, thank You for forgiving us, for loving us, and for encouraging us to keep growing. In Jesus' name, amen."

Option 2: Prepare a three-by-five card for each member with the following printed on it: "My struggle with sin involves _____." Tell the group to use a category of sin, not a specific sin. After a few moments, you may want to call on volunteers to confess. If you do, be sure as the leader you go first to "model" the confession. After a short while, read the "forgiveness prayer" in Option 1. Ask for three volunteers to read the Scriptures above. Then have class members write the Scripture reference on their card that best answers their need for forgiveness. Then pray the "prayer of thanksgiving" from above to close the class.

Be prepared to stay after class to answer specific questions from your students.

Let's Talk It Over

The questions on this page are designed to promote discussion of the lesson by the class and to encourage application of the lesson Scriptures. The answers provided are only discussion starters. Let your class talk it over from there.

1. What kinds of man-made, unwritten traditions have become "laws" in our church? What can we do about them?

Every congregation of believers becomes a subculture of its own. Each community develops its own personalities and preferences about the way things should be. In many congregations a certain style of music is preferred, and participants may begin to believe that it is the only type of music that can honor God. Most congregations and cultures and generations have certain expectations of what is appropriate dress—whether casual or formal. These are only two examples, and your students can list dozens more. But what do we do when someone "violates" our traditions? Can we see past our own comfort zone to allow a difference? Do we derive a sense of power from enforcing our traditions?

2. Like the Pharisees, many today pay "lip service" to the Lord but do not wholeheartedly follow Him. What are the dangers of such a practice, for those who do it and for those who observe them?

One of the obvious dangers is that we fall under the condemnation of both Isaiah and Jesus. Our hearts are "far from" the Lord, and that is a dangerous situation. We gain a false sense of security, trusting in our own righteousness instead of on God's grace. Ask your students to think about who is at risk from observing the example of such "lip servants." They will probably note the children of such people, who will grow up following their bad example. Other youth in the church and new believers are also at risk from such phony disciples. Just as the people in Judea and Galilee tended to follow the bad example of the Pharisees, so young believers may be led astray by church leaders who have this wrong view of discipleship.

3. As important as traditions are, how can we be sure they do not override Scriptural doctrines and precedents?

We have to keep in mind the purpose of our traditions. The sect of the Pharisees began as a group of people committed to the preservation of God's law. Their traditions were intended to safeguard the law. In their zeal to keep the law, they would deliberately demand of themselves more than the law required.

Unfortunately, this led to a very legalistic approach to righteousness. They began to focus on the externals, on the forms and structures they themselves had established, instead of on God's Word. When our own traditions become sacred to us, then we are in danger of falling into the same trap. We need to see past our traditions to the Lord. The traditions ought to help us to know and follow God's Word; they should not replace it. Ask your students for specific ways to keep that balance. Regular Bible study, for example, is one safeguard. What are some others?

4. What do people do today that you find similar to the Pharisees' use of the "Corban" law to avoid caring for their parents? What can be done to right these modern wrongs?

Perhaps the dependence on government programs and subsidies for the elderly is similar. Some believers think we ought to care for our parents at home, or that the church should take a more active role as it did in the first century. Does government do more and more to care for the elderly because the church does less, or does the church do less because the government is doing more?

But don't get caught up in care for the elderly. Jesus used that as an example. Using church attendance to mask immoral behavior is another situation. What others can your students suggest?

5. If the words that come from our mouths have the power to "defile" us, what safeguards ought we to take? How can we help one another to avoid such defilement?

While many of us may not use any type of profanity or blasphemy, are we guilty of criticizing others unfairly? Is our speech often cynical or sarcastic? If someone were listening to everything that came out of our mouths, what kind of character would that person assume we had? Perhaps we need to cultivate a more positive manner of speaking. We can look for ways to encourage and build up others instead of speaking the first critical thought that enters our minds. Perhaps we need to be sure we are feeding on that which is good (Philippians 4:8) so that good also comes out. If we focus on what goes into our hearts and then comes out of our mouths, we can experience a change in our character.

The Messiah Challenges the Corrupt

April 6
Lesson 6

DEVOTIONAL READING: Luke 19:28-40.

BACKGROUND SCRIPTURE: Mark 11:1–12:12.

PRINTED TEXT: Mark 11:1-9, 15-18.

Mark 11:1-9, 15-18

1 And when they came nigh to Jerusalem, unto Bethphage and Bethany, at the mount of Olives, he sendeth forth two of his disciples,

2 And saith unto them, Go your way into the village over against you: and as soon as ye be entered into it, ye shall find a colt tied, whereon never man sat; loose him, and bring him.

3 And if any man say unto you, Why do ye this? say ye that the Lord hath need of him; and straightway he will send him hither.

4 And they went their way, and found the colt tied by the door without in a place where two ways met; and they loose him.

5 And certain of them that stood there said unto them, What do ye, loosing the colt?

6 And they said unto them even as Jesus had commanded: and they let them go.

7 And they brought the colt to Jesus, and cast their garments on him; and he sat upon him.

8 And many spread their garments in the way; and others cut down branches off the trees, and strewed them in the way.

9 And they that went before, and they that followed, cried, saying, Hosanna; Blessed is he that cometh in the name of the Lord.

. . . .

15 And they come to Jerusalem: and Jesus went into the temple, and began to cast out them that sold and bought in the temple, and overthrew the tables of the money changers, and the seats of them that sold doves;

16 And would not suffer that any man should carry any vessel through the temple.

17 And he taught, saying unto them, Is it not written, My house shall be called of all nations the house of prayer? but ye have made it a den of thieves.

18 And the scribes and chief priests heard it, and sought how they might destroy him: for they feared him, because all the people was astonished at his doctrine.

GOLDEN TEXT: And they come to Jerusalem: and Jesus went into the temple, and began to cast out them that sold and bought in the temple, and overthrew the tables of the money changers, and the seats of them that sold doves.
—Mark 11:15.

Lesson Aims

After participating in this lesson, each student will be able to:

1. Summarize Mark's account of Jesus' triumphal entry into Jerusalem and the cleansing of the temple.

2. Explain how these events, which demonstrate Jesus' authority as the divine Son of God, challenge us to confront evil.

3. Suggest at least one specific way to detect and oppose corruption in society.

Lesson Outline

INTRODUCTION
 A. When the Secular Invades the Sacred
 B. Lesson Background
 I. THE KING'S PREPARATION (Mark 11:1-6)
  A. Receiving the Instructions (vv. 1-3)
  B. Bringing the Colt (vv. 4-6)
 II. THE KING'S ENTRY (Mark 11:7-9)
  A. Jesus Rides the Colt (v. 7)
  B. People Prepare the Way (v. 8)
  C. People Hail Jesus (v. 9)
   A Leader, Not a Publicity Hound
 III. THE KING'S ANGER (Mark 11:15-18)
  A. The Son of God Acts (vv. 15, 16)
   A Different Kind of Hoax
  B. The Son of God Explains (v. 17)
  C. The Religious Leaders React (v. 18)
CONCLUSION
 A. When Leaders Fail
 B. Prayer
 C. Thought to Remember

Introduction

A. When the Secular Invades the Sacred

Several years ago the U.S. government took action to recover a million and a half dollars in back taxes that it claimed was due from a certain religious order. This particular order was engaged in the manufacture and sale of wine. Some of this wine was sold for sacramental purposes, but much of it was sold on the market in competition with regular commercial producers of wine. The religious order claimed exemption from the tax levied on commercial producers on the basis that their product was "subject to the control of the Pope," and thus was "exempt as a church" from taxation.

Compare the activities of this religious order with those of the money changers in the temple of Jesus' day. In both cases, people were using religion to justify a profit-making activity. There is nothing wrong with making a profit, of course, but the similarity does not end there. In both cases the activities crossed the line into misconduct. In speaking to the money changers, Jesus said that they had made the temple into "a den of thieves." What would Jesus say today about the wine-making religious order?

B. Lesson Background

The first five lessons in this quarter have given us thumbnail sketches of Jesus' early life and ministry. Beginning with His baptism and temptation, we have studied some of His early conflicts including His rejection at Nazareth and some of His ethical teachings.

The three lessons of this unit bring His earthly life and ministry to its climax in His crucifixion and resurrection. Today's lesson begins what we have come to call the "Final Week."

Several months earlier Jesus had warned His disciples that He must go to Jerusalem and suffer many things, including His own death, at the hands of the elders, chief priests, and scribes (Mark 8:31-33). Peter strongly resisted such an idea. He even rebuked Jesus. The idea of Jesus' dying was completely foreign to what Peter and the other disciples understood Jesus' mission to be. When Jesus entered Jerusalem, the disciples must have believed that their hopes of establishing Jesus as an earthly Messiah were about to be realized. By the next day, those hopes must have dimmed considerably.

I. The King's Preparation (Mark 11:1-6)

A. Receiving the Instructions (vv. 1-3)

1, 2. And when they came nigh to Jerusalem, unto Bethphage and Bethany, at the mount of Olives, he sendeth forth two of his disciples, and saith unto them, Go your way into the village over against you: and as soon as ye be entered into it, ye shall find a colt tied, whereon never man sat; loose him, and bring him.

Just prior to this, Jesus had been in Jericho, where He had healed blind Bartimeus. Then Jesus and His disciples make the long, uphill walk to *Bethphage and Bethany*. While Bethphage (which means, "house of figs") has never been located, scholars believe that both villages were situated on the eastern slope of *the mount of Olives*. This arduous trip of about sixteen miles takes the better part of the day. We may assume that they arrive at Bethany late in the afternoon just before the beginning of the Sabbath. Jesus is no stranger at Bethany. That is where Mary, Martha, and Lazarus live.

On Sunday morning after Jesus and the apostles had spent Saturday resting in observance of the Sabbath Day, Jesus sent *two of his disciples* on a special mission. They are to go to the nearby *village* of Bethphage, where at the entrance of the village they will *find a colt* that has never been ridden. This is the fulfillment of a prophecy found in Zechariah 9:9.

3. And if any man say unto you, Why do ye this? say ye that the Lord hath need of him; and straightway he will send him hither.

Jesus' knowledge of the availability of the colt may have come supernaturally. But, on the other hand, it is entirely possible that the Lord has made prior arrangements for the use of the animal. In either event, Jesus certainly has the owner's approval for its use.

B. Bringing the Colt (vv. 4-6)

4. And they went their way, and found the colt tied by the door without in a place where two ways met; and they loose him.

The two disciples follow Jesus' instructions and find *the colt* just as He has told them. Matthew's version of this account informs us that there were two animals—"an ass tied, and a colt with her" (Matthew 21:2). A colt that has never been ridden could be difficult to manage. Perhaps this is the reason that Jesus sends two disciples on this errand instead of one.

5. And certain of them that stood there said unto them, What do ye, loosing the colt?

On the surface, this appears to be a case of good neighbors looking out for one another. *Certain* villagers, noting that the two disciples are strangers, immediately challenge their action. In a small village where everyone knows everyone else, this is what we might expect. But Luke 19:33 reveals that the colt's owners are present. We would be very surprised if the owners did not say something when two strangers began untying their animals!

6. And they said unto them even as Jesus had commanded: and they let them go.

The disciples may be startled when they are questioned, but they respond as Jesus has instructed them, telling the villagers that "the Lord hath need of him" (v. 3). These words may be a prearranged password that establishes the identity of the disciples with the villagers. Many commentators believe that the owner of the colt is quietly making a contribution to Jesus' ministry in his own way. There may be thousands of such

followers in Palestine at that time. The Lord needs some who serve publicly out in front, but He also uses many whose ministries are performed quietly behind the scenes. [See question #1, page 280.]

II. The King's Entry (Mark 11:7-9)

A. Jesus Rides the Colt (v. 7)

7. And they brought the colt to Jesus, and cast their garments on him; and he sat upon him.

Saddles as we know them are not commonly used in the ancient Orient. Instead, the disciples lay some of their clothing on the back of the animal to cushion Jesus' ride. Without a saddle or stirrups, Jesus probably has to be lifted onto the back of the animal. Amazingly, the colt remains docile as Jesus begins to ride it. Apparently this animal recognizes Jesus as the ruler of the universe and behaves accordingly.

B. People Prepare the Way (v. 8)

8. And many spread their garments in the way; and others cut down branches off the trees, and strewed them in the way.

The spontaneous response of the people to Jesus' ride from the Mount of Olives to Jerusalem is remarkable. At least we assume that it was spontaneous, for we have nothing to indicate that Jesus made any effort in advance to encourage the people to respond in this fashion.

But even without the benefit of our modern electronic media, word passes from person to person with amazing speed. Jerusalem at the time is crowded with many visitors who have come to the city to celebrate the Passover. (The number of people in the city perhaps triples during this celebration!) No doubt some of these visitors, especially those from Galilee, already know of Jesus. Only a short time before, Jesus had raised Lazarus from the dead and this word spread among the visitors, increasing their excitement and their desire to see Him.

How to Say It

BARTIMEUS. *Bar*-tih-*me*-us (strong accent on *me*).
BETHANY. *Beth*-uh-nee.
BETHPHAGE. *Beth*-fuh-gee.
GALILEE. *Gal*-uh-lee.
JEREMIAH. Jair-uh-*my*-uh.
JERICHO. *Jair*-ih-co.
MACCABEUS. Mack-uh-*bee*-us.
RABBI. *rab*-eye.
ZECHARIAH. *Zek*-uh-*rye*-uh (strong accent on *rye*).

In order to honor Jesus as He rides down the slope of the Mount of Olives, the people *spread their garments* on the road. They further demonstrate their respect for Him by cutting tree *branches* and laying them down on the road. John tells us that they also cut palm branches or fronds and wave these as they go out to meet Him (John 12:13). Normally this behavior is reserved for nobility. Crowds of people had welcomed the Jewish hero Simon Maccabeus in a similar manner some 110 years before (see 1 Maccabees 13:51). The people are demonstrating their belief that Jesus is more than just another prophet or rabbi: He is the "Son of David" (Matthew 21:9.)

Since palm fronds grow at the very top of the trees, the people must have gone to considerable effort to cut them for this occasion. This action is the basis for observing the day of Jesus' triumphal entry as "Palm Sunday." [See question #2, page 280.]

C. People Hail Jesus (v. 9)

9. And they that went before, and they that followed, cried, saying, Hosanna; Blessed is he that cometh in the name of the Lord.

All four Gospel accounts record Jesus' triumphal entry into Jerusalem. However, these separate accounts present some interesting variations. Both Matthew and Mark indicate that two groups make up the crowd that accompanied Jesus: those *that went before* are those who come out from Jerusalem to meet Him (cf. John 12:12, 13), while those *that followed* come from Bethany with Him.

Both groups join in shouting their praise, and the two phrases they use catch our attention. *Hosanna* originally meant "save now," as in Psalm 118:25. (See also 2 Samuel 14:4 and 2 Kings 6:26.) Over the centuries, however, this word came to be used as an expression of acclamation rather than a cry for help. The phrase *blessed is he that cometh in the name of the Lord* is found in Psalm 118:26. Verses 25 and 26 of that Psalm are used in the formal worship services of the major Jewish feasts, indicating that the people attach great significance to Jesus' entry into Jerusalem. Matthew 23:39 notes that Jesus will use the second phrase Himself a bit later.

The Gospel of John records that the crowd also hails Jesus as "King of Israel" (John 12:13). Luke also tells us that some of the religious leaders demand that Jesus silence the enthusiastic crowd. Jesus responds that "if these should hold their peace, the stones would immediately cry out" (Luke 19:40). Luke also informs us that Jesus stops before He enters the city and weeps as He predicts the tragic future that awaits Jerusalem (Luke 19:41-44).

Mark tells us in verse 11 (not in our text today) that after Jesus enters the city, He goes into the temple area and observes some of the activities there. As events of the following day will show, Jesus is displeased with some of the things He sees. But since it is already late in the day, He chooses to wait until the next day to confront those who are corrupting God's house. And so He leaves and returns to Bethany with His disciples. [See question #3, page 280.]

A LEADER, NOT A PUBLICITY HOUND

"Screaming Lord Sutch" was founder of Britain's Monster Raving Loony Party. When he died in June 1999, he was England's longest-serving political leader. He had run for parliament forty times without ever being elected. His campaign slogan was, "Vote for insanity—you know it makes sense!" His trademark "uniform" during his campaigns was an animal-skin print hat, gold lamé suit, and a gold megaphone.

Sutch was famed for such inane proposals as banning January and February in order to shorten winter, and forcing the unemployed to walk on a giant treadmill to generate cheap electricity. Appropriately, his countrymen saw his antics as publicity stunts more than efforts to bring positive change to the nation. However, he did have an effect on the British electoral process: the government drastically increased candidates' registration fees to keep people like him from running for office!

Skeptics may have seen Jesus' triumphal entry as a mere publicity stunt. However, unlike people's reaction to Screaming Lord Sutch and a multitude of his sort, the common people recognized that what Jesus said made sense, and they followed Him gladly. We'll always have "Loonies" vying for our attention, urging us to join their parades. But the only leader really worthy of a devoted following is Jesus. Even at their best, all others pale in comparison.   —C. R. B.

III. The King's Anger
(Mark 11:15-18)

A. The Son of God Acts (vv. 15, 16)

15. And they come to Jerusalem: and Jesus went into the temple, and began to cast out them that sold and bought in the temple, and overthrew the tables of the money changers, and the seats of them that sold doves.

The next morning *Jesus* returns to *the temple* area ready to confront the merchants and *money changers* in God's house. In the cleansing of the temple, Jesus challenges the corrupt practices of the religious leaders head on. At the beginning of His ministry Jesus had cleansed the temple in a similar manner (John 2:13-17), but in the three years that have passed since then, the merchants and money changers have returned to their lucrative practices.

At first glance, one might suppose that these merchants and money changers are rendering a service for the benefit of those who come to the temple to worship. Worshipers are allowed to bring their own sacrificial animals for their offerings, but bringing a sheep or even a dove all the way from Galilee can be inconvenient. So many people prefer to purchase an animal from the vendors in the temple area.

Further, those bringing their own animals often run into another problem: sacrificial animals have to be without blemish (Leviticus 22:21). Those who bring their own animals often have them rejected by the temple inspectors. Thus the worshipers have to purchase approved animals at inflated prices. Then to avoid having to take their own "unacceptable" animal all the way back home, the worshipers sell them at greatly reduced prices to merchants in Jerusalem. These merchants have "inside connections" through which they can get these rejected animals approved for worship. Using this trick, the religious leaders are able to make a nice profit on the side.

But the corruption doesn't stop there. Worshipers often make contributions to the temple treasury, a practice that is quite acceptable to the religious leaders. However, those who bring coins from foreign lands will have those coins rejected because they bear images of their rulers, a violation of the second (and possibly the first) of the Ten Commandments (Exodus 20:3, 4). For this reason, worshipers have to trade those coins for the proper "temple currency" (cf. Matthew 17:24-27). There is little doubt that the religious leaders profited from a lopsided "exchange rate"!

Quite apart from the corruption involved in these temple activities, another issue is involved. Worship ought to be kept holy and sacred, but these religious leaders are squeezing out the sacred as they pursue their commercial venture. Today we are immersed in a secular world that uses every opportunity to intrude into the most sacred moments. These intrusions are often subtle and may go unnoticed. Sometimes they are blatant and obvious. Although the practices noted here are carried on in the outer courts of the temple (the area that surrounds the temple building) the smell and noise of livestock directly adjacent to a solemn place of prayer has to be a distraction. From time to time we need spiritual leaders with keen insights to call our attention to the compromises we are making. That's what Jesus is doing when He cleanses the temple.

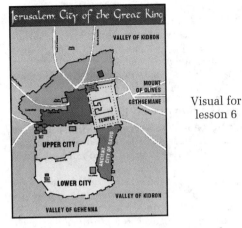

Visual for lesson 6

Use this map to locate sites in and around Jerusalem relevant to this and other lessons.

A DIFFERENT KIND OF HOAX

Hoaxes have often been perpetrated on a gullible public, but the increasing use of E-mail has resulted in an increase of the number of people who can be duped by a given hoax. For example, an E-mail that purported to come from a law firm in the Washington, D.C. area warned a few years ago that a bill before Congress, 602P, would add a five-cent tax to each E-mail message a person received. Even worse, Republican Congressman Tony Schnell was trying to get an even higher tax passed in order to help the U.S. Postal Service fight its electronic competition.

However, the bill, the law firm, and the Congressman do not exist! A distrustful public's willingness to believe the worst about government's appetite for tax income conspired with its naïve acceptance of what it reads in E-mail messages. The result was the rapid spread of the hoax.

But hoaxes are nothing new. In Jesus' day, religious leaders conspired with greedy merchants and crooked money changers to force worshipers at the temple into believing that God required a specific kind of money and preapproved sacrificial animals for their worship. Jesus' actions in cleansing the temple should remind us to keep a watchful eye on those who, in claiming to be God's authorities, would fool us about God's requirements for pleasing Him.   —C. R. B.

16. And would not suffer that any man should carry any vessel through the temple.
The temple area covers most of the eastern side of the city of Jerusalem. Anyone wishing to travel to points east of the city has to go through the temple area or take a much longer route either north or south of that area. Jesus does not object

to people taking a shortcut through the area, but He does condemn them for carrying *any vessel* with them. This word can signify a wide variety of things—from a dish, to a jar, to even a ship's gear. (Some modern translations render it "merchandise.") Thus a person carrying almost anything comes under Jesus' condemnation.

B. The Son of God Explains (v. 17)

17. **And he taught, saying unto them, Is it not written, My house shall be called of all nations the house of prayer? but ye have made it a den of thieves.**

Certainly many who witness Jesus' actions are astonished, so He explains what He is doing and why. As He so often does when challenged, Jesus turns to the Scriptures for support. Here He quotes both Isaiah 56:7 and Jeremiah 7:11. The offenders are turning God's *house of prayer* into *a den of thieves!* What God intends to be a holy place has been turned into a site where profits are more important than prayer. [See question #4, page 280.]

C. The Religious Leaders React (v. 18)

18. **And the scribes and chief priests heard it, and sought how they might destroy him: for they feared him, because all the people was astonished at his doctrine.**

Throughout much of His ministry Jesus has faced opposition from the religious leaders. Now the focused opposition is coming from *the scribes and chief priests,* who control both the temple and the policies concerning the nation's religious life. Even though the scribes are the recognized scholars, they are at a loss in knowing how to challenge Jesus when He uses the Scripture. Probably they don't respond because they do not want to risk a humiliating defeat in front of the people, who are *astonished at his* teaching. His teaching amazes the people, not only because it contradicts what they have been taught by the religious leaders, but also because He has boldly entered the leaders' own territory to confront them. His is a voice of authority!

The religious leaders have good reason to fear Him because He is a threat to their positions and their incomes (John 11:48). Thus they begin to plot *how they might destroy him.* Jesus' earlier critics had sought to discredit Him and to undermine His influence with the people. Realizing that these earlier efforts have only served to increase Jesus' popularity with the people, His enemies now resort to more drastic measures. [See question #5, page 280.]

Conclusion

A. When Leaders Fail

Unfortunately, corruption among religious leaders is not confined to the distant past. Over the last two decades we have been appalled at the moral failure of several religious leaders whose personal lives belied the messages they preached. Many were surprised at these moral disasters, but this is nothing new. Satan is always going about as a roaring lion, "seeking whom he may devour" (1 Peter 5:8). He cleverly concentrates his attacks on our leaders because he knows that their fall will have widespread consequences. Notice how Satan influences Judas to have Jesus killed (Luke 22:3; John 13:27).

To thwart Satan in these matters, we need to take some important steps. We should choose our leaders carefully, seeking to ensure that they are sound in the faith and experienced enough to ward off Satan's attacks. We need to insist on their accountability. And we must lift them up in our prayers. And as we support our leaders in these ways, we also take the same steps to make sure that we ourselves do not fall into sin (cf. 1 Corinthians 9:27; Hebrews 4:1).

B. Prayer

We thank You, Father, that Jesus did not turn aside from the mission that brought Him into the world. We pray that His example of facing corruption without hesitation will serve as a model for us when we face similar situations. Give us the wisdom to know how to oppose evil and defend the truth when Your standards are rejected. In our Master's name we pray, amen.

C. Thought to Remember

"Arm me with jealous care, / As in Thy sight to live, / And O, Thy servant, Lord, prepare, / A strict account to give."   —Charles Wesley

---

Home Daily Bible Readings

Monday, Mar. 31—Jesus Rides Into Jerusalem (Mark 11:1-11)

Tuesday, Apr. 1—The King Comes Riding a Donkey (Zechariah 9:9-12)

Wednesday, Apr. 2—The Stones Would Shout (Luke 19:28-40)

Thursday, Apr. 3—Jesus Cleanses the Temple (Mark 11:12-19)

Friday, Apr. 4—Have Faith in God (Mark 11:20-25)

Saturday, Apr. 5—By What Authority? (Mark 11:27-33)

Sunday, Apr. 6—The Story of Wicked Tenants (Mark 12:1-12)

Learning by Doing

This page contains an alternative lesson plan emphasizing learning activities.
Classes desiring such student involvement will find these suggestions helpful.

Learning Goals

After participating in this lesson, each student will be able to:

1. Summarize Mark's account of Jesus' triumphal entry into Jerusalem and the cleansing of the temple.

2. Explain how these events, which demonstrate Jesus' authority as the divine Son of God, challenge us to confront evil.

3. Suggest at least one specific way to detect and oppose corruption in society.

Into the Lesson

Begin this lesson by grouping class members in sixes. Each group is to plan a parade. Distribute the following questions to each group.

1. What is the purpose of your parade?

2. What items or units (bands, vehicles, and others) will make up the parade?

3. What permits will be necessary to allow the parade to take place?

4. Who will watch your parade?

Allow the groups eight minutes to outline this task. When all the groups are finished ask, "What do you like best about parades?" A variety of answers will be given. Next ask, "Why are parades held?" *Answers may include the celebration of historical events, celebrating present conquests, or the recognition of certain personalities.*

Introduce today's lesson by saying, "Today we will study a parade for Jesus. The response of the people seems to be spontaneous as Jesus rides into Jerusalem on the donkey colt. As we study, look for how people respond to Jesus and His authority."

Into the Word

(Option 1) One way to cover the details of today's text is to contact some of the children's class teachers to prepare a skit for each of the text sections. One group will do Mark 11:1-9, the second will prepare Mark 11:15-18.

(Option 2) Divide your class into three groups. Each group should have four to six members. If your class is larger, give some of the following assignments to more than one group. Provide Bible dictionaries, study Bibles, paper, markers, and other materials necessary.

Group 1: Read Mark 11:1-9. Prepare a short role play of the events. Provide a narrator who can define the word *Hosanna* and discuss the origin of Mark 11:9. (The teacher's commentary is helpful here.)

Group 2: Develop a short report on "money changers" in the Jewish temple. (Especially helpful is the article in *A Dictionary of the Bible* by James Hastings.)

Group 3: Read Mark 11:15-18. Prepare a short role play of the events. Provide a narrator to explain some of the corruption that had entered into this practice. (Use the commentary for help.)

Whichever options you use, call the class back together for reports or performances based on the projects. Lead a discussion using the following questions. (These are in the student book.)

1. How does the reaction of the people at Jesus' triumphal entry remind us of who He is? *(They give adoration and quote Psalm 118.)*

2. How does Jesus react to their worship? *(He accepts it.)*

3. What does Jesus' reaction to the money changers signify about Him? *(He has authority to confront activity that does not honor God.)*

4. What does the response of the leaders tell us about Jesus? *(He is powerful; He is feared; He is amazing.)*

5. What do the leaders seek to do? *(Kill Him.)*

Into Life

Have the class move back to their original groups. Distribute a large piece of poster paper, markers, glue or tape, scissors, and several newspapers or news magazines collected from the previous week.

Ask each group to select stories from the newspaper or magazines that reflect corruption in daily life. They should paste or tape pictures of the story to the poster paper. After ten minutes have each group explain its poster.

Ask each group the following questions:

1. How are Christians being affected by these events?

2. What should be a Christian's response to these events?

3. How can we be helpful to fellow Christians who oppose these events?

Direct your class to pair off for this closing activity. Say, "Choose an area of corruption that bothers you most. Share it with your partner, along with one step you will take this week to oppose it. Pray with each other for strength and courage to oppose this area."

Let's Talk It Over

The questions on this page are designed to promote discussion of the lesson by the class and to encourage application of the lesson Scriptures. The answers provided are only discussion starters. Let your class talk it over from there.

1. Whether by divine foreknowledge or personal interview, Jesus knew the owner of the colt would allow Him to use it on a moment's notice. What of your possessions would you find difficult to give up for the Lord's use? How can a believer release any and every possession to the Lord?

Giving our every possession to the Lord is the essence of stewardship. Have the class suggest some ways we do that, such as giving money, allowing our homes to be used for ministry, using our cars in a ministry of transportation, or willingly providing food or other tangible goods to the needy. Perhaps the greatest resource, and the one we tend to hoard, is time. Ask for specific ways we can make our time and other resources available to the Lord.

2. In Mark 11 many people exhibited an unplanned, uninhibited, unguarded response of praise to the lordship of Jesus. Why is it so hard for some of us to be spontaneous with our praise?

Most of us are creatures of habit. Our routines are comfortable. At the triumphal entry, Jesus broke with the routine. This was something the people had never seen before. Perhaps what we need to be spontaneous in our praise is a new sense of freshness in our faith. Have your students suggest some specific "new" situations: serving in a homeless shelter, a change in the order of worship, or a testimony from a new Christian. Of course, we don't have to wait for a program change or a special event. Talk about how an individual can find freshness from a deliberate change in attitude, an anticipation of God's glory, and a new determination to respond to His lordship.

3. Jesus noted the situation in the temple, and then He left. It wasn't until the next day that He took action to clean things up. What value is there in assessing a situation before reacting? What dangers do we risk when we fail to do so?

Some have accused Jesus of reacting in a fit of rage at what He saw in the temple. The record is clear that He checked it out, returned to Bethany, and then came to Jerusalem the next day ready to execute justice in the temple. No doubt what He had seen the evening before became a matter of prayer for Him before He returned. While He was angry, He was not acting in a fit of rage.

Such care is even more important for us, who do not have Jesus' divine knowledge of all things. We may need to study the situation, ask pertinent questions, and be sure we have all the facts. Certainly we want to be sure our emotions are in control. Failing to do these things may cause us to react to the wrong issues. It may also discredit us as credible spokesmen the next time we try to address some problem.

4. What social or religious injustices are opposed at your church? How do we decide whether one of our protests is shared by Jesus?

In many churches today, the sin of abortion is publicly spoken against. While this practice is legal, Scripture clearly tells us that murder is wrong, and that God values the lives of those in the womb. Many churches also take a public stand against immorality. While live-in partners (of the same or opposite sex) are being granted many of the same rights and privileges as married couples, the Bible is clear that fornication, adultery, and homosexuality are sin. Most churches, on the other hand, do not speak out about a variety of issues about which many of their members may have strong personal opinions. The church must be careful about taking public stands against those issues which Scripture does not address. Talk about the issues your church has addressed in the public forum. Do you need to do more?

5. Being aware of the dire consequences of moral failure in church leadership, how can we contribute to the spiritual health and purity of our church's leaders?

While each leader must answer to God about his own moral choices, congregations can take action to encourage moral purity among their church leaders. Positive feedback, regular words of encouragement, and the establishment of clear and concrete standards for leaders are helpful. Also, a congregation should demand that leaders observe times of rest, including going away for vacations and taking at least one night a week off for family. Finally, a congregation needs to show constant appreciation toward godly leaders, despite their shortcomings. Have your students suggest specific and tangible ways of providing these items—especially ways individuals can encourage their leaders.

Jesus Gives Passover New Meaning

Apr 13

DEVOTIONAL READING: Matthew 26:17-30.

BACKGROUND SCRIPTURE: Mark 14:1-25.

PRINTED TEXT: Mark 14:12-25.

Mark 14:12-25

12 And the first day of unleavened bread, when they killed the passover, his disciples said unto him, Where wilt thou that we go and prepare that thou mayest eat the passover?

13 And he sendeth forth two of his disciples, and saith unto them, Go ye into the city, and there shall meet you a man bearing a pitcher of water: follow him.

14 And wheresoever he shall go in, say ye to the goodman of the house, The Master saith, Where is the guest chamber, where I shall eat the passover with my disciples?

15 And he will show you a large upper room furnished and prepared: there make ready for us.

16 And his disciples went forth, and came into the city, and found as he had said unto them: and they made ready the passover.

17 And in the evening he cometh with the twelve.

18 And as they sat and did eat, Jesus said, Verily I say unto you, One of you which eateth with me shall betray me.

19 And they began to be sorrowful, and to say unto him one by one, Is it I? and another said, Is it I?

20 And he answered and said unto them, It is one of the twelve, that dippeth with me in the dish.

21 The Son of man indeed goeth, as it is written of him: but woe to that man by whom the Son of man is betrayed! good were it for that man if he had never been born.

22 And as they did eat, Jesus took bread, and blessed, and brake it, and gave to them, and said, Take, eat; this is my body.

23 And he took the cup, and when he had given thanks, he gave it to them: and they all drank of it.

24 And he said unto them, This is my blood of the new testament, which is shed for many.

25 Verily I say unto you, I will drink no more of the fruit of the vine, until that day that I drink it new in the kingdom of God.

GOLDEN TEXT: This is my blood of the new testament, which is shed for many.
—Mark 14:24.

Jesus: God's Power in Action
Unit 2: Jesus' Crucifixion and Resurrection
(Lessons 6-8)

Lesson Aims

After participating in this lesson, each student will be able to:

1. Describe the event that became the occasion for the institution of the Lord's Supper.

2. Explain the significance of the Lord's Supper both for the disciples and for Christians today.

3. Suggest some meditation thoughts that can help a participant have a more meaningful experience at the Lord's table.

Lesson Outline

INTRODUCTION
 A. Memories Bring Relief
 B. Lesson Background
 I. PREPARATIONS FOR THE PASSOVER (Mark 14:12-16)
 A. The Disciples' Query (v. 12)
 B. Jesus' Instructions (vv. 13-16)
 II. PREDICTION OF BETRAYAL (Mark 14:17-21)
 A. Assembly and Announcement (vv. 17, 18)
 B. Sorrow and Response (v. 19)
 The Price of a Good (Bad) Deed
 C. Treason and Implication (vv. 20, 21)
 III. INSTITUTION OF THE LORD'S SUPPER (Mark 14:22-25)
 A. The Bread (v. 22)
 B. The Cup (vv. 23, 24)
 A Reminder of a Heroic Sacrifice
 C. The Future (v. 25)
CONCLUSION
 A. Four Looks at the Lord's Supper
 B. Prayer
 C. Thought to Remember

Introduction

A. Memories Bring Relief

S. S. Lappin, a well-known preacher of an earlier generation, told of his growing up in humble surroundings. Their house was scarcely more than a shack. There were large cracks in the wall, which the family kept filled with clay to keep the wind out. On one occasion after they had packed fresh clay into the cracks, a younger brother about two years old pressed his little hands into the clay, leaving the imprint of his hands. The clay soon hardened, leaving the handprints permanently etched into the clay.

Tragedy struck the following spring when the little brother suddenly became ill and died. Dr. Lappin told how for many months afterward his mother, who was losing her eyesight, would feel her way along the wall until she found the little handprints. Then she would gently caress them, thus bringing back fond memories of her son and finding relief in her soul for her painful loss.

In a way, this is our mindset when we come to the Lord's Supper. Saddened by the burden of our sins, we reach for the loaf and the cup as a reminder of our Lord. Although He is no longer with us in His physical body, we can find relief for our troubled souls in remembering what the Communion signifies.

B. Lesson Background

The period between Jesus' triumphal entry and His resurrection the following Sunday is sometimes referred to as the "Final Week." This proved to be the busiest week in Jesus' ministry. In last week's lesson we studied His triumphal entry into Jerusalem and the cleansing of the temple. After that experience, Jesus left Jerusalem and spent the night in Bethany. On the following day (Tuesday) He returned to Jerusalem, where His enemies challenged His authority in a series of bitter attacks. Jesus was able to turn aside these challenges, leaving the religious leaders more determined than ever to destroy Him (Mark 11:27–12:34).

I. Preparations for the Passover
(Mark 14:12-16)

A. The Disciples' Query (v. 12)

12. And the first day of unleavened bread, when they killed the passover, his disciples said unto him, Where wilt thou that we go and prepare that thou mayest eat the passover?

The feast *of unleavened bread* was originally a festival of seven days beginning on the fifteenth day of the month of Nisan (formerly called "Abib"; see Exodus 23:15; 34:18; Leviticus 23:6). This corresponds to late March or early April. This feast became closely associated with the feast of *the passover* (see Numbers 28:16, 17; 2 Chronicles 35:17), which commemorates the deliverance of the Israelites from Egypt (Exodus 12).

In preparation for this Passover, the group has to have a place large enough to accommodate Jesus and the twelve disciples. Extensive arrangements have to be made for the food that is needed for the meal. (See Exodus 12:3, 8, 43-47; Numbers 9:11.) With Jesus' enemies looking to arrest Him (see Mark 14:1), the disciples may be concerned that meeting in a large room and the attendant preparations will draw unwanted attention to themselves. Yet even with security an obvious issue, their question is not whether they will observe the Passover, but *where*. [See question #1, page 288.]

B. Jesus' Instructions (vv. 13-16)

13. And he sendeth forth two of his disciples, and saith unto them, Go ye into the city, and there shall meet you a man bearing a pitcher of water: follow him.

As with the colt borrowed for His entry into Jerusalem, Jesus has either made prior arrangements or has used His supernatural abilities to know about the circumstances that will come together concerning His observance of the Passover. Just as He had sent *two of His disciples* to secure the colt, so He sends two to find the room and prepare it. (From Luke 22:8 we know that the two in this instance are Peter and John.)

Men normally carry water or wine in jugs or wineskin bottles. A Jewish woman, on the other hand, carries a pitcher or jar of water on her head. Even though the streets of Jerusalem are teeming with hundreds of visitors for this important feast, seeing a man carrying a jar in such a crowd will be certain to attract the disciples' attention.

14. And wheresoever he shall go in, say ye to the goodman of the house, The Master saith, Where is the guest chamber, where I shall eat the passover with my disciples?

The disciples are to follow this man to a *house*, where they are to speak to the *goodman*, or owner. In speaking to him, the disciples are to use certain words—*the Master saith*—to indicate to him that they come from Jesus.

15. And he will show you a large upper room furnished and prepared: there make ready for us.

Houses in this region often have a second story *room*, normally accessed by an outside stairway, that can be used for guests. The prophet Elijah had stayed in such a room (or "loft") when he was a guest of the widow of Zarephath (1 Kings 17:19; Luke 4:26). The fact that the room is *large* enough to accommodate the thirteen men indicates that the owner is a person of some means.

The room is *furnished*, but the furnishings are simple by today's standards—perhaps only a low table surrounded by pallets for reclining. Leonardo da Vinci's famous painting of *The Last Supper*, which shows Jesus and His disciples seated about a table, depicts a Renaissance Italian setting rather than the setting that would have been found in Jesus' day. The furnishings in the room do not include the food, which the disciples will have to provide.

16. And his disciples went forth, and came into the city, and found as he had said unto them: and they made ready the passover.

The two *disciples* do as Jesus instructs them and find the situation exactly *as he had said* it would be. Making *ready the passover* involves preparing or purchasing several things: the Passover lamb, which will take some time to kill and roast; unleavened bread—meaning bread made with no yeast—to remind them of the haste of the departure from Egypt; a bowl of salt water to remind them of the Red Sea; bitter herbs as a reminder of their bitter experience as slaves; a paste or sauce made of a mixture of fruit and nuts; and fruit of the vine to drink. All this preparation has to be finished on the fourteenth of Nisan within the space of just a few hours (see Exodus 12:6; Numbers 9:3; Deuteronomy 16:6).

II. Prediction of Betrayal (Mark 14:17-21)

A. Assembly and Announcement (vv. 17, 18)

17. And in the evening he cometh with the twelve.

When *evening* comes, Jesus and the ten disciples who have remained with Him walk from Bethany to join the other two in the upper room. Tradition holds that the upper room is in the western part of Jerusalem. Wherever this room is located, it must be somewhere within the walls of Jerusalem, since that is where the Passover meal must be eaten. A new day—the fifteenth of Nisan—begins in the evening at sundown, and the Passover meal can now begin.

18. And as they sat and did eat, Jesus said, Verily I say unto you, One of you which eateth with me shall betray me.

The Passover is a sacred and solemn occasion. But it is also a time to celebrate God's deliverance of the Jewish people from slavery in Egypt. As they eat the meal, however, Jesus makes an

---

How to Say It

ABIB. *A*-bib.
BETHANY. *Beth*-uh-nee.
DEUTERONOMY. Due-ter-*ahn*-uh-me.
ELIJAH. Ee-*lye*-juh.
EUCHARIST. *Yoo*-kuh-rust.
LEONARDO DA VINCI. Lee-uh-*nard*-oh duh *Vin*-chee.
NISAN. *Nye*-san.
PENTECOST. *Pent*-ih-kost.
RENAISSANCE. *Reh*-nuh-*sonts* (strong accent on *sonts*).
ZAREPHATH. *Zair*-uh-fath.

announcement that casts a pall over the celebration. These men had been together for three years, in all kinds of circumstances. That one of this number, His closest companions, will *betray* Him is unthinkable. [See question #2, page 288.]

B. Sorrow and Response (v. 19)

19. And they began to be sorrowful, and to say unto him one by one, Is it I? And another said, Is it I?

Jesus' announcement leads to a time of serious soul-searching. With sorrow, each in turn asks the same question: *Is it I?* Except for Judas, each one is convinced that he will not knowingly betray the Master. Yet each harbors a lingering doubt that he might unwittingly or accidentally betray the Lord. If they know this in advance, they might take steps to avoid this possibility.

Matthew's version of this incident indicates that after the others have responded to Jesus in this way, Judas also asks, "Master, is it I?" Jesus replies, "Thou hast said" (Matthew 26:25). The other disciples apparently do not hear or do not understand Jesus' response to Judas. While this is an affirmative response, it is also intentionally vague. It might mean no more than, "You're the one who said it, not I." Had the other disciples understood that Judas was to become the betrayer, they surely would have tried to stop him. [See question #3, page 288.]

THE PRICE OF A GOOD (BAD) DEED

A couple of years ago, a professional musician left his 1673 Stradivarius cello in a New York City taxicab. The cab driver later realized his passenger had left something in the car and tried to return it where he had let the man off. However, the doorman would agree only to pass on the driver's phone number to the owner. The next day the musician picked up his cello and gave the cabbie a $75 check. The cabbie said it wasn't good enough so the offer was raised to $1,000. But the cab driver decided a "finder's fee" of 1 percent was more appropriate. Thus he should get $40,000 for returning a cello valued at $4,000,000. How much is a good deed worth? It seems it depends on the greed of the person doing it!

Many people have speculated about Judas's reason or motive for betraying Christ—and for a mere thirty pieces of silver at that! How much is a *bad* deed worth? A currently popular theory is that Judas was trying to do good by forcing Jesus to become king. On the other hand, it may well have been greed; it's a common human sin. In either case, Judas missed the point of what Jesus was trying to do. When Jesus announced that one of His disciples would betray Him, the others

asked, "Is it I?" We who follow Christ today must ask ourselves, "Would I betray my Lord for money, or even deny Him for no tangible reward as the other disciples did?"   —C. R. B.

C. Treason and Implication (vv. 20, 21)

20. And he answered and said unto them, It is one of the twelve, that dippeth with me in the dish.

In this meal it is a common practice for those participating to dip their bread into *the dish* that contains the bitter herbs and fruit paste. Probably all of the disciples have dipped their bread into this dish at one time or another during the meal. In the ancient near East, sharing a meal with a host involves a sacred trust. It is considered most reprehensible for a person to violate that trust by harming the host in any way. This may have been Jesus' intent rather than an effort to identify Judas specifically as the traitor.

John's account of this event indicates that Jesus goes a step farther in identifying the traitor. When Peter presses John to ask Jesus specifically about the identity of the traitor, Jesus replies, "He it is, to whom I shall give a sop, when I have dipped it." Then He dips a piece of bread and gives it to Judas (John 13:26). The other disciples miss even this clear signal, however, because they think Jesus is giving instructions to Judas about money (13:28, 29). [See question #4, page 288.]

21. The Son of man indeed goeth, as it is written of him: but woe to that man by whom the Son of man is betrayed! good were it for that man if he had never been born.

In referring to what *is written of him*, Jesus may have Psalm 41:9 in mind. This passage speaks explicitly of a person who betrays a friend, even after sharing bread. Other possible references are Isaiah 53:7-9 and Daniel 9:26.

Even though Jesus predicts His death, which is necessary in God's plan for human salvation, that does not make the guilt of the betrayer any less. Judas has the freedom to make a different choice. But from eternity past, God has known the path Judas would choose (cf. John 17:12; Acts 1:16-18). Surely to have *never been born* would be preferable to the eternal destruction that awaits Judas! (See Acts 1:25.)

III. Institution of the Lord's Supper (Mark 14:22-25)

A. The Bread (v. 22)

22. And as they did eat, Jesus took bread, and blessed, and brake it, and gave to them, and said, Take, eat; this is my body.

Jesus injects a completely new element as the Passover meal approaches its conclusion. Taking some of the fruit of the vine and the *bread,* He gives them new meaning. With this new meaning in place, today we celebrate the Lord's Supper (or "Communion") rather than the Passover.

But exactly what the new meaning is has been a source of intense debate throughout church history. Various interpretations of the phrases *this is my body* and "this is my blood" (v. 24, below) have resulted in Christians' dividing themselves from one another. How sadly ironic this is: the Lord's Supper, which should bring Christians together, actually drives them apart! (See 1 Corinthians 10:17.)

Some teach that Jesus was speaking literally—that the bread and fruit of the vine in some miraculous way actually become His flesh and blood. But in His preaching and teaching Jesus often used figurative language to get His point across to His listeners. For example, in John 10:7 He said, "I am the door." No one who heard Him say these words supposed that He was actually a wooden door that swung on iron hinges! Why then should anyone assume that the bread and fruit of the vine must actually be His flesh and blood? Even as Jesus breaks the bread and hands it to the disciples, He is still right there before them in the flesh. The disciples know that drinking actual blood is against the Old Testament law (cf. Leviticus 7:26, 27), but we see them raising no objection.

B. The Cup (vv. 23, 24)

23. And he took the cup, and when he had given thanks, he gave it to them: and they all drank of it.

Just as the bread Jesus uses is a part of the usual Passover observance, so also is fruit of the vine. Typically the Passover meal features four cups, each to be used at a particular point to correspond with the four promises of Exodus 6:6, 7.

The particular *cup* Jesus uses here is probably the third of the four cups, known as "the cup of blessing." But before He passes the cup around, He gives *thanks.* When the Greek letters of this word are pronounced in English, the result is the familiar word *Eucharist,* which in some churches is the term used to denote the Lord's Supper.

24. And he said unto them, This is my blood of the new testament, which is shed for many.

The word *new* is not found in many of the ancient manuscripts and is thus omitted in many modern translations. However, "new" is found in the accounts of the Lord's Supper in Luke 22:20 and 1 Corinthians 11:25, revealing how appropriate the word is in this context. The word *testament* is easier to understand as a "covenant," which is a formal, solemn, and binding agreement. This understanding allows us to compare

Visual for lesson 7

"This is my blood of the new testament, which is shed for many." Mark 14:24

This classic illustration of the Lord's Supper is suitable for this lesson and for general use.

more easily the "Old Covenant" with the "New Covenant" (cf. Jeremiah 31:31, 32; see also Hebrews 8:7-13). Of course, the word *testament* has significance, too, in that it was put into effect with the "death of the testator" (Hebrews 9:16, 17).

Sacrificial *blood* was an important part of the Old Covenant. When Moses initiated the people into God's covenant, he took the blood from the sacrificial animals and sprinkled it on the people (Exodus 24:8; Hebrews 9:18-22). This lent solemnity to the occasion and symbolically committed them to live according to the terms of that covenant. Now as Jesus passes the cup from which all drink, He points the disciples toward the New Covenant. This is a covenant that Jesus will seal with His own blood (cf. John 6:53-56; Hebrews 10:10-18).

A REMINDER OF A HEROIC SACRIFICE

The Arizona State Hospital cemetery contains some twenty-four hundred gravestones marked only with numbers. Beneath one of those stones lies Corporal Isaiah Mays. He was born in 1858 and after emancipation he became a member of the U.S. Army's Tenth Cavalry, an all-black unit. While guarding a payroll wagon near Tucson in 1889, his unit was attacked by thieves. Most of the soldiers were driven off, but Mays fought back valiantly. Although wounded in both legs, he crawled two miles to sound a warning.

Mays was awarded the Medal of Honor for his heroic deeds. But the government refused to give him a pension, and he died in poverty at the hospital in 1925. No relatives claimed the body, so Mays was buried under one of those numbered stones. However, a therapist at the hospital has taken on the task of trying to identify the remains of those twenty-four hundred soldiers. She was able to match Mays's numbered stone with hospital records. Finally, in 2001, Mays's grave received a four-foot-high Medal of Honor headstone like those at Arlington National Cemetery.

The Lord's Supper is like that numbered gravestone. Both are such simple things, but both serve as reminders of courage and sacrifice. When we understand the nature of the Lord's Supper, this simple service beckons us to remember the heroic sacrifice that one Man made so long ago to pay sin's price.   —C. R. B.

C. The Future (v. 25)

25. Verily I say unto you, I will drink no more of the fruit of the vine, until that day that I drink it new in the kingdom of God.

Within six weeks of this meal, Jesus will return to His Heavenly home (Acts 1:3, 9). There is no indication that He shares the Lord's Supper with the disciples during this period. The first indication we have that the disciples, along with other Christians, observe the Lord's Supper comes after the Day of Pentecost in Acts 2. Thus, many understand Jesus to be saying that He is looking forward to the consummation of His kingdom in Heaven (cf. Isaiah 25:6; Matthew 8:11).

Others take this to mean that Jesus will participate in Communion with Christians each time they assemble to worship and meet around His table. Of course, He will not be with them in the flesh, but He will be with them spiritually. "For where two or three are gathered together in my name, there am I in the midst of them" (Matthew 18:20). Today when we participate in the Lord's Supper, Satan does his best to reduce this experience to a routine that becomes virtually meaningless. But when we realize that the Lord is present, our participation becomes a solemn, reverent experience that reminds us of Whose we are. [See question #5, page 288.]

Conclusion

A. Four Looks at the Lord's Supper

Christianity is a *historic* religion with its roots deep in the past, but it is also a *futuristic* religion, looking to eternity beyond this world. Christianity is a *personal* religion, encouraging its adherents to examine their hearts, but it is also a *social* religion, looking outside the individual to the larger human family. Nowhere are these four aspects of Christianity better illustrated than in the Lord's Supper.

First of all, the participant is encouraged to look backward to the suffering and death of Christ. We are deeply humbled when we pause to consider what a great price our Lord paid for our sins.

The Lord's Supper is also a look forward. Jesus has promised that He will "drink it new in the kingdom of God." Our hopes are not anchored permanently to the past or to the present but are free to reach out to eternity (cf. Ecclesiastes 3:11). Through His death Christians have the certain hope of eternal life.

Our participation in Communion challenges us to look inward. As we come together at His table, our thoughts are turned to our own failures. In those few moments we have the opportunity to examine our lives and compare them to the Biblical standards. To that point, Paul writes, "Let a man examine himself," before eating the bread and drinking of the cup (1 Corinthians 11:28). Paul goes on to warn of the dire consequences that will result when one does not conduct this self-examination.

Finally, the Lord's Supper is a look outward. The message of Christianity is a message for all humanity (Matthew 28:19, 20). In a way, Communion is this gospel message in a capsule form. Just as the Passover celebration had an important meaning to convey to future generations (Exodus 12:25-27), so also our observance of the Lord's Supper proclaims "the Lord's death till he come" (1 Corinthians 11:26).

B. Prayer

Gracious Father, as we participate in the Lord's Supper teach us to examine our hearts so that we may commune in a worthy manner. Let the Communion elements remind us of our Lord's suffering and death that purchased our eternal life. In Jesus' name we pray, amen.

C. Thought to Remember

"This do in remembrance of me."

—1 Corinthians 11:24

Home Daily Bible Readings

Monday, Apr. 7—A Woman Anoints Jesus (Mark 14:1-9)

Tuesday, Apr. 8—Plans Made for Passover (Mark 14:10-16)

Wednesday, Apr. 9—The Cup and the Bread (Mark 14:17-25)

Thursday, Apr. 10—Jesus Washes the Disciples' Feet (John 13:1-5)

Friday, Apr. 11—I Have Set You an Example (John 13:12-20)

Saturday, Apr. 12—Where I Go, You Cannot Come (John 13:31-35)

Sunday, Apr. 13—In Remembrance of Me (1 Corinthians 11:23-28)

Learning by Doing

This page contains an alternative lesson plan emphasizing learning activities.
Classes desiring such student involvement will find these suggestions helpful.

Learning Goals

After participating in this lesson, each student will be able to:

1. Describe the event that became the occasion for the institution of the Lord's Supper.

2. Explain the significance of the Lord's Supper both for the disciples and for Christians today.

3. Suggest some meditation thoughts that can help a participant have a more meaningful experience at the Lord's table.

Into the Lesson

As your students arrive today, put them in groups of four. Have the following materials ready (or you can use the student books for this activity): letter-size paper, pens or pencils, markers, envelopes.

Say, "Today I want you to design an invitation to a class dinner. Determine the menu and the guest list. Make a list of what you will need for decorating the room. We will plan this dinner to be in two weeks."

Encourage your class members to plan a meal that will be remembered by all participants. The invitation should include date and time, place, menu, and keynote speaker and the subject of the speech to be given (if any). They should also draw a floor plan with table seating, serving tables, speaker's podium, and decorations needed. This activity should take no more than fifteen minutes.

Call the class together by saying, "Keep your invitations and plans for later in the session. Today we are studying how Jesus prepared for and celebrated the Passover and then instituted the 'Lord's Supper.' As we study, think about how you might invite someone to the Lord's table on His behalf."

Into the Word

Use the Lesson Background on page 282 to prepare a brief introduction of the events leading up to today's text.

Copy the following matching list for each student, putting the numbered column on the left and the lettered column on the right. Be sure each person has a Bible or a copy of the printed Scriptures for today's study. (This matching activity also appears in *Adult Bible Class*.) The correct answers are 1-d; 2-e; 3-g; 4-a; 5-c; 6-f; 7-b.

___ 1. Disciples wonder where the Passover will be eaten.

___ 2. Jesus gives two disciples specific instructions for preparation.

___ 3. The disciples find things as Jesus had said.

___ 4. Jesus and the twelve disciples eat the Passover together.

___ 5. Jesus predicts His betrayal.

___ 6. Jesus institutes the Lord's Supper.

___ 7. The disciples sing a hymn and leave.

a. Mark 14:18a	e. Mark 14:13-15
b. Mark 14:26	f. Mark 14:22-25
c. Mark 14:18b-21	g. Mark 14:16
d. Mark 14:12	

Give your class approximately ten minutes to complete this activity. Review the correct answers and discuss the events. Your text commentary contains helpful materials.

Emphasize to your class members the significance of the Lord's Supper for today by using the material in "Four Looks at the Lord's Supper" in the commentary (page 286) and the following questions.

How does the Lord's Supper help us to look *backward?*

How does the Lord's Supper help us to look *forward?*

How does the Lord's Supper help us to look *inward?* (See also 1 Corinthians 11:28.)

How does the Lord's Supper help us to look *outward?* (See also 1 Corinthians 11:26.)

From our text today, why did Jesus institute the Lord's Supper? *(To solemnize the fact that the disciples were entering a covenant with Jesus.)*

Into Life

Refer to the introductory exercise (or to the student book). Each student will complete an invitation to the Lord's Supper, a first-century guest list, and a twenty-first century guest list. Help each student to realize that every Christian is invited to the Lord's table.

Distribute to each student a blank sheet of paper. Students may work in pairs as they write a brief Communion meditation outline based on today's text and 1 Corinthians 11:17-34. Ask volunteers to read their finished meditations.

Close the session with prayer and an appropriate hymn or song.

Let's Talk It Over

*The questions on this page are designed to promote discussion of the lesson
by the class and to encourage application of the lesson Scriptures. The answers
provided are only discussion starters. Let your class talk it over from there.*

1. The disciples were concerned for their safety, but they still wanted to observe the Passover as the law required. How different they are from the many today who abandon Scriptural precedents for the sake of convenience! How do we make sure that we, in attempting to be contemporary in our observance of Scriptural practice, do not change their essence?

Naturally, we want people of today to connect with the precedents of the past. The Lord's Supper, for example, was given by Jesus as a memorial to His sacrifice in our behalf. That must be continued, but there are disagreements over some of the details: who may "preside" at the table, and who may pass the emblems? One cup or many? A whole loaf or wafers? With any Scriptural precedent, we want to maintain the essence of the observance with an attitude that is pleasing to God. We do not make substitutions merely out of convenience. Our practices must communicate the meaning of the precedent to each new generation.

2. The original Passover celebration was both solemn and joyful. It represented the deaths of thousands of Egyptians and also God's deliverance of His people. How is Communion a combination of solemnity and rejoicing? How do those differing dynamics deepen your Communion experience?

Today, when we celebrate the Lord's Supper, we gather to commemorate the death of a close friend, and it could be accurately said that we caused Him to die. On the other hand, we celebrate the triumph of God over the grave and the forgiveness of sins made possible through the ultimate sacrifice. We humbly and sadly accept the tragic gift that God gave us at the cross, while we rejoice in the end result: our eternal salvation!

3. When Jesus predicted His betrayal, the disciples in turn asked, "Is it I?" Suppose a fellow believer tells you he feels like one of those disciples, afraid that he might someday unintentionally betray Jesus? What would you say?

All of us need to participate in periods of self-examination, where we consider where we are in our relationship with Christ, and in what areas of our life we may have let our old life creep in. We may realize that we have disappointed Christ.

We ask Him for forgiveness for such sins, and we repent and turn from those actions. When we have done so, our conscience and the Holy Spirit will be satisfied that we are again on the right track. Paul writes that nothing in all creation can separate us from the love of God; Jesus, however, tells us that it is our responsibility to choose to remain in His love. It is our responsibility to watch that we don't knowingly disappoint our Lord, but it would be a denial of God's grace to wonder if we might have unknowingly betrayed Him and lost our salvation.

4. How can we follow Jesus' example of graciousness in the presence of someone who has betrayed, hurt, or disappointed us?

Someone might say, in the words of the ad slogan, "Just do it!" Just follow Jesus' example. Of course, that is easier said than done, but it must be done. We need to resolve to do so. And we should also remember that we, unlike Jesus, are not perfect. We may have provoked the other person somehow. We also are guilty of offending Jesus at some point. We are not so different from the one who has hurt us. If Jesus, who was guilty of no offense, can forgive us, then we can forgive others. (See Colossians 3:13.)

5. What aspects of the Lord's Supper make it consistently meaningful for those of us who observe it frequently?

Several aspects of the Lord's Supper allow it to retain, or even increase, its meaning. First of all, time spent at the Lord's table is time spent with the Lord. As our relationship with Christ grows, our time with Him becomes more meaningful. Second, Communion time is a time of self-examination. If we are honest about where we are and where we should be, time at the Lord's table will not be boring or "the same as it always is." Third, time at the Lord's table is a memorial service in which we focus on Jesus' life and death. As our knowledge of Jesus grows, our sense of awe that He would die for us should likewise grow. Finally, the memorial service at the Lord's table commemorates the death of a person who is no longer dead! Time spent at the Lord's table is a time of joy and connection with other believers. It is a preparation for the marriage supper of the Lamb (Revelation 19:9) in His eternal kingdom.

Jesus Dies and Lives Again

DEVOTIONAL READING: John 20:11-18.

BACKGROUND SCRIPTURE: MARK 15:1–16:8.

PRINTED TEXT: Mark 15:21-25, 33-37; 16:1-8.

Mark 15:21-25, 33-37

21 And they compel one Simon a Cyrenian, who passed by, coming out of the country, the father of Alexander and Rufus, to bear his cross.

22 And they bring him unto the place Golgotha, which is, being interpreted, The place of a skull.

23 And they gave him to drink wine mingled with myrrh: but he received it not.

24 And when they had crucified him, they parted his garments, casting lots upon them, what every man should take.

25 And it was the third hour, and they crucified him.

. . . .

33 And when the sixth hour was come, there was darkness over the whole land until the ninth hour.

34 And at the ninth hour Jesus cried with a loud voice, saying, Eloi, Eloi, lama sabachthani? which is, being interpreted, My God, my God, why hast thou forsaken me?

35 And some of them that stood by, when they heard it, said, Behold, he calleth Elijah.

36 And one ran and filled a sponge full of vinegar, and put it on a reed, and gave him to drink, saying, Let alone; let us see whether Elijah will come to take him down.

37 And Jesus cried with a loud voice, and gave up the ghost.

Mark 16:1-8

1 And when the sabbath was past, Mary Magdalene, and Mary the mother of James, and Salome, had bought sweet spices, that they might come and anoint him.

2 And very early in the morning, the first day of the week, they came unto the sepulchre at the rising of the sun.

3 And they said among themselves, Who shall roll us away the stone from the door of the sepulchre?

4 And when they looked, they saw that the stone was rolled away: for it was very great.

5 And entering into the sepulchre, they saw a young man sitting on the right side, clothed in a long white garment; and they were affrighted.

6 And he saith unto them, Be not affrighted: ye seek Jesus of Nazareth, which was crucified: he is risen; he is not here: behold the place where they laid him.

7 But go your way, tell his disciples and Peter that he goeth before you into Galilee: there shall ye see him, as he said unto you.

8 And they went out quickly, and fled from the sepulchre; for they trembled and were amazed: neither said they any thing to any man; for they were afraid.

GOLDEN TEXT: Be not affrighted: ye seek Jesus of Nazareth, which was crucified: he is risen; he is not here: behold the place where they laid him.—Mark 16:6.

Lesson Aims

After participating in this lesson, each student will be able to:

1. Cite the significant details concerning Jesus' crucifixion and resurrection.

2. Tell why the crucifixion and resurrection are vital to the Christian faith.

3. Prepare an answer for someone who might deny the resurrection.

Lesson Outline

INTRODUCTION
 A. "Bought for all Time"
 B. Lesson Background
I. JESUS' CRUCIFIXION (Mark 15:21-25)
 A. The Heaviness of the Cross (v. 21)
 B. The Place of the Skull (v. 22)
 C. The Activities of the Soldiers (vv. 23-25)
II. JESUS ON THE CROSS (Mark 15:33-37)
 A. The Darkness of Judgment (v. 33)
  History's Darkest Day
 B. The Cry of Desolation (vv. 34-36)
 C. The Death of Jesus (v. 37)
III. THE EMPTY TOMB (Mark 16:1-8)
 A. The Women (vv. 1-4)
 B. The Angel (vv. 5-8)
  A New Reality
CONCLUSION
 A. "Descend Now From the Cross"
 B. Prayer
 C. Thought to Remember

Introduction

A. "Bought for All Time"

Many years ago, a German nobleman determined to build a tomb that would stand against the ravages of time. Workmen fashioned the structure from huge blocks of granite that interlocked in such a way that once set in place they were almost impossible to move. When the nobleman died, his body was sealed in the tomb with this inscription on the outside: "This grave, bought for all time, must never be opened."

Within a few years a seed from a nearby tree fell into a small crevice between two of the stones. With the help of rain and sunshine, the seed germinated and sent its rootlets down into the microscopic cracks between the stones. The years passed and the seedling continued to grow. This growth, along with the freezing and thawing, eroded the granite and began to force apart the huge blocks. Eventually a large tree grew up through the middle of the tomb.

Those who thought that killing Jesus and placing Him in a stone tomb "bought for all time" would eliminate Him permanently didn't count on the power of God. If God, working through the forces of nature, could destroy a tomb of granite, what chance did a man-made tomb have of containing the body of Jesus against a far greater power? It is Jesus' *empty* tomb that is "bought for all time"!

B. Lesson Background

When the meal in the upper room had been concluded, Jesus and His disciples sang a hymn and went out to the Garden of Gethsemane on the western slope of the Mount of Olives (Mark 14:26). Jesus, seeking privacy, left the disciples and went deeper into the garden. There He fervently poured out His heart in prayer to the Father: "Take away this cup . . . nevertheless, not what I will, but what thou wilt" (14:36).

Shortly afterward, the forces of the religious leaders, led by Judas, seized Jesus. As Jesus was led away for trial, the disciples fled. In a series of trials before the Sanhedrin, Herod Antipas, and Pilate, Jesus was condemned to die on the cross. Today's lesson begins at this point.

I. Jesus' Crucifixion (Mark 15:21-25)

A. The Heaviness of the Cross (v. 21)

21. And they compel one Simon a Cyrenian, who passed by, coming out of the country, the father of Alexander and Rufus, to bear his cross.

Crucifixions and other methods of capital punishment are conducted outside the city walls (cf. Leviticus 24:14; Numbers 15:35, 36; 1 Kings 21:13; Acts 7:58; Hebrews 13:12, 13). As Jesus is led to the place of the crucifixion (supposedly along the *Via Dolorosa*—the "Way of Sorrow"), He is forced to carry His own *cross* (John 19:17).

But Jesus has gone sleepless from the night before, probably has been denied food, and has been brutally tortured (Mark 15:16-20). It is little wonder that the weight of the cross becomes more than He can bear. Thus a certain *Simon*, from the province of Cyrene, is compelled to carry the cross as he comes into the city. Since Mark mentions this man by name along with the fact that he is *the father of Alexander and Rufus*, some propose that Simon is the father of the Rufus mentioned in Romans 16:13. [See question #1, page 296.]

B. The Place of the Skull (v. 22)

22. And they bring him unto the place Golgotha, which is, being interpreted, The place of a skull.

Mark interprets the Aramaic term *Golgotha* for his Greek-speaking readers. Tourists today are shown a little mound north of Jerusalem's walls that does indeed resemble *a skull*. Another tradition holds that the crucifixion occurred near the modern site of the Church of the Holy Sepulchre. This place was near the city in the first century (John 19:20), but is located inside the city walls today. Of course, there is no way of knowing with certainty whether either of these spots is the actual location of the crucifixion.

C. The Activities of the Soldiers (vv. 23-25)

23. And they gave him to drink wine mingled with myrrh: but he received it not.

Myrrh is a gum resin from trees that grow in Arabia and eastern Africa. It is highly prized as a perfume, as an embalming agent (cf. Matthew 2:11; John 19:39), and as a medicine. Some students think it was for this medicinal value that the soldiers offer the drink to Jesus—that it has some narcotic effect that will relieve some of Jesus' pain. They believe Jesus refuses it because He has committed Himself to drink the full measure of the cup of suffering and He wants to have a clear mind when He speaks His last words.

Other students note, however, that myrrh is very bitter in taste. *Wine mingled with myrrh*, they say, would be undrinkable. The soldiers know that this mixture is too bitter to drink; they are merely adding to Jesus' torture by offering it (cf. Psalm 69:20, 21). We cannot say for certain which view is correct. However, it does seem more in keeping with the soldiers' hardened character that they would tease their victims with undrinkable wine than offer pain-relieving medicine.

24. And when they had crucified him, they parted his garments, casting lots upon them, what every man should take.

To be *crucified* means to be either tied or nailed to a crossbeam, which is then fastened to an upright support. (In Jesus' case, He was nailed; see John 20:25.) In the Roman Empire, crucifixion is usually reserved for slaves or those who have committed the most heinous crimes. It is especially feared because it prolongs for hours (or even days) the agony of death, which eventually comes by exposure, infection, and/or asphyxiation. As in the case of those who are executed alongside Jesus, measures such as breaking the victim's legs are sometimes used to hasten death (cf. John 19:32).

The soldiers assigned to the execution are hardened to suffering. Once the condemned prisoners are on the crosses, the soldiers' interest turns to what personal gain they can get. And so they cast *lots*—using something like dice—to divide Jesus' meager earthly possessions among themselves. Jesus may have had an inner garment, an outer robe or tunic, a belt or sash, sandals, and perhaps a headpiece. This is a fulfillment of Psalm 22:18. [See question #2, page 296.]

25. And it was the third hour, and they crucified him.

The ancient Jews count their days from sunrise to sunrise. Under this system, *the third hour* would be about 9:00 A.M. But John 19:14 indicates that the trial is still in progress at "the sixth hour." How could Jesus have been crucified at the "third" hour if the trial lasted past the "sixth" hour? There is more than one possible solution to this puzzle. One well-known suggestion holds that John, addressing a Roman audience, used a different means of counting time. In certain instances, the Romans count time from midnight rather than sunrise. Thus, John's "sixth hour" was 6:00 A.M., three hours before the crucifixion.

II. Jesus on the Cross
(Mark 15:33-37)

A. The Darkness of Judgment (v. 33)

33. And when the sixth hour was come, there was darkness over the whole land until the ninth hour.

The *darkness* that comes *over the whole land* at *the sixth hour* (noon) cannot be a normal eclipse. The moon is full during the Passover period. We can only conclude that this is a tremendous miracle, visible to thousands of people.

No doubt the darkness at midday strikes fear in the hearts of those watching the crucifixion. During this time, the veil in the temple is torn in two from top to bottom, the earth shakes, many godly people rise from their graves, and a pagan Roman centurion confesses that Jesus is indeed "the Son of God" (Matthew 27:51-54).

HISTORY'S DARKEST DAY

At 8:32 A.M. on May 18, 1980, volcanologist David A. Johnston yelled his last words as he radioed his colleagues: "Vancouver, Vancouver, this is it!" A fiery-hot cloud of gas was rolling toward him at three hundred miles per hour. Mount Saint Helens had just "blown its top." Johnston was camped five miles from the peak when the mountain erupted with the destructive force of a twenty-four-megaton nuclear bomb. Nearly four billion cubic yards of earth were blown off the north face of the mountain. Enough trees to build two hundred thousand homes were burned instantly by the 660-degree wind.

How to Say It

AFFRIGHTED. uh-*frite*-ud.

ARAMAIC. *Air*-uh-*may*-ik (strong accent on *may*).

ARIMATHEA. *Air*-uh-muh-*thee*-uh (strong accent on *thee* as in *thin*).

CYRENE. Sigh-*ree*-nee.

CYRENIAN. Sigh-*ree*-nee-un.

DEUTERONOMY. Due-ter-*ahn*-uh-me.

ELIJAH. Ee-*lye*-juh.

ELOI, ELOI, LAMA SABACHTHANI (Aramaic). Ee-*lo*-eye, Ee-*lo*-eye, *lah*-mah suh-*back*-thuh-nee.

GETHSEMANE. Geth-*sem*-uh-nee.

GOLGOTHA. *Gahl*-guh-thuh.

HEROD ANTIPAS. *Hair*-ud *An*-tih-pus.

MYRRH. mur.

RENAISSANCE. *Reh*-nuh-*sonts* (strong accent on *sonts*).

SANHEDRIN. *San*-huh-drun or San-*heed*-run.

SEPULCHRE. *sep*-ul-kur.

VIA DOLOROSA. *Vye*-uh (or *Vee*-uh) *Doe*-luh-*row*-suh (strong accent on *row*).

Some of the ash that roiled thousands of feet into the air came down as far away as Oklahoma. Closer to the scene, it darkened the earth as if it were night. Jay Thomas was a logger working in the forest more than twenty miles from the mountain that morning. He said, "It got quiet, eerie quiet—not a bird chirping, a frog croaking. And it got dark, midnight dark."

The afternoon Christ died must have been something like that: the silence of creation interrupted only by the terrified screams of people wondering if the end of their world had come. And the darkness that day—what an awesome symbol of God's judgment on sin! How terrifying the silence and blackness must have been when God bent creation to His will on the darkest day in human history!   —C. R. B.

B. The Cry of Desolation (vv. 34-36)

34. And at the ninth hour Jesus cried with a loud voice, saying, Eloi, Eloi, lama sabachthani? which is, being interpreted, My God, my God, why hast thou forsaken me?

At the ninth hour, or about 3:00 P.M., Jesus raises His voice in a dramatic cry of desolation. The Aramaic words that Mark interprets for his readers come from the first part of Psalm 22:1.

This is one of the most difficult of all of Jesus' sayings. At first glance it may seem that the "human part" of Jesus is being critical of God because God has forsaken Him. We are not capable with our mere human minds to comprehend fully how the human and the divine could be combined in the Christ. There seemed to be a struggle between Jesus' human and divine parts as He prayed in the Garden of Gethsemane—a struggle that reaches its climax on the cross.

Jesus' ordeal is physically painful beyond imagination. But the agony of bearing the weight of the sins of all humanity must be even more extreme than the physical torture. Suspended between Heaven and earth, He takes on the curse of God for our sake (Galatians 3:13). And yet, God is still present. If we read to the end of Psalm 22, we find the psalmist reaffirms God's presence and God's victory in his life. This, too, is prophetic of Jesus' experience on the cross.

35. And some of them that stood by, when they heard it, said, Behold, he calleth Elijah.

Because of His parched throat and tongue, Jesus may not be able to speak clearly. Apparently some people take *Eloi* for *Elijah.* Jewish tradition holds that Elijah will return someday to save his nation, and the people seem to make this connection. Malachi 4:5, 6 does predict the return of Elijah as a forerunner of the "great and dreadful day of the Lord," a prediction fulfilled in the ministry of John the Baptist (Matthew 17:10-13).

36. And one ran and filled a sponge full of vinegar, and put it on a reed, and gave him to drink, saying, Let alone; let us see whether Elijah will come to take him down.

Jesus, suffering shock and the loss of blood, is undoubtedly quite thirsty. But whether this offer of a *drink* is an act of mercy or an act of mockery is hard to say. The *vinegar* mentioned here is a cheap, sour wine often drunk by laborers and foot soldiers. As with Mark 15:23 above, there is a tie-in to Psalm 69:21. The fact that the sponge soaked in wine has to be put *on a reed* in order for it to reach His mouth indicates that the cross that suspends Him is some height above the ground.

If the offer of this drink is designed to prolong Jesus' life—and His agony—then it is not an act of mercy. *Let alone* means "Now let's leave Him alone." With a morbid curiosity, the enemies of Christ want to wait and see if Elijah *will come to take him down* from the cross.

C. The Death of Jesus (v. 37)

37. And Jesus cried with a loud voice, and gave up the ghost.

Jesus still has enough strength to cry *with a loud voice.* Mark does not tell us the words He speaks, but Luke informs us that He says, "Father, into thy hands I commend my spirit" (23:46). John tells us that just after He tastes the wine, He also utters, "It is finished" (19:30).

These may have been His very last words. Jesus has now died as "a ransom for many" (Mark 10:45). [See question #3, page 296.]

III. The Empty Tomb (Mark 16:1-8)

A. The Women (vv. 1-4)

1, 2. And when the sabbath was past, Mary Magdalene, and Mary the mother of James, and Salome, had bought sweet spices, that they might come and anoint him. And very early in the morning, the first day of the week, they came unto the sepulchre at the rising of the sun.

Joseph of Arimathea, "an honorable counselor" and follower of Jesus, has secured permission from Pilate to bury the body of Jesus (Mark 15:43). The burial place is a tomb cut out of rock (Mark 15:46), probably a tomb that Joseph has prepared for himself and members of his family. The tomb is conveniently close by (John 19:41), so they are able to bury Jesus before *the sabbath* begins (Mark 15:42). After Jesus' burial, a large stone is rolled across the mouth of the tomb, a common practice in that day (15:46).

Some of the women followers of Jesus watched as Joseph and Nicodemus buried Jesus, so they know where the tomb is located (15:47; John 19:38-42). Early Sunday morning, after *the sabbath* has *past* and there is enough sunlight to find their way in the retreating darkness (John 20:1), several women go to the tomb with *spices* to complete the burial process.

3. And they said among themselves, Who shall roll us away the stone from the door of the sepulchre?

As the women travel to the tomb with the sunlight just making its way over the horizon, it occurs to them that they have a problem. How will they be able to move *the stone* that covers the mouth of the tomb? Such a stone is usually quite large, round in shape, and resting in a channel. To move it will require several people equipped with poles for levers. The women also apparently do not know that Roman soldiers have been stationed at the tomb to guard it (Matthew 27:62-66).

4. And when they looked, they saw that the stone was rolled away: for it was very great.

As it turns out, however, they have no need to worry! There has been a "great earthquake" (Matthew 28:2) and an angel of the Lord has *rolled* the stone *away*.

B. The Angel (vv. 5-8)

5. And entering into the sepulchre, they saw a young man sitting on the right side, clothed in a long white garment; and they were affrighted.

The entrance of a tomb in this era usually opens into a central room, making the tomb large enough to walk into. Bodies are placed in niches or shelves cut into the walls of this room. Several bodies—perhaps a whole family—can thus be buried in one tomb.

When they enter the tomb, the women receive a shock. The body of Jesus is missing, and *a young man . . . clothed in a long white garment* is sitting *on the right side* where the body formerly had been. Matthew tells us that he was an angel and that his "countenance was like lightning" (28:3-5). Luke informs us that there are two angels (24:4); Matthew and Mark apparently mention only the one who speaks.

6. And he saith unto them, Be not affrighted: ye seek Jesus of Nazareth, which was crucified: he is risen; he is not here: behold the place where they laid him.

It should come as no surprise that the women are frightened—so frightened that they bow their faces to the ground (Luke 24:5). But the angel quickly assures them that they have nothing to fear and gives them the good news that *Jesus has risen*. We can only imagine their conflicting emotions as they experience fear one moment and then unbelievably good news the next.

A NEW REALITY

Some years ago, James Burke wrote a book entitled *The Day the Universe Changed*. In it he proposed that when our ideas about reality change, reality itself changes. Whether or not his thesis is true, Burke makes a case for the fact that the late Middle Ages was one of those critical points in history at which significant change took place in the way we understand the physical world about us. Because of the great minds of the Renaissance, who broke free from medieval notions, we live in a world governed by physical

Visual for lesson 8. *This poster is meant to spark some discussion. Ask, "How is the presence of Christ evident in our homes—and in our lives?"*

laws rather than the world of ancient times in which superstition reigned supreme.

The day Jesus rose from the dead was a day unlike any other before or since. Because of what happened that day, there is a new reality in the universe. The power of Satan had been in control of human life from the time of the first sin, which we read about in Genesis 3. On the day of the crucifixion, Satan seemed to have taken complete control. Yet three days later that power was broken, and the world has been different ever since. The angel's words, "He is not here; he is risen," changed our way of looking at the world. Now the power of God is at work, redeeming and renewing the creation in anticipation of the day when Christ comes again to make all things new. It really *is* a new world since Christ arose!   —C. R. B.

7. But go your way, tell his disciples and Peter that he goeth before you into Galilee: there shall ye see him, as he said unto you.

When God sends an angel to deliver a message to a person, that message is important. This case is certainly no exception. The women have seen the empty tomb and now it is their responsibility to carry that word to the *disciples*. There are good reasons for Jesus to meet His followers in *Galilee*. First of all, this fulfills a prophecy Jesus made before His death (see Mark 14:28). Further, the disciples will be safer there in case Jesus' enemies seek to follow up His killing by persecuting His followers. We know that Jesus does indeed visit Galilee after His resurrection (see John 21:1), but most of His recorded appearances are in and around Jerusalem.

8. And they went out quickly, and fled from the sepulchre; for they trembled and were amazed: neither said they any thing to any man; for they were afraid.

Home Daily Bible Readings

Monday, Apr. 14—The Place of the Skull (Mark 15:21-32)
Tuesday, Apr. 15—Why Have You Forsaken Me? (Mark 15:33-41)
Wednesday, Apr. 16—Joseph Asks for Jesus' Body (Mark 15:42-47)
Thursday, Apr. 17—He Is Not Here (Mark 16:1-8)
Friday, Apr. 18—Jesus Joins Two on the Road (Luke 24:13-27)
Saturday, Apr. 19—The Lord Has Risen Indeed! (Luke 24:28-35)
Sunday, Apr. 20—Touch Me and See (Luke 24:36-49)

Torn between fear and hope, the women do not linger to discuss or debate what they have experienced. They do not stop to talk to anyone else as they hurry to find the disciples and report what they have witnessed. But Matthew tells us that Jesus meets them along the way. As they hold Him by the feet and worship Him, He repeats the instructions they had received from the angel at the tomb (Matthew 28:9, 10). [See question #4, page 296.]

Conclusion

A. "Descend Now From the Cross"

Mark 15:31 and 32 tell how the chief priests and the scribes mocked Jesus, saying, "He saved others; himself he cannot save." They challenged Him to come down from the cross—then they would believe in Him. In the wilderness, Satan had challenged Jesus to perform miracles to prove that He was indeed the Son of God (Matthew 4:1-11). Even though the forty days in the wilderness left Him hungry and weakened, Jesus consistently resisted the temptations to play by Satan's rules.

Now Jesus' enemies want Him to play by their rules. They certainly have had every opportunity to know of His miraculous power. Surely some of them have witnessed at least a few of these miracles. But because Jesus doesn't meet their expectations of who they think the Messiah ought to be, they are not convinced that Jesus is the divine Son of God.

Jesus knew very well that even if He came down from the cross, they would still find a way to reject Him. More importantly, coming down from the cross would thwart His very reason for coming to earth—to give His life as a ransom for our sins (Mark 10:45).

Modern skeptics are much like these religious leaders. God has ensured that sufficient evidence exists to establish the truth of Jesus' identity and the resurrection. When Jesus' enemies rejected His claims and that evidence, they eventually paid a terrible (eternal) price for their decision. In the same way, those today who reject Jesus' claims face an eternity of shame and contempt (Daniel 12:2). [See question #5, page 296.]

B. Prayer

O Holy God, we thank You for sending Your Son to die for our sins, unworthy though we are. We further thank You for the resurrection that offers us the hope we have for eternal life. In the name of the resurrected Lord we pray, amen.

C. Thought to Remember

"He is risen; he is not here" (Mark 16:6).

Learning by Doing

This page contains an alternative lesson plan emphasizing learning activities.
Classes desiring such student involvement will find these suggestions helpful.

Learning Goals

After participating in this lesson, each student will be able to:

1. Cite the significant details concerning Jesus' crucifixion and resurrection.

2. Tell why the crucifixion and resurrection are vital to the Christian faith.

3. Prepare an answer for someone who might deny the resurrection.

Into the Lesson

In the ancient world, roads were often marked by milestones, similar to interstate highway mile markers. They were used so the traveler could be aware of his direction and know where he was. Distribute to each learner a piece of paper with several "milestones" drawn on it. They can look like small stones or tablets. (A similar activity appears in the student book, *Adult Bible Class*.)

Students are to write on each "milestone" a significant event in their lives that has helped define who they are today. These events could be such occasions as graduations, conversion to Christ, marriage, birth of children, career moves, or others. They should write where they were at each time and who observed each event.

Ask the students to form pairs and share their milestones with one another. Partners may ask questions for clarification. Call the class together and ask for two or three volunteers to share their milestones. Be sure to ask each one who their "witnesses" were.

Say, "When significant life-changing events happen in our lives, it is important that we have others who observe and can corroborate them. Today, as we study the greatest life-changing event ever, we want to be aware of how many witnessed it."

Into the Word

To set the stage and tie this week's lesson to last week, use the "Lesson Background" from page 290 in a brief lecture.

Form groups of six and designate each as either Group One or Group Two. (More than one group can work on each of the two assignments.)

Group One will survey the relevant Bible texts to compile a list of five to seven details about the crucifixion. Write the following Scripture references on the chalkboard or on individual sheets of paper for this group to use: Matthew 27:11-61;

Mark 15:2-47; Luke 23:1-56; John 18:28; 19:42. (This activity is in the student book.)

Group Two will survey the assigned Bible texts to compile a list of five to seven details about the resurrection. Provide the following Scripture references for the group to use: Matthew 28:2-20; Mark 16:1-20; Luke 24:1-53; John 20:1-31. (This activity is also in the student book.)

Ask each group to report its conclusions. Compile a class list on a poster or chalkboard. Be prepared to clear up any misunderstandings by using notes from the commentary pages. Emphasize to the class how many witnessed the events. You may also want to refer to 1 Corinthians 15:6, 7 and Acts 1:1-18.

Into Life

Brainstorm. Ask each group to brainstorm reasons why the crucifixion and resurrection are vital to the Christian faith. They should appoint a secretary to record the results. To discuss all the groups' suggestions, ask one student to record the answers on a large poster. Have the groups take turns in calling out reasons. Go around the groups until all of the reasons they have listed are given. Keep this list on display for the remainder of the class time.

Statement of Faith. Keep the students in their small groups and ask each group to create a list of the most-often-used reasons for not believing in the resurrection of Jesus. This list could include such entries as the following: "It's never happened before" or "He wasn't really dead." Then ask the students to list and discuss the reasons why they do believe in the resurrection. Suggest that each write down a personal response to the statement, "I believe in the resurrection of Jesus because. . . ."

After a brief discussion, have each student write the name of one friend with whom he or she needs to share the truth of the resurrection. Each person will be directed to use his or her brief statement of faith in the resurrection using facts from today's study. (This activity is in the student book.)

Suggest a closing prayer for boldness to confront those who deny the resurrection and strength to endure their opposition: "God, I do believe in Your Son's resurrection. Strengthen my faith. Give me both opportunity and courage to tell my friend, _____, of my resurrection faith."

Let's Talk It Over

The questions on this page are designed to promote discussion of the lesson by the class and to encourage application of the lesson Scriptures. The answers provided are only discussion starters. Let your class talk it over from there.

1. Some students believe that Simon of Cyrene was the father of the Rufus mentioned in Romans 16:13. If that is correct, how much influence do you think carrying Jesus' cross had on Simon to lead him to become a Christian? Why? How can Christians today be good witnesses even when experiencing extreme circumstances?

Jesus' personality amazed people around Him. The crowds were struck by the authority of His teaching (Matthew 7:28, 29). Even the temple guards were struck by His words (John 7:45, 46). His demeanor in the face of capital charges made Pilate marvel (Mark 15:4, 5). So we would not be surprised if His behavior on the way to Golgotha made an impression on Simon. No anger, no cursing, no threats—none of the actions typically associated with condemned criminals. Instead, Jesus comforted the women who cried for Him (Luke 23:27-31). Even today, when Christians bear suffering with more concern for others than for themselves, when they refuse to seek revenge, non-Christians will notice. Some of them may be led to faith.

2. The lesson writer notes that the soldiers assigned to the execution were interested in what personal gain they could get out of it. Who today displays such an interest even in the midst of spiritually significant events? What can we do to change their focus?

These soldiers were present at the pivotal event of all history and closer to Jesus than anyone else. But they were not focused on who He was, what He was doing, or what He might mean for their lives. They were "putting in their time," seeing what they could get out of the deal. In today's society, we find many who "put in their time" in the church pews, who are there primarily to be entertained. While we cannot identify everyone who has this "what's in it for me" attitude, we need to discourage it in every way we can. We need to examine our own lives to see if we approach worship as entertainment and act as if everything in worship should entertain us. We need to address the issue publicly in preaching and to change the focus from what one receives to what one can give by being in the presence of Jesus.

3. Even as death arrived, Jesus still was able to utter a victory cry. Have you ever known some follower of Jesus who could see the "big picture" and have confidence of God's victory even in the face of what may have looked like defeat? How does one develop such overcoming faith?

Surely your learners know several examples. A believer with a severe disability refuses to feel sorry for herself, but ministers to others. Someone with a terminal illness keeps his focus on helping and even comforting others. Such a perspective comes from a consistent walk with the Master, always looking beyond the temporal to the eternal.

4. What evidence of Jesus' resurrection in the first eight verses of Mark 16 give you confidence that the resurrection account is authentic and not manufactured?

Many items might reassure your learners. First, there is harmony among the Gospel writers: the account of the women going to the tomb early on Sunday morning is in agreement with the other Gospel accounts. Second, the Gospel writers give credit to women for first discovering the resurrection of Jesus; a made-up tale in that culture would have used male witnesses. Third, the presence of an angel is another element of the story that would have been unnecessary if Mark simply had manufactured a wishful thinking story of the resurrection of Jesus. Finally, the reaction of the women is yet another detail that indicates the authenticity of Mark's account. The women were clearly shaken by what had gone on, having no understanding and explanation of what had been told them and how it could be possible. A manufactured story might have portrayed confident, poised women who "knew all along" that this would happen. Instead, they were very scared.

5. The reality of Jesus' crucifixion and resurrection is absolutely essential to the Christian faith. How can we convince a "postmodern" culture of this great truth?

Postmoderns value experience, and there is plenty of that in this account. Eyewitnesses testify to the event's reality. This testimony becomes authoritative (something postmoderns are not comfortable with). It blends with prophecy and later Scripture to declare not only the reality of the event, but its significance as well. To relieve the nihilistic mind-set of postmoderns, significance is desperately needed!

Faith Conquers Fear

DEVOTIONAL READING: Hebrews 11:1-6.

BACKGROUND SCRIPTURE: Mark 5:21-43.

PRINTED TEXT: Mark 5:22-36, 41, 42.

Mark 5:22-36, 41, 42

22 And, behold, there cometh one of the rulers of the synagogue, Jairus by name; and when he saw him, he fell at his feet,

23 And besought him greatly, saying, My little daughter lieth at the point of death: I pray thee, come and lay thy hands on her, that she may be healed; and she shall live.

24 And Jesus went with him. And much people followed him, and thronged him.

25 And a certain woman, which had an issue of blood twelve years,

26 And had suffered many things of many physicians, and had spent all that she had, and was nothing bettered, but rather grew worse,

27 When she had heard of Jesus, came in the press behind, and touched his garment.

28 For she said, If I may touch but his clothes, I shall be whole.

29 And straightway the fountain of her blood was dried up; and she felt in her body that she was healed of that plague.

30 And Jesus, immediately knowing in himself that virtue had gone out of him, turned him about in the press, and said, Who touched my clothes?

31 And his disciples said unto him, Thou seest the multitude thronging thee, and sayest thou, Who touched me?

32 And he looked round about to see her that had done this thing.

33 But the woman fearing and trembling, knowing what was done in her, came and fell down before him, and told him all the truth.

34 And he said unto her, Daughter, thy faith hath made thee whole; go in peace, and be whole of thy plague.

35 While he yet spake, there came from the ruler of the synagogue's house certain which said, Thy daughter is dead; why troublest thou the Master any further?

36 As soon as Jesus heard the word that was spoken, he saith unto the ruler of the synagogue, Be not afraid, only believe.

· · · · · · · · · · · ·

41 And he took the damsel by the hand, and said unto her, Talitha cumi; which is, being interpreted, Damsel, (I say unto thee,) arise.

42 And straightway the damsel arose, and walked; for she was of the age of twelve years. And they were astonished with a great astonishment.

Apr 27

GOLDEN TEXT: [Jesus] saith unto the ruler of the synagogue, Be not afraid, only believe.—Mark 5:36.

Jesus: God's Power in Action
Unit 3: Jesus' Responses to Faith
(Lessons 9-13)

Lesson Aims

After participating in this lesson, each student will be able to:

1. Recall the details of Jesus' healing of the woman with the issue of blood and of Jairus's daughter.

2. Compare the anxiety of Jairus and the woman with the fears and uncertainties people bring to Jesus today.

3. In faith, give a specific fear to Jesus and allow Him to give the victory.

Lesson Outline

Introduction

A. The Action Gospel

All of our lessons this quarter have been from the Gospel of Mark. For the first five weeks we studied the opening chapters. Then for the resurrection season we studied the closing chapters, celebrating again the heart of the great good news: the King's entry into Jerusalem and His death and resurrection. Now we return to the central section of the Gospel record and the earlier days of Christ's ministry.

All along the way we are struck again by Mark's crisp style. His record doesn't start with the birth or early life of Jesus. It begins when Jesus started His ministry, when He began to "do" things. The Gospel of Luke, according to the opening verses of the book of Acts (Luke's other correspondence), reports what Jesus began to do and teach. Matthew spent a lot of time on the teaching part. John gives us his uniquely personal perspective on who Jesus was, as only "the disciple whom Jesus loved" might have understood. Mark majors on the "do." He launches right in to various encounters and healings after a very brief introduction.

It may be pure imagination, but some of us have wondered if Mark's approach had to do with his youthfulness. In the early years of school, it is hard to write a long paper, hard to think of "what else" there might be to say. Many of us, when we began to preach, finished a sermon in five minutes, and stretched it into ten by repeating ourselves—and we had gone from Genesis to Revelation! How much more could there be to say? Mark was younger than the others who presented Gospel records. Perhaps he listened to Peter's reports—it is generally believed that Mark recorded the apostle Peter's perspective on Jesus' life and teaching—pared away some of Peter's typical enthusiasm and tendency to talk, and acted rather like Sgt. Joe Friday of the old TV show *Dragnet*, who wanted "just the facts, Ma'am."

So Mark didn't waste any time getting to the heart of the matter. Jesus made a difference everywhere He went. Just watch what He did with people who were sick and dying. In the early chapters of Mark we see numerous encounters with Jesus in which people were healed, but that just seems to scratch the surface. Early in the record the evangelist reports, "And he healed many that were sick of divers diseases, and cast out many devils" (Mark 1:34).

Lesson Background

Jesus conducted much of the early part of His ministry around the Sea of Galilee. Specifically, much of the ministry was on the north end, in and around the village of Capernaum (Peter's hometown). And Jesus had begun to teach His lessons about life and about the kingdom of God in the rural areas and towns along the western side of the sea. It didn't take long for the crowds to follow Him everywhere. His teaching was pointed. His spirit was magnetic. And having already healed so many people, His reputation had spread far and wide.

Jesus was building up His team of apostles, who gave up their occupations to follow Him. He also was attracting a regular following of those who didn't believe in Him and who wanted to find reasons to eliminate Him. Everything He did was watched—either with loving appreciation or with suspicion.

In search of a little rest, and maybe in search of a new opportunity, Jesus had crossed to the eastern shore of the sea. There He cured a demon-possessed man who had been terrorizing the whole community. As a result, Jesus made some farmers who had lost their pigs very unhappy (Mark 5:2-17; see lesson 3). After certain people told Jesus that He was no longer welcome there, Jesus crossed back over into familiar territory. The news that He was coming had arrived ahead of Him, and the crowds were waiting (Mark 5:21).

I. Expectant Faith (Mark 5:22-24)

A. A Humble Ruler (v. 22)

22. And, behold, there cometh one of the rulers of the synagogue, Jairus by name; and when he saw him, he fell at his feet.

Jairus, as a *synagogue* ruler, is in a position of great influence (cf. Acts 13:15). Although he is not a priest, he is a religious leader—surely respected and counted on. But he is not arrogant or self-important to the point that he cannot go for help when he needs it. So he bows in respect before Jesus. Many of his contemporaries see the power of Jesus as a threat. Jairus sees the power of Jesus as a great hope, a potential blessing. It is evident that to him truth and life are more important than position and tradition. When your child is at the point of death, you go for genuine help. This is no time to posture or to play religious games. [See question #1, page 304.]

B. A Dying Child (v. 23)

23. And besought him greatly, saying, My little daughter lieth at the point of death: I pray thee, come and lay thy hands on her, that she may be healed; and she shall live.

Clearly, Jairus has heard about Jesus. It is also clear that Jairus believes in Jesus' power to heal. Jairus is unlike some others in his position who are following Jesus as critics—watching for a lapse in His popularity or hoping that He will make a big mistake. Had Jairus been in need of healing himself, he might not have gone to the Master. Such an action surely would draw the ire of his fellow authorities. But when it is his *little daughter*, there is no hesitation. It is time for help, time for action. And he believes that Jesus can heal.

Jairus wants Jesus to touch his daughter. Ah! The healing power of touch! With Jesus it is something enormous. With us touch counts, too.

It counts for a lot. Watch the eyes of the next person that you lovingly, respectfully touch.

And one teacher really hit a piece of truth squarely on the head when he said, "When Jesus is allowed to *lay* His hand on a family, it lives." That's a thought to give a lot of attention. Are the hand of Jesus, the heart of Jesus, and the manner of Jesus on your family?

C. The Responsive Christ (v. 24)

24. And Jesus went with him. And much people followed him, and thronged him.

Probably some of the friends of Jairus are certain that the Master will not go *with him*. But the great physician makes house calls. And, as usual, everywhere He goes a mob *followed*. It isn't only curiosity. It isn't always that they have someone who needs to be healed. They want to be part of the good things that are happening.

You may have heard that the chickens follow the one who is plowing up the worms. If your church is a place where good things are happening, where lives are being changed, where spiritual nourishment is being offered, then all kinds of people will want to take part. [See question #2, page 304.]

II. Excited Faith (Mark 5:25-33)

A. A Suffering Woman (vv. 25, 26)

25, 26. And a certain woman, which had an issue of blood twelve years, and had suffered many things of many physicians, and had spent all that she had, and was nothing bettered, but rather grew worse.

Along the way to Jairus's house, another need presents itself. But the need of this *woman* is not just medical. Her chronic flow *of blood* has made her ceremonially "unclean" for *twelve years* (cf. Leviticus 15:25-33). This means she is ostracized

---

How to Say It

CAPERNAUM. Kuh-*per*-nay-um.

CENTURION. sen-*ture*-ee-un.

GALILEE. *Gal*-uh-lee.

JAIRUS. *Jye*-rus or *Jay*-ih-rus.

NAIN. Nane.

NOSTRUMS. *nahs*-trumz.

PSYCHOSOMATIC. *sigh*-koe-suh-*ma*-tik (strong accent on *ma*).

SEPPHORIS. Sep-*for*-is.

SYNAGOGUE. *sin*-uh-gog.

SYROPHOENICIAN. *Sigh*-roe-fih-*nish*-un (strong accent on *nish*).

TALITHA CUMI. *Tal*-ih-thuh (or Tuh-*lee*-thuh) *koo*-me.

from Jewish society, much like a leper. She is not supposed to be here with the crowd, since touching other people will make them "unclean" as well. If the bleeding is from her womb, which is likely, then she is probably barren as well—an added stigma for a woman in her day.

This woman has tried everything—doctor after doctor. But after the money is gone she is *worse*, not better. She is also desperate.

B. A Hopeful Touch (vv. 27, 28)

27, 28. When she had heard of Jesus, came in the press behind, and touched his garment. For she said, If I may touch but his clothes, I shall be whole.

Being ritually unclean, this woman cannot approach Jesus directly. Thus she attempts to slip in unnoticed. This is more than "I'll try just one more thing." She has heard of Jesus. She believes in His power. He doesn't even have to speak to her, see her, or touch her. She is confident that, if she can just *touch* Him, or even the corner of *His clothes*, her hemorrhage will stop. [See question #3, page 304.]

C. A Power Transfer (vv. 29-33)

29. And straightway the fountain of her blood was dried up; and she felt in her body that she was healed of that plague.

Right away this woman can feel that she has been healed! (If you had hemorrhaged for a dozen years, you would know right away when it stopped, too.) If she expected Jesus' garment to have some magical power, then she was wrong about that. But she was absolutely right to believe. In a moment Jesus will clear up any possible misconception and make it clear that her faith in Him has worked the healing. She has been healed because she believed in Him. She expected to be *healed*, and *she was*. Just that quickly!

30. And Jesus, immediately knowing in himself that virtue had gone out of him, turned him about in the press, and said, Who touched my clothes?

This is the only place recorded in Scripture where Jesus feels an outflow of power. This is noteworthy, it seems, because He has not planned to do the healing, and He Himself has "done" nothing. At other times He might very well have had the sense of power—what the *King James Version* calls *virtue*—passing from Him to another person. But in those cases He purposefully gives the gift. Here, the woman's faith taps into His power without Jesus' having initiated it.

But He knows when it happens. This proves that this is not some kind of "psychosomatic" healing. There is something more here than a

woman having believed so strongly that she was going to be well that she actually "wills" herself to be well. Because Jesus feels the power go *out of Him*, that possibility cannot be true. Her faith has facilitated the healing, but the healing power comes from outside her.

We sometimes call Jesus the "Great Physician." But He is more than a great doctor who knows how to treat and cure diseases. There is power in Jesus, power that eradicates disease. There is the power of life in Jesus—power for life now and for eternity.

SEEKING *REAL* POWER

The New Age movement has brought some strange beliefs and practices with it. Many people have fantasized about the assumed mystical nature of crystals and are convinced that crystals have a magic power to heal. So it could be expected that someone would expand the theory a bit (not to mention make some money off of other people's gullibility).

In California, a musician who is a pet lover laminated some three-fourths-inch-long crystals to a copper heart and attached the devices to her two dogs and seven cats. She claims her animals are now in good health: the formerly lazy ones energetic and the previously excitable ones calm. So far her eleven turtles and nine-hundred-pound pig named Popcorn have escaped her ministrations, but she has plans to tape a crystal to a turtle she says "has been acting kind of hectic lately." (Just how does a "hectic" turtle behave, anyway?) She is also offering her combination copper and crystal hearts to the public for only ten dollars apiece.

Although the woman who called on Jesus' healing power may have had a bit of superstition mixed in with her faith, she wasn't seeking New Age nostrums. She was looking for the real thing. For a long time she had been trying every type of help she could find, but to no avail. Now she saw in Jesus the person who had *real* power—power that would heal her at long last. He is *still* our greatest source of power. —C. R. B.

31. And his disciples said unto him, Thou seest the multitude thronging thee, and sayest thou, Who touched me?

Dozens of people probably touch Jesus every few minutes with such a large crowd milling about. This fact makes the disciples' question seem very reasonable. Even so, the Twelve don't always seem to be as respectful or attentive as Jesus deserves for them to be. Every now and then it becomes apparent that they are a little slow and have not caught much of His spirit. The problem is usually that they have an agenda that doesn't match Jesus' own. In this case, the disciples apparently are focused on the urgency of the life-and-death situation that awaits them at Jairus's home. But Jesus has a spiritual sensitivity they do not have. Indeed, on a certain level, they are not able to have His sensitivity.

32, 33. And he looked round about to see her that had done this thing. But the woman fearing and trembling, knowing what was done in her, came and fell down before him, and told him all the truth.

Jesus is not dissuaded by the disciples' question. When it becomes apparent to the woman that Jesus' searching eyes cannot be avoided, she comes forward, bows down, and tells her story.

Why is she afraid? And what is the connection between her fear and her decision to step forward? Is she afraid because she knows *what was done in her?* That is reasonable. Her healing is evidence that Jesus acts with divine authority. There is always a sense of holy fear when the human meets the divine. Or is she afraid of the crowd? Is she still fearful of the stigma of her uncleanness? If so, her healing may be what emboldens her now to step forward. God has accepted her; He has healed her! Now she can face the hostile crowd.

Visual for lesson 9

Today's visual is an attractive illustration of the Golden Text—and a timely encouragement.

III. Rewarded Faith
(Mark 5:34-36, 41, 42)

A. Wholeness (v. 34)

34. And he said unto her, Daughter, thy faith hath made thee whole; go in peace, and be whole of thy plague.

It is a *faith* lesson for the crowd! Trust Jesus, and *be* made *whole,* be healed, have peace.

It's interesting that Jesus repeats the comment about wholeness. The woman's crippling disease had been cured. But surely this was not all that Jesus wanted to say. If faith in Jesus guided her life, she would be a *whole* person. And the same thing is true of us, isn't it? In the case of the man carried to Jesus by four others and let down through the roof before Jesus, sinfulness was addressed first (see Mark 2:5; lesson 2). It is forgiveness that really makes us whole. Physical health is a bonus. [See question #4, page 304.]

B. Message (vv. 35, 36)

35. While he yet spake, there came from the ruler of the synagogue's house certain which said, Thy daughter is dead; why troublest thou the Master any further?

Apparently the healing encounter with the woman has delayed Jesus' arrival at the home of the synagogue *ruler.* Now, it appears, it is too late to continue the journey. But that is not an "unfortunate circumstance." There is no accident

that has spoiled Jesus' intent. The delay actually offers Him an even better opportunity to demonstrate His power. Rather than healing a little girl who is ill, He will bring her back from the dead!

36. As soon as Jesus heard the word that was spoken, he saith unto the ruler of the synagogue, Be not afraid, only believe.

One writer suggests that the art of ignoring, here illustrated by Jesus, is one of the fine arts of faith. A human conclusion, even one that sounds reasonable and authoritative, is never the last word. God has the last word. Jesus' counsel to *only believe* is good advice yet today! [See question #5, page 304.]

C. Resurrection (vv. 41, 42)

41. And he took the damsel by the hand, and said unto her, Talitha cumi; which is, being interpreted, Damsel, (I say unto thee,) arise.

Not much drama! Jesus doesn't make a big show. He merely reaches down, takes her *hand,* and speaks to her. The Aramaic phrase *Talitha cumi* is not a magic incantation of some kind. It is evident that Jesus speaks that language as His own. Including it for color and emphasis, Mark uses this forceful phrase to underline a significant moment. Even so, Mark is careful to translate Aramaic phrases for his readers. See Mark 7:34 and 15:34. For *Damsel,* an old English word not heard so much today, we probably would say something like "Little girl" or "Young lady."

42. And straightway the damsel arose, and walked; for she was of the age of twelve years. And they were astonished with a great astonishment.

The witnesses in the room are Peter, James, and John, plus the child's parents (see vv. 37, 40, not in the printed text). Even though the disciples already had seen Jesus raise from the dead the widow's son at Nain (Luke 7:11-17), *they* are greatly *astonished* nonetheless.

The simplicity of Jesus' healing is striking. After Jesus' words and touch, this *twelve*-year-old immediately *arose* and *walked.* Jesus didn't rage and shout, use dramatic props, or call attention to Himself. When the power of life is there, all these other things are not necessary. And God is glorified.

THE MAN FOR ALL PEOPLE

The popular image of Jesus among many skeptics of the Bible is that He was a small-town, "backwoods hick" who appealed to His followers because they, too, were simple people. This view took a solid hit a few years ago when an archeological excavation at Sepphoris revealed something about the area in which Jesus grew up. Sepphoris was the Roman capital of Galilee for much of the first century A.D.

Eric Myers of Duke University, a leader of the Sepphoris excavation, says "Galilee [was] an enormously cosmopolitan urban area." Researchers have found that 80 percent of Jewish tombs in the area had inscriptions written in Greek. Other artifacts suggest that the Galilee of New Testament times was a very pluralistic society. These findings coincide with recent literary discoveries indicating the strong probability that Jesus was fluent in Greek, the cosmopolitan language of His day.

These discoveries offer us a partial explanation for why such a large variety of people were so at ease with Jesus and felt they could call upon Him in their time of need. The poor woman and the ruler of the synagogue we read of in today's text, plus the Syrophoenician woman (Mark 7:24-30), the Roman centurion (Matthew 8:5-13), and a host of others we read about elsewhere all testify that Jesus was a man for all people. Today, He still is able to cure the ills of all societies and cultures, if only we will let Him.

—C. R. B.

Conclusion

A. It's About Faith

Faith is the one thing that stands out in today's text. The woman with the issue of blood believed in Jesus' power and was healed. The synagogue ruler also believed in Jesus' power, and his daughter came back to life.

But the faith in this passage is not the same as the common conception of faith today. It is much more than mere positive thinking, hope against hope, or petitioning the fates. We are concerned with faith in Jesus, the Son of the living God. Trust Jesus! Trust Jesus with your family! Trust Jesus with your destiny! Trust Jesus for your eternal wellness and wholeness! Sometimes He even will grant you physical wellness and emotional wholeness as an added blessing.

B. It's About Jesus' Love

In your Bible studies, surely you have noticed that the only "favorites" that Jesus has are those who love His Father and who respond to Him. If we do that, we are His family (Matthew 12:50).

Jesus is eager to call men into service and to be in their company. He respects and expects many good things from women. Some were His financial supporters, and others were among His close friends. Jesus has a heart for children. His gospel is for all peoples. There are no first- and second-class citizens, as defined by age, gender, or race. Today, we have seen Him respond to a father, raise a girl, heal a woman, and use a teachable moment to train His disciples. It is surely in the spirit of Jesus that Paul writes, "For as many of you as have been baptized into Christ have put on Christ. There is neither Jew nor Greek, there is neither bond nor free, there is neither male nor female: for ye are all one in Christ Jesus" (Galatians 3:27, 28).

C. Prayer

Father God, we are thankful above all for the sending of Your Son and the eternal life He brings. Forgive our seasons of non-faith and of half-hearted discipleship. We rejoice in His power and in His love and are constantly amazed at His willingness to come to our house and heal. In Jesus' name, amen.

D. Thought to Remember

Bring your fears to Jesus.

Home Daily Bible Readings

Monday, Apr. 21—A Woman Touches Jesus' Cloak (Mark 5:21-34)

Tuesday, Apr. 22—Do Not Fear; Only Believe (Mark 5:35-43)

Wednesday, Apr. 23—Believe in God, Believe in Me (John 14:1-7)

Thursday, Apr. 24—Do You Not Believe? (John 14:8-14)

Friday, Apr. 25—The Conviction of Things Not Seen (Hebrews 11:1-6)

Saturday, Apr. 26—A Faithless Generation (Matthew 17:14-20)

Sunday, Apr. 27—Increase Our Faith (Luke 17:1-6)

Learning by Doing

This page contains an alternative lesson plan emphasizing learning activities.
Classes desiring such student involvement will find these suggestions helpful.

Learning Goals

After participating in this lesson, each student will be able to:

1. Recall the details of Jesus' healing of the woman with the issue of blood and of Jairus's daughter.

2. Compare the anxiety of Jairus and the woman with the fears and uncertainties people bring to Jesus today.

3. In faith, give a specific fear to Jesus and allow Him to give the victory.

Into the Lesson

Say to your class, "Today's lesson deals with Jesus' ability to overcome the fears of people who were sick or had loved ones who were sick. Scripture tells us not to fear. Let's look for the strong reasons we who believe in Jesus should not be afraid."

In pairs, have your students answer the following questions. "Who is your favorite doctor? Why?" and "What was your longest stay in the hospital?" Allow the pairs about five minutes for this exchange.

Say, "Several of us have experienced illnesses and physical difficulties of serious import. In some cases we have been or are afraid of the future. In today's text we study how Jesus answered the requests of individuals and conquered their fears."

Into the Word

Distribute the following true/false quiz based on today's text. In groups of two to four, students are to read Mark 5:22-43 and complete the quiz. (Answers and reasons for the answers are printed in italics to help the teacher discuss the material further.)

1. The ruler ordered Jesus to come with him. *(False; he fell at Jesus' feet and begged, vv. 22, 23.)*

2. The ruler asked Jesus to touch his daughter. *(True, v. 23.)*

3. The woman with bleeding had been ill twelve years. *(True, v. 25.)*

4. The woman had never been to a doctor. *(False; she had seen many doctors and had spent much money, v. 26.)*

5. Jesus touched the woman to heal her. *(False; the woman touched Jesus' garment, vv. 27-29.)*

6. Jesus was unaware of what had happened. *(False; He realized someone had touched Him and that "virtue"—i.e., power—had gone out of Him, v. 30.)*

7. Before Jesus arrived at the ruler's home, word came that the girl had died. *(True, v. 35.)*

8. Jesus encouraged the man not to be afraid. *(True, v. 36.)*

9. Jesus only spoke to the girl; He did not touch her. *(False; He took her by the hand and spoke to her, v. 41.)*

10. Jesus accomplished both healings immediately. *(True, vv. 29, 42.)*

Into Life

Ask, "If you had been any one of the participants in these healings, how do you think you would you have felt? What would you have thought? How does this help you understand how Jesus conquers our fears?" Use the comments for Mark 5:29-33, 36, 41, 42 to address concerns.

During the week before this class collect newspaper and magazine articles concerning things people fear: sickness, financial problems, unemployment, crime, and others. Distribute these articles to your groups, asking them to identify the situation and the concerns raised. For example, you may have an article about a robbery and the concern for physical safety and the loss of something valued.

Prepare a poster with the following headings: "Fearful Situation" and "How Jesus Might Answer." Involve the group by writing their suggestions under each heading.

Have each class member choose a situation in which he or she has a fear. These might include an operation, a diagnosis, a family matter, or personal employment. Distribute a three-by-five card to each student. The student is to describe the situation and compose a brief prayer asking Jesus to remove the fear and give victory to the student.

Using the pairs originally formed, have the two pray for their mutual concerns. When the prayers are completed, read 1 Peter 5:7, "Casting all your care upon him; for he careth for you." Have a trash bag available to be passed among the students, and encourage all to cast their cares away literally, even as they do the three-by-five cards.

Let's Talk It Over

The questions on this page are designed to promote discussion of the lesson by the class and to encourage application of the lesson Scriptures. The answers provided are only discussion starters. Let your class talk it over from there.

1. The critical illness of a child or other loved one has quite an impact on a person. How could such an illness change one's perspective of Jesus today? How can we enter the open door that such an occasion may provide?

Jairus was willing to risk his reputation and possibly his career by approaching Jesus because of his love for his daughter. Today, when a person is concerned for a critically ill loved one, he or she might pray for the first time. One who previously doubted God's existence begins to wonder, "What if He does exist, and what if He does care, and what if He could help me in my weakness?" We must be ready to reach out to minister to any person who finally might be willing to look to Jesus because of his or her love for a loved one. We must be careful not to exploit the person in a time of need. That happens when we are more concerned with getting a "decision" than with truly ministering. But in ministering to the apparent needs of a person, we may receive natural opportunities to minister to one's not-so-apparent spiritual needs.

2. In the crowds that followed Jesus, there were some who were devoted disciples. Others were looking for entertainment—wanting to see what miracle Jesus would do next. Others were critics, looking for a way to throw cold water on the enthusiasm Jesus generated. How are the same three groups seen in the attendance of a vibrant church? What should we do about it?

Exciting churches do draw crowds. "If your church is a place where good things are happening," the lesson writer says, "all kinds of people will want to take part." Some are looking for spiritual nourishment, and they are blessed if they are in a church that provides it. Some are looking for mere entertainment. Unfortunately, some churches have found that providing entertainment is a way to draw a crowd. If that is all they provide, they have compromised their purpose. And every program has its critics. We just need to be sure the criticisms are not justified, and we need to take corrective action when they are!

3. Like the bleeding woman, many people have obstacles to overcome in trying to reach out to Jesus. What are some of them, and how can we eliminate such barriers?

The woman had to get through crowds, work through embarrassment, and ignore a serious social taboo. Today, some people are hindered by a harsh past. While they have been told that Jesus has the power to forgive anything, a part of them believes that their sins are too bad for God to love them. For others, close friends or relatives with no faith—or with a ritualistic, empty form of faith—discourage them from approaching the living Lord. Crowded schedules and preoccupations prevent many from finding Jesus. And, of course, pride stands in the way of many, many people. Coming to Jesus means admitting that they've messed up, that they don't have all the answers, and that they have needs. Our job as disciples is to try to "clear the path" to Jesus. Ask for specific ways to do that for each obstacle mentioned.

4. There is more to being "whole" than simply being free of disease. What is wholeness? What traits are typical of one who is "whole"?

Your discussion may focus on the meaning of the word *whole*. It means undivided. As such, it is related to the word *integrity,* which comes from the Latin word for whole or entire. A whole person is a person of integrity, honest, not one person in some situations and another when the circumstances change.

Or you might note that the woman was made whole by her faith. What else comes by faith? Justification (Romans 5:1), purity of heart (Acts 15:9), and God's righteousness (Philippians 3:9), to name a few. Discuss how these traits are related to being "whole."

5. The lesson writer says, "The art of ignoring . . . is one of the fine arts of faith." What beliefs or voices must we ignore to have faith in Jesus?

Jairus had to ignore the voices of his servants. Today many voices argue against our faith and must be ignored: the voice of the atheistic scientist who says science "proves" there is no God, the voice of the postmodernist who says there is no absolute truth, the voice of the secular humanist who says we are here to serve ourselves, that we're our own form of a god, and that success is achieved through stepping on others and climbing to the top. For many, ignoring the voices of the past is essential to faith. With each "voice" cited, suggest ways to ignore that voice.

Jesus Honors Bold Faith

Devotional Reading: Luke 7:1-10.

Background Scripture: Mark 7:24-37.

Printed Text: Mark 7:24-37.

Mark 7:24-37

24 And from thence he arose, and went into the borders of Tyre and Sidon, and entered into a house, and would have no man know it: but he could not be hid.

25 For a certain woman, whose young daughter had an unclean spirit, heard of him, and came and fell at his feet:

26 The woman was a Greek, a Syrophoenician by nation; and she besought him that he would cast forth the devil out of her daughter.

27 But Jesus said unto her, Let the children first be filled: for it is not meet to take the children's bread, and to cast it unto the dogs.

28 And she answered and said unto him, Yes, Lord: yet the dogs under the table eat of the children's crumbs.

29 And he said unto her, For this saying go thy way; the devil is gone out of thy daughter.

30 And when she was come to her house, she found the devil gone out, and her daughter laid upon the bed.

31 And again, departing from the coasts of Tyre and Sidon, he came unto the sea of Galilee, through the midst of the coasts of Decapolis.

32 And they bring unto him one that was deaf, and had an impediment in his speech; and they beseech him to put his hand upon him.

33 And he took him aside from the multitude, and put his fingers into his ears, and he spit, and touched his tongue;

34 And looking up to heaven, he sighed, and saith unto him, Ephphatha, that is, Be opened.

35 And straightway his ears were opened, and the string of his tongue was loosed, and he spake plain.

36 And he charged them that they should tell no man: but the more he charged them, so much the more a great deal they published it;

37 And were beyond measure astonished, saying, He hath done all things well: he maketh both the deaf to hear, and the dumb to speak.

May 4

Golden Text: [Jesus] hath done all things well: he maketh both the deaf to hear, and the dumb to speak.—Mark 7:37.

Jesus: God's Power in Action
Unit 3: Jesus' Responses to Faith
(Lessons 9-13)

Lesson Aims

After participating in this lesson, each student will be able to:

1. Tell how Jesus rewarded the faith of two people in non-Jewish territory by healing disability and demon possession.

2. Tell how faith was more important than nationality, and remains so today.

3. Suggest one specific way to demonstrate boldness in his or her personal faith.

Lesson Outline

INTRODUCTION
  A. Time to Speak—or Not
  B. Lesson Background
 I. THE FAITH OF A MOTHER (Mark 7:24-30)
  A. Jesus Seeks Refuge (v. 24)
    The "Goldfish Bowl" Syndrome
  B. Faith Crosses Barriers (vv. 25, 26)
  C. Jesus Resists (v. 27)
  D. Faith Persists (vv. 28-30)
    The Value of "Spunk"
 II. THE FAITH OF GOOD FRIENDS (Mark 7:31-37)
  A. A Disabled Man (vv. 31, 32)
  B. A Thoughtful Master (vv. 33-35)
  C. An Excited People (vv. 36, 37)
CONCLUSION
  A. We're Prone to Get It Backward
  B. He Needs Our Voice
  C. Prayer
  D. Thought to Remember

Introduction

A. Time to Speak—or Not

As you study this lesson, contrast it with a healing by Jesus from lesson 3. It took place on the eastern shore of the Sea of Galilee, where Jesus drove demons from a man who lived in the tombs and terrorized the people of the region. When the man was freed, clothed, and in his right mind, Jesus told him to go home to his friends and tell them what the Lord had done for him. In today's lesson, however, we will read about a healing where Jesus asked people *not* to tell anyone. Why the difference?

The Bible notes that there are times when people are supposed to be vocal and times when they are supposed to be quiet (see Ecclesiastes 3:7 and Amos 5:13). God gave the prophet Ezekiel specific times to speak out and to hold his tongue (cf. Ezekiel 3:26; 33:22). So when are we supposed to talk, and when are we supposed to be quiet?

Consider the demon-possessed man whom Jesus told to go home and tell his friends what had happened. Fewer people knew about Jesus in that region. The cured man could introduce the Master and draw others to His kingdom. Not only that, but Jesus really didn't have any enemies there yet who would try to find something negative in everything He did.

When Jesus told the deaf man (today's lesson) and the family of the little girl raised from the dead (last week's lesson) not to talk about their miracles, He had a good reason. By the time those two miracles occurred, Jesus' fame had spread to the north and west of the Sea of Galilee (cf. Matthew 4:24; Mark 1:28). With the fame came opposition, and people had even tried to kill Him (Luke 4:29). Jesus knew that the building opposition eventually would result in His death—that was according to God's plan. But it was not yet God's time for that to happen. So it was important to slow down the mounting fame and the spreading visibility.

Followers of Jesus are to do what He says to do and stop what He says to stop. But knowing which is which can sometimes be a problem! However, if we read our Bibles carefully with a discerning spirit, it is usually not too difficult to know His will in this regard. The Bible is full of divine guidance. A failure to obey causes pain and trouble. A readiness to listen and to do what He says causes joy.

B. Lesson Background

A lot of things happened between the time of the events that we studied last week and those of our current lesson. Jesus went to His hometown, where His ministry was discounted. He did some teaching and a little bit of healing; but they could hardly imagine that Mary's son, the local carpenter's boy, would have much to offer (Mark 6:1-6).

He sent out the Twelve to do several kinds of ministry: healing, teaching, and encouraging (6:7-13). He directed them to depend on the hospitality of the people they served. His cousin, John the Baptist, was beheaded by Herod, after Herod had made a rash and foolish promise to his stepdaughter (6:14-29). He fed about five thousand men (plus families) with just five loaves and two fish (6:30-44) and then walked on the sea and calmed it (6:45-52). Landing in the area of Gennesaret, He was thronged by people seeking healing. After that He was confronted by some Pharisees from Jerusalem, and He chided them for their hypocrisy (7:1-13). He told the people that immorality defiles them, but that ceremonial matters are not nearly so important; and He taught them that right and wrong actions spring from right and wrong motives—things within us (7:14-23). Of course, that wasn't going to make Him any more popular with the Pharisees, either. Tradition and ceremony were just about all there was to great religion, so far as they were concerned.

Now we follow Jesus into new territory, this time to the north.

I. The Faith of a Mother
(Mark 7:24-30)

As we have noted already, the popularity of Jesus is growing around Galilee. Everywhere He goes, the crowds follow. And most of them are looking for healing. He is glad to do that, but the healing dimension of His ministry is secondary. His primary concern is to introduce the kingdom of God, urging people to become part of it. His compassion makes Him quite willing to give healing, which will bless and enrich lives for some years to come. But His passion is to offer spiritual healing, which is eternal! That speaks to the priorities of the church, doesn't it? "Seek ye first the kingdom of God, and his righteousness" (Matthew 6:33). But we ensure people's physical needs are met as well (cf. Matthew 25:35, 36).

A. Jesus Seeks Refuge (v. 24)

24. And from thence he arose, and went into the borders of Tyre and Sidon, and entered into a house, and would have no man know it: but he could not be hid.

There are times when Jesus needs to slow down the aggressive adulation of the crowds and to find some time to renew Himself. So now He goes back into Gentile territory in order to separate from the crowds for a time. He travels to the northwest, from the regions around the Sea of Galilee up to the coastal cities of *Tyre and Sidon.*

Tyre is a city with a fine natural harbor (on the end of a land bridge) and is important for the commercial shipping business on the eastern end of the Mediterranean Sea. Sidon is another seacoast town about twenty-five miles farther north. God had condemned both cities centuries earlier (cf. Isaiah 23; Jeremiah 27:1-7; Ezekiel 28), but now Jesus considers them to be agreeable places for travel (cf. Matthew 11:21, 22).

Somewhere in that region Jesus finds a receptive home and apparently He intends to spend some quiet time to plan and reflect. But since *he could not be hid,* it doesn't work exactly as He had hoped. [See question #1, page 312.]

THE "GOLDFISH BOWL" SYNDROME

Public figures often pay a price for their high visibility. They sometimes become too visible, as if their lives are lived in a great "goldfish bowl" where everyone can observe them and there's no place to hide. Some revel in the publicity, but almost everyone wants some privacy at some time.

For entertainers, the problem is that everything they do is "news." What styles they wear, what they do with their hair, whom they see—the public wants to know all this. For political figures it's what they can offer. Private interests besiege them with requests for their support of, or opposition to, every item on the political agenda. And for religious figures, it's how they behave. And if they fall—committing the very sins they have publicly denounced—they lose their credibility. Sometimes they all just want to get out of the goldfish bowl and be "like other people."

Jesus also needed to get out of the goldfish bowl from time to time. So we find Him in today's text trying to isolate Himself so He could be at least somewhat "like other people" for a time. But He couldn't be, and we find Him accepting the responsibility that comes with His position. Of course, this is the ultimate solution for all of us who are looked upon as role models.
—C. R. B.

B. Faith Crosses Barriers (vv. 25, 26)

25, 26. For a certain woman, whose young daughter had an unclean spirit, heard of him, and came and fell at his feet: the woman was a Greek, a Syrophenician by nation; and she besought him that he would cast forth the devil out of her daughter.

Greek is the same as "Gentile." *The woman* who finds Jesus is not Jewish. Her nationality is Phoenician (Phoenicia is the nation that occupies that part of the Mediterranean coast). She lives in an area that is part of the larger regional designation, Syria. So she is Syrian and Phoenician—Syrophoenician. The people who live in this area are ancient enemies of Israel (see Joel 3:4-6). But such issues are not important to her. Whatever barrier her nationality or background may have posed is shattered as she seeks help for her daughter. (Notice that *an unclean spirit,* v. 25, is the same as a *devil* or demon, v. 26.)

C. Jesus Resists (v. 27)

27. But Jesus said unto her, Let the children first be filled: for it is not meet to take the children's bread, and to cast it unto the dogs.

Jesus' reply is startling to us. It sounds harsh. It sets us back a little bit to hear Jesus strongly implying that this anxious woman is one of the *dogs.* That simply doesn't sound like something

Home Daily Bible Readings

Monday, Apr. 28—A Gentile Woman Seeks Out Jesus (Mark 7:24-30)

Tuesday, Apr. 29—He Has Done Everything Well (Mark 7:31-37)

Wednesday, Apr. 30—Do You Not Understand? (Mark 8:11-21)

Thursday, May 1—A Centurion's Faith (Luke 7:1-10)

Friday, May 2—Peter and John Show Boldness (Acts 4:5-14)

Saturday, May 3—We Cannot Keep From Speaking (Acts 4:15-22)

Sunday, May 4—Prayer for Boldness (Acts 4:23-31)

that would come from the lips of Jesus! But He uses a word that describes a little dog, a puppy. That softens it somewhat for us. In the New Testament the word *dog* is used five times, and each time it is used in a negative fashion. But here, and in the parallel passage in Matthew 15 (just these two times), the word for "little dog" is used. Still, a puppy is a far cry from a child. We still puzzle over Jesus' choice of wording.

In our puzzling, however, let's not miss the "bigger picture." Jesus is using an illustration of *children* and dogs to teach a lesson in priority. The *bread* that He is talking about is His attention, His gracious healing, and His message. The children who are to come *first* are the children of Israel—the Jews (cf. Matthew 10:5, 6; John 4:22). Paul, the apostle to the Gentiles, later will express the same priority. The gospel of Christ, the power of God for salvation, is "to the Jew first, and also to the Greek" (Romans 1:16). However surprised or shocked we are by Jesus' words, they apparently do not surprise or offend the woman, as her reply shows. [See question #2, page 312.]

D. Faith Persists (vv. 28-30)

28. And she answered and said unto him, Yes, Lord: yet the dogs under the table eat of the children's crumbs.

If you have house dogs, you can visualize this very easily. You feed the children, but while you're at it you feed the *dogs*, too. And the first course of the dogs' meal often comes from the floor under the baby's booster seat. Homes in first-century Syria probably are more hospitable to animals and *crumbs* than are ours, but it is an easy picture for us to understand.

This woman recognizes the age-old distinction between Jew and Gentile. Even so, she believes that Jesus has enough love, power, and kindness

to spare. After He feeds the needs of the children of Israel, the leftovers will be plenty for her. And Jesus honors her humility.

29, 30. And he said unto her, For this saying go thy way; the devil is gone out of thy daughter. And when she was come to her house, she found the devil gone out, and her daughter laid upon the bed.

Jesus admires her faith and her spunk. She is persistent, creative, quick thinking, courageous, and humble. Her faith does not even require Jesus' personal presence with her *daughter* (cf. Matthew 8:8). It is plain to Him that she has the faith to accept His simple assurance. Unlike the long and involved "exorcisms" that one sees in the movies and on TV, Jesus merely says the word, and *the devil* is *gone out*.

THE VALUE OF "SPUNK"

"Spunk" is that indefinable something that enables some people to attempt to do what others will not. When told, "It can't be done," or "No one will listen to you," they go ahead and try anyway.

That describes Nancy Wright. Her first motorcycle ride came when she was seventy-one. Shortly after that she bought one of her own. No doubt family and friends assured her of the dangers and (especially) the folly of someone her age trying to act like a kid again. Seven years later she had ridden her Honda Gold Wing all over the United States, even to the Yukon and Alaska and back! When she was seventy-seven she fell down some stairs. She got on her Gold Wing and rode twenty-five miles before she realized she had fractured her hip. Two months later she was out of the hospital and back on her motorcycle. Nancy Wright has spunk! She explains what drives her: "I lost my husband, and my kids are grown, so I found something interesting and challenging to do. . . . It's extended my life."

Another woman with spunk is the one in our lesson today. She was not a Jew, and people probably told her that Jesus wouldn't have time for her. She went looking for Jesus anyway, and when He challenged her faith, she replied with such spunkiness that Jesus admiringly granted her request. Do we possess the spiritual spunkiness that will bring us the spiritual blessings that God has waiting for us?   —C. R. B.

II. The Faith of Good Friends (Mark 7:31-37)

Jesus is now on the move again. Since He has just stressed the priority of Israel in receiving the gospel (7:27), we might expect Him to return to Jewish territory. But He does not. He goes instead to the Gentile region known as the Decapolis. His decision to remain in Gentile territory may be a lesson in "balance" for the disciples: although Gentiles do not receive *priority*, they are not *excluded*. [See question #3, page 312.]

A. A Disabled Man (vv. 31, 32)

31. And again, departing from the coasts of Tyre and Sidon, he came unto the sea of Galilee, through the midst of the coasts of Decapolis.

Leaving *Tyre and Sidon* for the *Decapolis* means that Jesus is now back in the general area where He had healed the demon-possessed man earlier (Mark 5:1-20). The name *Decapolis* means "ten cities." East and southeast of the Sea of Galilee, ten cities had banded together, including the region surrounding them, to form what might be called a "league" of cities. Ancient lists of the ten cities that comprise the Decapolis vary, so the name applies more to the general area than to ten specific cities.

32. And they bring unto him one that was deaf, and had an impediment in his speech; and they beseech him to put his hand upon him.

A good English teacher might rebuke Mark for using the pronoun *they* without telling his readers who *they* are! We assume the reference is to growing crowds, which always seem to show up when Jesus is around.

The man *they bring* to Jesus is *deaf* and partially mute. We are not certain whether *the impediment in his speech* is due to the man's deafness or has a physical cause all its own. Some students take the reference to loosing "the string of his tongue" in verse 35 to mean there was a physical defect. They may be right, or the reference may be figurative, suggesting that he spoke as if his tongue were tied down.

B. A Thoughtful Master (vv. 33-35)

33, 34. And he took him aside from the multitude, and put his fingers into his ears, and he spit, and touched his tongue; and looking up into heaven, he sighed, and saith unto him, Ephphatha, that is, Be opened.

In taking *him aside*, perhaps Jesus wants to heal without calling unnecessary attention to the miracle. This is the same concern that we have noted before: avoiding the mounting visibility that draws mounting opposition. But some of us see it as a thoughtful gesture on the part of Jesus. This man may have had to endure the laughter of unthinking people who make fun of the unusual sounds he makes. He has endured enough of that unwanted attention. The next time the townspeople see him he will be different. They will meet a new man, able to hear and to speak clearly.

Jesus, of course, is able to heal without any touch whatsoever. But in this case He uses a bit

of drama to communicate something to the deaf man. In pressing *his fingers into* the man's *ears* and touching *his tongue* with saliva, Jesus leaves no doubt as to the source of the healing. The same is true of His *looking up into heaven* and His sigh, which could be part of a prayer. [See question #4, page 312.]

As we have seen before, Mark translates Jesus' use of Aramaic for his readers. As Jesus speaks the word *Ephphatha*, the man being healed is unable to hear it since he does not regain his hearing until after the word is spoken. This means that Jesus is speaking for the benefit of the disciples and whatever witnesses happen to be close by.

35. And straightway his ears were opened, and the string of his tongue was loosed, and he spake plain.

As before, the healed person needs no lengthy series of treatments to get better. This is a miracle by the power of God! Problems of both *ears* and *tongue* are solved immediately.

C. An Excited People (vv. 36, 37)

36, 37. And he charged them that they should tell no man: but the more he charged them, so much the more a great deal they published it; and were beyond measure astonished, saying, He hath done all things well: he maketh both the deaf to hear, and the dumb to speak.

Jesus tries again: "Please don't spread this word around!" But again, it doesn't work. Surely Jesus doesn't mind if people spread the news that "the kingdom of God is at hand" (Mark 1:15). It's the news of the miracles He wants kept quiet. But the more He asks them to be quiet, the

---

How to Say It

DECAPOLIS. Dee-*cap*-uh-lis.

ECCLESIASTES. Ik-*leez*-ee-*as*-teez (strong accent on *as*).

EPHPHATHA (Aramaic). *Ef*-uh-thuh.

EZEKIEL. Ee-*zeek*-ee-ul or Ee-*zeek*-yul.

GALILEE. *Gal*-uh-lee.

GENNESARET. Geh-*ness*-uh-ret (*G* as in *get*).

HEROD. *Hair*-ud.

MEDITERRANEAN. *Med*-uh-tuh-*ray*-nee-un (strong accent on *ray*).

PHARISEES. *Fair*-ih-seez.

PHOENICIA. Fuh-*nish*-uh.

PHOENICIAN. Fuh-*nish*-un.

SIDON. *Sigh*-dun.

SYRIAN. *Sear*-ee-un.

SYROPHOENICIAN. *Sigh*-roe-fih-*nish*-un (strong accent on *nish*).

TYRE. Tire.

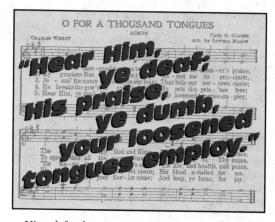

Visual for lesson 10. *This hymn reminds us, who have received far more from the Lord than mere hearing and speech, to praise Him.*

more they talk. It is just too good to keep to themselves, just too remarkable not to express. We might say it "blew their minds." That they would have a hard time keeping the news to themselves is easy to understand.

But Jesus' concern is also easy to see. Jesus has indeed *done all things well!* But the people (including the disciples) don't really understand who He is or the true nature of His mission. Like the crowds across the sea a few months earlier, these people would gladly make Jesus their earthly king (John 6:15). But were they ready to submit to a King whose kingdom is "not of this world" (John 18:36)? Are we? [See question #5, page 312.]

Conclusion

A. We're Prone to Get It Backward

Jesus asked these people to wait, to keep from spreading the information about His power to heal and to change their earthly lives. He is glad to address their physical needs. He cared about them. And it is not as though He didn't care about all of those other people—their friends and neighbors who had illnesses or who are near death. But the more they talked, the angrier His opponents became. And the angrier those religious authorities grew, the more active they would be in putting together whatever kind of coalition it would take to get rid of Him.

But it just wasn't time for that yet. The people who had been healed or who had seen loved ones healed are well intentioned, but they are actually doing more harm than good. By broadcasting the fame of Jesus, they are potentially shortening the length and the breadth of His ministry. Consequently, He would be limited in where He could go and to whom He could speak. Fewer would hear about the kingdom, and fewer, actually, would have access to Him.

Today, Jesus commands us *not* to be quiet. Some of His final words to His disciples are also His words to us: "Go ye therefore, and teach all nations, baptizing them in the name of the Father, and of the Son, and of the Holy Ghost: teaching them to observe all things whatsoever I have commanded you: and, lo, I am with you alway, even unto the end of the world" (Matthew 28:19, 20).

B. He Needs Our Voice

What a remarkable thing that God has done! He does not send angels down to evangelize. He depends on His church instead. He does not address men and women caught in the bonds of sin—who are candidates for eternal death and Hell!—by using angels. The modern television drama *Touched by an Angel* has created a very positive sensitivity to spiritual things and has some great and encouraging moments. But what we see on that program is not the way it works in reality.

The gospel of Christ is, instead, spread by people: men and women who speak for Jesus. They are empowered by the Holy Spirit, who lives in and works with Christians. They are guided and instructed by the Bible, the Word of God, through which the Holy Spirit of God also works by inspiration. But the relationships are established, eternal life is demonstrated, and the words are spoken by everyday people. Those to whom they speak will respond to a reasonable message with a faith grounded in the evidence of history. It will not be confirmed by angelic beings who materialize, then disappear. As strange as it sounds, God needs our voices.

C. Prayer

Dear Father God, we bow before Your wisdom and grace, and we celebrate with great gratitude the personal fulfillment of Your grace, Jesus the Christ, Your Son. We affirm with the crowds in the Decapolis that He has "done all things well." We have watched Him bless and heal our families, as He did the Syrophoenician woman's daughter. He has brought us healing, not only in physical things, but also in many other ways for which families need healing. We have seen Him change our friends, as He did the deaf man whose friends found Jesus. We are grateful also for the privilege of praying in His name; amen!

D. Thought to Remember

The time for silence is past.
The time to speak is now!

Learning by Doing

This page contains an alternative lesson plan emphasizing learning activities.
Classes desiring such student involvement will find these suggestions helpful.

Learning Goals

After participating in this lesson, each student will be able to:

1. Tell how Jesus rewarded the faith of two people in non-Jewish territory by healing disability and demon possession.

2. Tell how faith was more important than nationality, and remains so today.

3. Suggest one specific way to demonstrate boldness in his or her personal faith.

Into the Lesson

As class members arrive, have them participate in an informal fellowship time, perhaps with coffee and pastries. During the week before this session ask a Christian of a different nationality to attend your class. Be sure you do not alert the class to this person's attendance. Observe how your class responds to the "outsider." (If you do not invite a person of another nationality, have someone "dress up" as an unkempt outsider and attend the class.)

After a few minutes call the class to order and ask the learners to sit in groups of four. Draw attention to your "outsider" and ask the person how he or she felt. Was this person welcomed by the group or treated as an outsider? Then ask the following questions: "In today's text Jesus meets and deals with both a woman and a man who were outsiders to the Jewish religion. When have you felt like an outsider? What can you do to make visitors and new people feel more welcome and comfortable? Have you ever reached out to an 'outsider' in a situation where you saw uneasiness in the person? How did it make you feel?"

Say, "In today's lesson we will see how Jesus treated outsiders and responded to them."

Into the Word

Select someone in your class earlier in the week to review the introductory remarks in today's commentary (pp. 306, 307). Ask this person to prepare and present a five-minute report on the events leading up to today's text.

Create three groups with up to six students in each and give them the following assignments. (If you have more students, create more groups and repeat assignments.) Each will make a short presentation to the class.

Group 1. Use Bible dictionaries, encyclopedias, and other helps to research the relationship of Jews to non-Jews. Look particularly at the differences of the Greeks and Jews and those of Decapolis and Jerusalem. (Have such reference books available.)

Group 2. Read Mark 7:24-37 and Matthew 15:21-31. Prepare a short drama on the events told here. Develop props and the characters from what the Scripture describes.

Group 3. Read Mark 7:24-37 and Matthew 15:21-31. Prepare a short drama putting these events into contemporary terms of a different nationality from your own as it relates to missionary work. Decide on what characters need to be present and what particular hurdles are present; then write the dialog.

After fifteen minutes call the groups together. Have Group 2 present its drama. If any questions arise from the presentation, refer to the commentary for answers.

Ask Group 1 to present the results of its research. Ask the class, "How easy is it for us to ignore certain groups when it comes to sharing the gospel? Who are some of those groups? Why is it hard for us to reach out to them?"

Then say, "With our Biblical drama and our research about groups, it is reasonable to assume that there were some large hurdles to overcome in carrying the gospel to other nations."

Into Life

Ask Group 3 to present its drama, then ask, "How do you think most people feel when asked to talk about Jesus with someone of a different nationality? How would most people react if they had been the 'outcast'? What does this passage tell us about the need to carry the gospel to all 'people groups'? What are some examples of how faith transcends nationality lines?"

Provide stationery and envelopes for each student. The students are to write personal letters to themselves. In their letters they are to challenge themselves to share the gospel with others in a bold manner. Each should write specific goals and procedures for sharing within the next four weeks. (This activity is in the *Adult Bible Class.*) Collect the letters after class members seal them in envelopes addressed to themselves. After four weeks, return the letters to the students as an accountability device.

Close this study session with a prayer for building personal faith.

Let's Talk It Over

The questions on this page are designed to promote discussion of the lesson by the class and to encourage application of the lesson Scriptures. The answers provided are only discussion starters. Let your class talk it over from there.

1. Jesus was looking to escape the crowds and to "renew Himself." What can we do to renew ourselves for ministry? How can we be sure to allow our Christian leaders to have opportunities to renew themselves?

Everyone needs a change of pace from time to time. Reading a book, sharing in a small group, attending a convention are all examples of ways to renew oneself. Church members should respect their ministers' need for such activities as well. Honoring the minister's day off, insisting on reasonable vacations, and paying for the minister to attend retreats and conventions are some ways to help their leaders get the time they need to renew themselves. Of course, emergencies may sometimes intrude, even as they did in Jesus' experience. But we need to make sure we do not intrude on our leaders' time for anything less than an emergency.

2. Though Jesus' remark might seem "cold" to us, the woman did not take offense. How can we be sure we do not take offense at remarks that are not meant to be offensive but that some people might think are offensive?

Sometimes we take offense at innocent remarks because we are unsure of ourselves or have a low self-image. Likewise, people who are confident can take remarks meant to be offensive and not take offense! Jesus commended this woman for her faith, and surely that is a trait that helps us keep our thoughts focused in the right direction. If we live by faith, confident we are doing what we can to advance the cause of Christ, then we can take the remarks of others and not be offended at any criticism or rebuke.

3. Jesus' remaining in Gentile territory may be a "lesson in 'balance' for the disciples." What do we today need to keep in "balance"? How do we do that?

For many, keeping a balance between work and family or work and church involvement is difficult. Today's culture values workplace accomplishments and advancements so much that people feel pressured to excel at all costs. As a result, their families suffer and they are unable to be involved in ministry and worship opportunities provided by the church. One has to make a conscious decision and firm commitment to keep the job from overpowering other responsibilities. Have students tell how they decide where to draw the line at work to preserve family and ministry time.

The proper use of money is another balance issue. How does one balance the acquisition of material wealth with the need to invest in eternal treasures? How much is too much when so many have so little? Again, ask students to tell how they decide such issues. Encourage them to support their positions with Scripture.

4. It has been suggested that taking the deaf man aside privately was a "thoughtful gesture." How can we be sensitive to the feelings of those who have disabilities or special needs?

Jesus would not allow the deaf man to become an object of curiosity or entertainment for the crowds. People with disabilities can become that in our churches if we do not plan for their presence and comfort. Making our buildings and facilities accessible to people with physical limitations is one way of doing that. Cheerfully offering to help—as one friend might offer to help another—also will be appreciated.

Take a few moments to evaluate how friendly your facilities are to people with disabilities. What improvements can be made? If people with disabilities feel welcome in your facility, what makes that so? What decisions were made in the past to make the present what it is?

5. What does it mean that Jesus does "all things well"? What encouragement does that offer?

The people in our text were awed by the miracles Jesus did. But we know so much more than did they. We know of His death, burial, and resurrection. We know He died as the ransom for our sin and to provide the means of eternal life. We know He is the One who works "all things . . . together for good to them that love God" (Romans 8:28). We find comfort, then, that even when things seem dark, the One who "does all things well" is looking out for our best interests. We find encouragement that the One who "does all things well" is the One who has begun a good work in us and will bring it to completion (Philippians 1:6). If He does all things well, then He will do well in and for us!

Putting Faith in Jesus Alone

DEVOTIONAL READING: Philippians 2:5-11.

BACKGROUND SCRIPTURE: Mark 8:27–9:8.

PRINTED TEXT: Mark 8:27-36; 9:2-8.

Mark 8:27-36

27 And Jesus went out, and his disciples, into the towns of Caesarea Philippi: and by the way he asked his disciples, saying unto them, Whom do men say that I am?

28 And they answered, John the Baptist: but some say, Elijah; and others, One of the prophets.

29 And he saith unto them, But whom say ye that I am? And Peter answereth and saith unto him, Thou art the Christ.

30 And he charged them that they should tell no man of him.

31 And he began to teach them, that the Son of man must suffer many things, and be rejected of the elders, and of the chief priests, and scribes, and be killed, and after three days rise again.

32 And he spake that saying openly. And Peter took him, and began to rebuke him.

33 But when he had turned about and looked on his disciples, he rebuked Peter, saying, Get thee behind me, Satan: for thou savorest not the things that be of God, but the things that be of men.

34 And when he had called the people unto him with his disciples also, he said unto them, Whosoever will come after me, let him deny himself, and take up his cross, and follow me.

35 For whosoever will save his life shall lose it; but whosoever shall lose his life for my sake and the gospel's, the same shall save it.

36 For what shall it profit a man, if he shall gain the whole world, and lose his own soul?

Mark 9:2-8

2 And after six days Jesus taketh with him Peter, and James, and John, and leadeth them up into a high mountain apart by themselves: and he was transfigured before them.

3 And his raiment became shining, exceeding white as snow; so as no fuller on earth can white them.

4 And there appeared unto them Elijah with Moses: and they were talking with Jesus.

5 And Peter answered and said to Jesus, Master, it is good for us to be here: and let us make three tabernacles; one for thee, and one for Moses, and one for Elijah.

6 For he wist not what to say; for they were sore afraid.

7 And there was a cloud that overshadowed them: and a voice came out of the cloud, saying, This is my beloved Son: hear him.

8 And suddenly, when they had looked round about, they saw no man any more, save Jesus only with themselves.

GOLDEN TEXT: [Jesus] saith unto them, But whom say ye that I am? And Peter answereth and saith unto him, Thou art the Christ.—Mark 8:29.

Lesson Aims

After participating in this lesson, each student will be able to:

1. Cite evidence from today's texts that Jesus is the Christ, the Son of God.

2. Compare people's wrong ideas about Jesus in his own day with modern misconceptions about Him.

3. Make a statement of faith in Jesus Christ, and give a way to live out that faith.

Lesson Outline

Introduction

A. About Slow (and Non-) Learners

Jesus' disciples were a rather unlikely team of followers. But Jesus was preparing them to step up and provide dynamic leadership for God's people when His own work on earth was finished. Peter, Andrew, James, and John were fishermen. Matthew had been a tax collector—considered a traitor by most Jewish people. Peter was clearly the leader—at least he said the most! James and John, Zebedee's sons, were rather impetuous (Luke 9:54). Simon the Zealot was part of a group of patriotic militants (Acts 1:13). Nathanael was prejudiced against people from Nazareth (John

1:46). All of them were slow to accept eyewitness testimony of the Lord's resurrection (Luke 24:11).

Some were outgoing; others were introverted. Of some we know very little. All of those personalities! But a blend like that can make a creative and productive team. They can balance and supplement each other.

That's the way it works in the church. Each member contributes the personality and spiritual gifts built in by God and developed by the Holy Spirit. Some have strengths in the areas where the others are weak. Together we are much more than any one of us would be without the others. Paul said, "And he gave some, apostles; and some, prophets; and some, evangelists; and some, pastors and teachers; for the perfecting of the saints, for the work of the ministry, for the edifying of the body of Christ" (Ephesians 4:11, 12). Different personalities, perspectives, and gifts, when they are used together, can be a very good thing.

But the thing that puzzles us about the disciples is that even though they were right there and saw so many things that Jesus did, they often were slow to get the point. How could they watch Him heal so many people and not know that there wasn't anyone else like Him? How could they listen to His peerless teaching and miss the fact that He had divine insight? Why did they continue to fret about small things? In our look at the Lesson Background (below), we will see a perfect illustration of that blindness.

Another group that leaves us scratching our heads is that of the Pharisees and religious leaders who showed up so often to check on Jesus. No matter what Jesus did, they were never convinced. Mark 8:11, 12 says that He sighed deeply in His spirit to at least one of their requests for an additional sign. Such skeptics abound even today. Nothing is enough to satisfy them; they always seek another sign. When we are determined not to see, we just don't see, do we?

But the Christian faith is based on sufficient and reasonable evidence. God has done dramatic things in the world to illustrate His power. Jesus lived and did mighty works. The Bible, contemporary secular literature, and archaeology attest to these things. The faith that our salvation requires is a faith that trusts God to keep His promises for *the future* because of what He has done in *the past.*

B. Lesson Background

Today we will see Jesus ask His disciples a very important question about His identity. But behind that question stands a prime illustration of just how slow they have been on the uptake. A short time before, they had been aboard a small ship, crossing from one side of the Sea of Galilee to the other (Mark 8:13). But the disciples had forgotten to bring along any lunch. Among them they just had one loaf of bread, and they were beginning to fret.

As Jesus listened to them, He asked them some questions. Do you remember when we fed the five thousand? How much food did we start with? Do you remember the twelve baskets of scraps left over? So how can you be worrying about having just one loaf of bread? "How is it that ye do not understand?" (Mark 8:21). If they don't understand that, they don't understand Him.

But now it's time for Jesus to clear up their confusion. It's not time for everyone in the country to understand yet; but it is time for the Twelve to know just who Jesus is.

I. Jesus the Christ (Mark 8:27-33)

A. Mistaken Identity (vv. 27, 28)

27, 28. And Jesus went out, and his disciples, into the towns of Caesarea Philippi: and by the way he asked his disciples, saying unto them, Whom do men say that I am? And they answered, John the Baptist: but some say, Elijah; and others, One of the prophets.

Jesus and *His disciples* will stay a little longer in Gentile territory. It is still time to keep a lower profile, time to train His disciples, time to spread His love a little farther. *Caesarea Philippi* is a city north of the land of Galilee. Herod Philip named it in honor of Caesar Augustus. This city is located near the modern Golan Heights.

The question Jesus asks marks a turning point in His ministry as He affirms to the disciples His identity and just what will soon happen to Him. As a natural consequence, they will begin to understand the real meaning of faith and of discipleship. In asking who *men say that I am*, Jesus is not requesting information from the disciples. He already knows the various beliefs the people hold about Him. The question is intended to start a conversation.

The disciples' answer starts with Herod Antipas's frightened concern. He is nervous that this Jesus is *John the Baptist*—the man he had beheaded—back from the dead (Mark 6:16). That would have been a fairly logical conclusion for some people. Jesus has the same forceful personality that John had. The people turn out in droves to listen to Him as well. So it must be John. Interestingly, some had asked John if he were the Christ (John 1:19, 20). Now there are some who were thinking that the Christ was John. Jesus just doesn't fit the pattern of what they have come to expect from the Messiah. He shows no evidence that He is about to take charge of the empire.

Others thought that Jesus could be *Elijah*—or perhaps *one of the* other *prophets* who has been dead for many centuries (Mark 6:15). They remember that the Old Testament prophetic book of Malachi (4:5) predicts that Elijah will return to precede the arrival of the Messiah (cf. Matthew 17:10-13). The prophets, like Jesus, were wise men with powerful messages.

None of these guesses is unflattering. People think very highly of Jesus. But they do not recognize who He is. [See question #1, page 320.]

B. The Expected One (vv. 29, 30)

29. And he saith unto them, But whom say ye that I am? And Peter answereth and saith unto him, Thou art the Christ.

Jesus addresses His next question to the group as a whole, since *them* and *ye* are plural. Peter answers for the group. He is always the first one to speak. Sometimes he speaks rashly, but here he speaks perfectly. Of course, he just barely knows what he is talking about, but he does say exactly the right thing. Now, every week, men and women who would be saved announce the same thing, in full faith. Jesus is the Christ!

The Christ! Messiah! The anointed one! The expected one! The one who has come from God! The only one in whom salvation can be found (Acts 4:12).

30. And he charged them that they should tell no man of him.

Jesus still does not want His identity broadcast. By saying what He does, it is clear that He is confirming Peter's statement. Now Jesus will accelerate His teaching schedule. He will bring the rest of the disciples to this same point. When the time comes for His death, His resurrection, and His ascension, these men will be equipped

Lesson	He is	Text from Mark's Gospel
1	Son of God	1:9-26
2	Friend of Sinners	2:3-17
3	Master Over Wind and Sea	4:36-41; 5:2-13
4	Prophet	6:1-13
5	Authority on the Law	7:1-15
6	Messiah	11:1-9, 15-18
7	Passover Lamb	14:12-25
8	Suffering Servant	15:21-25, 33-37; 16:1-8
9	Victor Over Death	5:22-36, 41, 42
10	Savior for All Nations	7:24-37
11	The Christ	8:27-36; 9:2-8
12	Master Over Demons	9:14-29
13	King	10:35-52

Who Is Jesus?

Visual for lessons 2 and 11

Who is Jesus? Use this poster to note how this entire quarter has answered that question.

with the message and courage they need. But they are not ready yet. It is not yet God's time. But it is coming soon.

C. The Unexpected Truth (vv. 31, 32)

31. And he began to teach them, that the Son of man must suffer many things, and be rejected of the elders, and of the chief priests, and scribes, and be killed, and after three days rise again.

Son of man seems to be Jesus' favorite designation for Himself. He may be identifying His divine nature by drawing on a phrase that the prophet Daniel had used (see Daniel 7:13). Mark sometimes quotes Jesus' use of this phrase in such a way as to underline His divine nature (see Mark 8:38; 13:26; and 14:62).

The disciples must be shocked to hear these words. They are the exact opposite of what they expect for the Messiah. From this point on, Jesus gets increasingly clear about His future and about the nature of their discipleship (cf. Mark 9:31; 10:29-31, 33, 34, 45). He will not want them to carry on with Him under false pretenses. His way will be a way of suffering. There is going to be a high cost to Him, and there will be significant costs associated with following Him.

The disciples know that *the elders, . . . the chief priests, and scribes* have opposed Jesus to this point. But they certainly don't expect things to turn out so grimly. Jesus will *suffer?* He will die? By the time Jesus gets to the part about *after three days rise again*, the disciples probably have stopped hearing, their minds numb from what He has just told them.

We might say that Jesus' prediction should not be such a big surprise. The prophet Isaiah had written about "a man of sorrows, and acquainted with grief" (Isaiah 53:3), and had said "he was wounded for our transgressions, he was bruised for our iniquities: the chastisement of our peace was upon him; and with his stripes we are healed" (Isaiah 53:5). And the rest of the fifty-third chapter clearly describes what happened to Jesus. But most of the Jews of Jesus' day do not see the Messiah in Isaiah 53. A "suffering servant" is not the Christ they are anticipating. After Jesus' resurrection, the leaders of the first-century church will demonstrate that they have come to a profound understanding of Isaiah 53, as much of the New Testament shows. [See question #2, page 320.]

32. And he spake that saying openly. And Peter took him, and began to rebuke him.

Peter again speaks first, and his response is perfectly natural. It stands to reason that the One anointed by God to come to His people will not be abused and killed. What Jesus has just said doesn't seem to make sense!

D. God's Reality (v. 33)

33. But when he had turned about and looked on his disciples, he rebuked Peter, saying, Get thee behind me, Satan: for thou savorest not the things that be of God, but the things that be of men.

Peter's mistake is to think and talk from a worldly point of view. When he (or anyone else) doesn't embrace *the things that be of God,* he is automatically in league with *Satan.* Peter has stepped out of line. Jesus knows that if He takes the easy way—Peter's way, Satan's way, the way that the Jews have in mind—it will not be God's way. Satan had offered Jesus a kingship without suffering once before (Matthew 4:8, 9). Jesus had rejected that false path (4:10). Now He rejects it again: "Don't try to lead me, Peter. Follow me. *Get behind me.*"

II. The Followers of Christ (Mark 8:34-36)

A. Following and Self-Denial (v. 34)

34. And when he had called the people unto him with his disciples also, he said unto them, Whosoever will come after me, let him deny himself, and take up his cross, and follow me.

The concept of self-denial is rather easy to understand, although not many seem to practice it. Daily we are confronted with all kinds of enticements from others, and temptation to assert ourselves. When we begin to grow as Christians, we can also understand how foolish it is to say "no" to God and "yes" to ourselves.

Taking up the *cross* is a harder idea to grasp. Jews of the era know that being condemned to death by crucifixion also means carrying the burden of one's own cross on the way to the place of execution. So Jesus is talking about martyrdom as well as "death to self" (cf. John 12:24-26). Even if we are not called on to die because of our stand with Christ, Jesus still requires that we die to our old, sinful selves (Romans 6:6). Carrying a cross means more than merely "bucking up" when tough times come—enduring the normal challenges of life or working through personal failure. It means death to an old way, a way never to be followed again. [See question #3, page 320.]

THE ORDEAL AHEAD

The annual Race Across America is a bicycle race of three thousand grueling miles, covered in about eleven days. Riders pedal through nighttime temperatures near freezing in eleven-thousand-foot mountain passes; daytime in the desert brings scorching temperatures well above one hundred degrees. Their strength will be sapped by the muggy heat of the Gulf states after they have gone nearly a week on two or three hours of sleep out of every twenty-four. Heat exhaustion, hallucinations, saddle sores, and the constant threat of accidents are all part of the ordeal.

Yet year after year, thirty to thirty-five men and women train rigorously for months, pay an entrance fee of several hundred dollars, and endure a week-and-a-half of agony with the prospect of a few thousand dollars as a reward *if they win!* Half will drop out along the way with torn ligaments, strained muscles, and more severe physical problems.

Most people have no sense of what it means to endure such hardship. Perhaps that's the reason Jesus' announcement of what lay ahead of Him and the disciples caused such a strong reaction from Peter. But Jesus knew what He must face if He were to accomplish what He had been called to do. He also knew the hardships His disciples would face. When we answer His call to discipleship, none of us knows what lies ahead. Agonies of body and spirit may await us, but our Lord will help us to victory at the finish line.—C. R. B.

B. Losing to Win (vv. 35, 36)

35, 36. For whosoever will save his life shall lose it; but whosoever shall lose his life for my sake and the gospel's, the same shall save it. For what shall it profit a man, if he shall gain the whole world, and lose his own soul?

Elsewhere in the Gospels, Jesus illustrates the folly of accumulating wealth at the cost of one's *own* eternal *soul* (e.g., Luke 12:18-21). If I lose my soul I lose my very essence—all that I am. If I am in Christ, who I am will be His forever and ever. If I simply lose my life, I don't lose who I am. Many of the followers to whom Jesus is speaking will face this very choice.

III. The Transfigured Christ (Mark 9:2-8)

A. The Best of the Best (vv. 2-6)

2. And after six days Jesus taketh with him Peter, and James, and John, and leadeth them up into a high mountain apart by themselves: and he was transfigured before them.

No one knows for sure exactly which *high mountain* this is. The fact that it is within a journey of *six days* doesn't help much in narrowing down the choices! A good candidate is Mount Hermon, which is about 9,166 feet high.

Peter, James, and *John* traditionally are referred to as "the inner circle" of disciples whose support and partnership Jesus wants and needs on certain occasions. James will be the first to be martyred (Acts 12:2), leaving the other two to be the clear leaders of the original Twelve.

The Greek verb for *transfigured* sounds like the word "metamorphosis" when pronounced in English. It means Jesus was changed in His outward form. This change underlines the most important point that has just been made by Peter's confession in verse 29.

3. And his raiment became shining, exceeding white as snow; so as no fuller on earth can white them.

Jesus' clothes appear to grow whiter, the whitest thing the disciples have ever seen (*no fuller,* or cloth dresser, could ever get them that *white*). This dramatizes the character of the One who is wearing them. It gives these disciples a peek at the glory Jesus had before He came to earth as a man (cf. John 1:14; 17:5).

4. And there appeared unto them Elijah with Moses: and they were talking with Jesus.

God has brought back two important leaders from Israel's history for the three disciples to see. *Elijah* had lived over eight hundred years before the time of Jesus and was the foremost of the prophets. *Moses,* who lived some fourteen hundred years before Christ, was God's specially selected and prepared giver of the law—the law Jesus would fulfill. The apostles are dazed by all of this, but somehow they know who these men are (as Peter's next remark shows). The presence of Elijah and Moses with Jesus is powerful; but the point that God will make in taking them away (v. 8, below) is the far more powerful one.

5, 6. And Peter answered and said to Jesus, Master, it is good for us to be here: and let us make three tabernacles; one for thee, and one for Moses, and one for Elijah. For he wist not what to say; for they were sore afraid.

In stressful situations, some people "clam up" while others run off at the mouth. Apparently,

---

How to Say It

ANTIPAS. *An*-tih-pus.

AUGUSTUS. Aw-*gus*-tus.

CAESAR. *See*-zur.

CAESAREA PHILIPPI. Sess-uh-*ree*-uh Fih-*lip*-pie or *Fil*-ih-pie.

ELIJAH. Ee-*lye*-juh.

GALILEE. *Gal*-uh-lee.

GOLAN. *Go*-lahn.

HERMON. *Her*-mun.

HEROD. *Hair*-ud.

MESSIAH. Meh-*sigh*-uh.

NATHANAEL. Nuh-*than*-yull (*th* as in *thin*).

NAZARETH. *Naz*-uh-reth.

PHARISEES. *Fair*-ih-seez.

ZEALOT. *Zel*-ut.

ZEBEDEE. *Zeb*-eh-dee.

Peter is one of the latter, and is speaking out of fear. Before he stops to think, he suggests putting up *three tabernacles* (or tents), so that Elijah and Moses might stay awhile. It sounds like a good idea: he wants to freeze that moment in time. He wants to honor all three. [See question #4, page 320.]

MONUMENTAL TRUTH

Paris has its Eiffel Tower, New York has the Statue of Liberty, St. Louis has the Gateway Arch, Kuala Lumpur has the Petronas Towers, Jerusalem has the Western Wall of the ancient temple mount, and London has Big Ben (although the London Bridge somehow escaped and ended up in Arizona!). Every major city in the world seems to have a piece of architecture that says, "This is _____" [insert city name].

Los Angeles's thirty-two-story City Hall was once recognized wherever its image was broadcast because it appeared in the old TV series *Dragnet*. But other, commercial buildings have long since surpassed it in prominence. So a few years ago, a grandiose scheme was hatched by an artist best known for his sculptures of Hollywood personalities. His $3.6 billion idea includes a 750-foot tower with a skeletal steel frame, topped by a winged angel. Skeptics derided the proposal as simply a ploy for fame and fortune. (Did someone say, "What else is new?")

Peter had no such grandiose concept in mind when he enthusiastically suggested that tabernacles or tents—memorials or monuments of sorts—be erected at the site of the transfiguration. But Jesus knew a monumental truth: such physical things have only a fleeting existence. Only spiritual realities will stand the test of time and eternity. Is that the testimony of our lives as well?

—C. R. B.

Home Daily Bible Readings

Monday, May 5—Who Do You Say I Am?
(Mark 8:27-33)
Tuesday, May 6—Take Up Your Cross
(Mark 8:34—9:1)
Wednesday, May 7—This Is My Son
(Mark 9:2-8)
Thursday, May 8—You Have the Words of Life (John 6:60-69)
Friday, May 9—Zaccheus Sees Jesus
(Luke 19:1-10)
Saturday, May 10—Every Tongue Shall Confess (Philippians 2:5-11)
Sunday, May 11—Confess That Jesus Is Lord (Romans 10:5-13)

B. The First of the Rest (vv. 7, 8)

7. And there was a cloud that overshadowed them: and a voice came out of the cloud, saying, This is my beloved Son: hear him.

The cloud indicates the presence of God and that He has something to say (cf. Psalm 97:2; Isaiah 4:5). The disciples are privileged to hear God's direct *voice*. The message is similar to the one at the baptism of Jesus (Mark 1:11). It is a message of confirmation. God wants to make the message clear to the three apostles: the law (represented by Moses) and the prophets (represented by Elijah) point to His *beloved Son,* Jesus, and He is the One you now are to listen to. Jesus is primary!

8. And suddenly, when they had looked round about, they saw no man any more, save Jesus only with themselves.

The fact that Elijah and Moses now are gone is an important illustration in God's elaborate drama. The law and the prophets these two represent have done what they were supposed to do. They have prepared the way. Now Jesus is the fulfillment of everything. Acknowledge Him and listen to Him. [See question #5, page 320.]

Conclusion

A. Jesus the Only Way

We can't improve on the declaration that Peter made. We can't improve on the drama that God orchestrated on the mountain. Jesus Himself put it into the words that John, one of the primary observers to this scene, later recorded: "I am the way, the truth, and the life: no man cometh unto the Father, but by me" (John 14:6).

People will have wrong opinions about Jesus. Some will count Him to be a fraud. Others will view Him as no more than a nice, wise man. Some will consider Him to be one of the prophets, along with other historic world leaders. But these ideas are all inadequate. Today, He confronts us with the truth of His identity as He asks us the same question He asked of Peter: "Who do you say that I am?"

B. Prayer

Lord, our proper prayer today will be a heartfelt confession of Your Son. Each of us individually, and all of us together as a church, make a commitment that Jesus' words will guide our minds and that Jesus' spirit will be the guide for our spirits. Jesus is Lord! And it is in His name we pray, amen.

C. Thought to Remember

No one comes to the Father except through Jesus.

Learning by Doing

This page contains an alternative lesson plan emphasizing learning activities.
Classes desiring such student involvement will find these suggestions helpful.

Learning Goals

After participating in this lesson, each student will be able to:

1. Cite evidence from today's texts that Jesus is the Christ, the Son of God.

2. Compare people's wrong ideas about Jesus in his own day with modern misconceptions about Him.

3. Make a statement of faith in Jesus Christ, and give a way to live out that faith.

Into the Lesson

As students enter the classroom, have chairs arranged in groups of six. On each chair place these written instructions: "Take three things from your wallet or purse that will prove who you are. Arrange them in order from least convincing to most convincing."

Each group is to be sure all are introduced and the "proofs" given. Ask, "What was most convincing about the proof presented? Who gave the best proof? Why was it so?"

Ask, "What one word would your best friend use to define or describe you? Why?" Each person will need a short time to think and then share it with the group. Allow two to four minutes.

Say, "In today's lesson we will see how evidence is given of Jesus' true identity. We will see how clear the teaching is. This evidence will help us grow in our faith in Jesus."

Into the Word

Ask one volunteer to read Mark 8:27-36 and another to read Mark 9:2-8. Provide copies of the following questions, and allow students several minutes to answer. Use these as a guide to discussion in studying the passage. (You will want to be familiar with the commentary material for difficult questions that may arise during the study.)

1. What do you judge to be the most important thought in each of these passages?

2. From your perspective, what is the key verse in these passages?

3. How did Jesus teach this lesson?

4. What is the most practical teaching in this text for you?

5. If you had been one of the disciples with Jesus, what would you have asked Him?

After discussing the students' findings, ask, "What do these two passages teach us about the identity of Jesus? Why is this important to us today?" As this discussion develops, students will see that Jesus' identity is central to His mission. Only the divine Son of God could accomplish the task of salvation.

Into Life

Prepare a chart with the following three headings: "Opinions of Jesus—Then," "Opinions of Jesus—Now," and "Biblical Teachings of Who Jesus Is."

Say, "Suppose we were developing an evangelism program for our congregation. For it to be effective we need to be able to communicate who Jesus is. We want to be able to anticipate peoples' responses to 'Who is Jesus?' Using this chart, what would you include?"

Note how this chart helps us to anticipate objections people might have to the teaching that Jesus is the Christ, the Son of God. How would it help a person recognize the Biblical teaching concerning the identity of Jesus?

Now provide paper and pencil for each student. Supply hymnals or songbooks also. Ask each individual to write a statement of belief. It can be a simple statement, such as the one Peter made in Mark 8:29 or a more elaborate one using other Scriptures and hymns or songs. As teacher you may need to help your students get started in this activity. Allow several minutes for completion. (A similar activity is in the student book, *Adult Bible Class.*)

Have volunteers read their statements of faith to the class. After each statement, answer the student with Jesus' words in Matthew 16:17, "Blessed are you, *(name)*, for this was not revealed to you by man, but by [the] Father in heaven" *(New International Version)*.

Recognize that this may be difficult for students who are not yet confessed and obedient believers. Be sensitive to their situation, but encourage them to write what they presently believe about Jesus.

Mark 9:7 reminds us that we are to listen to Jesus' teaching. After listening to the written statements of faith, have each student write the one or two things that keep him or her from listening to Jesus and share the answer with one other person in the group. Have the pairs close in prayer concerning their steadfastness in following Jesus.

Let's Talk It Over

*The questions on this page are designed to promote discussion of the lesson
by the class and to encourage application of the lesson Scriptures. The answers
provided are only discussion starters. Let your class talk it over from there.*

1. While it may be flattering that some people think highly of Jesus, what is the major problem with someone believing that He's simply some kind of prophet?

Any view of Jesus that portrays Him as less than the Son of God is simply wrong. It might be partially correct; there might be some truth in the estimation. But if it does not see the whole picture, it is incomplete. The famous trilogy credited to C.S. Lewis sums it up best: Jesus is "Lord, Liar, or Lunatic." He claimed to be the Son of God—Lord of the universe. If He is not, then He either lied or He was deluded.

2. The disciples had a blind spot about the Messiah, which kept them from understanding Isaiah's prophecy. How do we know whether our understanding of Scripture is blocked by a blind spot? How should we respond to "new" interpretations of Bible passages—interpretations that differ from our understanding?

It is very difficult to know that we have a blind spot because it *is* a blind spot. We might begin to suspect it when someone challenges our understanding—as Jesus challenged the disciples' thinking. We can react like Peter and simply reject the new concept, or we can evaluate it carefully to see whether we have missed something. We need to keep the passage in context and compare it with other Scriptures. We can talk to careful Bible students whom we respect, and we can look up the passage in some commentaries or other Bible study helps. Ask your students for the names of Bible teachers or study guides that they respect and count on to keep their thinking straight.

3. What has following Christ cost you? What "cross-bearing" experiences have you endured? What has been the result?

Until Jesus began to make predictions about His own upcoming death, the disciples apparently had not even addressed the fact that He would, or even could, die. When Jesus began to speak of His death, the disciples were introduced first to the idea that He Himself would die. Then as He began to address the concept of carrying one's cross, He introduced them next to the idea that they, too, could possibly die. The disciples were beginning to see in Jesus a self-sacrifice, a

sense of purpose, and a love for God that would take Him to the cross. That same sense of purpose, love for God, and willingness to sacrifice must characterize His followers. Encourage your students to tell, without self-consciousness, how they keep these things in balance. What specifically have they sacrificed? Have they given up the wealth of a high-stress job in order to focus on ministry and/or family? Did some of them have to choose between pleasing unbelieving family members and serving Christ?

4. What do you do when you have spoken without thinking and made a foolish or even hurtful remark? What do you do when someone else does?

Too often, when we find someone has taken offense at a remark we have made, we become defensive. They shouldn't feel that way, we think. And we dig in our heels and refuse to admit we could have used better judgment. Perhaps one kind of self-sacrifice that we can practice is the sacrifice of pride. Even if another party shouldn't have taken offense, if we have hurt someone's feelings, we need to be mature enough to apologize and seek resolution. Ask students to tell how they discern when they have made an ill-timed remark and need to make amends. At the same time, we need to be mature enough to ignore foolish remarks by others. (See Proverbs 15:1; 26:4.)

5. What voices rival that of Jesus today? How can we be sure the message of Jesus is heard?

Many voices appeal for supremacy in our world today. There is the voice of the secular humanist, who claims mankind can solve its own problems and set its own destiny—without any help from God. There is the postmodernist, who claims there is no absolute authority. There is the New Ager, who claims you can be your own god. All these voices are easy to recognize and to reject. But some voices are harder to discern as that of the enemy. The religious leader who twists Scripture to suit his own desires is one example. Another is the one who claims to have a word from the Lord but whose message is not consistent with the Scripture. We must be sure to measure each message by the Word of God and let it be our only rule of faith and practice.

Expressing Honest Faith

DEVOTIONAL READING: John 16:25-33.

BACKGROUND SCRIPTURE: Mark 9:14-37.

PRINTED TEXT: Mark 9:14-29.

Mark 9:14-29

14 And when he came to his disciples, he saw a great multitude about them, and the scribes questioning with them.

15 And straightway all the people, when they beheld him, were greatly amazed, and running to him saluted him.

16 And he asked the scribes, What question ye with them?

17 And one of the multitude answered and said, Master, I have brought unto thee my son, which hath a dumb spirit;

18 And wheresoever he taketh him, he teareth him; and he foameth, and gnasheth with his teeth, and pineth away: and I spake to thy disciples that they should cast him out; and they could not.

19 He answereth him, and saith, O faithless generation, how long shall I be with you? how long shall I suffer you? bring him unto me.

20 And they brought him unto him: and when he saw him, straightway the spirit tare him; and he fell on the ground, and wallowed foaming.

21 And he asked his father, How long is it ago since this came unto him? And he said, Of a child.

22 And ofttimes it hath cast him into the fire, and into the waters, to destroy him: but if thou canst do any thing, have compassion on us, and help us.

23 Jesus said unto him, If thou canst believe, all things are possible to him that believeth.

24 And straightway the father of the child cried out, and said with tears, Lord, I believe; help thou mine unbelief.

25 When Jesus saw that the people came running together, he rebuked the foul spirit, saying unto him, Thou dumb and deaf spirit, I charge thee, come out of him, and enter no more into him.

26 And the spirit cried, and rent him sore, and came out of him: and he was as one dead; insomuch that many said, He is dead.

27 But Jesus took him by the hand, and lifted him up; and he arose.

28 And when he was come into the house, his disciples asked him privately, Why could not we cast him out?

29 And he said unto them, This kind can come forth by nothing, but by prayer and fasting.

GOLDEN TEXT: Straightway the father of the child cried out, and said with tears, Lord, I believe; help thou mine unbelief.—Mark 9:24.

Lesson Aims

After participating in this lesson, each student will be able to:

1. Tell how Jesus healed the demon-possessed boy just after the transfiguration.

2. Compare and contrast modern levels of faith with that of the disciples, whom Jesus chided for their inability to cast out the demon, and of the boy's father, who believed but prayed for help with his unbelief.

3. Commit to Jesus one specific area of weak faith with the prayer, "Lord, I believe; help thou mine unbelief."

Lesson Outline

INTRODUCTION
    A. Up the Mountain . . . and Down Again
    B. Lesson Background
  I. CRISIS ARISES (Mark 9:14-18)
    A. A Religious Struggle (vv. 14-16)
    B. A Failed Attempt (vv. 17, 18)
      The Limits of Human Resources
 II. CRISIS MEETS THE CHRIST (Mark 9:19-27)
    A. The Master Shows Irritation (v. 19)
    B. The Demon Reacts to the Master (vv. 20-22)
    C. The Master Solves Two Problems (vv. 23-27)
III. CHRIST EXPLAINS THE CRISIS (Mark 9:28, 29)
    A. The Question (v. 28)
    B. The Answer (v. 29)
      Spiritual Navigation
CONCLUSION
    A. How Long?
    B. Prayer
    C. Thought to Remember

Introduction

A. Up the Mountain . . . and Down Again

A summer week at Christian service camp has always been a terrific time for a lot of the kids in the church. They love the team competition. Swimming and softball, funny new games, great music, and, in some places, even the old Bible drama nights are almost too exciting to bear. It's hard to settle down at night. Sleep deprivation is "the norm in the dorm."

One of the great things at camp is studying the Bible every day. In addition to Bible classes, there are vesper services and other worship times each night. Every camper has to examine his or her faith in the light of all that is being said. It is two months of Sunday school every day! And at week's end there are always young people ready to give their lives to Christ, eager to be baptized. It is a "mountaintop experience."

From the time we were children, a lot of us have heard about (and have had) mountaintop experiences. Frequently, adults used that description when talking to us as children about Christian service camp. They also cautioned us, however, to be aware that down in "the valley" (after leaving "the mountain") things wouldn't be the same as they had been during that glorious week. The idyllic experience of the songs and the swimming pool, thoughtful counselors and lots of laughter, God's Word and great hopes—these would not be much in evidence back in the old neighborhood. But on the mountaintop many wonderful things happened. And, properly embraced, they prepared us for the valley.

The "mountaintop experience" near Caesarea Philippi in last week's lesson is the model for that expression. There, three disciples began to understand Jesus' true nature. They had seen something of Jesus' Heavenly glory. They had remembered how God worked through the law and the prophets. And God had confirmed that Jesus, their Master and Teacher, was His one and only Son. They were beginning to put the pieces together. And until Jesus' resurrection, this would be the crowning event that clinched their understanding. From that point onward, they would know who their Master was.

But then they came down from the mountain. As soon as they reached its foot, they heard an argument. They encountered illness. They heard about the failure of their colleagues. The harsh reality of everyday life in a sin-scarred world took about a minute to strike them. It was back to the grind. But they had new equipment, a new assurance. We rather suppose that as soon as things settled down that night, they told their fellow disciples all they had seen and heard. While Jesus had told them not to tell anyone (Mark 9:9), it seems reasonable that He meant no one outside the group of the Twelve.

B. Lesson Background

As they were coming down the mountain, Peter, James, and John, who comprised the inner circle of the disciples and who had just been treated to that majestic drama, were on sensory overload. They understood, but just barely. Jesus had told them not to broadcast the news of this event until after He had "risen from the dead" (Mark 9:9). This "rising from the dead" business troubled them (v. 10). And then there was the question of Elijah—wasn't he supposed to precede the Messiah (v. 11)? Jesus' explanation (vv. 12, 13) probably left them with even more questions, but with a measure of understanding as well. (See Matthew 17:13.)

So, with the experience on the mountaintop in their hearts and with these issues still in their minds, they came to the foot of the hill. Immediately they were in the midst of a squabble.

I. Crisis Arises (Mark 9:14-18)

A. A Religious Struggle (vv. 14-16)

14, 15. And when he came to his disciples, he saw a great multitude about them, and the scribes questioning with them. And straightway all the people, when they beheld him, were greatly amazed, and running to him saluted him.

The *disciples* mentioned here are the nine whom Jesus left behind when He went up on the mountain with Peter, James, and John. It is evident that there is some excitement surrounding them. And it is pretty clear that something is wrong. We can almost hear the confusion of near-Eastern voices debating with each other as *the scribes* challenge the disciples. As we will see in verses 17 and 18 below, the debate is undoubtedly due to a certain failure on the disciples' part. The religious leaders, always alert for an opening, are quick to find fault.

The crowd plays a big part here. *The people* are listening to everything that is said—watching everything that happens. It seems as though they really don't expect to see Jesus; they are *amazed* when He appears. While it seems natural but amazing that Jesus would rejoin His disciples, there must be something in the timing of His arrival that seems more than coincidental. The people run *to Him* immediately. If anyone can resolve this problem, He can.

16. And he asked the scribes, What question ye with them?

Jesus looks at *the scribes* and challenges them to tell Him why they are confronting His disciples. He knows that they have been arguing. With divine insight He also knows the issue at the heart of the argument. He wants to point up the foolishness of their dispute.

It's typical! It happens in the world; and more often than we like, it happens in the church. There is a child (or an adult or a family) in great need. And some who are unwilling or unable to meet the need go to war with others who are unable to meet the need. They discuss. They fight. They blame. And the need just sits there.

B. A Failed Attempt (vv. 17, 18)

17, 18. And one of the multitude answered and said, Master, I have brought unto thee my son, which hath a dumb spirit; and wheresoever he taketh him, he teareth him; and he foameth, and gnasheth with his teeth, and pineth away: and I spake to thy disciples that they should cast him out; and they could not.

The scribes don't answer, but the father of a demon-possessed boy does. This is the most detailed description of a case of demon possession in the Gospels. This is unusual for Mark, whose record is usually more concise. Perhaps the event struck Peter with special significance. Jesus' unique authority, affirmed by the Father on the mountain, is now demonstrated. Mark picks up on it and is moved to write of the event fully.

Previously, Jesus had given His *disciples* power over such spirits (see Mark 6:7). But for some reason, the disciples could not release this demon's hold on the boy. The fierce demon, bent on destruction, lets its tenacious and angry actions speak for it as it tears at the boy and causes him to foam at the mouth and gnash his *teeth*.

One thing that strikes us is the controlled way that the father speaks to Jesus. He does not seem to be hostile about the fact that the disciples are unable to cure his son. He doesn't speak bitterly. But he is disappointed and discouraged. Even so, he still can come to Jesus in hope. [See question #1, page 328.]

THE LIMITS OF HUMAN RESOURCES

Lloyd's of London was long a "rock solid" company. It started in 1688 as a coffeehouse where merchants and ship owners came to insure their cargoes and ships. Eventually Lloyd's became an insurer of many enterprises, from the

Home Daily Bible Readings

Monday, May 12—They Could Not Cast It Out (Mark 9:14-18)

Tuesday, May 13—Help My Unbelief (Mark 9:19-27)

Wednesday, May 14—This Kind Comes Out Through Prayer (Mark 9:28-32)

Thursday, May 15—Do You Now Believe? (John 16:25-33)

Friday, May 16—Jesus Prays for Future Believers (John 17:20-24)

Saturday, May 17—One Healed Leper Returns (Luke 17:11-19)

Sunday, May 18—Whoever Believes Has Eternal Life (John 6:43-48)

How to Say It

CAESAREA PHILIPPI. Sess-uh-*ree*-uh Fih-*lip*-pie or *Fil*-ih-pie.
ELIJAH. Ee-*lye*-juh.
EXXON VALDEZ. *Ex*-on Val-*deez*.
MESSIAH. Meh-*sye*-uh.
MOSQUE. mosk.
SCEVA. *See*-vuh.

---

risky to the mundane. Movie star Betty Grable even bought a Lloyd's insurance policy on her legs—legs that were as much a source of her celebrity status as was her acting ability!

But in 1987, Lloyd's began to lose money because of catastrophic losses on policies held by companies who suffered major disasters. In just two years' time, a petroleum drilling platform in the North Sea exploded; terrorists blew up Pan Am Flight 103 over Lockerbie, Scotland; the *Exxon Valdez* spilled its load of oil off the coast of Alaska; a refinery exploded in Texas; and the 1989 San Francisco earthquake struck—the one the world saw live during a World Series telecast. Lloyd's covered them all, and by the early 1990s it was questionable whether the fabled insurance company could survive.

The disciples seemed at one time to have everything they needed for a rock-solid ministry. After Jesus gave them power over demonic spirits earlier, it seemed the ministry of the disciples would be unstoppable. But like the disasters just mentioned, the demon in our text presented itself as an unrelenting disaster—wreaking havoc on its victim and pointing to the inadequacy of the disciples' resources for all to see. Whatever the source of evil, human power is often unable to solve our problems. God Himself doesn't always make our problems go away, but ultimately only He can help us deal with them. —C. R. B.

II. Crisis Meets the Christ
(Mark 9:19-27)

A. The Master Shows Irritation (v. 19)

19. He answereth him, and saith, O faithless generation, how long shall I be with you? how long shall I suffer you? bring him unto me.

Jesus sounds almost angry. That may surprise us. There are not many times in His ministry when Jesus sounds this agitated. His strongest actions are directed against the cheats and profiteers who turn the temple into a thieves' market. His strongest words are directed toward the religious pretenders, scribes, and Pharisees who twisted the laws and traditions to make life easy

for themselves and hard for everyone else.

At first glance, we might think that Jesus is irritated with the father of the boy. Upon reflection, though, Jesus' primary frustration seems to be with His own disciples. They have reason to understand more about faith by now than they are giving evidence of using. *How long* is He going to have to put up with their slowness? How many illustrations is He going to have to give? How many miracles will they have to see? When will they understand and show evidence of that understanding? He could ask me the same things—and probably you, too! [See question #2, page 328.]

Jesus teaches good lessons about anger. His anger is not out of control. It is controlled; it is directed. It has a purpose. He does not get angry about things that are done to Him—such as rude slights or insults. He gets angry when His anger can make a difference. Here it makes a point about faith, whole-hearted faith; about trust, which depends on God for what is beyond ourselves. No, men, you can't handle this on your own. Why will you even try? Jesus had given them authority over unclean spirits (Mark 6:7), and already they had cast out demons (Mark 6:13). But when this tough one came along they did not believe enough, and they did not depend enough—on God's power.

B. The Demon Reacts to the Master
(vv. 20-22)

20. And they brought him unto him: and when he saw him, straightway the spirit tare him; and he fell on the ground, and wallowed foaming.

This is a resistant, insistent demon. He won't give up voluntarily, even when facing Jesus directly. This unholy *spirit* takes its rage out on the boy in very visible ways.

There has to be a lesson here, doesn't there? The devil won't give up on you either. He will scratch and tear and try to toss you around. Jesus scares him, but you don't. And it may be that you will not trust Jesus. He'll still get you.

21, 22. And he asked his father, How long is it ago since this came unto him? And he said, Of a child. And ofttimes it hath cast him into the fire, and into the waters, to destroy him: but if thou canst do any thing, have compassion on us, and help us.

Jesus, of course, does not need to ask any questions. As the Son of God, He is able to know the answer in advance. But in asking *how long* this problem has persisted, Jesus opens a way to test the man's faith.

The father's devotion to his son obviously is profound. He has had to keep an eye on his son continually since early childhood in order to be able to rescue him immediately any time the demon would throw the boy into *fire* or *waters.* Notice the plural as the father asks Jesus to *have compassion on us* and to *help us.* This is not just the child's problem. It is a family problem.

The plea *if thou canst do anything* shows discouragement. The disciples have already tried and failed. But it is not an insult for the father to ask Jesus to help *if* He can. Everyone can see that this is the most awful kind of affliction that can be imagined. The father is aware that Jesus has done great things, but maybe this is too much. Anything that Jesus can do will be greatly appreciated. [See question #3, page 328.]

C. The Master Solves Two Problems (vv. 23-27)

23. Jesus said unto him, If thou canst believe, all things are possible to him that believeth.

Jesus immediately responds to the father's "if" with an *if* of His own. The father's "if" in verse 22 has raised the issue of Jesus' power or ability. But Jesus turns the tables and says, in effect, that this isn't an issue of His own power, but of the father's faith. I can do it, if you can *believe,* Jesus answers. What Jesus is talking about, of course, is not just some general kind of belief, some hoping against hope, some power of positive thinking. Rather, it is an absolute trust in Him. That's the only kind of faith that can yield results.

24. And straightway the father of the child cried out, and said with tears, Lord, I believe; help thou mine unbelief.

We understand! We *believe,* too, but imperfectly. We are a strange combination of believing and unbelieving. Please help me, despite my incomplete and imperfect faith, the man says. We know how that is. And probably we will pray that prayer to God as long as we live. *I believe!* I really do! But my confidence and my follow-through are both flawed. Please accept my heart and my intentions, and *help* me. [See question #4, page 328.]

25. When Jesus saw that the people came running together, he rebuked the foul spirit, saying unto him, Thou dumb and deaf spirit, I charge thee, come out of him, and enter no more into him.

The crowd (v. 14) is growing, as more people are *running together.* Before the commotion gets out of hand, Jesus decides to act. He does it from compassion for the boy. He does it in recognition of the faith of the father. He does it to underline for the crowd the fact that they can depend on Him, and that He has that kind of power. He does it because He is not about to let demons have the last word against His disciples! So He rebukes the *foul spirit*—and it's over!

26. And the spirit cried, and rent him sore, and came out of him: and he was as one dead; insomuch that many said, He is dead.

One last surge! The *spirit* tears at the child again, a death-gasp this time. In the crowd, *many* jump to the logical (but wrong) conclusion that the boy *is dead.* Although Jesus has done His best, they think, this one was just too strong!

27. But Jesus took him by the hand, and lifted him up; and he arose.

Jesus' healing of this boy certainly solves that young fellow's immediate problem. But more importantly, this healing demonstrates to the disciples, the father, and the crowd the importance of faith. Even so, the disciples won't really "get it" until they ask Jesus about it privately.

III. Christ Explains the Crisis (Mark 9:28, 29)

A. The Question (v. 28)

28. And when he was come into the house, his disciples asked him privately, Why could not we cast him out?

The *disciples* had driven out demons before (Mark 6:13), but for some reason this one was different.

B. The Answer (v. 29)

29. And he said unto them, This kind can come forth by nothing, but by prayer and fasting.

Jesus sometimes speaks to His disciples in public, but also instructs them in private, as now (cf. Mark 13:3; Luke 10:23).

Matthew's account of this event includes a gentle rebuke of the disciples. They could not cast out the demon "because of [their] unbelief" (Matthew 17:20). They suffer the same problem

"Lord, I believe; help thou mine unbelief." — Mark 9:24

Visual for lesson 12

Today's visual powerfully illustrates the Golden Text and is an apt reminder of our need to pray.

as the boy's father—they believe, but there is still unbelief. Both faith and *prayer* are vital to ministry. Apparently the disciples hadn't exercised much of either. Instead, they had drawn on their previous experience and depended on themselves. Perhaps they had tried to use their God-given power (Mark 6:7) as if it were some kind of "magic," requiring nothing but their own desires. (Later, the seven sons of Sceva would find out the hard way just how dangerous such a practice could be! See Acts 19:13-16.)

But faith and prayer acknowledge that we are inadequate by ourselves. When we exercise them, we admit that we must depend on God. And the kind of prayer that Jesus is talking about is not a few words spoken with head bowed. It is a life of dependent communion with God, a life of sustained communication. [See question #5, page 328.]

Our *King James Version* of the Bible has Jesus adding *fasting* to the requirement as well. Many other translations do not include this call to fasting, since quite a number of the early Greek manuscripts do not mention it. Jesus did expect His followers to fast, however (Matthew 6:16-18), and the early church practiced it (see, for example Acts 13:2, 3; 14:23). We'll leave to the scholars the debate over whether or not the reference to fasting was in the original. But let us note that fasting is a good Biblical discipline. As it shows a dependence on the Lord, it is consistent with the point Jesus is making here.

SPIRITUAL NAVIGATION

On a tiny island off the eastern coast of Africa in the Indian Ocean, archaeologists have found the remains of eight Islamic mosques, buried one on top of another. Islamic practice is to have mosques situated so that they point to Mecca, the Muslim holy city. Mecca is almost exactly due north of this small island.

The archaeologists discovered that as new mosques were built on top of older ones, the orientation changed. A mosque built in A.D. 780 pointed toward 310 degrees on the compass (roughly northwest); one built 120 years later was pointed at 329 degrees; and one built in A.D. 1000 was pointed at 342 degrees. (Mecca would be at 360 degrees from the island.) Apparently, Muslim navigators sailing the Gulf of Aden and the Indian Ocean gradually, over time, refined their ability to plot true directions. They used this improved knowledge in building each successive mosque.

Christians have no need to orient their church buildings toward Jerusalem (or any other city). But we are under obligation to orient our lives so that they point more and more toward Christ. Yet the process of increasingly accurate spiritual navigation is one that takes time, effort, and commitment on the part of the person who would serve God. We work through this process by deepening our levels of faith and prayer. This is an obligation each of us must take seriously as we plot a true direction for our life.   —C. R. B.

Conclusion

A. How Long?

Jesus asked how long He was going to have to be with His disciples until they caught on, how long He was going to have to suffer with their obtuseness. How long would He have to teach before they learned the lessons?

Can't you hear Him asking us the same kind of questions today? Some of us have studied in Sunday school for years. We have been through the International Sunday School Lesson series six or seven times. It's okay for us to continue to learn. It is understandable that every time we go through the Bible, we see things that we have not seen before. That's fine—we all overlook some things occasionally. But sadly, sometimes we choose not to see. As a result, we do not obey (cf. James 1:22-25).

We have so often missed the Spirit of Jesus. We have heard His words, but unlike the wise man who built his house on the rock, we have not put them into practice. How long is He going to have to wait for us to practice what He has preached?

Some of our debates over music styles in worship services have caught us not having listened. Those of us who have been longest in the church of Jesus seem to be the most frightened by any change. We are most resistant to some things to which other generations are responding—changing music style, levels of formality, and ways of addressing human need that are making them dynamic and enthusiastic Christians. They seem different from us. That seems to be most important. But are we, and are they, listening to the orders of Jesus and walking in His ways, copying His style? That's what is important. How long will He have to wait for us to understand that?

B. Prayer

Our Father, it is our prayer that we will have learned with the close disciples of Jesus the lessons in faith and prayer that He is eager to teach them. And we are thrilled to celebrate again the power of Your Son, through Whom we pray, amen!

C. Thought to Remember

"Lord, I believe; help thou mine unbelief."

Learning by Doing

This page contains an alternative lesson plan emphasizing learning activities.
Classes desiring such student involvement will find these suggestions helpful.

Learning Goals

After participating in this lesson, each student will be able to:

1. Tell how Jesus healed the demon-possessed boy just after the transfiguration.

2. Compare and contrast modern levels of faith with that of the disciples, whom Jesus chided for their inability to cast out the demon, and of the boy's father, who believed but prayed for help with his unbelief.

3. Commit to Jesus one specific area of weak faith with the prayer, "Lord, I believe; help thou mine unbelief."

Into the Lesson

Have your classroom decorated this week with a number of "snapshots": photos, newspaper or magazine pictures, or drawings. As the students arrive, give each a blank sheet of paper. (Or refer them to the appropriate page in the *Adult Bible Class* student book.)

Ask the students to sketch pictures of "mountaintop" experiences they have had in their spiritual lives. Rather than drawing, if they choose, they may write brief descriptions of the events. Ask students to tell about their creations to each other in groups of four.

Say, "Each of us has had 'mountaintop' experiences in the Lord. Today's lesson comes right after the disciples had experienced a special message from God. They struggled to obey Him. As we study, we will see how we need to trust God more after the 'mountaintops.'"

Into the Word

Use the introductory remarks of the commentary for a brief lecture to remind students of what the disciples had experienced with Jesus.

Form two groups, each no larger than six. (If you have more people, assign the following to more than one group.) Give each group a white poster board or an overhead transparency with markers. One person in each group will be asked to serve as secretary.

Group One: Read Mark 9:14-29. Complete an acrostic of the word FAITH with as many words, phrases, or ideas that describe the practice of faith in the text. *Examples include Focuses on Christ, Accepts Christ's authority, Inspires action, Trusts, Heavenly oriented.* (This activity is in the student book.)

Group Two: Read Mark 9:14-29. List event-by-event the major circumstances in this healing. Start with the crowd's approaching Jesus. *The list should include: Jesus challenges the teachers of the Law, the father approaches Jesus, Jesus rebukes the crowd for disbelief, the boy is brought to Jesus, Jesus questions the father, the father responds, Jesus teaches the father, the father believes, Jesus rebukes the evil spirit, the spirit departs leaving the boy in bad shape, Jesus helps the boy to his feet and responds to the disciples' questions.*

Call the groups together to present their findings. Discuss any difficult points using the lesson commentary for answers. Ask the following series of questions:

1. What do we learn about Jesus? *(He is greater than evil spirits and seeks to encourage faith in Himself.)*

2. What do we learn about the disciples? *(At times they were slow to understand Jesus' teaching. They often relied upon themselves and not on Jesus.)*

3. What is faith? *(Believing and trusting Jesus to accomplish His will.)*

4. How does Jesus help the man in his unbelief? *(Jesus shows the man that He has the power to do God's will.)*

Into Life

Ask the class to return to their original groups of six. Have each group discuss situations or examples of present-day individuals who exercise faith in Jesus' power. They may recall a missionary's presentation, a co-worker's challenge, a neighbor's friendly conversation, or a relative's concern. Encourage them to share some common denominators in each example. Examples may include trust in God, a willingness to admit personal frailty, or an openness to God's will. How are these similar to and different from the disciples' and the man's experiences?

Have the class form pairs. Give a blank three-by-five card to each class member. Say, "Just as the man asked Jesus to help him in his unbelief, so we will ask Jesus to help us. Choose an area in which you believe yourself to be weak in faith. Write it on your card. Under that write, 'Lord, I believe. Help me in my unbelief.' Share the circumstance with your partner and pray together for strength."

Let's Talk It Over

The questions on this page are designed to promote discussion of the lesson by the class and to encourage application of the lesson Scriptures. The answers provided are only discussion starters. Let your class talk it over from there.

1. The disciples had failed in their attempts to minister. Of course, there were critics on hand to point the finger and blame. How should we respond to failure in our ministry efforts—and to those who criticize our failed efforts?

If we keep an open mind, we can learn much from our failures. Was it the wrong program or bad timing? Were the people involved up to the task? Was it a real need, or did we have a need to be needed? Were we acting in God's strength or our own? Perhaps some of your students can tell of failed efforts that taught them valuable lessons. Ask them how they rose above the failure and how they analyzed the critical issues to make their experiences productive.

Then there are the critics. Sometimes they may be right! If we set aside our pride, we might learn something from them—even if their intentions are less than honorable. Otherwise, we simply need to be gracious, express our desire to learn from our mistakes, and then ignore the critics.

2. In what areas of the church might Jesus be wondering about us, "How long until they 'get it'?"

Be careful with this question. If there are issues causing strife in the church, this may provide an excuse to blast the "other side." But if your class is mature, the students may profit from a little self-examination. In many churches the issue of how to worship—particularly what music styles to employ—is causing division. Someone is "not getting it." Jesus has told the woman at the well that true worshipers worship the Father in spirit and in truth. Discuss how that should be the issue instead of personal preference.

Another area is that of race relations. What is your church doing about bridging the gap that exists between races today? How about showing mercy? Jesus reached out to the lost, sick, and hurting. Are we keeping evangelism and social concerns in balance?

3. The father said, "If you can." He wasn't sure Jesus could handle his son's problem. Which problems do we have trouble trusting Jesus to handle today?

Of course, your students will protest, "We believe Jesus can handle *any* problem!" But our actions sometimes conflict with what our words

say. We do not demonstrate faith that Jesus can handle our problems. When the medical experts say, "There's no chance," is our faith strong? When God's answer to our prayers is "No," is our faith strong? Sometimes the way God handles our problem is not exactly as we have hoped or expected. Can we still have faith?

4. The boy's father confessed both faith and weakness. Where might we make this same admission?

Probably most of us who have been Christians for some time would have to make the same kind of admission if we were honest about our own trust in Jesus. We may be weak in our view of society's problems. We know that God holds the answer to everything, but we look at our local, national, and world news and see that our society is layered with complex issues, complicated by our own self-inflicted problem of legalized sin. We must ask God to help us in our unbelief when it comes to what He can do. We may be weak in our faith in God's ability to help us rear our children. We know that God wants to be the most important parent in the lives of our young and innocent family members, but our unbelief says, "If I don't take this into my own hands and figure it out on my own, He won't reach them in time." Let's ask God to help us in our unbelief when it comes to what He can do.

5. In what extremely difficult areas of our society is it absolutely essential that serious, focused prayer be concentrated?

Ephesians 6 makes it clear that we are in a spiritual battle, and prayer is one of our weapons. Like the "foul spirit" of our text, some issues in our society are especially resistant to our efforts to shine the light of Christ on them. Consider legalized abortion—perhaps what lobbying efforts and peaceful protests have failed to do could be accomplished through intense prayer. How about the problem of drug abuse? What good have increased penalties and reports by subcommittees done? Have we tried intense prayer? What issues are problematic in your area? Is it the homosexual agenda, pornography, corrupt political leadership, or something else? What if some of your students committed themselves to intense prayer over one or more of these issues?

Faith Becomes Sight

DEVOTIONAL READING: John 20:24-31.

BACKGROUND SCRIPTURE: Mark 10:32-52.

PRINTED TEXT: Mark 10:35-52.

Mark 10:35-52

35 And James and John, the sons of Zebedee, come unto him, saying, Master, we would that thou shouldest do for us whatsoever we shall desire.

36 And he said unto them, What would ye that I should do for you?

37 They said unto him, Grant unto us that we may sit, one on thy right hand, and the other on thy left hand, in thy glory.

38 But Jesus said unto them, Ye know not what ye ask: can ye drink of the cup that I drink of? and be baptized with the baptism that I am baptized with?

39 And they said unto him, We can. And Jesus said unto them, Ye shall indeed drink of the cup that I drink of; and with the baptism that I am baptized withal shall ye be baptized:

40 But to sit on my right hand and on my left hand is not mine to give; but it shall be given to them for whom it is prepared.

41 And when the ten heard it, they began to be much displeased with James and John.

42 But Jesus called them to him, and saith unto them, Ye know that they which are accounted to rule over the Gentiles exercise lordship over them; and their great ones exercise authority upon them.

43 But so shall it not be among you: but whosoever will be great among you, shall be your minister:

44 And whosoever of you will be the chiefest, shall be servant of all.

45 For even the Son of man came not to be ministered unto, but to minister, and to give his life a ransom for many.

46 And they came to Jericho: and as he went out of Jericho with his disciples and a great number of people, blind Bartimeus, the son of Timeus, sat by the highway side begging.

47 And when he heard that it was Jesus of Nazareth, he began to cry out, and say, Jesus, thou Son of David, have mercy on me.

48 And many charged him that he should hold his peace: but he cried the more a great deal, Thou Son of David, have mercy on me.

49 And Jesus stood still, and commanded him to be called. And they call the blind man, saying unto him, Be of good comfort, rise; he calleth thee.

50 And he, casting away his garment, rose, and came to Jesus.

51 And Jesus answered and said unto him, What wilt thou that I should do unto thee? The blind man said unto him, Lord, that I might receive my sight.

52 And Jesus said unto him, Go thy way; thy faith hath made thee whole. And immediately he received his sight, and followed Jesus in the way.

GOLDEN TEXT: Jesus said unto him, Go thy way; thy faith hath made thee whole. And immediately he received his sight, and followed Jesus in the way.
—Mark 10:52.

Jesus: God's Power in Action
Unit 3: Jesus' Responses to Faith
(Lessons 9-13)

Lesson Aims

After participating in this lesson, each student will be able to:

1. Summarize the story of James and John's asking for the chief seats of the kingdom as well as the account of the healing of Bartimeus.

2. Tell why "blind" people sometimes see more clearly than others and why supposed leaders sometimes need to learn to follow.

3. Decide which "blind spot" he or she needs to work on most in order to follow the Lord more closely.

Lesson Outline

INTRODUCTION
  A. "When E. F. Hutton Speaks"
  B. Lesson Background
I. AN UNINFORMED FAITH (Mark 10:35-40)
  A. The Questioners' Immaturity (vv. 35-37)
    Sweet Seduction
  B. The Questioners Questioned (vv. 38, 39a)
  C. The Questioners Instructed (vv. 39b, 40)
II. AN INFORMED FAITH (Mark 10:41-45)
  A. The World's Way (vv. 41, 42)
  B. The Kingdom Way (vv. 43-45)
III. A VICTORIOUS FAITH (Mark 10:46-52)
  A. A Blind Man Asks (vv. 46-48)
    Seeing What God Wants to Show Us
  B. A Blind Man Receives (vv. 49-52)
CONCLUSION
  A. Seeing Like the Blind Man
  B. Serving Like the Great Man
  C. Prayer
  D. Thought to Remember

Introduction

A. "When E. F. Hutton Speaks"

In the early 1980s, the large Wall Street brokerage firm of E. F. Hutton came to be identified with its series of clever TV commercials. These ten commercials featured people in various social situations talking about the status of their financial portfolios. At a certain point, someone would always say something like, "Well, my broker is E. F. Hutton, and E. F. Hutton says—" Immediately dead silence would fall, as everyone in the place turned his or her ears to the speaker to find

out just *what* E. F. Hutton had to say! The commercial would then end with a hushed voice saying, "When E. F. Hutton speaks, people listen!"

By 1985, however, no one was listening to E. F. Hutton! That was the year that the company pleaded guilty to two thousand federal charges concerning manipulation of accounts. As a result of that plea, the firm agreed to pay two million dollars in fines and to reimburse defrauded banks as much as eight million dollars. In early 1988, E. F. Hutton ceased to exist when it was absorbed by another brokerage house.

Jesus is different. His timeless, living message never disappoints. But we must make sure that we are actually hearing *His* message. When we contaminate that message with our own expectations, disappointment will follow.

Today, we will see some disciples who allowed their own expectations to color what Jesus was saying. We will also see a crowd that tried to shout down a poor blind man because of their wrong understanding of Jesus and His message. As we examine their thinking, it will be a good time to examine our own!

B. Lesson Background

Between the healing of the demon-possessed boy of last week's lesson and the events of today's text, a great deal has happened. Most of the intervening events are recorded in Luke 10–18 and John 7–11. These events include incidents of Jesus' later Judean ministry (e.g., the mission of the seventy) and of Jesus' later Perean ministry (e.g., the healing of ten lepers).

Now Jesus and His disciples have started on the way to Jerusalem—the way to betrayal and the cross. Every day He was teaching. Every day the Pharisees were attacking. Not always were His followers learning. Sometimes it seemed they were not listening at all.

I. An Uninformed Faith
(Mark 10:35-40)

A. The Questioners' Immaturity (vv. 35-37)

35. And James and John, the sons of Zebedee, come unto him, saying, Master, we would that thou shouldest do for us whatsoever we shall desire.

In the two verses just before this one Jesus has again predicted His death—this time in very specific terms. Now Mark shows us that the disciples still "just don't get it." They have a plan of their own.

John's wisdom and maturity will be evident later in the five New Testament books he writes. We will see the spiritual maturity of his brother *James* in the martyrdom he will be willing to undergo (Acts 12:2). But right now both seem almost like children. This is the way a child speaks to his parents when he is about to ask something unreasonable. He seeks assurance first. "Tell me that you will give me whatever I ask!"

The parallel in Matthew 20:20 notes that it is their mother who asks the favor for them. Putting the two reports together, we can reasonably conclude that the two disciples have cooked up this idea, and their mother acts as the spokesperson. (Some students believe her to be Jesus' "mother's sister" of John 19:25. Perhaps the disciples believe Jesus will not refuse His own aunt!) Since the other ten disciples will be indignant with these two brothers (Matthew 20:24; Mark 10:41, below), the source of the problem is James and *John*.

36. And he said unto them, What would ye that I should do for you?

Jesus doesn't promise them, of course, that they can have whatever they want. But He is willing to listen to their request. Earlier, He had heard the disciples talking as they walked along the road. He knew that they were arguing among themselves about who was the best (Mark 9:33-37). It may be that He now just wants them to hear themselves make their selfish request out loud. This will be another opportunity to teach.

37. They said unto him, Grant unto us that we may sit, one on thy right hand, and the other on thy left hand, in thy glory.

The seats on the *right* and *left* sides of a king's throne are the places of highest honor, the places for the king's most trusted and respected aides. Despite all that Jesus has said about the nature of the spiritual kingdom over which He reigns, the disciples still think in terms of a physical and political kingdom. And here they are eager to have not only a reward for their partnership, but also position, rank, and preference.

That's so wrong! It's so selfish! And it proves they have not been listening to what Jesus has just recently been saying about His approaching death (Mark 9:31). [See question #1, page 336.]

SWEET SEDUCTION

The search for love potions is a historic one: humans have long desired to find a magic substance that can arouse amorous passions in another person. Chocolate has found a place in Western culture as one such substance. That's the reason we see all those chocolate hearts for sale around Valentine's Day.

One story has it that the sixteenth-century Aztec emperor Montezuma daily drank fifty cups of a potion made from the cacao bean. It was called *chocoatl*. Rumors spread that this substance was what made the king a very virile man. From the New World to Spain to England to Switzerland, the substance made its way, being refined with the addition of sugar and milk to the recipe as it went along. Today, chemists tell us Montezuma may have been on the right track: a chemical found in chocolate is also produced by the brain when one falls in love!

But there are other kinds of seduction as well. One that is perhaps subtler than that plied by the givers of chocolate is the seduction into which James and John had fallen: they wanted the glory of sitting on thrones beside Jesus in the glory of His kingdom. They could almost *taste* the sweetness of the honor. The temptation is with us yet. The glory of exalted positions still seduces many Christians who should know better.   —C. R. B.

B. The Questioners Questioned (vv. 38, 39a)

38. But Jesus said unto them, Ye know not what ye ask: can ye drink of the cup that I drink of? and be baptized with the baptism that I am baptized with?

What Jesus really asks here is whether they can give their lives. The *cup* that He is talking about relates to judgment and suffering (cf. Psalm 75:8; Jeremiah 25:15-28). Later, in the garden as He prays to His father, Jesus will ask that the cup (of suffering) be taken from Him if possible. He knows that His death and the terrible things leading up to it are in God's design. But it will be very hard nonetheless. This suffering will come upon Jesus as a deluge, or *baptism*.

39a. And they said unto him, We can.

James and John surely are sincere. In their enthusiasm they are ready to commit to anything. They think they can do it. They know the result will be great because Jesus is great. They have already seen that the way is hard. But for one who could raise the dead and drive out demons, how hard could it really be? [See question #2, page 336.]

C. The Questioners Instructed (vv. 39b, 40)

39b. And Jesus said unto them, Ye shall indeed drink of the cup I drink of; and with the baptism that I am baptized withal shall ye be baptized.

These two and the others *indeed* will suffer for their discipleship. In the early days after Pentecost, Peter and John will be thrown into jail for preaching about the resurrection and healing (Acts 4:1-22). A few years later, Herod will have James executed. This will draw a good response from the Jewish leaders, so Herod will become more aggressive in pursuing and jailing other apostles (12:1-4). Tradition says that the enemies of Jesus tried once to boil John in oil, but failed. Subsequently, John is sent into exile on the tiny island of Patmos (Revelation 1:9).

Visual for lesson 13. *Use today's visual to sum-marize and review the lessons of the quarter. Note some relevant application of each lesson as well.*

40. But to sit on my right hand and on my left hand is not mine to give; but it shall be given to them for whom it is prepared.

After sharing His cup and baptism of suffer-ing, the disciples will indeed share in His king-dom. But it will be a kingdom different from the one they expect. Jesus cannot make a commit-ment to them about a place of prominence in His "court." God the Father has certain prerogatives that the Son does not have (Mark 13:32; John 14:28).

II. An Informed Faith
(Mark 10:41-45)
A. The World's Way (vv. 41, 42)

41. And when the ten heard it, they began to be much displeased with James and John.

The other *ten* are *displeased* because they are sorry that they hadn't thought of asking first! Their displeasure here is consistent with the adolescent conversation they recently had car-ried on along the road (Mark 9:33, 34). It is very unlikely that these ten have a better understand-ing of the Lord's way than do *James and John.*

42. But Jesus called them to him, and saith unto them, Ye know that they which are accounted to rule over the Gentiles exercise lordship over them; and their great ones exer-cise authority upon them.

Jesus understands. The Twelve are acting like products of what is around them. Greatness in the secular Gentile culture (the Romans in par-ticular) means authority, superiority, the giving of orders. For the upper classes and those in po-sitions of power, control, perks, and pomp are important. Such thinking still predominates today. [See question #3, page 336.]

B. The Kingdom Way (vv. 43-45)

43, 44. But so shall it not be among you: but whosoever will be great among you, shall be your minister: and whosoever of you will be the chiefest, shall be servant of all.

The world's way is not Christ's way. (Nor is it the church's way.) Greatness is related to service. The one who is in first place is like a lowly *ser-vant.* Since the Greek word for *servant* here liter-ally means "slave," such thinking is undoubtedly a shock to the Twelve. But how many times have we heard Jesus turn human values on their head? His followers are in the world, but they don't belong there. We are not defined by the world (cf. Galatians 6:14; Colossians 2:8, 20).

The same is true of leadership in the church. Paul says that an elder must not be a novice, lest he succumb to pride (1 Timothy 3:6). There is a significant level of authority in the elder's task (Hebrews 13:17). A new Christian might not be able to handle such authority without its "going to his head." And Peter reminds the elders that they are not to act like lords over the flock, but rather to be examples to them (1 Peter 5:3).

45. For even the Son of man came not to be ministered unto, but to minister, and to give his life a ransom for many.

Jesus Himself models the service He expects from His followers. And He models service and sacrifice to the point of giving *his life* as *a ran-som for many.* The ultimate object of His life as a man is that very service: His death as ransom to recover prisoners and to free slaves. That's what Jesus' sacrifice does as it pays the price to release us from God's wrath (Romans 3:21-26). The price is paid for all who will accept it (Acts 2:38, 39). [See question #4, page 336.]

III. A Victorious Faith
(Mark 10:46-52)
A. A Blind Man Asks (vv. 46-48)

46. And they came to Jericho: and as he went out of Jericho with his disciples and a great number of people, blind Bartimeus, the son of Timeus, sat by the highway side begging.

Mark has one more healing encounter to tell us about before he reports the final week that ends with the cross and the empty tomb. Once more he wants to underscore a theme of his Gospel: Jesus is all-powerful. He rules over all ill-ness, forces of nature, and spirits. He is able to protect us in every way. He is the Messiah, the Son of Man, the Son of David.

Jesus moves His base of operations for the final part of the ministry. Up north, His "head-quarters" had been in Capernaum. Now to the south, He will spend valuable time teaching in

Bethany (John 12:1-11). He and His disciples will travel the road from *Jericho* (about seventy miles south of Capernaum) to get there before entering Jerusalem. But right now, a poor, *blind* man, *the son of* a certain *Timeus*, hears a crowd approach.

47. And when he heard that it was Jesus of Nazareth, he began to cry out, and say, Jesus, thou Son of David, have mercy on me.

Bartimeus apparently has heard about *Jesus of Nazareth*. The reports of all of those healings, which caused the multitudes to follow Him all over Galilee, have made their way to Jericho (about eighteen miles northeast of Jerusalem, where the Jordan River meets the Dead Sea). For a blind man, Bartimeus can "see" with remarkable clarity.

We have noted already how slow Jesus' own disciples have been to understand Jesus' true identity. He has shown them many miracles. He has called their attention to Isaiah's description of the one who is coming, who would suffer. Peter eventually was able to put it into words: "Thou art the Christ" (Mark 8:29). Then three of the disciples had seen Him transfigured on the mountain and had heard the voice of God expressing His approval (9:7). Now here is a blind man, who knows Jesus only by reputation, referring to Jesus by the messianic title *Son of David* (cf. Ezekiel 34:23, 24). Bartimeus knows who Jesus is. [See question #5, page 336.]

SEEING WHAT GOD WANTS TO SHOW US

The story is probably the same in every major city: thousands, perhaps millions of people hurry about their business unaware of places of beauty around them. In Long Beach, California, the El Dorado Park Nature Center is such a place. It is a 102-acre sanctuary of plants and wildlife right next to Interstate 605, one of the busiest freeways in the metropolitan Los Angeles area. Its meadows, brooks, and two lakes are home to a fascinating variety of flora and fauna. The garden is a quiet refuge in the midst of the noisy, teeming city. All it takes for anyone to enjoy it is the willingness to take the time to stroll, sit, look at, and listen to God's creation.

But from time immemorial, multitudes of people have considered themselves too busy (or perhaps too important) to take time out, stop, and appreciate the handiwork of God. This isn't a new problem. In Jesus' day, many were apparently too engrossed in their own plans and expectations to appreciate God's greatest piece of handiwork: the work His Son was doing in their very midst. But a certain blind man could "see" what so many others failed to notice: this Jesus was the messianic Son of David. Sometimes we have to stop the hurry of our lives and listen to

God's voice and see what He is trying to show us. Bartimeus can teach us a profound lesson if we are willing to learn!   —C. R. B.

48. And many charged him that he should hold his peace: but he cried the more a great deal, Thou Son of David, have mercy on me.

Bartimeus annoys many in the crowd. So they tell him to shut up. Jesus has better things to do than to deal with a pesky blind man. Obviously, these are people who have plans and expectations that are very different from those of Jesus. But this is nothing new! Even so, the blind man is persistent in crying out *the more a great deal.*

B. A Blind Man Receives (vv. 49-52)

49. And Jesus stood still, and commanded him to be called. And they call the blind man, saying unto him, Be of good comfort, rise; he calleth thee.

To *Jesus,* the *blind man* is not a hindrance to His mission, but a reason for it. Jesus always sees "little" people differently from the way others see them. Many in the crowd probably believe the man deserves to be blind because of sin (cf. John 9:1, 2). But Jesus stops and asks that the man be brought to Him.

50. And he, casting away his garment, rose, and came to Jesus.

This report has an unusual amount of detail! Mark not only gives the man's name, but also the name of his father. Mark describes the persistence of his call. He relates the title that the blind

---

How to Say It

AZTEC. *Az*-teck.
BARTIMEUS. *Bar*-tih-*me*-us (strong accent on *me*).
BETHANY. *Beth*-uh-nee.
CACAO. Kuh-*kay*-oh.
CAPERNAUM. Kuh-*per*-nay-um.
CHOCOATL. *cho*-co-*aht*-ul (strong accent on *aht*).
GADARENES. Gad-uh-*reenz*.
GALILEE. *Gal*-uh-lee.
GENTILE. *Jen*-tyle.
HEROD. *Hair*-ud.
JERICHO. *Jair*-ih-co.
JORDAN. *Jor*-dun.
JUDEAN. Joo-*dee*-un.
MESSIANIC. mess-ee-*an*-ick.
MONTEZUMA. Mon-tuh-*zoo*-muh.
NAZARETH. *Naz*-uh-reth.
PEREAN. Peh-*ree*-un.
TIMEUS. Ty-*me*-us.
ZEBEDEE. *Zeb*-eh-dee.

man uses for Jesus and tells us that the man is a beggar. Now, Mark even describes the man's quick jump to his feet and the fact that he tosses his cloak aside.

Matthew 20:30 tells us there were actually two blind men. Mark mentions only one—apparently to focus on the spokesman. We saw the same thing with his description of Jesus' casting out the legion of demons from the man in the region of the Gadarenes (Mark 5, lesson 3). Matthew's account included a second man (Matthew 8:28).

51. And Jesus answered and said unto him, What wilt thou that I should do unto thee? The blind man said unto him, Lord, that I might receive my sight.

Jesus already knows, of course, what Bartimeus wants. But Jesus doesn't provide the healing right away. He questions *the blind man* to give him a chance to express his hope and his trust. Here the word for *Lord* that he uses is "rabbi," "my master." No beating around the bush! No reluctance to repeat what was surely so plain! "My master, I would like to have *my sight.*"

52. And Jesus said unto him, Go thy way; thy faith hath made thee whole. And immediately he received his sight, and followed Jesus in the way.

He identifies Jesus. He asks for help. He believes that Jesus can give him his sight. Jesus doesn't waste any time. Bartimeus receives *his sight.*

In an interesting conclusion to this healing encounter, Bartimeus immediately becomes part of the crowd that *followed Jesus.* He doesn't take his healing for granted. He doesn't head off to use his newfound sight to do all of the things that he had always wanted to do, but couldn't. He uses his gift for the one who has given him the gift. That's a stewardship idea worth pursuing, isn't it?

Home Daily Bible Readings

Monday, May 19—Can You Drink the Cup? (Mark 10:32-40)

Tuesday, May 20—The Great Must Become Servant (Mark 10:41-45)

Wednesday, May 21—Jesus Gives Bartimeus Sight (Mark 10:46-52)

Thursday, May 22—Believing Without Seeing (John 20:24-31)

Friday, May 23—Abraham's Faith Did Not Weaken (Romans 4:16-22)

Saturday, May 24—Promises Seen From a Distance (Hebrews 11:8-16)

Sunday, May 25—Looking Ahead to the Reward (Hebrews 11:23-28)

This is unlike other healings in that Jesus does not forbid him from following as He has done elsewhere. For example, in Mark 5:18, 19 a man cured of demon possession was told instead to go tell his friends the good things that Jesus had done. But now, as the trip to the cross is very close, the crowds around Him and all of the publicity that will relate to this healing will not matter. Let them talk. Let these throngs of people frustrate the Pharisees. It is time.

Conclusion

A. Seeing Like the Blind Man

Maybe you know individuals who have been without one of their senses, particularly sight or hearing, who say that their other senses are sharpened. Such sharpening isn't automatic, however. Some people who suffer handicaps give up. Everything goes. They are not able to make much of a contribution. But others refuse to let one loss lead to many others. They make a remaining sense stand for two. That seems to be what this man did. Without his eyesight, his hearing sharpened. He listened. He processed what he heard. He understood. When Jesus came by, he was ready. He reached out. He trusted the Master.

Christians know that a loss doesn't have to be total or final. If one avenue is cut off, there are others to find. Christ is there. Sometimes He helps us be restored. Sometimes He helps us use very well what we have left.

B. Serving Like the Great Man

Jesus also teaches us that greatness doesn't come from being the boss or exercising authority. It comes from being a servant—a slave. Jesus had time for people whom society ignored. He had time for blind men. He had time for people who recognized their need and put their trust in Him.

In the days ahead, His disciples would watch Him act out His service. He would make the ultimate sacrifice. They would soon understand how much they needed that sacrifice for their own sin. They would understand how much they needed to be servants themselves (cf. John 21:15-17). Is that true of you?

C. Prayer

Lord, thank You for teaching us about faith and love this quarter, through the life of Your Son and through the record of Your servant Mark. Thank You for empowering Jesus to make such an eternal difference in so many lives. Through Him we pray, amen.

D. Thought to Remember

Blindness can be temporary—or eternal.

Learning by Doing

This page contains an alternative lesson plan emphasizing learning activities. Classes desiring such student involvement will find these suggestions helpful.

Learning Goals

After participating in this lesson, each student will be able to:

1. Summarize the story of James and John's asking for the chief seats of the kingdom and also the story of the healing of Bartimeus.

2. Tell why "blind" people sometimes see more clearly than others and why supposed leaders sometimes need to learn to follow.

3. Decide which "blind spot" he or she needs to work on most in order to follow the Lord more closely.

Into the Lesson

To begin, distribute copies of the following agree-disagree exercise. Ask your students to circle the response that best reflects their opinion for each statement. This activity is in *Adult Bible Class* student book.

1. Leaders should be more highly paid than followers. Agree/Disagree

2. Leaders get more benefits than those they lead. Agree/Disagree

3. Leaders are more important than their followers. Agree/Disagree

4. Leaders should never do the tasks their followers do. Agree/Disagree

5. A servant's attitude is necessary for a good leader. Agree/Disagree

(If your class enjoys more activity, place an "Agree" sign on one wall of the classroom and a "Disagree" sign on the opposite wall. Read each statement and have the students move to the side of the room that corresponds to their answer. If your students don't like to move around, ask them to raise their hands if they agree.)

Discuss your students' responses. Tell the class that today's lesson deals with attitudes and actions that communicate a servant's heart as a leader. We will also "see" how things may be different from what they appear.

Into the Word

Prepare an eight-minute overview for today's lesson using the introductory remarks from page 330. Then divide your class into three groups of six. (More groups can be used if necessary.) Copy the following directions for groups and assign one to each group. If a group completes its exercise early, assign another. You will need poster paper, markers, blank paper, and pens or pencils.

Exercise 1: Read Mark 10:35-52. Develop a chart with column one titled "The Disciples" and column two titled "The Blind Man." Under each column write these categories: 1. Title used for Jesus; 2. Persistence of person(s); 3. Question Jesus asked; 4. Request of person(s); 5. Result of encounter. Compare and contrast the encounters in your report to the class. (This exercise is in *Adult Bible Class* student book.)

Exercise 2: Read Mark 10:35-45. Compose a summary of the encounter and the lesson Jesus taught the disciples. Present the summary to class.

Exercise 3: Read Mark 10:46-52. Compose a summary of the encounter and the lesson Jesus taught the blind man and the witnesses to the event. Present the summary to class.

Plan for this exercise to take about twenty minutes.

Into Life

Distribute copies of the six questions below. Allow each group to discuss and determine its best answer for each question. (These questions appear in the student book for convenience.)

1. Compare Mark 9:35 and Mark 10:31 with this episode. Why are James and John's request and the reaction of the ten so amazing?

2. How does Jesus teach the concept again and what is His ultimate conclusion? (See Mark 10:45.)

3. Why do you think the apostles had to learn this lesson again?

4. How does Bartimeus get Jesus' attention? How is this different from James and John?

5. Why do you think Jesus asked both James and John and Bartimeus, "What do you want me to do for you?"

6. What do you think Bartimeus "saw" that the apostles did not?

After some discussion, encourage class members to pick a partner. Ask, "If Jesus were here right now and He asked you to determine a 'blind spot' in your walk with Him, what would you tell Him?" After a moment, ask them to reveal their responses to their partners. Then say, "If Jesus asked, 'What do you want me to do for you?' how would you respond? Tell your partner. Then tell Jesus in prayer."

After three minutes, close the class with your prayer for strength, asking God to answer class members' prayers.

Let's Talk It Over

The questions on this page are designed to promote discussion of the lesson by the class and to encourage application of the lesson Scriptures. The answers provided are only discussion starters. Let your class talk it over from there.

1. The lesson writer says the disciples' desire for "position, rank, and preference" was "so wrong!" Is it wrong, then, for a Christian to seek advancement, leadership, and higher pay? Why or why not?

If many of your students hold management-level jobs, you may get an immediate chorus of no's. Play a little "devil's advocate" and make them defend their position Biblically. Whatever your students' experience, challenge them to think Biblically and not to generalize their own experience as the norm.

The Bible's position is that consuming desire for wealth is wrong. See 1 Timothy 6:6-11. Stewardship is the proper management of whatever resources God gives us—whether great or small. As long as one keeps his or her priorities in order (Matthew 6:33), wealth is not an issue. The reason so few rich people will enter the kingdom (Mark 10:23) is that it is so hard for them to keep those priorities straight.

2. James and John naïvely stated that they would be willing and able to drink from the same cup that Jesus would drink. How have you seen God transform the naïve overconfidence of a new believer into a mature faith that's truly willing to take up any cross for Jesus?

For someone who is seriously committing his whole life to Jesus today, it is natural to make the promise without realizing what kinds of challenges Satan will throw and without realizing what a commitment that is. While some of those tone down such promises as they grow in Christ, others—simply by being in the presence of Jesus and understanding the harsh nature of commitment to Him—end up following through on their promises to give their whole lives to Him. Ask the class to tell of specific people—perhaps young people from the church's past—who have become significant leaders in the Lord's work.

3. Jesus warned the Twelve against following the cultural pattern of leadership. What kinds of selfish values from our culture sometimes creep into the way that the church approaches leadership and greatness?

One area in which this can be a problem is in leadership selection. Do we bend some of the Scriptural qualifications to fit the culture's views

on such issues as gender, wealth, and business savvy? Do we encourage servant leadership or privileged leadership? How about the way we choose and "un-choose" ministers? Do we treat ministers the way sports teams treat coaches? If he's had a "losing season," he may as well kiss his job good-by! Our churches must commit to re-examining the spirit of leadership that Jesus presented, and weeding out worldly definitions and processes. Ask the class to suggest specific ways your church can do that.

4. Can you think of someone who imitates Jesus' teaching on servanthood? How does following His pattern work out in "real life"?

Your students probably know several committed saints whose hearts are for the kingdom and not for personal gain. Encourage them to tell of such people. People who follow Jesus' pattern are generous. Whether they have much or little, they are always using their resources to bless others. They are often quiet, not seeking attention or having to be heard. But when they do speak, their words are carefully selected and poignant. They would be embarrassed to have their names mentioned in this context, but they are very worthy of it.

5. How is Bartimeus's cry to Jesus for mercy the basic prayer that every lost and blind person needs to pray before coming to Jesus?

Bartimeus is not too complex of a figure in the Bible. Yet his example is an amazing parallel to the steps necessary for any lost or blind person to take in order to receive the healing power of Jesus. When Bartimeus cries out to Jesus, we find that his cry is not complex either: it's a simple cry for mercy. "Jesus, thou Son of David, have mercy on me." By crying for mercy, he was demonstrating a belief that Jesus would not allow him to continue in blindness and would not ignore his need. Even when rebuffed by others who were more capable than he, he cried for it even more loudly. Every lost and blind person needs to realize that blindness and the state of being lost are just symptoms of the consequences of sin in a fallen world. It is necessary that we not come to Jesus as people who deserve what He has to offer, but as people who need His mercy in order to overcome and be set free.

Summer Quarter, 2003

God Restores a Remnant
(Return From Exile)

Special Features

Lessons

Unit 1: Return

Unit 2: Renewal

Unit 3: Repentance

About These Lessons

With this quarter we conclude the chronological study of the Old Testament begun in the summer of 1999. We have seen how God created the world and in that world blessed a special nation, Israel. We have seen how Israel was at times faithful to God, and how God blessed her in response. But we have seen sad times of disobedience, ultimately resulting in exile. Now we see the nation returned and reestablished to be ready to bring about the ultimate fulfillment of God's promises: the coming of the Messiah. May we prepare our own hearts to receive Him as King of kings and Lord of our lives.

Jun
1

Jun
8

Jun
15

Jun
22

Jun
29

Jul
6

Jul
13

Jul
20

Jul
27

Aug
3

Aug
10

Aug
17

Aug
24

Aug
31

Return! Renewal! Repentance!

by Lloyd M. Pelfrey

THE THREE WORDS IN THE CAPTION above are the titles for the three units of study during the months of June, July, and August. Each word represents the theme for one month in this unusual quarter that has fourteen lessons.

These studies bring to a close the history of Old Testament Israel. God's faithful people will be presented as they return from exile in Babylon to face the challenge of restoring their nation.

Unit 1: June
Return

Nebuchadnezzar, king of Babylon, destroyed Jerusalem in 586 B.C. In turn, Cyrus, king of the Medo-Persian Empire, conquered Babylon in 539 B.C. He then proclaimed that all captives could return to their native lands. Almost seventy years had passed since the first Jewish captives had arrived from Judah in 605 B.C. The fall of Jerusalem had convinced the people that the prophets were right: it would be a long stay. After becoming comfortable, would anyone want to "return"?

Lesson 1: The Exiles Return. The Lord's prompting (through Cyrus) motivated about fifty thousand people to return. They brought back with them many of the vessels of the temple.

Lesson 2: Beginning to Rebuild. The returnees wanted God's blessing, so one of their first acts was to rebuild the altar for burnt offerings. To be able again to offer sacrifices to God was exciting!

Lesson 3: Returning to the Work. After the rebuilding stopped, God raised a prophet, Haggai, to challenge the people to evaluate their priorities. His preaching got them back to work.

Lesson 4: God Gives Hope for the Future. The prophet Zechariah then teamed with Haggai to assure the people of God's concern for them. The nation would be an example of God's blessings.

Lesson 5: The Exiles Dedicate the Temple. Under the prodding of prophets and decrees of kings, the people finally completed the temple. The dedication of their new place of assembly was a time for celebration.

Unit 2: July
Renewal

Another seventy-year period elapsed between the completion of the temple and the next positive action by God concerning His city, Jerusalem. God needed a man who was a capable leader, could administrate a large project, could motivate others to help, and would persevere in spite of opposition. He also had to be a man of prayer. That man was Nehemiah!

Lesson 6: Nehemiah Begins Work. Nehemiah was serving in the palace of the king of Persia when the distressing news came: Jerusalem needed walls! Nehemiah prayed and got busy.

Lesson 7: Nehemiah Completes the Wall. Every building project has those who oppose it. But Nehemiah prayed, resisted the enemies, and completed the project in record time.

Lesson 8: Ezra Reads the Law. After dedicating the rebuilt temple, Ezra led in the reading of God's Word. The people wept as they realized their sin. Then their weeping turned into a joyful obedience.

Lesson 9: The People Renew the Covenant. A thousand years had passed since the Israelites had received God's covenant. But they had broken it many times. Now they promised again to obey the terms of God's covenant.

Unit 3: August
Repentance

Exhortations to repent by four prophets conclude the summer's lessons. Repentance involves examining the past and deciding again to do what it takes to keep God's Word.

Lesson 10: Message of Condemnation. Obadiah's thrust is that Edom will be destroyed because of its prideful attitude and actions. God is concerned with what nations and individuals do, and the time to repent is *now*.

Lesson 11. Call for Repentance. Joel portrays dreaded invasions of locusts as God's discipline. The underlying motive is God's concern and love for His people.

Lesson 12: Promise to the Faithful. Ezra and Nehemiah receive additional support from Malachi's prophetic voice. His words remind the people that both judgment and blessings are in God's plans.

Lesson 13: Prophecy of an Eternal Kingdom. As a captive in Babylon, Daniel interpreted a dream involving four great kingdoms. None of those were to last, but God's kingdom will!

Lesson 14: Prediction of the End. In his final vision Daniel gives a veiled look at events of "the end." Simply to know that God is sovereign over all history and that all things are moving according to His plan enables us to experience a "return" to God for the "renewal" that only He can provide after our genuine "repentance."

The Exiles Return

June 1
Lesson 1

DEVOTIONAL READING: Isaiah 52:7-12.

BACKGROUND SCRIPTURE: Ezra 1.

PRINTED TEXT: Ezra 1.

Ezra 1:1-11

1 Now in the first year of Cyrus king of Persia, that the word of the LORD by the mouth of Jeremiah might be fulfilled, the LORD stirred up the spirit of Cyrus king of Persia, that he made a proclamation throughout all his kingdom, and put it also in writing, saying,

2 Thus saith Cyrus king of Persia, The LORD God of heaven hath given me all the kingdoms of the earth; and he hath charged me to build him a house at Jerusalem, which is in Judah.

3 Who is there among you of all his people? his God be with him, and let him go up to Jerusalem, which is in Judah, and build the house of the LORD God of Israel, (he is the God,) which is in Jerusalem.

4 And whosoever remaineth in any place where he sojourneth, let the men of his place help him with silver, and with gold, and with goods, and with beasts, besides the freewill offering for the house of God that is in Jerusalem.

5 Then rose up the chief of the fathers of Judah and Benjamin, and the priests, and the Levites, with all them whose spirit God had raised, to go up to build the house of the LORD which is in Jerusalem.

6 And all they that were about them strengthened their hands with vessels of silver, with gold, with goods, and with beasts, and with precious things, besides all that was willingly offered.

7 Also Cyrus the king brought forth the vessels of the house of the LORD, which Nebuchadnezzar had brought forth out of Jerusalem, and had put them in the house of his gods;

8 Even those did Cyrus king of Persia bring forth by the hand of Mithredath the treasurer, and numbered them unto Sheshbazzar, the prince of Judah.

9 And this is the number of them: thirty chargers of gold, a thousand chargers of silver, nine and twenty knives,

10 Thirty basins of gold, silver basins of a second sort four hundred and ten, and other vessels a thousand.

11 All the vessels of gold and of silver were five thousand and four hundred. All these did Sheshbazzar bring up with them of the captivity that were brought up from Babylon unto Jerusalem.

GOLDEN TEXT: Who is there among you of all his people? his God be with him, and let him go up to Jerusalem, which is in Judah, and build the house of the LORD God of Israel, (he is the God,) which is in Jerusalem.—Ezra 1:3.

God Restores a Remnant

Unit 1: Return

(Lessons 1-5)

Lesson Aims

After participating in this lesson, the students will be able to:

1. Narrate the highlights of the initial return of devout Jews from their Babylonian exile to their Judean homeland.

2. Explain the historical and spiritual significance of this return.

3. Develop a list of principles that can guide their reactions to new ventures or projects in the church.

Lesson Outline

INTRODUCTION
  A. Moving Day!
  B. Lesson Background
 I. THE KING'S DECREE (Ezra 1:1-4)
  A. Divine Aspect (v. 1)
    Fulfilled Prophecy
  B. Royal Proclamation (vv. 2-4)
 II. THE PEOPLE'S DECISIONS (Ezra 1:5, 6)
  A. Decisions to Return (v. 5)
    Decisions Have Consequences
  B. Decisions to Share (v. 6)
III. THE VESSELS RETURNED (Ezra 1:7-11)
  A. Endowed by Cyrus (v. 7)
  B. Entrusted to Sheshbazzar (v. 8)
  C. Enumerated by Ezra (vv. 9-11)
CONCLUSION
  A. Longing for Home?
  B. Prayer
  C. Thought to Remember

Introduction

A. Moving Day!

The obituary revealed that she had had quite a past. Having been born in 1898 and dying in 2001, she had lived in three centuries. Her past included a six-hundred-mile move in a covered wagon when her parents decided to relocate to an area where there might be more opportunities.

The logistics of such a move are mind-boggling. Back then, there were no paved roads for travel. (In 1900, the United States had only 144 miles of such roads.) The arrangements for food and sanitation were far different from what is considered "normal" today. In addition, the time required for

such a move stands in stark contrast to what the "now generation" expects. Such journeys took months, not one or two days. Obviously, one did not decide to undertake such a move lightly.

Today's lesson relates the circumstances behind the decision of many Israelites to make a nine-hundred-mile move from their settled situations in Babylon. This journey would take them back to Judah, the land of their roots.

B. Lesson Background

Last November we concluded a three-month study that considered God's prophecies of judgment against Judah as well as the conquest of that country by the Babylonians. Nebuchadnezzar destroyed Jerusalem in the summer of 586 B.C. Before that, he already had taken captives from Jerusalem in 605 B.C. (including Daniel and his friends) and in 597 B.C. (including the prophet Ezekiel). The Babylonian Empire was a great empire, reaching its peak with King Nebuchadnezzar, who reigned from 605–562 B.C. It was just twenty-three years after Nebuchadnezzar's death that the troops of Cyrus, on October 29, 539 B.C., gained entrance to the city of Babylon and brought the Babylonian Empire to an end. As the Persian troops of Cyrus entered the city, Belshazzar was having a feast with a thousand of his nobles. He knew that the Persian troops were approaching, but he felt secure. Babylon was considered impregnable, and the city was ready for a long siege.

Then the appearance of fingers writing on the wall of his banquet hall petrified Belshazzar. The prophet Daniel was called to provide the meaning of the strange words. The ominous message that the kingdom would be given to the Medes and Persians was fulfilled that very night (see Daniel 5).

I. The King's Decree
(Ezra 1:1-4)

The opening words of the Book of Ezra are of great importance. God is ready to act again in a mighty way to bring His people to the promised land for a second time. The importance can be seen in the fact that the last two verses of the previous book, 2 Chronicles, match the first verses of Ezra almost verbatim. Regardless of which book is being read, the reader must know that the sovereign Lord was directing these historical actions.

In addition, the return of God's people to Judah was necessary to bring about the fulfillment of certain prophecies about the Messiah. For example, He would be born in Bethlehem (Micah 5:2), and it was imperative that David's descendants be in the right place.

A. Divine Aspect (v. 1)

1. Now in the first year of Cyrus king of Persia, that the word of the LORD by the mouth of Jeremiah might be fulfilled, the LORD stirred up the spirit of Cyrus king of Persia, that he made a proclamation throughout all his kingdom, and put it also in writing, saying.

Cyrus king of Persia is a special person in the plan of God. Approximately 150 years before Cyrus's birth, the prophet Isaiah recorded his name as one chosen by God (see Isaiah 44:28; 45:1, 13). Cyrus is God's "shepherd" and God's "anointed." Isaiah prophesied that Cyrus would speak the words that Jerusalem would be built and that the temple's foundations would be laid. [See question #1, page 346.]

The prophecies about Cyrus are amazingly precise. Isaiah wrote that God would "subdue nations before him" and that gates would be opened to him. Cyrus had become a minor king within the nation of Media in 559 B.C. In a remarkable series of events, he became the ruler of all Media, conquering the nation of Lydia, Croeses its king, and his capital city of Sardis. The forces of Cyrus then marched on Babylon, ready for the long siege. To their amazement, the city's gates were opened by those who were unhappy with King Belshazzar. The siege never occurred.

Cyrus gives his "emancipation *proclamation*" in the spring of 538 B.C., in his first year of rule over Babylon. A possible reconstruction of the events indicates that he had left Babylon, turning it over to Darius the Mede (see Daniel 5:31), and later returned and issued this proclamation.

This act by Cyrus also fulfills prophecies that had been given by the prophet *Jeremiah*, who said that the desolation would last for seventy years (Jeremiah 25:1, 11, 12; 29:10; 2 Chronicles 36:21). Those same predictions also served as the background for one of Daniel's prayers (Daniel 9:2).

FULFILLED PROPHECY

The Bible is filled with a pattern of fulfilled prophecies about people, cities, nations, and events. What are the odds of all this happening by accident?

Consider just the case of Cyrus. Isaiah made his prophecies concerning that ruler some 150 years before he was even born! In 1996, Dr. Hugh Ross calculated the probability of chance fulfillment of the prophecies of Isaiah 44:28; 45:1, 13 at one in one quadrillion! To get a perspective on how large a quadrillion really is, picture it this way: that many silver dollars would cover the entire surface of the state of Texas more than twice! Imagine having that many coins, marking one with a big X, and mixing it in. Then blindfold someone and put him in the middle of that twice-covered state with this instruction: "Go anywhere you wish, and pick a single coin." The odds of his picking the coin having the X on it are about the same as a chance fulfillment of the prophecy about Cyrus.

Cyrus, king of Persia, didn't know it, but he was God's errand boy for the fulfillment of Jeremiah's prophecy that the captivity of Judah would end after seventy years. The fulfilled prophecies of the Bible are testimony to God's sovereignty and the Bible's trustworthy nature as the Word of God. Fulfilled prophecy strengthens our faith. —J. A. M.

B. Royal Proclamation (vv. 2-4)

2. Thus saith Cyrus king of Persia, The LORD God of heaven hath given me all the kingdoms of the earth; and he hath charged me to build him a house at Jerusalem, which is in Judah.

The expression *God of heaven* is popular among the writers of the closing days of the Old Testament. It emphasizes the sovereignty of God. He is the God who made the heavens and the earth. He is in the heavens directing the course of all history to His desired end. In fact, the phrase is used so often in Daniel 2 that many students

---

How to Say It

ASSYRIANS. Uh-*sear*-e-unz.
BABYLON. *Bab*-uh-lun.
BABYLONIAN. Bab-ih-*low*-nee-un.
BELSHAZZAR. Bel-*shazz*-er.
CROESES. *Kree*-sus.
CYRUS. *Sigh*-russ.
DARIUS. Duh-*rye*-us.
EZEKIEL. Ee-*zeek*-ee-ul or Ee-*zeek*-yul.
EZRA. *Ez*-ruh.
ISAIAH. Eye-*zay*-uh.
JEREMIAH. Jair-uh-*my*-uh.
JERUSALEM. Juh-*roo*-suh-lem.
JUDAH. *Joo*-duh.
JUDEAN. Joo-*dee*-un.
LEVI. *Lee*-vye.
LEVITES. *Lee*-vites.
LYDIA. *Lid*-ee-uh.
MEDIA. *Meed*-ee-uh.
MEDE. Meed.
MITHREDATH. *Mith*-ree-dath.
NEBO. *Nee*-bo.
NEBUCHADNEZZAR. *Neb*-yuh-kud-*nez*-er (strong accent on *nez*).
PERSIA. *Per*-zhuh.
SARDIS. *Sar*-dis.
SHENAZAR. Sheh-*naz*-ar.
SHESHBAZZAR. Shesh-*baz*-ar.
ZERUBBABEL. Zeh-*rub*-uh-bul.

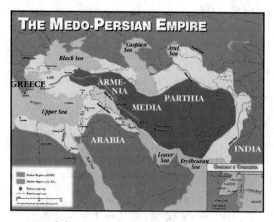

THE MEDO-PERSIAN EMPIRE

Visual for lessons 1 and 10. *Use this map to locate the various places that relate to the events you will be studying this quarter.*

believe Daniel may have been the one who actually penned the document on behalf of Cyrus.

The opening words of Cyrus's statement emphasize that it is *the Lord* who has *given* him *all the kingdoms of the earth,* and that it is He who has commissioned Cyrus to *build* the temple *at Jerusalem.* When Cyrus reflects on the ease by which he conquered Media, Lydia, and Babylon, he may conclude that it was not by his own might that he was able to do these things, but by God's. [See question #2, page 346.]

The rebuilding of the *house* at Jerusalem (i.e., the temple) is extremely important for Israel. Their worship is not considered complete without the temple and its facilities.

3. Who is there among you of all his people? his God be with him, and let him go up to Jerusalem, which is in Judah, and build the house of the LORD God of Israel, (he is the God,) which is in Jerusalem.

Cyrus is apparently impressed with the God of the Jews! This does not mean, however, that he has surrendered his pagan concepts about what "other" gods there may be. A famous archaeological find known as the "Cyrus Cylinder," a historical record written on baked clay in about 536 B.C., ends with this prayer of Cyrus: "May all the gods whom I have resettled in their sacred cities ask daily Bel and Nebo for a long life for me." (Bel and Nebo are Babylonian deities.) The mention of so many "gods" makes it clear that Cyrus is not a convert to the one true God.

According to this decree, each person is free to choose whether or not to make the nine-hundred-mile trip to Jerusalem. The time in Babylon has permitted the roots to grow deep. Pulling up those roots will demand a price that some will not want to pay.

Obviously, such a decision is monumental. Those who make that choice will never see certain of their family members again. There are no telephones for maintaining contact, and any postal deliveries depend on knowing someone who is planning to travel that direction.

Such a decision is similar to that made by those who decide to serve the Lord in foreign nations. While jet planes and E-mail have made it much easier to stay in contact with family back home, the separation is real and not always easy to endure. Wise churches will make special efforts to lessen the pain of separation for the missionaries they support.

4. And whosoever remaineth in any place where he sojourneth, let the men of his place help him with silver, and with gold, and with goods, and with beasts, besides the freewill offering for the house of God that is in Jerusalem.

The final part of Cyrus's edict addresses the people who will choose not to return to Judah. Every Israelite can have a part in the rebuilding programs of *Jerusalem* and its temple. A project of this scope demands great resources, and each person must do his or her part, either by going or by giving *silver, gold,* and *goods,* plus livestock for sacrifices and food. [See question #3, page 346.]

The sharing of provisions by those who stay behind invites comparison with the exodus from Egypt a thousand years before. On that occasion, the Israelites asked their neighbors for silver, gold, and clothing (Exodus 12:35). Those items were used in the building of the tabernacle (25:1-9; 35:4-9, 20-29).

II. The People's Decisions (Ezra 1:5, 6)

The proclamation of the new king was made known throughout the land. It would be fascinating to know more about the discussions that were held by people of all ages. There was much to be considered. Would anyone be willing to return? Was the price too great to pay?

A. Decisions to Return (v. 5)

5. Then rose up the chief of the fathers of Judah and Benjamin, and the priests, and the Levites, with all them whose spirit God had raised, to go up to build the house of the LORD which is in Jerusalem.

As *God* had stirred the heart of Cyrus, so He prompts the leaders of three tribes—*Judah, Benjamin,* and Levi—to go up to *Jerusalem* in order to build the house of the Lord. [See question #4, page 346.]

The mention of just three tribes is understandable. The Assyrians had taken the northern nation of Israel, with its ten tribal territories, into captivity in 722 B.C. The southern nation of Judah consisted primarily of just the two tribes of Judah and Benjamin. Many of the priestly *Levites* (who had no tribal territory) had lived in Judah where the temple was located. (See 2 Chronicles 11:13-17.) It will be imperative to have *priests* as a part of the group who will return; the priests are the ones who will officiate in offering sacrifices to God.

The number of people who decide to return totals nearly 50,000 (see Ezra 2:64, 65). While that seems small compared with the 603,550 adult males who came out of Egypt with Moses (Exodus 38:26), it still staggers the imagination when the factors such as transportation, food, and sanitation are considered. The emotions in the case at hand undoubtedly are quite mixed since the people are leaving their "home" in Babylon to return voluntarily to their "home" in Judah.

DECISIONS HAVE CONSEQUENCES

The 1981 Academy Award-winning film *Chariots of Fire* focused on decisions and their consequences. The film's main character, Eric Liddell, was a Scotch Presbyterian minister who believed that Sunday was the "Sabbath" and should not be used for any secular purpose. Liddell was also a gifted athlete who qualified to compete in the 1924 Olympics. For years he had set his heart on running in the games and winning a gold medal for England. He was considered the best sprinter in the world.

But Liddell was in for a surprise. For the first time in history, some Olympic events were scheduled on Sunday—including the sprint race in which he was to compete. Forced to choose between a potential medal and his principles, he decided to come down on the side of his faith.

In one of the film's decisive scenes, Harold Abrahams, a Jewish athlete friend, asked Liddell, "Do you have any regrets?" Eric Liddell responded, "Regrets, yes. Doubts, no."

Sometimes we shy away from making decisions, uncertain if we can handle the regrets and the consequences. Sometimes we stand at a crossroad and realize that each path leads to a different destination, but we aren't sure where. In either case, decision-making can be agonizing.

In Ezra's day, God's people faced a choice— stay in the security and certainty of the only home most had ever known, or follow the call of God and step into an uncertain tomorrow. What choice would you have made?   —J. A. M.

B. Decisions to Share (v. 6)

6. And all they that were about them strengthened their hands with vessels of silver, with gold, with goods, and with beasts, and

with precious things, besides all that was willingly offered.

This outpouring of spiritual patriotism provides those returning with everything they need. They have resources for a temple (Ezra 2:68, 69), animals for sacrificing, and wealth to sustain them until they can establish themselves again in Judah. This is different from the conquest of Canaan in the days of Joshua some 950 years before. This time God moves His people to enter the promised land not as conquerors, but to reclaim what is still theirs.

III. The Vessels Returned (Ezra 1:7-11)

Nebuchadnezzar had taken items from the temple during each of the three major deportations: in 605 B.C. (Daniel 1:2), 597 B.C. (2 Kings 24:13), and 586 B.C. (25:14). The major articles of furniture for the temple were destroyed (25:13). These items were taken to Babylon to be stored in the house of Nebuchadnezzar's gods. Some have conjectured that they were in a temple that was built to honor the Babylonian god Marduk.

It was during this time that the famous ark of the covenant disappeared from history. Some believe it was destroyed by the Babylonians; others suggest that it was hidden by devout Jews. It is impossible to say which—if either—of these ideas is correct.

A. Endowed by Cyrus (v. 7)

7. Also Cyrus the king brought forth the vessels of the house of the LORD, which Nebuchadnezzar had brought forth out of Jerusalem, and had put them in the house of his gods.

Cyrus seems to want to be loved by his people, and this charitable deed will encourage a certain loyalty to him. Perhaps Daniel, who lives in Babylon, has a considerable influence on Cyrus and his decision.

B. Entrusted to Sheshbazzar (v. 8)

8. Even those did Cyrus king of Persia bring forth by the hand of Mithredath the treasurer, and numbered them unto Sheshbazzar, the prince of Judah.

This was not a casual gift. It was carefully overseen by *Mithredath the treasurer*. (The name of this official is a frequent Persian name. The word for his title is also a Persian word, found nowhere else in the Bible.) As he looks on, the items are counted as they are given into the hands of a certain *Sheshbazzar, the prince of Judah*. The identity of Sheshbazzar has given rise to much speculation. His title could be translated as "leader," so he may or may not be an actual member of the royal family. Several possibilities have been put forth, but it is not certain that any of them is correct. Some believe he is a Persian official who is in charge of the entire project. Others think this is the Persian name for Zerubbabel (see Ezra 2:2) or that this is a variant name for Shenazar, a member of the royal family (1 Chronicles 3:18)—who actually would be a prince. We also see Sheshbazzar mentioned in Ezra 1:11; 5:14, 16. [See question #5, page 346.]

C. Enumerated by Ezra (vv. 9-11)

9. And this is the number of them: thirty chargers of gold, a thousand chargers of silver, nine and twenty knives.

A *charger* is a large flat platter or dish. The exact meaning of twenty-nine *knives*, the final items in this verse, is unknown. Some believe they are actually censors (fire pans) or just pans.

10. Thirty basins of gold, silver basins of a second sort four hundred and ten, and other vessels a thousand.

Today we might refer to *basins* as "bowls." The content of the thousand *vessels* or articles is not specified, but the summary statement in the next verse indicates that all the returned items were *gold* or *silver*.

11. All the vessels of gold and of silver were five thousand and four hundred. All these did Sheshbazzar bring up with them of the captivity that were brought up from Babylon unto Jerusalem.

The number of items listed in the two previous verses total 2,499, not 5,400. The most logical explanation for this difference is that many smaller items are not listed, but they are counted in with the grand total of 5,400. When the people return from their *captivity*, it will be in the context of returning items to place in the temple that they will rebuild. The important thing is that they make the trip! It will be a gigantic undertaking, and they will do it for the glory of God!

Conclusion

A. Longing for Home?

Many of the comments above are offered from the perspective that the decision to leave Babylon to return to Jerusalem was almost traumatic. While there must surely have been some trauma in the event, that must not be overstated.

Psalm 137 relates the emotions of a captive in Babylon, and the early verses indicate that the author longs for Jerusalem. For some, then, the decision to return may have been reached eagerly and quickly. They had been waiting for just such an opportunity. Those most eager to return were probably the older folks who had seen the temple before its destruction (Ezra 3:12).

The obvious question is this: for what do we long today? Where are our treasures and our hearts? Are we so attached to the familiar surroundings of our "earthly" home that we might say "maybe later" if Jesus offered us the option to go home with Him today? On another level, do we have a longing or thirsting for the Word and things of God? If we were given the opportunity to serve God more completely, would we jump eagerly and quickly to take advantage of the opportunity, or would our decision entail a lengthy searching of the heart?

Jesus addressed this issue when He said, "But seek ye first the kingdom of God, and his righteousness; and all these things shall be added unto you" (Matthew 6:33).

B. Prayer

Our God in Heaven, help us to recognize the opportunities that we have to serve You, even if they are not noticed by others. And may we have the courage to make the right decisions when the challenges of life are placed before us. In the name of Jesus Christ, Your Son, amen.

C. Thought to Remember

Kings, prophets, and large groups are not the only ones whose hearts may be stirred to make important decisions for God.

Learning by Doing

This page contains an alternative lesson plan emphasizing learning activities.
Classes desiring such student involvement will find these suggestions helpful.

Learning Goals

After participating in this lesson, the students will be able to:

1. Narrate the highlights of the initial return of devout Jews from their Babylonian exile to their Judean homeland.

2. Explain the historical and spiritual significance of this return.

3. Develop a list of principles that can guide their reactions to new ventures or projects in the church.

Into the Lesson

Display these instructions: Think about a time when you have been homesick—for your hometown or family or home congregation or for a special period of time in your life. Turn to the person beside you and complete this sentence: "I wish I could go back to _____ because. . . ."

After pairs talk, ask for two or three volunteers to complete the sentence for the whole class. Say, "It is not unusual for us to want to return to a special time or place. The people in today's study decided whether they wanted to return to their homeland for a spiritual reason."

Into the Word

ADVANCE PREPARATION. To prepare for the lecture, borrow some teaching pictures of the people and events in this quarter's lessons from the children's department. Post or show them when appropriate.

Lecture. Present a lecture that gives the historical and spiritual background for the quarter. Include the destruction of Jerusalem, relocation of the Jews, the captivity, and prophets of the time. Use the commentary, map (visual 1; see page 342), chart (visual 2; see page 351), and any teaching pictures that you have.

Group Study. Divide the class into five small study groups, giving each group one of the following assignments. (Assignments are also in the student book in an individual study form.)

Group 1. Read Psalm 137. Identify the emotions that are expressed by the captives; suggest how those feelings could motivate a person to return to the homeland.

Group 2. Read these prophetic passages and prepare a report summarizing what the prophets said: Jeremiah 25:1, 11, 12; 29:10-14; Isaiah 44:28–45:7.

Group 3. Read the following narrative passages about Cyrus and prepare a report of the events: 2 Chronicles 36:22, 23; Ezra 1:1-8.

Group 4. Read Ezra 1:5, 6 and Ezra 2. Summarize what these verses tell you about the people involved in the return.

Group 5. Read Micah 5:2; Isaiah 9:1, 2; Zechariah 9:9. Tell how this return of Jews to their homeland relates to messianic prophecies.

Summarize their reports, pinpointing the historical events that fulfilled prophecy. Supplement the groups' discoveries with insights from the your study of the commentary and other sources.

Preview future lessons by saying, "Our study this summer will take us from the return of this first group of Jews to the building of the walls of Jerusalem, with a study of their leaders and two prophets. This period of history and spiritual pilgrimage concludes the Old Testament era and sets the foundation for the development of the nation of people from whom would come the Messiah. As Ezra and Nehemiah would say, we will see the 'hand of God' at work. Finally, we will look to the future return of Jesus."

Into Life

Have the students return to their small groups. Then suggest the following scenario: "Imagine you are part of a family who hears about the plan to return to the homeland. What do you say to one another? What pros and cons can you list for making the trip? What could be the deciding factor to motivate you to give up everything and go back? If you choose not to return, what pros and cons are there for offering support to those going back?"

After the groups make their reports, make this assignment: "When church leaders today suggest a big project or new program to the congregation, what gets said by people in the hallways, the classrooms, and homes? What pros and cons are given? What is often the deciding factor? What could we learn from the Jews in Babylon that could help us step out with courage for God?" (If your leaders are contemplating a special project, apply the discussion to it.)

List the suggestions and select those that class members think are appropriate to follow. Ask a volunteer to make a poster of the ideas to be displayed for future reference. To conclude, read aloud the selected principles and ask God's help in carrying out such responses to church plans.

Let's Talk It Over

The questions on this page are designed to promote discussion of the lesson by the class and to encourage application of the lesson Scriptures. The answers provided are only discussion starters. Let your class talk it over from there.

1. The text says that God "stirred" Cyrus—a pagan ruler—to a specific action. What significance, if any, do you find in that fact as you consider religious, political, and other leaders today? How should this affect us?

God's stirring of Cyrus is especially interesting because Cyrus was a foreign king who held the power to control the destinies of the exiled Jews. The fact that God moved Cyrus may encourage us to pray boldly for God to move in the hearts of those in authority over us. God is able to accomplish His purposes through our employers, government officials, judges, and parents, even when those authorities are hostile to Christianity.

God has established the governing authorities (Romans 13:1). The Bible is clear that we have a duty to obey them (1 Peter 2:13-17)—except, of course, when the authorities command us to do something in direct violation of God's Word (see Acts 4:19). In any case, we should always pray for our leaders.

2. King Cyrus attributed his success to God. What does this say about the proper way to react to God's work in our own achievements?

King Cyrus demonstrates an admirable humility in the face of his considerable military success. He knew better than to assume that his own strength, cunning, and leadership skill had made him ruler of such a vast empire. (Compare this with the arrogance of Nebuchadnezzar in Daniel 4:30 and Herod in Acts 12:21-23.) When we are tempted to congratulate ourselves on some long-desired achievement, we might remember that it is God who grants us the power, the resources, the mental and physical abilities, and the opportunity necessary for every accomplishment.

3. Why was it right for the Jews who stayed in Babylon to give gifts to those who went to rebuild Jerusalem? How does their example apply to our practice of supporting missionaries who serve in distant places?

The rebuilding of the temple and the renewal of temple worship were important to the covenant relationship between God and Israel. *Every* Jew had an obligation to that covenant and a personal interest in the restoration. Some of the Jews could respond by going to Jerusalem to participate directly, but there would be great personal cost involved. It was only fair that those who chose to stay in Babylon share that burden by giving gifts to those who went.

Today every Christian has an obligation to the Great Commission to make disciples of all nations (Matthew 28:19, 20). Some respond by preparing to go and share the gospel with other cultures, sometimes at a great distance and at great personal sacrifice. Those who do not leave their familiar culture must participate by giving material support to those who do. (See also 2 Corinthians 8:1-15; 9.)

4. How do we know when the promptings we feel are truly from the Lord and not just our own personal desires?

We can imagine that it was difficult for some of the ancient Jews to obey the prompting of God to return to Jerusalem, especially if other family members or cherished friends did not experience the same prompting. Deferred obedience, however, is the same as disobedience, especially when the opportunity to obey is lost.

At the same time, however, we must realize that just because someone has a feeling that, "the Lord told me to do such-and-such" doesn't mean that the Lord really has! (See Jeremiah 23:26; Ezekiel 13:1-17; and 1 John 4:1-3.) The Lord will never prompt Christians to do anything that violates Scripture.

5. There was leadership and organization to the party that left for Jerusalem. How do good organization and good leadership make it easier for you to commit to a risk-filled decision?

Sound strategic planning, an accounting of available resources, and trustworthy leadership all help inspire confidence. In the face of calculated risk and long odds, even when God is prompting the action, good organization and leadership help motivate people and ensure a successful result. Even Jesus referred to the wisdom of "counting the cost" before choosing to build or to enter a battle (Luke 14:28-32).

Organization, leadership, administration, strategic plans, and budgets can be effective tools to accomplishing tasks that help us fulfill the Great Commission. Such tools should not be viewed as a failure of faith unless they become an excuse for disobedience or endless delay in obedience.

Beginning to Rebuild

DEVOTIONAL READING: Psalm 100:1-5.

BACKGROUND SCRIPTURE: Ezra 3, 4.

PRINTED TEXT: Ezra 3:1-3, 6b, 7, 10-13.

Ezra 3:1-3, 6b, 7, 10-13

1 And when the seventh month was come, and the children of Israel were in the cities, the people gathered themselves together as one man to Jerusalem.

2 Then stood up Jeshua the son of Jozadak, and his brethren the priests, and Zerubbabel the son of Shealtiel, and his brethren, and builded the altar of the God of Israel, to offer burnt offerings thereon, as it is written in the law of Moses the man of God.

3 And they set the altar upon his bases; for fear was upon them because of the people of those countries: and they offered burnt offerings thereon unto the LORD, even burnt offerings morning and evening.

6b The foundation of the temple of the LORD was not yet laid.

7 They gave money also unto the masons, and to the carpenters; and meat, and drink, and oil, unto them of Zidon, and to them of Tyre, to bring cedar trees from Lebanon to the sea of Joppa, according to the grant that they had of Cyrus king of Persia.

10 And when the builders laid the foundation of the temple of the LORD, they set the priests in their apparel with trumpets, and the Levites the sons of Asaph with cymbals, to praise the LORD, after the ordinance of David king of Israel.

11 And they sang together by course in praising and giving thanks unto the LORD; because he is good, for his mercy endureth for ever toward Israel. And all the people shouted with a great shout, when they praised the LORD, because the foundation of the house of the LORD was laid.

12 But many of the priests and Levites and chief of the fathers, who were ancient men, that had seen the first house, when the foundation of this house was laid before their eyes, wept with a loud voice; and many shouted aloud for joy:

13 So that the people could not discern the noise of the shout of joy from the noise of the weeping of the people: for the people shouted with a loud shout, and the noise was heard afar off.

GOLDEN TEXT: All the people shouted with a great shout, when they praised the LORD, because the foundation of the house of the LORD was laid.—Ezra 3:11.

God Restores a Remnant
Unit 1: Return
(Lessons 1-5)

Lesson Aims

After participating in this lesson, each student will be able to:

1. Give evidence of unity and worship in at least three distinct places in the text.

2. Understand that corporate worship is multi-dimensional and unifying.

3. Identify a new personal dimension of worship that will have a positive effect on the church body.

Lesson Outline

INTRODUCTION
  A. The Architect
  B. Lesson Background
  I. REBUILDING THE ALTAR (Ezra 3:1-3)
    A. Gathering in Jerusalem (v. 1)
    B. Constructing the Altar (vv. 2, 3a)
      Be a Leader
    C. Using the Altar (v. 3b)
 II. PREPARING FOR THE FOUNDATION (Ezra 3:6b, 7)
    A. Problem Stated (v. 6b)
    B. Provisions Made (v. 7)
III. CELEBRATING TOGETHER (Ezra 3:10-13)
    A. Preparations (v. 10)
    B. Praises (v. 11)
      Celebrate!
    C. Emotions (v. 12)
    D. Sounds (v. 13)
CONCLUSION
  A. In This Mountain!
  B. Prayer
  C. Thought to Remember

Introduction

A. The Architect

Somehow it seems fitting that the lesson for today involves building, because June 8 is the birthday of one of the premier architects of the twentieth century: Frank Lloyd Wright (1867–1959). The underlying philosophy that governed Wright's designs became known as "organic architecture." By this he meant that a building should seem to be a part of its natural surroundings. Houses and other buildings with his name attached often have become attractions for tourists.

On an infinitely grander scale, the name of the Ultimate Architect and Master Builder is attached to the universe itself (cf. Psalm 19:1). The writer of Hebrews describes Abraham as having "looked for a city which hath foundations, whose builder ['architect' in most modern translations] and maker is God" (Hebrews 11:10). Abraham was not looking for just any city. He was looking for the city that had been designed by God Himself.

Abraham focused his attention on the Heavenly Jerusalem, the final abode for all of God's people. In fact, the context of the word *looking* implies that Abraham continued to seek this city throughout his life. There may have been times when his attention was diverted briefly, but his focus always returned to the city that has God as its Architect and Builder.

Like Abraham, many other people in the Old Testament also maintained their faith and faithfulness. Today's lesson is about some of those people. We will see their faith as they return from their Babylonian captivity to the earthly Jerusalem, which gives its name to the Heavenly city for which we long—the New Jerusalem (cf. Hebrews 12:22; Revelation 3:12; 21:2, 10).

B. Lesson Background

The book of Ezra is divided into two major parts. In the first six chapters, Ezra describes the first return from captivity. That major event, occurring around 538 to 536 B.C., involved almost fifty thousand people. Ezra 7–10 tells of the return of a much smaller group. Ezra himself led that return about eighty years after the first, in 458 B.C.

Last week's lesson concluded by noting the first group's arrival in Jerusalem (Ezra 1:11). Ezra 2 lists the groups that were a part of that initial return. The final verses of the chapter reveal that the people wanted to rebuild the temple and that they gave generously to that end: about eleven hundred pounds of gold and three tons of silver!

I. Rebuilding the Altar
(Ezra 3:1-3)

Genuine worship at the central sanctuary ceased when the Babylonians destroyed the temple in 586 B.C. So it has been almost fifty years since any Israelite has been able to participate in worship that involves the continual offerings to God both morning and evening. The returnees desperately want to restore such worship.

A. Gathering in Jerusalem (v. 1)

1. And when the seventh month was come, and the children of Israel were in the cities, the people gathered themselves together as one man to Jerusalem.

Some have conjectured that *the seventh month* refers to the seventh month since the exiles left Babylon or since they arrived in Judah. Since it is the custom for the Israelites to refer to the months of the year by numerical designations instead of the names of the months, however, it seems more likely that this refers to the seventh month on the ancient Israelite calendar. (This is the month "Tishri." In postbiblical Judaism, Tishri will remain the seventh month on the "religious calendar," but will become the first month of the "civil calendar.") This equates to late September and early October.

The seventh month is a special month in the Israelites' calendar. The first day of the month is the day the Feast of Trumpets begins (Leviticus 23:23-25). The high day of the entire year is the tenth day of this month. This is the Day of Atonement. While the tabernacle or temple stood, the Day of Atonement was the only day in the entire year when the high priest could enter the Holy of Holies. This day involves special sacrifices and the sending of the scapegoat into the wilderness (16; 23:26-32).

The Feast of Tabernacles (or Booths), one of Israel's major festivals, is also a part of the seventh month. This seven-day event starts on the fifteenth day of the month. Its purpose is to remind the Israelites of their forty years of camping during the wilderness wanderings (Leviticus 23:33-36). Ezra 3:4 (not in our text for today) notes that the Israelites observed this feast after rebuilding the altar of burnt offerings.

One of the outstanding features that Ezra cites is the unity of the returning Israelites: the people are *as one man!* If there is a time for "rugged individualism," this is not it. The sense of community overcomes negative attitudes that could have stifled or divided them. At last they are all together again in *Jerusalem*, the city of David, and they are ready to begin the work of restoration. [See question #1, page 354.]

B. Constructing the Altar (vv. 2, 3a)

2. Then stood up Jeshua the son of Jozadak, and his brethren the priests, and Zerubbabel the son of Shealtiel, and his brethren, and builded the altar of the God of Israel, to offer burnt offerings thereon, as it is written in the law of Moses the man of God.

Jeshua and *Zerubbabel* hold impressive credentials for leadership. Jeshua is in the lineage of the high *priests*. His grandfather Seraiah had been the chief priest and was executed by the Babylonians when Nebuchadnezzar destroyed Jerusalem (2 Kings 25:18, 21). *Jeshua* is spelled "Joshua" in Haggai 1:1, and there he is called the high priest. His father *Jozadak* apparently was high priest during most of the Babylonian captivity. (Jozadak is the same as "Jehozadak" in 1 Chronicles 6:14 and 15, and "Josedech" in Haggai 1:1.)

Zerubbabel is a grandson of Jehoiachin, one of the last kings of Judah. They are listed in the genealogy for the Messiah in Matthew 1:12, where Jehoiachin is called "Jeconiah." The returning captives thus have qualified leaders in two important areas: they have a religious leader who is a priest, and they had a civil leader who is of the Davidic line. (Zerubbabel may be another name for Sheshbazzar of Ezra 1:8, 11; 5:14, but this is not certain.) [See question #2, page 354.]

The two leaders in view here are not left to do the work by themselves. Constructing *the altar of the God of Israel* is a community project. Undoubtedly, this new altar is built on the precise spot where the former altar for the temple had been. David had built an altar there even before it became the site for the temple (2 Samuel 24:25). Such sites were considered very sacred, and its location would have been easily determined.

We are not given the dimensions of the new altar, so we remain curious about the altar's size. If Solomon's bronze altar is the pattern, then this altar is about fifteen feet in height and thirty feet in length and width (see 2 Chronicles 4:1). However, this was probably a more modest enterprise than the construction of Solomon's temple. The altar was probably smaller. The wooden altar constructed at Mt. Sinai was less than a third the size of Solomon's altar (cf. Exodus 27:1).

BE A LEADER

Those of you who are late-night channel surfers may have run across the 1952 black-and-white movie classic *Viva Zapata!* It is the story of one of Mexico's best-known political families. There is a dramatic deathbed scene in the film where the elderly Zapata is speaking his final words to his son. "Trouble is coming," the old man says. "Find a leader. If you cannot find a leader, be a leader." That challenge motivated his son to become one of Mexico's greatest and most colorful political leaders.

Zapata's insight that troubled times demand effective leaders rings true in every generation and nation. Be a leader! In ancient Jerusalem, Joshua and Zerubbabel recognized and responded to Israel's need for godly leaders. Centuries later, Jesus will look upon the multitude and have great compassion for them because He sees them "as sheep having no shepherd" (Matthew 9:36). There is still a tremendous leadership void in many churches today.

J. Oswald Sanders, in his book *Spiritual Leadership*, writes, "The overriding need of the church, if it is to discharge its obligation to the rising generation, is for a leadership that is authoritative, spiritual, and sacrificial." If you cannot find such a leader, be one! —J. A. M.

3a. And they set the altar upon his bases; for fear was upon them because of the people of those countries.

The Israelites' *fear* is understandable, as subsequent events demonstrate (Ezra 4). Some commentators suggest that the *altar* site has been used by others during the fifty years since the temple was destroyed. As the Israelites clear away all semblance of pagan worship, their religious neighbors resent the intrusion. [See question #3, page 354.]

But those returning are convinced that there is only one God and that this altar is only for Him.

How to Say It

ABRAHAM. *Ay*-bruh-ham.
ASAPH. *Ay*-saff.
BABYLONIANS. Bab-ih-*low*-nee-unz.
CYRUS. *Sigh*-russ.
DAVIDIC. Duh-*vid*-ick.
DEUTERONOMY. Due-ter-*ahn*-uh-me.
GERIZIM. *Gair*-ih-zeem or Guh-*rye*-zim.
HAGGAI. *Hag*-eye or *Hag*-ay-eye.
ISRAELITE. *Iz*-ray-el-ite.
JECONIAH. Jek-o-*nye*-uh (strong accent on *nye*).
JEHOIACHIN. Jeh-*hoy*-uh-kin.
JEHOZADAK. Jeh-*ho*-zuh-dak.
JEREMIAH. Jair-uh-*my*-uh.
JESHUA. *Jesh*-you-uh.
JOPPA. *Jop*-uh.
JOSEDECH. *Jahss*-uh-dek.
JOSHUA. *Josh*-yew-uh.
JOZADAK. *Joz*-uh-dak.
JUDAISM. *Joo*-duh-izz-um or *Joo*-day-izz-um.
LEBANON. *Leb*-uh-nun.
LEVITES. *Lee*-vites.
MEDITERRANEAN. Med-uh-tuh-*ray*-nee-un (strong accent on *ray*).
MICHAL. *My*-kal.
NEBUCHADNEZZAR. Neb-yuh-kud-*nez*-er (strong accent on *nez*).
PERSIA. *Per*-zhuh.
SERAIAH. Seh-*ray*-yuh or Seh-*rye*-uh.
SHEALTIEL. She-*al*-tee-el.
SHESHBAZZAR. Shesh-*baz*-er.
TISHRI. *Tish*-ree.
TYRE. Tire.
VIVA ZAPATA (Spanish). *Vee*-vuh Zuh-*paht*-uh.
ZERUBBABEL. Zeh-*rub*-uh-bul.
ZIDON. *Zye*-dun.
ZION. *Zye*-un.

Their forefathers had attempted to blend the worship of God with pagan worship, and captivity was the result. This captivity accomplished one very important thing: it cured the Israelites of being tempted by idolatry. The Israelites now are convinced that there is only God. They will now have no other gods, just as the First Commandment instructs (Exodus 20:3; Deuteronomy 5:7).

C. Using the Altar (v. 3b)

3b. And they offered burnt offerings thereon unto the LORD, even burnt offerings morning and evening.

What a thrill it must be for these former exiles to see the smoke rise to heaven from the very first sacrifice on the new altar! The Mosaic Covenant decreed that *burnt offerings* are to be made each *morning and evening*, one animal each time. On the Sabbath Day, two animals are sacrificed in the morning and two in the evening (Numbers 28:1-10).

II. Preparing for the Foundation (Ezra 3:6b, 7)

A. Problem Stated (v. 6b)

6b. The foundation of the temple of the LORD was not yet laid.

With the construction of the altar, the Israelites have made a bold beginning. But those two little words *not yet* are a vivid reminder that there is more to be done. The old temple is gone. The fact that sacrifices now can be offered is a great thing, but some of the prescribed rituals cannot be carried out until a new *temple* is in place. This becomes the theme through Ezra 6. [See question #4, page 354.]

The Israelites who have returned have many financial blessings (see page 348). But they cannot supply resources as did Solomon for the glorious temple that he constructed (2 Chronicles 2, 3). The new altar only starts the restoration. Can they complete it?

B. Provisions Made (v. 7)

7. They gave money also unto the masons, and to the carpenters; and meat, and drink, and oil, unto them of Zidon, and to them of Tyre, to bring cedar trees from Lebanon to the sea of Joppa, according to the grant that they had of Cyrus king of Persia.

The organizing necessary to build the second temple now begins. Surely there are architects, planners, and an overall superintendent. Someone also has to be the treasurer in order to be able to distribute *money* to the stonemasons and *carpenters* who will do the work. Verses 8 and 9 (not in our text for today) offer at least a partial listing of those who lead in this endeavor. Undoubtedly many of the Israelites have acquired in Babylon the skills that they need for this undertaking.

Some of the stone necessary for the construction may be on the site already, depending on how thorough the Babylonians were in their destruction of the city and its temple. But all the wood of the previous temple had been burned when the temple was destroyed, so they need the *cedar* timbers that are available from the mountains of *Lebanon,* far to the north.

The similarities of this construction to that of Solomon some 430 years before are striking (see 1 Kings 5:1-11). In both instances the logs are taken from the mountains to the Mediterranean Sea, formed into giant rafts, and floated to *Joppa,* Israel's primary seaport. From there they are transported overland to the hills of Jerusalem, a distance of about forty miles. And in each case the workers in *Tyre* are paid with food.

This exchange between two nations has been pre-approved by *Cyrus king of Persia.* (See Ezra 6:3-5.) Cyrus's order suggests the method of construction. He surely has some input from Daniel or a knowledgeable Israelite about these matters.

III. Celebrating Together (Ezra 3:10-13)

A. Preparations (v. 10)

10. And when the builders laid the foundation of the temple of the LORD, they set the priests in their apparel with trumpets, and the Levites the sons of Asaph with cymbals, to praise the LORD, after the ordinance of David king of Israel.

Verse 8 (not in our text for today) notes that it is now the second month of the second year since the arrival from Babylon. This is late April or early May of 536 B.C. Interestingly, the building of Solomon's temple also began in "the second month" of the Jewish year (1 Kings 6:1).

The cultural climate for religion for the people of the Middle East lends itself to noise. The *priests* with their special garments use *trumpets* according to the law of Moses (Numbers 10:8). *Levites* who are *the sons of Asaph* provide percussion accompaniment (cf. Nehemiah 12:27).

The mention of Asaph and *David* has a certain significance: when David moved the ark of the covenant to Jerusalem, it is Asaph who sounded the *cymbals* (1 Chronicles 16:5). That was about 1000 B.C. It is now over 450 years later, and the sons of Asaph are still playing the cymbals! Twelve of the psalms have Asaph in the superscriptions as the author, so he must have been a capable musician.

The fact that they *laid the foundation* means that this is only the beginning of the building

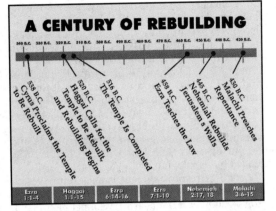

Visual for lesson 2. *This chart will help your students understand the chronology of this quarter's lessons.*

project. Unfortunately, the work will progress very slowly, as we will see in next week's lesson.

B. Praises (v. 11)

11. And they sang together by course in praising and giving thanks unto the LORD; because he is good, for his mercy endureth for ever toward Israel. And all the people shouted with a great shout, when they praised the LORD, because the foundation of the house of the LORD was laid.

This is a day of great joy! The hopes, prayers, and dreams of the captives are being fulfilled before their very eyes. There is genuine worship again in Jerusalem, and it is a time to celebrate to *the Lord.* The language used indicates that the singing is antiphonal: two groups answering each other as *they sang.* The singing includes the important concepts of praise and thankfulness as the people recognize God's goodness and *mercy.* This event may be the fulfillment of a prophecy given by Jeremiah during the last days of Jerusalem before its destruction (see Jeremiah 33:11). Similar phrases are also seen in the book of Psalms (100:4, 5; 106:1; 107:1, etc.).

CELEBRATE!

C. S. Lewis once commented on the lack of emotion in the worship of his denomination. He said, "We have a terrible concern about good taste."

Too many are more concerned with what looks good to others than with what looks good to God. King David didn't make that mistake. On the day the ark of God returned to Jerusalem, King David was a man caught up in worship. His celebration included leaping and dancing and music and praise and joy (2 Samuel 6). Michal, David's wife, didn't like it, but God did.

I remember the first time I saw people raising their hands in worship. It shocked me. I wondered, "What are they doing? Is the roof leaking?" I felt a mild revulsion, but my revulsion had nothing to do with their worship. Since then I have learned the value of upraised hands in praise. This spirit of surrender and praise is something God encourages and desires. Don't be concerned with pleasing people. Please God.

David's attitude should be our own. When we worship we need to get our eyes off people and get our eyes on God. Our worship is not to be judged by people, but by the Master.

Ezra 3:11 records ancient Israel's return to the spirit and action of David in worship. Celebration was alive in the hearts of the people of God. Is that spirit of celebration alive in you? To come into His presence is to enter into joy. We are the beloved of the Father. He delights and takes pleasure in our praise. Let's celebrate!   —J. A. M.

C. Emotions (v. 12)

12. But many of the priests and Levites and chief of the fathers, who were ancient men, that had seen the first house, when the foundation of this house was laid before their eyes, wept with a loud voice; and many shouted aloud for joy.

Men and women of all ages are present for this joyful dedication. Just as the ages vary, so do the emotions. Some of the older people had seen the temple of Solomon prior to its destruction some fifty years before. Now on this special occasion, they are the ones weeping *with a loud voice*.

The text does not say why these older *men* are weeping, but it is likely that they are reflecting on the sin that caused the temple to be destroyed. Perhaps they are overwhelmed by the knowledge that there will be a temple again. They have painful memories of Jerusalem's destruction, of

the deaths of loved ones, and of the long trek to Babylon when they were young. Now they have survived the journey back to Jerusalem, back to the places of their ancestral homes. Being able to worship at the temple site again makes for a very emotional moment. [See question #5, page 354.]

D. Sounds (v. 13)

13. So that the people could not discern the noise of the shout of joy from the noise of the weeping of the people: for the people shouted with a loud shout, and the noise was heard afar off.

So, which sound does God prefer, *the noise* of *joy* or *the noise of the weeping*? The answer is simple: both! (See Psalm 126:5.) Sometimes God delights in the "sound" of a broken heart—broken in repentance as a person participates in the Lord's Supper and reflects on the agony of the Son of God on the cross. This type of "blended worship" is not a new thing. It is part of the fabric of the Old Testament, and it is relevant today. There is a time to weep and a time to laugh (Ecclesiastes 3:4).

On this occasion, the sound is so *loud* that people in the surrounding area know that something special is happening. Genuine worship does make an impact! Others are watching, and they can determine whether your worship is sincere.

Conclusion

A. In This Mountain!

There is a missionary message in today's lesson. Is Jerusalem the place to worship? Yes! Is it the only place? No! Jesus stated to the woman at the well that worship in the future would not be confined to Mt. Gerizim or Mt. Zion. What really matters is whether the worship is in spirit and in truth (John 4:21, 23).

The sounds of joy and the sounds of weeping may be heard throughout the entire planet whenever worshipers assemble to exalt God, examine themselves, exhort others, and determine to evangelize the lost. This type of "blended worship" is always pleasing to God.

B. Prayer

Heavenly Father, we come to You in the name of Your Son. Thank You for comfortable buildings in which we can assemble to hear and study the history of Your people, and for the challenges that it makes to our hearts. Please give us the strength to respond as You desire. In the Son's name, amen.

C. Thought to Remember

Whatever you do for the Lord, do it with all your heart, soul, mind, body, and strength.

Home Daily Bible Readings

Monday, June 2—The People Worship in Jerusalem (Ezra 3:1-5)

Tuesday, June 3—Worship the Lord With Gladness (Psalm 100:1-5)

Wednesday, June 4—The People Build the Foundation (Ezra 3:6-13)

Thursday, June 5—Adversaries Discourage the People (Ezra 4:1-5)

Friday, June 6—Adversaries Write to the Persian King (Ezra 4:6-16)

Saturday, June 7—The King Orders the Work Stopped (Ezra 4:17-24)

Sunday, June 8—Your Foundation Shall Be Laid (Isaiah 44:24-28)

Learning by Doing

This page contains an alternative lesson plan emphasizing learning activities.
Classes desiring such student involvement will find these suggestions helpful.

Learning Goals

After participating in this lesson, each student will be able to:

1. Give evidence of unity and worship in at least three distinct places in the text.

2. Understand that corporate worship is multidimensional and unifying.

3. Identify a new personal dimension of worship that will have a positive effect on the church body.

Into the Lesson

Before the class arrives, display a poster for all to see. On the poster write, "Major Events in Our Church's History." As students arrive, ask them to write down, on their own or in pairs, some of the major events in the history of the congregation. Allow the students time for response. Ask volunteers to share what they have written, and write those ideas on the poster. Draw attention to the relationship between what may be perceived as negative events and positive events. It is not unusual for a seemingly negative event to be followed by a positive event.

Say, "It often happens that upheaval precedes change and growth in a church. The people in our text have just experienced significant upheaval in the exile, yet it resulted in a tremendous opportunity to enhance their worship."

Into the Word

Ask a student to read Ezra 3. Divide the class into two groups. Ask the students of one group to read through the text and record places they see *unity* demonstrated. Ask those in the other group to read through the text and record places they see *worship* demonstrated. After the groups have completed this task, ask a representative from each to report on its findings.

Some places where unity is demonstrated are the gathering together (3:1), the setting up of the altar (3:3), the celebrating of the Feast of Tabernacles (3:4), the providing for the temple (3:7), the working on the temple (3:8-10), the praising of the Lord (3:11-13). Note especially the consistent use of the plural *they* throughout the text, indicating unified effort. Also, recognize that this text begins with an explicit reference to unity, in gathering "as one man," and ends with an explicit reference to unity, in the different responses of the people being indistinguishable.

Places where worship is demonstrated are the gathering together in the seventh month (3:1; be prepared to explain the significance of the seventh month in the people's worship life according to the commentary), the offering of sacrifices (3:2-6), the providing for the temple (3:7), the working on the temple (3:8-10), the praising of the Lord (3:11-13). Help the students consider the work on the temple as a valid means of worship. Share this definition of *worship* to clarify the point: "to regard with great—even extravagant—respect, honor, or devotion."

Draw attention to the fact that the unity texts and worship texts are the same. Point out that "Corporate worship and unity go together."

Into Life

ADVANCE PREPARATION: Collect copies of your church newsletters from time periods significant to the history of the church. Ask several long-time members for help with this or consult someone in the church office for copies.

Have the students return to their groups. Distribute church newsletters from significant points in the church's history. Ask each group to write down ways they notice worship and unity as indicated in the church newsletters they view. Direct the students to consider acts of service similar to those seen in the Ezra text. For example, a member who has consistently provided service through repair work may be seen as someone who regards God "with great—even extravagant—respect, honor, or devotion" so that he or she gives time and effort dependably.

Ask for volunteers to present the various ways worship and unity have been demonstrated throughout the history of the church. Discuss how many of the individual acts of service have facilitated worship and unity for the church. For example, you might ask, "How has the person who prepares the sanctuary each Sunday morning contributed to the worship experience?"

Ask the students to think of areas in their lives that can be considered worship. These may include specific acts not often considered worshipful. Tell the students to list these. Finally, have each student select one item from the list as an area he or she will approach with an attitude of worship and would consider worshipful. Remind them of the definition, "to regard with great—even extravagant—respect, honor, or devotion."

Let's Talk It Over

The questions on this page are designed to promote discussion of the lesson by the class and to encourage application of the lesson Scriptures. The answers provided are only discussion starters. Let your class talk it over from there.

1. How important is a common vision to a group of people trying to complete a major project? Can you give an example of how a group has been moved to action by a compelling vision? Can you give an example where a project floundered because of an unclear vision?

The Israelites who had returned to Jerusalem faced a huge task in rebuilding the temple and then their city. It would require a sacrificial effort from everyone, and then it would be accomplished only as they cooperated toward agreed goals. If a group is not agreed on what is to be accomplished, individuals may apply their efforts toward their private objectives or argue for their favored outcome. Without a unifying vision, some good work may be done, but it will be only a fraction of what can be accomplished when everyone is pulling toward the same desired outcome. Hopefully you have had the experience of working with a group that came together "as one man."

2. Israel's rebuilding project had leaders who were qualified (by birth), who were willing to take initiative, and who had the support of their "brethren." How do potential leaders gain acceptance today? What happens when leadership is lacking?

Today, people often will not follow a leader unless they trust the leader's character and have confidence in the leader's competency. Mounting significant efforts and completing major projects are difficult if the designated leaders do not have the general trust and acceptance of the group.

An expected function of leadership is to "set the course," "blaze the trail," and "point the way." A necessary component of successful leadership is followers. John Maxwell says, "If no one is following you, you are not leading, you are just taking a walk."

3. For the returning Jews to build an altar in Jerusalem, faith had to overcome fear. What does it take today for you to act on faith in spite of fear? Give an example of a time in your life when your faith overcame your fear.

It took courage for the Israelites to erect an altar to the one true God in the midst of people who worshiped a variety of gods. Their recent exile in Babylon, however, was a judgment against previous idolatry. Now their interest in being faithful and obedient to God was stronger than their fear of reprisal from their neighbors.

Today, people have been known to do unethical or immoral things in order to please their employers. Such people fear that they will lose their jobs unless they give in to the bosses' demands. But mature Christians realize that there are times when we must choose to obey God rather than people (cf. Acts 4:19). These are the times when our faith and trust in God must outweigh our fear of people.

4. For over fifty years it had been impossible for the Jews to offer sacrifices on the temple mount in Jerusalem. What are some religious privileges that we may take for granted, but that are denied to Christians in some places? What would you do if these privileges were prohibited in your own culture?

Freedom to assemble for Christian worship, to observe Communion together, and to perform public baptisms are denied in some places. Activities aimed at converting others to Christ may be politically incorrect in some quarters, and they are outright illegal in some countries. These activities may not be outlawed where you live, but for some they may still become impossible as the frailty of old age keeps them housebound. What is your class doing for older members of the congregation who cannot assemble with you?

5. The worship in our text included both shouts of joy and weeping. How does worship in our church give place to either expression?

Our text explains that some of the "ancient men" wept loudly, while others shouted for joy. Both emotions are easy to understand, as noted in the commentary.

Today, there should be room for both emotions in our worship. Churches that focus exclusively on somber, sorrowful reflection or on emotional exuberance are out of balance. When we draw near to God in worship, we should be overwhelmed at times by a sense of our unworthiness before a holy God. We may want to weep in sorrow for our sin. At other times we may be overcome by the majesty, grace, and love of our God. Both weeping and joy together are particularly appropriate when we meet around the Lord's table for Communion.

Returning to the Work

DEVOTIONAL READING: 1 Corinthians 3: 10-17.

BACKGROUND SCRIPTURE: Haggai; Ezra 5:1, 2.

PRINTED TEXT: Haggai 1:2-14.

Haggai 1:2-14

2 Thus speaketh the LORD of hosts, saying, This people say, The time is not come, the time that the LORD's house should be built.

3 Then came the word of the LORD by Haggai the prophet, saying,

4 Is it time for you, O ye, to dwell in your ceiled houses, and this house lie waste?

5 Now therefore thus saith the LORD of hosts; Consider your ways.

6 Ye have sown much, and bring in little; ye eat, but ye have not enough; ye drink, but ye are not filled with drink; ye clothe you, but there is none warm; and he that earneth wages, earneth wages to put it into a bag with holes.

7 Thus saith the LORD of hosts; Consider your ways.

8 Go up to the mountain, and bring wood, and build the house; and I will take pleasure in it, and I will be glorified, saith the LORD.

9 Ye looked for much, and, lo, it came to little; and when ye brought it home, I did blow upon it. Why? saith the LORD of hosts. Because of mine house that is waste, and ye run every man unto his own house.

10 Therefore the heaven over you is stayed from dew, and the earth is stayed from her fruit.

11 And I called for a drought upon the land, and upon the mountains, and upon the corn, and upon the new wine, and upon the oil, and upon that which the ground bringeth forth, and upon men, and upon cattle, and upon all the labor of the hands.

12 Then Zerubbabel the son of Shealtiel, and Joshua the son of Josedech, the high priest, with all the remnant of the people, obeyed the voice of the LORD their God, and the words of Haggai the prophet, as the LORD their God had sent him, and the people did fear before the LORD.

13 Then spake Haggai the LORD's messenger in the LORD's message unto the people, saying, I am with you, saith the LORD.

14 And the LORD stirred up the spirit of Zerubbabel the son of Shealtiel, governor of Judah, and the spirit of Joshua the son of Josedech, the high priest, and the spirit of all the remnant of the people; and they came and did work in the house of the LORD of hosts, their God.

GOLDEN TEXT: Is it time for you, O ye, to dwell in your ceiled houses, and this house lie waste?—Haggai 1:4.

God Restores a Remnant
Unit 1: Return
(Lessons 1-5)

Lesson Aims

After participating in this lesson, each student will be able to:

1. Summarize the people's actions, God's actions, and the results of these actions in this text.

2. Recognize the ongoing interaction that God has with His people.

3. Prepare a godly response to an upcoming event by carefully considering the consequences of two previous events (one considered positive, one negative) in his or her life.

Lesson Outline

INTRODUCTION
  A. Prioritize!
  B. Lesson Background
  I. THREE MESSAGES (Haggai 1:2-11)
    A. To the Leaders (v. 2)
    B. To the People, Part 1 (vv. 3-6)
    C. To the People, Part 2 (vv. 7-11)
      Examine Your Ways
  II. TWO RESPONSES (Haggai 1:12, 13)
    A. The People's Resolve (v. 12)
      Truly Free?
    B. The Prophet's Reassurance (v. 13)
  III. TWO POSITIVE ACTIONS (Haggai 1:14)
    A. The Lord's Stirring (v. 14a)
    B. The People's Working (v. 14b)
CONCLUSION
  A. Principles and Precepts
  B. Prayer
  C. Thought to Remember

Introduction

A. Prioritize!

The student came home from the university with a new word that he learned sprinkled regularly into his conversations. The word was *prioritize,* and it really was a new word at the time.

The dictionary indicates that the date for the earliest recorded use of the word *prioritize* is 1964, just thirty-nine years ago. It was easily recognized, for the noun form, *priority,* had been in use for a long time. Making a verb of the noun did sound strange at first, but it made good sense to use it, for it reduced to one word what had formerly been said in a phrase. A popular way of saying it was, "putting first things first." Illustrations of prioritizing are very familiar. Parents have often said, "Eat your spinach, and then you may have dessert," or "You cannot go out to play until your homework is done."

A man in a hospital was dying of cancer. Just a few days before he died, he uttered a five-word sentence that indicated that his priorities had been wrong: "I see it all now." He continued by saying that he had been determined that his children would not be deprived as he had been when he was a child. He worked two jobs, quit attending church (even though he had been baptized as a young person), and gave his children all that they wanted. He concluded by saying that if he had his life to live over, he would have put Jesus first and given his children what they really needed—salvation. His spoiling them had resulted in lives that embarrassed him and other family members.

The study for today is about priorities. The Israelites who had returned from Babylonian exile had started well, but then they found reasons to rearrange their priorities. They prioritized, but they put first things last!

B. Lesson Background

The study from Ezra 3 last week ended with a tumultuous rejoicing. In the spring of 536 B.C., after the Jews returned from Babylon, they had laid the foundation of the temple. They had great resources. They had made arrangements for the material and the laborers to continue the task until the house of God was finished—but it wasn't.

What happened? The next five verses in the book of Ezra (4:1-5) reveal that the "fear" that gripped them "because of the people of those countries" (3:3) was based in reality. At first their enemies offered to help build, but the Jews were not about to risk mingling their worship with neighbors who served other gods. When the Jews rejected their neighbors' offer, those neighbors began active opposition, which lasted from about 536 to 520 B.C. In 520, when both Haggai and Zechariah received the word of the Lord and proclaimed it to the people of Jerusalem, they finally returned to the work.

Little is known about Haggai. He simply calls himself "the prophet." He uses that title five times—more than any other "minor" prophet (Haggai 1:1, 3, 12; 2:1, 10). He is mentioned also in the book of Ezra (5:1; 6:14) in connection with the historical record of the rebuilding and dedication of the temple.

Haggai was careful to date the four sermons that he gave. Each has a precise date, and it is therefore possible to provide the equivalent dates according to the calendar methods in use today.

I. Three Messages (Haggai 1:2-11)

The first date is August 29, 520 B.C. (1:1), and something amazing is about to happen: God is ready to break His silence. So far the people who have returned to Judah and Jerusalem have been responding on their own, armed only with a personal devotion to the Lord and His Word. This has led them from Babylon. It has inspired them to build the altar for the burnt offerings and to lay the foundation of the temple. Since their return in about 538 B.C., it almost has seemed that God has abandoned the Israelites. But now God speaks through Haggai.

A. To the Leaders (v. 2)

2. Thus speaketh the LORD of hosts, saying, This people say, The time is not come, the time that the LORD's house should be built.

The verse just before this (not in our text for today) indicates that this message is addressed to Zerubbabel and Joshua, the governor and high priest respectively. Since their arrival, Zerubbabel evidently has been appointed as the governor by the Persian king (cf. Ezra 2:2).

The *Lord of hosts* begins His message with a stinging rebuke in the form of two words: *this people*. We can feel the sense of contempt here. At this particular time, the Israelites do not deserve to be called "my people," a phrase of endearment that God uses so often (see Hosea 2:23; Romans 9:25).

God reminds Zerubbabel and Joshua that the people are saying that it is not the right *time* to build *the Lord's house*. But God has a different opinion. The people undoubtedly have a variety of alibis to justify the sentiment that they express. If a person does not wish to perform a task, he or she can find many excuses not to do it. But it's now been sixteen years since the foundation was laid!

The context of the chapter provides various possibilities for the procrastination. "It's harvest time, and we are too busy." Or, "The crops are bad, and we cannot afford it" (vv. 10 and 11). They might have added that their neighbors would not like it, or that the new king, Darius, had not endorsed the project. [See question #1, page 362.]

B. To the People, Part 1 (vv. 3-6)

3, 4. Then came the word of the LORD by Haggai the prophet, saying, Is it time for you, O ye, to dwell in your ceiled houses, and this house lie waste?

The verb *ceil* means to furnish with a lining. What we call a "ceiling," then, is the overhead lining (covering the joists or rafters) in a room. The Jews' *ceiled houses* were probably "paneled," or lined with boards, to cover the stone or other material used to form the walls.

To live in comfort is not wrong in and of itself. To do so at the expense of the Lord's *house* that still lies in ruins, however, indicates that they have not prioritized correctly. Some commentators propose that cedar logs from Lebanon had been diverted to personal use, instead of being a part of the construction of the temple (Ezra 3:7). First Kings 7:7 notes that Solomon's palace had walls covered with cedar. That wood has a better appearance than bare stone, but it is costly, supposedly reserved for royalty and the wealthy.

Attitudes about such matters do make a difference spiritually. Many people buy only the top-of-the-line items for themselves, but think that the economy model is good enough for the Lord's work. When some folks buy a new microwave oven for their own house, they sometimes donate their old one to the church. But if the old one isn't good enough for them anymore, then why do they think it's good enough for the Lord? (See Malachi 1:8.) [See question #2, page 362.]

5. Now therefore thus saith the LORD of hosts; Consider your ways.

The Israelites are commanded to examine their *ways*. Haggai likes to use the word *consider*, and it appears four more times in his short book (1:7; 2:15; and twice in 2:18). The idea is that everyone should take a good, hard look at what they have been doing, and what the results have been.

6. Ye have sown much, and bring in little; ye eat, but ye have not enough; ye drink, but ye are not filled with drink; ye clothe you, but there is none warm; and he that earneth wages, earneth wages to put it into a bag with holes.

"Is it time for you, O ye, to dwell in your ceiled houses, and this house lie waste?" —Haggai 1:4

Visual for lesson 3. *Use this visual to illustrate verse 4. Call attention to it also as you discuss question #2 on page 362.*

Haggai lists five essential areas in which the people are lacking. The first has a certain irony to it. They are really trying to have good harvests in that they sow *much*, but ultimately they are able to harvest only *little*. Their expenditures of time, energy, and seed seem to be wasted.

The next three deal with the physical necessities of life: food, *drink*, and clothing. They never seem to have enough of any. To use familiar imagery, they go to bed hungry and cold every night. Keeping warm means putting on more clothing. But in their nicely furnished houses (Haggai 1:4), they never seem to be warm enough.

The final item of this five-fold observation is that their *wages* seemed to be going *into a bag with holes*. It takes all of their resources for what necessities they do have, and there is nothing left over (cf. Isaiah 28:20). The second part of the message that follows offers even more for the people to consider.

C. To the People, Part 2 (vv. 7-11)

7. Thus saith the LORD of hosts; Consider your ways.

This repetition of the expression *Consider your ways* could mean that this is part of a new message, or it may be intended to capture the attention of the hearers who are allowing their minds to wander. Hope is a part of the message, and the next verse offers a positive note. It will comfort those who are seriously "considering their ways."

8. Go up to the mountain, and bring wood, and build the house; and I will take pleasure in it, and I will be glorified, saith the LORD.

Three commands are given for the people: *go*, *bring*, and *build*. If the commands are obeyed, two results will follow. First, the Lord *will take pleasure* in obedience to His commands and in the restoration of the special worship that is possible only when the temple is completed. Second, the Lord *will be glorified* in the sight of other peoples because of the obedience of the Israelites. This also will point to the glory that is in the future when the Messiah will come. In Jesus' final discourses to the apostles, He affirmed that the Holy Spirit would glorify Him (John 16:14). Ultimately, God desires that all people glorify Him.

EXAMINE YOUR WAYS

Every June the National Basketball Association wraps up its playoffs by crowning a new champion. Years ago, a fan in Portland, Oregon, went to the airport to greet the Trailblazers following a victory over the Los Angeles Lakers.

At the airport this fan attempted to make some money by scalping two tickets to the next game. He spotted a well-dressed man and made his move.

"How much?" asked the gentleman.

"One hundred fifty," he replied. "Not a cent less."

"Sir, do you realize you're talking to a plain-clothes officer of the law?" the man asked the scalper. "I'm a detective. What you are doing is illegal and I'm going to turn you in."

Suddenly the seller began to backpedal. He talked about his large family and his financial need. He promised never to do it again.

Looking both ways the well-dressed man said, "Just hand over the tickets and we'll call it even." And he did. "Now get out of here and I better never catch you here again!"

What a close call! But that well-dressed man was no compassionate cop. He was just a quick-thinking opportunist who used imagination and guts to land two choice seats to the next playoff game. He anonymously admitted it in the local newspaper a few days later.

It hurts when others deceive us. But to live in the blindness of self-deception is even worse. God called Israel to examine their ways. Haggai 1:6 makes it clear that many in Israel were robbing themselves by their lack of self-examination. Take an honest look at your life. Any holes in your bag?

—J. A. M.

9. Ye looked for much, and, lo, it came to little; and when ye brought it home, I did blow upon it. Why? saith the LORD of hosts. Because of mine house that is waste, and ye run every man unto his own house.

Haggai now informs the people of the real reason behind their hardship. They are suffering because the Lord's *house* is still in ruins! Because each man preferred to *run* to *his own house*, God has withdrawn His blessings. *Mine house that is waste* speaks of an unfinished building, an eyesore, and all that goes with such a situation.

We need a word of caution here. The doctrine of "divine retribution" is not absolute or universal in its earthly application. Often there is a cause-and-effect relationship between one's sin and subsequent suffering in his or her life. This may be simply a natural consequence of the behavior, as when an alcoholic develops liver disease. Or the penalty may be imposed by judgment. In the Old Testament, for example, famine, the sword, and/or captivity often came about because of the people's sin. The record of Job, however, establishes that humans may not be aware of all the circumstances. In a fallen world, bad things do happen to good people. It is important to remember the lesson from another Old Testament prophet: "the just shall live by his faith" (Habakkuk 2:4; cf. Romans 1:17; Galatians 3:11). We must do this regardless of what happens.

10. Therefore the heaven over you is stayed from dew, and the earth is stayed from her fruit.

The dry season in Israel is from April to October. During this period, crops depend on heavy, overnight *dew* to be sustained in their growth. The prophet makes clear that the absence of the dew is not just a random weather condition. It actually is an act of God. [See question #3, page 362.]

11. And I called for a drought upon the land, and upon the mountains, and upon the corn, and upon the new wine, and upon the oil, and upon that which the ground bringeth forth, and upon men, and upon cattle, and upon all the labor of the hands.

In Moses' farewell discourse, he warned the people of Israel that disobedience to God would bring about these kinds of disasters (Deuteronomy 28:23, 24, 38-40). As that nine-hundred-year-old warning has come true before, so now it is coming true again.

A drought affects everything. A bad crop of grain means that neither *men* nor *cattle* eat well. (The word given as *corn* refers to any grain; what we call *corn* today was not grown in that region.) The three food items mentioned here—grain, *new wine*, and olive *oil*—are the foundation items in their diets. There is no prosperity without these three. Since the people are now at the end of their agricultural year, the results of the drought are impossible to miss.

II. Two Responses
(Haggai 1:12, 13)

The combination of the catastrophes and the preaching of Haggai has gained the attention of the people. But after they "considered their ways," what next?

A. The People's Resolve (v. 12)

12. Then Zerubbabel the son of Shealtiel, and Joshua the son of Josedech, the high priest, with all the remnant of the people, obeyed the voice of the LORD their God, and the words of Haggai the prophet, as the LORD their God had sent him, and the people did fear before the LORD.

Haggai is a successful communicator. The backdrop of drought and famine allows him to preach a great, one-sermon revival with immediate results. The entire *remnant of the people obeyed the voice of the Lord their God*. [See question #4, page 362.]

The use of the word *remnant* has special meaning. It tends to be reserved for the faithful few who are willing to serve the Lord, regardless of what the majority do. In this case, the reference is to the people who came back from captivity, as had been prophesied. In the New Testament, it is

applied by Paul to those who are saved (Romans 9:27; 11:5).

The end of the verse introduces a very important concept: the people now have a proper reverence toward God that transcends any fear they have of their neighbors (cf. Ezra 4:4, 5). They now have a godly *fear* that produces godly living. Perhaps they realize that famine is only one of the punishments that God can bring about. Things could be worse! While they had not been bowing to any idols lately, and they may have been proud of themselves, they had their priorities all wrong.

TRULY FREE?

On December 18, 1865, the United States ratified the Thirteenth Amendment to its Constitution. With this amendment's adoption, slavery officially ended. What a wonderful day for America that was!

But then something strange happened: slaves were free to decide their own futures, but the vast majority voluntarily stayed in slavery. The war was over, blood had been shed, and the price of freedom had been paid. Yet little actual change took place as slavery continued to be the *de facto* practice. Yes, slaves were legally free, but to live out their new freedom in a practical way was something new and foreign. They had trouble living free lives.

Israel faced a similar challenge following years of captivity. When the people finally returned home, Haggai makes it clear that the Israelites had difficulty using their freedom to bless themselves and to serve God. They had trouble thinking in a new way. At Haggai's instruction, people finally learned to use their freedom to obey.

Christians today can identify with those slaves. Set free from sin—yes! Jesus is Savior. Transformed living? That can be a different story.

How to Say It

COLOSSIANS. Kuh-*losh*-unz.

DARIUS. Duh-*rye*-us.

DEUTERONOMY. Due-ter-*ahn*-uh-me.

EZEKIEL. Ee-*zeek*-ee-ul or Ee-*zeek*-yul.

HABAKKUK. Huh-*back*-kuk.

HAGGAI. *Hag*-eye or *Hag*-ay-eye.

JEREMIAH. Jair-uh-*my*-uh.

JOSEDECH. *Jahss*-uh-dek.

JOSHUA. *Josh*-yew-uh.

LEBANON. *Leb*-uh-nun.

PERSIAN. *Per*-zhun.

SHEALTIEL. Shee-*al*-tee-el.

ZECHARIAH. Zek-*uh*-rye-*uh*.

ZERUBBABEL. Zeh-*rub*-uh-bul.

Galatians 5:1 says, "Stand fast therefore in the liberty wherewith Christ hath made us free." Second Corinthians 3:17 makes clear that "where the Spirit of the Lord is, there is liberty." Have we learned what it means to live a life that is truly free to serve Christ as He wants? —J. A. M.

B. The Prophet's Reassurance (v. 13)

13. Then spake Haggai the LORD's messenger in the LORD's message unto the people, saying, I am with you, saith the LORD.

The positive actions on the part of the people bring forth a *message* of assurance from the prophet. Here he is called *the Lord's messenger,* and that is a rare, special title in the Old Testament (cf. Malachi 2:7; Matthew 11:10).

The message by God's messenger is short but powerful: *I am with you!* Other faithful servants through the centuries who had that same assurance were Moses (Exodus 3:12), Gideon (Judges 6:16), and Jeremiah (Jeremiah 1:8). How much greater this same assurance is to us now that Christ—Immanuel—has come (Matthew 1:23)! [See question #5, page 362.]

III. Two Positive Actions (Haggai 1:14)

The last verse of chapter 1 gives us another precise date. Converted to modern reckoning, it is September 21, 520 B.C. The twenty-three-day interval allowed time for two things to happen.

A. The Lord's Stirring (v. 14a)

14a. And the LORD stirred up the spirit of Zerubbabel the son of Shealtiel, governor of Judah, and the spirit of Joshua the son of Josedech, the high priest, and the spirit of all the remnant of the people.

Home Daily Bible Readings

Monday, June 9—Time to Rebuild (Haggai 1:1-6)

Tuesday, June 10—God Stirs the People's Spirits (Haggai 1:7-15)

Wednesday, June 11—Take Courage; I Am With You (Haggai 2:1-9)

Thursday, June 12—They Did Not Stop (Ezra 5:1-5)

Friday, June 13—We Are the Servants of God (Ezra 5:6-12)

Saturday, June 14—From That Time Until Now (Ezra 5:13-17)

Sunday, June 15—From This Day I Will Bless (Haggai 2:13-23)

The spirits of the people and their leaders are bolstered by a divine stirring. Everyone now has to make changes in daily routines. When was the last time you saw God work at your church in such a way that the spirits of the people were stirred so that they started changing "the way we've always done things"?

B. The People's Working (v. 14b)

14b. And they came and did work in the house of the LORD of hosts, their God.

Whereas the first temple in Solomon's day had been built by conscripted labor (2 Chronicles 2:2), the completion of the temple this time seems to have been by these eager volunteers. The three-week interval allows the people time to organize their *work* and gather the required material and tools. As the title for today's lesson says, they are "returning to the work."

Conclusion

A. Principles and Precepts

A lesson on building the temple for worship in Israel lends itself to comparisons with the buildings used by churches today, but there are two major differences. First, the Lord commanded the construction of the tabernacle through Moses and the temple through David and Solomon, but there are no precepts that buildings must be constructed to use when Christians assemble. Second, the Old Testament temple was God's distinctive "holy place" on earth (2 Chronicles 5:13, 14; 33:7), but in New Testament times our bodies now are the temple of God's Spirit (1 Corinthians 3:16, 17; 6:19).

Is having a building wrong, because God did not command it? Absolutely not! The example of the early church is that the people met in different places. God left it up to each generation to determine the best way for a body of believers to come together. Changes in circumstances, cultures, and climates are to be considered when congregations make such decisions, but this is an area that is guided by principles, not by divine precepts. The most important thing to remember is that we are commanded to build His church— His holy people.

B. Prayer

Almighty God, we want to have a reverence for You so that the things we do will always have You at the center of them. In the name of Your Son, Jesus Christ, amen.

C. Thought to Remember

The righteous must continue to live by faith— no matter what.

Learning by Doing

This page contains an alternative lesson plan emphasizing learning activities. Classes desiring such student involvement will find these suggestions helpful.

Learning Goals

After participating in this lesson, each student will be able to:

1. Summarize the people's actions, God's actions, and the results of these actions in this text.

2. Recognize the ongoing interaction that God has with His people.

3. Prepare a godly response to an upcoming event by carefully considering the consequences of two previous events (one considered positive, one negative) in his or her life.

Into the Lesson

After students arrive, say, "Think of two events in your life in which your actions had a direct impact on the outcome. One of these should be a positive event and the other one, negative. One example of an event with a positive outcome might be the decision to attend Sunday school regularly. Examples of an event with a negative outcome might be to gossip about a particular person or to buy something on impulse." Encourage students to think of situations that did not have drastic outcomes, if they would be more comfortable.

Say, "What sort of thoughts and actions contributed to the positive and negative outcomes of these two events? Consider your ways."

Allow time for the students to ponder these past events. Then enter into the Word by saying, "The returning exiles started strong, as we saw last week, but they have begun to fade. In today's passage God commands that they consider their ways and tells them the consequences of their actions or lack of action."

Into the Word

Assemble the students into three small groups (or multiples of three). Assign one group to read the text and record the actions of the people. Assign another group to read the text and record the consequences of the actions of the people. Assign a third group to read the text and record the actions of God.

God's actions begin the assigned text by responding to "this people's" decision that it was not the right time for them to build the Lord's house. (Note the reference on page 357 to God's change in tone toward the people, as signalled by the term this *people.) The people's actions are clearly discerned from the Lord's rebuke of them*

in Haggai 1:4-6, 9. God's actions are seen again in verse 11 and in verses 13, 14. The consequences of the people's actions may be found in verses 10, 11, and 13.

Have students share their findings. Make special note of the comforting, yet convicting, truth that God is with us (v. 13). This truth allows for God's ongoing interaction with His people despite their fading spiritual lives. Also, emphasize that God's actions in verse 14 stirred the people to do the work He required. Say, "It is often helpful to recognize God's involvement in the events and decisions of our lives."

Into Life

Ask students to recall the events they were asked to consider when they entered the class. Have them write down the events and the decisions and actions made prior to and during each event.

Ask students to compare (and contrast) the decisions and actions of the event with a negative outcome with those of the event with a positive outcome. Ask students to reveal these comparisons and contrasts to a partner. They may include making a selfish decision *versus* making a Christ-centered decision, listening to others *versus* listening to God's Word, thinking in the short-term *versus* long-term considerations, and others. Be aware that the events the students consider will vary in their degree of significance in the person's life. Write on the board any common themes you hear. Raise the ideas of God-focused decisions *versus* self-focused decisions, as this is evident in the text.

After completing this, have the students think of upcoming events in their lives. These events may be different events, unique to each individual, or you may have the learners work in groups on a public event known to be coming in the church or community. Ask them to anticipate their ways and list what they will do in order to ensure a godly response to the upcoming event. If considering a public event, ask the class to work in groups; then draw their responses together in a single list at the end of the lesson. If individual events are to be considered, allow time for each student to work through the task. Conclude by drawing out any similarities in the individual responses by asking for volunteers to tell of their individual events.

Let's Talk It Over

The questions on this page are designed to promote discussion of the lesson by the class and to encourage application of the lesson Scriptures. The answers provided are only discussion starters. Let your class talk it over from there.

1. What are some of the reasons that believers today give for postponing obedience to God? How do we guard our hearts against these?

Some sample excuses include the following: "I am too young (old); no one will take me seriously." "My job is very demanding right now; I don't have time." "When you have young children to care for, your time is not your own." "I do not feel prepared to . . . (make a decision; serve in that role; accept a leadership position; grow personally)." "Since we bought that property at the lake, we just don't have a spare minute or a spare dollar."

Perhaps you have heard some of these excuses or even have used them yourself. The reasons we give for postponed obedience reveal a lot about our priorities and values. It is entirely possible for very good personal objectives to interfere with the greatest objective: honoring and obeying the Lord. Being honest here is the first step to guarding our hearts against this danger. Jesus had some important things to say about right priorities in Luke 9:59-62; 14:15-24.

2. How can believers decide how much luxury to allow themselves relative to the needs and condition of their church building?

Our text shows that many Israelites were guilty of neglecting the temple construction in favor of providing beautiful and comfortable houses for themselves. But Jesus cautions that "where your treasure is, there will your heart be also" (Matthew 6:21). If believers extend themselves financially to provide themselves the most comfortable homes possible but disregard the condition of their church building, that reveals something significant about their hearts.

Modern church buildings do not serve the same purpose as the temple did for the ancient Israelites. (Today, our bodies serve as God's temple; see 1 Corinthians 3:16, 17). Even so, our worship facilities visibly represent God's people to the surrounding community. The unchurched whom we are trying to reach will form impressions about the level of commitment in a congregation by the condition of the church building relative to the condition of the members' homes.

3. What is the outcome of being stingy with God? Do you believe that God withholds bless-

ing today from those who put their own interests above His? Why or why not?

In spite of all the attention they were giving to personal fortune, the Israelites addressed by Haggai were experiencing drought instead of bounty. They had disregarded the needs of God's temple in favor of their own needs, but their efforts had not yielded the outcome they had hoped. Is there any reason to suppose that God will deal with His people any differently today? "Give, and it shall be given unto you; . . . For with the same measure that ye mete withal it shall be measured to you again" (Luke 6:38).

4. God called on the Israelites for obedience in building the temple. What is the obedience from believers today that would cause God the greatest pleasure and glory?

The temple, in particular the Holy of Holies, was considered the seat of God's glory on the earth. The temple was a symbol of God's presence among the people. In Christ we are promised that the Holy Spirit resides in us. The church as the body of Christ, as well as individual Christians, represents God's presence on earth. God is most glorified by people who are submitted to His will and who are being built up in the image of Christ (John 15:9, 10; Colossians 3:9, 10). Talk about ways your students can participate in your church's efforts in evangelism.

5. During what times or circumstances have you felt that God was especially *with* you or *with* your church? Why do you suppose God chose especially to bless those instances?

The most favorable words we can hear from God are, "I am with you." The most unfavorable words are, "I am against you" (cf. Jeremiah 21:13; Ezekiel 21:3). The Israelites knew all too well what it was like to incur God's disfavor, so their response to Haggai's message of rebuke was to repent and obey God by resuming the construction of the temple. Perhaps you have had the experience of being involved in a project that you believed was clearly mandated by God—a mission venture, an evangelistic outreach, or a benevolence effort. God blesses us when we yield to His will in such undertakings. But when they become the means to further our own agendas, God can just as quickly withdraw His blessing!

God Gives Hope for the Future

DEVOTIONAL READING: Psalm 48:1-14.

BACKGROUND SCRIPTURE: Zechariah 8.

PRINTED TEXT: Zechariah 8:1-13.

Zechariah 8:1-13

1 Again the word of the LORD of hosts came to me, saying,

2 Thus saith the LORD of hosts; I was jealous for Zion with great jealousy, and I was jealous for her with great fury.

3 Thus saith the LORD; I am returned unto Zion, and will dwell in the midst of Jerusalem: and Jerusalem shall be called A city of truth; and the mountain of the LORD of hosts, The holy mountain.

4 Thus saith the LORD of hosts; There shall yet old men and old women dwell in the streets of Jerusalem, and every man with his staff in his hand for very age.

5 And the streets of the city shall be full of boys and girls playing in the streets thereof.

6 Thus saith the LORD of hosts; If it be marvelous in the eyes of the remnant of this people in these days, should it also be marvelous in mine eyes? saith the LORD of hosts.

7 Thus saith the LORD of hosts; Behold, I will save my people from the east country, and from the west country;

8 And I will bring them, and they shall dwell in the midst of Jerusalem: and they shall be my people, and I will be their God, in truth and in righteousness.

9 Thus saith the LORD of hosts; Let your hands be strong, ye that hear in these days these words by the mouth of the prophets, which were in the day that the foundation of the house of the LORD of hosts was laid, that the temple might be built.

10 For before these days there was no hire for man, nor any hire for beast; neither was there any peace to him that went out or came in because of the affliction: for I set all men every one against his neighbor.

11 But now I will not be unto the residue of this people as in the former days, saith the LORD of hosts.

12 For the seed shall be prosperous; the vine shall give her fruit, and the ground shall give her increase, and the heavens shall give their dew; and I will cause the remnant of this people to possess all these things.

13 And it shall come to pass, that as ye were a curse among the heathen, O house of Judah, and house of Israel; so will I save you, and ye shall be a blessing: fear not, but let your hands be strong.

GOLDEN TEXT: I am returned unto Zion, and will dwell in the midst of Jerusalem: and Jerusalem shall be called A city of truth; and the mountain of the LORD of hosts, The holy mountain.—Zechariah 8:3.

Lesson Aims

After participating in this lesson, each student will be able to:

1. Explain how God's jealousy for His people motivates Him to provide hope for the future.

2. Understand the Biblical concept of hope.

3. Develop a plan for providing one person eternal hope, which is in Christ.

Lesson Outline

INTRODUCTION
  A. The Need for Encouragement
  B. Lesson Background
 I. PROMISES FOR JERUSALEM (Zechariah 8:1-8)
  A. The Lord's Passion and Presence (vv. 1-3)
  B. The Lord's Peace and Power (vv. 4-6)
  C. The Lord's People (vv. 7, 8)
II. PROMISES FOR THE PEOPLE (Zechariah 8:9-13)
  A. Retrospect (vv. 9, 10)
    Hard Work
  B. Prospect (vv. 11, 12)
    Peace
  C. Respect (v. 13)
CONCLUSION
  A. Those Who Help Themselves
  B. Prayer
  C. Thought to Remember

Introduction

A. The Need for Encouragement

Someone has said that life may be compared to walking through a minefield, for disaster or death may come at any moment. We see this possibility in all the current fears that the media feels compelled to share in somber tones: air and water pollution, energy shortages, global warming, AIDS, cancer-causing products, heart diseases, overpopulation—not to mention threats of terror somewhere on the planet. The list seems to go on and on.

As we have noted previously, the Biblical response to all these threats is to live by faith, regardless of what God allows to happen. However, the people around us often need to be encouraged and reminded of the hope that Christians have.

One Sunday school class has the right idea: it has designated itself *The Encouragers*. The teacher is taking the lead in providing encouragement to others. He may not be the official "greeter" for the congregation, but each Sunday he is at his post to welcome visitors and friends. His genuine interest in others is shared by his wife, who prepares a variety of cards to be sent through the class each week so that the members may sign them.

Behind acts of encouragement are the Biblical concepts of thankfulness and the fruit of the Spirit as given in Galatians 5:22, 23. Every family, church, or other social group could benefit if its members would minimize the negatives and publicize the positives with encouragement.

B. Lesson Background

God was speaking again through the prophets after the exile! It started with Haggai on August 29, 520 B.C. (last week's lesson). Slightly over two months later, the voice of Zechariah was also heard in Jerusalem (Zechariah 1:1). Both men provided encouragement to those who were building the temple (Ezra 5:1). The temple was finished and dedicated on March 12, 515 B.C., and the people prospered under the preaching of these two prophets.

The name Zechariah means "Yahweh remembers" or "Yahweh has remembered." Combining the information in Zechariah 1:1 with Nehemiah 12:12 and 16, we conclude that this Zechariah was a priest, and that he was much younger than Haggai. Zechariah came to a tragic end (see Matthew 23:35).

The four messages in Zechariah 7 and 8 involve a delegation from Bethel, which is about twelve miles north of Jerusalem. The delegation arrived on December 7, 518 B.C., to pose some questions on the subject of fasting (7:1-3). The Jews had added days of fasting to their religious calendar to memorialize events associated with the fall of Jerusalem, which had occurred some sixty-eight years earlier. Specifically, the delegation was concerned about a fast in the fifth month (late July and early August), to remember the destruction of Jerusalem, and a fast in the seventh month (late September and early October) to remind them of the murder of governor Gedaliah in a civil uprising after Jerusalem was destroyed (Zechariah 7:3, 5; Jeremiah 41:1, 2).

The Jews also had added two other fasts. One memorialized the month that the siege of Jerusalem had begun, and another was a reminder of when the Babylonians broke through the walls of the city (Zechariah 8:19). The Jews probably had been keeping these fast days during all the time that they were in Babylon (7:5). Now they wondered whether they should continue to observe these traditions (7:3).

The lesson today is from the first part of the third message that Zechariah gave to the men from Bethel. (The four messages begin at 7:4, 8; 8:1, and 18.) Zechariah's words were encouraging words for people who wondered about the future.

I. Promises for Jerusalem (Zechariah 8:1-8)

One hundred years ago, an English scholar wrote that Zechariah 8 contains a "decalogue of promises." These are messages of "hope," as the title for the lesson indicates. Our printed text covers several of these promises that concern Jerusalem.

A. The Lord's Passion and Presence (vv. 1-3)

1, 2. Again the word of the LORD of hosts came to me, saying, Thus saith the LORD of hosts; I was jealous for Zion with great jealousy, and I was jealous for her with great fury.

Throughout this chapter, Zechariah emphasizes that his words are from the Lord (cf. vv. 1 and 2, 3, 4, 6, 7, 9, 14, 18, 20, 23). All but one of the "ten promises" begins by stating that this is from *the Lord of hosts.* (The promise in v. 3 does not include the word "hosts.") There is no doubt that the message is from God Himself! [See question #1, page 370.]

Many centuries earlier, the Lord had stated in the Second Commandment that He is a *jealous* God (Exodus 20:5). *Jealousy* is a very strong emotion or passion. For humans, it can be good or bad; with God, however, this emotion is always for our benefit. To be *jealous for Zion*, jealous *with great fury*, means that God is passionate about restoring His people (cf. Zechariah 1:14). [See question #2, page 370.]

3. Thus saith the LORD; I am returned unto Zion, and will dwell in the midst of Jerusalem: and Jerusalem shall be called A city of truth; and the mountain of the LORD of hosts, The holy mountain.

This promise involves the Lord's returning His presence to *Jerusalem. Zion* is one of the hills on which Jerusalem stands. The term became a synonym for Jerusalem itself and is used interchangeably with it. [See question #3, page 370.]

When Solomon dedicated the temple in about 950 B.C. (1 Kings 6:38), a special glory prevented the priests from entering (see 2 Chronicles 7:2, 3). There is no record of any such event this time—just the assurance that God *will dwell in* His *city* (cf. Zechariah 1:16; 2:10). Before the city's destruction God's glory had withdrawn because of wickedness within her (see Ezekiel 9:3; 10:4, 18, 19; 11:23).

Two new descriptive names now are assigned to the city: *city of truth* and *the holy mountain.* Before Jerusalem was destroyed by the Babylonians in 586 B.C., the city had become "full of perverseness" (Ezekiel 9:9). Now it is to be holy, a city that is set apart for the Lord. Isaiah 62:4 prophesies still another name for Jerusalem: "Hephzibah," which means "my delight is in her."

B. The Lord's Peace and Power (vv. 4-6)

4. Thus saith the LORD of hosts; There shall yet old men and old women dwell in the streets of Jerusalem, and every man with his staff in his hand for very age.

This promise begins with assurance of a peaceful existence. Things are still difficult for the hardy remnant that has been back in their land and their city for less than twenty years. Although not describing their present situation, this verse gives them hope for the future. To have a time without the ravages of war, which had been so much a part of Jerusalem's past, will be a joy. *Jerusalem* will be a place where one can walk *the streets* in safety.

Our historical perspective teaches us that this type of tranquility for Jerusalem seems to come and go. Today, the threat of terrorism lurks around every corner in modern Jerusalem. Such uncertainty makes us look forward to the Heavenly Jerusalem, where perfect peace will exist (Revelation 3:12; 21:2, 10-27). Only there will this prophecy find ultimate fulfillment.

5. And the streets of the city shall be full of boys and girls playing in the streets thereof.

This verse depicts the other end of the age spectrum. In times of danger, *boys and girls* sometimes are compelled to play behind locked doors, with bars on the windows. That is not a

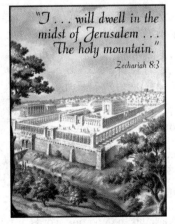

"I . . . will dwell in the midst of Jerusalem . . . The holy mountain."

Zechariah 8:3

Visual for lessons 4 and 5

Use this poster to illustrate verse 8 of the text. Keep it on display for next week's lesson as well.

How to Say It

ABRAHAM. *Ay*-bruh-ham.
BABYLONIANS. Bab-ih-*low*-nee-unz.
BETHEL. *Beth*-ul.
CORINTHIANS. Kor-*in*-thee-unz (th as in *thin*).
DECALOGUE. *dek*-uh-log.
EPHESIANS. Ee-*fee*-zhunz.
EZEKIEL. Ee-*zeek*-ee-ul or Ee-*zeek*-yul.
GEDALIAH. *Ged*-uh-*lye*-uh. (G as in get; strong accent on *lye*).
YAHWEH (Hebrew). *Yah*-weh.
HAGGAI. *Hag*-eye or *Hag*-ay-eye.
HEPHZIBAH. *Hef*-zih-bah.
ISAIAH. Eye-*zay*-uh.
JEREMIAH. Jair-uh-*my*-uh.
MICAH. *My*-kuh.
NEHEMIAH. *Nee*-huh-*my*-uh (strong accent on *my*).
ZECHARIAH. Zek-uh-*rye*-uh.

pleasant childhood. (See Isaiah 65:19-25.) The imagery suggests that the children can play happily outside. Young people can grow old and not have their lives taken by the ravages of war, with dreams unfulfilled.

6. Thus saith the LORD of hosts; If it be marvelous in the eyes of the remnant of this people in these days, should it also be marvelous in mine eyes? saith the LORD of hosts.

The implied answer to the question *should it also be marvelous in mine eyes?* is to be a firm negative. To the people, that which seems marvelous to the point of being impossible is certainly not impossible with God. With God all things are possible (Matthew 19:26; Mark 10:27).

A similar question arose in the days of Abraham and Sarah. When the Lord promised that this aged woman would have Abraham's son the following year, her disbelief produced laughter. God then asked, "Is any thing too hard for the Lord?" (Genesis 18:14). The implied answer is that the God who made the heavens and the earth could bring about this event. In Romans 4:18-22 the apostle Paul affirms that this is one of the events that demonstrated Abraham's faith.

In a similar hopeless situation Jeremiah the prophet expressed the same type of faith in a prayer. In his case, Jerusalem was under siege by the Babylonians, and he was instructed to buy a field. His symbolic act was intended to show that "Houses and fields and vineyards shall be possessed again in this land" (Jeremiah 32:15). He then voiced a prayer, and the opening words are the inspiration for a contemporary song: "Ah Lord God! behold, thou hast made the heaven

and the earth by thy great power . . . there is nothing too hard for thee" (32:17). [See question #4, page 370.]

C. The Lord's People (vv. 7, 8)

7. Thus saith the LORD of hosts: Behold, I will save my people from the east country, and from the west country.

This section concludes the brief messages of hope. The two opposite directions *east* and *west* express totality in signifying that God will regather His *people* from "the ends of the earth." Although this prediction is nothing new (see Isaiah 43:5-7 and Jeremiah 31:7, 8), it needs to be restated for a new generation.

8. And I will bring them, and they shall dwell in the midst of Jerusalem: and they shall be my people, and I will be their God, in truth and in righteousness.

Isaiah 2:1-4 and Micah 4:1-3 prophesy that the journey to *Jerusalem* is for all of God's *people*. Most students agree that "Jerusalem" is not confined to the physical city. Rather, it includes all of spiritual Israel, all who are God's people in Christ (cf. Romans 9:24; 1 Peter 2:9, 10). The prophet foretold of a new covenant (Jeremiah 31:31-34), and the writer of Hebrews states that it is fulfilled in Christ now as He serves as the high priest for this new covenant (Hebrews 8:8-11). That writer adds that we already have come to the Heavenly Jerusalem (Hebrews 12:22-24). The expression *my people* is a special concept in both Old and New Testaments (see last week's lesson).

II. Promises for the People (Zechariah 8:9-13)

Zechariah again brings a message directly from the Lord. The people need encouragement as they continue to work on the temple in the year 518 B.C.

A. Retrospect (vv. 9, 10)

9. Thus saith the LORD of hosts; Let your hands be strong, ye that hear in these days these words by the mouth of the prophets, which were in the day that the foundation of the house of the LORD of hosts was laid, that the temple might be built.

Encouragement comes from looking to the past. The *Lord of hosts* wants to remind the people of the way things were, but He prefaces the reminder with a strong admonition: *Let your hands be strong.*

In an era before power tools, almost everything would be accomplished by the work of the hands. For this reason, "hands" frequently serves as a figure of speech in the Bible (e.g., 2 Samuel

16:21). Approximately seventy years after Zechariah's prophecy, Nehemiah will ask the Lord to strengthen his hands (Nehemiah 6:9) as he prepares to lead the work in rebuilding the walls of Jerusalem. (This will be a part of the study on July 13.) Zechariah will repeat this phrase in verse 13, below.

The prophet reminds the delegation from Bethel to look back to how the Lord has already blessed them. *The foundation of the house of the Lord of hosts was laid* in 536 B.C. (see Ezra 3:8-10). The work on the temple was resumed in 520 B.C., and both Haggai and Zechariah were eyewitnesses (Ezra 5:1, 2).

HARD WORK

Colonel Sanders, Kentucky's favorite son, said, "Hard work beats all the tonics and vitamins in the world." The chicken king knew the truth!

A good work ethic is not an American invention. It's Biblical! Hard work pays. In Zechariah 8, the prophet challenged his hearers to have strong hands—to work hard! Hard work is God's high calling. God called Israel to work hard at rebuilding the temple. He calls us to greater energy in working for His kingdom.

Listen to the commands of God. "Whatsoever ye do, do it heartily" (Colossians 3:23). "Show [yourself] . . . a workman that needeth not to be ashamed" (2 Timothy 2:15). "Not slothful in business; fervent in spirit; serving the Lord" (Romans 12:11). These are verses that cut across every aspect and activity of our lives.

Years ago, doctors at New York's Montifiore Hospital advertised for volunteers to study the impact of complete bed rest. They were swamped with volunteers! A life without hard work seems the ambition of many. Is this a good thing? Not according to God.

Robert Frost said, "The world is full of willing people. Some willing to work, the rest willing to let them." Which category best describes you?

—J. A. M.

10. For before these days there was no hire for man, nor any hire for beast; neither was there any peace to him that went out or came in because of the affliction: for I set all men every one against his neighbor.

Before these days is roughly the years 530–520 B.C. Haggai 1:6-11; 2:15-19 describe the economic conditions of that time period (see last week's lesson). The work on the temple had come to a halt. That happened in part because the economic situation did not provide for any extra funds for this major project. A certain physical and spiritual "slackness" on the part of the people also was a factor (see Haggai 1:9), as was opposition by their

enemies (see Ezra 4:23, 24). To move *out* of the city or back *in* does not improve the situation. The Lord has allowed the tensions to rise, which they do in such crises. It is God Himself who has brought these conditions about in order to accomplish His larger purpose (cf. Haggai 2:17).

B. Prospect (vv. 11, 12)

11. But now I will not be unto the residue of this people as in the former days, saith the LORD of hosts.

The first two words *but now* offer a sharp contrast. The *former* circumstances are over. Those were the *days* between the laying of the foundation and the resumption of the work on the temple.

The prospect for the future will continue to be different for the *residue* (remnant) of the *people* who have returned from Babylon. The prophet Haggai already has confirmed this in his final sermon on December 18, 520 B.C. At that time (just about two years before Zechariah's message here) he had passed along the Lord's promise that "from this day I will bless you" (Haggai 2:19c).

12. For the seed shall be prosperous; the vine shall give her fruit, and the ground shall give her increase, and the heavens shall give their dew; and I will cause the remnant of this people to possess all these things.

The future for Israel will include prosperity. All the necessary ingredients will come together to achieve it. These include *the heavens* (the atmosphere, to provide the *dew* during the dry season) and *the ground*. The ground would not be as hard as iron, but would provide the essential nutrients for growth (see Haggai 1:10, 11 in last week's lesson for the disastrous situation that the people had been experiencing).

Home Daily Bible Readings

Monday, June 16—I Will Return to Zion (Zechariah 8:1-6)

Tuesday, June 17—Let Your Hands Be Strong (Zechariah 8:7-12)

Wednesday, June 18—You Shall Be a Blessing (Zechariah 8:13-17)

Thursday, June 19—Many People Will Seek the Lord (Zechariah 8:18-23)

Friday, June 20—Great Is the Lord (Psalm 48:1-8)

Saturday, June 21—Let Zion Be Glad (Psalm 48:9-14)

Sunday, June 22—Sing Praises Among the Nations (Psalm 57:7-11)

One additional factor is necessary for such growth: peace, or freedom from conflict. The opening words in the Hebrew literally read, "For the seed of peace, the vine, will give its fruit." Scholars differ on whether it is *the vine* itself that is *the seed* of peace, or if this is a reference to the absence of conflict. Most translations ignore the issue and give the basic idea: the prospect for the faithful *remnant* is bright!

PEACE

People want peace. In the 1980s a retired couple was alarmed by the threat of war, so they undertook a serious study of all the inhabited places on the globe. Their goal: find the place in the world least likely to experience war, especially nuclear war.

They studied and traveled and finally found the *ideal* place. And on Christmas they sent their pastor a card from their new home, a little known and isolated place called the Falkland Islands. But in just days their paradise became a battle zone as Great Britain and Argentina fought for control of those islands.

The Encyclopedia of Military History by Dupuy and Dupuy lists over four thousand battles and sieges since 3,500 B.C. The most destructive wars of the twentieth century were fought by the most "educated" countries in human history! Today, armed conflicts continue to pop up on every continent on the earth except Antarctica—and people would probably be fighting there if it weren't so cold! Our world still needs peace.

Peace isn't found in a property, no matter where it's located. Peace is found in a Person, Jesus Christ. Do you know Him?   —J. A. M.

C. Respect (v. 13)

13. And it shall come to pass, that as ye were a curse among the heathen, O house of Judah, and house of Israel; so will I save you, and ye shall be a blessing: fear not, but let your hands be strong.

In the past the nation of *Judah* had suffered greatly by having its capital razed and its temple destroyed. People in other lands knew about these tragedies, so when they wanted to call down evil on a person or a nation—often using the name of a pagan deity in the expression—then either Judah or *Israel* could be an example in the *curse* or oath (cf. Jeremiah 26:6; 44:8, 22).

God's promises have an inclusive ring in mentioning both Judah and Israel. Two positive outcomes are stated for them: the Lord will *save* them, and they will *be a blessing*. That will be the opposite of their previous experiences when they had been used in curses. (Compare Jeremiah 31:1-31; Ezekiel 37:11-28; Romans 9–11.)

The conditional factor is in the final phrase *but let your hands be strong.* The Lord has the ability to do these things by Himself, but He considers it essential for Judah to demonstrate her faith by cooperating with God in a genuine, sincere way. When people work with God, then "God gives hope for the future." [See question #5, page 370.]

Conclusion

A. Those Who Help Themselves

God in His compassion reaches out to help the helpless (e.g., Psalm 12:5). Even so, the final statement in the printed text, "but let your hands be strong," could well serve as the basis for the popular saying, "The Lord helps those who help themselves." That exact phrase is not in the Bible. (It has been variously attributed to Thomas Jefferson, Benjamin Franklin, and Algernon Sidney.) But although the exact words in that particular order may not be in the Bible, the concept is present in several places.

For example, Noah's righteous life enabled him to find favor in the eyes of the Lord. The Lord could have saved Noah from the flood in some other way than having him build the ark. Certainly that would have been much easier for Noah, for it was a major project for him and his sons with the primitive tools at their disposal. But the Lord did not choose some other way. He commanded Noah to build an ark. And Noah obeyed.

On the other hand, there are faithful Christians in some nations today who work diligently in many ways. Their hands indeed are "strong," but they will never experience prosperity in physical things.

We must conclude that the Lord really wants us to apply ourselves diligently to the spiritual aspects of life. This is expressed well in 2 Timothy 2:15: "Study to show thyself approved unto God, a workman that needeth not to be ashamed, rightly dividing the word of truth." When we are diligent for God, we will discover, as Paul did, that His grace is sufficient for us (2 Corinthians 12:9).

B. Prayer

Our Father in Heaven, You have no other hands but ours to use in taking Your message to humanity. Today I resolve to strengthen my hands to do what I can to help give a bright hope for the future to others. In the name of Your Son, amen.

C. Thought to Remember

"According to the power that worketh in us, unto him be glory" (Ephesians 3:20, 21).

Learning by Doing

This page contains an alternative lesson plan emphasizing learning activities.
Classes desiring such student involvement will find these suggestions helpful.

Learning Goals

After this lesson each student will be able to:

1. Explain how God's jealousy for His people motivates Him to provide hope for the future.

2. Understand the Biblical concept of hope.

3. Develop a plan for providing one person eternal hope, which is in Christ.

Into the Lesson

Before class, write the word *jealousy* on the chalkboard. Ask the students to cite different kinds or examples of jealousy that they have observed. *(Responses may include a reference to a "jealous husband," "jealous of my neighbors' car," and others.)*

Say, "*Jealousy* is a word that usually carries a negative connotation. However, as Paul indicates in 2 Corinthians 11:2, godly jealousy is positive, not negative." Ask the students to read Zechariah 8:2. Note that the concept of jealousy with reference to God almost always involves people, and very frequently occurs in the prophetic books. Have the students answer this question: "What is the first thing that comes to mind when you think of personally being jealous?" Then ask, "For whom are you jealous with a godly jealousy?" *(Likely responses here will be anyone loved by the student: a child, a spouse, a close friend.)* Finally, ask, "How do you demonstrate this godly jealousy?" *(Jealousy may be demonstrated by being with the person often, providing growth opportunities for the person, and others.)*

Say, "In today's text we'll see that God's jealousy for His people gives us hope."

Into the Word

Read Zechariah 8:1-13 aloud to the students. After verse 2, stop and say, "These first two verses are unlike the rest of the text; they are not speaking of the future. As a result, these verses give the motivation for the rest of the text." Emphasize God's jealousy for His people as a motivating force by saying, "Because of God's jealousy He makes promises for the future in the remainder of the text." Continue reading the text and vocally emphasize the words *shall* and *will*.

After the reading note that the word *hope* is not used in this text. Yet it is difficult to miss the concept of hope that is present. The future tense of the "Thus-saith-the-Lord" promises indicates God's distinct provision of hope.

Three words are most often translated *hope* in the Old Testament. These three carry meanings of "waiting for with tension or confident expectation" and "being firmly rooted in a foundation." This understanding of hope refers to something that transcends the temporary. Moreover, it is not based only in the future. It has a foundation of trust and strength in the past and present. In this text, God provides the foundation. Christ ultimately transcends the temporary.

Into Life

Say, "It has been said that hopelessness has become pervasive in much of the world." Ask the students to suggest ways they encounter hopelessness. Responses may include suicide attempts, increasing violence, high rates of depression, and a lack of faith in political, educational, and other institutions.

In his book, *The Baby Bust*, William Dunn points out that the lack of absolutes diminishes hope in people, especially children. Say, "There is a concept known as 'dying without death' that was first named by Cecil Brown during World War II. It is a malady in which a person resigns himself to circumstances because he believes that he cannot possibly change those circumstances. This is the sense of hopelessness that many people feel today."

Say, "Yet, God's jealousy for His people moves Him to provide them with hope. The hope He will provide is more than temporary. It is indeed eternal." Ask the students to think of another person they are jealous "for," not "of," reminding them about the nature of God's jealousy for them. This person should be someone who is in need of hope that goes beyond the temporary. This may mean salvation for a person who is lost or a renewal of hope for someone who has become cynical.

Indicate that eternal hope is ultimately found in Jesus Christ. Guide the students in developing a step-by-step plan for providing hope to a person for whom they are jealous. The first step may be to strengthen the relationship by spending more time each week with the person. The second step may be to determine what the person values at his or her core.

Finish by having pairs pray for one another and the one for whom each is jealous. Focus on providing eternal hope to the "chosen" people.

Let's Talk It Over

The questions on this page are designed to promote discussion of the lesson by the class and to encourage application of the lesson Scriptures. The answers provided are only discussion starters. Let your class talk it over from there.

1. Why is it important for us to know that the promises of the Bible are from God? How do we know that they are indeed from God and are not merely fanciful inventions?

The words *thus saith the Lord of hosts* established the source of authority and provided the first hearers reason to believe the promises that followed. If the words of our text were only the personal opinions or speculations of the prophet Zechariah, there would be no reason for the hearers to put trust in them. This is true, as well, for the promises of the Bible directed to believers in the New Testament era. We know the promises are from God because of the remarkable pattern of prophecy and fulfillment that spans human history. The God we trust to keep His promises is the same God Who always *has* kept His promises!

2. Why would the fact that the Lord is "jealous" be a comfort? Why could it be a frustration to others? How does one move from the "frustration" category to the "comfort" category?

Jealousy is usually a sign of possessiveness. People react negatively to possessiveness whenever it exceeds the level of commitment they have in a given relationship. A friendship or dating relationship does not give someone an exclusive claim upon us. A spouse, however, may be expected to be jealous if he or she perceives a threat to the exclusive commitment expressed in the marriage vows.

The "fury" of God's jealousy speaks to the intensity of His love and care for those with whom He has established an exclusive covenant relationship. The only reason someone might feel frustrated at that is if he or she is interested in compromising that relationship by giving attention to competing gods (idols)—and an idol is anything that takes first place in our lives. Christians find God's jealousy to be a comfort rather than a frustration when they realize that His jealousy results in our salvation!

3. What assurance do Christian believers have of God's presence? How do you experience that presence in your life?

In our text God promised to dwell in Jerusalem and to make the temple mountain holy by His presence. No physical manifestation of God's presence, such as the pillars of cloud or fire of former times, was promised (see Exodus 13:21). Christians have the promise of the indwelling presence of God's Spirit that those under the Old Covenant did not have (John 14:16, 17; Acts 2:38; Romans 8:9). The bestowing of the Spirit may not be accompanied by "tongues of fire" as on the Day of Pentecost or by visible power, but we are reassured of His presence by the fruit of a changed life (Galatians 5:16-26). Remember that *Immanuel* means "God with us" (Matthew 1:23).

4. Recount a time in your life when God intervened in a situation that appeared hopeless.

It is one thing to believe that God has done wonderful things in the past or in someone else's life. It requires a more intense, personal faith to believe that God is willing and able to do wonderful things in one's own life! God's providential care was part of the heritage of the ancient Israelites. They had heard how God had provided for their nation in amazing ways in the past. In Zechariah's day, they were asked to believe that He would do so again.

Without divine revelation, however, identifying specific acts of God is not entirely possible. Looking back on certain events, however, we may believe strongly that God's hand was at work. Perhaps you or your church undertook something for God that was so big it could be accomplished only if He blessed it. Maybe you prayed for His help in a situation that appeared doomed, beyond your ability to remedy.

5. What are some tasks or objectives for which God may call believers today to "strengthen their hands"? How much or how little attention do you consider that believers generally have given to those callings?

Believers in Christ are called to live lives of holiness (1 Peter 1:13-16), lives of love (Ephesians 5:1, 2), and lives of witness (Matthew 5:16). We are called to evangelize "all nations" (Matthew 28:19, 20). We are called to exhibit the fruit of the Spirit (Galatians 5:22-26).

Undergirding all of these challenges is the need for prayer, worship, sacrificial giving, and Bible study. Churches can help their members "strengthen their hands" in these areas through small groups that assist people in being accountable to one another.

The Exiles Dedicate the Temple

DEVOTIONAL READING: Psalm 96:1-13.

BACKGROUND SCRIPTURE: Ezra 5, 6.

PRINTED TEXT: Ezra 6:13-22.

Ezra 6:13-22

13 Then Tatnai, governor on this side the river, Shethar-boznai, and their companions, according to that which Darius the king had sent, so they did speedily.

14 And the elders of the Jews builded, and they prospered through the prophesying of Haggai the prophet and Zechariah the son of Iddo. And they builded, and finished it, according to the commandment of the God of Israel, and according to the commandment of Cyrus, and Darius, and Artaxerxes king of Persia.

15 And this house was finished on the third day of the month Adar, which was in the sixth year of the reign of Darius the king.

16 And the children of Israel, the priests, and the Levites, and the rest of the children of the captivity, kept the dedication of this house of God with joy,

17 And offered at the dedication of this house of God a hundred bullocks, two hundred rams, four hundred lambs; and for a sin offering for all Israel, twelve he goats, according to the number of the tribes of Israel.

18 And they set the priests in their divisions, and the Levites in their courses, for the service of God, which is at Jerusalem; as it is written in the book of Moses.

19 And the children of the captivity kept the passover upon the fourteenth day of the first month.

20 For the priests and the Levites were purified together, all of them were pure, and killed the passover for all the children of the captivity, and for their brethren the priests, and for themselves.

21 And the children of Israel, which were come again out of captivity, and all such as had separated themselves unto them from the filthiness of the heathen of the land, to seek the LORD God of Israel, did eat,

22 And kept the feast of unleavened bread seven days with joy: for the LORD had made them joyful, and turned the heart of the king of Assyria unto them, to strengthen their hands in the work of the house of God, the God of Israel.

GOLDEN TEXT: The children of Israel, the priests, and the Levites, and the rest of the children of the captivity, kept the dedication of this house of God with joy.
—Ezra 6:16.

God Restores a Remnant
Unit 1: Return
(Lessons 1-5)

Lesson Aims

After participating in this lesson, each student will be able to:

1. Describe the special events that followed the completion and dedication of the temple.

2. Imagine the joy of people who worship God during a special event or religious holiday.

3. Select an event in the life of the class or church and help plan a celebration that will include all ages.

Lesson Outline

INTRODUCTION
  A. Summer Soldier
  B. Lesson Background
 I. COMPLETING THE TEMPLE (Ezra 6:13-15)
  A. Compliance (v. 13)
  B. Commands (v. 14)
    Teamwork
  C. Completion (v. 15)
II. CONSECRATING THE TEMPLE (Ezra 6:16-18)
  A. Delight of the Remnant (v. 16)
  B. Determination of the Sacrifices (v. 17)
  C. Delegation of Duties (v. 18)
III. CELEBRATING THE FEASTS (Ezra 6:19-22)
  A. Passover Observed (v. 19)
  B. Purification of the Priests (v. 20)
  C. Purification of the People (v. 21)
    Project Exile
  D. Praises Continued (v. 22)
CONCLUSION
  A. Here to Stay?
  B. Prayer
  C. Thought to Remember

Introduction

A. Summer Soldier

On Friday, July fourth, the United States will celebrate another birthday. It will be 227 years since July 4, 1776.

But the winter of 1776–77 was very difficult for General George Washington and his men. The war was not going well. On December 23 of that year, Thomas Paine published the first chapter of his work *The Crisis*. After reading it, Washington gave orders that it be read to his discouraged men, especially the opening words: "These are the times

that try men's souls. The summer soldier and the sunshine patriot will, in this crisis, shrink from the service of their country; but he that stands it now, deserves the love and thanks of man and woman." Those words had a positive effect on Washington's troops, and the rest is history.

Do you think that the final success in the War for American Independence had more meaning to the men who suffered through those cold winters? Did Joseph in Egypt have a greater appreciation for his position over all Egypt because of the trials he suffered? Was the dedication of the second temple in 515 B.C. more meaningful to the people who had lived through the exile and return?

What if everything had gone smoothly for the exiles after their return? What if they had been able to complete the temple without any interruptions or opposition? Would the dedication of the temple have become more of a ho-hum event? James, the brother of our Lord, has written thoughtful words that have application to these situations. "My brethren, count it all joy when ye fall into divers temptations; knowing this, that the trying of your faith worketh patience. But let patience have her perfect work, that ye may be perfect and entire, wanting nothing" (James 1:2-4).

Any faith that has been tested and has passed the test is a stronger, maturer faith. How's your faith today?

B. Lesson Background

The temple of Solomon, which had stood for over 360 years, had been burned by the troops of Nebuchadnezzar in 586 B.C. The Jews have been without their temple for over seventy years.

But that is just part of the story. The people who had returned from exile in Babylon had been back in Jerusalem for twenty years—since about 536 B.C. Enemies without and selfishness within have combined to delay the project. The people have provided well for their own homes, but the temple of God has been neglected (Haggai 1:4, 9).

Finally, the preaching of Haggai and Zechariah had motivated the people again to put first things first—to give first place to the things of God. As a result they resumed building on September 21, 520 B.C. (Ezra 5:1, 2; Haggai 1:14, 15).

That action brought questions from the Persian officials in the area. A project of such proportions could have subversive designs. The situation was explained to the regional governor, and he was told that permission for the construction had been received from Cyrus shortly after he conquered Babylon in 539 B.C. (Ezra 5:3-17).

The new king, Darius, upon hearing the report, ordered that a search be made for the original decree. It was located in the summer home of the Persian rulers, in Achmetha (Ecbatana in modern versions; cf. Ezra 6:2), in the mountains of Media, almost three hundred miles northeast of Babylon. Darius then ordered that the work must continue and that the royal revenues of the area be used to assist in the project (Ezra 6:6-12).

I. Completing the Temple
(Ezra 6:13-15)
A. Compliance (v. 13)

13. Then Tatnai, governor on this side the river, Shethar-boznai, and their companions, according to that which Darius the king had sent, so they did speedily.

The identity of *Shethar-boznai* is unknown. He is probably an assistant to the governor. The rulers know how to do their part in the political system, so they comply with the king's order.

B. Commands (v. 14)

14. And the elders of the Jews builded, and they prospered through the prophesying of Haggai the prophet and Zechariah the son of Iddo. And they builded, and finished it, according to the commandment of the God of Israel, and according to the commandment of Cyrus, and Darius, and Artaxerxes king of Persia.

As Ezra writes this account, perhaps up to eighty years after the events he is describing, he records the fact that many people are responsible for the rebuilding of the temple. It involved the work of *the elders of the Jews* as well as the forceful exhortations of *Haggai the prophet and Zechariah*, but behind them all was *the God of Israel*. Everything went *according to the* plan that He had revealed to Isaiah many years before.

The influence of three Persian kings is also cited. They include *Cyrus* (who gave the original decree for the project in 538 B.C.), *Darius* (who enforced the decree of Cyrus when it was found), and *Artaxerxes*. The mention of Artaxerxes is a surprise, for his reign is much later, from 464 to 424 B.C., in the time of Ezra and Nehemiah. Ezra, however, makes a very wise gesture by including the name of the king of his own time, for Artaxerxes provides significant assistance to the Jews (Ezra 7:11-28; Nehemiah 2:1-8). This also serves to introduce Artaxerxes in preparation for his part in the remainder of the book.

TEAMWORK

Herman Ostry, of Bruno, Nebraska moved a barn by hand! But, he didn't do it alone. Not long after he had bought a farm, a nearby creek swelled out of its banks and a barn on the property was flooded. Ostry half-jokingly said to his family, "I bet if we had enough people, we could pick up that barn and carry it to higher ground."

His remark prompted Ostry's son Mike to think. He counted the number of boards, timbers, and nails and estimated the barn's weight to be about nineteen thousand pounds. Mike figured 344 people would have to lift only about fifty-five pounds each to carry the barn to higher ground.

But how do that many people get a grip on the barn to lift it? Mike designed a grid of steel and attached it to the barn. This provided handles for the barn raisers. Herman Ostry then suggested a "barn raising" as part of the Bruno centennial celebration. Word of the "barn raising" spread far beyond Bruno. On July 30, 1988, nearly four hundred thousand people from eleven states showed up. When everything was ready, Herman gave the signal and 344 people lifted together. The barn rose like nothing at all! The crowd cheered as the nine-ton barn walked fifty yards up a hill in just three minutes.

How did it happen? Teamwork! When enough people work together with one heart, one mind, one purpose, and one direction, they can accomplish the impossible. Teamwork was necessary for rebuilding the temple, and teamwork is vital to build God's kingdom today. Are you part of a healthy team for God? —J. A. M.

C. Completion (v. 15)

15. And this house was finished on the third day of the month Adar, which was in the sixth year of the reign of Darius the king.

The precise date is given for the completion of this lengthy project. *Adar* is the twelfth *month* of the year in the Jewish calendar. As stated above, the date is equivalent to March 12, 515 B.C. [See question #1, page 378.]

The date given is actually a Sabbath Day, so the implication of the passage is that the new temple is used in the prescribed way for the very

---

Home Daily Bible Readings

Monday, June 23—A Decree to Rebuild (Ezra 6:1-5)

Tuesday, June 24—Adversaries Must Let the Work Alone (Ezra 6:6-12)

Wednesday, June 25—A Joyous Dedication (Ezra 6:13-18)

Thursday, June 26—Sing to the Lord (Psalm 96:1-6)

Friday, June 27—Ascribe to the Lord Glory (Psalm 96:7-13)

Saturday, June 28—God Has Done Marvelous Things (Psalm 98:1-6)

Sunday, June 29—Extol the Lord Our God (Psalm 99:1-5)

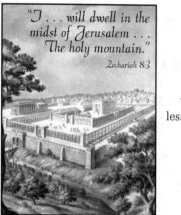

"I . . . will dwell in the midst of Jerusalem . . . The holy mountain."

Zechariah 8:3

Visual for
lessons 4 and 5

Display the same poster as was used last week. Use it to illustrate verse 15 of the text.

first time on a Sabbath. That is a special Sabbath in the history of the nation of Israel.

Now that the temple *is finished*, what is it like? Some other ancient works refer to the temple, but they give few details. They indicate that this temple is probably about the same size as the one Solomon built, but its furnishings are inferior. For example, the new temple has just one seven-branched candelabrum; Solomon's temple had ten. The ark of the covenant is missing from this temple. Josephus, the first-century Jewish historian, notes that in the Holy of Holies (where the ark of the covenant had been) "there was nothing at all."

II. Consecrating the Temple
(Ezra 6:16-18)

A. Delight of the Remnant (v. 16)

16. And the children of Israel, the priests, and the Levites, and the rest of the children of the captivity, kept the dedication of this house of God with joy.

Everyone joins in the celebration. The work itself has been a cooperative effort, and *the dedication* is for all. Whenever new buildings for worship and service are dedicated, usually the *joy* is so contagious that even those who did not participate become enthusiastic supporters. Yet the purpose is not just to build, but to use the facility to fulfill its intended purposes. Continued support is therefore essential.

When the foundations of the temple were laid, two sounds had been heard: joy and weeping (Ezra 3:12, 13). This time only the emotion of joy is expressed. The entire nation is delighted that the temple is completed (cf. Nehemiah 8:12). [See question #2, page 378.]

B. Determination of the Sacrifices (v. 17)

17. And offered at the dedication of this house of God a hundred bullocks, two hundred rams, four hundred lambs; and for a sin offering for all Israel, twelve he goats, according to the number of the tribes of Israel.

The celebration involves animal sacrifice. The *twelve goats* are noted as being *sin* offerings, *according to the* total *number of the tribes of Israel.* Most of the people present are from only the tribes of Judah and Benjamin. But Israel in its fullness has twelve tribes. No doubt many faithful Israelites relocated from the north to Judah when Jeroboam set up the idols in Bethel and Dan. (Luke 2:36 notes that Anna, the elderly woman present at the dedication of Jesus, was of the tribe of Asher; see also Acts 26:7.) [See question #3, page 378.]

The other animals probably were offered for two purposes: as burnt offerings and as peace (fellowship) offerings. The latter type would have been the larger portion. Such offerings primarily are eaten by the people present. This is a very big picnic for the entire community!

In the dedication of Solomon's temple, 22,000 oxen and 120,000 sheep and goats were offered (1 Kings 8:63). The great difference in the numbers shows that there are fewer people in the nation when the second temple is dedicated.

Two additional differences are interesting. When Solomon finished his dedicatory prayer, fire descended from Heaven and consumed the portions of the animals on the altar, and the special glory of the Lord filled the area (2 Chronicles 7:1). Neither is recorded as recurring for the second dedication.

C. Delegation of Duties (v. 18)

18. And they set the priests in their divisions, and the Levites in their courses, for the service of God, which is at Jerusalem; as it is written in the book of Moses.

The captivity had convinced the Israelites of one necessity: they must be obedient to the commands of God given through *Moses*. The consequences of experimentation with other gods and religions had led to disastrous results, just as the Lord had promised through Moses in one of his farewell addresses (Deuteronomy 28:15-68).

Moses, however, did not organize the *priests* into *divisions* in his own time, for the priests consisted of only his brother Aaron and two of Aaron's sons (Numbers 3:1-4). King David was the primary person who organized the priests and *Levites* into their groups (1 Chronicles 23–26). This became necessary in his time because of the major spiritual renewal that was a part of his reign. The Levites—the tribe from which the priests after Aaron would come—originally had been set apart and commissioned by God through Moses to meet the needs of Israel in the wilderness (Numbers 3:5-10; 8:5-14). The implications of worship at the temple demand that an organizational pattern now be employed again.

III. Celebrating the Feasts (Ezra 6:19-22)

A. Passover Observed (v. 19)

19. And the children of the captivity kept the passover upon the fourteenth day of the first month.

The *passover* is always a special event, but at this particular time it is even more meaningful to the Israelites. They must be feeling some of the same exhilaration as the devout Israelites did in the early years after the nation had achieved its independence from Egypt. It is a celebration in which they look to the past, to the time when the destroyer (Exodus 12:23) had gone through the land of Egypt. The firstborn of every household that did not have the blood of the lamb on the door frames was slain. The Israelite households, however, had an obedient faith that motivated them to apply the blood at the entrances of their homes and thus save them from that tragedy.

Moses had commanded all Israel to celebrate the Passover on the *fourteenth day of the first month* into the indefinite future (Exodus 12:24, 25). As this Passover is observed on April 21, 515 B.C., it now has been more than nine hundred years since that first Passover celebration.

B. Purification of the Priests (v. 20)

20. For the priests and the Levites were purified together, all of them were pure, and killed the passover for all the children of the captivity, and for their brethren the priests, and for themselves.

The original specifications in Exodus were for the heads of families to sacrifice the prescribed animals. In the intervening years, *the priests and the Levites* had assumed the task of slaying the animals for the worshipers.

The Passover in the time of Hezekiah (2 Chronicles 30) had to be deferred a month because too few of the priests had cleansed themselves ceremonially for the occasion. This time the Israelites were ready. Perhaps the people were being extra careful to do things properly. They had learned the consequences of careless, insincere worship.

We should note that the word *passover* is used in two ways in verses 19, 20. In verse 19 it refers to the feast itself. But here in verse 20, it refers to the animals that are slain. Problems in interpretation may arise if that distinction is ignored.

C. Purification of the People (v. 21)

21. And the children of Israel, which were come again out of captivity, and all such as had separated themselves unto them from the filthiness of the heathen of the land, to seek the LORD God of Israel, did eat.

The identity of those who *were come again out of captivity* (exile) is obvious. But who are the people who *had separated themselves* in order to be able to participate in the celebration? Two possibilities are usually given. The first is that it is a reference to Israelites who had been able to stay in the land (cf. Jeremiah 52:16). The other possibility is that it refers to Gentile converts to Judaism.

In either case, two definite actions are described for those people who had not come out of captivity. First, they separated and purified themselves from pagan *filthiness* in order to be able to join in the festive event. This uncleanness is mainly idol worship (cf. Ezekiel 22:4; 36:18, 25). [See question #4, page 378.]

Their second action is *to seek the Lord.* In other words, they recognize that demands are made on those who would serve God. In some cases today, this message has been modified to say that the Lord requires no changes in the lives of those who decide to follow Him. Such an idea suggests

---

How to Say It

AARON. *Air*-un.
ACHMETHA. Ock-*mee*-thuh.
ADAR. *Ay*-dar.
ARTAXERXES. Are-tuh-*zerk*-sees.
ASSYRIA. Uh-*sear*-e-uh.
BABYLON. *Bab*-uh-lun.
CYRUS. *Sigh*-russ.
DARIUS. Duh-*rye*-us.
ECBATANA. Ek-buh-*tahn*-uh.
GENTILE. *Jen*-tyle.
HAGGAI. *Hag*-eye or *Hag*-ay-eye.
HEZEKIAH. Hez-ih-*kye*-uh.
IDDO. *Id*-do.
ISRAELITE. *Iz*-ray-el-ite.
JEROBOAM. Jair-uh-*boe*-um.
JOSEPHUS. Jo-*see*-fus.
JUDAISM. *Joo*-duh-izz-um or *Joo*-day-izz-um.
LEVITES. *Lee*-vites.
NEBUCHADNEZZAR. *Neb*-yuh-kud-*nez*-er (strong accent on *nez*).
NEHEMIAH. *Nee*-huh-*my*-uh (strong accent on *my*).
PERSIA. *Per*-zhuh.
SHETHAR-BOZNAI. *She*-thar-*boz*-nye (strong accent on *boz*).
TATNAI. *Tat*-nye or *Tat*-eh-nye.
ZECHARIAH. Zek-uh-*rye*-uh.

that such a person may believe or do whatever he or she wants, and still be a member of the community of the redeemed. The Bible certainly does not support this concept! (See John 14:15.)

PROJECT EXILE

The city of Richmond, Virginia, had a problem. For more than a decade, gun violence had plagued her streets to the point where she was usually among the top five U.S. cities having the worst per capita murder rates.

But all that began to change in 1997 when the U.S. Attorney's Office in Richmond developed and implemented a program called "Project Exile." Aggressive federal prosecution, stiffer bond rules, and tougher sentencing guidelines resulted in the imposition of mandatory minimum prison sentences for individuals convicted of firearm violations. In effect, these felons were sent "into exile." The resulting drop in Richmond's homicide rate was so impressive that one hundred fifty cities are expected to adopt similar "exile" programs by October 1, 2003.

The long-term effects on those who serve their sentences and return from this "exile," however, are unknown. Undoubtedly, they will all rejoice when they are released, but how will they choose to rebuild their shattered lives from then on? Will they resolve to separate themselves permanently from the filthiness of their sinful past? Will they devote themselves to seeking the Lord for the rest of their lives? Only time will tell for them—and for us. —R. L. N.

D. Praises Continued (v. 22)

22. And kept the feast of unleavened bread seven days with joy: for the LORD had made them joyful, and turned the heart of the king of Assyria unto them, to strengthen their hands in the work of the house of God, the God of Israel.

The *feast of unleavened bread* immediately follows the Passover (Leviticus 23:5, 6). It prolongs the festivities for another *seven days*. The two events are connected so closely that they are usually considered to be a part of the same celebration (cf. Mark 14:1). [See question #5, page 378.]

The Feast of Unleavened Bread also has a distinctive purpose. Doing without leavened bread for seven days reminds the Lord's people of the exodus in the days of Moses. They had left Egypt quickly, so unleavened bread was standard fare as the Israelites fled. There was no time to leaven the bread and allow it to raise.

This celebration is therefore intended to remind the people that the generations in the past were compelled to experience self-denial and to be prepared for action before they were able to enjoy the blessings of freedom.

The reference to *the king of Assyria* is somewhat surprising at first. The Assyrian Empire had come to an end for all practical purposes in 612 B.C. (about a hundred years before this time) when it was conquered by the Babylonians. The Babylonian kingdom was followed in turn by the Persian kingdom. (The latter two kingdoms are found in the prophecies of Daniel 2 and 7.)

Many kings, however, prefer using different titles to show the greatness of their power. The Persians controlled the region that had been the heart of Assyria, and it is very likely that this is just one of the titles being used in the time of Darius (or in the time of Artaxerxes when the book is being written by Ezra). Note that Artaxerxes is also called "king of Babylon" in Nehemiah 13:6.

The word *joy* reveals to us that the spring of 515 B.C. is a time of great spiritual enthusiasm for the renewed nation of Israel. The same emotion was part of the dedication of the temple a few weeks before (Ezra 6:16), and its presence carried over to the first feasts of the New Year. There may be a time for sadness and remorse in worship, but it is joy that is a fruit of the Spirit (Galatians 5:22), not sadness.

Conclusion

A. Here to Stay?

This rebuilt, second temple stood for close to six hundred years. But its destruction by the Romans under Titus in A.D. 70 showed that it, too, was temporary. (It had a total refurbishing in the days of Herod the Great, but it was essentially the same structure.)

This brings up a question. When a congregation, a church building, a place of higher education, or a home is established in the name of Christ, how long will it retain its original purpose? The answer is always the same: it depends!

When a nation celebrates a birthday, and that nation clearly refers to divine providence in the document that called it into existence, the question must be asked again: how long will it remain in existence? The answer is still the same: it depends—and the choice is ours.

B. Prayer

Heavenly Father, today we dedicate ourselves again to the service of Your Son in all that we do or say. We commit ourselves to return to Your Word, as the Israelites of old returned to the law of Moses. May we remain faithful to the end. In the name of our Redeemer, amen.

C. Thought to Remember

"But the fruit of the Spirit is . . . joy . . . against such there is no law" (Galatians 5:22, 23).

Learning by Doing

This page contains an alternative lesson plan emphasizing learning activities.
Classes desiring such student involvement will find these suggestions helpful.

Learning Goals

After this lesson each student will be able to:

1. Describe the special events that followed the completion and dedication of the temple.

2. Imagine the joy of people who worship God during a special event or religious holiday.

3. Select an event in the life of the class or church and help plan a celebration that will include all ages.

Into the Lesson

Before class, think of a recent accomplishment or special event in the life of your church. To begin class ask, "When we celebrated _____, what feelings did you hear people express?" After students answer, note the answers that reflect joy, commitment, and unity. "It is exciting to celebrate accomplishments together. In today's text the people around Jerusalem enjoyed a celebration for over two months."

Into the Word

From study of the background material in the commentary (pages 372, 373), present a lecture to review briefly the last four lessons and the chapters skipped. Fill in, as it were, the twenty years since the captives returned.

To further prepare students for their reflection on the passage, describe the feasts of Passover and Unleavened Bread. (If you have students who enjoy research, contact them early and ask them to prepare lectures on the two feasts.)

Use the journaling technique to get your students to reflect on this lesson's events (the dedication of the new temple, the Passover, and the Feast of Unleavened Bread). To write an imaginary journal entry, students must "get inside the heads of the participants" to write about events from their perspective. If you want to ensure a variety of entries, ask for volunteers for each of the groups that would have been present: priest, Levite, elder, older person who came back from Babylon, young adult, parent, child. Let volunteers read their journal entries.

Into Life

Ask, "As you listened to one another's journal entries, what common themes, attitudes, or emotions did you hear?"

Write answers on the chalkboard. Mark and add anything that you want to emphasize, such as repentance for their delay in building the temple, satisfaction for getting priorities right, appreciation for the role of Darius, awareness of God's provision, or joy from being in the temple.

Say: "Everyone was present for this special time of renewing obedience and purification. From your reflection as you wrote your journal entries, what impact do you think these three special events had on the various groups: priests, Levites, adults who returned from Babylon, adults who had always lived in Jerusalem, parents and children? How were they going to be different?"

Allow some time for discussion. Then say: "Sociologists have discovered that when people share in the same unifying event or activity, it becomes a bonding experience. Faith development research is confirming that the congregation in which children live contributes to their spiritual growth. Catherine Stonehouse writes, 'In the elementary school years, children begin to take ownership of the stories, beliefs, and religious rituals valued by those who belong to their faith communities. Their identity in the community grows as they learn the stories, recite some of the beliefs, and participate in the rituals—when they can say, "This is what we believe, what we do. This is our story"' (*Joining Children on the Spiritual Journey*; Grand Rapids: Baker Books, 1998, page 162).

"The events in Ezra 6 allowed Jews of all ages to experience joy and commitment together. They would be bonded with the children who were learning from the adults and rituals."

Challenge your class to support an intergenerational event that is being planned or to initiate and plan an event, either for class members and their families or for the whole church. Guide class members to commit to providing such an opportunity to help people of all ages to experience joy and commitment to God together.

Option for Individual Action: Give your learners a copy of these three questions as they ponder their own worship joy: (1) "What do I think and feel when I worship in God's house?" (2) "What can I do to begin to experience the joy of the people described in Ezra 6?" (3) "How can I express my joy in Christ to others, especially my children and/or grandchildren?"

Cut index cards lengthwise in half to distribute as bookmarks. Have students write the Golden Text from Ezra 6:16 on them as a reminder to worship God with joy.

Let's Talk It Over

The questions on this page are designed to promote discussion of the lesson by the class and to encourage application of the lesson Scriptures. The answers provided are only discussion starters. Let your class talk it over from there.

1. How do you respond when you hear a report of how vision, faith, and obedience led to a great accomplishment? How has others' success inspired you to greater endeavors for God?

We occasionally hear reports of a church that is experiencing rapid growth, of the dedication of a new church building, of a wonderful response to some evangelistic effort, or the commissioning of a group for the mission field. Some people feel personally threatened by others' success and react critically. That is a shame! Most will find these reports to be cause for rejoicing. Some may even be personally challenged and motivated!

Conventions and conferences often feature the testimonies of those whose faith-filled efforts have been richly blessed. Their courage, obedience, and successful result (as God counts success) inspire others to new levels of devotion and activity.

2. What feelings come to mind when you recall successfully completing a large-group project? What nonmaterial rewards did you enjoy?

Depending on how much you had invested personally, you probably felt a great relief, a sense of fulfillment, satisfaction, joy, and even a certain degree of pride upon completing the project. The pride was probably tempered, however, by the acknowledgment that you could not have accomplished the project alone. When you realize that God ultimately was the One who brought the success, you have the type of pride that honors Him.

Strong personal bonds are created between partners who have learned to lean on and trust one another. No one appreciates the required sacrifices more than those who shared in the effort. Mutual admiration and a willingness to serve one another in other areas are by-products of this kind of experience.

3. What is the value in celebration when God blesses faithful obedience? Do you believe your church is too extravagant in celebration, or not extravagant enough? Give an example.

There were a lot of cattle, sheep, and goats slaughtered as a part of the celebration of the rebuilt temple. This was a very expensive event. The size of the celebration made it memorable to the people. The celebration validated the significance of the temple in the life of Israel. This cele-

bration may have been the most lavish and important that those present would ever witness!

Perhaps that is a key to evaluating the celebrations we plan. What kind of celebration is warranted by the baptism into Christ of one person? of five people? Does the retirement of a minister after many years of effective and faithful service warrant a "fatted calf"? What about the dedication of a new church building? Remember, sometimes Jesus doesn't mind if we "break the perfume bottle" (see Mark 14:3-9).

4. What would it take in today's world to separate oneself from "the filthiness of the heathen"? How important is that for Christians in preparation for worship?

Jesus and the New Testament writers spent much effort warning about the allure of this world (e.g., Matthew 16:26; 1 John 2:15). The challenge is to separate ourselves mentally and morally from the "filthiness" of the world without altogether withdrawing ourselves from the people who need to hear the gospel. Jesus spent time with sinners, but did not engage in their sinful practices. If we engage in the corruption and immorality of the pagans who disregard God, it will blight our attempts to encounter Him in worship as those attitudes and practices begin to leak into our worship (cf. 1 Corinthians 10:14–11:34).

5. Which Christian rites or worship observances are most precious to you? How can Christians best preserve the sense of wonder and joy in worship?

Believers of different eras cherish different things. Some of the elderly people present at the dedication of the second temple in Jerusalem cherished worship there because they had experienced worship in the former temple. For the younger folks, however, observing Passover in Jerusalem was brand new—something they may only have heard their parents wish for. Today, some cherish the old hymns while others embrace newer praise choruses. All should cherish the observances of the Lord's Supper.

Wonder and joy probably are best preserved by our personal preparation and frame of mind for worship. If reading the Sunday newspaper before church is a distraction for your worship preparation, then save the paper for after church!

Nehemiah Begins Work

DEVOTIONAL READING: Isaiah 26:1-9.

BACKGROUND SCRIPTURE: Nehemiah 1, 2.

PRINTED TEXT: Nehemiah 1:1-4; 2:4, 5, 13, 16-18.

Nehemiah 1:1-4

1 The words of Nehemiah the son of Hachaliah. And it came to pass in the month Chisleu, in the twentieth year, as I was in Shushan the palace,

2 That Hanani, one of my brethren, came, he and certain men of Judah; and I asked them concerning the Jews that had escaped, which were left of the captivity, and concerning Jerusalem.

3 And they said unto me, The remnant that are left of the captivity there in the province are in great affliction and reproach: the wall of Jerusalem also is broken down, and the gates thereof are burned with fire.

4 And it came to pass, when I heard these words, that I sat down and wept, and mourned certain days, and fasted, and prayed before the God of heaven.

Nehemiah 2:4, 5, 13, 16-18

4 Then the king said unto me, For what dost thou make request? So I prayed to the God of heaven.

5 And I said unto the king, If it please the king, and if thy servant have found favor in thy sight, that thou wouldest send me unto Judah, unto the city of my fathers' sepulchres, that I may build it.

. . . .

13 And I went out by night by the gate of the valley, even before the dragon well, and to the dung port, and viewed the walls of Jerusalem, which were broken down, and the gates thereof were consumed with fire.

. . . .

16 And the rulers knew not whither I went, or what I did; neither had I as yet told it to the Jews, nor to the priests, nor to the nobles, nor to the rulers, nor to the rest that did the work.

17 Then said I unto them, Ye see the distress that we are in, how Jerusalem lieth waste, and the gates thereof are burned with fire: come, and let us build up the wall of Jerusalem, that we be no more a reproach.

18 Then I told them of the hand of my God which was good upon me; as also the king's words that he had spoken unto me. And they said, Let us rise up and build. So they strengthened their hands for this good work.

GOLDEN TEXT: They said, Let us rise up and build. So they strengthened their hands for this good work.—Nehemiah 2:18.

God Restores a Remnant
Unit 2: Renewal
(Lessons 6-9)

Lesson Aims

After participating in this lesson, each student will be able to:

1. Retell the account of Nehemiah's conviction and commission.

2. Suggest actions and attitudes of Nehemiah that could help anyone carry out God's work.

3. Select a work project or ministry in which he or she will participate as an individual or with the rest of the class.

Lesson Outline

INTRODUCTION
    A. The Pioneer Life
    B. Lesson Background
  I. REQUEST FOR NEWS (Nehemiah 1:1-4)
    A. Who, When, Where, What, and Why (vv. 1-3)
    B. Weeping and Wanting (v. 4)
 II. REQUESTS FOR HELP (Nehemiah 2:4, 5)
    A. To God (v. 4)
    B. To the King (v. 5)
      Plan and Act
III. REQUEST FOR ACTION (Nehemiah 2:13, 16-18)
    A. Secret Survey (vv. 13, 16)
    B. Public Recommendation (vv. 17, 18a)
    C. Right Response (v. 18b)
      Cooperate!
CONCLUSION
    A. Nehemiah's Way Repeated
    B. Our Own Needs
    C. Prayer
    D. Thought to Remember

Introduction

A. The Pioneer Life

My grandfather and his bride moved to Nebraska when the Homestead Act of 1862 made land available there. Neighbors they left behind said those two were too young to have good sense, and perhaps they were right. In their new homeland it seemed that everything had to be done at once. The apple trees they had brought from Ohio had to be planted immediately. Their chickens needed a chicken house to keep them safe from coyotes at night. Humans, too, must have shelter before winter. They cut building blocks from the tough prairie sod and made a tiny house with a fireplace in one of its walls. No less urgent was the task of breaking up that tough sod and planting a little field of wheat that fall. This would supply them with bread when the flour barrel they had brought was empty. Naturally the Indians of that area resented the invasion of their hunting ground. Each night the settlers went to sleep wondering if they would have their scalps in the morning.

Similar problems faced the Jews when they returned from captivity in Babylon. They went to their ancient homeland, but they were like pioneers in a new country. They had to build houses, plant grapevines and fruit trees, wheat and barley, gardens of vegetables. They had to establish flocks of sheep and herds of cattle. They had to face the bitter opposition of people living nearby. In spite of all these problems, they wanted to build a fitting temple for the Lord.

Through the month of June, our lessons have focused on those pioneers in their homeland, their problems, and their successes. This week's lesson brings us first to the Eastern country, the land of captivity; but then it brings us back to that ancient homeland where the Jews are pioneers, where their troubles are not yet over.

C. Lesson Background

When Cyrus conquered Babylon and set the captives free in 538 B.C., the majority chose to stay right where they were. That is not surprising, for most had been born there. They had their work and their friends there. They had "put down roots." Even so, the Jews who stayed behind in the East had kinsmen and friends among the pioneers who moved back west to Palestine. They liked to hear from them. But the distance was long and travel was slow. News was hard to come by.

I. Request for News
(Nehemiah 1:1-4)

Some of the Jews in the East became prominent there. Daniel is the most evident example. He was high in the government of Babylon (Daniel 2:48). Then when the Persians conquered Babylon, they promptly gave him a high place among them (6:1-3). Nehemiah had less power than Daniel had, but he was even closer to the king of Persia.

A. Who, When, Where, What, and Why (vv. 1-3)

1. The words of Nehemiah the son of Hachaliah. And it came to pass in the month Chisleu, in the twentieth year, as I was in Shushan the palace.

The account of Nehemiah's life on the stage of world history begins as autumn is turning to winter, for *the month Chisleu* corresponds to the last part of November and the first part of December on our calendars. The *twentieth year* of Artaxerxes, king of Persia (2:1) means that this is either 445 or 444 B.C. As a personal cupbearer (1:11), *Nehemiah* has close access to this king. Nehemiah is *in Shushan* (sometimes called Susa), which is the winter capital of Persia.

More than ninety years have now passed since the Jews were released from captivity in Babylon. Seventy years have passed since the completion of the temple in Jerusalem (see last week's lesson).

2. That Hanani, one of my brethren, came, he and certain men of Judah; and I asked them concerning the Jews that had escaped, which were left of the captivity, and concerning Jerusalem.

At some point, *Hanani*, one of Nehemiah's brothers, had chosen to make the nine-hundred-mile trip to Jerusalem and back again along with a few others. Nehemiah had chosen to stay in the East, and Hanani's return offers the opportunity to get some news *concerning Jerusalem*. Nehemiah is keenly interested in the progress of the Jewish pioneers there.

3. And they said unto me, The remnant that are left of the captivity there in the province are in great affliction and reproach: the wall of Jerusalem also is broken down, and the gates thereof are burned with fire.

The answer Nehemiah receives is discouraging. The Jews, now in their old homeland, are *in great affliction*, trouble, and distress. They are a *reproach* (or disgrace) in the eyes of the peoples around them. God had promised this as part of their punishment (Jeremiah 24:9; 29:18), but He had also promised a time when such scorn would disappear (Ezekiel 36:15). But when would that promise be fulfilled?

Nebuchadnezzar's troops had destroyed the city wall nearly a century and a half earlier. Now it remains as they had left it: disorderly heaps and scattered stones. Nothing is left of the wooden *gates* that had been *burned*.

B. Weeping and Wanting (v. 4)

4. And it came to pass, when I heard these words, that I sat down and wept, and mourned certain days, and fasted, and prayed before the God of heaven.

Nehemiah's concern for the land of his forefathers is profound. Notice that his weeping, fasting, and mourning doesn't last for hours, but for *days!* Some believe that Nehemiah is ashamed because he has stayed in the East to live in the king's palace instead of going to help restore the ancient homeland. The text gives no hint of this,

however. In fact, from his prayer for "mercy in the sight of this man," (i.e., the king, v. 11), it could be assumed that the decision for Nehemiah to stay had not been his own.

II. Requests for Help (Nehemiah 2:4, 5)

Nehemiah's time of mourning, praying, and planning lasts four months, from the month Chisleu to the month Nisan (1:1; 2:1). When the right time comes, he is ready to move decisively. His opportunity presents itself when the king notices his mournful countenance and asks the reason for it. Anyone in the presence of the king is expected to be happy to have that privilege. A man who displeases the king by looking sad might well lose his head! So Nehemiah was "very sore afraid" (2:2) at the king's question, but he explained bravely that he was mourning over the plight of Jerusalem (2:3).

A. To God (v. 4)

4. Then the king said unto me, For what dost thou make request? So I prayed to the God of heaven.

Since Nehemiah is mourning over the poor condition of Jerusalem (v. 3), *the king* supposes he has some idea for improving that condition. But Nehemiah first prays *to the God of Heaven* before responding. No doubt it is a very short prayer and a silent one, but God values sincerity more than many loud words. Perhaps Nehemiah repeats the prayer that he might have mercy from the king (1:11). Nehemiah relies on prayer often (see 4:4, 9; 5:19; 6:9, 14; 13:14).

B. To the King (v. 5)

5. And I said unto the king, If it please the king, and if thy servant have found favor in thy sight, that thou wouldest send me unto Judah, unto the city of my fathers' sepulchres, that I may build it.

Nehemiah wants to go to Jerusalem, to go as the king's emissary with the king's authority to rebuild the ruined *city*. When *the king* asks how long that will take, Nehemiah makes an estimate and the king is pleased to send him (v. 6). [See question #1, page 386.]

Then Nehemiah adds some details. He wants letters to the governors of provinces west of the Euphrates, ordering them to give him safe conduct (v. 7). He wants a letter ordering "the keeper of the king's forest" to supply the timber that will be needed (v. 8). Nehemiah obviously has thought all this out in advance, and in addition requests a military escort to ensure a safe journey (v. 9). The king grants all these requests and appoints Nehemiah as governor (5:14; 12:26). [See question #2, page 386.]

Thus when Nehemiah comes to Jerusalem (v. 11), he comes as the highest official of the province. Clay seal impressions reveal that since the times of governors Sheshbazzar (538 B.C., Ezra 1:8; 5:14) and Zerubbabel (515 B.C., Haggai 1:1, 14), there have been three other governors before him. But Nehemiah does not behave as recent governors have behaved (see Nehemiah 5:14-18).

PLAN AND ACT

While heading Montgomery Ward & Co. Sewell Avery was responsible for leading Ward's to amass $607 million in cash. His plan? Avoid risk. Get all you can, can all you get, sit on the can!

Avery's cash accumulation plan was Montgomery Ward's most monumental mistake. This huge cash reserve earned the retailer a dubious Wall Street nickname: "the bank with the department store front." From 1941 to 1957, during his reign as CEO, Ward's failed to open a single new store.

Why didn't Avery join in the nation's postwar expansion by following Americans to the suburbs? He was afraid of uncertain circumstances. He believed that a depression had followed every major war since the time of Napoleon.

On the other side of Chicago, Ward's rival, Sears, Roebuck & Co., had a different idea. Sears took a risk and in 1946 began a costly expansion into suburbia. Sears' bold plan doubled its revenues. Sears never looked back and Ward's never caught up. In fact, in 1997 it went bankrupt.

Hearing of the situation in Jerusalem, Nehemiah had good reason to be cautious and to sit tight. The times were uncertain. But he was bold. He was willing to act in spite of uncertainty. He prayed long and hard, and determined a course

of action, and then he went to the king. And the king granted him his desire, as Nehemiah himself put it, "according to the good hand of my God upon me" (Nehemiah 2:8). Make God your planning partner and count on Him for success.

—J. A. M.

III. Request for Action (Nehemiah 2:13, 16-18)

The trip to Jerusalem takes several weeks, giving Nehemiah time to think and pray about a plan of action. He does not announce his intention as soon as he arrives in Jerusalem. He first wants to examine the ruined city and estimate how big the job of rebuilding will be.

After arriving, Nehemiah takes three days to rest and otherwise "settle in" after the long journey (v. 11). He makes his investigation by night with a few trusted men, perhaps those who had come with him from Persia (v. 12). Nehemiah probably chooses a bright, moonlit night for his inspection tour.

A. Secret Survey (vv. 13, 16)

13. And I went out by night by the gate of the valley, even before the dragon well, and to the dung port, and viewed the walls of Jerusalem, which were broken down, and the gates thereof were consumed with fire.

This verse and the two that follow (not in our text for today) trace the course of Nehemiah's inspection trip. We cannot identify all the places that are named, but the direction of the trip is clear. Nehemiah and his few men go outside the city near the southwest corner. Outside the city they move eastward to the southeast corner, where they turn north in the Kidron Valley. The men then move on to the northeast corner of the city where they turn back (v. 15). Nehemiah does not make a complete circuit of the walls—he has seen enough!

What he sees is not encouraging. The former walls are *broken down*. Nothing is left of the wooden *gates* that had been *consumed with fire*. More than two miles of rebuilt wall probably will be needed. This new wall will have to be high enough so it cannot be scaled easily. It will have to be strong enough to resist battering rams. The scattered stones of the former wall will provide at least part of the building material. But more stones, freshly quarried and unbroken probably will be needed as well. And there is no machinery to move or lift such stones. They will have to be moved and raised by muscles and rope. It looks like a hard job. [See question #3, page 386.]

16. And the rulers knew not whither I went, or what I did; neither had I as yet told it to the

Jews, nor to the priests, nor to the nobles, nor to the rulers, nor to the rest that did the work.

The moonlight survey is still secret. No one knows about it except Nehemiah and the few trusted men who have made the inspection with him. Perhaps Nehemiah wants a chance to contemplate without a lot of "Negative Nellies" constantly interrupting his train of thought!

B. Public Recommendation (vv. 17, 18a)

17, 18a. Then said I unto them, Ye see the distress that we are in, how Jerusalem lieth waste, and the gates thereof are burned with fire: come, and let us build up the wall of Jerusalem, that we be no more a reproach. Then I told them of the hand of my God which was good upon me; as also the king's words that he had spoken unto me.

Now is the time to end the secrecy. When Nehemiah speaks *unto them,* he is addressing all the classes or groups named in verse 16, perhaps in a mass meeting.

His presentation is in three parts. First is the need: *Ye see the distress that we are in.* Until the rubble of the old wall is cleared away and a new wall is built, Jerusalem cannot have the dignity, respect, and protection of an important city. Second is the remedy: *Come, and let us build up the wall of Jerusalem.* The Jews will not have a wall unless they go to work and build it. Third is the result of rebuilding: *that we be no more a reproach.* This will fulfill the promise of Ezekiel 36:15 and other prophecies.

Nehemiah cites two things to encourage the building: God's providential care and the favor of King Artaxerxes. If God and the king both want the people of Judah to build that wall, it would be dangerous not to build it, and quickly! [See question #4, page 386.]

C. Right Response (v. 18b)

18b. And they said, Let us rise up and build. So they strengthened their hands for this good work.

The decision apparently is reached without a dissenting voice. Indeed, how could anyone of Judah dissent? God and the king are in favor of that wall. Building stone is already at the site, so the work can be started immediately. Timber is freely available in the king's forest. Nothing else is needed except a lot of "elbow grease" by the people who will benefit from the wall. With thinking like this, the people *strengthened their hands for this good work.* [See question #5, page 386.]

COOPERATE!

The Kentucky state flag captures a Biblical principle when it shows two men clasping hands

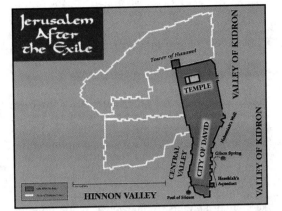

Visual for lesson 6. *Use this map to trace Nehemiah's inspection tour of the walls of the city of Jerusalem (vv. 13-16).*

ringed by this motto: "United we stand. Divided we fall." Nehemiah cultivated cooperation to ensure success.

Cooperation lightens the load and increases effectiveness. Nehemiah 2:18 says the people of Jerusalem said, "Let us rise up and build," and that "they strengthened their hands for this good work." Nehemiah 3 lists seventy-nine leaders and contributors to the enterprise of rebuilding the walls and gates of Jerusalem. Seventy-nine are mentioned, but thousands shared in the work.

"Many hands make light work," the old saying goes. Rebuilding this city was an impossible task for Nehemiah alone. But, he wasn't alone. Nearly everyone cooperated. And because of the participation of all, the monumental task was completed in an amazing time. In fifty-two days the wall was completely rebuilt.

I cannot do the work of the church alone nor can you. No one person can meet every need and fill every role. Rather, the body grows as each part does its work.

Here is God's challenge: Cooperate! Let's each determine to do his or her part. When any one of us fails to cooperate and contribute, the load becomes a little heavier for all the rest. When we work together, everything is lighter.

Cooperation is essential for success in God's work. Does a harmonious, cooperative spirit always carry the day in your congregation? United we stand.   —J. A. M.

Conclusion

Nehemiah was a capable investigator, planner, politician, and man of prayer. He presented his plan to the people, along with encouragement to think it would work. The people accepted the plan enthusiastically, and with God's blessing it worked.

A. Nehemiah's Way Repeated

In Riverside, the church outgrew its building. The young married couples wanted a class of their own, but they had to meet in the auditorium along with the older adults. Both the high school and the college-career classes were put in that huge class with all the adults—and they were not happy about it. At the other end of the age scale, the keepers of the nursery were not happy to have toddlers in the nursery.

The elders of the congregation knew something had to be done. But like Nehemiah, they kept such thoughts to themselves while they investigated and planned. From those working with the children, the elders learned how much room was needed to accommodate the present attendance plus a 50 percent increase. With that information they sought out the architect who had designed their existing building. He now was retired, but he readily agreed to plan a new wing. One of the church members was a reputable builder. He looked at the architect's plan and estimated the cost. The elders consulted their banker. Finally, they examined the church's income. It would have to increase 8 percent to pay for the thirty-year loan on that addition.

Then it was time to end the secrecy. Everyone's help was needed. The elders summoned the entire congregation to a Sunday afternoon meeting to talk about enlarging the church house. All the members could see the need, and most of them came to the meeting.

The elders showed the architect's drawing of the proposed addition. They said it would accommodate a growing church and Sunday school for many years. They said each elder already had agreed to increase his contribution by 10 percent. They asked each member to follow the elders.

They did not ask for commitment that moment. They asked each member to think, pray, and remember that this was for God's church. Then they were to make their commitments to the future of the church. Nearly every member agreed to the 10 percent increase. Later, when the church gathered in the enlarged house for the first time, the feeling was pure joy. Not one grumble was heard.

B. Our Own Needs

What is the outstanding need in your church right now? A larger worship area? More parking? More people in the room you already have? More teachers in the Sunday school? More dedication and hard work among the people? A greater emphasis on prayer and spirituality? Exactly what is the most important "wall" in your church that needs to be built?

And how will you approach the need that is most pressing? Ask everyone for suggestions? Follow the elders? Appoint a committee? And where does prayer fit into the overall approach?

If it's facility improvements that your church needs, how will you pay for them? Hold bake sales, carnivals, and other such fund-raisers? Ask local businesses for donations? (Nehemiah, after all, solicited a pagan king!) Go door-to-door requesting contributions? Or will you and the people in your church sacrificially alter your spending and dig into personal bank accounts? Will there be a trust in God to help today as He helped the ancient Israelites to rebuild first their temple and then their wall? (See 3 John 7.)

C. Prayer

Thank You, Father, for entrusting some of Your work to us. We want to see Your church grow in size and goodness and influence, and we know its progress depends on us as well as You. For that progress we promise a worthy portion of our time, energy, and money. Grant us wisdom for our planning and strength for our doing. We pray in Jesus' name, amen.

D. Thought to Remember

With God's help we can do what He wants us to do.

How to Say It

ARTAXERXES. Are-tuh-*zerk*-seez.
BABYLON. *Bab*-uh-lun.
CHISLEU. *Kiss*-loo.
CYRUS. *Sye*-russ.
EUPHRATES. You-*fray*-teez.
EZEKIEL. Ee-*zeek*-ee-ul or Ee-*zeek*-yul.
EZRA. *Ez*-ruh.
HAGGAI. *Hag*-eye or *Hag*-ay-eye.
HACHALIAH. Hack-uh-*lye*-uh.
HANANI. Huh-*nay*-nye.
KIDRON. *Kid*-ron.
NEBUCHADNEZZAR. *Neb*-yuh-kud-*nez*-er (strong accent on *nez*).
NEHEMIAH. *Nee*-huh-*my*-uh (strong accent on *my*).
NISAN. *Nye*-san.
PERSIA. *Per*-zhuh.
SEPULCHRES. *sep*-ul-kurz.
SHESHBAZZAR. Shesh-*baz*-ar.
SHUSHAN. *Shoo*-shan.
SUSA. *Soo*-suh.
ZERUBBABEL. Zeh-*rub*-uh-bul.

Learning by Doing

This page contains an alternative lesson plan emphasizing learning activities.
Classes desiring such student involvement will find these suggestions helpful.

Learning Goals

After this lesson each student will be able to:

1. Retell the account of Nehemiah's conviction and commission.

2. Suggest actions and attitudes of Nehemiah that could help anyone carry out God's work.

3. Select a work project or ministry in which he or she will participate as an individual or with the rest of the class.

Into the Lesson

ADVANCE PREPARATION: Investigate potential short-term projects and continuing ministries available in your church with ideas for both groups and individuals. Include projects for both active people and quieter people. Church staff may already have such a list. If not, such a handout could be a short-term project for someone in the class. Get enough details so that people will recognize tasks they want to investigate. Or ask someone who has done such a short-term project to prepare a testimony or report. These activities will be explained more in the "Into Life" section.

ADVANCE PREPARATION: Before class ask two actors from the class or congregation to prepare a brief skit in which they are discouraged because no one will do anything.

Let the actors present their skit. Then say, "Many of us have felt that way, haven't we? Today we are studying a man who heard about a sad situation in Jerusalem. It grieved him, but he took action that solved the problem."

Into the Word

Read chapters 1 and 2 as students follow along. Ask students for their impressions of Nehemiah, and write the descriptors on the board. Ask small groups to outline what happens from the time Nehemiah hears the need through the people's response. If your students are not comfortable with outlining the passage, give them the following outline of main points and let them add subpoints or a summary for each main point. (Or you may scramble the points and have students put them in chronological order.)

A. Nehemiah learns of the condition of Jerusalem.

B. Nehemiah mourns, fasts, and prays for four months.

C. Nehemiah and the king talk.

D. Nehemiah returns to Jerusalem.

E. Nehemiah surveys the city at night.

F. Nehemiah presents the challenge to the Jews, priests, nobles, and rulers.

G. The people accept the challenge.

"Do you have other words to describe Nehemiah, now that we have studied him more?" Make additions to the list. "What else did you learn about Nehemiah and how he operated?" Add those insights. *(Learners will discover Nehemiah was prayerful, patient, persistent, a man of action with the right priority, realistic, sharp, a planner, willing to serve and lead, able to bring fresh perspective, aware of God's hand on him, an effective presenter, and perceived as a leader.)*

Add any concepts from your own study that the class missed.

Into Life

To make the lesson more personal say, "We have good observations about Nehemiah. Let's draw from our list character qualities and principles that apply to all who want to serve God."

Guide students in stating such principles. See the commentary and the list in "Into the Word."

Continue the discussion by saying, "How could developing such character traits or following such principles help prevent some of the frustrations in congregational life when it seems no one is willing to work?"

Direct the application to meet your students' needs. If you have leaders, talk about using these principles when they are leading. If you have potential leaders, challenge them to consider taking a leadership position and using the principles. Encourage people to consider how they can follow a leader in a short-term project or join an existing ministry (such as teaching a Sunday school class).

To encourage your students to get involved in serving, ask someone to give a testimony about the joys of serving. Distribute the handout(s) you obtained from a church staff member or copies of the list of projects you developed.

If in lesson 5 your class planned an event, apply the principles to that planning and work.

Conclude the session by asking students to mark a short-term project or a continuing ministry that interests them. Suggest that they contact project leaders to get more information and then pray during the week about how they could serve God in such a short-term project.

Let's Talk It Over

The questions on this page are designed to promote discussion of the lesson by the class and to encourage application of the lesson Scriptures. The answers provided are only discussion starters. Let your class talk it over from there.

1. What are some causes for which you would risk personal position, fortune, and comfort? What is the value of thinking about such situations ahead of time?

Most probably have never thought seriously about the situations in which they would risk security, welfare, and reputation. As a culture, we revel in comfort—and personal comfort is the deadly enemy of risk-taking. But if there's one "category" of things that should cause us to take risks, it is matters of faith and obedience to God (e.g., Acts 4:19). God always honors risk-taking that is in accordance with His will. But unless we think through such situations in advance, when "the pressure is off," we might not make the right decision when "the pressure is on." Ask the students to try to be specific about the situations that may call forth that kind of sacrifice.

2. The response of the king to Nehemiah's request must have encouraged Nehemiah that he was doing the right thing. Give examples of times when God has confirmed plans by provision of resources or by opening doors of opportunity.

God called my father into ministry when he was in his thirties, married, with three children. Dad has some wonderful stories of how God provided during very difficult times. I used to marvel at those modern-day examples of God's providence, but now I have my own stories. I can tell how God provided for my wife and me during my own years of seminary so that we did not have to take out any educational loans. We were able to become homeowners at an early age when an elder in our church offered to lend us the down payment at passbook rates.

Tell of your own experiences, and ask the students to tell of specific occasions when God's providence confirmed their faith. Often, the providence may not have been apparent until later. The experience may have included trial and required patience—but in the end, it was clear that God had seen them through!

3. Why was it important to Nehemiah to examine the condition of the city wall personally before announcing his plans publicly? In what circumstances should we follow his example?

Nehemiah could not rebuild the city walls by himself. He would have to motivate the people to follow his leadership, and he would have to organize them to complete the task. In order to win their confidence, he needed more than courage and enthusiasm. He needed a thorough understanding of the conditions at hand. The citizens of Jerusalem certainly were familiar with the piles of stone that were once the city walls. Nehemiah would not be a credible leader for the construction project if he did not have a realistic personal assessment of what was required.

4. Nehemiah had impressive credentials for leadership. What qualities inspire you to follow a leader at work? in government? at church?

Leadership can be assigned and authority conferred, as in the commission given Nehemiah by the king of Persia. The most effective leaders, however, lead by reputation (cf. Galatians 2:2). People endorse and follow such leaders regardless of their actual position or status. People follow leaders they can trust, and trust is built by demonstrated competency and character. If you think about the leaders you enjoy working with (following), you probably can give illustrations of their proven competency and their character. How sad it is to see people following leaders of low character simply because the people agree with those leaders' viewpoints on various issues!

5. Nehemiah's proposal met with strong agreement from the people. What are the projects or causes in your church or community that could be accomplished given a passionate and capable leader? What could be your role in pursuing one of those projects or causes?

The broken down walls of Jerusalem were obvious to everyone who lived or visited there. It should have been easy to get agreement that something should be done. Even without the king's timber, there was plenty of material (stones) lying about. But until Nehemiah came, no one had been willing to take responsibility. Perhaps your church needs an overhaul of its Sunday school program. Perhaps your church needs leadership in casting a vision for world missions. Maybe your church facility needs updating. Your local school may need more parent-volunteer involvement. Are you the one to give leadership to such projects? If you do not lead, who will? Some causes just need a good leader.

Nehemiah Completes the Wall

DEVOTIONAL READING: Isaiah 49:13-18.

BACKGROUND SCRIPTURE: Nehemiah 6.

PRINTED TEXT: Nehemiah 6:1-9, 15, 16.

Nehemiah 6:1-9, 15, 16

1 Now it came to pass, when Sanballat, and Tobiah, and Geshem the Arabian, and the rest of our enemies, heard that I had builded the wall, and that there was no breach left therein; (though at that time I had not set up the doors upon the gates;)

2 That Sanballat and Geshem sent unto me, saying, Come, let us meet together in some one of the villages in the plain of Ono. But they thought to do me mischief.

3 And I sent messengers unto them, saying, I am doing a great work, so that I cannot come down: why should the work cease, whilst I leave it, and come down to you?

4 Yet they sent unto me four times after this sort; and I answered them after the same manner.

5 Then sent Sanballat his servant unto me in like manner the fifth time with an open letter in his hand;

6 Wherein was written, It is reported among the heathen, and Gashmu saith it, that thou and the Jews think to rebel: for which cause thou buildest the wall, that thou mayest be their king, according to these words.

7 And thou hast also appointed prophets to preach of thee at Jerusalem, saying, There is a king in Judah: and now shall it be reported to the king according to these words. Come now therefore, and let us take counsel together.

8 Then I sent unto him, saying, There are no such things done as thou sayest, but thou feignest them out of thine own heart.

9 For they all made us afraid, saying, Their hands shall be weakened from the work, that it be not done. Now therefore, O God, strengthen my hands.

. . . .

15 So the wall was finished in the twenty and fifth day of the month Elul, in fifty and two days.

16 And it came to pass, that when all our enemies heard thereof, and all the heathen that were about us saw these things, they were much cast down in their own eyes: for they perceived that this work was wrought of our God.

GOLDEN TEXT: When all our enemies heard thereof, and all the heathen that were about us saw these things, they were much cast down in their own eyes: for they perceived that this work was wrought of our God.
—Nehemiah 6:16.

God Restores a Remnant
Unit 2: Renewal
(Lessons 6-9)

Lesson Aims

After this lesson each student will be able to:
1. List the types of opposition Nehemiah and the people of Judah met while completing the wall.
2. Describe appropriate, godly ways to handle opposition.
3. Publicly commit to persevere dutifully in one area of his/her spiritual life in which he/she is experiencing opposition.

Lesson Outline

INTRODUCTION
  A. Real Hostility
  B. Lesson Background
I. CRAFTY OPPOSITION (Nehemiah 6:1-4)
  A. Call Issued (vv. 1, 2)
  B. Call Rejected (v. 3)
  C. Cycle Repeated (v. 4)
    Priorities
II. OVERT THREAT (Nehemiah 6:5-9)
  A. False Gossip (vv. 5-7)
  B. Nehemiah's Answer (vv. 8, 9)
III. ULTIMATE TRIUMPH (Nehemiah 6:15, 16)
  A. Wall Completed (v. 15)
    Don't Stop!
  B. Enemies Dismayed (v. 16)
CONCLUSION
  A. Fear and Leadership
  B. Fear and Followership
  C. Prayer
  D. Thought to Remember

Introduction

My great-uncle was an itinerant preacher on the American frontier. One day he and a friend were walking across the prairie when they spotted an Indian war party on the distant horizon. Cautiously the two hid in a buffalo wallow and waited for the danger to pass. But when they peeked out an hour later, the war party had not moved an inch. It was not a war party at all—just a clump of natural growth. Ashamed but relieved, the travelers went on their way.

A. Real Hostility

Hostile neighbors were real when the Jews went back to their homeland after their captivity in Babylon. More than a century before that captivity began, conquering Assyrians had deported most of the people of north Israel and had brought in immigrants to take their place (2 Kings 17:1-6, 24). Descendants of those immigrants quickly became enemies of the Jews who came back from captivity (Ezra 4:1-5). Those enemies were scornful when Nehemiah came and started to build a city wall (Nehemiah 2:19, 20). But the Jews organized their workers, and the wall began to rise (Nehemiah 3). The enemies then planned to stop the building by force (4:7, 8). But the Jews prayed and armed themselves for defense, and the enemies gave up that plan (4:9, 13-15).

B. Lesson Background

The Jews went on with their work, but they did it without letting down their guard (Nehemiah 4:16-23). Since they were so well prepared to fight, and since they were now protected by a wall built to half its intended height (4:6), the enemies were afraid to launch a violent attack. Instead, they resorted to the strategy described in our text.

I. Crafty Opposition
(Nehemiah 6:1-4)

Communication was so open and constant between the Jews and their enemies that neither could make a secret move. When the enemies were gathering their forces for a violent attack, they hoped it would be a surprise; but it was reported to the Jews (Nehemiah 4:11, 12). When the Jews then prepared to repel such an attack, that resolve was promptly told to the enemies (4:13-15). Then the enemy leaders thought it was time for a person-to-person talk with Nehemiah.

A. Call Issued (vv. 1, 2)

1. Now it came to pass, when Sanballat, and Tobiah, and Geshem the Arabian, and the rest of our enemies, heard that I had builded the wall, and that there was no breach left therein; (though at that time I had not set up the doors upon the gates;).

These three leading enemies illustrate the fact that people of different nations now live in the area that once had belonged to Israel. Nehemiah 2:19 reveals a bit more information about the nationalities of these three. There, *Sanballat* is called "the Horonite." He is probably a native of Beth Horon, in the land from which northern tribes of Israel had been evicted (see Joshua 10:10; 16:3, 5). On the other hand, some students think that he comes from the city of Horonaim in Moab, a country east of the Dead Sea (see Jeremiah 48:34). *Tobiah* is from Ammon, east of the Jordan River. He is called "the servant" in Nehemiah 2:10, which some take to mean a "servant" of Sanballat. If so, it seems he had become a friend and coworker as well as a slave. Many students think that Tobiah, like Nehemiah, is a "servant" of the king of Persia; perhaps he has been appointed to an official position in that western land. (The term *servant* in 2:10 may also be translated "official.") *Geshem the Arabian* is the third enemy. He comes from the area that is still called Arabia today.

These three *and the rest of* Nehemiah's *enemies* are chagrined to learn that the wall now extends all the way around Jerusalem. It is only half as high as it eventually will be (4:6), but there is *no breach* through which armed forces might enter. The gateways are still open, but the enemies dare not attack through them when they know armed men are on guard there. So the enemies turn to diplomacy rather than to battle.

2. That Sanballat and Geshem sent unto me, saying, Come, let us meet together in some one of the villages in the plain of Ono. But they thought to do me mischief.

Ono lies on the coastal plain near Joppa, nearly thirty miles from Jerusalem (cf. 1 Chronicles 8:12). Some Jews returning from exile had settled there (Nehemiah 7:37; 11:35). The enemies pick this place to lure Nehemiah far away from the protection of his people who are working with their weapons at hand (4:16-18). No doubt the enemies are saying that they desire peaceful coexistence.

But Nehemiah records with full confidence that *they thought to do me mischief.* Considering the open communication between the enemy groups, we wonder if Nehemiah has learned this from some informant who has heard the plotting of the enemies. We know for certain that Nehemiah has enemy spies in his own midst (see 6:10-13, 17, 18), so the reverse probably is true as well. [See question #1, page 394.]

We wonder what kind of mischief the enemies have in mind. Do they plan to assassinate Nehemiah? Will they hold him hostage to gain an advantage in negotiation with his people? Or are they thinking merely of slowing the work in Jerusalem by depriving the workers of their best leader? The Bible provides no answers to these questions.

B. Call Rejected (v. 3)

3. And I sent messengers unto them, saying, I am doing a great work, so that I cannot come down: why should the work cease, whilst I leave it, and come down to you?

Understanding the insincerity of the request, Nehemiah's answer is a flat refusal—he is just too busy. Accepting the invitation would be a

waste of time at least, and a death trap at most. The *work* he is doing is so important that he cannot *leave it* at that time. Nehemiah does not even bother to suggest an alternative, "safer" location for the meeting. [See question #2, page 394.]

C. Cycle Repeated (v. 4)

4. Yet they sent unto me four times after this sort; and I answered them after the same manner.

Nehemiah's reply does not discourage his enemies from repeating their "invitation." Perhaps they argue reasonably that it is important to avoid any hostility between their groups, that they want to be friendly neighbors, that it is better to talk than to fight. Whatever argument they use, Nehemiah is not fooled. He simply cannot take time for such a pointless conference.

PRIORITIES

Chris Spielman played middle linebacker for the Ohio State University and then in the NFL for the Buffalo Bills. He was tough, strong, smart, passionate, committed, and loyal. He played the entire 1995 season with a torn pectoral muscle sustained in the season opener. He was a leader.

But life took a different turn during the 1998 season. He didn't play at all—and that by choice. His priorities had shifted. Instead he cooked, took care of his kids, and cared for his wife. Stephanie Spielman was battling breast cancer. During her fight, Chris was at her side. He lived out his priorities—"family before job."

A reporter from the *Rochester Democrat and Chronicle* asked if he'd return to the Bills late in

---

How to Say It

AMMON. *Am*-mun.
ASSYRIANS. Uh-*sear*-e-unz.
BABYLON. *Bab*-uh-lun.
BETH HORON. Bayth (or bait) *Hoe*-ron.
ELUL. *Ee*-lull or *Eh*-lool.
GASHMU. *Gash*-moo.
GESHEM. *Gee*-shem.
HORONAIM. *Hor*-oh-*nay*-im (strong accent on *nay*).
HORONITE. *Hor*-oh-night.
JOPPA. *Jop*-uh.
MOAB. *Mo*-ab.
NEHEMIAH. *Nee*-huh-*my*-uh (strong accent on *my*).
ONO. *Oh*-no.
PERSIA. *Per*-zhuh.
SANBALLAT. San-*bal*-ut.
SHUSHAN. *Shoo*-shan.
TOBIAH. Toe-*bye*-uh.

the season. Spielman said, "I'd play in a heart-beat, but what kind of man would I be if I backed out on my word to her? I wouldn't be a man at all."

Football fans saw Spielman as a man because of his aggressive toughness. But what really makes him a man? His priorities are in order. Personal sacrifice, unending commitment, and loyalty to his wife define him.

Nehemiah left behind the luxury, influence and access to power that were his in Persia. In Jerusalem he faced challenge and uncertainty. But when tempted away from his work on the wall he replied, "Why should the work cease, whilst I leave it, and come down to you?" Nehemiah knew what was important and he invested his energy there.

Are your priorities in order? What are you doing with your life that will last forever?

—J. A. M.

II. Overt Threat
(Nehemiah 6:5-9)

Four times the enemies have sent an apparently friendly invitation for a chat. Just as often Nehemiah has declined it. Still, Sanballat persists in inviting Nehemiah to join him for a talk. But the fifth invitation carries a clear threat of serious trouble if the request is declined again.

A. False Gossip (vv. 5-7)

5. Then sent Sanballat his servant unto me in like manner the fifth time with an open letter in his hand.

To emphasize the serious nature of his request, *Sanballat* puts this communication in writing. The fact that the *letter* is *open* means that it is unsealed. This procedure is unusual and may mean that Sanballat wants all the people to know of the letter's contents.

6. Wherein was written, It is reported among the heathen, and Gashmu saith it, that thou and the Jews think to rebel: for which cause thou buildest the wall, that thou mayest be their king, according to these words.

Sanballat relates to Nehemiah what (supposedly) is being said *among the* peoples of the surrounding nations. Sanballat tries to improve the credibility of the rumor by attaching to it the name of a prominent pagan leader. This person, *Gashmu*, is probably the same as "Geshem"—one of the leaders of the Jews' enemies (Nehemiah 2:19; 6:1, 2).

With mock concern, Sanballat passes along the anxiety that others supposedly have regarding Nehemiah's motives: fortifying *the wall* can mean only defense against the Persian troops

that will soon come to put down the rebellion. A rumor of sedition could undo all of Nehemiah's work on the wall if such innuendo were credible and found its way back to the Persian king. We know already, of course, that Nehemiah is a loyal servant of that king. The king has authorized him to build the wall he is constructing.

7. And thou hast also appointed prophets to preach of thee at Jerusalem, saying, There is a king in Judah: and now shall it be reported to the king according to these words. Come now therefore, and let us take counsel together.

This verse falls naturally into three parts. First comes another accusation. The use of false prophets is nothing new in Jewish history. (See Jeremiah 14:14; 50:36.) Usually such "prophets" tell the leader what he wants to hear (e.g., 1 Kings 22:6). In this case, Nehemiah allegedly has *appointed prophets* to announce *at Jerusalem* that he is no longer a mere governor of a Persian province, but is now *king* of independent *Judah*. [See question #3, page 394.]

Then comes the threat to report *these words* to *the king*. If Nehemiah does not agree to confer with Sanballat and his cronies, these enemies will tell the king that Nehemiah is proclaiming Judah's independence and is preparing to support that proclamation with a well-fortified city. If the king believes this report, overwhelming numbers of Persian troops soon will arrive to dispose of Nehemiah. So why go on building a wall that will just be battered down again anyway?

The last sentence of the verse is a repetition of the invitation already given and refused four times. But now that invitation is backed by the threat. This is nothing short of blackmail!

B. Nehemiah's Answer (vv. 8, 9)

8. Then I sent unto him, saying, There are no such things done as thou sayest, but thou feignest them out of thine own heart.

Sometimes gossip contains truth, but it is spread maliciously nonetheless. Sanballat's report, however, is a pure fabrication, and Nehemiah knows it. He is not frightened enough to give in to the demand for a conference. The king has been his supporter. Nehemiah is doing exactly what the king has told him to do. Very likely, Nehemiah does not think the king now will accept such accusations at face value without an investigation. And any royal investigation will undoubtedly vindicate Nehemiah.

A previous king had promised death to anyone attempting to stop the rebuilding of the temple (cf. Ezra 6:11). The current king may not take kindly, either, to those who would spread false rumors to stop the rebuilding of the walls. Nehemiah, in effect, calls Sanballat's bluff.

9. For they all made us afraid, saying, Their hands shall be weakened from the work, that it be not done. Now therefore, O God, strengthen my hands.

Nehemiah is not frightened enough to give in (v. 8). Even so, it is sobering to think of the consequences that will follow if the king believes the lies the enemies said they would tell. But Nehemiah knows the solution to fear: he must trust in *God.* So Nehemiah prays for strength and keeps on working without a pause.

III. Ultimate Triumph (Nehemiah 6:15, 16)

Try to imagine the pressure that was on those builders of the wall. What would be the result if killers really would sneak in and murder Nehemiah as he slept (6:10)? What would happen if liars really could convince the Persian king that his trusted cupbearer was now a traitor, leading a rebellion? What would happen if the enemies plucked up enough courage to swarm into Jerusalem through the open gateways with swinging swords to slaughter the defenders? None of these things happened, and the people of Israel put their fears behind them and pressed on to a triumphant finish.

A. Wall Completed (v. 15)

15. So the wall was finished in the twenty and fifth day of the month Elul, in fifty and two days.

Now imagine the rejoicing among the people who had been toiling overtime for fifty-two days! Continuously haunted by the fear of what terrible thing the enemies might do, the job finally is done. And now the wise timing for the work is seen. It began in the middle of July. The busy, busy time of barley and wheat harvest is over. Some of the grain had been milled into flour; it is ready to be baked into bread for the hungry builders. And the wall is finished early in September, leaving time—though only a short time—for the ingathering of grapes and other fruit before the autumn festival, the Feast of Tabernacles. This is a harvest festival as well as a memorial of Israel's time in the wilderness as the nation was moving from Egypt to the promised land. [See question #4, page 394.]

DON'T STOP!

Art Chen was a fighter pilot for the Chinese in the 1930s, when Japan was determined to conquer China. Duane Schultz records his story in his book *The Maverick War.*

On one occasion Chen "took on three Japanese fighters and shot one down before running out of ammunition. He deliberately rammed the second Japanese plane and then bailed out. He landed close to the wreckage of his plane and salvaged one of the machine guns, which he carried eight miles back to the airfield. Presenting the heavy gun to his commanding officer, Chen allegedly asked, 'Sir, can I have another airplane for my machine gun?'"

What spirit! What dedication to the cause! Art Chen is remembered because he refused to quit.

Nehemiah 4:6-23 reports a time of discouragement and intense opposition when the wall "was joined together to half its height." The most difficult part of any project seems to be "halfway." The work is hard, the hours long, the obstacles are real and the outcome is uncertain. But victory comes to those who refuse to quit. The Jerusalem wall was completed because the workers didn't quit.

Are you halfway through some project? Sometimes success is achieved simply because of dogged determination, an unwillingness to quit. Someone said, "By determination the snail reached the ark!"

Are you ready to quit? To give up? To surrender? To resign? It's too soon to quit! —J. A. M.

B. Enemies Dismayed (v. 16)

16. And it came to pass, that when all our enemies heard thereof, and all the heathen that were about us saw these things, they were much cast down in their own eyes: for they perceived that this work was wrought of our God.

The *enemies* of the Jewish people feel disappointed, defeated, humiliated, and disgraced. The impudent immigrants from the East seem to be beyond the control of the earlier inhabitants. Short of all-out military action, there is nothing

In Spite of Enemies

"This Work Was Wrought of Our God." —from Nehemiah 6:16

Visual for lesson 7

Display this poster and discuss some of the victories God has "wrought" in your church.

more those earlier inhabitants can do. Military action might be unsuccessful, for those Jews who have worked so hard probably would fight hard, too. And any attempt to exterminate the newcomers would likely be punished by the king of Persia.

Interestingly, the enemies give *God* credit for their defeat. They know the people of Israel have not been victorious by their own effort alone. Perhaps that was the main reason *they were much cast down in their own eyes:* they realize they have been fighting against God all along! [See question #5, page 394.]

Conclusion

Jerusalem would have had no wall in that century if Nehemiah had chosen to live on in luxury in the king's palace in far-off Shushan. But Nehemiah knew what needed to be done, he knew how to put a plan in motion, and he knew how to pray. He secured the support of the king in Shushan, he secured the support of the people in Jerusalem, but most importantly he secured the support of God!

A. Fear and Leadership

In English-speaking countries where this book is read, people probably do not fear armed intervention to stop the work of Christianity. But our hands may be weakened by another kind of fear. When someone proposes a great, challenging work, voices may cry out, "No, no! We can't do it! It's too big!" We shall not accomplish anything very great for God unless we ignore such voices and press on with courage and determination.

But courage needs to be balanced with common sense. Sometimes the fear-mongers are right. Mistaking folly for faith, eager Christians

Home Daily Bible Readings

Monday, July 7—The People Had Minds to Work (Nehemiah 4:1-6)
Tuesday, July 8—Enemies Plot Against the Workers (Nehemiah 4:7-14)
Wednesday, July 9—A Guard Is Set (Nehemiah 4:15-23)
Thursday, July 10—O God, Strengthen My Hands (Nehemiah 6:1-9)
Friday, July 11—The Wall Is Finished (Nehemiah 6:10-19)
Saturday, July 12—Gates and People Are Purified (Nehemiah 12:27-31b)
Sunday, July 13—Jerusalem's Joy Is Heard Far Away (Nehemiah 12:43-47)

may plunge into an enterprise far beyond their resources or with very little time spent in prayer. The result may be an unfinished church building standing through the years as a silent rebuke of their folly (cf. Luke 14:28-30). Wiser Christians may build a basement with a roof and simply meet in it until God grants them the resources to finish the interior. Such Christians have the faith to say, "If this is what God wants us to do, He will give us the ability to do it." No less true is the converse: "If God does not enable able us to undertake this project, then this is not what God wants us to do." When we prayerfully and fearlessly trim each dream to fit God's providence, we end up doing everything He wants us to do, and nothing that He doesn't.

B. Fear and Followership

Imagine what would have happened if the people of Jerusalem had answered Nehemiah's appeal by saying, "Forget it! We don't need a wall as much as we need to get along with our neighbors. If we build that wall, they will just see us as an even greater threat."

There are many reasons why people do not follow leaders who are worthy of being followed, but *fear* is one of the most damaging. Fear accepts "what is" because "what might be" *could* be even worse. This is paralysis at its worst! If the people had allowed themselves to be immobilized by fear, in effect they would have been saying, "The situation as it stands now is not ideal. But we've lived with it for quite some time, and we've adjusted. Things could be better, but we're getting by. Why rock the boat? Who knows what would happen after building that wall?!"

But the fear of earthly enemies has no place in God's program today any more than it did in Nehemiah's day. Our modern-day Nehemiahs cannot do it alone. They need thousands of godly followers. We follow our godly leaders today with full confidence that the gates of Hell shall not prevail against the church (Matthew 16:18).

C. Prayer

Thank You, gracious Father, for entrusting us with the greatest work in all the world—not the work of building a wall, but the work of building Your church by leading the lost to salvation and leading the saved to understand Your Word and obey it. For that work may we have consecration and courage and common sense and success in Jesus' name, amen.

D. Thought to Remember

Bring your plans before God, and listen carefully to His response.

Learning by Doing

This page contains an alternative lesson plan emphasizing learning activities.
Classes desiring such student involvement will find these suggestions helpful.

Learning Goals

After this lesson each student will be able to:

1. List the types of opposition Nehemiah and the people of Judah met while completing the wall.

2. Describe appropriate, godly ways to handle opposition.

3. Publicly commit to persevere dutifully in one area of his/her spiritual life in which he/she is experiencing opposition.

Into the Lesson

Prior to the arrival of the students, rearrange your classroom. Place the furniture in ways that make it difficult to interact, or turn a writing board around so that it faces away from the students. The object is to place obstacles in the way of the students. As students arrive, they may take the initiative to move items back to their usual places. Allow them to do this without much comment. If they do not work to restore the room, make sure it is back to its usual appearance just before beginning the lesson.

Begin by saying, "Our room today was not set up as it usually is." Ask the students how the room's awkward setup could have affected learning. Allow for a variety of responses. Help the students to notice a theme of opposition. Say, "In today's text, the Jews faced opposition to their task in completing the wall. This was not typical violent opposition, but more covert and subtle."

Into the Word

Ask for two volunteers to read. Assign the first volunteer Nehemiah 4:1-3. Assign Nehemiah 6:1, 2 to the second. Alert the class to listen for similarities and differences in these two brief texts. Have the first volunteer read, followed immediately by the second. Let students list the similarities (Sanballat and Tobiah are involved; the wall is the subject at hand) and differences (4:1-3—Sanballat ridicules; 6:1, 2—Sanballat seeks a meeting; 4:1-3—dismissal; 6:1, 2—scheming).

Ask the first volunteer to read Nehemiah 4:7, 8, 11, 12. The second volunteer should then read Nehemiah 6:2, 5, 9, and 13. Again, notice some similarities (opposition) and differences (4:11, 12—violent opposition, 6:2, 9, 13—subtle opposition). Ask the students to identify the different types of opposition that Nehemiah and his associates faced while building the wall. These types

may be as simple as violent and covert or more specific types including slander, threatening to kill the leader, entrapment, or others.

Into Life

Say, "Having identified the types of opposition faced by the people in rebuilding the wall, we will now consider the types of opposition faced in our own spiritual lives." If your church is undertaking a major project, you might suggest that this be the "rebuilding of the wall" for your class. If this does not fit your church or if it is not an appropriate subject to discuss in class, have the students identify an individual "rebuilding-of-the-wall" spiritual life issue. These could include prayer life, Sunday school attendance, or evangelism. Have the students identify either a church issue or individual issue to address as the lesson continues.

Assemble the class into groups. Have half of the groups read Nehemiah 4:4, 5, 13, 14, 19-23. Have the other half read Nehemiah 6:3, 4, 8, 9b, 11-13. Ask each group to report what the people did in response to the various oppositions they faced. Answers should include the following: 4:4, 5—pray; 4:13, 14—stand guard and protect one another; 4:19-23—remind one another of God's power, be diligent in the work; 6:3, 4—be steadfast; 6:8—identify the lie; 6:9b—pray; 6:11-13—exhibit fearlessness, identify slander.

While the students are thinking about these various oppositions, ask what specific opposition they have faced in their personal lives and ministries. Write these on the chalkboard. Ask, "What are some typical responses to these types of opposition?" These may include appropriate (as seen in the text) and inappropriate responses (such as ways all of us have responded to opposition at times). Write these on the board also.

Remind the students that no type of opposition from the enemy dissuaded the people responsible for rebuilding the wall from their God-given task. Have each student publicly commit either to the entire class or to a partner to persevere dutifully in the "rebuilding-of-the-wall" spiritual life issue chosen earlier. This commitment should include an identification of a specific opposition and an appropriate response to such opposition. Give each a card on which to record the decisions and to carry with them in pocket or purse for a time.

Let's Talk It Over

The questions on this page are designed to promote discussion of the lesson by the class and to encourage application of the lesson Scriptures. The answers provided are only discussion starters. Let your class talk it over from there.

1. When is it appropriate to question the motives of someone who proposes negotiating resolution of a conflict?

Nehemiah had no reason to trust those who were self-declared enemies of his people. If someone has opposed us or our objectives from the beginning, and if that person's cooperation is not necessary to the completing of a worthy and desired goal, there seems little reason to agree to sit down for a chat—particularly if the work stops while the talking is going on. On the other hand, opposition to our plans comes often from brothers and sisters who share a vital interest in the project. We must be careful not to question the motives of such people without a fair hearing. Our coworkers are not our enemies!

2. Why is the kind of firm resolve exhibited by Nehemiah so important in a leader? in a parent? Give an example of a time when you had to be similarly firm—or when you should have been.

"If the trumpet give an uncertain sound, who shall prepare himself to the battle?" (1 Corinthians 14:8). Followers want to have confidence in their leader, confidence that the leader knows what needs to be done and has the determination and the know-how to succeed. The completion of the walls of Jerusalem required persistence. If Nehemiah had not modeled that persistence, he could not have expected it from his people.

Parents cannot afford to equivocate in what is important. Children need to see consistency in the values that their parents pursue. If parents are sincere and unwavering in what they hold dear, children will generally follow their lead.

Encourage your learners to tell of personal experiences that model this important quality.

3. Why are leaders often targets for a charge of improper motives? How can they prepare for those attacks?

Leaders, literally and figuratively, are the ones out in front—they are highly visible. Critics and enemies rightly perceive that leaders are setting the direction and the pace of movement. If the leader can be derailed, the entire group may lose its momentum and possibly its will.

A leader can do several things to prepare against attack: (1) expect it; do not be surprised when it comes; (2) maintain accountability and do not give reason for reproach; and (3) remember that anytime you attempt anything noteworthy, someone will be ready to throw stones.

It is also important to keep "a clear conscience, so that those who speak maliciously against your good behavior in Christ may be ashamed of their slander" (1 Peter 3:16, *New International Version*). Nehemiah was willing to live by the record of his deeds. He had no fear of the lies of his enemies. If we aim at noble character and are quick to confess our failings, then it will be nearly impossible for slander to stick to us. Often we will not even have to respond to unfair criticisms; our record and reputation will speak for us. If, however, we have mixed motives, secret sin, or character defects, then we are vulnerable and have reason to be anxious.

4. What do you think were the chief reasons that the rebuilding of the walls—delayed some ninety years—could be accomplished in just *fifty-two days*? What principles here can we apply to completing projects today?

God's supernatural blessing was certainly on this effort, but God also worked through human factors as well. Nehemiah's role cannot be overestimated! He was a visionary, determined, wise, and self-sacrificing leader. He cast a clear vision of what needed to be done and then effectively used delegation and shared ownership in the project. His effective planning and cooperative execution overcame fear. His early success and progress engendered hope and encouraged further effort. And, most importantly, he was a man of prayer. These are dynamics that continue to apply to group accomplishment.

5. It is hard to admit that you have been on the wrong side of an issue. What would have been the most constructive response of Nehemiah's enemies to the completion of the walls?

Interestingly, Nehemiah's enemies concluded that the work was accomplished through the help of God. Yet instead of celebrating, they were downcast. Instead of admitting that perhaps the God of Israel is the true God, and instead of worshiping Him and seeking His favor, these enemies responded with sulking. Human pride so often blocks our access to God! When a project that we opposed succeeds, how should *we* respond?

Ezra Reads the Law

DEVOTIONAL READING: Psalm 119:33-40.

BACKGROUND SCRIPTURE: Nehemiah 8.

PRINTED TEXT: Nehemiah 8:1-12.

Nehemiah 8:1-12

1 And all the people gathered themselves together as one man into the street that was before the water gate; and they spake unto Ezra the scribe to bring the book of the law of Moses, which the LORD had commanded to Israel.

2 And Ezra the priest brought the law before the congregation both of men and women, and all that could hear with understanding, upon the first day of the seventh month.

3 And he read therein before the street that was before the water gate from the morning until midday, before the men and the women, and those that could understand; and the ears of all the people were attentive unto the book of the law.

4 And Ezra the scribe stood upon a pulpit of wood, which they had made for the purpose; and beside him stood Mattithiah, and Shema, and Anaiah, and Urijah, and Hilkiah, and Maaseiah, on his right hand; and on his left hand, Pedaiah, and Mishael, and Malchiah, and Hashum, and Hashbadana, Zechariah, and Meshullam.

5 And Ezra opened the book in the sight of all the people; (for he was above all the people;) and when he opened it, all the people stood up:

6 And Ezra blessed the LORD, the great God. And all the people answered, Amen, Amen, with lifting up their hands: and they bowed their heads, and worshipped the LORD with their faces to the ground.

7 Also Jeshua, and Bani, and Sherebiah, Jamin, Akkub, Shabbethai, Hodijah, Maaseiah, Kelita, Azariah, Jozabad, Hanan, Pelaiah, and the Levites, caused the people to understand the law: and the people stood in their place.

8 So they read in the book in the law of God distinctly, and gave the sense, and caused them to understand the reading.

9 And Nehemiah, which is the Tirshatha, and Ezra the priest the scribe, and the Levites that taught the people, said unto all the people, This day is holy unto the LORD your God; mourn not, nor weep. For all the people wept, when they heard the words of the law.

10 Then he said unto them, Go your way, eat the fat, and drink the sweet, and send portions unto them for whom nothing is prepared: for this day is holy unto our Lord: neither be ye sorry; for the joy of the LORD is your strength.

11 So the Levites stilled all the people, saying, Hold your peace, for the day is holy; neither be ye grieved.

12 And all the people went their way to eat, and to drink, and to send portions, and to make great mirth, because they had understood the words that were declared unto them.

GOLDEN TEXT: So they read in the book in the law of God distinctly, and gave the sense, and caused them to understand the reading.—Nehemiah 8:8.

God Restores a Remnant
Unit 2: Renewal
(Lessons 6-9)

Lesson Aims

After participating in this lesson, each student will be able to:

1. Explain the reverence that the people had for God's presence through the reading of His Word.

2. Show respect for the Bible as God's Word.

3. Implement one way in which respect for the Word of God might be increased.

Lesson Outline

INTRODUCTION
  A. Bible Teaching?
  B. Lesson Background
 I. PURPOSEFUL MEETING (Nehemiah 8:1-3)
  A. By Popular Demand (vv. 1, 2)
    Watergate
  B. A Long Reading (v. 3)
 II. WORSHIPFUL MEETING (Nehemiah 8:4-6)
  A. Important Occasion (v. 4)
  B. Reverent Attention (v. 5)
  C. Emotional Worship (v. 6)
III. INSTRUCTIVE MEETING (Nehemiah 8:7, 8)
  A. The Teachers (v. 7)
  B. Their Method (v. 8)
    Hearing and Knowing
IV. JOYOUS HOLY DAY (Nehemiah 8:9-12)
  A. Call to Joy (vv. 9, 10)
  B. End of Mourning (v. 11)
  C. Celebration of Learning (v. 12)
CONCLUSION
  A. Do We Teach Properly?
  B. Do We Make Things Plain?
  C. Prayer
  D. Thought to Remember

Introduction

A. Bible Teaching?

Going to church was not easy when I was a boy on the farm. Church was more than six miles away. After the morning chores were done, there was not enough time to harness the team, dress in our best, and travel those miles in the old surrey.

Although we seldom went to church, we boys went to Sunday school every Sunday. Grandma saw to that. She subscribed to a children's weekly magazine that included a Sunday school lesson, and she led my brother and me through the lesson every week. Besides that, the children's books in our home had more Bible stories than fairy tales. That background forms a vitally important part of my Christian identity today.

B. Lesson Background

When the Jews went back to their homeland after their captivity in Babylon, the grandmas among them had no magazines with Sunday school lessons. They had no children's books full of Bible stories. They did not even have Bibles in their homes. Jewish men were overworked with the tasks of building houses, tilling gardens, plowing, planting, and harvesting the fields, tending flocks of sheep and herds of cattle—not to mention the rebuilding of the temple and the city walls! It is not surprising to learn that Bible teaching was neglected.

About eighty years after the first Jews returned from Babylon, a priest, scribe, and scholar named Ezra (cf. Ezra 7:11) led a second group from the East back to Jerusalem in 458 B.C. Ezra was shocked to see how God's law was being ignored. Some men had even taken wives from among the pagans who lived nearby (Ezra 9). That was forbidden by God's law (Deuteronomy 7:3, 4). Ezra's first arrival and his teaching about the law had brought reform that was painful to those who agreed that they must give up the pagan wives whom they had cherished for years (Ezra 10:3, 14).

Many students think Ezra soon must have gone back to the Eastern country, and injustice and lawbreaking increased while he was away. When Nehemiah came to rebuild Jerusalem's walls in 444 B.C., he found widespread injustice in the commercial life of the nation. He had to establish justice in Jerusalem even while he was building walls around the city (Nehemiah 5:1-13). After the walls were finished, however, Ezra was in Jerusalem again, and the people eagerly looked to him for more teaching about the law. It is to the credit of the people that they now wanted to learn more, though they must have suspected it would require further reforms that would be painful or costly. Today we see people who wanted to do God's will!

I. Purposeful Meeting (Nehemiah 8:1-3)

A. By Popular Demand (vv. 1, 2)

1. And all the people gathered themselves together as one man into the street that was before the water gate; and they spake unto Ezra the scribe to bring the book of the law of Moses, which the LORD had commanded to Israel.

This isn't the first time *all the people* gather *together as one man* (see Ezra 3:1). The place where they meet, *the water gate,* is in the east wall of Jerusalem. It has that name because the people go through it to bring water from a spring outside the wall. *The street* leading to that gate widens into a square inside the wall. A great number of armed men can gather there to oppose enemies who might try to smash the gate with a battering ram. The same square provides space for a peaceful assembly when no enemy is in sight.

The people gather because they want *Ezra the scribe* to teach them more about the law. [See question #1, page 402.] Literally, the word *scribe* means "writer." But when a writer painstakingly makes copies of the Scriptures by hand, naturally he comes to know those Scriptures very well and can teach them to others. Therefore the word *scribe* came to signify a scholar and teacher. That is what Ezra has proved himself to be, and now the people are eager to hear him teach the law.

The *book of the law* is not hundreds of flat pages bound between hard covers like a modern book. Rather, it is a long strip, probably of parchment, and perhaps about eighteen inches wide. It can be rolled up for storage and unrolled for reading. *Moses* had received the law from God and had written it down some one thousand years before. Although very old, that *which the Lord had commanded to Israel* is still mandatory in Ezra's day.

WATERGATE

On June 17, 1972, the word "Watergate" began to become part of the American psyche. That was the night that burglars broke into the offices of the Democratic National Committee, located in the Watergate office complex in Washington, DC.

The two-year investigation that followed uncovered a trail of corruption and abuse of power that pointed to the highest levels of the executive branch of government, and eventually to President Richard M. Nixon himself. Under threat of impeachment, President Nixon resigned from office on August 9, 1974.

Since that time, the very mention of the word *Watergate* has conjured up negative images of the arrogance of power and the dangers of having ethical blinders. For those who choose to look on the bright side, however, the outcome of the Watergate scandal reaffirms the concept of "the rule of law" upon which the United States of America was founded.

The gathering "before the water gate" in Jerusalem was a pivotal point in Israel's history. As the crowd of people heard the law read, negative thoughts swept through their minds concerning how the law had been broken so often, and they wept.

But Nehemiah and Ezra also made sure that the people had positive images because of the holiness of the day and the joy of forgiveness. From that day forward, any Israelites who had been there would only have to say, "Remember the water gate," and they would bring back both negative and positive emotions of recommitment. What causes you to renew your commitment to Christ each day?   —R. L. N.

2. And Ezra the priest brought the law before the congregation both of men and women, and all that could hear with understanding, upon the first day of the seventh month.

Now we see that *Ezra* is a *priest* as well as a scribe. The inclusion of *women, and all that could hear with understanding* (i.e., older children) shows the seriousness of the occasion in that culture (see Deuteronomy 31:12, 13; Joshua 8:35; 2 Kings 23:2). [See question #2, page 402.]

Last week we read that the city wall was finished on the twenty-fifth day of the sixth month (Nehemiah 6:15). If we now are reading of the same year, the assembly occurs only a few days after that big construction job ended. The timing of this gathering (Nehemiah 7:73b) coincides with the Feast of Trumpets (Leviticus 23:23-25; Numbers 29:1-6).

B. A Long Reading (v. 3)

3. And he read therein before the street that was before the water gate from the morning until midday, before the men and the women, and those that could understand; and the ears of all the people were attentive unto the book of the law.

This is no twenty-minute sermon! *From the morning until midday* is at least five hours. Perhaps all the people are attentive because God is very prominent in their thoughts as they look around with amazement at their newly rebuilt walls. [See question #3, page 402.]

II. Worshipful Meeting (Nehemiah 8:4-6)

A. Important Occasion (v. 4)

4. And Ezra the scribe stood upon a pulpit of wood, which they had made for the purpose; and beside him stood Mattithiah, and Shema, and Anaiah, and Urijah, and Hilkiah, and Maaseiah, on his right hand; and on his left hand, Pedaiah, and Mishael, and Malchiah, and Hashum, and Hashbadana, Zechariah, and Meshullam.

The biggest part of the preparation for this event probably is the building of *a pulpit of wood.* In today's English we would call it a "platform"

How to Say It

AHAB. *Ay*-hab.

AKKUB. *Ak*-ub.

ANAIAH. Uh-*nye*-uh.

AZARIAH. Az-uh-*rye*-uh.

BANI. *Bay*-nye.

GOMORRAH. Guh-*more*-uh.

HANAN. *Hay*-nuhn.

HASHBADANA. Hash-*bad*-uh-nuh.

HASHUM. *Hay*-shum.

HILKIAH. Hill-*kye*-uh.

HODIJAH. Ho-*dye*-juh.

JAMIN. *Jay*-min.

JESHUA. *Jesh*-you-uh.

JEZEBEL. *Jez*-uh-bel.

JOZABAD. *Jaws*-ah-bad.

KELITA. *Kel*-ih-tuh.

MAASEIAH. May-uh-*see*-yuh.

MALCHIAH. Mal-*kye*-uh.

MATTITHIAH. Mat-ih-*thigh*-uh.

MESHULLAM. Me-*shul*-am.

MISHAEL. *Mish*-a-el.

NEHEMIAH. *Nee*-huh-*my*-uh (strong accent on *my*).

NISAN. *Nye*-san.

PEDAIAH. Peh-*day*-yuh.

PELAIAH. Pe-*lay*-yuh or Pe-*lye*-uh.

SHABBETHAI. *Shab*-ee-thigh.

SHEMA. *She*-muh.

SHEREBIAH. *Sher*-ee-*bye*-uh (strong accent on *bye*).

TIRSHATHA. Tur-*shay*-thuh.

URIJAH. Yu-*rye*-juh.

ZECHARIAH. Zek-uh-*rye*-uh.

Apparently most of the people have been sitting on the ground while Ezra and his companions assemble on the stage. Then Ezra holds the sacred scroll on which the law is written and starts to unroll it. *All the people* rise to their feet to show respect for the Word of God.

C. Emotional Worship (v. 6)

6. And Ezra blessed the LORD, the great God. And all the people answered, Amen, Amen, with lifting up their hands: and they bowed their heads, and worshipped the LORD with their faces to the ground.

To bless *the Lord* is to praise Him. Often we open our own prayers in the way that Ezra does here. God is called *great* in other passages as well (see Deuteronomy 10:17; Nehemiah 9:32; Jeremiah 32:18; Daniel 9:4). Coupled with lifted *hands* and bowed *heads,* the people's response of *Amen, Amen* shows intense emotion. [See question #4, page 402.]

III. Instructive Meeting (Nehemiah 8:7, 8)

A. The Teachers (v. 7)

7. Also Jeshua, and Bani, and Sherebiah, Jamin, Akkub, Shabbethai, Hodijah, Maaseiah, Kelita, Azariah, Jozabad, Hanan, Pelaiah, and the Levites, caused the people to understand the law: and the people stood in their place.

The meeting begins with worship that is united, fervent, and reverent. But the people have come primarily to listen to the Word of God and learn from it. Well might their opening prayer be that of the psalmist: "Open thou mine eyes, that I may behold wondrous things out of thy law" (Psalm 119:18). That may well be our prayer, too.

In verse 4, we counted fourteen people on the stage. Now we see there are many more. (The phrase *and the Levites* probably refers to those listed here; compare the names listed in Nehemiah 10:9-13.) They fact that they *caused the people to understand the law* shows us the importance of the teaching function.

All of us need help in understanding the Bible at one time or another. The majestic *King James Version* was translated nearly four hundred years ago, and our English language has changed since that time. Some of the words we read are no longer in common use. Others are still in use, but their meanings have changed over the centuries. Moses wrote the law about a thousand years before Ezra read it to the people, so imagine how the Hebrew language has changed in that span of time! In fact, the Hebrew language is beginning to fade out of common use as Aramaic

rather than a "pulpit." It had to be big enough and strong enough to support Ezra and the other men listed in this chapter. We suppose the thirteen cited here are Ezra's fellow priests or other men of influence who take their place with Ezra to indicate their approval of what he is doing. With about half on *his right* and about half on *his left,* Ezra is the focal point of attention.

A huge supply of lumber had been procured to make the gates in the city wall. Probably enough of it was left over to build the big and sturdy stage on which Ezra and his companions are lifted so high that they can be seen by every person of that big throng in the square (v. 5). The appearance of so many leaders on that stage marks this as an important occasion.

B. Reverent Attention (v. 5)

5. And Ezra opened the book in the sight of all the people; (for he was above all the people;) and when he opened it, all the people stood up.

takes its place. The Jews need a lot of help understanding a book that is a thousand years old, and Ezra has a lot of help in explaining it. Do we do as well with the two-thousand-year-old phrases, terms, and concepts we use so freely in the church?

B. Their Method (v. 8)

8. So they read in the book in the law of God distinctly, and gave the sense, and caused them to understand the reading.

You may have noticed that some who read aloud are hard to understand because they do not read *distinctly:* they mumble, they slur short vowels, they run syllables together. The trained readers who help Ezra are easy to understand because they pronounce everything clearly. Perhaps these readers are also translating from Hebrew to Aramaic as they go.

The people *understand the reading* not only because the words are distinct and clear, but also because the readers give *the sense.* This is preaching and teaching at its finest! When we study and learn from godly teachers today and apply the Bible to our lives, then we are "rightly dividing the word of truth" (2 Timothy 2:15).

HEARING AND KNOWING

Romans 10:17 teaches, "Faith cometh by hearing, and hearing by the word of God." There ought to be in us an increasing desire to hear and know the Bible. However, most do not read the Bible regularly.

Research confirms it. Billy Graham reported a survey indicating only 12 percent of people who say they believe the Bible read it every day.

Television confirms it. On *Jeopardy* "The Bible" is almost always the last category chosen.

Cause Them to Understand
—from Nehemiah 8:8

Visual for lesson 8. *This poster illustrates verse 8. Discuss how the church can find new ways to help people understand the Bible.*

Experience confirms it. Two ladies were overheard talking about the Bible. One asked the other if she knew about the epistles. She replied, "Of course. The epistles are the wives of the apostles."

Honors students in Newton, Massachusetts, high school gave these astounding replies on a quiz for a Bible as Literature course.

Sodom and Gomorrah were lovers.

Jezebel was Ahab's donkey.

The four horsemen appeared on the Acropolis.

The Gospel writers were Matthew, Mark, Luther, and John.

Eve was created from an apple.

Jesus was baptized by Moses.

Golgotha was the giant who slew the apostle David.

Can anybody dispute that Bible reading has fallen on hard times? Ezra, Nehemiah, Paul, and others knew the importance of hearing and knowing God's Word. Do you?   —J. A. M.

IV. Joyous Holy Day
(Nehemiah 8:9-12)

A. Call to Joy (vv. 9, 10)

9. And Nehemiah, which is the Tirshatha, and Ezra the priest the scribe, and the Levites that taught the people, said unto all the people, This day is holy unto the LORD your God; mourn not, nor weep. For all the people wept, when they heard the words of the law.

The first day of any month is observed with special religious ceremonies (see Numbers 28:11-15). But the first day of the seventh month, known as Tishri (September-October), has added meaning because it marks the end of the agricultural and festival year. It eventually comes to be regarded as the "civil" New Year's Day, even after the Lord made Nisan (March-April) the first month of the "religious" year (Exodus 12:1, 2). Mourning is not appropriate for such a *holy* day. The command to stop mourning and weeping comes from both civil and religious leaders, namely *Nehemiah* the *Tirshatha* (governor) and *Ezra the priest.*

When the law is made clear to the people, many know they have been violating it. They are overcome with shame, grief, and fear. The reading of the law has convicted the people of their sin. But this is a time to celebrate God's forgiveness. There is a proper time for grief and a proper time for joy, and we must know the difference (cf. Ezra 3:12; 10:1; Nehemiah 1:4; 2 Corinthians 2:5-11; James 4:9). The teachers instruct the people in a better way, and that is the climax of this great day of teaching.

10. Then he said unto them, Go your way, eat the fat, and drink the sweet, and send portions

unto them for whom nothing is prepared: for this day is holy unto our Lord: neither be ye sorry; for the joy of the LORD is your strength.

From daybreak until noon the people have been listening attentively, becoming increasingly convicted in their hearts. Now *he* (probably Nehemiah) dismisses them to go home and use the rest of the day in joyous celebration. But they are not to be selfish—the finest of food and *drink* are to be shared with people too poor to prepare the best for themselves. And as the people resolve to leave sin behind, they are to remember that *the joy of the Lord is* their *strength* for avoiding future disobedience and its terrible consequences. [See question #5, page 402.]

B. End of Mourning (v. 11)

11. So the Levites stilled all the people, saying, Hold your peace, for the day is holy; neither be ye grieved.

The *Levites* mentioned in verse 7 comfort *all the people*. Perhaps they do this by going out in the crowd to give personal messages of encouragement to those most distressed. [See question #6, page 402.]

C. Celebration of Learning (v. 12)

12. And all the people went their way to eat, and to drink, and to send portions, and to make great mirth, because they had understood the words that were declared unto them.

Now the people follow the instructions that we read in verse 10. The fact that they *make great mirth* doesn't mean they celebrate in a frivolous, shallow, or profane manner (cf. Exodus 32:5, 6, 25). Rather, the idea is that they celebrate appropriately, with great joy, for what God has done. How delightful it is to understand what God has *declared* in His book!

Home Daily Bible Readings

Monday, July 14—The People Gather (Nehemiah 7:66–8:1)

Tuesday, July 15—Ezra Reads From the Law (Nehemiah 8:2-6)

Wednesday, July 16—This Day Is Holy (Nehemiah 8:7-12)

Thursday, July 17—The Study of the Law Continues (Nehemiah 8:13-18)

Friday, July 18—Teach Me Your Statutes (Psalm 119:33-40)

Saturday, July 19—Your Commandment Makes Me Wise (Psalm 119:97-104)

Sunday, July 20—I Long for Your Commandments (Psalm 119:129-136)

Conclusion

A. Do We Teach Properly?

Karen was twelve years old when she made Peter's confession her own when she said, "I believe that Jesus is the Christ, the Son of the living God." Later, someone asked her what the word *Christ* means. Karen said, "It's Jesus' other name." But the word *Christ* really is a title rather than a name. It is the accepted English form of a Greek word that means "anointed." The Christ is the Anointed One.

In the centuries before Jesus came to earth, prophets, priests, and kings were anointed when they were appointed to those offices. When we say that Jesus is the Christ, we are acknowledging that He is the supreme *Prophet* who makes God and His will known to us; we are saying He is the *Priest* who gave His own life as the only sacrifice that can win forgiveness for us by satisfying God's wrath; we are saying He is the eternal *King* whom we shall obey now and forever.

Should we have made all that plain to Karen before she made her confession?

B. Do We Make Things Plain?

Ezra, Nehemiah, and the teaching Levites all gave the same advice, and that advice turned a day of mourning into a day of joy. The weeping people raised their heads, wiped their eyes, and went home to celebrate. For us, too, it is good to grieve for a while because we have sinned. But eventually it is better to stop sinning and be glad.

Today we understand this transformation from sorrow to joy better than did Ezra's hearers, better even than Ezra himself. We have sinned, yes, and the wages of sin is death (Romans 3:23; 6:23). But we escape death because Jesus died in our place. He took the punishment we deserved, and we can live forever. In all the world there is no joy to compare with the joy of our salvation. And such great joy brings with it a great obligation. We ought to obey the Christ, our King, and we ought to be telling the good news of salvation far and wide. How can we not share our matchless joy?

C. Prayer

Thank You, Father, for giving us the Bible, a practical guide for our daily living and the words of eternal life. Thank You, also, for raising up godly teachers to bring Your Word to us and help us understand it. Today we promise that we will study to know it better, apply it to the full, and offer it to others. In Jesus' name, amen.

D. Thought to Remember

There is joy in knowing God's Word and obeying it.

Learning by Doing

This page contains an alternative lesson plan emphasizing learning activities.
Classes desiring such student involvement will find these suggestions helpful.

Learning Goals

After participating in this lesson, each student will be able to:

1. Explain the reverence that the people had for God's presence through the reading of His Word.

2. Show respect for the Bible as God's Word.

3. Implement one way in which respect for the Word of God might be increased.

Into the Lesson

Prior to class time, read Nehemiah 8:1-12 to become familiar with it, practicing proper pronunciation of names and noting any phrases that you want to emphasize vocally. After everyone has entered the room, read Nehemiah 8:1-5 while everyone remains seated. You, as the reader, should remain seated as well. Stumble through the names in verse 4. After concluding this first reading in a monotone, pause for a moment in silence. Then say, "Would everyone please stand for the reading of God's Word?" Stand and read the entire text (Nehemiah 8:1-12) with some intentional excitement, emphasizing the areas you planned in your preliminary reading.

Say, "You may be seated." Ask the students for their responses to the different presentations of the text. Listen for different thoughts and feelings. You may ask, "How did standing as opposed to sitting specifically affect your hearing of the Word of God?" Discuss the various responses from the students. At the conclusion of this brief discussion say, "This text presents a clear reverence for God's Word. Let's study the passage today with this reverence." (Assure the students that they will not have to stand throughout the lesson!)

Into the Word

Ask students to assemble into discussion groups of three to five. Each of these groups should read through the text again, writing down any elements that they see demonstrating reverence for the Word of God. *(These may include the following: publicly gathering as one, requesting the reading [8:1], the preparation for [see commentary on verse 3] and length of time of the reading [8:3—If this is raised, you may note that many people who have preached in cultures that do not have easy access to Scripture have asked preachers to continue to preach for hours], the*

building of a special platform [8:4], standing for the reading [8:5], and other obviously reverent behaviors.)

Into Life

During the week, find articles showing respect, or lack of respect, for the Bible. *Christianity Today*™ magazine is often a good source for these, as are some *Focus on the Family*™ newsletters, local newspapers, and other such material.

To begin the activity, say, "It is difficult to miss the respect that the people in this text have for the Word of God." Distribute the various articles you have compiled to individual students or to the small groups. Ask them to read through the articles to determine specific ways in which the Bible is shown to be either valued or disrespected. If you were unable to attain several articles, ask, "How does this culture demonstrate respect or a lack of respect for God's Word?" Allow ample time for students to respond.

Ask the students, "If our culture at large truly respected the Word of God, how would that be demonstrated?" Have them work in small groups to write down some responses. You may also ask them to share times when they have seen the Word treated more respectfully. Have the groups report their responses to the class.

Next, have the students brainstorm ways in which the church can demonstrate greater respect for the Word of God. Ask volunteers to share their responses. (You might note that some people consider an effective way of doing this is to have the congregation stand during the reading of Scripture prior to a sermon. In one church the preacher asks a different person each week to read Scripture on Sunday. The request is made during the preceding week, and the task is treated as a very important one. People in that congregation say the people who read have a position of honor, and that standing during the reading helps the people who hear better recognize the reading as truly being God's Word.)

Have the students agree on one way the church can show greater respect and value for God's Word. Have them make a plan toward implementing this idea. For individual application, have each student consider one way he or she can demonstrate greater respect and reverence for God's Word and commit to implementing this in his or her daily life.

Let's Talk It Over

The questions on this page are designed to promote discussion of the lesson by the class and to encourage application of the lesson Scriptures. The answers provided are only discussion starters. Let your class talk it over from there.

1. The people knew that hearing the law was important. How can we emphasize the importance of Scripture reading in our public worship and private devotions today?

Throughout church history, congregations have emphasized the importance of Scripture reading in various ways. Many use lectionaries— reading plans that include passages from different parts of the Bible, often organized around a theme. (These are often coordinated with a reading plan for individual use at home.) In some churches, the worshipers show respect for the Scripture by standing when it is read aloud.

At the very least, people who are called upon to read Scripture in public should practice reading it in advance in order to do the best job possible. Worshipers can discipline themselves to listen carefully or read along in their own Bibles when Scripture is read aloud.

2. Included in the Israelites' worship were "all that could hear with understanding" (i.e., older children). What, if anything, does this say to us today about age-graded worship?

Those who support age-graded worship say, "Children need to worship at their own level." This means that the younger children do not attend the same worship service as the adults. Instead, they go to a service geared to their own level of understanding. Some churches have only one children's worship while others offer several age-level services.

On the other hand, some believers say, "Families need to worship *together*, so children of all ages need to be with their parents." Emphasizing the importance of family units is important. Children were present on the day Ezra read the law, but the youngest children apparently were not.

3. "From morning until midday" shows that the people had a long attention span! How should the church adjust to the fact that people's attention spans today seem to be very short?

Paying attention is a learned behavior. Television, with its frequent commercial breaks and fast-moving images, undoubtedly has a role in training people to have shorter attention spans. In some churches this is accommodated with shorter songs and sermons, drama and a variety of other activities, and—in all—a rather

fast-paced service. In other congregations, however, the pace slows. Sermons may last an hour or more. The song service may be lively, or it may not be. If your class does not include leaders who can implement changes to the worship service, perhaps your discussion would be better aimed at how individuals can increase their attention spans. Taking notes on the sermon is one method. What are some others?

4. The text pays close attention to the worshipers' movements. What lessons can we learn from these descriptions?

The people's movements reflected their reaction to God and His Word. The movements expressed reverence, awe, contrition, humility, praise, and submission. We have many examples in Scripture of people standing up to show reverence, kneeling or bowing low to show submission or repentance, and lifting "holy hands" in praise and adoration. Our bodies are not isolated from our spirits and minds. Our body language can be a vital part of our public and private worship.

5. In what ways has "the joy of the Lord" been your strength, both as an individual and as a part of the church?

Often, we will find our greatest joy in *giving*, which can take the forms of money, invested time, or use of spiritual gifts to bless others (cf. Acts 20:35). Another theme in Scripture is that God blesses people when they follow His way (Matthew 6:33). We do not obey God to earn our salvation, so proper motives are important. God has promised that if we are faithful, He will strengthen us and provide for our needs. One way He may strengthen us is through the joy and encouragement we receive as we obey Him.

6. Verses 9-11 note that the day of the reading was "holy." Which days, if any, should be holy to us today? Why?

The first day of every week (Sunday) was special to the apostles, and it should be special to us as well (cf. Acts 20:7; 1 Corinthians 16:2). Beyond that, many Christians find great comfort in honoring God in special ways on Christmas, Easter, etc. Even so, we are to be careful not to impose on others a matter of conscience in this area (Romans 14:5, 6; Colossians 2:16, 17).

The People Renew the Covenant

DEVOTIONAL READING: Psalm 66:8-20.

BACKGROUND SCRIPTURE: Nehemiah 9:38–10:39.

PRINTED TEXT: Nehemiah 10:28-39.

Nehemiah 10:28-39

28 And the rest of the people, the priests, the Levites, the porters, the singers, the Nethinim, and all they that had separated themselves from the people of the lands unto the law of God, their wives, their sons, and their daughters, every one having knowledge, and having understanding;

29 They clave to their brethren, their nobles, and entered into a curse, and into an oath, to walk in God's law, which was given by Moses the servant of God, and to observe and do all the commandments of the LORD our Lord, and his judgments and his statutes;

30 And that we would not give our daughters unto the people of the land, nor take their daughters for our sons:

31 And if the people of the land bring ware or any victuals on the sabbath day to sell, that we would not buy it of them on the sabbath, or on the holy day: and that we would leave the seventh year, and the exaction of every debt.

32 Also we made ordinances for us, to charge ourselves yearly with the third part of a shekel for the service of the house of our God;

33 For the showbread, and for the continual meat offering, and for the continual burnt offering, of the sabbaths, of the new moons, for the set feasts, and for the holy things, and for the sin offerings to make an atonement for Israel, and for all the work of the house of our God.

34 And we cast the lots among the priests, the Levites, and the people, for the wood offering, to bring it into the house of our God, after the houses of our fathers, at times appointed year by year, to burn upon the altar of the LORD our God, as it is written in the law:

35 And to bring the firstfruits of our ground, and the firstfruits of all fruit of all trees, year by year, unto the house of the LORD:

36 Also the firstborn of our sons, and of our cattle, as it is written in the law, and the firstlings of our herds and of our flocks, to bring to the house of our God, unto the priests that minister in the house of our God:

37 And that we should bring the firstfruits of our dough, and our offerings, and the fruit of all manner of trees, of wine and of oil, unto the priests, to the chambers of the house of our God; and the tithes of our ground unto the Levites, that the same Levites might have the tithes in all the cities of our tillage.

38 And the priest the son of Aaron shall be with the Levites, when the Levites take tithes: and the Levites shall bring up the tithe of the tithes unto the house of our God, to the chambers, into the treasure house.

39 For the children of Israel and the children of Levi shall bring the offering of the corn, of the new wine, and the oil, unto the chambers, where are the vessels of the sanctuary, and the priests that minister, and the porters, and the singers: and we will not forsake the house of our God.

Jul
27

GOLDEN TEXT: Because of all this we make a sure covenant, and write it; and our princes, Levites, and priests, seal unto it.—Nehemiah 9:38.

God Restores a Remnant
Unit 2: Renewal
(Lessons 6-9)

Lesson Aims

After this lesson each student will be able to:

1. Describe the covenant made in Jerusalem under Ezra's leadership, identifying who signed it and who agreed to it.

2. Suggest aspects of the people's lives that were affected by the covenant and suggest how they might be worded today.

3. Begin a personal covenant with God.

Lesson Outline

INTRODUCTION

   A. The Value of Your Personal History

   B. Lesson Background

 I. OBEDIENCE PLEDGED (Nehemiah 10:28, 29)

   A. All the People (v. 28)

   B. All the Law (v. 29)

     Pledges, Solemn and Otherwise

 II. BEHAVIORS CHANGED (Nehemiah 10:30, 31)

   A. Holy People (v. 30)

   B. Holy Times (v. 31)

III. OFFERINGS RENEWED (Nehemiah 10:32-39)

   A. Temple Tax (v. 32)

   B. Daily Perishables (v. 33)

   C. Firewood (v. 34)

   D. First Parts (vv. 35-37a)

   E. Tithes (vv. 37b, 38)

     Giving

   F. Summary of Offerings (v. 39)

CONCLUSION

   A. Free From Law, Free to Obey

   B. Prayer

   C. Thought to Remember

Introduction

A. The Value of Your Personal History

Suppose you were to wake up tomorrow morning and couldn't remember anything about your past. Would you be able to function? I can safely predict that the answer would be a decisive *no*. It is your own personal history—with all its highs and lows, joys and sorrows, successes and failures—that will shape your today and all your tomorrows.

Each of us does indeed meet the world daily through our personal experiences of the past. If we are wise enough, we also meet the world

daily through the past experiences of other people. Those other people certainly would include our own family members and loved ones. But the experiences—the histories—of those who lived at other times and in other places should not be overlooked. When we learn from such people, we avoid repeating their mistakes and their sins.

B. Lesson Background

In several of our studies this summer, we have seen evidence that the returning exiles have truly "learned their lesson" concerning sin and punishment. That hard lesson comes from examining the experiences of their forefathers who neglected and violated God's law. Last week we saw the people of Judah assembled in a great mass meeting on the first day of the seventh month. They heard Ezra and others read and explain that law all morning long (Nehemiah 8:1-8).

The following day a group of leaders met for further study of the law. Among other things, they read about the Feast of Tabernacles (cf. Numbers 29:12-40). For a long time, this feast had not been celebrated as the law directed—and it was scheduled to begin in the middle of that very month. So preparations were made, and the people again observed this ancient festival in the proper way (Nehemiah 8:13-18).

When that happy festival was over, the people met again for a session that was not so joyous. They spent a quarter of the day in study of the law, and then a quarter of the day in mourning and confessing their disobedience (Nehemiah 9:1-3). The substance of their confession is recorded in 9:4-37. They said that they and their forefathers had often disobeyed the law, and that their disobedience had brought them many troubles. As a result, they had lost their national independence; because of disobedience they even then were subject to the Persians.

The climax of all this is recorded in our Golden Text. The people now would make a formal agreement to obey the law. They would put it in writing, and their leaders would make it official by putting their seals on it (Nehemiah 9:38).

Nehemiah 10:1-27 lists the leaders who sealed the covenant, and our printed text continues with what the rest of the people did.

I. Obedience Pledged (Nehemiah 10:28, 29)

In a single month, most of the people of Judah learned more about God's law than they had learned in all their lives before that time. After celebrating the Feast of Tabernacles, they are ready for commitment and action. They meant to honor that law!

A. All the People (v. 28)

28. And the rest of the people, the priests, the Levites, the porters, the singers, the Nethinim, and all they that had separated themselves from the people of the lands unto the law of God, their wives, their sons, and their daughters, every one having knowledge, and having understanding.

A covenant (or agreement) had been drawn up, a promise to obey the law. Leading citizens had affixed their seals to it (Nehemiah 9:38–10:27). Now the historian turns his attention to *the rest of the people*, and he names several different groups among them. *The priests* are in charge of public worship and teaching. *The Levites* (i.e., those of the historic tribe of Levi) are set apart to the service of God, and served in many ways, from janitor work to teaching and law enforcement. (All priests are Levites, but not all Levites are priests.) *The porters* are gatekeepers for the temple, and perhaps the city as well. *The singers* constitute the temple choir. *The Nethinim* are temple servants whose duties are not clearly described. Perhaps they did whatever the priests and Levites told them to do (cf. Ezra 8:20).

They that had separated themselves from the people of the lands may mean pagans from the area who had converted to Judaism. They include whole families: men, women, and children old enough to understand the law that the people now intend to obey. This listing of different groups among *the rest of the people* seems intended to indicate that the people of Judah are unanimous in making the same promise that leading citizens had written in a covenant. [See question #1, page 410.]

B. All the Law (v. 29)

29. They clave to their brethren, their nobles, and entered into a curse, and into an oath, to walk in God's law, which was given by Moses the servant of God, and to observe and do all the commandments of the LORD our Lord, and his judgments and his statutes.

All the people listed in verse 28 agree with the distinguished citizens who had put their seals on the contract. The distinguished ones are called *nobles* because they are specially honored as the heads of families or because they had won honor in some other way. Everyone takes an *oath* to keep the promise they make. They also place themselves under God's *curse* should they fail to keep it. (See similar promises in Ezra 10:5 and Nehemiah 5:12, 13.)

PLEDGES, SOLEMN AND OTHERWISE

Frivolous oaths and pledges seem to be common these days. A school principal makes the newspapers when he pledges to shave his head if his students read a certain number of books. When he actually carries through on his oath, the reporters and cameras turn out to cover the "news." College students "pledge" a fraternity or sorority through all kinds of inane activities. The list could go on.

The life-changing pledge made by Jonathan Edwards (1703–1758) could not have been more different. In his "Personal Narrative," Edwards relates that, "On January 12, 1723, I made a solemn dedication of myself to God, and wrote it down; giving up myself, and all that I had to God; to be for the future, in no respect, my own; to act as one that had no right to himself, in any respect. And solemnly vowed, to take God for my whole portion and felicity; looking on nothing else, as any part of my happiness, nor acting as if it were; and his law for the constant rule of my obedience: engaging to fight, with all my might, against the world, the flesh, and the devil, to the end of my life."

Jonathan Edwards went on to become one of the greatest revivalists in the history of New England. He also became a major figure in what came to be called Christianity's "Great Awakening" in the American colonies (1725–1760). Does anyone know what happened to that principal?
—R. L. N.

II. Behaviors Changed (Nehemiah 10:30, 31)

The general promise to do everything the law required may seem to be enough, but now some specific promises are added, promises to obey specific parts of the law. Perhaps these were parts that had been broken most frequently in the past.

A. Holy People (v. 30)

30. And that we would not give our daughters unto the people of the land, nor take their daughters for our sons.

The law forbade Jews to marry pagans (Deuteronomy 7:1-4). That law had been broken in the past. When Ezra first came to Jerusalem, he found that more than a hundred Jewish men had foreign wives. Skilled teacher that he was, Ezra convinced the nation that all those wives, with their children, must be sent back to the homes from which they had come (Ezra 9, 10). Imagine how terrible it was for the husbands to give up the wives and children they loved. The consequences of sin can be truly heart-wrenching.

Now it is about thirteen years later. Remembering that traumatic time of parting, the men of Israel write into their covenant the specific promise that never again would any of them consent to such illegal marriages. Unfortunately, Nehemiah will have to correct this problem again a few years later (Nehemiah 13:23-28). [See question #2, page 410.]

B. Holy Times (v. 31)

31. And if the people of the land bring ware or any victuals on the sabbath day to sell, that we would not buy it of them on the sabbath, or on the holy day: and that we would leave the seventh year, and the exaction of every debt.

The Ten Commandments require that the seventh day of every week be holy. No regular work is to be done on that day (Exodus 20:9, 10). God takes this law seriously, prescribing the death penalty for its violation (31:15). *The sabbath* is a memorial of the time when God finished His creation in six days and rested on the seventh (Genesis 2:1-3; Exodus 20:11). Failure to keep the Sabbath Day holy was one of the reasons for Jerusalem's destruction (see Jeremiah 17:19-27). When these Jews promise to obey the law, they go so far as to vow not even to *buy* food on the Sabbath or on any other *holy day*. But, as with the intermarriage problem, Nehemiah will have to provide more correction on this issue a few years later (see Nehemiah 13:15-22).

As every seventh day was to be a Sabbath, a time of rest, so also was every *seventh year*. In that year there was to be no sowing or reaping—the land was to lie fallow (Leviticus 25:1-5). In the harvest of the sixth year a little grain would be lost in the field. It would grow of itself in the seventh year, but it was not to be harvested by the landowner. It was for the poor and for animals (Exodus 23:10, 11). Frequent breaking of this law also was one of the reasons for the Babylonian captivity. (See 2 Chronicles 36:20, 21.) The land lay unused all the years of the captivity to make up for the Sabbath years that had been missed. But now the people rededicate themselves to keeping this ancient law and never again to sow and reap in the Sabbath year. The historical record in non-Biblical sources suggests that the Jews did indeed keep this promise faithfully (cf. 1 Maccabees 6:49, 53).

Before the people promised to stop *the exaction of every debt*, wealthy moneylenders had been charging heavy interest, which was against the law (Exodus 22:25). They had been foreclosing on the property of debtors who could not pay, and even making them slaves in order to get back what had been lent. Nehemiah had insisted earlier that such heartless practices be stopped (Nehemiah 5:3-13). Now the people agree that a moneylender will take a loss rather than take away a poor man's means of livelihood or his children (cf. Deuteronomy 24:6; Proverbs 14:31). [See question #3, page 410.]

III. Offerings Renewed (Nehemiah 10:32-39)

When we hear the word *offering*, we most often think of money or a check that can be put in the offering plate. But God's law for the Jews called for offerings of various kinds. Some of them are mentioned in our text.

A. Temple Tax (v. 32)

32. Also we made ordinances for us, to charge ourselves yearly with the third part of a shekel for the service of the house of our God.

The men agree to pay an annual tax for the materials and manpower needed in the temple services. A *third part of a shekel* is about one-eighth of an ounce of silver. What this equals in today's money is hard to say, but it is less than the half shekel required by the law (Exodus 30:11-16; 38:25, 26). The amount of money involved seems rather small for supporting *the service of the house of our God*. Perhaps the Persian government is still making generous contributions to the temple services (Ezra 6:8-10), or perhaps the financial situation of the people in Jerusalem justifies a reduced rate. In Jesus' day, the authorities ask about His payment of the "tribute" (Matthew 17:24). This "tribute" translates a term that literally means two drachmas, which is equal to half a shekel. [See question #4, page 410.]

B. Daily Perishables (v. 33)

33. For the showbread, and for the continual meat offering, and for the continual burnt offering, of the sabbaths, of the new moons, for the set feasts, and for the holy things, and for the sin offerings to make an atonement for Israel, and for all the work of the house of our God.

This verse lists some things involved in the temple services, and they are expensive. Some are provided by the tax mentioned in verse 32. Perhaps more are provided by the offerings mentioned in the following verses. If the Persian government is still making a contribution out of the tribute paid by its western provinces, that would be big help, too. (See Numbers 28:9-15.)

C. Firewood (v. 34)

34. And we cast the lots among the priests, the Levites, and the people, for the wood offering, to bring it into the house of our God, after the houses of our fathers, at times appointed year by year, to burn upon the altar of the LORD our God, as it is written in the law.

Plenty of firewood is needed for the big altar that stands before the temple. When all the meat of an animal is burned in sacrifice, a big fire has to be maintained for some time, for meat does not burn easily. Sacrifices are burned every day (Exodus 29:38-42), and large numbers of them on feast days. Besides, the altar fire is kept burning continually, even in hours when no sacrifices are being made (Leviticus 6:8-13).

The priests, the Levites, and the people all play a part in supplying needed wood. This even includes Nehemiah the governor (Nehemiah 13:31). *After the houses of our fathers* means that families take turns at this responsibility. It is not uncommon to see people cast *lots* in Biblical times to make decisions (e.g., Numbers 26:55; Joshua 14:2; 18:10; 1 Chronicles 24:5; 25:8; 26:13; Luke 1:9; Acts 1:26).

D. First Parts (vv. 35-37a)

35. And to bring the firstfruits of our ground, and the firstfruits of all fruit of all trees, year by year, unto the house of the LORD.

The very first part of every harvest belongs to the Lord (Exodus 23:19a). Bringing that part *unto the house of the Lord* means that these offerings are part of the support for the priests and Levites (Numbers 18:12, 13).

36. Also the firstborn of our sons, and of our cattle, as it is written in the law, and the firstlings of our herds and of our flocks, to bring to the house of our God, unto the priests that minister in the house of our God.

In Israel, the *firstborn* "both of man and of beast" (Exodus 13:2) belongs to God; but fathers "buy back" their firstborn *sons* by paying five shekels (Numbers 18:15, 16). Suitable firstborn animals are sacrificed; the fat is burned, and the lean meat becomes food for *the priests* (18:17, 18). This agreement certainly will cost the people more than the third of a shekel of Nehemiah 10:32! [See question #5, page 410.]

37a. And that we should bring the firstfruits of our dough, and our offerings, and the fruit of all manner of trees, of wine and of oil, unto the priests, to the chambers of the house of our God.

Dough and *wine* and olive *oil* are manufactured products. Freewill offerings have already been noted in Ezra 8:28 and will be noted again in Nehemiah 10:39, below. The temple *chambers* are the places where such things are stored until

the priests are ready to use them. Again, this attitude toward *firstfruits* means that the people promise to do just as the law directs them.

E. Tithes (v. 37b, 38)

37b. And the tithes of our ground unto the Levites, that the same Levites might have the tithes in all the cities of our tillage.

A tithe is 10 percent, or one-tenth. That part of each Israelite's income belongs to the Lord (Leviticus 27:30, 32). It is to be delivered to *the Levites* as payment for their services (Numbers 18:21, 24). We are not told just what their work is in the time of Ezra and Nehemiah. It seems reasonable to suppose that some of them are teachers of the law. But some are musicians and singers, and perhaps some even are carpenters and masons (cf. Nehemiah 10:28, above).

Whatever their duties are, the Levites are servants of God, and their pay comes from the tithes paid by other people of Israel.

38. And the priest the son of Aaron shall be with the Levites, when the Levites take tithes: and the Levites shall bring up the tithe of the tithes unto the house of our God, to the chambers, into the treasure house.

The Levites receive tithes for their support, but do they pay tithes as well? Indeed they do! Their *tithe of the tithes* goes right back into the treasury for supporting *the house of our God.* Everyone must give something!

GIVING

Think about some of the important key words from the Bible. By one student's count the word *believe* (or some form of the word) is used 275 times. The word *pray* (including variations) is used 371 times. Some form of the word *love* is used 714 times.

Home Daily Bible Readings

Monday, July 21—People Make Confession, Worship (Nehemiah 9:1-5)

Tuesday, July 22—Ezra Prays (Nehemiah 9:6-12)

Wednesday, July 23—Our Ancestors Did Not Obey (Nehemiah 9:16-21)

Thursday, July 24—Many Years You Were Patient (Nehemiah 9:26-31)

Friday, July 25—A Firm Agreement (Nehemiah 9:32-38)

Saturday, July 26—We Will Observe the Commandments (Nehemiah 10:28-34)

Sunday, July 27—We Will Not Neglect God's House (Nehemiah 10:35-39)

For the word *give* (with variations) the student counted 2,162 uses!

Incredibly, Jesus taught more about money than any other topic. How we handle money is very important to God. Everything we have belongs to God and is a gift from Him (1 Chronicles 29:10-14). As a response to God's generosity, we are called to be generous and cheerful givers of our financial resources. God loves a cheerful giver (2 Corinthians 9:7).

God commanded the Israelites to give tithes (10 percent) of everything they received, as well as additional gifts to maintain His temple, provide for the priests, and care for the poor (Leviticus 27:30; Numbers 18:26; Malachi 3:8-10). Israel recommitted themselves to that standard in Nehemiah 10.

In the New Testament Jesus taught about giving generously just as He gave generously. How much we give is a response to how God has given to us and changed our hearts.

Karl Menninger said giving "is a very good criterion of a person's mental health. Generous people are rarely mentally ill people." Have you discovered the joy of generous giving? —J. A. M.

F. Summary of Offerings (v. 39)

39. For the children of Israel and the children of Levi shall bring the offering of the corn, of the new wine, and the oil, unto the chambers, where are the vessels of the sanctuary, and the priests that minister, and the porters, and the singers: and we will not forsake the house of our God.

This verse summarizes all that *the children of Israel and the children of Levi* are to do to support *the house of our God.* All the Israelites, including the Levites, agree to bring to the temple all the offerings that were required by the law. (*Corn* in the *King James Version* means grain of any kind, in this case mainly wheat and barley.) The spacious storage *chambers* and big *vessels* in that facility are ready to receive the produce that is brought.

Conclusion

A. Free From Law, Free to Obey

Christians are not under the law given at Sinai, as the Jews were, but that is no excuse for doing wrong (Romans 6:15, 16). We are taught to do all that Jesus commanded (Matthew 28:20). Can that be any less than what God's law requires? We are to be holy, as God is holy (1 Peter 1:15, 16). Can that be any less than what the law requires? We are not under the law, but the law and the history of Israel were written for our instruction (Romans 15:4). So then, what lessons for our lives can we learn from the record we see in our text today?

The last verse in Nehemiah 10 ends by saying, "We will not forsake the house of our God." God's house today is not a building of stone; it is the church, a spiritual house built of living stones, and we ourselves are those stones (1 Peter 2:5). Shall we not then meet with our fellow Christians at every opportunity (Hebrews 10:25)?

The sacrifices we offer are not sheep and cattle, killed at the altar. They are our own bodies, living and serving God (Romans 12:1). What has your body been doing in the Lord's service this past week?

No law requires us to give to God a tenth of our income and some offerings beside. But God assures us of a living in this world (Matthew 6:31-33) and a matchless inheritance in another (1 Peter 1:4). Shall we not give Him more than the law required of the Jews? Shall we not give it gladly because "God loveth a cheerful giver" (2 Corinthians 9:7), and sacrificially (Mark 12:43, 44) in light of Jesus' sacrifice on the cross?

The list could go on! The work of Christ truly frees us from "the oldness of the letter" (Romans 7:6); the Son of God has taken the old code "out of the way, nailing it to his cross" (Colossians 2:14). Christ, in redeeming us "from the curse of the law" (Galatians 3:13), frees us to obey a better law (1 Corinthians 9:21; Galatians 6:2). This is "the perfect law of liberty" (James 1:25).

B. Prayer

How richly You have blessed us, Father! How grateful we are for a living in this world and treasure in Heaven! Like those Jews taught by Ezra, we who are taught by Jesus promise an earnest effort to do Your will all the days of our lives. In Jesus' name, amen.

C. Thought to Remember

Only our best is good enough.

Visual for lesson 9. *The terminology on today's poster comes from the Golden Text. Discuss how Jesus' death has given us a "sure covenant."*

Learning by Doing

This page contains an alternative lesson plan emphasizing learning activities.
Classes desiring such student involvement will find these suggestions helpful.

Learning Goals

After this lesson each student will be able to:

1. Describe the covenant made in Jerusalem under Ezra's leadership, identifying who signed it and who agreed to it.

2. Suggest aspects of the people's lives that were affected by the covenant and suggest how they might be worded today.

3. Begin a personal covenant with God.

Into the Lesson

Ask class members to brainstorm all the promises and contracts they can think of. *(They will name marriage, loan, business, employment, and possibly others.)* Then ask, "What does the contract accomplish?" Allow a few people to comment.

Say, "One dictionary says that a contract is 'an agreement that is usually formal, solemn, and intended as binding.' In today's study the Jews make such an agreement with God: formal, solemn, and binding."

Into the Word

Raymond Brown in his *The Message of Nehemiah* (Inter-Varsity Press, 1998, pp. 170, 171) describes the literary structure of political covenants that were made in the ancient Near East. An analysis of Nehemiah 9 and 10 reveals that the passage demonstrates just such a style. In our age of lack of commitment, it could provide a means for us Christians to step outside our culture and make a commitment, a covenant with God.

Give your students the outline of this literary style, as numbered in the following paragraph, and let them find the features in Nehemiah 9 and 10. (If your students have the *Adult Bible Class* student book, they have the outline there and can do this work in their books.)

Such a covenant usually included the following six features:

1. It began by outlining the historical relationship between the two parties in the agreement—paying special attention to the generosity of the stronger party. (This is the "prayer.")

2. This was followed by the covenant's basic stipulations (10:29).

3. Next came a description of the specific and practical ways in which this more general commitment is to be applied (vv. 30-39).

4. It often required that a copy of the written agreement be deposited in the temple of the god and that the covenant's terms be declared publicly on given occasions.

5. Those who signed (10:1-27) went on to agree to blessings and curses that would follow the keeping or breaking of the covenant (v. 29).

6. The covenant concluded with a brief summary of its terms (v. 39).

Into Life

Say, "When we study this covenant, we see that it was very specific and practical. Now that the people had heard God's law read again, they were changing their lifestyles. Although we are not under the Old Covenant, we can find in it relevant principles for living in today's world."

Either as a large group or in small groups, have students look again at the text and glean principles to apply. The list may include these entries:

9:5-38—Remind ourselves of God's generosity.

10:29—Promise to obey God's Word.

10:30—Teach children to marry someone who is also committed to God.

10:31—Honor God's day; care for God's world.

10:32-39—Support God's work.

As the people in Jerusalem made a public commitment to obey God's law, challenge your learners to begin private covenants. Point out our need to make a conscious decision whether we are willing to make a commitment in a world where so few want to make commitments.

Suggest that the students may follow the full six-point pattern or concentrate on promises and commitments in a variety of areas, such as the authority of Scripture, family life, relationships, finances, ministry for God, and witness in the midst of so many different worldviews. Encourage the learners to add promises in the weeks and months ahead as they participate in Bible studies and hear sermons.

Distribute a covenant form you have prepared and copied and let people begin working on their covenants. When the end of the class time approaches, pray for the commitments that have been made and will be made.

Suggest that each class member arrange with another to be accountability partners. Each partner will check with the other to confirm the status of covenant keeping after a week, a month, or some other agreed-on time period.

Let's Talk It Over

The questions on this page are designed to promote discussion of the lesson by the class and to encourage application of the lesson Scriptures. The answers provided are only discussion starters. Let your class talk it over from there.

1. In what ways are God's people today to be separate and distinct from their neighbors?

Reflecting on Christianity *vs.* the surrounding pagan culture of his day, the third-century church leader Tertullian asked, "What has Jerusalem to do with Athens?" Today, some Christians might well ask, "What has the church to do with Washington? or Hollywood? or Wall Street? or Nashville?" (See 1 John 2:15.) Entire groups of believers think that the way to holiness is isolation from the surrounding culture. Others, however, believe that Christians are free to participate in the wider culture.

Perhaps most Christians try to reach a middle ground of being "in the world, but not of the world," often wrestling with how to apply that phrase to everyday life. (Can Christians go to movies, invest in the stock market, or get tattoos?) Christians are indeed called to be different from their neighbors in significant ways—not as a matter of pride or superiority, but to live as the "salt and light" that help others find their way to Jesus Christ. Discuss how we can be different in ways that are attractive.

2. Where would you "draw the line" for yourself or your children about whom to marry?

The ancient Jews had, in one sense, an advantage over us today: they could tell with certainty who was Jewish and who wasn't. The problem can be more complex for us. Would we accept a marriage with someone who claimed faith in Christ but was from another denomination? with someone who shared our church background but didn't show any interest in worship or church work? with someone who was moral, loving, and dependable but not a Christian? Paul cautions us about being "unequally yoked together with unbelievers" (2 Corinthians 6:14), but application of this is not always clear-cut.

3. When the people reaffirmed their covenant with God, they pledged to change many areas of their lives, including their family structures, their schedules, their livelihood, and their personal finances. How should these areas of our lives be affected when we make a commitment to serving God?

A preacher is fond of saying, "Show me a person's checkbook and calendar, and I'll show you what's *really* important to him." How we spend our time and money does indeed indicate our true priorities. When we commit ourselves to the Lord, we should expect our spending habits to change (less for ourselves and more for the work of God). We should expect our relationships to change (from seeking to dominate to seeking to serve). We should expect our schedules to change (from spending Sundays on recreation to spending it in worship). We may even face a career change if we're involved in a business that is morally compromised. In other words, when we commit ourselves to God, any part of our lives might change. Encourage students who have made significant lifestyle changes because of their faith to tell of their experiences.

4. To what extent is the Israelites' support of their temple a model of how Christians are to support the church today? Explain.

Generally, the Jews were commanded to give a tenth to support the work of the temple and the Levites. We're not commanded a certain percentage today, but many Christians believe that the "law of love" should compel us to give even more as we support the work of the church. We give to pay the living of those who serve the church full time (1 Corinthians 9:7-11), to help people in need both inside and outside the church, and to spread the gospel.

5. In what ways can Christians offer the "firstfruits" our families and of our livelihoods today?

The law of firstfruits helped people remember that their lives and livelihoods depended first on God. We can remember the same truth in several ways. For example, we can set aside our offerings to the church first—before our other bills are paid. We can offer God the first moments of each day by cultivating the habit of morning Bible reading and prayer. We can dedicate ourselves to lead our families to God by including explicitly Christian content and teaching in marriage ceremonies, by praying for the faith and calling of our children (even yet to be born), or by offering prayers or special offerings in connection with the significant events of our children's lives. Ask the learners for specific ways that they demonstrably put God first.

Message of Condemnation

DEVOTIONAL READING: Isaiah 43:1-7.

BACKGROUND SCRIPTURE: Obadiah.

PRINTED TEXT: Obadiah 1-4, 10, 11, 15, 21.

Obadiah 1-4, 10, 11, 15, 21

1 The vision of Obadiah. Thus saith the Lord GOD concerning Edom; We have heard a rumor from the LORD, and an ambassador is sent among the heathen, Arise ye, and let us rise up against her in battle.

2 Behold, I have made thee small among the heathen: thou art greatly despised.

3 The pride of thine heart hath deceived thee, thou that dwellest in the clefts of the rock, whose habitation is high; that saith in his heart, Who shall bring me down to the ground?

4 Though thou exalt thyself as the eagle, and though thou set thy nest among the stars, thence will I bring thee down, saith the LORD.

. . . .

10 For thy violence against thy brother Jacob shame shall cover thee, and thou shalt be cut off for ever.

11 In the day that thou stoodest on the other side, in the day that the strangers carried away captive his forces, and foreigners entered into his gates, and cast lots upon Jerusalem, even thou wast as one of them.

. . . .

15 For the day of the LORD is near upon all the heathen: as thou hast done, it shall be done unto thee: thy reward shall return upon thine own head.

. . . .

21 And saviours shall come up on mount Zion to judge the mount of Esau; and the kingdom shall be the LORD'S.

Aug 3

GOLDEN TEXT: As thou hast done, it shall be done unto thee: thy reward shall return upon thine own head.—Obadiah 15.

God Restores a Remnant

Unit 3: Repentance

(Lessons 10-14)

Lesson Aims

After this lesson each student will be able to:

1. Relate Obadiah's verbal portrait of a nation whose hatred carried it down the road to its own destruction.

2. Explain how hatred can cause us to put our pride in the wrong things.

3. Identify personal feelings of hatred and plan ways to begin removing those feelings.

Lesson Outline

INTRODUCTION

  A. Red and Heelcatcher

  B. Lesson Background

 I. WARNING TO EDOM (Obadiah 1-4)

  A. Battle Is Coming (v. 1)

  B. Defeat Is Looming (v. 2)

  C. Edom's Foolish Pride (v. 3)

    Pride

  D. God's Certain Victory (v. 4)

 II. CHARGE AGAINST EDOM (Obadiah 10, 11)

  A. Violence Against Israel (v. 10)

  B. Help to Israel's Enemies (v. 11)

III. OVERTHROW OF EDOM (Obadiah 15, 21)

  A. Day of the Lord (v. 15)

    Moral Court

  B. Triumph of the Lord (v. 21)

CONCLUSION

  A. Nations Used and Punished

  B. Nations and People

  C. Prayer

  D. Thought to Remember

Introduction

A. Red and Heelcatcher

Red and Heelcatcher were twins, and their rivalry began before they were born. Their prenatal struggles made their mother's pregnancy difficult (Genesis 25:22). To her the Lord revealed not only that she would have twins, but also that each twin would become the father of a nation and that the nation springing from the younger twin would be dominant (25:23).

The firstborn twin had so much body hair that he was named "Hairy" (or "Esau" in the language of his parents; 25:25). The second followed quickly, for his baby hand was grasping his brother's heel. Appropriately he was named "Heelcatcher," or "Jacob" in his parents' language.

When the boys grew up, Jacob turned out to be a homebody, while Esau became a roving hunter (25:27, 28). Then the younger twin began to dominate, using methods more shrewd than just or right.

One day Esau came home from his hunting, and he was very hungry. He found Jacob cooking a stew of red lentils. Naturally the hungry man wanted some of that savory food. Jacob was willing to sell it, but the price he asked was Esau's birthright. Reckless Esau accepted that deal. With a solemn oath he delivered his birthright. That meant that Jacob, not Esau, would become head of the family at the father's death and would inherit a double portion of the estate. All that for a bowl of stew (25:29-34)!

The father of those twins was Isaac, son of Abraham. In his old age he lost his eyesight. Then his wife conspired with Jacob to make him give to Jacob the blessing he intended for Esau. In that chosen family, a father's dying blessing was a real prophecy. It told what actually was going to happen later. So Isaac, thinking he was talking to Esau, promised to Jacob prosperity and dominion over nations (27:1-40). In later years, that promise was fulfilled.

Because Esau was so eager for Jacob's red stew, he was given the nickname "Red" (25:30), or "Edom" in the language then spoken. That nickname clung so long that the nation descended from this man was called Edom as well as Esau. (See the two terms used interchangeably in Jeremiah 49:7, 8 and Obadiah 8.) In later years Jacob, "Heelcatcher," also received a new name. He was called "Israel," or God's contender (Genesis 32:28). So the nation descended from him was and is called Israel. This week our lesson brings us to those two nations at a time more than a twelve hundred years after the time of Esau and Jacob.

B. Lesson Background

The background to the book of Obadiah is a time of invasion and distress in Israel's history. But figuring out just which invasion Obadiah is referring to is a problem! There are at least six invasions or times of civil unrest between the breakup of Israel into two parts in 931 B.C. and the Babylonian exile in 586 B.C. Scholars have proposed as many theories for Obadiah as their were invasions!

Since the language of Obadiah 10-13 implies that the Jewish people have been carried off into captivity, it is most likely that Obadiah prophesies some time after 586 B.C. The first four verses of Obadiah look quite similar to Jeremiah 49:14-16, where the Babylonian exile has just become a reality. The condemnation of Edom in Lamentations 4:21, 22, which was written after the sobering events of 586 B.C., also supports this background for the book of Obadiah.

Before the Babylonian captivity, the Jewish people (descended from the younger twin Jacob) had lived in the country at the eastern end of the Mediterranean Sea. Edom (the nation descended from Esau) lived right next door, in the broad area south and east of the Dead Sea. As foretold in Genesis 25:23, the nation of the younger twin was stronger. King David subdued Edom in about 990 B.C. and added it to the Israelite empire (2 Samuel 8:14). After David's son Solomon died, that empire split apart in about 931 B.C. Edom eventually revolted in about 847 B.C. (2 Kings 8:20-22). For many years to follow there was more war than peace between Israel and Edom. In our text, we shall see the prophet Obadiah rebuking Edom for its enmity toward the nation God had chosen for His own.

I. Warning to Edom (Obadiah 1-4)

Obadiah means "servant of Yahweh." About this prophet we know only what we learn from this short book that bears his name. Nothing is said about his parents or his family, nothing about his birthplace or his home, nothing about how or when or where he delivered God's message to Edom. The prophet hides in the shadows; God's message stands in the spotlight.

A. Battle Is Coming (v. 1)

1. The vision of Obadiah. Thus saith the Lord GOD concerning Edom; We have heard a rumor from the LORD, and an ambassador is sent among the heathen, Arise ye, and let us rise up against her in battle.

The phrase *the vision of Obadiah* stands out as the title of the book. The clause *thus saith the Lord God concerning Edom* may be called a subtitle. *We have heard* indicates that Obadiah is not alone as he prophesies. But exactly who the "we" are is uncertain. It may indicate that Obadiah is part of a larger group of prophets.

What Obadiah and the others have heard is very important since it is a message *from the Lord.* No doubt the word *rumor* was a good translation when the *King James Version* was made nearly four hundred years ago. Today the word "rumor" means something like "idle gossip"—talk that is passed around without any reliable information about its source or authority. Here we know the Source of the message is God Himself. You can't get any more reliable than that!

The message is that of a coming *battle.* Just as God already has used pagan nations against Judah (e.g., Isaiah 8:1-10; Jeremiah 22:24-27), so He also promises to do against Edom (cf. Jeremiah 27:1-7).

The *ambassador* who *is sent* to the pagan nations perhaps is not literally a messenger walking from place to place. In some way not known to us, *the Lord* is stirring up the ungodly nations as instruments of destruction to attack Edom. Certainly those nations do not intend to serve the Lord. But God still uses them to punish people and nations that need punishment. Soon it will be Edom's turn on the chopping block.

B. Defeat Is Looming (v. 2)

2. Behold, I have made thee small among the heathen: thou art greatly despised.

Edom does not know it yet, but God has made that nation too *small* to stand against the pagan nations He is stirring up for the attack. This smallness leads Edom to be *greatly despised* by those nations. When battle comes, defeat is certain.

C. Edom's Foolish Pride (v. 3)

3. The pride of thine heart hath deceived thee, thou that dwellest in the clefts of the rock, whose habitation is high; that saith in his heart, Who shall bring me down to the ground?

The Bible often warns of the dangers of *pride* and arrogance. Solomon cautions, "Pride goeth before destruction, and a haughty spirit before a fall" (Proverbs 16:18). Certainly the Edomites ought to be enthusiastic about their nation, their civilization, and their accomplishments. But that attachment becomes a self-deceiving pride; the Edomites think they are stronger, wiser, and better than they really are. As a result, they probably

Visual for lessons 1 and 10. *Locate Edom on a more detailed map; then point out for your students its general location on this wall map.*

scorn Obadiah's warning. The Edomites have no fear of the nations around them.

The clefts of the rock, whose habitation is high describes Edom in a way that is both picturesque and accurate. Even today, visitors to that area are amazed at the rose-red city of Petra. It is not built of quarried stone; rather, it is carved out of the face of a towering cliff of solid rock. To approach it, one must go through a cleft of the rock too narrow for anything much wider than a single camel. It is small wonder that the inhabitants of such a place feel secure.

Only fifty miles from the Dead Sea, the mountain beside Petra rises a mile above that body of water. Edom's homeland is so high, so rough, and so difficult for the traveler, that the proud inhabitants feel immune to invasion. What natural defenses! "Surely no one *shall bring me down,*" they reason. But Edom reckons without God, and His viewpoint is different. See the next verse.

PRIDE

Five centuries ago in the city of Florence, a woman came day after day to worship and do homage before a statue of the Virgin Mary. "Look how she reverences the Virgin mother," said one priest to another.

"Don't be deceived by what you see," his colleague responded. "Many years ago an artist was commissioned to create a statue for the cathedral. He sought a young woman to pose as the model for his sculpture and found one who seemed to be the perfect subject. She was young, serenely lovely, and had a mystical quality to her face. The image of that young woman inspired his statue of Mary. The woman you now see worshiping the statue is the same one who served as its model years ago. Shortly after the statue was put in place, she began to visit it and has continued to worship there religiously ever since."

Pride is arrogant self-worship. Pride deludes its victims into believing that they have no peers and drives them to destroy anyone who takes recognition away from them. The proud are infatuated with themselves.

Centuries ago Edom was judged by God for a prideful heart and arrogant spirit (v. 3) Deceived by their own prideful illusions they became God's enemy.   —J. A. M.

D. God's Certain Victory (v. 4)

4. Though thou exalt thyself as the eagle, and though thou set thy nest among the stars, thence will I bring thee down, saith the LORD.

God is going to bring Edom *down*. Even if Edom could soar like an *eagle* far above those mile-high mountains, even if the Edomites could build their cities *among the stars* instead of carving them

from the lofty rock, God still is going to bring that nation down. It won't be by an earthquake, to crumble the solid rocks where they dwell. Rather, the destruction will come at the hands of human invaders (v. 1). Edom's allies will become enemies (v. 7). They will be God's instrument to destroy both the wise leaders and the mighty soldiers of Edom, "to the end that every one of the mount of Esau may be cut off by slaughter" (v. 9).

II. Charge Against Edom (Obadiah 10, 11)

Edom would fall for the same reason that many nations had fallen before and since that time: Edom would fall because of wickedness. Next we see exactly what type of wickedness it is that condemns Edom.

A. Violence Against Israel (v. 10)

10. For thy violence against thy brother Jacob shame shall cover thee, and thou shalt be cut off for ever.

As we noted in the Introduction, Esau and *Jacob* were twin brothers many centuries earlier. Those two should have acted in brotherly fashion. But Jacob resorted to deceit to get the blessing

---

How to Say It

ASSYRIA. Uh-*sear*-ee-uh.
BABYLON. *Bab*-uh-lun.
BABYLONIAN. Bab-ih-*low*-nee-un.
DEUTERONOMY. Due-ter-*ahn*-uh-me.
EDOM. *Ee*-dum.
EDOMITES. *Ee*-dum-ites.
ESAU. *Ee*-saw.
EZEKIEL. Ee-*zeek*-ee-ul or Ee-*zeek*-yul.
HABAKKUK. Huh-*back*-kuk.
HASMONEANS. *Haz*-mow-*nee*-unz (strong accent on *nee*).
HEROD. *Hair*-ud.
IDUMEANS. Id-you-*me*-unz.
ISAAC. *Eye*-zuk.
ISAIAH. Eye-*zay*-uh.
JEREMIAH. Jair-uh-*my*-uh.
MACCABEES. *Mack*-uh-bees.
MEDES. Meeds.
NABATEANS. *Nab*-uh-*tee*-unz (strong accent on *tee*).
NAHUM. *Nay*-hum.
NINEVEH. *Nin*-uh-vuh.
OBADIAH. O-buh-*dye*-uh.
PERSIANS. *Per*-zhunz.
PETRA. *Peh*-trah.
SYRIANS. *Sear*-ee-unz.
YAHWEH (Hebrew). *Yah*-weh.

their father meant to give to Esau as firstborn. To retaliate, Esau planned to kill Jacob, so Jacob had to flee the country to save his life (Genesis 27).

Likewise the two nations descended from those brothers should have maintained brotherly relations. Their people are blood relatives, and God expected civility between them (see Deuteronomy 2:1-8). But often they were hostile instead. [See question #1, page 418.] Edom shall be humbled by being *cut off for ever.* [See question #2, page 418.] In the next verse we see the Lord chose one example as a basis for His charge against Edom.

B. Help to Israel's Enemies (v. 11)

11. In the day that thou stoodest on the other side, in the day that the strangers carried away captive his forces, and foreigners entered into his gates, and cast lots upon Jerusalem, even thou wast as one of them.

In the critical time when *foreigners* invaded Israelite territory and looted Jerusalem, Edom, Israel's kin, took a stand *on the other side*—the side of the foreigners. The most disastrous of those invasions was that of the Babylonians, who destroyed Jerusalem and took most of its people into captivity. Therefore it is natural to suppose that the fall of Jerusalem to Babylon in 586 B.C. is in view here. [See question #3, page 418.]

That destruction by the Babylonian forces was total. Those *strangers carried away captive his forces.* The Hebrew word for "forces" also can be translated "wealth." The Babylonians completely eliminated Judah's forces (military power) and wealth—the Babylonians took it all! (See 2 Kings 25:11-21; 2 Chronicles 36:17-20; and Jeremiah 52:12-30.)

After crashing through Jerusalem's walls, the invaders had *entered into* the city's *gates* and burned them (Nehemiah 1:3). Invading soldiers in the ancient world often divided up the loot with games of chance, such as casting *lots* (cf. Luke 23:34). This had happened both to Nineveh (Nahum 3:10) and Jerusalem (Joel 3:3) when they fell to invaders. However this casting of lots was not for the purpose of showing favoritism or letting anyone "off the hook" (cf. Ezekiel 24:6). All of Jerusalem had suffered. And when it happened, Edom had shown no sympathy or compassion. Rather, inhabitants of that country had stood on the sidelines and gloated (see Psalm 137:7).

Not merely content to gloat, Edom actively helped the invaders as verses 12-14 (not included in our text) make clear. And when the Babylonians took their army away, the Edomites started moving into Israelite territory themselves (cf. Ezekiel 25:12-14).

III. Overthrow of Edom (Obadiah 15, 21)

The facts are stated clearly. First, God said proud Edom was to be brought low because of Edom's violence to Israel and help to Israel's enemies. Now the last two verses of our text relate the final outcome of all this.

A. Day of the Lord (v. 15)

15. For the day of the LORD is near upon all the heathen: as thou hast done, it shall be done unto thee: thy reward shall return upon thine own head.

The Bible speaks of *the day of the Lord* in many places. It is a foreboding phrase of judgment. It is a time of the Lord's victory and His enemies' defeat. That time is *near* for Edom. What Edom has *done* to others eventually is turned right back on that country's *own head.* Such is the ultimate fate of *all* nations that oppose God and His people. [See question #4, page 418.]

MORAL COURT

In the late 1990s, televised legal proceedings became all the rage. It began in 1981 when Judge Joseph Wapner became the star of "The People's Court." By the year 2000, there were at least ten "courtroom" programs on TV. Televised legal proceedings today can feature the deadly serious. Who can forget the O. J. Simpson trial from 1995? But at the other end of the spectrum stands the downright trivial, as with one case on the show "Moral Court" that featured a mother "suing" her live-in daughter over how often the daughter should wash her hair!

As we read Obadiah's prophecy against Edom, we get the distinct impression that we are witnessing a courtroom scene there as well. The Judge, the evidence, the verdict, and the sentence are all easy to recognize. But when we realize that it is God Himself who is the Judge, and that an entire nation is being condemned, we are reminded of how inconsequential many of today's "legal proceedings" really are.

The book of Obadiah also reminds us that a day is coming when we will be participants in God's "moral court." As John said, "I saw the dead, small and great, stand before God; and the books were opened: . . . and the dead were judged out of those things which were written in the books, according to their works" (Revelation 20:12). Will you be ready?   —R. L. N.

B. Triumph of the Lord (v. 21)

21. And saviours shall come up on mount Zion to judge the mount of Esau; and the kingdom shall be the LORD's.

In the time between the Old and New Testaments, the eastern part of Edom *(Esau)* is taken by the Nabateans, an Arabian tribe. That happens in about 325 B.C. And although Obadiah's short book deals mostly with the sin and punishment of Edom, the people of Israel are sinners, too. They are punished by captivity in Babylon. When they are allowed to go back home, they are subjects of the Persian Empire. When Alexander the Great subdues that empire, the people of Israel are then in his realm. When Alexander dies, they are ruled by Syrian tyrants.

Then the *saviours* come. Perhaps "rescuers" would better describe them in our day. They are a priestly family called Maccabees (or Hasmoneans), who lead a desperate revolt against the Syrians until Israel is independent again. Israel conquers the western part of Edom in a bloody campaign (2 Maccabees 10:14-23), and the Edomites (by then called Idumeans) are compelled to become Jews. (One of them, Herod the Great, even becomes a Jewish king.)

But then independent Israel is swallowed up by the growing Roman Empire. When the Romans destroy Jerusalem and scatter the Israelites in A.D. 70, Edom vanishes from the pages of history.

Yet it is also under Roman rule that the greater Savior comes to *mount Zion.* He is crucified as King of the Jews (Matthew 27:37), but His kingdom is not of this world (John 18:36). He is raised up to be King of kings (Revelation 19:16). His is the kingdom that "shall break in pieces and consume all these kingdoms, and it shall stand for ever" (Daniel 2:44; cf. Amos 9:12). [See question #5, page 418.]

Conclusion

A. Nations Used and Punished

Perhaps it seem strange that the Lord used Babylon to punish Israel (Jeremiah 25:9), and then rebuked Edom for helping in that punishment. But this is just another example of God's customary way of working with evil nations. He will use one wicked nation to punish another, and then turn around and punish the first nation for its own wickedness. (This is a major theme of the book of Habakkuk.)

Isaiah 10:5-12 plainly shows God's way in this regard. There we see God using Assyria to punish northern Israel. But Assyria does not intend to be used by God. Assyria's motives are selfish and malicious. The Assyrian rulers are greedy for wealth and power (vv. 7-11). Therefore God punishes Assyria in her turn (v. 12). History reveals that God used Babylon to destroy Assyria; then used the Medes and Persians to destroy Babylon. Next, God used the Greek empire under Alexander the Great to destroy the empire of the Medes and Persians.

These are lessons for all nations of the twenty-first century! Read history and learn. The God of all history still casts a watchful eye over all nations today.

B. Nations and People

What makes a nation wicked? Wicked people do. What makes a nation good? Good people do. Do we want our nation to be better? If we do, we must help its people to be better. Two things are necessary for that to happen.

The first thing is *repentance.* A bad person will not become good unless he or she wants to reject evil. But no one can be good enough by personal effort alone. Something else is needed.

That something else is *forgiveness.* Forgiveness is God's doing, not ours. Forgiveness comes when a person believes in the Savior who long ago came up on Mount Zion and who gave His life at Calvary. A person who truly believes in the Savior will submit to Peter's instructions to "Repent, and be baptized every one of you in the name of Jesus Christ for the remission of sins" (Acts 2:38). Jesus is the crucified King who now lives and rules forever. Forgiveness through Him enrolls us in His kingdom, the "kingdom, which shall never be destroyed" (Daniel 2:44).

C. Prayer

Forgive our sins, O Father, and guide us daily that we shall sin no more. By Your grace may we have our home forever in that kingdom that shall never be destroyed, the only kingdom that shall stand for all eternity. In Jesus' name, amen.

D. Thought to Remember

Trust the Lord and do right.

Home Daily Bible Readings

Learning by Doing

This page contains an alternative lesson plan emphasizing learning activities.
Classes desiring such student involvement will find these suggestions helpful.

Learning Goals

After participating in this lesson, each student will be able to:

1. Relate Obadiah's verbal portrait of a nation whose hatred carried it down the road to its own destruction.

2. Explain how hatred can cause us to put our pride in the wrong things.

3. Identify personal feelings of hatred and plan ways to begin removing those feelings.

Into the Lesson

ADVANCE PREPARATION: If you have the *Adult Visuals* that support these lessons, pull out this unit's map; get any pictures of the city of Petra that you can; and borrow appropriate teaching pictures from teachers of children's Bible classes. Recruit a good storyteller from the class to tell the historical background of Jacob and Esau from Genesis 25–33; provide the information from this lesson's commentary and other study sources.

Option One: As students arrive say, "Have you ever noticed how many movies and television shows revolve around the theme of revenge? Can you identify some?" Write the titles and plot lines on the chalkboard or a poster sheet as they are suggested.

Option Two: Provide markers or watercolor paints and brushes and invite students to paint images of "hatred" on poster board or banner paper. (You can offer students both options.)

Then say, "Revenge is a strong motive for many people to act hatefully. Our study in the prophecy of Obadiah today will reveal how far such hatred ultimately can take people."

Into the Word

An understanding of the historical background is imperative for your students to comprehend Obadiah's message. Using the unit map (or another map of Old Testament Palestine that clearly shows Edom) and teaching pictures, help your students understand the long legacy of hatred between the two nations and the false security that Petra's physical location gave.

With strong expression read the book of Obadiah to the class. Lecture on the contents of the commentary. You can use the outline given in it (see page 412) as your framework, or you can adapt the material to fit the following outline

suggested by Loren Deckard (*Minor Prophets*, Cincinnati: Standard Publishing, 1999, p. 33):

    I. Hateful thinking causes us to misunderstand who the enemy is (vv. 2, 4).

    II. Hateful thinking causes us to overestimate our own power.

    III. Hateful thinking leads us to take joy and pride in the wrong things.

To get students to look closely at the text of Obadiah, divide the twenty-one verses equally among your class members. If you have more than twenty-one, repeat assignments. Indicate you are going to read "paraphrases" of verses, and you want someone to identify and read the corresponding verse from the text. For example, "You can't get high enough above the ground to escape God's notice" (v. 4); "You should not stand across the street indifferent to a mugging going on on the other side" (v. 11). Write and use others.

Into Life

Guide students to make a comparison between the attitudes and actions of the people of Edom and of people today. This can be done individually or in small groups by giving the following questions to either. Write the students' answers on the board or an overhead transparency so that students can follow the progression.

Questions: "Edom hated Judah; which groups today express hatred for others?"

"Edom's hatred caused the people to rejoice and boast when God's people suffered; what is hatred causing people to do today?"

"The inhabitants of Petra felt secure in the city built into the face of a towering cliff; in what do we place our security today?"

"Edom's pride had deceived them; in what ways are we proud today? How could our pride be deceiving us?"

After this analysis, let students individually examine their own lives to determine whether they are harboring feelings of anger or hatred. If your students are comfortable in holding one another accountable, let partners confess such feelings to each other and talk together about how they could begin removing those feelings this week. If your students are not that comfortable with such an exercise, let them write down the first step, and then you follow with a prayer for God's strength and wisdom to be given in carrying out their plans.

Let's Talk It Over

The questions on this page are designed to promote discussion of the lesson by the class and to encourage application of the lesson Scriptures. The answers provided are only discussion starters. Let your class talk it over from there.

1. Edom stands condemned because of actions against "thy brother Jacob." Family relationships are important to God; what can we do to strengthen our own family relationships?

The first structure of human relationships God instituted was the family (Adam and Eve). Later, God developed His plan of salvation based on family, promising that Abraham would be the "father of many nations." In the New Testament, relationships in the church are compared to the family, beginning with God being "our Father."

The close bonds that normally form between family members benefit us in many ways. Families ensure that the youngest, oldest, and weakest members of society are taken care of. They pass down treasures from one generation to the next—skills for living, wisdom, and faith as well as property. They offer a sense of identity, belonging, and unconditional love. The home is the first place we learn how to live peacefully with other people. Parents need to model that kind of relationship for their children. They need to insist on the children's treating others in the family with love, courtesy, and respect. Consistent rules backed by a consistent example is critical to passing on godly family values.

2. How would you reconcile this passage with the Sermon on the Mount, in which Jesus tells us to pray for those who persecute us, bless our enemies, and turn the other cheek?

The main distinction between this passage and Jesus' teaching could be summed up by Paul: "avenge not yourselves, . . . for it is written, Vengeance is mine; I will repay, saith the Lord" (Romans 12:19). While Jesus often spoke of judgment, it was always the judgment of God, usually that which takes place at the end of the age. The parable of the wheat and the tares is a good example (Matthew 13:24-30). We are called to treat others with love and mercy. We leave matters of vengeance and condemnation to the Lord and the governing authorities (Romans 13:1-4).

3. God condemned Edom for standing "on the other side" when Judah fell. How are we sometimes guilty of standing aloof when someone is in trouble? In what ways should we—as individuals, as churches, and as nations—help those we see in trouble?

Jesus addressed this issue in the parable of the Good Samaritan (Luke 10:25-37). There, a priest and a Levite purposefully avoided a situation where they should have helped.

Individuals, churches, and nations have different roles in this regard. Christians should live by the "law of love," which says anyone in need should be considered our neighbor, not our enemy. Sometimes churches can do things that individual Christians cannot. And certain projects, such as feeding millions of starving refugees, are so daunting that only entire nations can make a significant difference. We can't always expect a secular nation to live by Christian values, but Christians and their churches can show that it is possible to offer service rather than self-interest.

4. Some people say the "God of the Old Testament" is vengeful and harsh, but the "God of the New Testament" is loving and merciful. How would you respond to such a statement?

At first glance, it might seem that there are indeed "two faces of God." That teaching, however, reflects a selective reading of Scripture. In truth, there are many tender words of love, mercy, patience, and compassion throughout the Old Testament (e.g., Joel 2:13, next week). At the same time, many warnings of judgment can be found throughout the New Testament, starting with Jesus Himself (e.g., Matthew 23, 24) and ending with the book of Revelation. A unifying theme between the testaments is that God hopes people will choose to walk faithfully with Him, because in Him—and only in Him—is there life.

5. The Lord promised that one day the kingdom would be His. What is our part in this?

The final words of Obadiah echo many promises of a coming Messiah and kingdom, including Jesus' prayer, "Thy kingdom come. Thy will be done in earth, as it is in heaven" (Matthew 6:10). Our part begins with submitting ourselves to God and allowing His will to dominate ours. We can also continue to pray for God's Spirit to work through fellow Christians in our churches, towns, and nations. By telling others the good news of Jesus and demonstrating His love, we all can help increase the reach of God's kingdom now, anticipating His complete reign yet to come.

Call for Repentance

DEVOTIONAL READING: Acts 2:14-23, 32, 33.

BACKGROUND SCRIPTURE: Joel 1, 2.

PRINTED TEXT: Joel 2:1, 2, 12-14, 28, 29.

Joel 2:1, 2, 12-14, 28, 29

1 Blow ye the trumpet in Zion, and sound an alarm in my holy mountain: let all the inhabitants of the land tremble: for the day of the LORD cometh, for it is nigh at hand;

2 A day of darkness and of gloominess, a day of clouds and of thick darkness, as the morning spread upon the mountains: a great people and a strong; there hath not been ever the like, neither shall be any more after it, even to the years of many generations.

. . . .

12 Therefore also now, saith the LORD, turn ye even to me with all your heart, and with fasting, and with weeping, and with mourning:

13 And rend your heart, and not your garments, and turn unto the LORD your God: for he is gracious and merciful, slow to anger, and of great kindness, and repenteth him of the evil.

14 Who knoweth if he will return and repent, and leave a blessing behind him; even a meat offering and a drink offering unto the LORD your God?

. . . .

28 And it shall come to pass afterward, that I will pour out my Spirit upon all flesh; and your sons and your daughters shall prophesy, your old men shall dream dreams, your young men shall see visions:

29 And also upon the servants and upon the handmaids in those days will I pour out my Spirit.

GOLDEN TEXT: Turn ye even to me with all your heart, and with fasting, and with weeping, and with mourning: and rend your heart, and not your garments, and turn unto the LORD your God: for he is gracious and merciful, slow to anger, and of great kindness, and repenteth him of the evil.
—Joel 2:12, 13.

God Restores a Remnant
Unit 3: Repentance
(Lessons 10-14)

Lesson Aims

After this lesson each student will be able to:

1. Describe the message of Joel to the people in Israel's southern kingdom (Judah).

2. Make a list of sins and define *repentance*.

3. Identify a sin in his or her life and plan a private time to repent of it.

Lesson Outline

INTRODUCTION

  A. When the Grasshoppers Came

  B. Lesson Background

  I. WARNING OF DESOLATION (Joel 2:1, 2)

    A. Announcing the Day of the Lord (v. 1)

      Intelligent Alarms

    B. Describing the Day of the Lord (v. 2)

  II. CALLING FOR REPENTANCE (Joel 2:12-14)

    A. The Call (vv. 12, 13a)

    B. The Lord (v. 13b)

    C. The Hope (v. 14)

      Repentance

  III. ANTICIPATING THE FUTURE (Joel 2:28, 29)

    A. Outpouring of God's Spirit (v. 28)

    B. Servants, Too (v. 29)

CONCLUSION

  A. Prophets in the New Testament

  B. Calling on the Name of the Lord

  C. Prophecy for Today

  D. Prayer

  E. Thought to Remember

Introduction

A. When the Grasshoppers Came

From my long-ago childhood on the farm, I carry a dim memory of the year the grasshoppers came. My brother and I picked our way with great care when we walked to the barn, for it was quite alarming to have a bare foot step on one of those squirming, scratching little creatures. On the wing, the insects would mindlessly smack us in the face, drop to the ground, and sit there looking stupefied. The chickens happily pounced on the invaders, but only for a time. When their gullets were full, they could only stand and watch the oversupply of food hopping around them.

We were all concerned with the crops, of course. So the county entomologist provided a recipe for poison bait, and the newspapers published it daily. We mixed bran with sorghum molasses to delight the grasshoppers' taste, and deadly poison to kill them. We spread the stuff in fields of corn and cotton, and the critters died by the millions.

We dared not poison the garden, however, lest we die with the bugs! So our growing beans and peas and turnips vanished. We ate the last of the vegetables Mom had canned the year before, and then we bought tin cans at the store.

The next year we watched with bated breath as "grasshopper time" approached, but the little pests came in their normal numbers. Only the chickens paid them any attention.

As bad as our grasshopper infestation had been, a plague of locusts in a Mediterranean country is worse. Exodus 10:12-15 provides a brief description of locusts as one of the famous ten plagues upon Egypt. Clouds of those insects blocked the sun and darkened the whole land. Those hordes devoured every green thing that grew.

The first chapter of Joel also describes a locust plague, but this description is not so short and literal as the one in Exodus 10. Joel's account is long, poetic, and compelling. The locusts there are "a nation . . . strong, and without number, whose teeth are the teeth of a lion" (Joel 1:6). Vividly this account describes the devastation; poignantly it calls the people to mourn (vv. 7-20).

B. Lesson Background

Other than his father's name (Joel 1:1), we know little about Joel himself. As with Obadiah from last week, the spotlight is on God's message. The dating of Joel's message is even more uncertain than that of Obadiah. Some scholars think Joel to be among the earliest of the writing prophets; others think he was one of the latest. If we must guess about this, perhaps a date of about 780 B.C. would be good—during the time of Isaiah and King Uzziah. The prophet Amos, who definitely does live in the time of Uzziah (Amos 1:1), also speaks of locusts (Amos 4:9; 7:1-3).

That was a time of immorality and sloth in Israel's history. Here we use the name *Israel* to refer to the southern part of divided Israel—the part with its capital at Jerusalem, the part composed of the tribes of Judah and Benjamin, the part often called Judah. We use the name *Israel* to help us remember that this nation was descended from Jacob, whom God renamed Israel (cf. Joel 2:27; 3:2, 16). If our dating is correct, Joel was preaching heroically to a people so at ease in their "good times" that they paid little heed to the true meaning of that heritage or predictions of doom. God has decided to correct the problem.

I. Warning of Desolation
(Joel 2:1, 2)

Before we reach this point in Joel, the prophet already has painted a foreboding picture of locusts and great mourning. A call to repentance has been offered (1:13-20). Now the cycle repeats.

A. Announcing the Day of the Lord (v. 1)

1. Blow ye the trumpet in Zion, and sound an alarm in my holy mountain: let all the inhabitants of the land tremble: for the day of the LORD cometh, for it is nigh at hand.

Mount *Zion* is God's *holy mountain*, the site of Jerusalem, the capital of God's holy people. Now *the day of the Lord* is coming, and soon. This is a day of "destruction" (Joel 1:15). It will be "terrible" (2:11, 31), a day of "decision" (3:14). In Bible times, trumpets are used to *sound* alarms (e.g., Jeremiah 4:5, 19; 6:1, 17). Why would the announcement be *an alarm* to *the inhabitants of the land?* Because the people supposed to be His were not His at all. By their sinning, they have made themselves His enemies: His victory will be their defeat. [See question #1, page 426.]

The day of the Lord is any time when the Lord's victory and His enemies' defeat are clearly seen. The Lord's true people long for such a time; His enemies should dread it. In the Old Testament we see that God chose the people of Israel to be His people; but all too often they chose to disobey Him, and so they become His enemies by their sinning. Consequently, this is not good news for them, as the next verse will make clear. [See question #2, page 426.]

INTELLIGENT ALARMS

People try various gadgets to keep their cars from being stolen. One of the most irritating is the car alarm. These things produce so many *false* alarms that people largely ignore them when they go off. The really irritating part comes when those devices awaken us at 3:00 A.M.!

But now enter the "intelligent" car alarm, announced in a story by the BBC March 7, 2001. When this alarm is installed, numerous sensors are placed within the car to detect break-in or towing. If the sensors notice questionable activity, the car's transceiver actually telephones the owner to warn of the theft in progress! The whole idea is to make car alarms viable again by overcoming the problem of "bystander apathy."

Throughout the history of His people, God has encountered a lot of human apathy in response to His alarms. This has been true regardless of how many alarms He has sounded. But no matter how "intelligent" He makes those alarms, they won't do any good if people are not discerning enough to hear them. Today, do we hear God's warning and take right action, or are we among those who are so apathetic that we cannot "discern the signs of the times" (Matthew 16:3)?   —R. L. N.

B. Describing the Day of the Lord (v. 2)

2. A day of darkness and of gloominess, a day of clouds and of thick darkness, as the morning spread upon the mountains: a great people and a strong; there hath not been ever the like, neither shall be any more after it, even to the years of many generations.

The *day* of the Lord will bring no bright joy to Israel. It will be a time of *darkness and of gloominess*—a time of loss, trouble, and sorrow. The imagery of *clouds* and *thick darkness* recalls Exodus 10:21, 22 and Deuteronomy 4:11. Most students agree that the imagery here describes the people's mood rather than the weather.

The reason for this gloominess is that the day of the Lord will bring upon Israel *a great people and a strong.* Joel may be using a double reference here. In addition to the literal locusts described in chapter 1, this "great people" may refer to an invading army of human soldiers. (Judges 6:5 and 7:12 use "grasshoppers" figuratively for "people.")

The description of these invaders—whether they are insects or human or even both—is continued in verses 3-11 (not included in our printed text). They spread like a wildfire, transforming fruitful land into "a desolate wilderness" (v. 3). They seem to be unstoppable (v. 4). Their noise is deafening (v. 5). At their coming "the people shall be much pained" (v. 6). No place is safe from them (vv. 7-9). They shake the earth and sky, darken the sun and moon. Perhaps this is a figurative way of saying the people are so shaken that nothing seems secure any more (v. 10; cf. Jeremiah 15:9). The Lord lets His voice be

---

How to Say It

AMOS. *Ay*-mus.
BABYLON. *Bab*-uh-lun.
DEUTERONOMY. Due-ter-*ahn*-uh-me.
ENTOMOLOGIST. en-tuh-*mawl*-uh-jist.
EZEKIEL. Ee-*zeek*-ee-ul or Ee-*zeek*-yul.
ISAIAH. Eye-*zay*-uh.
JEREMIAH. Jair-uh-*my*-uh.
MALACHI. *Mal*-uh-kye.
OBADIAH. O-buh-*dye*-uh.
PENTECOST. *Pent*-ih-kost.
SIMEON. *Sim*-ee-un.
SORGHUM. *sor*-gum.
UZZIAH. Uh-*zye*-uh.
ZION. *Zye*-un.

heard. Perhaps by this very prophet He lets it be known that people who persist in evil will have to face this "great and very terrible" day of the Lord (Joel 2:11).

II. Calling for Repentance (Joel 2:12-14)

That terrible day of the Lord, bringing an army of locusts and/or soldiers to punish the people of Israel for their stubborn sin—that day is near, not yet present (v. 1). Could it be avoided if the people would repent and change their evil ways, and walk in a path of sincere obedience? (See 2 Chronicles 7:13, 14.) Or was that day too near to be avoided? (Compare Jeremiah 7:16-20; 11:14-17; 14:11, 12.) Must the people endure that coming judgment in order to be motivated to repent and avoid some worse catastrophe in the future? Ultimately, we need not try to decide that question. In either case, God by His prophet is calling Israel to repent.

A. The Call (vv. 12, 13a)

12. Therefore also now, saith the LORD, turn ye even to me with all your heart, and with fasting, and with weeping, and with mourning.

Turning to God means turning away from disobedience and sin. It means humble and obedient service to the Lord. That is repentance. That is what it takes for a sinner to avoid judgment and punishment. No pretended repentance will do. People may be fooled by outward appearance and lying words, but God sees the heart (1 Samuel 16:7). Repentance may be expressed *with fasting, and with weeping, and with mourning;* but those things are worthless unless you repent sincerely, *with all your heart.* (See Isaiah 58:2-5.)

Visual for lesson 11. *Today's visual illustrates verse 13. Talk about the changes in one's life that are produced by such a rending of the heart.*

13a. And rend your heart, and not your garments.

Tearing one's own clothing is a time-honored way of expressing deep sorrow (e.g., Ezra 9:3-5; Esther 4:1-3). But such a visible sign can tell a lie as easily as words can. As David wrote, "a broken and a contrite heart, O God, thou wilt not despise" (Psalm 51:17; see also Isaiah 1:11-17; 58:3b-12; Amos 5:21-24; Micah 6:6-8). [See question #3, page 426.]

B. The Lord (v. 13b)

13b. And turn unto the LORD your God: for he is gracious and merciful, slow to anger, and of great kindness, and repenteth him of the evil.

The Bible stresses in several places that *the Lord is slow to anger* (e.g., Psalms 86:15; 103:8; 145:8). He is never vindictive, never malicious. He has no pleasure in the death of one who dies in his or her own sin (Ezekiel 18:32). He cannot forgive a sinner who scorns His mercy and goes on stubbornly in willful sin, but He is eager to forgive one who truly repents. When true repentance takes place, the person turns away from doing evil, so God turns away from sending the punishment that He warned would come. That is how God *repenteth him of the evil.* [See question #4, page 426.]

C. The Hope (v. 14)

14. Who knoweth if he will return and repent, and leave a blessing behind him; even a meat offering and a drink offering unto the LORD your God?

If people will reject their sin and turn back to God with faith and obedience, perhaps the Lord will *leave a blessing* instead of the promised punishment. Instead of destroying the produce of the land, perhaps He will leave it so the people can make to Him the offerings required by the law. (See also Exodus 32:14; 2 Samuel 24:16.)

REPENTANCE

Early in the 1989 basketball season, Michigan's Rumeal Robinson stepped to the foul line for two shots late in the fourth quarter. His team trailed Wisconsin by one point. With the game on the line, Rumeal could regain the lead for Michigan. He missed both shots. Michigan was defeated.

Robinson felt awful about costing his team the game, but his sorrow went beyond feelings. He changed his behavior, adding one hundred extra foul shots after each practice for the rest of the season.

Months later Rumeal Robinson stepped to the foul line again. There were just three seconds left in overtime in the game that would decide the national championship. This time he was ready.

Swish went the first shot. Swish went the second. Two made free throws made Michigan the national champions!

Rumeal Robinson demonstrated an important element of genuine repentance. Repentance is not just regret. It is a change of mind and heart that leads to a change in behavior. Genuine sorrow motivated him to work so that he would never make that mistake again.

Paul wrote, "Godly sorrow worketh repentance" (2 Corinthians 7:10). God's call to repentance in Joel 2:12, 13 involved both emotions and actions. God wants an internal transformation that is marked by an external reformation. Such repentance opens the door to God's forgiveness and the presence and power of His Spirit. How has repentance changed your life?   —J. A. M.

III. Anticipating the Future (Joel 2:28, 29)

Verses 15-17, not in our printed text, continue the call to repent. The people should gather in solemn assembly to make their repentance known (vv. 15, 16). The priests should weep and pray fervently for mercy on the nation (v. 17). Verses 18-20 promise that the Lord then will bless His people with abundant harvests and protect them from enemies. Verses 21-27 call the people to rejoice and to praise the Lord. Prosperity could continue as long as the people would continue to obey the Lord, enjoy His blessing, and give Him praise. Then the final verses of our text tell what would follow afterward, centuries later.

A. Outpouring of God's Spirit (v. 28)

28. And it shall come to pass afterward, that I will pour out my Spirit upon all flesh; and your sons and your daughters shall prophesy, your old men shall dream dreams, your young men shall see visions.

The ideal conditions portrayed in verses 18-27 do not materialize in the time of Joel. Despite the warnings of prophets such as Isaiah and (later) Jeremiah, the Jewish people slide farther and farther down the slope that leads to exile. A succession of bad kings and false prophets brings the people to such disobedience that God places them under the domination of Babylon for seventy years. When they return from captivity in Babylon, again they waver between serving God and turning away from Him. Consequently He sometimes blesses them and sometimes punishes them. After the time of Malachi, it seems that there are no inspired prophets in Israel for about four hundred years. Verse 28 of our text points to a time *afterward*, a time when prophecy again will be abundant.

God's promise to *pour out* His *Spirit upon all flesh* certainly does not mean that God will send His Spirit to make every person a prophet. But some people of every kind would be so gifted: both men and women, *your sons and your daughters*, both *old men* and *young men*. Sometimes God used *dreams and visions* to convey truths (Obadiah 1; Matthew 1:20). Sometimes He imparted His messages using other methods (1 Kings 19:15; Daniel 5:5, 6; Joel 1:1; Luke 2:8-12). But now He promises a time when His people will be blessed by many prophets who will make His will and His truth known. Even so, Zechariah 13:1-6 also promises that there will come a time when there are no more prophets.

B. Servants, Too (v. 29)

29. And also upon the servants and upon the handmaids in those days will I pour out my Spirit.

When God pours out His *Spirit*, it will not be just on those of high position and power. The lowly servants and handmaids will receive this gift, too. This outpouring truly is for "all flesh" (v. 28). As history unfolds, this outpouring will not occur until some eight hundred years after Joel's time. But it will happen—on the Day of Pentecost. [See question #5, page 426.]

Conclusion

A. Prophets in the New Testament

Very early in the New Testament we begin to read of prophets inspired by God. Before John the Baptist was born, his mother was "filled with the Holy Ghost" and inspired to pronounce on Mary the blessing that is recorded in Luke 1:41-45. It is not stated that Mary's response was specially inspired by God, but who will doubt that it was? (See Luke 1:46-55.) After John was born, his father "was filled with the Holy Ghost, and prophesied" as recorded in Luke 1:67-79. John the Baptist was a prophet, and more; he was the messenger foretold by Malachi 3:1, the one who would prepare the way for the Christ (Matthew 11:7-10). Simeon was an inspired prophet when he spoke at the infant Jesus' circumcision (Luke 2:25-35). Anna is plainly called a prophetess (Luke 2:36-38).

Perhaps the most notable record that the Spirit of God was poured out on people is the one recorded in Acts 2:1-12. God poured out His Spirit on the apostles of Jesus, poured the Spirit out so abundantly that the apostles were overwhelmed. They were under the Spirit's influence so completely that the Spirit used their voices to talk in human languages (Acts 2:8-11) that the apostles had not previously studied. Thus controlled completely by God's Spirit, Peter explained, "This is that which was spoken by the prophet Joel"; and he quoted the last verses of our text and several more from that prophet (Joel 2:28-32; Acts 2:16-21).

God poured out His spirit on others, too, and the Spirit guided them so fully that they spoke God's word, not their own. Read about some of them in Acts 11:27, 28; 15:32; 21:10, 11. These are mentioned so casually that we feel sure there were many others who received the same gift and were recognized as prophets.

We can hardly conclude this lesson without a glance at the rest of those few words of Joel that are quoted by Simon Peter (Joel 2:30-32; Acts 2:19-21). Joel's prophecy sweeps past the centuries of the Christian era to "the great and the terrible day of the Lord," the day of final judgment (Joel 2:31; Acts 2:20). That day will be heralded by wonders in earth and sky, by the darkening of sun and moon (Joel 2:30, 31; Mark 13:24, 25; Acts 2:19, 20). Then people on earth will see Jesus "coming in the clouds of heaven with power and great glory" (Matthew 24:30). He will send His angels to reap the harvest of humanity (Matthew 24:31). He will "gather his wheat into the garner; but he will burn up the chaff with unquenchable fire" (Matthew 3:12). And "whosoever shall call on the name of the Lord shall be saved" (Joel 2:32; Acts 2:21).

B. Calling on the Name of the Lord

Of course, calling on the name of the Lord includes more than just shouting for help. To the people of Joel's time the Lord said, "Turn ye even to me with all your heart, and with fasting, and with weeping, and with mourning" (Joel 2:12). That means a sincere change in the way of living. It means genuine sorrow for past sins and steadfast determination not to repeat them. It means deciding to do right and doing it.

To the people of his time and ours, Simon Peter says, "Repent" (Acts 2:38). That means turning to God with the whole heart as the people of Joel's time were told to do. Peter also adds, "And be baptized every one of you in the name of Jesus Christ for the remission of sins." If one is sincere in repentance, his or her sins are washed away at the time of baptism (Acts 22:16). Those sins are not removed by water, of course, but by God's gracious forgiveness that is available to us because Christ has paid sin's penalty. From the water of baptism the sincere penitent rises to walk in a new way of life, a way of doing right instead of wrong (Romans 6:4).

The result of repentance and baptism is that "ye shall receive the gift of the Holy Ghost" (Acts 2:38). Of course, God's Spirit, the Holy Ghost, does not make every baptized person a prophet like the apostles. But if one's baptism is accompanied by real repentance, the Holy Spirit comes to live within that person (1 Corinthians 3:16). With the Spirit's help he or she can overcome every temptation (1 Corinthians 10:13; James 4:7). And if he or she carelessly fails to follow the Spirit's leading slips again into sin, fresh forgiveness is available (1 John 1:9).

C. Prophecy for Today

Do we have prophecy now? Indeed we do. We have the same prophecy the Christians had in New Testament times. We do not see the prophets of that era walking among us, but we hear their voices from the pages of the New Testament. Matthew, Mark, Luke, and John are prophets, so are Peter, Paul, and the other New Testament writers. The messages they give us are God's messages. Let's treasure them always, read them over and over, and obey them moment by moment.

D. Prayer

Father in Heaven, what a gracious Father You are! How often You have healed our new sin with new forgiveness, that we may be Your children still! Grateful for the Word You have given through Your prophets, we promise a constant effort to obey it. Grateful for Your Spirit living in us, we promise a constant effort to do Your will, depending on His help. So in the last great and terrible day of the Lord, may we by Your grace escape the everlasting fire and be gathered into Your blessed garner forever. In Jesus' name, amen.

E. Thought to Remember

With the Holy Spirit helping me, I can do right today.

Home Daily Bible Readings

Monday, Aug. 4—Sound the Alarm (Joel 2:1-11)

Tuesday, Aug. 5—Return to the Lord (Joel 2:12-17)

Wednesday, Aug. 6—God Had Pity on the People (Joel 2:18-22)

Thursday, Aug. 7—I Will Pour Out My Spirit (Joel 2:23-29)

Friday, Aug. 8—God Is a Stronghold (Joel 3:16-21)

Saturday, Aug. 9—The Day of Pentecost (Acts 2:14-23)

Sunday, Aug. 10—God Has Made Jesus Lord (Acts 2:29-36)

Learning by Doing

This page contains an alternative lesson plan emphasizing learning activities.
Classes desiring such student involvement will find these suggestions helpful.

Learning Goals

After participating in this lesson, each student will be able to:

1. Describe the message of Joel to the people in Israel's southern kingdom (Judah).

2. Make a list of sins and define *repentance*.

3. Identify a sin in his or her life and plan a private time to repent of it.

Into the Lesson

ADVANCE PREPARATION: Gather the following supplies: roll of banner paper, markers, index cards, pencils, and pens. Print the key verse on poster board or an overhead transparency.

Describe a situation in which someone does something wrong (breaks something valuable, steals a parking place) and then says, "I'm sorry." Say, "Imagine that someone started a false rumor about you. When the person says, 'I'm sorry,' what do you think and feel?" Many students probably are frustrated by the ease with which so many people use this phrase with no remorse. Our culture has lost the concept of sin; saying "I'm sorry" is supposed to excuse one's mistake.

In today's lesson Joel the prophet calls the people of Israel to repent of their sins to avoid the calamity coming.

Into the Word

Use the commentary to prepare a lecture on the background for this passage, Joel's call to repentance. Explain "the day of the Lord," Judah, Israel, southern kingdom, Zion, and repentance.

Say, "The call to repentance is strong and clear. The people had sinned. The corporate nature of the call reflects how widespread the sin was, and the actions required reflect the culture of Israel. How would a prophet state the call today?" Let students individually or in pairs paraphrase 1:13, 14; 2:12-14. *(They might write sentences such as, "Ministers and church leaders, put on dark clothing and cry to show your sadness. Call everyone to the church building where you will announce a time of fasting" [from Joel 1:13, 14]. "God says, 'Come back to me. Fast and cry. Looking sad or saying "I'm sorry" is not enough. Let your hearts break.' God is kind, merciful, slow to get angry, and loving. He would rather forgive than punish. Perhaps He will change His mind and you will be able to give an offering of thanksgiving" [from Joel 2:12-14].)*

Invite volunteers to read their paraphrases with prophet-like strong voices!

Into Life

Say, "Israel and Judah comprised the chosen nation of God, yet they had turned away from Him and were sinning so much that they were being called to repent as a community. Joel is talking about national repentance for a nation that was a theocracy. Whether corporate or individual, the dynamics of repentance are the same.

"We twenty-first-century Christians also commit sins that could prompt someone to call for repentance—perhaps with the words you wrote as your paraphrase. Since our culture is no longer calling sin by that name, let's identify actions that God would call sin."

Form small groups and give Bibles and concordances to each. If your students need help, select some passages from the following to stimulate their thinking. These familiar passages can help them find both sins of commission and sins of omission: Matthew 5-7; Matthew 18:1-9; Matthew 22:34-40; Matthew 28:18-20; Luke 12:22-40; John 17:20-26; Romans 12; Romans 13; 1 Corinthians 13; 2 Corinthians 5:14-21; Galatians 5:19-26; Galatians 6:1-10; Ephesians 4:17-32; Ephesians 5:1, 2; Philippians 2:1-4; Philippians 2:14-16; Colossians 3; 1 Thessalonians 5:12-22; Titus 2:1-10; Hebrews 10:19-31; Hebrews 13:1-6; James 1:19-27; 2:1-13; James 3:9; 4:13-17; 1 Peter 1:13-16. Add other passages that should be considered. Give each group a piece of banner paper to record its list.

Display Joel 2:12, 13: "Therefore also now, saith the Lord, turn ye even to me with all your heart, and with fasting, and with weeping, and with mourning: and rend your heart, and not your garments, and turn unto the Lord your God: for he is gracious and merciful, slow to anger, and of great kindness, and repenteth him of the evil."

Distribute the index cards. Tell students to write a sin on the card in pencil and then copy the verse on the card. They should also write a time that they will go to God in repentance. Tell them that when they have repented of that sin and confessed it to God, they may erase the sin from the card. Suggest that they keep their cards in a place where they can read the verse when they are tempted to commit that sin again.

Let's Talk It Over

The questions on this page are designed to promote discussion of the lesson by the class and to encourage application of the lesson Scriptures. The answers provided are only discussion starters. Let your class talk it over from there.

1. How has God used disasters ("natural" and otherwise) to communicate with people? Does he send disasters today to punish people for sin? Defend your answer.

The Bible relates many accounts of God's using forces of nature to communicate His displeasure (e.g., Exodus 8). We know that God brought these things about because the Bible specifically tells us so.

In the time since Jesus, however, it is very dangerous to interpret a disaster as a judgment of God. The reason is simple: we have no explicit Scripture that tells us so. Revelation warns in general of disasters as judgments of God. But to say, for example, that the cause of someone's sickness, poverty, or loss of something of value is God's judgment on the person is mere human speculation. (See Luke 13:1-5.)

2. What emotions would you have if you knew that the ultimate "day of the Lord"—the final judgment—were tomorrow?

Ideally, Christians eagerly anticipate the return of the Lord. When Jesus returns in glory, all the sin, corruption, and flaws of a fallen creation will be set right for eternity—and who wouldn't want that? But many of us are frightened of the unknown. While the current world has its flaws, it is familiar, and almost everyone feels more secure in familiar (if imperfect) surroundings. Perhaps our best response is to pray for that day to come, asking God to help us live in a way that will keep us prepared and eager to see His face.

3. What happens when we "repent"? How do we demonstrate that we have done so?

When the Lord told the people, through Joel, to rend their hearts and not their garments, He was saying they needed a change of attitude and action, not just an outward, symbolic display. When we repent, our hearts sincerely grieve over the pain that our sins have caused to God. Our heart change then results in a change in thoughts and behavior. Changed behavior may include restitution (e.g., Luke 19:8) and reconciliation (e.g., Matthew 5:23, 24). Remission of sins does not come without repentance (Acts 2:38).

4. What effects do our prayers have on the will of God? Can we actually change His mind?

Two ideas in Biblical teaching seem to be in conflict: God's ability to know all things beforehand and the power of prayer. On the one hand, if God already knows everything and what He is going to do in advance, then how can He "change His mind"? On the other hand, if "the die is already cast" in terms of God's decisions, then why should we bother praying at all? Our text suggests that humbly coming before God can change His mind about judgment and He "may relent." Other Bible accounts suggest that God does indeed alter His plans in response to prayer (e.g., Exodus 32:9-14).

The solution to our apparent conflict is to realize that God not only knows in advance what He is going to do, He also knows in advance what our prayers will be. He already has taken our prayers into account from eternity past. We should also recognize that a primary reason God calls us to pray is for the benefit of increasing our faith.

5. How can believers who have never had a "vision" or a prophetic "dream" participate in the fulfillment of Joel's prophecy?

Christians generally agree that God poured out His Spirit on the Day of Pentecost, providing the first-century Christians with gifts of prophecy, tongues, etc., as miraculous signs that confirmed the message they preached. Peter says as much as he explains the unique event that occurred that day (Acts 2:16-18). The apostles and a few other "prophets" received divine revelation and inspiration in order to deliver God's Word to all succeeding generations.

But what of those of us who do not have that gift? Do we not share in the promise? We certainly do! As recipients of the the Word that has been passed down to us, now translated into our own language, we receive the benefit of the outpouring of God's Spirit on the prophets. Paul explained that the gift of prophecy was given to edify the whole church (1 Corinthians 14:3, 4). That edification can extend beyond a single time and place.

In addition, every believer receives the "gift of the Holy Ghost" (Acts 2:38) when he or she responds to the gospel according to the New Testament pattern. The Spirit gifts us for a variety of ministries, even if prophecy is not one of them.

Promise to the Faithful

August 17
Lesson 12

DEVOTIONAL READING: Psalm 90:1-17.

BACKGROUND SCRIPTURE: Malachi 3, 4.

PRINTED TEXT: Malachi 3:1-4, 16-18; 4:1-6.

Malachi 3:1-4, 16-18

1 Behold, I will send my messenger, and he shall prepare the way before me: and the Lord, whom ye seek, shall suddenly come to his temple, even the messenger of the covenant, whom ye delight in: behold, he shall come, saith the LORD of hosts.

2 But who may abide the day of his coming? and who shall stand when he appeareth? For he is like a refiner's fire, and like fullers' soap:

3 And he shall sit as a refiner and purifier of silver: and he shall purify the sons of Levi, and purge them as gold and silver, that they may offer unto the LORD an offering in righteousness.

4 Then shall the offering of Judah and Jerusalem be pleasant unto the LORD, as in the days of old, and as in former years.

. . . .

16 Then they that feared the LORD spake often one to another: and the LORD hearkened, and heard it, and a book of remembrance was written before him for them that feared the LORD, and that thought upon his name.

17 And they shall be mine, saith the LORD of hosts, in that day when I make up my jewels; and I will spare them, as a man spareth his own son that serveth him.

18 Then shall ye return, and discern between the righteous and the wicked, between him that serveth God and him that serveth him not.

Malachi 4:1-6

1 For, behold, the day cometh, that shall burn as an oven; and all the proud, yea, and all that do wickedly, shall be stubble: and the day that cometh shall burn them up, saith the LORD of hosts, that it shall leave them neither root nor branch.

2 But unto you that fear my name shall the Sun of righteousness arise with healing in his wings; and ye shall go forth, and grow up as calves of the stall.

3 And ye shall tread down the wicked; for they shall be ashes under the soles of your feet in the day that I shall do this, saith the LORD of hosts.

4 Remember ye the law of Moses my servant, which I commanded unto him in Horeb for all Israel, with the statutes and judgments.

5 Behold, I will send you Elijah the prophet before the coming of the great and dreadful day of the LORD:

6 And he shall turn the heart of the fathers to the children, and the heart of the children to their fathers, lest I come and smite the earth with a curse.

Aug
17

GOLDEN TEXT: Then shall ye return, and discern between the righteous and the wicked, between him that serveth God and him that serveth him not.—Malachi 3:18.

God Restores a Remnant
Unit 3: Repentance
(Lessons 10-14)

Lesson Aims

After this lesson each student will be able to:

1. Explain the day of the Lord's coming, summarizing the outcomes for the evildoers and the outcomes for those who fear God's name.

2. Recognize the Messianic nature of this text.

3. Pray, throughout the week, for one person who is an evildoer and one person who is apathetic toward the future.

Lesson Outline

INTRODUCTION
 A. Whose Side Are You On?
 B. Lesson Background
 I. THE LORD'S COMING (Malachi 3:1-4)
 A. With Preparation (v. 1)
 B. With Power (v. 2)
 C. With Purpose (vv. 3, 4)
 II. THE LORD'S PEOPLE (Malachi 3:16-18)
 A. Speaking to Each Other (v. 16)
 B. Secured by the Lord (v. 17)
  Securing an Infrastructure
 C. Separated From the Wicked (v. 18)
 III. THE LORD'S PLAN (Malachi 4:1-6)
 A. For the Wicked (v. 1)
 B. For the Righteous (vv. 2, 3)
 C. Final Challenge (vv. 4-6)
  Proper Focus
CONCLUSION
 A. "Faithful to the Promise"
 B. Prayer
 C. Thought to Remember

Introduction

A. Whose Side Are You On?

The story is told of an elderly gentleman who, in spite of failing health, did his best to attend Sunday morning services in his church. Regardless of how poorly he felt or how bad the weather was, he never missed a Sunday. Out of a concern for the man's health and safety, someone in the church approached him one day and told him, "People realize how hard it is for you to get out some Sunday mornings. They would understand if you missed worship occasionally." The elderly man replied, "Perhaps they would. But I want to make it clear to everyone whose side I'm on."

God always has desired a relationship with humanity. Our sin has severed that relationship. It has put us on the wrong side. Malachi called the people of God back to God's side. His message calls to us with the same plea.

B. Lesson Background

Unlike most of the other prophetic books in the Old Testament, the book of Malachi does not mention the name of any king at the beginning that would help us date the book. In order to arrive at the time of Malachi's ministry, it is necessary to search for clues within the book itself.

Those clues point to the days of Nehemiah, primarily because many of the sins highlighted in the book of Malachi are the same sins that Nehemiah had to confront. These include indifference toward the kind of sacrifices required by the Lord (Malachi 1:6-14; Nehemiah 10:37-39), disregard for the Lord's teaching concerning marriage (Malachi 2:14-16; Nehemiah 13:23-27), and the bringing of tithes and offerings to support the Lord's work (Malachi 3:8-10; Nehemiah 10:37-39; 13:10-13). In addition, the mention of a "governor" (Malachi 1:8) fits well with this time, since that was a title given to Nehemiah (Nehemiah 5:14).

From our studies so far this quarter we know that Nehemiah journeyed to Jerusalem in the twentieth year of Artaxerxes (445 B.C.). He came primarily to spearhead efforts to rebuild the wall of the city (Nehemiah 2:1-3, 11). This was almost one hundred years after the Jews had first returned from captivity in Babylon. After a twelve-year period of service, Nehemiah returned to Babylon (13:6). Following an unspecified length of time, he received permission to return to Jerusalem. Upon his arrival, he learned of the abuses noted above.

Exactly where Malachi's ministry fits with Nehemiah's is difficult to determine. Regardless of the specific time or number of years involved in Malachi's service, his ministry may be dated to approximately 430 B.C. This makes him the last of the Old Testament prophets. While he addressed the problems of his own day, Malachi, like other prophets, was used by the Spirit of God to foretell what God would bring to pass. This "promise to the faithful" is the heart of today's lesson.

I. The Lord's Coming (Malachi 3:1-4)

A. With Preparation (v. 1)

1. Behold, I will send my messenger, and he shall prepare the way before me: and the Lord, whom ye seek, shall suddenly come to his temple, even the messenger of the covenant, whom

ye delight in: behold, he shall come, saith the LORD of hosts.

God's promise to *send* His *messenger* calls attention to the name *Malachi*, which in Hebrew means "my messenger." Thus, while Malachi serves as God's spokesman to communicate His will to His people, he is also pointing toward another messenger who *shall prepare the way before* the Lord. The Christian cannot read these words without thinking of the ministry of John the Baptist, who called himself "The voice of one crying in the wilderness, Prepare ye the way of the Lord, make his paths straight" (Luke 3:4; cf. Isaiah 40:3).

This promise highlights the failure of certain contemporary "messengers" of the Lord to fulfill the task He has given them. Some of Malachi's sternest words are directed toward the priests of his day, who are supposed to be models of uprightness and holiness (Malachi 2:7). But what ought to have been and what really was are two different matters (2:8). So God planned to send another messenger, one who would not fail in accomplishing the task given him.

Once he had fulfilled his assigned role, the promised messenger would yield to the One for whose coming he had prepared. Then *the Lord, whom ye seek, shall suddenly come to his temple.* Nearly one hundred years earlier, the prophet Haggai had used similar language in his own prediction of the Messiah's coming (see Haggai 2:7). Those who had returned from captivity in Babylon had built the very temple that Jesus would enter when He came to Jerusalem (though by then it would be embellished significantly with the support of King Herod the Great). The word *suddenly* implies a time or manner that is unexpected and often accompanied by disastrous consequences for those caught unprepared (Mark 13:35, 36).

In addition, Malachi describes the Lord as *the messenger of the covenant.* Malachi is referring to two covenants made by the Lord. The first was with Levi (that is, the priesthood), a covenant that had been "corrupted" by the priests of Malachi's day (Malachi 2:8). The second is found in 2:10, where Malachi asks, "Why do we deal treacherously every man against his brother, by profaning the covenant of our fathers?" Apparently this refers to the covenant God had made with Israel at Mount Sinai, which was now being "profaned." Clearly a new covenant is in order. [See question #1, page 434.]

Jesus came to usher in that New Covenant— one far superior to the old one. This is the theme of the book of Hebrews. Thus we are presented with a threefold "messenger" emphasis: the messenger Malachi, who announced the coming of the messenger John the Baptist, who in turn prepared the way for the messenger Jesus.

B. With Power (v. 2)

2. But who may abide the day of his coming? and who shall stand when he appeareth? For he is like a refiner's fire, and like fullers' soap.

These questions are to be considered "rhetorical"—that is, they are more of a challenge to think than to give a verbal response. Those who have so flippantly asked, "Where is the God of judgment?" (2:17) will see what it is like to have their question answered. The refining *fire* is used to burn away impurities from precious metals. A "fuller" is one who cleanses, bleaches, and sometimes dyes cloth. *Soap,* at this time, is an alkaline lye used to bleach dirty garments white.

The message of these word pictures is that when the Lord comes, He will come to make changes in people's lives. (Compare Mark 9:3; Revelation 3:5.) He will want to purify and cleanse them, with the purpose of obtaining the results described in the next two verses. [See question #2, page 434.]

C. With Purpose (vv. 3, 4)

3, 4. And he shall sit as a refiner and purifier of silver: and he shall purify the sons of Levi, and purge them as gold and silver, that they may offer unto the LORD an offering in righteousness. Then shall the offering of Judah and Jerusalem be pleasant unto the LORD, as in the days of old, and as in former years.

The Lord's refining and cleansing ministry will focus primarily on the Levites. They already have been exposed as violators of the covenant that the Lord made with their ancestor *Levi* (Malachi 2:1-5). As noted in the Introduction, one of the concerns of both Nehemiah and Malachi was the abuses of the sacrificial system. Here the Lord cites the real problem: it is not just the offerings that are defective, it is also those who bring them!

An important characteristic of the New Covenant is that everyone who is part of the covenant has Levitical duties to fulfill. Everyone is considered a priest (1 Peter 2:9; Revelation 1:6). All Christians are called to offer the sacrifices of praise and of good works (Hebrews 13:15, 16). Participating in the New Covenant will make *the offering of Judah and Jerusalem . . . pleasant unto the Lord.* The situation will be radically different from Malachi's day, when God declared, "I have no pleasure in you, saith the Lord of hosts, neither will I accept an offering at your hand" (Malachi 1:10). The term *Jerusalem* should be understood in its New Covenant sense; the "heavenly Jerusalem" is the "church of the firstborn" (Hebrews 12:22, 23).

II. The Lord's People
(Malachi 3:16-18)

A. Speaking to Each Other (v. 16)

16. Then they that feared the LORD spake often one to another: and the LORD hearkened, and heard it, and a book of remembrance was written before him for them that feared the LORD, and that thought upon his name.

Some of the people have spoken "stout" (or harsh) words against God (Malachi 3:13). But there apparently are those among God's people who do not agree with those naysayers. The Lord always has had those among His people who have refused to bow to the spirit of negativity and pessimism, whether it be the seven thousand in Elijah's day (1 Kings 19:18) or those in Malachi's day. Here, those who fear *the Lord spake often one to another*, perhaps offering words of mutual encouragement. As a result, *the Lord hearkened, and heard it.*

The mention of a *book of remembrance* calls to mind the familiar book of life, which God is described as opening at the final judgment (Revelation 20:12, 15). Here it appears to be a way for those who fear the Lord to commemorate their commitment and express their loyalty to Him. What joy this book must have brought to the Lord—and to His messenger Malachi!

B. Secured by the Lord (v. 17)

17. And they shall be mine, saith the LORD of hosts, in that day when I make up my jewels; and I will spare them, as a man spareth his own son that serveth him.

God then gives a special promise to those who have chosen to honor His name: *they shall be mine, . . . in that day when I make up my jewels.*

"Discern...
between
him that
serveth God

and him
that
serveth
him not."
–Malachi 3:18

Visual for
lesson 12

This visual illustrates Malachi 3:18. Challenge students to think of specific ways they "serve God."

The Hebrew word translated "jewels" is the same word used in Exodus 19:5, when God spoke to His people at Mount Sinai and called them to be His "peculiar treasure." Here Malachi's words seem to anticipate the *day* of judgment when the Lord will make a clear distinction between the righteous and the wicked, as the next verse shows.

SECURING AN INFRASTRUCTURE

Following the terrorist attacks of September 11, 2001, *security* was something that everyone desperately wanted but nobody seemed to have. Suddenly, all of America seemed vulnerable. Even the parts that weren't attacked, such as the Internet, did not seem as secure as they once appeared to be.

In truth, America's computer networks have never been very secure. Yet the disruptions in air traffic control, delivery of electrical power, and financial services that could result from a successful "cyberterrorism" attack are massive! In 1997, the President's Commission on Critical Infrastructure Protection noted how much the world's economy increasingly depends on the Internet and its data lines.

So government and industry leaders are working hard to protect that vital infrastructure. But nothing in this world ever will be 100 percent "secure." By contrast, what a comfort it is to have God's secure promise, "they shall be mine"! But this promise is only for those whose "spiritual infrastructure" is grounded in Jesus Christ.

Is yours?   —R. L. N.

C. Separated From the Wicked (v. 18)

18. Then shall ye return, and discern between the righteous and the wicked, between him that serveth God and him that serveth him not.

One of Jesus' most striking images of the judgment day is that of a shepherd dividing the sheep from the goats (Matthew 25:31-46). There clearly is no middle ground; no "hybrids" will be found before God's judgment throne! Concerning that day, the task of Christians is clear: to prepare people for Jesus' second coming, just as John the Baptist prepared people for His first one. [See question #3, page 434.]

III. The Lord's Plan
(Malachi 4:1-6)

A. For the Wicked (v. 1)

1. For, behold, the day cometh, that shall burn as an oven; and all the proud, yea, and all that do wickedly, shall be stubble: and the day that cometh shall burn them up, saith the LORD

How to Say It

ABRAHAM. *Ay*-bruh-ham.

ARTAXERXES. Are-tuh-*zerk*-sees.

BABYLON. *Bab*-uh-lun.

ELIJAH. Ee-*lye*-juh.

HAGGAI. *Hag*-eye or *Hag*-ay-eye.

HEROD. *Hair*-ud.

HOREB. *Ho*-reb.

JEREMIAH. Jair-uh-*my*-uh.

JERUSALEM. Juh-*roo*-suh-lem.

LEVI. *Lee*-vye.

LEVITES. *Lee*-vites.

LEVITICAL. Leh-*vit*-ih-kul.

MALACHI. *Mal*-uh-kye.

MESSIANIC. Mess-ee-*an*-ick.

NEHEMIAH. *Nee*-huh-*my*-uh (strong accent on *my*).

SINAI. *Sigh*-nye or *Sigh*-nay-eye.

ZECHARIAH. *Zek*-uh-*rye*-uh (strong accent on *rye*).

---

of hosts, that it shall leave them neither root nor branch.

This verse elaborates on what will happen to the wicked who are mentioned in Malachi 3:18. Whereas God will spare those who have served Him (3:17), the *proud* and *all that do wickedly* will be treated as *stubble* and will not be spared from the Lord's wrath (cf. Matthew 3:12).

Interestingly, previous judgments on God's people usually had left a "root" or a "branch," which became one of the names for the promised Messiah (Isaiah 4:2; 11:1; Jeremiah 23:5). But this judgment declared by Malachi will be so complete as to *leave . . . neither root nor branch.*

B. For the Righteous (vv. 2, 3)

2. But unto you that fear my name shall the Sun of righteousness arise with healing in his wings; and ye shall go forth, and grow up as calves of the stall.

Many will recognize these words as part of one of the verses in the Christmas carol, "Hark! the Herald Angels Sing." Whereas the wicked will experience the burning heat associated with the Lord's wrath, the righteous will experience another kind of heat from Heaven: the warmth of God's *Sun of righteousness.* Jesus is that "Sun" who will *arise with healing in his wings.* The term *wings* refers to the rays of the sun, as in Psalm 139:9.

Similar language is used by Zechariah, father of John the Baptist, when, in the Spirit-filled proclamation that followed the naming of his son, he speaks of the coming of the "dayspring [i.e. sunrise] from on high" (Luke 1:78). Like newborn *calves* just released from their stall into the bright sunlight, God's people will rejoice in all the Lord has done for them. [See question #4, page 434.]

3. And ye shall tread down the wicked; for they shall be ashes under the soles of your feet in the day that I shall do this, saith the LORD of hosts.

Often in this fallen, sinful world it appears that the *wicked* are those who have the upper hand (or foot, in this case). They *tread* upon the righteous with the utmost scorn. That situation will be reversed, however, in God's own time. In keeping with the image of fire and burning, the wicked are described as harmless *ashes under the soles* of the *feet* of the righteous. (Compare Micah 2:12, 13.)

C. Final Challenge (vv. 4-6)

4. Remember ye the law of Moses my servant, which I commanded unto him in Horeb for all Israel, with the statutes and judgments.

While God's prophets in the Old Testament spoke of the glorious things that He would do for His people in the future, they also called their hearers to recall their historical roots as a people—to *remember . . . the law of Moses,* given to him at *Horeb* (another name for Mount Sinai). The neglect of those roots—the failure to obey the *statutes and judgments* received from God through Moses—had produced nothing but chaos and heartache for God's people. They do not need a new message from Heaven; they need to renew their allegiance to the one they have ignored. [See question #5, page 434.]

5. Behold, I will send you Elijah the prophet before the coming of the great and dreadful day of the LORD.

This promise is similar to the one of the "messenger" who would prepare the way for the Lord (cf. Malachi 3:1). Here that messenger is called *Elijah.* Jesus' words in Matthew 17:10-13 make it clear that this prophecy of Malachi was fulfilled in John the Baptist. The angel Gabriel told Zechariah that his son John would serve "in the spirit and power of Elijah" (Luke 1:17). This would take place *before the coming of the great and dreadful day of the Lord.* Malachi already has highlighted the judgment events associated with that day. Now he states that this day will not come without proper warning. However, it is the duty of God's people today (the church) to sound the warning and prepare sinners for the great and dreadful day that will surely come.

If we do not, who will?

6. And he shall turn the heart of the fathers to the children, and the heart of the children to their fathers, lest I come and smite the earth with a curse.

Here Malachi describes what "Elijah" will achieve when he comes. Luke 1:17 links these same words to the ministry of John the Baptist.

While the term *fathers* may be used in a parental sense, it is also possible to see it as a reference to the forefathers or ancestors of Israel. There was a huge gap between these godly men and religious leaders in John the Baptist's day. Those leaders, while claiming to be children of Abraham, were really children of the devil (John 8:33, 39, 44). John came to appeal to such resistant hearts in order to prepare them for the coming of Jesus.

Many Bible students have called attention to the fact that the Old Testament ends with the word *curse*. This word well summarizes humanity's plight under the law of Moses. Although holy and just, that law was not able to provide salvation for sinners "in that it was weak through the flesh" (Romans 8:3). Thus the conclusion of the Old Testament set the stage for the One who would come to deliver us from the curse of sin and death (cf. Galatians 3:10-13). Because of Jesus, the New Testament concludes, not with a curse, but with a blessing (see Revelation 22:14). True, there is a warning at the end of the New Testament as well (22:18, 19), but it is grace that has the final say.

PROPER FOCUS

Before he became what *Newsweek* called a "commercial supernova," John Grisham was an unknown, small-town lawyer. Then his novels *The Firm, Pelican Brief, The Client,* and others catapulted him to celebrity status. Grisham works to keep a proper focus on meaningful things, particularly his faith in God.

As a young law student Grisham was confronted with the inevitability of death. One of his

best friends in college died of cancer at age twenty-five. Shortly before his death, Grisham's buddy took him to lunch and revealed his disease.

John Grisham asked his friend, "What do you do when you realize you are about to die?"

"It's real simple," he said. "You get things right with God, and you spend as much time with those you love as you can. Then you settle up with everybody else."

Finally he said, "You know, really, you ought to live every day like you have only a few more days to live." Those words were never forgotten.

Malachi's prophecy spells out several promises God makes to the faithful. His return and judgment are certain. How should we live in light of God's promises?

Death is a certainty. So is the return of Jesus. These realities call us to evaluate. Are you living your life with the proper focus?   —J. A. M.

Conclusion

A. "Faithful to the Promise"

In thinking about how to apply today's lesson, "Promise to the Faithful," it may be helpful to reverse the words and think about the phrase "Faithful to the Promise." Do we, like the people in Malachi's day, need to return to our roots? Have we forgotten the promise we made when we first gave our lives to Christ? Have we lost the zeal we possessed when that happened? (If so, can we determine why that has happened?) Is it clear whose side we are on? As someone once asked, "If you were arrested and charged with being a Christian, would there be enough evidence to convict you?"

Skeptics sometimes have stated, rather defiantly, "If I had the chance to speak with God, here's what I would say to Him." They then proceed to list all the complaints that they would lodge about various issues. It is far more profitable to consider what God will say to us when we face Him at the Day of Judgment. We want to hear Him say, "Well done, thou good and *faithful* servant" (Matthew 25:21).

Therefore, "Let us hold fast the profession of our faith without wavering; for he is faithful that promised" (Hebrews 10:23).

B. Prayer

Father, help us to make each day count in Your service. May it be clear to all that we are on Your side and that we have no regrets for having chosen to follow Jesus. In His name, amen.

C. Thought to Remember

The best way to be ready for the day of the Lord is to be faithful to the Lord of that day.

Home Daily Bible Readings

Monday, Aug. 11—A Priest Should Guard Knowledge (Malachi 2:1-9)

Tuesday, Aug. 12—The Lord's Messenger Will Refine (Malachi 3:1-5)

Wednesday, Aug. 13—Return to Me (Malachi 3:6-12)

Thursday, Aug. 14—The Lord's Special Possession (Malachi 3:13-18)

Friday, Aug. 15—The Sun of Righteousness Shall Rise (Malachi 4:1-6)

Saturday, Aug. 16—God's Steadfast Love (Psalm 89:19-29)

Sunday, Aug. 17—God Will Keep His Covenant (Psalm 89:30-37)

Learning by Doing

This page contains an alternative lesson plan emphasizing learning activities.
Classes desiring such student involvement will find these suggestions helpful.

Learning Goals

After participating in this lesson, each student will be able to:

1. Explain the day of the Lord's coming, summarizing the outcomes for the evildoers and the outcomes for those who fear God's name.

2. Recognize the Messianic nature of this text.

3. Pray, throughout the week, for one person who is an evildoer and one person who is apathetic toward the future.

Into the Lesson

Prior to the beginning of the lesson ask a person who is not in your class to enter the classroom about five minutes after class starts. Have him dress as a contemporary courier (a bike messenger perhaps), an Old Testament prophet (Malachi), or even as John the Baptist.

Before the "messenger's" arrival, ask students to respond to this question: "What does the future hold for you?" Enter into a discussion that addresses many different time horizons (immediate future, distant future) and social contexts (individual, family, community, national, and others).

When the "messenger" enters your class, he should read the assigned text, Malachi 3:1-4, 16-18; 4:1-4. Recalling lesson 8, the "messenger" may ask the students to stand for this important message.

Into the Word

Direct students to read quickly through today's text. Ask one student to read Exodus 23:20-26. Have the students list on paper the similarities they see and hear between the Exodus passage and the text being studied today (especially Malachi 3:1). The list will include such items as the fact that God will send a messenger or angel and that He will guard or prepare the way. Note that the language—very similar in Hebrew—ties these texts closely together. The Exodus passage promises a victory that God provides for His people. The Malachi text, by parallel, does the same thing. However, the Malachi text promises an eternal victory through Jesus. The Malachi passage is clearly Messianic in nature.

Ask students to tell about the nature of Christ's coming and what will happen to those who do evil and those who fear God's name according to this text. Ask them to identify similar ideas in the Gospels.

Into Life

Ask students to identify several high-profile people throughout history who can be identified as primarily good or evil in their actions. These may include political, religious, or business leaders, or others. *(Some examples associated with evil behavior are Hitler, Stalin, Timothy McVeigh, Osama bin Laden. Examples of those associated with good behavior are Mother Theresa, Christian missionaries, and others.)* Write these on a display board. Next to the names, place three columns headed "short-term," "long-term," and "eternity."

Ask the students what consequences each of the people or groups listed have experienced as a result of their behaviors. (Stalin lived a life of relative luxury and authority until his death; McVeigh died exactly as he wanted to; Mother Theresa suffered hardships during her life of service.) Comparing these people's actions with Matthew 25:31-46, speculate as to what the eternal consequences for each person may be, based on what we know of their lives. Place a "+" sign in the appropriate column for positive consequences, a "–" sign for negative consequences, and a "?" for unknown consequences (or those for which a consensus is not reached).

Say, "It is common for evildoers to reap short-term benefits while God-fearers seem to suffer, or at least not benefit, from the world's perspective." Ask for personal examples at this point. Point out that we can judge the behaviors and short- and long-term consequences, but that we are not in a position to judge eternal consequences.

Finally, prepare for a time of prayer. Ask each student to write down the name of someone he or she knows who is an evildoer and the name of someone who is apathetic or arrogant with regard to the eternal future. Provide a short time for the students to pray for these individuals silently. Close with a prayer for all who are behaving in such a way as to be outside God's kingdom for eternity. At the close of the lesson ask the students to commit to praying for one week for the two people whom they chose. Remind the students that just as God protected the way of His people in Exodus and promised (in Malachi) to prepare the way for Christ, Jesus promised to prepare a place in His Father's house for those who trust in God (fear His name). Read John 14:1-6, emphasizing verses 2, 3.

Let's Talk It Over

The questions on this page are designed to promote discussion of the lesson by the class and to encourage application of the lesson Scriptures. The answers provided are only discussion starters. Let your class talk it over from there.

1. The Lord mentions His covenant several times in Malachi. What significance do you see in that?

A covenant is an agreement between two parties. It is meant to provide a sense of clearly defined expectations in the relationship. God is reminding His people that we can rely on Him to fulfill His part of the pledge. He is not like a parent who makes idle promises or threats to his children. He is more like the parent who carefully tells his children the expectations of being in the family, and then metes out appropriate rewards and punishment to encourage the children to behave correctly. So if we live within the covenant, we can rest assured that God will bless us, just as He promised. Likewise, if we don't fulfill our part, we can be sure that "the day of the Lord" will be terrible.

2. What can we do to prepare for "the day of [the Lord's] coming"?

Christians are often pulled to one of two extremes. Some virtually ignore the promise of Jesus' return and the coming kingdom, while others become so fascinated by "end time" prophecies and interpretations that they neglect other aspects of the Christian life. Neither extreme honors God. Instead, we must daily "walk in the Spirit" (Galatians 5:25) to please God. This walk includes prayer, worship, Bible study, evangelism, and acts of benevolence and ministry—things that help us mature as God desires, anticipating the final coming of His kingdom. See especially 2 Peter 3:11, 12.

Part of our Bible study should focus on the age to come. The Scriptures are packed with teachings about that age; some descriptions are clear and some are highly symbolic. Jesus Himself spent much of His time teaching about the future. It is important for our encouragement and hope as believers to understand what God is planning for us. Remember, however, that we find more teaching in the Bible about living in the here and now. Our study of the coming age must be in balance with that designed to guide us in this one.

3. How were God's people to distinguish between "righteous and wicked" in Old Testament times? How can we use this pattern in the New Testament era?

God reminded His people continually that they were to be a holy people and were not to imitate the practices of the surrounding pagans. In the Old Testament, God gave His people over six hundred laws so they could distinguish between holiness and unholiness.

This call to holiness has not changed. The command to be holy in Leviticus 11:44, 45 is repeated in 1 Peter 1:15, 16. We live in a fallen world and we interact with non-Christians, trying to win them for Christ. But in the process, we are to be careful not to be "unequally yoked together with unbelievers" (2 Corinthians 6:14), lest we corrupt our holiness and endanger our salvation in the process. Our concerns are not the same as those of the pagans (Matthew 6:31, 32).

4. Think about a situation that made you wonder whether God really cared about the righteous. How can people maintain their faith in God during such times?

Most of us don't need to think very hard to recall situations or events that made life seem unfair or cruel: a trustworthy employee is laid off while less capable workers are promoted; terrorists crash airplanes into skyscrapers; a mother of young children dies from complications of "routine" surgery. At times like these, we may wonder, with the psalmist, whether God is paying attention or cares about us (Psalm 73:1-14).

But we should remember that God rarely "balances the books" immediately. Instead, He usually allows people to live with the consequences of their actions (and the actions of others). He also allows time for His followers to step into situations with loving actions and truthful words. We live with the assurance that God promises to set everything right when the "day of the Lord" arrives.

5. What things are we to "remember" in the New Testament era? Why?

The death of Christ is one of the most important things we are to remember throughout our lives (1 Corinthians 11:24, 25). The Lord's Supper helps us to do that regularly. We also are to remember His resurrection (2 Timothy 2:8). These are just two among many! When we remember what God has done for us, we are able to renew our commitment to lifelong service.

Prophecy of an Eternal Kingdom

DEVOTIONAL READING: **Revelation 21:1-7.**

BACKGROUND SCRIPTURE: **Daniel 2.**

PRINTED TEXT: **Daniel 2:26, 36-45.**

Daniel 2:26, 36-45

26 The king answered and said to Daniel, whose name was Belteshazzar, Art thou able to make known unto me the dream which I have seen, and the interpretation thereof?

· · · · · · · · · · · · ·

36 This is the dream; and we will tell the interpretation thereof before the king.

37 Thou, O king, art a king of kings: for the God of heaven hath given thee a kingdom, power, and strength, and glory.

38 And wheresoever the children of men dwell, the beasts of the field and the fowls of the heaven hath he given into thine hand, and hath made thee ruler over them all. Thou art this head of gold.

39 And after thee shall arise another kingdom inferior to thee, and another third kingdom of brass, which shall bear rule over all the earth.

40 And the fourth kingdom shall be strong as iron: forasmuch as iron breaketh in pieces and subdueth all things: and as iron that breaketh all these, shall it break in pieces and bruise.

41 And whereas thou sawest the feet and toes, part of potters' clay, and part of iron, the kingdom shall be divided; but there shall be in it of the strength of the iron, forasmuch as thou sawest the iron mixed with miry clay.

42 And as the toes of the feet were part of iron, and part of clay, so the kingdom shall be partly strong, and partly broken.

43 And whereas thou sawest iron mixed with miry clay, they shall mingle themselves with the seed of men: but they shall not cleave one to another, even as iron is not mixed with clay.

44 And in the days of these kings shall the God of heaven set up a kingdom, which shall never be destroyed: and the kingdom shall not be left to other people, but it shall break in pieces and consume all these kingdoms, and it shall stand for ever.

45 Forasmuch as thou sawest that the stone was cut out of the mountain without hands, and that it brake in pieces the iron, the brass, the clay, the silver, and the gold; the great God hath made known to the king what shall come to pass hereafter: and the dream is certain, and the interpretation thereof sure.

Aug 24

GOLDEN TEXT: The God of heaven [shall] set up a kingdom, which shall never be destroyed.—Daniel 2:44.

God Restores a Remnant
Unit 3: Repentance
(Lessons 10-14)

Lesson Aims

After participating in this lesson, each student will be able to:

1. Retell Nebuchadnezzar's dream and its interpretation.

2. Explain God's eternal kingdom and His role in history.

3. Describe God's role in history to a non-Christian.

Lesson Outline

INTRODUCTION
  A. Homesickness
  B. Lesson Background
 I. A KING'S EXPECTATION (Daniel 2:26)
II. DANIEL'S EXPLANATION (Daniel 2:36-45)
  A. The Head of Gold (vv. 36-38)
  B. Two Inferior Kingdoms (v. 39)
  C. A Kingdom Strong as Iron (v. 40)
  D. Iron Mixed With Clay (vv. 41-43)
    Do You See Where You're Standing?
  E. A Superior Kingdom (vv. 44, 45)
CONCLUSION
  A. Homesickness Revisited
  B. Prayer
  C. Thought to Remember

Introduction

A. Homesickness

During a ministry with a church in Indiana, I served occasionally as dean for a "Beginner Week" at an area Christian service camp. This week was for children going into the third grade of school, and it lasted for only two-and-a-half days—from Sunday afternoon until Tuesday evening after dinner.

For some of the children, this experience was the first time they had ever been away from home for any length of time. Some had never spent even one night away from home. So there was always the possibility that some would begin to suffer pangs of homesickness—in some cases, even before it was time to go to bed on Sunday night. Camp counselors did their best to encourage the timid to "hang in there." We figured that if we could get a child past Sunday night and into Monday morning, we probably

were "over the hump," because then we could assure them, "Tomorrow night you'll be home."

Just imagine a child (or anyone, for that matter) being taken from home and having to face the possibility of *never* returning! This was the bitter prospect faced by Daniel and his three companions as they were taken from their home in Judah to become captives in Babylon. True, they were probably older than third-graders (some believe they were around age fifteen or sixteen), but the ordeal they had to endure would have been nightmarish for anyone.

What kept these youths from giving in to despair and gloom? How were they able to rise above their circumstances? They knew that although they had been taken captive, their God could not be. He was still King, even in Babylon.

B. Lesson Background

Last week's lesson was drawn from the book of the prophet Malachi, whom we suggested was serving as God's prophet during the time of Nehemiah (around 430 B.C.). The book of Daniel, from which the final two lessons in this quarter are taken, records events that took place before Malachi's time. The first date mentioned in the book is the "third year of the reign of Jehoiakim king of Judah," or about 605 B.C. (Daniel 1:1).

We should note that *"the Lord* gave Jehoiakim king of Judah into [Nebuchadnezzar's] hand" (1:2). From a purely secular standpoint, Nebuchadnezzar's efforts might be seen as a demonstration of Babylon's military superiority over the ill-equipped forces of Judah. But in truth, the Lord was bringing His promise of judgment to pass against a disobedient, rebellious people.

While the Babylonians were known for their brutal treatment of the peoples whom they overpowered, there was also a more rational or practical side to their conquests. This involved taking young men who had great potential for service in the Babylonian administration and "educating" them in the culture of the Babylonians. This was the position in which Daniel and his three friends found themselves.

Right from the start of their captivity, Daniel and his friends demonstrated exemplary faith in their God. Daniel 1:17 records God's special provision for them: "God gave them knowledge and skill in all learning and wisdom: and Daniel had understanding in all visions and dreams."

This unique ability to understand visions and dreams brought Daniel to prominence in a culture where dreams were thought to communicate significant messages. When King Nebuchadnezzar had a dream on one occasion, he first consulted his own "wise men" to get the interpretation. They requested that the king tell the contents of the dream so that they could concoct an "interpretation" of it (2:4). The king refused—he expected the "wise men" to give him the content of the dream as well as the interpretation (2:5-9).

When Daniel learned of the king's dilemma and of his intention to kill all the wise men (including Daniel and his friends), he spoke with his friends. Together they brought the matter to God in prayer. That night "was the secret revealed unto Daniel in a night vision" (2:19). Armed with what the real King had shown him, Daniel requested an audience with Nebuchadnezzar.

I. A King's Expectation
(Daniel 2:26)

26. The king answered and said to Daniel, whose name was Belteshazzar, Art thou able to make known unto me the dream which I have seen, and the interpretation thereof?

Daniel received the Babylonian name *Belteshazzar* soon after his arrival in Babylon (1:7). It means, "O Bel, protect his life!" (Bel is one of the fictitious Babylonian gods.) *Belteshazzar* is not to be confused with *Belshazzar*, the king who saw the handwriting on the wall in Daniel 5. [See question #1, page 441.]

King Nebuchadnezzar is troubled, and he wants to be sure that Daniel can address two issues. First, is Daniel able to know the content of *the dream?* Second, what does the dream mean?

Before giving the content and *interpretation* that God had revealed to him, Daniel wants the king to know about the source of the information about to be conveyed. Six times within verses 27-30, Daniel uses either a form of the word "reveal" or a form of *make known* to emphasize that neither he nor any human being is responsible for what the king is about to hear. Only the "God in heaven that revealeth secrets" (v. 28) can do what the king has asked. [See question #2, page 441.]

II. Daniel's Explanation
(Daniel 2:36-45)

A. The Head of Gold (vv. 36-38)

36. This is the dream; and we will tell the interpretation thereof before the king.

After describing *the dream* itself in verses 31-35, Daniel undoubtedly has the king's full attention. By saying *we will tell the interpretation thereof* Daniel makes clear that he is not performing a "solo" *before the king*. It is the one true God who has revealed both the contents of the king's dream and its interpretation.

37. Thou, O king, art a king of kings: for the God of heaven hath given thee a kingdom, power, and strength, and glory.

The title *king of kings* is one that we normally give to Jesus (Revelation 19:16). Here Daniel uses it to call attention to Nebuchadnezzar's status as one of the most renowned rulers of the ancient world. Nebuchadnezzar's achievements in expanding Babylonian power and in enhancing the splendor of Babylon itself are impressive. Yet in spite of such credentials, this great man is only a steward. Whatever he has accomplished and whatever he has become have been *given* to him by *the God of heaven*—the same God who has revealed to Daniel the content and the meaning of his dream. [See question #3, page 441.]

38. And wheresoever the children of men dwell, the beasts of the field and the fowls of the heaven hath he given into thine hand, and hath made thee ruler over them all. Thou art this head of gold.

This verse calls to mind David's declaration of God's provisions for humanity in Psalm 8:6-8. The God of Heaven is the one who abundantly blesses Nebuchadnezzar, though often he sees himself as the primary reason for his power and success (see Daniel 4:30-37).

Nebuchadnezzar's dream consists of a "great image" (2:31) or statue. One can wonder at the king's reaction to find out that he himself is that statue's *head of gold*. Some suggest that Nebuchadnezzar's later construction of a golden image (3:1) is the result of his pride causing him to misapply the message of his dream.

B. Two Inferior Kingdoms (v. 39)

39. And after thee shall arise another kingdom inferior to thee, and another third kingdom of brass, which shall bear rule over all the earth.

How to Say It

ALEXANDER. Al-ex-*an*-der.
BABYLON. *Bab*-uh-lun.
BABYLONIAN. Bab-ih-*low*-nee-un.
BELSHAZZAR. Bel-*shazz*-er.
BELTESHAZZAR. Bel-tih-*shazz*-er.
CYRUS. *Sigh*-russ.
GRECO-MACEDONIAN. *Greck*-oh-Mass-uh-*doe*-nee-un (strong accent on *doe*).
JEHOIAKIM. Jeh-*hoy*-uh-kim.
MALACHI. *Mal*-uh-kye.
MEDES. Meeds.
MEDO-PERSIAN. *Me*-doe-*per*-zhun (strong accent on *per*).
NEBUCHADNEZZAR. *Neb*-yuh-kud-*nez*-er (strong accent on *nez*).
NEHEMIAH. *Nee*-huh-*my*-uh (strong accent on *my*).
PERSIAN. *Per*-zhun.

Beside having a head of gold, the statue in the dream has a chest and arms made of silver (2:32) and a belly and thighs made of *brass*. (The word for *brass* here describes what we would call bronze.) Instead of representing a king, as the head of gold had done, each of these metals stands for *another kingdom*. As silver and bronze are *inferior* metals to gold, so each of these kingdoms will be inferior to Nebuchadnezzar's.

The kingdom represented by the chest and arms of silver is the Medo-Persian empire, which took control from Babylon in 539 B.C. under Cyrus (cf. Isaiah 45:1). The two arms may represent the two major peoples who joined to form this empire: the Medes and the Persians (cf. Daniel 6:8, 12, 15).

The bronze kingdom represents the Greco-Macedonian kingdom established by Alexander the Great (cf. 8:20, 21), who dies in 323 B.C. Through Alexander's relentless efforts, his empire expands *over all the earth*—at least, as far as the earth is believed to extend at the time.

C. A Kingdom Strong as Iron (v. 40)

40. And the fourth kingdom shall be strong as iron: forasmuch as iron breaketh in pieces and subdueth all things: and as iron that breaketh all these, shall it break in pieces and bruise.

Legs of *iron* also are part of the statue in Nebuchadnezzar's dream (2:33). The *fourth kingdom* represented by this portion of the statue is the Roman Empire. Iron is an appropriate symbol for the might of Rome, which breaks *in pieces* all the existing kingdoms and ultimately incorporates them under Roman control.

D. Iron Mixed With Clay (vv. 41-43)

41. And whereas thou sawest the feet and toes, part of potters' clay, and part of iron, the kingdom shall be divided; but there shall be in it of the strength of the iron, forasmuch as thou sawest the iron mixed with miry clay.

The *mixed* nature of the feet and toes means that the *kingdom* of iron described in verse 40— the kingdom of brute strength—will become *divided* and thus weakened significantly. Such a picture is an accurate representation of what happens to the seemingly invincible Roman Empire. The next verse elaborates on this thought.

42, 43. And as the toes of the feet were part of iron, and part of clay, so the kingdom shall be partly strong, and partly broken. And whereas thou sawest iron mixed with miry clay, they shall mingle themselves with the seed of men: but they shall not cleave one to another, even as iron is not mixed with clay.

During the latter years of its existence, the Roman Empire expands by conquering peoples in lands that are now part of Europe. This may be the meaning of the phrase *they shall mingle themselves with the seed of men*. At the same time this is occurring, the emperors grow increasingly self-serving and decadent, making it more and more difficult to maintain a strong, united empire. As is often noted, the Roman Empire does not collapse because it was overpowered by enemies from without; rather, it rots from within. (We still use the term "feet of clay" to call attention to an individual's weaknesses, primarily in the area of personal character.) The growing instability of the earthly kingdoms sets the stage for the special kingdom described in the next two verses.

"DO YOU SEE WHERE YOU'RE STANDING?"

In the 1983 movie *The Scarlet and the Black*, Gregory Peck plays the part of Vatican priest Hugh O'Flaherty. The setting is the city of Rome during the Nazi occupation of 1944. O'Flaherty is busy helping prisoners of war escape, and a German colonel is trying to put a stop to that activity.

But as the city is about to fall to the approaching American army, the German colonel believes that his own wife and children are in danger, so he contacts O'Flaherty for help. The two meet at night in the ruins of the Roman Coliseum, where the German begins bragging about the invincibility of Hitler's "Thousand Year Reich." Incredulous, O'Flaherty exclaims, "Do you see where you're standing?" What irony—there they were, surrounded by ruins that witnessed to the long-gone power of the Roman Empire, and the arrogant German officer couldn't "see" it!

There is only one kingdom that lasts. God's Word and the unfolding events of history will teach us about it, but only if we have the eyes to see (cf. Mark 8:18).   —R. L. N.

Home Daily Bible Readings

Monday, Aug. 18—The King Has a Dream (Daniel 1:18—2:6)

Tuesday, Aug. 19—Daniel Agrees to Interpret (Daniel 2:7-16)

Wednesday, Aug. 20—Daniel Prays for Wisdom (Daniel 2:17-23)

Thursday, Aug. 21—God Reveals Mysteries (Daniel 2:24-28)

Friday, Aug. 22—Daniel Tells the Dream (Daniel 2:29-35)

Saturday, Aug. 23—This Kingdom Will Last Forever (Daniel 2:36-45)

Sunday, Aug. 24—The Alpha and Omega (Revelation 21:1-7)

Visual for
lesson 13

"The God of
heaven [shall] set
up a kingdom,
which shall never
be destroyed."
Daniel 2:44

*Today's visual connects the prophecy of today's
text with that of John in Revelation.*

E. A Superior Kingdom (vv. 44, 45)

**44. And in the days of these kings shall the
God of heaven set up a kingdom, which shall
never be destroyed: and the kingdom shall not
be left to other people, but it shall break in
pieces and consume all these kingdoms, and it
shall stand for ever.**

In contrast to the increasing weakness and instability of earthly *kingdoms,* the *kingdom* that
the God of heaven sets up *shall stand for ever.*
The real King (the God of Heaven) will do something that earthly *kings* are incapable of doing.

During the era of Roman rule, just before Jesus
begins His ministry, John the Baptist speaks of
the kingdom that is "at hand." This is the kingdom that *shall never be destroyed, shall not be
left to other people,* and *shall break in pieces and
consume all* of the earthly *kingdoms.* God's kingdom will outlast, and triumph over, all human
governments, no matter how hostile to God and
His purposes they may be.

The words *shall stand for ever* bring to mind
the title of today's study, "Prophecy of an Eternal
Kingdom." Throughout the history of the church,
many rulers have attempted to silence forever
the voice of Jesus and His followers. In every
case it is the rulers who have been silenced. The
voice of Jesus and His church remains strong. So
it will be when He returns (see Revelation 11:15).

**45. Forasmuch as thou sawest that the stone
was cut out of the mountain without hands, and
that it brake in pieces the iron, the brass, the
clay, the silver, and the gold; the great God hath
made known to the king what shall come to
pass hereafter: and the dream is certain, and
the interpretation thereof sure.**

The phrase *without hands* highlights once more
that this great kingdom is not of human origin (cf.

v. 34). Human effort will have nothing to do with
its establishment. (Human hands often wanted to
prevent its establishment.) God is in control! See
Psalm 118:23. [See question #4, page 441.]

Like the kingdom Daniel has just described,
his interpretation of the king's dream is not of
human origin, either. God has *made known* the
contents and the meaning of the dream to Daniel;
he, in turn, has conveyed that knowledge to King
Nebuchadnezzar. That information is not subject
to the king's approval or disapproval. The God of
Heaven has spoken; everything that Daniel has
declared would (and did) happen. Without a
doubt, *the dream is certain, and the interpretation thereof sure.* It is to the king's credit that he
falls upon his face before Daniel and confesses,
"Of a truth it is, that your God is a God of gods,
and a Lord of kings, and a revealer of secrets,
seeing thou couldest reveal this secret" (v. 47).
[See question #5, page 441.]

Conclusion

A. Homesickness Revisited

In the Introduction we thought about homesickness, using the example of children being
away from home. Eventually most children become more comfortable with the idea of spending
the night somewhere and are much less prone to
homesickness. (Often the parents are the ones
who wish their children didn't get quite so excited about being away from Mom and Dad!)

The term *homesickness* takes on a new meaning when one becomes a Christian and begins to
see things from an eternal perspective. With the
passing of time, we who are Christians find ourselves becoming "homesick for Heaven." This is
especially so if we begin to experience physical
ailments that are accompanied by constant pain
or discomfort. How thankful we are that we belong to the eternal kingdom of which Daniel
spoke! How encouraging to realize that each day
that passes brings us one day closer to our arrival
at our real home.

Let us press on faithfully in the Father's service, knowing that we are part of a "kingdom
which cannot be moved" (Hebrews 12:28).

B. Prayer

Father, we thank You for Your kingdom and
for the promise that it can never be destroyed.
May we be faithful in doing the work You have
for us to do, until the King Himself, the Lord
Jesus Christ, returns to take us home. In His
name we ask, amen.

C. Thought to Remember

Remember which kingdom you serve.

Learning by Doing

This page contains an alternative lesson plan emphasizing learning activities.
Classes desiring such student involvement will find these suggestions helpful.

Learning Goals

After this lesson each student will be able to:

1. Retell Nebuchadnezzar's dream and its interpretation.

2. Explain God's eternal kingdom and His role in history.

3. Describe God's role in history to a non-Christian.

Into the Lesson

Begin class by asking, "Name a regime or kingdom that rose and fell during the twentieth century." *(Students will probably mention the Third Reich, the Soviet Union, Romania, Poland, some of the African countries, or revolutionary leaders.)*

Say, "As we grew up, we learned about many kingdoms in our world, only to watch them fall. Only God's kingdom will stand forever."

Into the Word

Briefly tell the background for today's passage up to the moment Daniel comes before the king. Ask students to identify the parts of the statue. Make a handout with a rough sketch of a statue with five lines on either side of it, spaced to align with the different sections of the statue identified in the text. Reproduce this image on the chalkboard or an overhead transparency. Ask students to work individually or in small groups to explain the statue. On the lines to the left of the statue they should identify the parts of the statue (head of gold, chest and arms of silver, etc.). On the lines to the right they are to identify the interpretation (Nebuchadnezzar, Medo-Persian Empire, etc.).

Allow time for the groups to work; then ask for someone from each group to tell you what to write on the lines on the image on the chalkboard or overhead projection. Add a rock rolling toward the statue and ask what it is going to do. What does this rock represent? Supplement with information from the commentary.

Briefly contrast the earthly kingdoms of the statue and the kingdom of God, using commentary material for verse 44. Write key phrases on the board or reveal them on an overhead transparency so you can later refer to the contrast.

Into Life

Say, "Daniel's interpretation reminds us that God's kingdom is eternal. God is in control. He is in charge of history itself. No government is above God's control."

Find and play for your class the song "God Is in Control" by Twila Paris. Instruct students to listen carefully for phrases that demonstrate the truth of today's lesson. The verses talk about God's ultimate purpose, which will not be stopped by culture or deception.

If you cannot get a recording of Twila Paris's song, use the song "Onward, Christian Soldiers." Distribute hymnals and direct students to the song. If you can, play a recording and let them do the same search described above. (If your hymnal does not include the following stanza, make a handout and distribute it. It expresses well the truth Daniel was telling.)

Crowns and thrones may perish, kingdoms rise and wane,
But the Church of Jesus, constant will remain;
Gates of hell can never 'gainst that Church prevail;
We have Christ's own promise, and that cannot fail.

Ask, "When we say, 'God is in control,' just what do we mean? How does that affect our own decision-making?" (Or ask question #4 on the next page.) As you discuss this, observe that some people think that God wants them to marry only a specific person, take a specific job, get involved in a specific ministry, or buy a specific house. In other words, for every decision, there is only one right decision (God's will), and any other decision would be wrong. Others believe God's control is usually limited to what we might call the "big picture" of history. For God's big picture to occur, it is not necessary for God to decide every event in an individual's day.

When non-Christians hear us say God is in control, they may assume that we mean God killed their child or caused their terrible automobile accident or brought about the terrible terrorist attacks of recent history. But that is not true. Discuss how the Christian can respond to such misunderstandings.

Say, "It is not easy to remember everything we want to say when someone asks us questions, so we are going to practice explaining God's eternal kingdom and His role in history." Let partners practice with each other. Let two or three volunteers make their explanations for the class.

Play again the song you used, letting your students sing along as an expression of praise and thanksgiving to God.

Let's Talk It Over

*The questions on this page are designed to promote discussion of the lesson
by the class and to encourage application of the lesson Scriptures. The answers
provided are only discussion starters. Let your class talk it over from there.*

1. Daniel was prepared to serve a pagan king in a pagan culture without compromising his faith. How is this an example for us today?

Many Christians believe that we should try to avoid the world's "seats of power." Government, mass media, and other powerful influences are so corrupt, they claim, that we only risk our relationship with God by getting involved with them.

However, the Lord calls Christians to be "salt and light" to the world (Matthew 5:13-16). Daniel's life showed that it is possible for a person who follows God above all to live a faithful and obedient life while serving at the highest levels of a pagan government—even at the risk of life. Daniel chose to serve faithfully in the situation in which he found himself, and God saw to it that he was placed in a position to instruct a king and influence a massive empire.

2. Daniel was careful to give God the credit for his ability to tell Nebuchadnezzar what the king wanted to know. How can we be more vocal about giving God credit for His role in our lives?

We do not have to have some miraculous ability (as Daniel did) to appreciate the fact that God is at work in our lives. Paul says, "He which hath begun a good work in you will perform it until the day of Jesus Christ" (Philippians 1:6). In the same letter he says, "It is God which worketh in you both to will and to do of his good pleasure" (2:13). Sometimes we talk easily about God's role in our lives when we are with other Christians. To follow Daniel's example, we must testify of our faith in God's work in our lives before unbelievers. Nebuchadnezzar was a pagan; he believed in many gods. He probably believed his Babylonian gods had defeated Daniel's God and enabled him to take Daniel and others as captives. Daniel's words were bold ones indeed!

3. Nebuchadnezzar was a great king, and no one could doubt his accomplishments. Still, our lesson writer calls him a "steward" of what had been given to him by the God of Heaven. How can understanding that we are stewards help us to live as Christians today?

First, it should humble us. It is not by our own ability that we have accomplished whatever we have done. Paul asked the Corinthians, in effect, "What do you have that was not given to you by God? And if God gave it to you, why do you boast about it?" (See 1 Corinthians 4:7.)

Second, it should relieve us. We are called to be faithful in our stewardship (1 Corinthians 4:2). The results do not depend on us, but on God (cf. 1 Corinthians 3:6, 7).

Finally, it should encourage us. Our efforts (cf. Philippians 2:12) work with God's efforts in our lives (Philippians 2:13) to do God's good pleasure.

4. Suppose a fellow believer said to you, "If God is in control, what does He need me for?" How would you respond?

With the psalmist we may wonder, "What is man, that thou art mindful of him?" (Psalm 8:4). And yet, He is mindful of us, and He has chosen to use us as His instruments of ministry in the world. Nowhere has God or an angel delivered the gospel to a human—that responsibility is always given to someone else. The angel that appeared to Cornelius told him to send for Peter (Acts 10:5). Jesus appeared to Saul of Tarsus on the road to Damascus—and told him to go into the city where a man named Ananias would come to him (Acts 9:6, 11, 12). The Holy Spirit spoke on the road to Gaza where an unsaved Ethiopian was traveling, but He spoke to Philip and told him to join up with the traveler (Acts 8:29). We are "earthen vessels," but we contain the most valuable "treasure" there is (2 Corinthians 4:7). We have the Word of God. We have the Holy Spirit. Why does God need us? Because He has chosen to need us. Let's be faithful.

5. Nebuchadnezzar seemed comforted by the interpretation Daniel gave. How does God's Word give you comfort today?

People often fear the unknown. While the dream foretold disturbing events (at least from an earthly point of view), Nebuchadnezzar may have been relieved to have a clear interpretation. We also have no need to fear the unknown. While we do not know what will happen tomorrow (James 4:14), we know Who does! God has revealed enough about the future to us to assure us that we are safe in His care. While believers have many different views about end times, we agree that Jesus will return, and that we will be with Him for eternity (John 14:2, 3). However He brings that to pass will be marvelous in our eyes!

August 31
Lesson 14

Prediction of the End

DEVOTIONAL READING: **Revelation 7:9-17.**

BACKGROUND SCRIPTURE: **Daniel 12.**

PRINTED TEXT: **Daniel 12:1-9.**

Daniel 12:1-9

1 And at that time shall Michael stand up, the great prince which standeth for the children of thy people: and there shall be a time of trouble, such as never was since there was a nation even to that same time: and at that time thy people shall be delivered, every one that shall be found written in the book.

2 And many of them that sleep in the dust of the earth shall awake, some to everlasting life, and some to shame and everlasting contempt.

3 And they that be wise shall shine as the brightness of the firmament; and they that turn many to righteousness, as the stars for ever and ever.

4 But thou, O Daniel, shut up the words, and seal the book, even to the time of the end: many shall run to and fro, and knowledge shall be increased.

5 Then I Daniel looked, and, behold, there stood other two, the one on this side of the bank of the river, and the other on that side of the bank of the river.

6 And one said to the man clothed in linen, which was upon the waters of the river, How long shall it be to the end of these wonders?

7 And I heard the man clothed in linen, which was upon the waters of the river, when he held up his right hand and his left hand unto heaven, and sware by him that liveth for ever, that it shall be for a time, times, and a half; and when he shall have accomplished to scatter the power of the holy people, all these things shall be finished.

8 And I heard, but I understood not: then said I, O my Lord, what shall be the end of these things?

9 And he said, Go thy way, Daniel: for the words are closed up and sealed till the time of the end.

GOLDEN TEXT: Many of them that sleep in the dust of the earth shall awake, some to everlasting life, and some to shame and everlasting contempt.
—Daniel 12:2.

God Restores a Remnant
Unit 3: Repentance
(Lessons 10-14)

Lesson Aims

After participating in this lesson, each student will be able to:

1. Summarize the brief account of the end times found in Daniel 12.

2. Know that "everlasting" applies to both the saved and unsaved.

3. Write down and commit to changing one aspect of his or her life that would be different if Jesus were known to be returning within thirty days.

Lesson Outline

INTRODUCTION
    A. "The End"
    B. Lesson Background
  I. FUTURE EVENTS (Daniel 12:1-4)
    A. Distress, Deliverance, Drama (vv. 1-3)
    B. Command to Daniel (v. 4)
 II. FURTHER INFORMATION (Daniel 12:5-7)
    A. Two by a River (v. 5)
    B. Question Raised (v. 6)
    C. Answer Given (v. 7)
III. DANIEL'S RESPONSE (Daniel 12:8, 9)
    A. Confusion (v. 8)
    Inquiring Minds Want to Know!
    B. Closed Up (v. 9)
CONCLUSION
    A. Hold On!
    B. Prayer
    C. Thought to Remember

Introduction

A. "The End"

Whenever those two words appear on a movie screen, we know it's time to leave the theater. For many, however, "the end" is a topic of great fascination, particularly the topic of the end of the world. They sense that current events seem to be leading toward some kind of climax. Some have gone as far as attempting to attach specific dates to certain end-time events—despite Jesus' clear warning that such efforts are futile (Matthew 24:36, 42, 44).

Amid the current abundance of discussions and writings on the end times, it is easy to forget that ours is by no means the only generation to have a keen interest in such matters. Prior generations have interpreted certain wars, natural disasters, or other catastrophes as signs that "the end" was indeed at hand. There is a normal curiosity about these topics and a desire to possess some degree of understanding about them. Jesus' own disciples were very curious about such things (see Acts 1:6). Jesus' answer to them in Acts 1:7, 8 clearly indicates that the study of "the end" should not distract us from doing the will of the One in charge of the end.

This same perspective can be seen in today's study from the book of Daniel. That prophet received a lengthy description of future events affecting God's people. When Daniel asks, "O my Lord, what shall be the end of these things?" (Daniel 12:8), the reply he received is similar to Jesus' response to His disciples' inquiry about restoring the kingdom (see Acts 1:7; Daniel 12:9).

Why does God seem to "dangle the carrot" in front of us and then withhold information that might prove useful in understanding what He is saying? Does He want to keep us guessing? No, but He does want to keep us *trusting* and fully assured that no matter how perplexing the circumstances of our lives or our times may be, He remains firmly in control—until "the end."

B. Lesson Background

The book of Daniel can be divided into two main sections, and they are very different from each other! Chapters 1–6 include some of the most familiar stories in the Bible. Chapters 7–12 consist of some of the more unfamiliar portions of Scripture, or, at least, portions that are among the most puzzling in the Bible. Unlike last week's lesson, which featured both a dream *and* its interpretation, today we consider part of a vision with very little aid in the way of interpretation.

The background for today's lesson takes us to Daniel 10. There we are told that in the third year of Cyrus king of Persia (536 B.C.), Daniel received a vision from the Lord. The description of future events begins with 11:2 and includes today's lesson text from 12:1-9. In order to have a better grasp of this text, a survey of the contents of Daniel 11 is useful.

Daniel 11:2-4 notes the appearance of four Persian kings. The fourth king, Xerxes I, tries to conquer Greece in 480 B.C., but fails. The "mighty king" of verses 3 and 4 is Alexander the Great, who dies in 323 B.C.

Daniel 11:5-20 traces the history of God's people following the division of Alexander's empire. The "king of the south" (Egypt) and the "king of the north" (Syria) had great significance for God's people (who were caught right in the middle).

Many of them that sleep in the dust of the earth shall awake, some to everlasting life, and some to shame and everlasting contempt. —Daniel 12:2

Visual for lesson 14. *Use today's visual to illustrate verse 2. Ask, "In what situations do you lean most heavily on this promise?"*

Daniel 11:21-35 calls attention to a "vile person" (v. 21). This is most likely Antiochus Epiphanes, the Syrian ruler whose persecution of the people of God was particularly repulsive. He ruled from 175–163 B.C. (see 1 Maccabees 1–6).

Daniel 11:36-45 continues to chronicle the history of God's people during the time between the Testaments. It begins with a description of a king who "shall speak marvelous things against the God of gods" (v. 36). This is most likely Herod the Great, who sought to kill the infant Jesus. This brings us to today's lesson.

I. Future Events
(Daniel 12:1-4)

A. Distress, Deliverance, Drama (vv. 1-3)

1a. And at that time shall Michael stand up, the great prince which standeth for the children of thy people: and there shall be a time of trouble, such as never was since there was a nation even to that same time.

Jude 9 refers to *Michael* as one of the archangels (apparently a designation of a higher rank of angel). Earlier in the book of Daniel, Michael's name is mentioned by the one who said that he had come to tell Daniel what would befall his people in the latter days (10:13, 14).

In the verse before us, Michael's future action is linked with *a time of trouble, such as never was since there was a nation even to that same time.* The words of this verse are strikingly similar to what Jesus says in addressing His disciples' question about the destruction of the temple in Jerusalem (Matthew 24:1, 2, 21). Great distress does indeed come in A.D. 70, when the city falls to the Romans. According to the Jewish historian Josephus, the atrocities the Romans commit upon the Jews on this occasion are unparalleled in history. Such an interpretation describes the next major event in the history of God's people (following the reign of Herod the Great, covered at the end of Daniel 11). [See question #1, page 448.]

1b. And at that time thy people shall be delivered, every one that shall be found written in the book.

There is, however, a ray of hope. Along with Jesus' warning of the disaster coming upon Jerusalem, He provides a way of escape to His followers: anyone who sees "the abomination of desolation, spoken of by Daniel the prophet" should flee to the mountains to escape the imminent destruction (Matthew 24:15, 16). Those Jewish Christians who take the words of their Master seriously *(every one that shall be found written in the book)* will see the approaching Roman armies in A.D. 70 and leave the city. By doing so, they are spared the brutal treatment Josephus describes.

2. And many of them that sleep in the dust of the earth shall awake, some to everlasting life, and some to shame and everlasting contempt.

Many students see this as a prediction of the bodily resurrection to occur when Jesus returns (Acts 24:15). Certainly that is part of what is described here. However, it is also possible to interpret these words in a more spiritual sense, as highlighting the abundant *life* (John 10:10) that Jesus came to bring us. Jesus spoke of passing from death to life in John 5:24. Those who oppose this message bring only *shame and everlasting contempt* upon themselves—a fact that will become especially clear at the resurrection and final judgment. [See question #2, page 448.]

3. And they that be wise shall shine as the brightness of the firmament; and they that turn many to righteousness, as the stars for ever and ever.

Christians are to *"shine* as lights in the world" as a testimony to the grace of God (Philippians 2:15; cf. Matthew 5:14). And when this present life is complete, they will shine even brighter (Matthew 13:43). The description of Christians as *stars* calls attention to this truth: no matter how dark death may seem to be, it only serves as a backdrop against which the Christian's hope shines ever more brightly.

B. Command to Daniel (v. 4)

4. But thou, O Daniel, shut up the words, and seal the book, even to the time of the end: many shall run to and fro, and knowledge shall be increased.

A document of the time is "sealed" by impressing upon a piece of wax the identifying mark of the person(s) responsible for its contents. Any text thus sealed is not to be tampered with. The command for Daniel to *seal the book* may be symbolic of the fact that the events revealed to Daniel concerning *the time of the end* are unchangeable; they most certainly will come to pass. (Compare Revelation 5:1-5.)

There are two ways to understand the statement that *many shall run to and fro, and knowledge shall be increased.* From a positive standpoint, the "knowledge" may refer to the understanding of Daniel's message gained by God's faithful people as they go "to and fro" in fulfillment of the Great Commission. Negatively, the verse may describe the efforts of people scurrying "to and fro" to understand Daniel's message, yet having no success because they are relying on their own skill and insight, not God's. Either interpretation has merit.

II. Further Information
(Daniel 12:5-7)

A. Two by a River (v. 5)

5. Then I Daniel looked, and, behold, there stood other two, the one on this side of the bank of the river, and the other on that side of the bank of the river.

Once again Daniel has the opportunity to participate in a celestial conversation, as the *two* individuals are apparently angels. This river is undoubtedly the river mentioned earlier in Daniel 10:4, there called "Hiddekel." It is known today as the Tigris River (located in modern Iraq). Thus, Daniel is standing by the Tigris River when he begins to receive the revelation recorded in chapters 10–12.

B. Question Raised (v. 6)

6. And one said to the man clothed in linen, which was upon the waters of the river, How long shall it be to the end of these wonders?

The *man clothed in linen* is first mentioned in Daniel 10:5, in connection with the beginning of Daniel's vision. The manner in which he is described (10:5, 6) brings to mind the description of the glory of God in Ezekiel 1:13-16 and the appearance of Jesus to the apostle John in Revelation 1:13-15.

One of the two individuals mentioned in verse 5 raises a question of the man in linen: *How long shall it be to the end of these wonders?* It appears that, just like human beings, these two angelic beings are curious as to the timetable for the events described previously. [See question #3, page 448.]

C. Answer Given (v. 7)

7. And I heard the man clothed in linen, which was upon the waters of the river, when he held up his right hand and his left hand unto

heaven, and sware by him that liveth for ever, that it shall be for a time, times, and a half; and when he shall have accomplished to scatter the power of the holy people, all these things shall be finished.

Often in the Bible, if someone desires to state an oath, he raises one hand in a symbolic gesture, much as a person does in court today. (See Genesis 14:22-24 and Ezekiel 20:5, 6.) After stating the oath *by him that liveth for ever* (i.e., the Lord), the man utters the puzzling words in answer to the question that had been raised: *that it shall be for a time, times, and a half.*

The words "time, times, and a half" appear earlier in Daniel 7:25, where a period of oppression of God's people is described. (See also Revelation 12:14.) If the unit for measuring the time should be a year, then "time, times, and a half" would equal three and a half years. (This seems to be the most likely way to understand the word "times" in Daniel 4:25.)

Others take a more symbolic understanding, believing that the phrase designates simply a limited period of time (half the number seven, which generally symbolizes completeness in the Bible). If this understanding of the numbers is taken, then the message and its application are more general, being meant to speak to God's people in any situation where they are undergoing persecution. Such persecution is only temporary, it is never the final outcome for God's people. If they persevere and continue to be faithful to Him, they will be blessed.

The power of the holy people (the Jews) is broken in A.D. 70 when the Romans destroy Jerusalem (Daniel 12:1; Matthew 24:2).

How to Say It

ALEXANDER. Al-ex-*an*-der.
ANTIOCHUS EPIPHANES. An-*tie*-oh-kus Ih-*piff*-uh-neez.
CYRUS. *Sigh*-russ.
HEROD. *Hair*-ud.
HIDDEKEL. *Hid*-eh-kell.
JOSEPHUS. Jo-*see*-fus.
MACCABEES. *Mack*-uh-bees.
MICHAEL. *Mike*-ul.
NEBUCHADNEZZAR. *Neb*-yuh-kud-*nez*-er (strong accent on *nez*).
PERSIA. *Per*-zhuh.
SYRIAN. *Sear*-ee-un.
TAROT. *Tare*-oh.
THESSALONICA. *Thess*-uh-lo-*nye*-kuh (strong accent on *nye*; *th* as in *thin*).
TIGRIS. *Tie*-griss.
XERXES. *Zerk*-seez.

III. Daniel's Response
(Daniel 12:8, 9)

A. Confusion (v. 8)

8. And I heard, but I understood not: then said I, O my Lord, what shall be the end of these things?

Daniel *heard* the explanation given but does not understand it. His position is similar to ours as we try to understand certain prophetic passages in the Bible—such as the one before us now! Bible students continue to wrestle with the interpretation of this text. How can we possibly understand all the images and symbols that are both here and in the book of Revelation?

Daniel raises a question similar to the one asked of the man clothed in linen in verse 6: *what shall be the end of these things?* The question in verse 6 seems to deal more with the time element concerning future events; Daniel wants to know about the consequences or the impact of these events. [See question #4, page 448.]

INQUIRING MINDS WANT TO KNOW!

Several years ago, a supermarket tabloid popularized the phrase, "Inquiring minds want to know!" They used that phrase in their TV commercials to try and convince people of the need to buy the gossip sheet being promoted.

But think about how true the phrase itself is! Many today have an insatiable desire for more knowledge, especially knowledge about the future. Horoscopes, Tarot cards, and psychic readings abound. Even Christians can get obsessed with trying to figure out "Bible codes" and the precise meaning of the imagery in the books of Daniel and Revelation.

But God has given us just the amount of information that He knows we need concerning future events—more information than what Daniel had, but less than what we eventually will have when the Lord returns. How hard we push God for "more" information reveals something about our level of trust in Him.

          —R. L. N.

B. Closed Up (v. 9)

9. And he said, Go thy way, Daniel: for the words are closed up and sealed till the time of the end.

Daniel is informed once more (cf. v. 4) that *the words are closed up and sealed till the time of the end.* He will have to trust the Lord. He will have to make certain that even though his understanding remains incomplete, he will determine to be the kind of person that God wants him to be— "purified, and made white [clean], and tried [tested or refined]" (v. 10).

This must be our attitude as well. We may not possess the detailed understanding we would like, but we know who holds the future and we must trust Him to work out His purposes in His time. Both Daniel and Revelation conclude with a pronouncement of blessing upon a certain kind of person. It is not the person who has a complete understanding of all the contents in the books; rather, it is the one who waits for the end (Daniel 12:12) and who faithfully keeps the Lord's commandments (Revelation 22:14). [See question #5, page 448.]

Conclusion

A. Hold On!

Perseverance is a quality that God *always* has required of His people. Whether it is Noah building the ark, the children of Israel traveling toward the promised land, or Jesus who "endured" the cross (Hebrews 12:2), the standard has never changed. There is no room for the "faint-hearted," only the "faith-hearted" (Luke 9:57-62). The language of Daniel and Revelation should not cause us to look at our calendars or at current world events, but at our hearts. If we are faithful, then it will not matter when "the end" comes—whether by our own deaths or with Jesus' return. Either way, we will be ready.

B. Prayer

Father, help us to be faithful stewards of all we have so that when Jesus returns, His coming will be a time of joy for us, not embarrassment and dread. We are so thankful to know that the future, and the future of every Christian, is in Your hands. In Jesus' name, amen.

C. Thought to Remember

"I love Thy kingdom, Lord."—Timothy Dwight

Home Daily Bible Readings

Monday, Aug. 25—The Sealed Book (Daniel 12:1-7)

Tuesday, Aug. 26—Happy Are Those Who Persevere (Daniel 12:8-13)

Wednesday, Aug. 27—I Will Make You a Pillar (Revelation 3:7-13)

Thursday, Aug. 28—Inherit the Imperishable (1 Corinthians 15:50-56)

Friday, Aug. 29—The Multitude Before God's Throne (Revelation 7:9-17)

Saturday, Aug. 30—The Lord Will Be Their Light (Revelation 22:1-7)

Sunday, Aug. 31—Come, Inherit the Kingdom (Matthew 25:31-40)

Learning by Doing

This page contains an alternative lesson plan emphasizing learning activities.
Classes desiring such student involvement will find these suggestions helpful.

Learning Goals

After participating in this lesson, each student will be able to:

1. Summarize the brief account of the end times found in Daniel 12.

2. Know that "everlasting" applies to both the saved and unsaved.

3. Write down and commit to changing one aspect of his or her life that would be different if Jesus were known to be returning within thirty days.

Into the Lesson

ADVANCE PREPARATION: Collect a variety of articles, books, and commentaries purporting to give details of the end times. These may be found in virtually any context, from a church library to a popular newsmagazine. Highlight segments of articles that tell the supposed details of the end times.

Prior to class, post a large sign that says, "The End" and scatter around the room the various articles, books, and commentaries you have gathered. Be sure to have enough of these to draw attention to them and to the subject matter. Tab appropriate segments with stick-on notes. As students arrive, ask them to pick up one of the items and skim through it (highlighted sections of articles, brief description on book jackets). Have a few students concisely report what the item they have says about the end times.

Say, "Throughout history there has been an abundance of speculation on the end times. Dates have been given. Specific events have been said to be the precursors to the last days. Appropriately, today's text concludes the quarter by addressing the matter of the end."

Into the Word

Ask students to read Daniel 12:1-9 individually. At the conclusion of this reading, ask several students to provide their immediate impressions of the text, noting anything specific it indicates about the end times. You should be familiar with the commentary material in order to facilitate these reports. There likely will be different approaches to this text. For example, some will take the first verse as pointing to the end times, while others may interpret it as referring to the destruction of Jerusalem in A.D. 70. Say, "It is often true that when, out of individual curiosity or intrigue,

we get caught in the details of end times texts, we miss the basic point."

Ask students to work together in pairs to determine what the basic point of this text concerning the end times is. You may give the hint that the answer is alluded to in a phrase repeated in the text. Ask for volunteers to share their ideas. Direct the class to Daniel 12:4, 9. Like many of us, Daniel asks a question concerning the details, and he is given the answer by God that they will not be known.

Draw attention to the consequences indicated in Daniel 12:2. (You may also recall the distinction between the righteous and the wicked seen in the lesson text in Malachi 3 and 4 two weeks ago.) Say, "There are many different views of the afterlife today. Two of the primary ones are reincarnation and annihilation. Reincarnation presupposes an eternity that can get progressively better with each life. Annihilation assumes that death results in a person's ceasing to exist." Ask a student to read Acts 24:15. Then take time to compare this with the idea in Daniel 12:2. Say, "The idea of 'everlasting' applies to both the just and the unjust. The basic point of our text is that the end times will come with consequences, and we must be prepared regardless of how it comes about."

Into Life

Say, "Now imagine that you know that Jesus will return within the next thirty days. Ignore any details about His coming. Just think about the fact that He is coming." After allowing some quiet time for pondering this, ask the students to return to their pairs and describe the thoughts and emotions this exercise raised in each of them. Ask for volunteers to present their reactions to the class.

Say, "Dwight Moody was once asked what he would do if he knew Jesus was coming the next day. He replied that he would not change anything he does. It would be good if we were all able to say that honestly, but most of us would likely change something. Most of us would move something up our priority list." Have each student write down one thing that he or she would change if it could be known that Jesus would be coming in thirty days. Ask students to return to their earlier pairs, and direct the students to pray for one another in committing to this change.

Let's Talk It Over

The questions on this page are designed to promote discussion of the lesson by the class and to encourage application of the lesson Scriptures. The answers provided are only discussion starters. Let your class talk it over from there.

1. The prophecy predicts tribulation. Throughout history God's people—either Israel or the church—have never escaped the troubles that generally affect other people. Often they have had to endure special troubles because they were/are God's people. What gives you the determination to remain faithful in spite of troubles? How can you be sure your faith will hold up if the tribulation becomes intense?

To be forewarned is to be forearmed, as they say, and Jesus certainly warned us (e.g., John 16:33), as did Peter (1 Peter 4:12). The Bible teaches that enduring troubles can help us to grow in our faith (James 1:2-4, 12). Further, when we live through troubles with other people we are more likely to be empathetic and compassionate to their needs and more likely to share the love and comfort of Christ with them. And knowing that this life with its troubles is only temporary surely helps keep us on track (Romans 8:18; 2 Corinthians 4:16-18).

2. How can our faith be strengthened by thinking about the end times? How can we be distracted or discouraged in our faith by thinking about the end times?

Ironically, some Christians become so fascinated by visions of the future that they neglect what they should be doing in the present. Various groups throughout history have made this error. The church at Thessalonica had become distracted by end time concerns (2 Thessalonians 2:1-12), and their distraction apparently resulted in idleness (3:6-12).

Our faith is strengthened by realizing one important thing: in the end, our side wins. It is strengthened by knowing others have already made the trip and that we will join them someday (Hebrews 11:39, 40).

3. Why do we have this urge to know the *when* of future events? What should we do about this desire?

The fascination is human nature itself (and apparently angelic nature besides). So-called "psychics," fortune-tellers, and New Age false prophets exploit this desire. Earnest Christians search the Scriptures to understand better what God has planned for the world and how to prepare for what is to come.

Sometimes we want to know the future for selfish reasons. Students ask, "Will this be on the test?" (They don't want to study any more than is necessary!) Uncommitted believers would like to know when the end will be so they can "live it up" for a while and then "clean up their act" in the nick of time. Such a view shows they completely misunderstand the grace of God!

Sincere believers recognize the predictions of the future give us hope. Knowing that this world is not our home helps us endure until that time when we can go to that place that is our home!

4. What would be different in your walk with Christ if you knew nothing about the end times?

Having an eye on the future makes all the difference in every aspect of earthly life. A young woman studies hard, spends long hours in classrooms, and pays a lot of tuition so that one day she will be a physician. A couple will save money, change their schedules, and redecorate their house in anticipation of their first child. It's no different for us as Christians as we consider the end of time, and eternity to follow. Bible prophecies encourage us, spurring us on when we feel tired or disillusioned. They are also written to warn us of what we may face in the future, so we won't be caught off guard.

5. What are some ways we can "wait" in a way that pleases God?

The Bible's glimpses of the future should not detract us from living faithful lives now. Those glimpses are only part of the story. Alongside them we see a wealth of practical advice and moral teaching about day-to-day living; the book of Proverbs and the Sermon on the Mount are examples. God wants us to be dependable, productive, and loving people in the here-and-now, even while we keep an eye open for what is to come. God also wants us to have healthy human relationships, knowing that these are but a foretaste of the perfect relationships we'll experience in Heaven. He wants us to worship in spirit and in truth, keeping in mind that this is only a warm-up for worship in eternity.

We honor God by leading productive, holy lives while realizing that our final goal transcends anything this world has to offer. Remember: eternity is what lies beyond the "end times"!